MACMILLAN ANTHOLOGIES
OF ENGLISH LITERATURE

THE
TWENTIETH
CENTURY
(1900–present)

Edited by
Neil McEwan

MACMILLAN

First published 1989

Published by
MACMILLAN EDUCATION LTD
Houndmills, Basingstoke, Hampshire RG21 2XS
and London
Companies and representatives
throughout the world

Typeset by Wessex Typesetters
(Division of The Eastern Press Ltd)
Frome, Somerset

Printed in Hong Kong

British Library Cataloguing in Publication Data
The twentieth century (1900–present)
— (Macmillan anthologies of English
literature; V.5)
1. English literature, 1900 — Anthologies
I. McEwan, Neil
820.8′00912
ISBN 0–333–39273–6
ISBN 0–333–36477–X pbk

Contents

Acknowledgements	xv
General Introduction	xx
Introduction	xxii
Note on Annotation and Glossing	xxvii
Note on Dates	xxvii
THOMAS HARDY	1
I Said to Love	1
The Darkling Thrush	2
The Dark-Eyed Gentleman	3
Shut Out That Moon	4
'When I set out for Lyonnesse'	5
The Year's Awakening	6
My Spirit Will Not Haunt the Mound	6
The Haunter	7
The Going	8
After a Journey	9
At Castle Boterel	10
The Oxen	11
During Wind and Rain	12
The Glimpse	13
The Shadow on the Stone	14
Afterwards	15
If It's Ever Spring Again	15
The Sundial on a Wet Day	16
When Oats Were Reaped	17
He Never Expected Much	17
Family Portraits	18
HENRY JAMES	20
Fordham Castle	20
GEORGE BERNARD SHAW	38
From *Major Barbara*	
[Proper Names]	38
JOSEPH CONRAD	49
From *Typhoon*	
[Bad Weather]	49

From *The Secret Agent*   56
[England is Absurd]
A. E. HOUSMAN   74
Others, I am Not the First   74
On Wenlock Edge   75
The Chestnut Casts His Flambeaux   75
The Oracles   76
Could Man Be Drunk For Ever   77
The First of May   78
When I Would Muse in Boyhood   79
In Valleys Green and Still   79
Stars, I Have Seen Them Fall   80
Parta Quies   80
W. B. YEATS   82
Down by the Salley Gardens   82
The Lake Isle of Innisfree   83
The Fiddler of Dooney   83
Never Give all the Heart   84
Words   85
No Second Troy   85
A Coat   86
The Scholars   86
The Fisherman   86
An Irish Airman Foresees his Death   88
The Second Coming   88
Leda and the Swan   89
Sailing to Byzantium   90
Among School Children   91
Swift's Epitaph   93
Byzantium   93
Coole Park and Ballylee, 1931   95
Lapis Lazuli   96
Beautiful Lofty Things   98
Why Should Not Old Men Be Mad?   98
The Circus Animals' Desertion   99
Under Ben Bulben   101
RUDYARD KIPLING   104
From *Kim*
[Friend of All the World]   104
The Song of the Little Hunter   124

Recessional 125
Sussex 126
Harp Song of the Dane Women 129
Cities and Thrones and Powers 129
If ... 130
The Land 131
Gethsemane 1914–18 134
H. G. WELLS 135
The New Accelerator 135
ARNOLD BENNETT 147
From *The Old Wives' Tale*
Elephant 147
JOHN GALSWORTHY 162
From *Strife*
[Breaking the Men] 162
H. H. MUNRO ('SAKI') 173
Sredni Vashtar 173
HILAIRE BELLOC 178
Lord Lundy 178
From 'Epigrams' 180
WALTER DE LA MARE 182
Autumn 182
All That's Past 182
The Ghost 183
FORD MADOX FORD 185
From *The Good Soldier*
[The Ashburnhams] 185
G. K. CHESTERTON 194
The Praise of Dust 194
The Secret People 195
The House of Christmas 197
Variations of an Air 198
WINSTON CHURCHILL 201
A Speech to the House of Commons,
13 May 1940 201
The Dunkirk Evacuation, 4 June 1940 203
The Finest Hour, 18 June 1940 204
A Broadcast Speech, 11 September 1940 205
JOHN MASEFIELD 208
Sea-Fever 208
Cargoes 209

EDWARD THOMAS 210
Adlestrop 210
Swedes 211
The Owl 211
As the Team's Head Brass 212
Lights Out 213
Home 214
Good-night 215
HAROLD MONRO 216
Great City 216
Street Fight 217
Living 218
E. M. FORSTER 220
From *A Room With a View*
[Not Truly Refined] 220
LYTTON STRACHEY 229
From *Eminent Victorians*
Dr Arnold 229
P. G. WODEHOUSE 241
From *The Inimitable Jeeves*
The Great Sermon Handicap 241
VIRGINIA WOOLF 257
From *To the Lighthouse*
[Loneliness] 257
Letters
To Gerald Brenan, Christmas Day
1922 262
To V. Sackville-West, 16 March 1926 264
JAMES JOYCE 269
From *A Portrait of the Artist as a Young
Man*
[Mortal Beauty] 270
From *Ulysses*
[Hades] 277
JAMES ELROY FLECKER 291
The Parrot 291
To a Poet a Thousand Years Hence 292
The Old Ships 293

D. H. LAWRENCE   294
From *Women in Love*
  Classroom   294
The Bride   304
Snake   304
The Mosquito   307
Kangaroo   309
Innocent England   311
The Ship of Death   312
Bavarian Gentians   316
SIEGFRIED SASSOON   317
The General   317
To Any Dead Officer   317
Everyone Sang   319
RUPERT BROOKE   320
Heaven   320
Clouds   321
Peace   322
The Dead   322
The Soldier   323
EDWIN MUIR   324
The Covenant   324
The Labyrinth   324
The Horses   326
EDITH SITWELL   329
Still Falls the Rain   329
T. E. LAWRENCE   331
From *Seven Pillars of Wisdom*
  [Death was Cheap]   331
T. S. ELIOT   337
The Love Song of J. Alfred Prufrock   337
Sweeney Among the Nightingales   342
From *Four Quartets*
  Little Gidding   343
ISAAC ROSENBERG   350
God Made Blind   350
Break of Day in the Trenches   351
Louse Hunting   352
Returning, We Hear the Larks   352
Dead Man's Dump   353

IVY COMPTON-BURNETT   356
From *A House and Its Head*
[Father]   356
WILFRED OWEN   363
Anthem for Doomed Youth   363
Dulce et Decorum Est   364
Strange Meeting   365
ALDOUS HUXLEY   367
From *Brave New World*
[Suggestions from the State]   367
ROBERT GRAVES   374
The Cool Web   374
Sick Love   375
Welsh Incident   375
CHARLES SORLEY   377
To Germany   377
When You See Millions of the Mouthless
Dead   377
EDMUND BLUNDEN   379
The Pike   379
Forefathers   380
The Midnight Skaters   381
October Comes   382
BASIL BUNTING   383
On the Fly-leaf of Pound's *Cantos*   383
A thrush in the syringa sings   384
Three Michaelmas daisies   384
Gone to hunt   384
You idiot!   385
STEVIE SMITH   386
The Singing Cat   386
Not Waving But Drowning   387
EVELYN WAUGH   388
From *The Ordeal of Gilbert Pinfold*
Portrait of the Artist in Middle Age   388
GEORGE ORWELL   398
From *Nineteen Eighty-Four*
[The Principles of Newspeak]   398

GRAHAM GREENE 408
From *The Honorary Consul*
[The Hostage] 408
ANTHONY POWELL 420
From *At Lady Molly's*
[General Conyers] 420
SAMUEL BECKETT 430
From *Waiting for Godot*
[Magicians] 430
JOHN BETJEMAN 436
In Westminster Abbey 436
Senex 438
May-Day Song for North Oxford 439
Sunday Morning, King's Cambridge 439
W. H. AUDEN 441
This Lunar Beauty 441
On this Island 442
Lullaby 443
Gare du Midi 444
Musée des Beaux Arts 444
In Memory of W. B. Yeats 445
Law Like Love 447
The Shield of Achilles 449
Et in Arcadia Ego 451
WILLIAM EMPSON 453
To an Old Lady 453
Homage to the British Museum 454
Missing Dates 455
KATHLEEN RAINE 456
Shells 456
Rock 457
STEPHEN SPENDER 458
The Truly Great 458
An Elementary School Classroom in a
Slum 459
NORMAN MacCAIG 461
Feeding Ducks 461
Nude in a Fountain 461
Celtic Cross 463

WILLIAM GOLDING   464
From *The Inheritors*
[Pictures]   464
ROY FULLER   473
The Barber   473
The Family Cat   474
At a Warwickshire Mansion   475
F. T. PRINCE   477
Soldiers Bathing   477
R. S. THOMAS   480
Evans   480
A Welsh Testament   481
HENRY REED   483
Naming of Parts   483
Chard Whitlow   484
DYLAN THOMAS   486
The Force that through the Green Fuse
   Drives the Flower   486
And Death Shall Have No Dominion   487
Fern Hill   488
CHARLES CAUSLEY   490
Timothy Winters   490
JOHN HEATH-STUBBS   492
Not Being Oedipus   492
To a Poet a Thousand Years Hence   493
Hornbills in Northern Nigeria   494
IRIS MURDOCH   496
From *The Fire and the Sun*
[Praising Art to Plato]   496
D. J. ENRIGHT   504
University Examinations in Egypt   504
History of World Languages   505
KEITH DOUGLAS   506
On a Return from Egypt   506
Simplify Me When I'm Dead   507
Vergissmeinnicht   508
KINGSLEY AMIS   509
From *Lucky Jim*
[Ordeal by Music]   509

DONALD DAVIE 518
The Garden Party 518
PHILIP LARKIN 520
Church Going 520
Lines on a Young Lady's Photograph
Album 522
Toads 523
At Grass 525
Toads Revisited 526
The Whitsun Weddings 527
Vers de Société 529
The Explosion 530
JAMES KIRKUP 532
Rugby League Game 532
JOHN MORTIMER 534
From *A Voyage Round My Father*
[Words into the Darkness] 534
PATRICIA BEER 545
Spanish Balcony 545
ELIZABETH JENNINGS 547
San Paolo Fuori Le Mura, Rome 547
The Novice 548
WILLIAM TREVOR 549
From *Lunch in Winter*
The Bayeux Lounge 549
JOHN OSBORNE 553
From *Look Back in Anger*
[Damn them All] 553
TED HUGHES 564
The Jaguar 564
Pike 565
HAROLD PINTER 567
From *The Caretaker*
[Worries] 567
GEOFFREY HILL 575
Genesis 575
Canticle for Good Friday 577
'*Domaine Public*' 578
TONY HARRISON 579
A Kumquat for John Keats 579

Bringing Up	582
GILLIAN CLARKE	584
The Sundial	584
Plums	585
TOM STOPPARD	587
From *Jumpers*	
[What to Believe?]	587
IAN HAMILTON	600
Pretending Not to Sleep	600
Now and Then	601
SEAMUS HEANEY	602
The Otter	602
The Skunk	603
Holly	604
DOUGLAS DUNN	605
The Clear Day	605
A Summer Night	606
JAMES FENTON	608
The Killer Snails	608
Bibliography	609
Index of First Lines	611
Index of Authors	616
Source List	618

Acknowledgements

The editor and publishers wish to thank the following for permission to use copyright material: **Kingsley Amis**, for an extract from *Lucky Jim* (1965), pp. 36–46, by permission of Victor Gollancz Ltd; **W. H. Auden**, for 'Law Like Love', 'The Shield of Achilles', 'On this Island', '*Musée des Beaux Arts*', '*Gare du Midi*', 'In Memory of W. B. Yeats', 'This Lunar Beauty' and '*Et in Arcadia Ego*' from *Collected Poems* (1976), by permission of Faber and Faber Ltd; **Samuel Beckett**, for an extract from *Waiting for Godot* (1965), pp. 65–71, by permission of Faber and Faber Ltd; **Patricia Beer**, for 'Spanish Balcony' from *Collected Poems*, by permission of Carcanet Press Ltd; **Hilaire Belloc**, for 'Lord Lundy', 'On Lady Poltagrue', 'The Statue', 'On Mundane Acquaintances', 'On a General Election' and 'On a Sleeping Friend' from *Sonnets and Verse*, Gerald Duckworth & Co. Ltd (1954), by permission of A. D. Peters & Co. Ltd on behalf of the Estate of the author; **John Betjeman**, for 'In Westminster Abbey', '*Senex*', 'May-Day Song for North Oxford' and 'Sunday Morning, Kings Cambridge' from *John Betjeman's Collected Poems* (1958), by permission from John Murray (Publishers) Ltd; **Edmund Blunden**, for 'The Pike', 'Forefathers', 'October Comes', 'The Midnight Skaters' from *Poems of Many Years* (1957), by permission of Collins Publishers; **Basil Bunting**, for 'A Thrush', 'Three Michaelmas Daisies', 'Gone to Hunt', 'You Idiot!' and 'On the Fly-Leaf of Pound's Cantos' from *Collected Poems* (1978), by permission of Oxford University Press; **Charles Causley**, for 'Timothy Winters' from *Collected Poems* (Macmillan), by permission of David Higham Associates Ltd on behalf of the author; **Winston Churchill**, for extracts from *Into Battle Speeches of Sir Winston Churchill, May 1938–Nov. 1940*, ed. Randolph Churchill (1941), by permission of Curtis Brown Ltd on behalf of the Estate of the author. Copyright © The Estate of Sir Winston Churchill; **Gillian Clarke**, for 'Plums' from *Selected Poems* (1985), by permission of Carcanet Press Ltd, and 'The Sundial' from *The Sundial* (1978), by permission of the author and J. D. Lewis & Sons Ltd; **Ivy Compton-Burnett**, for an extract from *A House and its Head* (1951, Eyre and Spottiswoode), pp. 88–97, by permission of Curtis Brown Ltd on behalf of the Estate of the author. Copyright © 1935 by Ivy Compton-

Burnett; **Donald Davie**, for 'The Garden Party' from *Collected Poems* (1972, Routledge and Kegan Paul), by permission of the author; **Keith Douglas**, for '*Vergissmeinnicht*', 'On a Return from Egypt' and 'Simplify Me When I'm Dead' from *The Complete Poems of Keith Douglas*, ed. Desmond Graham (1978), by permission of Oxford University Press. Copyright © 1978 Marie J. Douglas; **Douglas Dunn**, for 'The Clear Day' and 'A Summer Night' from *Elegies* (1985), by permission of Faber and Faber Ltd; **T. S. Eliot**, for 'The Love Song of J. Alfred Prufrock' and 'Sweeney Among the Nightingales'; and 'Little Gidding' from *Four Quartets*, from *Collected Poems 1909–1962* (1963), by permission of Faber and Faber Ltd; **William Empson**, for 'To an Old Lady', 'Missing Dates' and 'Homage to the British Musuem' from *Collected Poems* (1955), by permission of Chatto & Windus Ltd; **D. J. Enright**, for 'University Examinations in Egypt' and 'History of World Languages' from *Collected Poems* (1981), by permission of Watson, Little Ltd on behalf of the author; **James Fenton**, for 'The Killer Snails' from *The Memory of War* (1982), The Salamander Press and Penguin Books, by permission of A. D. Peters & Co. Ltd on behalf of the author; **Ford Madox Ford**, for an extract from *The Good Soldier*, Chap. 3, by permission of The Bodley Head; **E. M. Forster**, for an extract from *A Room With a View* (1908), pp. 124–33, by permission of Edward Arnold (Publishers) Ltd; **Roy Fuller**, for 'The Barber', 'The Family Cat' and 'At a Warwickshire Mansion' from *New and Collected Poems 1934–84*, by permission of the author and Secker and Warburg Ltd; **William Golding**, for an extract from *The Inheritors* (1955), pp. 31–43, by permission of Faber and Faber Ltd; **Robert Graves**, for 'The Cool Web', 'Sick Love' and 'Welsh Incident' from *Collected Poems* (1975), by permission of A. P. Watt Ltd on behalf of the Executors of the Estate of the author; **Graham Greene**, for an extract from *The Honorary Consul* (1974), Chap. 3, by permission of Laurence Pollinger Ltd on behalf of the author; **Ian Hamilton**, for 'Pretending Not to Sleep' and 'Now and Then' from *The Visit* (1970), by permission of Faber and Faber Ltd; **Tom Harrison**, for 'A Kumquat for John Keats' and 'Bringing Up' from *Selected Poems* (1984, Viking Penguin), by permission of Fraser & Dunlop Scripts Ltd on behalf of the author; **Seamus Heaney**, for 'The Otter' and 'The Skunk' from *Field Work* (1979), and 'Holly' from *Station Island* (1984), by permission of Faber and Faber Ltd; **John Heath-Stubbs**, for 'Not Being Oedipus' from *Selected Poems* (1965, Oxford University Press), and 'Hornbills in Northern Nigeria' and 'To a Poet

A Thousand Years Hence' from *The Watchman's Flute* (Carcanet Press), by permission of David Higham Associates Ltd, on behalf of the author; **Geoffrey Hill**, for 'Genesis', 'Canticle for Good Friday' from *For the Unfallen 1952–8* (1968), and *'Domaine Public'* from *King Log* (1970), by permission of Andre Deutsch Ltd; **Ted Hughes**, for 'The Jaguar' from *The Hawk in the Rain*, and 'Pike' from *Lupercal*, by permission of Faber and Faber Ltd; **Aldous Huxley**, for an extract from *Brave New World* (Penguin), pp. 27–34, by permission of Mrs Laura Huxley and Chatto and Windus Ltd; **Elizabeth Jennings**, for 'Sao Paulo Fiora Le Mura, Rome' and 'The Novice' from *Collected Poems* (1967, Macmillan), by permission from David Higham Associates Ltd on behalf of the author; **James Joyce**, for extracts from *Ulysses* (1937), pp. 93–107, by permission of The Bodley Had on behalf of the Executors of the Estate of the author; and *A Portrait of the Artist* (1968), Chap. 4, by permission of Jonathan Cape Ltd on behalf of the Executors of the Estate of the author; **James Kirkup**, for 'Rugby League Game' from *Refusal to Confirm* (1963, Oxford University Press), by permission of the author; **Philip Larkin**, for 'Church Going', 'Lines on a Young Lady's Photograph Album', 'Toads' and 'At Grass' from *The Less Deceived* (1955), by permission of The Marvell Press; and 'Toads Revisited' and 'The Whitsun Weddings' from *The Whitsun Weddings* (1964), and *'Vers de Société'* and 'The Explosion' from *High Windows* (1974), by permission of Faber and Faber Ltd; **Norman MacCaig**, for 'Feeding Ducks', 'Nude in a Fountain' and 'Celtic Cross' from *Selected Poems* (1971), by permission of the author and The Hogarth Press; **Walter de la Mare**, for 'Autumn', 'All That's Past' and 'The Ghost' from *The Collected Poems of Walter de la Mare* (1979, Faber and Faber), by permission of The Society of Authors on behalf of the Literary Trustees of the author; **John Masefield**, for 'Sea-Fever' and 'Cargoes' from *Poems*, by permission of The Society of Authors on behalf of the Estate of the author; **John Mortimer**, for an extract from *A Voyage Round My Father* (1971, Methuen & Co.), pp. 36–48, by permission of A. D. Peters & Co. Ltd on behalf of the author; **Edwin Muir**, for 'The Covenant', 'The Labyrinth' and 'The Horses' from *The Collected Poems of Edwin Muir* (1960), by permission of Faber and Faber Ltd; **Iris Murdoch**, for an extract from *The Fire and the Sun* (1978, Oxford University Press), pp. 79–89, by permission of the author; **George Orwell**, for an extract from *Nineteen Eighty-Four* (1984, Penguin and Secker and Warburg), pp. 257–63, by permission of A. M. Heath on behalf of the Estate of the late Sonia Brownell Orwell and Secker and Warburg Ltd; **John Osborne,** for an extract from *Look Back in Anger* (1957), pp. 10–22, by permission of Faber and Faber Ltd; **Wilfred Owen,** for 'Anthem for Doomed Youth', *'Dulce et Decorum Est'* and 'Strange Meeting' from *The Collected Poems of Wilfred Owen,* ed. C. D. Lewis, by permission of the Estate of the author, editor and Chatto and Windus Ltd; **Harold Pinter,** for an extract from *The Caretaker* (1967), pp. 48–57, by permission of Methuen, London; **Anthony Powell,** for an extract from *At Lady Molly's* (1957), pp. 224–36, by permission of William Heinemann Ltd; **F. T. Prince,** for 'Soldiers Bathing' from *Collected Poems* (1979, The Menard Press), by permission of Anvil Press Poetry Ltd; **Henry Reed,** for 'Chard Whitlow' and 'Naming of Parts' from *A Map of Verona* (1946), by permission of Jonathan Cape Ltd on behalf of the Estate of the author; **Siegfried Sassoon,** for 'The General', 'Dead Officer' and 'Everyone Sang' from *The Collected Poems of Siegfried Sassoon 1908–1956* (1956, Faber ad Faber), by permission of George Sassoon; **George Bernard Shaw,** for an extract from *Major Barbara* (1958, Longman), pp. 78–90, by permission of The Society of Authors on behalf of the Estate of the author; **Edith Sitwell,** for 'Still Falls the Rain' from *Collected Poems* (1965, Macmillan), by permission of David Higham Associates Ltd on behalf of the Estate of the author; **Stevie Smith,** for 'The Singing Cat' and 'Not Waving But Drowning' from *The Collected Poems of Stevie Smith* (Penguin Modern Classics), by permission of James MacGibbon; **Stephen Spender,** for 'I Think Continually of Those Who Were Truly Great' and 'An Elementary School Classroom in a Slum' from *Collected Poems 1938–53* (1955), by permission of Faber and Faber Ltd; **Tom Stoppard,** for an extract from *Jumpers* (1972), pp. 57–71, by permission of Faber and Faber Ltd; **Dylan Thomas,** for 'The Force that through the Green Fuse Drives the Flower', 'And Death Shall Have No Dominion' and 'Fern Hill' from *Collected Poems 1934–52* (1952, Dent), by permission of David Higham Associates Ltd on behalf of the Estate of the author; **R. S. Thomas,** for 'A Welsh Testament' and 'Evans' from *Selected Poems 1946–68* (1973), Hart-Davis, by permission of Collins Publishers; **William Trevor,** for an extract from 'Lunch in Winter' in *The News From Ireland* (1986), pp. 80–84b by permission of A. D. Peters & Co. Ltd on behalf of the author; **Evelyn Waugh,** for an extract from *The Ordeal of Gilbert Pinfold* (1973, Chapman and Hall), pp. 121–33, by permission of A. D. Peters & Co. Ltd on behalf of the author;

H. G. Wells, for an extract from 'The New Accelerator' in *In the Days of the Comet and Seventeen Stories* (1925, T. Fisher Unwin), pp. 435–55, by permission of the Estate of the author and The Hogarth Press; **P. G. Wodehouse**, for an extract from 'The Great Sermon Handicap' in *Inimitable Jeeves* (1953, Penguin), pp. 122–40, by permission of A. D. Peters & Co. Ltd on behalf of the Trustees of the Wodehouse Trust; **Virginia Woolf**, for extracts from *To the Lighthouse* (1964, Penguin), pp. 230–7; and *The Letters of Virginia Woolf, Vols. II & III*, ed. Norman Nicholson (1976), by permission of the author's Literary Estate, the editor and The Hogarth Press; **W. B. Yeats**, for 'Down by the Salley Gardens', 'The Lake Isle of Innisfree', 'The Fiddler of Dooney', 'Never Give all the Heart', 'Words', 'No Second Troy', 'A Coat', 'The Scholars', 'The Fisherman', 'An Irish Airman Foresees his Death', 'The Second Coming', 'Leda and the Swan', 'Sailing to Byzantium', 'Among School Children', 'Swift's Epitaph', 'Byzantium', 'Coole Park and Ballylee, 1931', 'Lapis Lazuli', 'Beautiful Lofty Things', 'Why Should Not Old Men be Mad?', 'The Circus Animals' Desertion' and 'Under Ben Bulben' from *The Collected Poems of W. B. Yeats* (1965, Macmillan), by permission of A. P. Watt Ltd on behalf of Michael Yeats and Macmillan London Ltd.

Every effort has been made to trace all the copyright holders but if any have been inadvertently overlooked the publishers will be pleased to make the necessary arrangement at the first opportunity.

General Introduction

There can often be a gulf between the restricted reading required by a school, college or university syllabus and the great expanse of English literature which is there to be explored and enjoyed. There are two effective ways of bridging that gulf. One is to be aware of how authors relate or have related to their contemporary situations and their contemporaries, how they accept, develop or react against what has been written by their predecessors or older contemporaries, how, in short, they fit into the long history of English literature. Good histories of literature – and there is a welcome increase of interest in them – serve to place authors in their context, as well as giving a panoptic view of their careers.

The second way is to sample their work, to discover the kind or kinds of writing they have produced. Here is where the anthology contributes to an enjoyment of reading. It conveys the flavour of an author as nothing but reading that author can. And when an author is compared to his or her fellow writers – a thing a good anthology facilitates – the reader gains several extra dimensions, not least an insight into what thoughts, what fears, what delights have occupied writers at different times. To gain such insights is to see, among other things, the relevance of past authors to the present, to the reader. Reading an anthology shows something of the vast range of our literature, its variety of form and outlook, of mood and expression, from black despair to ecstatic happiness; it is an expansive experience widening our horizons, enhancing specialised study, but also conveying its own particular pleasures, the joy of finding familiar pieces among unfamiliar, of reacting to fresh stimuli, of reaching new conclusions about authors, in short, of making literature a part of oneself.

Anthologies also play a part in the life of a literature. If we are the beneficiaries of our literary inheritance, we are also trustees for it, and the maintenance of the inheritance for future generations requires new selections of properly edited texts. The Macmillan Literary Anthologies, which have followed on from the Macmillan Histories of Literature, are designed to present these texts with the essential pertinent information. The selection made of poetry, prose and plays has been wide and inclusive, authors appear in the order of their dates of birth, texts – with the exception of the Middle English section – are modernised and footnotes are kept to a minimum. A broadly representative policy has been the aim of the general editors, who have maintained a similar format and proportion in each volume, though the medieval volume has required more annotation.

ANJ
MJA

Introduction

Many of those who knew what was happening felt the 1914–18 war to be the end of an era. News of the death toll on the Western Front caused profound dismay. Henry James feared that 'the treacherous years' had betrayed all nineteenth-century hopes of 'betterment' – a disillusionment 'too tragic for any words'. National sentiment among intelligent members of the ruling classes was altered by the carnage at the battles of Mons, the Somme and Passchendale: the soldier-poet Wilfred Owen condemned 'the old lie' that it is sweet and fitting to die for one's country. Fastidious readers found Rudyard Kipling's tone wrong, in the Imperialist hymn 'Recessional', when it was published in 1897; after the war it became fashionable to mock such an unquestioning patriotism, especially for those who welcomed the Russian Revolution of 1917. Poems such as Kipling's 'The Land', which celebrated a serene unchanging rural England, came to seem naïvely 'pre-war', another old lie in a country where millions lived in urban poverty. The idea spread that the Victorian age and its Edwardian aftermath had been founded on lies.

The apocalyptic mood of the war years added impetus to the effect of discoveries in science and philosophy, as they gradually filtered into the awareness of educated people. Sigmund Freud's *Interpretation of Dreams* (1901) undermined nineteenth-century common sense about the workings of the mind, and Albert Einstein's *Special Theory of Relativity* (1905) upset assumptions about external reality. Various schools of philosophy tended to weaken confidence in reliable knowledge. The human mind, it was argued, imposes structures which we take for reality, so that the world is man-made and might be remade. Such ideas were dizzying. The Russian and Italian Futurists called for the 'abolition' of almost everything in previous culture. Spokesmen of the Swiss Dada movement declared that we can only be sure that everything is meaningless. Just at the time when technology, by producing motor-cars and aeroplanes, showed the power of reason when applied to things, 'advanced' thought denied its value when applied to human life. The Modernist movement in the visual arts thrived in this revolutionary atmosphere. The Post-Impressionist exhibition in London in 1910 presented a demanding challenge to

English popular taste, but Modernists knew that Cubism, then three years old, was even more radical and believed the new painting conveyed something profoundly new in twentieth-century sensibilities. Virginia Woolf announced that 'human nature changed' in 1910. She and others of the *avant-garde* looked to literature to catch up.

Several gifted writers thought in terms of such a challenge. D. H. Lawrence saw the war as the end of 'everything', and was full of dreams of a better world to be reborn like the phoenix. He argued for a new creed to emancipate 'the whole man – and woman – alive' from ugly industrialisation and Victorian respectability, and for fiction, free from 'the old stable ego of character', able to show the passionate, aggressive undercurrents of human nature. His finest works, *The Rainbow* (1915) and *Women in Love* (New York, 1920), are, none the less, recognisable as novels. James Joyce's *Ulysses* (Paris, 1922) makes far more drastic departures from traditionally realistic story-telling. T. S. Eliot's *Prufrock and Other Observations* (1917), *Poems* (1920) and *The Waste Land* (1922), difficult poems in which there is no evident interrelationship among the parts, looked equally revolutionary. Eliot knew Joyce's work and followed his example in drawing on the widest resources of language and varying style, from lyrical verse to scraps of public-house conversation; like Joyce, he mixed, as unpredictably as possible, fragmentary allusions to history, past literature and myth with vignettes of contemporary life, to convey a sense of deracinated and unreal modernity.

These writers were not only original but very good indeed. Eliot's control of rhythm and concentration of effect – in which he was aided by the American proponent of 'Imagist' terseness, Ezra Pound – are startlingly beautiful, even for readers who find modern life less hopelessly disintegrated than *The Waste Land* says it is. The richness and inventive energy of Joyce's prose and the fluent verve of D. H. Lawrence are compelling. It is natural for British literature to claim Eliot, who was an American citizen until 1928, the Irish Joyce, and the Anglo-Irishman W. B. Yeats, who figures with them in accounts of the Modernist movement. It is not necessary to sympathise with Yeats's eccentric mystical and political system of thought in order to admire the wide range of his mature poetry, intensely evocative in symbolist lyrics, sometimes frankly angry about old age. One of his finest short poems, 'The Second Coming' (1921), expresses the worst modern fears, as the slouching beast replaces Christ, in words which sound natural and tremendous. Another symbolist, Virginia Woolf, abandoned conventional story-telling and realism (which she called 'infantile') in her later novels; she wrote with delicate vivacity, in them and in essays and letters too. All these innovators in the literature of the second and third decades of the century had difficulty in establishing the validity of their work; Joyce and Lawrence were banned for indecency. They succeeded because they wrote so well.

The academic community which, since the 1920s, has become an influential arbiter of literary judgement, soon welcomed them as the principal authors of a new phase in literature. They were especially attractive because they offer such rich opportunities for rival interpretations, and for annotation: Eliot, Joyce and Yeats are more densely associative than any mainstream English writers since the seventeenth century. Newly created departments of English literature formed a canon in which Lawrence and Eliot, Joyce and Yeats are central; and 'new' critics valued ambiguity rather than clarity, symbolism rather than realism, and radical experiment rather than discreet modification of narrative and verse techniques. Major Victorians still productive after 1900 were, if possible, claimed for the 'Movement': Henry James and Joseph Conrad benefited, gaining wider attention than they had in their lifetimes. There was a tendency to dismiss from serious consideration such writers as Arnold Bennett who could not be assimilated, and to purvey the belief that superior new writing must be 'difficult'. This has been unfortunate, because much of the best modern literature cannot be judged by Modernist criteria.

English writers born between 1900 and 1914 – the first generation for whom twentieth-century conditions were normal – include Evelyn Waugh, George Orwell, Graham Greene, Anthony Powell, John Betjeman, W. H. Auden, Stephen Spender, William Golding and Roy Fuller. Most were at school during the First World War. Growing up, they were likely to meet ideas too new to be met in the classroom. When Graham Greene, for example, ran away from his public school, his parents sent him to a Freudian psycho-analyst. When these men began writing in the later 1920s and the 1930s, Modernism was a fact of contemporary literature; their elders had been the iconoclasts. Theirs was a natural response; they admired, and wrote differently.

There were other examples of new work by older writers. Thomas Hardy had completed his career as a Victorian novelist before 1900. His honesty and pessimism sounded up-to-date to young people in the 1920s determined to be unVictorian. His elegies for his wife Emma –

of which 'The Going' is the finest – are timeless in their appeal. A. E. Housman, too, expressed private unhappiness with grandeur: 'The troubles of our proud and angry dust / Are from eternity, and shall not fail'. W. H. Auden, who was to be *the* poet for most of his contemporaries, found encouragement in them to abandon the style of his early imitations of Eliot. He was able to revitalise traditional verse forms in crisp, idiomatic language, informal but authoritative. For the enigmatic, alienated voices of Eliot's *Prufrock* and *Sweeney*, he substituted the voice of a man speaking to men and women – of contemporary events (with a sympathy for Left-Wing convictions in the 1930s) and of the classic themes of lyric poetry. After 1939, when he moved to America, Auden grew in fluency and versatility, leaving a body of poems which are distinctly of our time, and good by old criteria. There have been various developments in English verse since 1945. William Empson (among older writers) and Geoffrey Hill are tough, erudite and oblique; Roy Fuller, Philip Larkin, D. J. Enright and others vaguely grouped as 'the Movement' are lucid, colloquial, and unafraid of old-fashioned disciplines.

There has been no radical, Joycean break with the past in English prose, despite the Modernist assertion that realism and story-telling were discredited. Ramshackle English society remained, after 1918, too worrying, amusing and interesting for new writers to ignore, and they portrayed it with a zestful sense of emancipation from Victorian restrictions. Lytton Strachey's *Eminent Victorians* (1918), elegant and ironic, implied that the culture of the last century had been bogus and stuffy, verbose and vulgar. This limited view became, for a while, very influential. But eras retreat rather than end; Victorian beliefs and doubts persisted into the age of motor-cars and votes for women, and relations between modern and older values are complicated. One of the liveliest advocates of social and political change was George Bernard Shaw, whose plays urging that poverty is the only crime were founded on Fabian Society assumptions of the late nineteenth century. The idea of a complete end to old ways was alarming as well as exciting. Despite Virginia Woolf's confidence about change, human nature was much the same after 1910 and, freed from civilised restraints in Germany and Russia between the wars, returned to ancient follies and brutality. Aldous Huxley's novel *Brave New World* (1932) and George Orwell's *Nineteen Eighty-Four* (1949) imagine future Englands where scientific progress has resulted in barbarism. The satires of Evelyn Waugh imply that this has happened already.

Another idiosyncratic novelist, Graham Greene, who made an art from the conventions of the thriller, assumes the modern world to be totally estranged from safe and solid Victorianism, but Anthony Powell's great novel in twelve volumes, *A Dance to the Music of Time*, published between 1951 and 1975, discovers comedy in the interaction of surviving nineteenth-century institutions and manners with modern ways. Waugh, Greene and Powell saw late James, Conrad and Ford Madox Ford as the modern masters of artistic rendering in fiction; they can be seen as followers of James in their concern with form and their respect for the claims of a good story. Among new writers of the 1950s, the novelist Kingsley Amis and the playwright John Osborne, known then as 'angry young men', made fresh attempts to dispel anachronistic stuffiness in British life. For those who think Samuel Beckett's *Waiting for Godot*, performed in London in 1955, authentically modern in its vision of a purposeless wasteland, such writers as Amis and Osborne can seem unsatisfactory. But Beckett progressed towards silence; most recent English prose literature has been talkative and interesting about what remains of our civilisation.

The most obvious strength of modern British literature is its diversity. Stubborn individuality, in authors who refuse to conform to any movement, is still characteristic. A remarkable number of them have been Christian. It was disconcerting to ideas about the Modern when T. S. Eliot's *Four Quartets* (1943) made him one of the most distinguished of Anglican poets. Throughout the century, writers have been healthily unpredictable. Ivy Compton-Burnett's novels of dialogue will not fit into any rigid literary historical scheme, and neither will the lyrics of Dylan Thomas, the wartime oratory of Winston Churchill, the light but not lightweight verses of John Betjeman or the brilliant prose fantasies of P. G. Wodehouse. This anthology aims to illustrate the diversity rather than to impose a theory, and to entice new readers into the work of authors – H. H. Munro, Arnold Bennett, T. E. Lawrence – who are not often 'set' for study. It has tried to show too that English writing has retained the power to entertain, without which literature will never achieve anything else.

Note on Anglo-Irish writers

W. B. Yeats, James Joyce and Samuel Beckett have been included in this anthology of British literature on the grounds that they were born before Irish independence. William Trevor (see p. 549) has also been considered to have a place in British as well as in Anglo-Irish literature.

Note on Annotation
and Glossing

An asterisk * at the end of a word indicates that such words are glossed in the margin.

A dagger † at the end of a word or phrase indicates that the word or phrase is annotated, or given a longer gloss, at the foot of the page.

Note on Dates

Where dates appear at the end of extracts, that on the left denotes the date of composition, that on the right, the date of publication.

Thomas Hardy
1840–1928

Thomas Hardy, the son of a stonemason, was born at Upper Bockhampton, Dorset. He went to school in Dorchester and was apprenticed to an architect when he was sixteen. He worked as an architect, read very widely, lost his religious faith, and started his career as a novelist with *Desperate Remedies* (1871), followed by *Under the Greenwood Tree* (1872). He stopped writing novels after *Jude the Obscure* (1895) had been widely condemned for obscenity, because he had written himself out. Hardy had composed poems since the 1860s; he now devoted himself to verse (writing nearly a thousand poems). *Wessex Poems* appeared in 1898, followed by *Poems of the Past and Present* (1902), *Time's Laughingstocks* (1909), *Satires of Circumstance* (1914), *Moments of Vision* (1917), *Late Lyrics and Earlier* (1922), *Human Shows* (1925), *Winter Words* (1928) and the *Collected Poems* (1930). *The Dynasts* (1904, 1906, 1908) is a long drama in prose and verse. The death in 1912 of Hardy's first wife, Emma Gifford (whom he met at St Juliot, Cornwall, in 1868, and married in 1874) prompted several of his finest poems. He wrote inventively in many verse forms and aimed to keep close to ordinary speech. The lyricism, imagination and honesty of his poetry were soon admired by the best judges; widespread recognition gradually followed. Hardy was awarded the Order of Merit in 1913; he is buried in Westminster Abbey.

I SAID TO LOVE

I said to Love,
'It is not now as in old days
When men adored thee and thy ways
All else above;
5 Named thee the Boy, the Bright, the One
Who spread a heaven beneath the sun,'
I said to Love.

I said to him,
'We now know more of thee than then;
10   We were but weak in judgment when,
With hearts abrim,
We clamoured thee that thou would'st please
Inflict on us thine agonies,'
I said to him.

15   I said to Love,
'Thou art not young, thou art not fair,
No elfin darts, no cherub air,
Nor swan, nor dove
Are thine; but features pitiless,
20   And iron daggers of distress,'
I said to Love.

'Depart then, Love! . . .
— Man's race shall perish, threatenest thou,
Without thy kindling coupling-vow?
25   The age to come the man of now
Know nothing of? —
We fear not such a threat from thee;
We are too old in apathy!
Mankind shall cease. — So let it be,'
30   I said to Love.

1902

THE DARKLING† THRUSH

I leant upon a coppice gate
When Frost was spectre-gray,
And Winter's dregs made desolate
The weakening eye of day.
5   The tangled bine-stems† scored the sky
Like strings of broken lyres,
And all mankind that haunted nigh
Had sought their household fires.

Darkling   in the dark   *bine stems*   shoots of a climbing plant

The land's sharp features seemed to be
10   The Century's corpse outleant,
His crypt the cloudy canopy,
        The wind his death-lament.
The ancient pulse of germ and birth
        Was shrunken hard and dry,
15 And every spirit upon earth
        Seemed fervourless as I.

At once a voice arose among
        The bleak twigs overhead
In a full-hearted evensong
20   Of joy illimited;
An aged thrush, frail, gaunt, and small,
        In blast-beruffled plume,
Had chosen thus to fling his soul
        Upon the growing gloom.

25 So little cause for carolings
        Of such ecstatic sound
Was written on terrestrial things
        Afar or nigh around,
That I could think there trembled through
30   His happy good-night air
Some blessed Hope, whereof he knew
        And I was unaware.

31 December 1900   1902

THE DARK-EYED GENTLEMAN

I

I pitched my day's leazings† in Crimmercrock Lane,
To tie up my garter and jog on again,
When a dear dark-eyed gentleman passed there and said,
In a way that made all o' me colour rose-red,
5   'What do I see —
            O pretty knee!'
And he came and he tied up my garter for me.

---

leazings   wheat from gleaning

II

'Twixt sunset and moonrise it was, I can mind:
Ah, 'tis easy to lose what we nevermore find! –
10 Of the dear stranger's home, of his name, I knew nought,
But I soon knew his nature and all that it brought.
    Then bitterly
    Sobbed I that he
Should ever have tied up my garter for me!

III

15 Yet now I've beside me a fine lissom lad,
And my slip's nigh forgot, and my days are not sad;
My own dearest joy is he, comrade, and friend,
He it is who safeguards me, on him I depend;
    No sorrow brings he,
20   And thankful I be
That his daddy once tied up my garter for me!

1909

SHUT OUT THAT MOON

Close up the casement,* draw the blind,   window
    Shut out that stealing moon,
She wears too much the guise she wore
    Before our lutes were strewn
5 With years-deep dust, and names we read
    On a white stone were hewn.

Step not forth on the dew-dashed lawn
    To view the Lady's Chair,†
Immense Orion's glittering form,
10   The Less and Greater Bear:
Stay in; to such sights we were drawn
    When faded ones were fair.

Brush not the bough for midnight scents
    That come forth lingeringly,
15 And wake the same sweet sentiments
    They breathed to you and me
When living seemed a laugh, and love
    All it was said to be.

the Lady's Chair   the constellation of Cassiopeia

Within the common lamp-lit room
20   Prison my eyes and thought;
Let dingy details crudely loom,
        Mechanic* speech be wrought: *lifeless
Too fragrant was Life's early bloom,
        Too tart the fruit it brought!

1904   1909

'WHEN I SET OUT FOR LYONNESSE'†

When I set out for Lyonnesse,
        A hundred miles away,
        The rime was on the spray,
And starlight lit my lonesomeness
5   When I set out for Lyonnesse
        A hundred miles away.

What would bechance at Lyonnesse
        While I should sojourn there
        No prophet durst declare,
10 Nor did the wisest wizard guess
What would bechance at Lyonnesse
        While I should sojourn there.

When I came back from Lyonnesse
        With magic in my eyes,
15   All marked with mute surmise
My radiance rare and fathomless,
When I came back from Lyonnesse
        With magic in my eyes!

1870   1914

Lyonnesse legendary region between Land's   King Arthur and of Tristram
    End and the Scilly Isles, the earliest home of

THE YEAR'S AWAKENING

How do you know that the pilgrim track
Along the belting zodiac
Swept by the sun in his seeming rounds
Is traced by now to the Fishes'† bounds
5   And into the Ram,† when weeks of cloud
Have wrapt the sky in a clammy shroud,
And never as yet a tinct of spring
Has shown in the Earth's apparelling;
    O vespering† bird, how do you know,
10   How do you know?

How do you know, deep underground,
Hid in your bed from sight and sound,
Without a turn in temperature,
With weather life can scarce endure,
15   That light has won a fraction's strength,
And day put on some moments' length,
Whereof in merest rote† will come,
Weeks hence, mild airs that do not numb;
    O crocus root, how do you know,
20   How do you know?

February 1910   1914

MY SPIRIT WILL NOT HAUNT THE MOUND†

My spirit will not haunt the mound
    Above my breast,
But travel, memory-possessed,
To where my tremulous being found
5   Life largest, best.

Fishes . . . Ram   the sun moves through the
  constellation of the Fishes (Pisces) into the
  Ram (Aries) in March
vespering   evening singing
in merest rote   in the course of nature

My Spirit Will Not Haunt . . .   the poem was
  composed soon after the death of Hardy's
  first wife, Emma. The following four poems
  were written in memory of her

My phantom-footed shape will go
      When nightfall grays
Hither and thither along the ways
I and another used to know
10   In backward days.

And there you'll find me, if a jot
      You still should care
For me, and for my curious† air;
If otherwise, then I shall not,
15   For you, be there.

1912   1914

THE HAUNTER

He does not think that I haunt here nightly:
      How shall I let him know
That whither his fancy sets him wandering
      I, too, alertly go? –
5 Hover and hover a few feet from him
      Just as I used to do,
But cannot answer the words he lifts me –
      Only listen thereto!

When I could answer he did not say them:
10   When I could let him know
How I would like to join in his journeys
      Seldom he wished to go.
Now that he goes and wants me with him
      More than he used to do,
15 Never he sees my faithful phantom
      Though he speaks thereto.

Yes, I companion him to places
      Only dreamers know,
Where the shy hares print long paces,
20   Where the night rooks go;
Into old aisles where the past is all to him,
      Close as his shade can do,

curious because a phantom

Always lacking the power to call to him,
     Near as I reach thereto!

25 What a good haunter I am, O tell him!
     Quickly make him know
If he but sigh since my loss befell him
     Straight to his side I go.
Tell him a faithful one is doing
30   All that love can do
Still that his path may be worth pursuing,
     And to bring peace thereto.

1912   1914

THE GOING

Why did you† give no hint that night
That quickly after the morrow's dawn,
And calmly, as if indifferent quite,
You would close your term here, up and be gone
5   Where I could not follow
           With wing of swallow
To gain one glimpse of you ever anon!

           Never to bid good-bye,
           Or lip me the softest call,
10 Or utter a wish for a word, while I
Saw morning harden upon the wall,
           Unmoved, unknowing
           That your great going
Had place that moment, and altered all.

15 Why do you make me leave the house
And think for a breath it is you I see
At the end of the alley of bending boughs
Where so often at dusk you used to be;
           Till in darkening dankness
20   The yawning blankness
Of the perspective sickens me!

you Emma Hardy

You were she who abode
By those red-veined rocks far West,
You were the swan-necked one who rode
25   Along the beetling Beeny Crest,†
And, reining nigh me,
Would muse and eye me,
While Life unrolled us its very best.

Why, then, latterly did we not speak,
30   Did we not think of those days long dead,
And ere your vanishing strive to seek
That time's renewal? We might have said,
'In this bright spring weather
We'll visit together
35   Those places that once we visited.'

Well, well! All's past amend,
Unchangeable. It must go.
I seem but a dead man held on end
To sink down soon. . . . O you could not know
40   That such swift fleeing
No soul foreseeing –
Not even I – would undo me so!

December 1912   1914

AFTER A JOURNEY

Hereto I come to view a voiceless ghost;
    Whither, O whither will its whim now draw me?
Up the cliff, down, till I'm lonely, lost,
    And the unseen waters' ejaculations awe me.
5   Where you will next be there's no knowing,
      Facing round about me everywhere,
        With your nut-coloured hair,
And gray eyes, and rose-flush coming and going.

Yes: I have re-entered your olden haunts at last;
10   Through the years, through the dead scenes I have tracked you;

Beeny Crest   near Boscastle, on the north coast of Cornwall

What have you now found to say of our past –
   Scanned across the dark space wherein I have lacked you?
Summer gave us sweets, but autumn wrought division?
    Things were not lastly as firstly well
15   With us twain, you tell?
But all's closed now, despite Time's derision.

I see what you are doing: you are leading me on
   To the spots we knew when we haunted here together,
The waterfall, above which the mist-bow shone
20   At the then fair hour in the then fair weather,
And the cave just under, with a voice still so hollow
   That it seems to call out to me from forty years ago,
     When you were all aglow,
And not the thin ghost that I now fraily follow!

25 Ignorant of what there is flitting here to see,
   The waked birds preen and the seals flop lazily;
Soon you will have, Dear, to vanish from me,
   For the stars close their shutters and the dawn whitens hazily.
Trust me, I mind not, though Life lours,
30   The bringing me here; nay, bring me here again!
    I am just the same as when
Our days were a joy, and our paths through flowers.

Pentargan Bay† 1913   1914

AT CASTLE BOTEREL†

As I drive to the junction of lane and highway,
   And the drizzle bedrenches the waggonette,
I look behind at the fading byway,
   And see on its slope, now glistening wet,
5   Distinctly yet

Myself and a girlish form benighted
   In dry March weather. We climb the road
Beside a chaise. We had just alighted

Pentargan Bay   below Beeny Cliff, in Cornwall
Castle Boterel   Hardy's name for Boscastle, Cornwall

To ease the sturdy pony's load
10   When he sighed and slowed.

What we did as we climbed, and what we talked of
    Matters not much, nor to what it led, –
Something that life will not be balked of
    Without rude reason till hope is dead,
15   And feeling fled.

It filled but a minute. But was there ever
    A time of such quality, since or before,
In that hill's story? To one mind never,
    Though it has been climbed, foot-swift, foot-sore,
20   By thousands more.

Primaeval rocks form the road's steep border,
    And much have they faced there, first and last,
Of the transitory in Earth's long order;
    But what they record in colour and cast
25   Is – that we two passed.

And to me, though Time's unflinching rigour,
    In mindless rote, has ruled from sight
The substance now, one phantom figure
    Remains on the slope, as when that night
30   Saw us alight.

I look and see it there, shrinking, shrinking,
    I look back at it amid the rain
For the very last time; for my sand is sinking,
    And I shall traverse old love's domain
35   Never again.

March 1913   1914

THE OXEN†

Christmas Eve, and twelve of the clock.
    'Now they are all on their knees,'

Oxen for the legend that oxen kneel in prayer
   on Christmas Eve, see *Tess of the D'Urbervilles*, XVII

An elder said as we sat in a flock
  By the embers in hearthside ease.

5 We pictured the meek mild creatures where
    They dwelt in their strawy pen,
Nor did it occur to one of us there
    To doubt they were kneeling then.

So fair a fancy few would weave
10   In these years! Yet, I feel,
If someone said on Christmas Eve,
    'Come; see the oxen kneel

'In the lonely barton* by yonder coomb*   farmyard   valley
    Our childhood used to know,'
15 I should go with him in the gloom,
    Hoping it might be so.

1915   1917

DURING WIND AND RAIN

    They[†] sing their dearest songs –
    He, she, all of them – yea,
    Treble and tenor and bass,
      And one to play;
5   With the candles mooning each face. . . .
      Ah, no; the years O!
How the sick leaves reel down in throngs!

    They clear the creeping moss –
    Elders and juniors – aye,
10   Making the pathways neat
      And the garden gay;
    And they build a shady seat. . . .
      Ah, no; the years, the years;
See, the white storm-birds wing across!

They Hardy is thinking of Emma's
  reminiscences of her family and their home in Cornwall

15 They are blithely breakfasting all –
    Men and maidens – yea,
    Under the summer tree,
        With a glimpse of the bay,
    While pet fowl come to the knee. . . .
20   Ah, no; the years O!
And the rotten rose is ript from the wall.

    They change to a high new house,
    He, she, all of them – aye,
    Clocks and carpets and chairs
        On the lawn all day,
25 And brightest things that are theirs. . . .
        Ah, no; the years, the years;
Down their carved names the rain-drop ploughs.

?1916   1917

THE GLIMPSE

She* sped through the door   Emma
And, following in haste,
And stirred to the core,
I entered hot-faced;
5   But I could not find her,
    No sign was behind her.
    'Where is she?' I said:
    – 'Who?' they asked that sat there;
    'Not a soul's come in sight.'
10 – 'A maid with red hair.'
    – 'Ah.' They paled. 'She is dead.
    People see her at night,
    But you are the first
    On whom she has burst
15 In the keen common light.'

    It was ages ago,
    When I was quite strong:
    I have waited since, – O,
    I have waited so long!
20 – Yea, I set me to own

The house, where now lone
I dwell in void rooms
Booming hollow as tombs!
But I never come near her,
25   Though nightly I hear her.
And my cheek has grown thin
And my hair has grown gray
With this waiting therein;
  But she still keeps away!

1917

THE SHADOW ON THE STONE

    I went by the Druid stone
  That broods in the garden white and lone,
And I stopped and looked at the shifting shadows
  That at some moments fall thereon
5   From the tree hard by with a rhythmic swing,
  And they shaped in my imagining
To the shade that a well-known head and shoulders
  Threw there when she was gardening.

    I thought her behind my back,
10   Yea, her I long had learned to lack,
And I said: 'I am sure you are standing behind me,
  Though how do you get into this old track?'
  And there was no sound but the fall of a leaf
  As a sad response; and to keep down grief
15 I would not turn my head to discover
  That there was nothing in my belief.

    Yet I wanted to look and see
  That nobody stood at the back of me;
But I thought once more: 'Nay, I'll not unvision
20   A shape which, somehow, there may be.'
  So I went on softly from the glade,
  And left her behind me throwing her shade,
As she were indeed an apparition –
  My head unturned lest my dream should fade.

Begun 1913: finished 1916   1917

AFTERWARDS

When the Present has latched its postern† behind my tremulous stay,
    And the May month flaps its glad green leaves like wings,
Delicate-filmed as new-spun silk, will the neighbours say,
    'He was a man who used to notice such things'?

5   If it be in the dusk when, like an eyelid's soundless blink,
    The dewfall-hawk comes crossing the shades to alight
Upon the wind-warped upland thorn, a gazer may think,
    'To him this must have been a familiar sight.'

If I pass during some nocturnal blackness, mothy and warm,
10   When the hedgehog travels furtively over the lawn,
One may say, 'He strove that such innocent creatures should come to
      no harm,
    But he could do little for them; and now he is gone.'

If, when hearing that I have been stilled at last, they stand at the door,
    Watching the full-starred heavens that winter sees,
15   Will this thought rise on those who will meet my face no more,
    'He was one who had an eye for such mysteries'?

And will any say when my bell of quittance is heard in the gloom,
    And a crossing breeze cuts a pause in its outrollings,
Till they rise again, as they were a new bell's boom,
20   'He hears it not now, but used to notice such things'?

                                    1917

IF IT'S EVER SPRING AGAIN

(Song)

If it's ever spring again,
    Spring again,
I shall go where went I when
Down the moor-cock splashed, and hen,
5   Seeing me not, amid their flounder,

---

postern   back door or gate, here representing death

Standing with my arm around her;
If it's ever spring again,
        Spring again,
I shall go where went I then.

10   If it's ever summer-time,
        Summer-time,
With the hay crop at the prime,
And the cuckoos – two – in rhyme,
As they used to be, or seemed to,
15   We shall do as long we've dreamed to,
If it's ever summer-time,
        Summer-time,
With the hay, and bees achime.

1922

THE SUNDIAL ON A WET DAY

I drip, drip here
In Atlantic rain,
Falling like handfuls
Of winnowed grain,
5   Which, tear-like, down
My gnomon† drain,
And dim my numerals
With their stain, –
Till I feel useless,
10   And wrought in vain!

And then I think
In my despair
That, though unseen,
*He** is still up there,   the sun
15   And may gaze out
Anywhen, anywhere;
Not to help clockmen
Quiz and compare,

---

gnomon   the upright part of the dial

But in kindness to let me
20   My trade declare.

St Juliot†   1925

WHEN OATS WERE REAPED

That day when oats were reaped, and wheat was ripe, and barley
            ripening,
        The road-dust hot, and the bleaching grasses dry,
            I walked along and said,
While looking just ahead to where some silent people lie:

5   'I wounded one who's there, and now know well I wounded her;
        But, ah, she does not know that she wounded me!'
            And not an air stirred,
Nor a bill of any bird; and no response accorded she.

August 1913   1925

HE NEVER EXPECTED MUCH
[or]
[A Consideration†] on My Eighty-Sixth Birthday

Well, World, you have kept faith with me,
        Kept faith with me;
Upon the whole you have proved to be
        Much as you said you were.
5   Since as a child I used to lie
Upon the leaze and watch the sky,
Never, I own, expected I
        That life would all be fair.

'Twas then you said, and since have said,
10   Times since have said,
In that mysterious voice you shed

St Juliot Emma's family home in Cornwall   *Consideration* reflection

From clouds and hills around:
'Many have loved me desperately,
Many with smooth serenity,
15   While some have shown contempt of me
Till they dropped underground.

'I do not promise overmuch,
Child; overmuch;
Just neutral-tinted haps and such,'
20   You said to minds like mine.
Wise warning for your credit's sake!
Which I for one failed not to take,
And hence could stem such strain and ache
As each year might assign.

1923   1928

FAMILY PORTRAITS

Three picture-drawn people† stepped out of their frames –
The blast, how it blew!
And the white-shrouded candles flapped smoke-headed flames;
– Three picture-drawn people came down from their frames,
5   And dumbly in lippings they told me their names,
Full well though I knew.

The first was a maiden of mild wistful tone,
Gone silent for years,
The next a dark woman in former time known;
10   But the first one, the maiden of mild wistful tone,
So wondering, unpractised, so vague and alone,
Nigh moved me to tears.

The third was a sad man – a man of much gloom;
And before me they passed
15   In the shade of the night, at the back of the room,
The dark and fair woman, the man of much gloom,
Three persons, in far-off years forceful, but whom
Death now fettered fast.

---

people   Hardy seems to have had no particular   refer to his ancestors
people in mind, although line 24 appears to

They set about acting some drama, obscure,
20   The women and he,
With puppet-like movements of mute strange allure;
Yea, set about acting some drama, obscure,
Till I saw 'twas their own lifetime's tragic amour,
       Whose course begot me;

25   Yea – a mystery, ancestral, long hid from my reach
       In the perished years past,
That had mounted to dark doings each against each
In those ancestors' days, and long hid from my reach;
Which their restless enghostings, it seemed, were to teach
30   Me in full, at this last.

But fear fell upon me like frost, of some hurt
       If they entered anew
On the orbits they smartly had swept when expert
In the law-lacking passions of life, – of some hurt
35   To their souls – and thus mine – which I fain would avert;
       So, in sweat cold as dew,

'Why wake up all this?' I cried out. 'Now, so late!
       Let old ghosts be laid!'
And they stiffened, drew back to their frames and numb state,
40   Gibbering: 'Thus are your own ways to shape, know too late!'
Then I grieved that I'd not had the courage to wait
       And see the play played.

I have grieved ever since: to have balked future pain,
       My blood's tendance foreknown,
45   Had been triumph. Nights long stretched awake I have lain
Perplexed in endeavours to balk future pain
By uncovering the drift of their drama. In vain,
       Though therein lay my own.

                                              1928

Henry James
1843–1916

Henry James, son of the philosopher Henry James (1811–82) and brother of the philosopher and scientist William James (1842–1910), was born in New York. He was educated at private schools in Switzerland, France and England, and at Harvard College. In 1876, after many prolonged visits to Europe, he settled in England where – apart from travels – he lived for the rest of his life. He became a British subject in 1915 and was awarded the Order of Merit in 1916. In novels such as *The American* (1877), *The Europeans* (1878) and *Portrait of a Lady* (1881), James 'dramatised' (his term) encounters between Americans and Europeans, contrasting the moral integrity of Puritan New England and the appeal of the older, broader civilisation of upper-class society in Europe. His novels of the 1890s examine English characters and settings with scrupulous subtlety. In his novels and stories after 1900 he returned to his 'international theme', exploring, in very elaborate prose, relations between Americans and Europeans. In the Prefaces to the New York edition of his works (1907–) he expounded views on the theory and practice of fiction which were very influential. For many younger writers, notably Joseph Conrad and Ford Madox Ford, James was 'the master' – the most dedicated and artistically rigorous of novelists.

FORDHAM CASTLE

Sharp little Madame Massin, who carried on the pleasant pension and who had her small hard eyes everywhere at once, came out to him on the terrace and held up a letter addressed in a manner that he recognised even from afar, held it up with a question in her smile, or a smile,
5 rather a pointed one, in her question – he could scarce have said which. She was looking, while so occupied, at the German group engaged in the garden, near by, with aperitive beer and disputation – the noonday luncheon being now imminent; and the way in which she could show prompt lips while her observation searchingly ranged might have
10 reminded him of the object placed by a spectator at the theatre in the seat he desires to keep during the entr'acte. Conscious of the cross-

currents of international passion, she tried, so far as possible, not to
mix her sheep and her goats. The view of the bluest end of the Lake of
Geneva – she insisted in persuasive circulars that it *was* the bluest –
15 had never, on her high-perched terrace, wanted for admirers, though
thus early in the season, during the first days of May, they were not so
numerous as she was apt to see them at midsummer. This precisely,
Abel Taker could infer, was the reason of a remark she had made him
before the claims of the letter had been settled. 'I shall put you next the
20 American lady – the one who arrived yesterday. I know you'll be kind
to her; she had to go to bed, as soon as she got here, with a sick-
headache brought on by her journey. But she's better. Who isn't better
as soon as they get here? She's coming down, and I'm sure she'd like
to know you.'
25 Taker had now the letter in his hand – the letter intended for 'Mr
C. P. Addard'; which was not the name inscribed in the two or three
books he had left out in his room, any more than it matched the initials,
'A. F. T.' attached to the few pieces of his modest total of luggage.
Moreover, since Madame Massin's establishment counted, to his still
30 somewhat bewildered mind, so little for an hotel, as hotels were mainly
known to him, he had avoided the act of 'registering,' and the missive
with which his hostess was practically testing him represented the very
first piece of postal matter taken in since his arrival that hadn't been
destined to some one else. He had privately blushed for the meagreness
35 of his mail, which made him look unimportant. That however was a
detail, an appearance he was used to; indeed the reasons making for
such an appearance might never have been so pleasant to him as on
this vision of his identity formally and legibly denied. It was denied
there in his wife's large straight hand; his eyes, attached to the envelope,
40 took in the failure of any symptom of weakness in her stroke; she at
least had the courage of his passing for somebody he wasn't, of his
passing rather for nobody at all, and he felt the force of her character
more irresistibly than ever as he thus submitted to what she was doing
with him. He wasn't used to lying; whatever his faults – and he was
45 used, perfectly, to the idea of his faults – he hadn't made them worse
by any perverse theory, any tortuous plea, of innocence; so that
probably, with every inch of him giving him away, Madame Massin
didn't believe him a bit when he appropriated the letter. He was quite
aware he could have made no fight if she had challenged his right to it.
50 That would have come of his making no fight, nowadays, on any
ground, with any woman; he had so lost the proper spirit, the necessary
confidence. It was true that he had had to do for a long time with no
woman in the world but Sue, and of the practice of opposition so far
as Sue was concerned the end had been determined early in his career.
55 His hostess fortunately accepted his word, but the way in which her

momentary attention bored into his secret like the turn of a gimlet gave him a sense of the quantity of life that passed before her as a dealer with all comers – gave him almost an awe of her power of not wincing. She knew he wasn't, he couldn't be, C. P. Addard, even though she
60 mightn't know, or still less care, who he was; and there was therefore something queer about him if he pretended to be. That was what she didn't mind, there being something queer about him; and what was further present to him was that she would have known when to mind, when really to be on her guard. She attached no importance to his
65 trick; she had doubtless somewhere at the rear amid the responsive underlings with whom she was sometimes heard volubly, yet so obscurely, to chatter her clever French amusement about it. He couldn't at all events have said if the whole passage with her most brought home to him the falsity of his position or most glossed it over. On the whole
70 perhaps it rather helped him, since from this moment his masquerade had actively begun.

Taking his place for luncheon, in any case, he found himself next the American lady, as he conceived, spoken of by Madame Massin – in whose appearance he was at first as disappointed as if, a little, though
75 all unconsciously, he had been building on it. Had she loomed into view, on their hostess's hint, as one of the vague alternatives, the possible beguilements of his leisure – presenting herself solidly where so much else had refused to crystallise? It was certain at least that she presented herself solidly, being a large mild smooth person with a
80 distinct double chin, with grey hair arranged in small flat regular circles, figures of a geometrical perfection; with diamond earrings, with a long-handled eye-glass, with an accumulation of years and of weight and presence, in fine, beyond what his own rather melancholy consciousness acknowledged. He was forty-five, and it took every year of his life, took
85 all he hadn't done with them, to account for his present situation – since you couldn't be, conclusively, of so little use, of so scant an application, to any mortal career, above all to your own, unless you had been given up and cast aside after a long succession of experiments tried with you. But the American lady with the mathematical hair which
90 reminded him in a manner of the old-fashioned 'work,'[†] the weeping willows and mortuary urns represented by the little glazed-over flaxen or auburn or sable or silvered convolutions and tendrils, the capillary flowers, that he had admired in the days of his innocence – the American lady had probably seen her half-century; all the more that before
95 luncheon was done she had begun to strike him as having, like himself, slipped slowly down over its stretched and shiny surface, an expanse as insecure to fumbling feet as a great cold curved ice-field, into the

---

work   embroidery

comparatively warm hollow of resignation and obscurity. She gave him from the first – and he was afterwards to see why – an attaching impression of being, like himself, in exile, and of having like himself learned to butter her bread with a certain acceptance of fate. The only thing that puzzled him on this head was that to parallel his own case she would have had openly to consent to be shelved; which made the difficulty, here, that that was exactly what, as between wife and husband, remained unthinkable on the part of the wife. The necessity for the shelving of one or the other was a case that appeared often to arise, but this wasn't the way he had in general seen it settled. She made him in short, through some influence he couldn't immediately reduce to its elements, vaguely think of her as sacrificed – without blood, as it were; as obligingly and persuadedly passive. Yet this effect, a reflexion of his own state, would doubtless have been better produced for him by a mere melancholy man. She testified unmistakeably to the greater energy of women; for he could think of no manifestation of spirit on his own part that might pass for an equivalent, in the way of resistance, of protest, to the rhythmic though rather wiggy† water-waves that broke upon her bald-looking brow as upon a beach bared by a low tide. He had cocked up† often enough – and as with the intention of doing it still more under Sue's nose than under his own – the two ends of his half-'sandy' half-grizzled moustache, and he had in fact given these ornaments an extra twist just before coming in to luncheon. That however was but a momentary flourish; the most marked ferocity of which hadn't availed not to land him – well, where he was landed now.

His new friend mentioned that she had come up from Rome and that Madame Massin's establishment had been highly spoken of to her there, and this, slight as it was, straightway contributed in its degree for Abel Taker to the idea that they had something in common. He was in a condition in which he could feel the drift of vague currents, and he knew how highly the place had been spoken of to *him*. There was but a shade of difference in his having had his lesson in Florence. He let his companion know, without reserve, that he too had come up from Italy, after spending three or four months there: though he remembered in time that, being now C. P. Addard, it was only as C. P. Addard he could speak. He tried to think, in order to give himself something to say, what C. P. Addard would have done; but he was doomed to feel always, in the whole connexion, his lack of imagination. He had had many days to come to it and nothing else to do; but he hadn't even yet made up his mind who C. P. Addard was or invested him with any distinguishing marks. He felt like a man who, moving in this, that or the other direction, saw each successively lead him to some danger; so

wiggy crinkled like a wig   *cocked up* refers to waxed moustaches

140   that he began to ask himself why he shouldn't just lie outright, boldly
and inventively, and see what that could do for him. There was an
excitement, the excitement of personal risk, about it – much the same
as would belong for an ordinary man to the first trial of a flying-
machine; yet it was exactly such a course as Sue had prescribed on his
145   asking her what he should do. 'Anything in the world you like but talk
about *me*: think of some other woman, as bad and bold as you please,
and say you're married to *her*.' Those had been literally her words,
together with others, again and again repeated, on the subject of his
being free to 'kill and bury' her as often as he chose. This was the way
150   she had met his objection to his own death and interment; she had
asked him, in her bright hard triumphant way, why he couldn't defend
himself by shooting back. The real reason was of course that he was
nothing without her, whereas she was everything, could be anything in
the wide world she liked, without him. That question precisely had
155   been a part of what was before him while he strolled in the projected
green gloom of Madame Massin's plane-trees; he wondered what she
was choosing to be and how good a time it was helping her to have.
He could be sure she was rising to it, on some line or other, and that
was what secretly made him say: 'Why shouldn't I get something out
160   of it too, just for the harmless fun –?'
       It kept coming back to him, naturally, that he hadn't the breadth of
fancy, that he knew himself as he knew the taste of ill-made coffee, that
he was the same old Abel Taker he had ever been, in whose aggregation
of items it was as vain to feel about for latent heroisms as it was useless
165   to rummage one's trunk for presentable clothes that one didn't possess.
But did that absolve him (having so definitely Sue's permission) from
seeing to what extent he might temporarily make believe? If he were to
flap his wings very hard and crow very loud and take as long a jump
as possible at the same time – if he were to do all that perhaps he
170   should achieve for half a minute the sensation of soaring. He knew
only one thing Sue couldn't do, from the moment she didn't divorce
him: she couldn't get rid of his name, unaccountably, after all, as she
hated it; she couldn't get rid of it because she would have always sooner
or later to come back to it. She might consider that her being a thing
175   so dreadful as Mrs Abel Taker was a stumbling-block in her social path
that nothing but his real, his official, his advertised circulated demise
(with 'American papers please copy') would avail to dislodge: she would
have none the less to reckon with his continued existence as the drop
of bitterness in her cup that seasoned undisguiseably each draught. He
180   might make use of his present opportunity to row out into the lake
with his pockets full of stones and there quietly slip overboard; but he
could think of no shorter cut for her ceasing to be what her marriage
and the law of the land had made her. She was not an inch less Mrs

Abel Taker for these days of his sequestration, and the only thing she
185 indeed claimed was that the concealment of the source of her shame,
the suppression of the person who had divided with her his inherited
absurdity, made the difference of a shade or two for getting honourably,
as she called it, 'about.' How she had originally come to incur this
awful inconvenience – *that* part of the matter, left to herself, she would
190 undertake to keep vague; and she wasn't really left to herself so long
as he too flaunted the dreadful flag.

This was why she had provided him with another and placed him out
at board, to constitute, as it were, a permanent *alibi*; telling him she should
quarrel with no colours under which he might elect to sail, and promising
195 to take him back when she had got where she wanted. She wouldn't mind
so much then – she only wanted a fair start. It wasn't a fair start – *was* it?
she asked him frankly – so long as he was always there, so terribly cruelly
there, to speak of what she *had* been. She had been nothing worse, to his
sense, than a very pretty girl of eighteen out in Peoria,[†] who had seen at
200 that time no one else she wanted more to marry, nor even any one who
had been so supremely struck by her. That, absolutely, was the worst that
could be said of her. It was so bad at any rate in her own view – it had
grown so bad in the widening light of life – that it had fairly become more
than she could bear and that something, as she said, had to be done about
205 it. She hadn't known herself originally any more than she had known
him – hadn't foreseen how much better she was going to come out, nor
how, for her individually, as distinguished from him, there might be the
possibility of a big future. He couldn't be explained away – he cried out
with all his dreadful presence that she *had* been pleased to marry him;
210 and what they therefore had to do must transcend explaining. It was
perhaps now helping her, off there in London, and especially at Fordham
Castle – she was staying last at Fordham Castle, Wilts – it was perhaps
inspiring her even more than she had expected, that they were able to try
together this particular substitute: news of her progress in fact – her
215 progress on from Fordham Castle, if anything could be higher – would
not improbably be contained in the unopened letter he had lately pocketed.

There was a given moment at luncheon meanwhile, in his talk with
his countrywoman, when he did try that flap of the wing – did throw
off, for a flight into the blue, the first falsehood he could think of. 'I
220 stopped in Italy, you see, on my way back from the East, where I had
gone – to Constantinople' – he rose actually to Constantinople – 'to
visit Mrs Addard's grave.' And after they had all come out to coffee in
the rustling shade, with the vociferous German tribe at one end of the
terrace, the English family keeping silence with an English accent, as it

---

Peoria   a town in Illinois

225 struck him, in the middle, and his direction taken, by his new friend's
side, to the other unoccupied corner, he found himself oppressed with
what he had on his hands, the burden of keeping up this expensive
fiction. He had never been to Constantinople – it could easily be
proved against him; he ought to have thought of something better,
230 have got his effect on easier terms. Yet a funnier thing still than this
quick repentance was the quite equally fictive ground on which his
companion had affected him – when he came to think of it – as
meeting him.

'Why you know that's very much the same errand that took me to
235 Rome. I visited the grave of my daughter – whom I lost there some
time ago.'

She had turned her face to him after making this statement, looked
at him with an odd blink of her round kind plain eyes, as if to see how
he took it. He had taken it on the spot, for this was the only thing to
240 do; but he had felt how much deeper down he was himself sinking as
he replied: 'Ah it's a sad pleasure, isn't it? But those are places one
doesn't want to neglect.'

'Yes – that's what I feel. I go,' his neighbour had solemnly pursued,
'about every two years.'

245 With which she had looked away again, leaving him really not able
to emulate her. 'Well, I hadn't been before. You see it's a long way.'

'Yes – that's the trying part. It makes you feel you'd have done
better –'

'To bring them right home and have it done over there?' he had
250 asked as she let the sad subject go a little. He quite agreed. 'Yes – that's
what many do.'

'But it gives of course a peculiar interest.' So they had kept it up. 'I
mean in places that mightn't have so *very* much.'

'Places like Rome and Constantinople?' he had rejoined while he
255 noticed the cautious anxious sound of her 'very.' The tone was to
come back to him, and it had already made him feel sorry for her, with
its suggestion of her being at sea like himself. Unmistakeably, poor
lady, she too was trying to float – was striking out in timid convulsive
movements. Well, he wouldn't make it difficult for her, and
260 immediately, so as not to appear to cast any ridicule, he observed that,
wherever great bereavements might have occurred, there was no place
so remarkable as not to gain an association. Such memories made at
the least another object for coming. It was after this recognition, on
either side, that they adjourned to the garden – Taker having in his
265 ears again the good lady's rather troubled or muddled echo: 'Oh yes,
when you come to all the *objects* – !' The grave of one's wife or one's
daughter was an object quite as much as all those that one looked up

in Baedeker[†] – those of the family of the Castle of Chillon[†] and the
Dent du Midi,[†] features of the view to be enjoyed from different parts
270   of Madame Massin's premises. It was very soon, none the less, rather
as if these latter presences, diffusing their reality and majesty, had
taken the colour out of all other evoked romance; and to that degree
that when Abel's fellow guest happened to lay down on the parapet of
the terrace three or four articles she had brought out with her, her fan,
275   a couple of American newspapers and a letter that had obviously come
to her by the same post as his own, he availed himself of the accident
to jump at a further conclusion. Their coffee, which was 'extra,' as he
knew and as, in the way of benevolence, he boldly warned her, was
brought forth to them, and while she was giving her attention to her
280   demi-tasse he let his eyes rest for three seconds on the superscription of
her letter. His mind was by this time made up, and the beauty of it was
that he couldn't have said why: the letter was from her daughter,
whom she had been burying for him in Rome, and it would be
addressed in a name that was really no more hers than the name his
285   wife had thrust upon him was his. Her daughter had put *her* out at
cheap board, pending higher issues, just as Sue had put him – so that
there was a logic not other than fine in his notifying her of what coffee
every day might let her in for. She was addressed on her envelope as
'Mrs Vanderplank,' but he had privately arrived, before she so much
290   as put down her cup, at the conviction that this was a borrowed and
lawless title, for all the world as if, poor dear innocent woman, she
were a bold bad adventuress. He had acquired furthermore the moral
certitude that he was on the track, as he would have said, of her true
identity, such as it might be. He couldn't think of it as in itself either
295   very mysterious or very impressive; but, whatever it was, her duplicity
had as yet mastered no finer art than his own, inasmuch as she had
positively not escaped, at table, inadvertently dropping a name which,
while it lingered on Abel's ear, gave her quite away. She had spoken,
in her solemn sociability and as by the force of old habit, of 'Mr
300   Magaw,' and nothing was more to be presumed than that this
gentleman was her defunct husband, not so very long defunct, who
had permitted her while in life the privilege of association with him,
but whose extinction had left her to be worked upon by different
ideas.
305   These ideas would have germed, infallibly, in the brain of the young
woman, her only child, under whose rigid rule she now – it was to be
detected – drew her breath in pain. Madame Massin would abysmally

Baedeker   Karl Baedeker (1801–59) founded a
very successful series of guide books
Castle of Chillon   on Lake Geneva. Byron's
poem 'The Prisoner of Chillon' (1816) made
the castle famous
Dent du Midi   Swiss mountain group

know, Abel reflected, for he was at the end of a few minutes more
intimately satisfied that Mrs Magaw's American newspapers, coming
310 to her straight from the other side and not yet detached from their
wrappers, would not be directed to Mrs Vanderplank, and that, this
being the case, the poor lady would have had to invent some pretext
for a claim to goods likely still perhaps to be lawfully called for. And
she wasn't formed for duplicity, the large simple scared foolish fond
315 woman, the vague anxiety in whose otherwise so uninhabited and
unreclaimed countenance, as void of all history as an expanse of Western
prairie seen from a car-window, testified to her scant aptitude for her
part. He was far from the desire to question their hostess, however –
for the study of his companion's face on its mere inferred merits had
320 begun to dawn upon him as the possible resource of his ridiculous
leisure. He might verily have some fun with her – or he would so have
conceived it had he not become aware before they separated, half an
hour later, of a kind of fellow-feeling for her that seemed to plead for
her being spared. She *wasn't* being, in some quarter still indistinct to
325 him – and so no more was he, and these things were precisely a reason.
Her sacrifice, he divined, was an act of devotion, a state not yet
disciplined to the state of confidence. She had presently, as from a
return of vigilance, gathered in her postal property, shuffling it together
at her further side and covering it with her pocket-handkerchief –
330 though this very betrayal indeed but quickened his temporary impulse
to break out to her, sympathetically, with a 'Had you the misfortune
to *lose* Magaw?' or with the effective production of his own card and
a smiling, an inviting, a consoling 'That's who *I* am if you want to
know!' He really made out, with the idle human instinct, the crude
335 sense for other people's pains and pleasures that had, on his showing,
to his so great humiliation, been found an inadequate outfit for the
successful conduct of the coal, the commission, the insurance and, as a
last resort, desperate and disgraceful, the book-agency business – he
really made out that she didn't want to know, or wouldn't for some
340 little time; that she was decidedly afraid in short, and covertly agitated,
and all just because she too, with him, suspected herself dimly in
presence of that mysterious 'more' than, in the classic phrase, met the
eye. They parted accordingly, as if to relieve, till they could recover
themselves, the conscious tension of their being able neither to hang
345 back with grace nor to advance with glory; but flagrantly full, at the
same time, both of the recognition that they couldn't in such a place
avoid each other even if they had desired it, and of the suggestion that
they wouldn't desire it, after such subtlety of communion, even were it
to be thought of.
350 Abel Taker, till dinner-time, turned over his little adventure and
extracted, while he hovered and smoked and mused, some refreshment

from the impression the subtlety of communion had left with him. Mrs
Vanderplank was his senior by several years, and was neither fair nor
slim nor 'bright' nor truly, nor even falsely, elegant, nor anything that
Sue had taught him, in her wonderful way, to associate with the
American woman at the American woman's best – that best than which
there was nothing better, as he had so often heard her say, on God's
great earth. Sue would have banished her to the wildest waste of the
unknowable, would have looked over her head in the manner he had
often seen her use – as if she were in an exhibition of pictures, were in
front of something bad and negligible that had got itself placed on the
line, but that had the real thing, the thing of interest for those who
knew (and when didn't Sue know?) hung above it. In Mrs Magaw's
presence everything would have been of more interest to Sue than Mrs
Magaw; but that consciousness failed to prevent his feeling the appeal
of this inmate much rather confirmed than weakened when she
reappeared for dinner. It was impressed upon him, after they had again
seated themselves side by side, that she was reaching out to him
indirectly, guardedly, even as he was to her; so that later on, in the
garden, where they once more had their coffee together – it *might* have
been so free and easy, so wildly foreign, so almost Bohemian – he lost
all doubt of the wisdom of his taking his plunge. This act of resolution
was not, like the other he had risked in the morning, an upward flutter
into fiction, but a straight and possibly dangerous dive into the very
depths of truth. Their instinct was unmistakeably to cling to each other,
but it was as if they wouldn't know where to take hold till the air had
really been cleared. Actually, in fact, they required a light – the aid
prepared by him in the shape of a fresh match for his cigarette after he
had extracted, under cover of the scented dusk, one of his cards from
his pocket-book.

'There I honestly am, you see – Abel F. Taker; which I think you
ought to know.' It was relevant to nothing, relevant only to the grope
of their talk, broken with sudden silences where they stopped short for
fear of mistakes; but as he put the card before her he held out to it the
little momentary flame. And this was the way that, after a while and
from one thing to another, he himself, in exchange for what he had to
give and what he gave freely, heard all about 'Mattie' – Mattie Magaw,
Mrs Vanderplank's beautiful and high-spirited daughter, who, as he
learned, found her two names, so dreadful even singly, a combination
not to be borne, and carried on a quarrel with them no less desperate
than Sue's quarrel with – well, with everything. She had, quite as Sue
had done, declared her need of a free hand to fight them, and she was,
for all the world like Sue again, now fighting them to the death. This
similarity of situation was wondrously completed by the fact that the
scene of Miss Magaw's struggle was, as her mother explained, none

other than that uppermost walk of 'high' English life which formed the
present field of Mrs Taker's operations; a circumstance on which Abel
presently produced his comment. 'Why if they're after the same thing
in the same place, I wonder if we shan't hear of their meeting.'

400   Mrs Magaw appeared for a moment to wonder too. 'Well, if they do
meet I guess we'll hear. I will say for Mattie that she writes me pretty
fully. And I presume,' she went on, 'Mrs Taker keeps *you* posted?'

'No,' he had to confess – 'I don't hear from her in much detail. She
knows I back her,' Abel smiled 'and that's enough for her. 'You be
405   quiet and I'll let you know when you're wanted' – that's her motto;
I'm to wait, wherever I am, till I'm called for. But I guess she won't be
in a hurry to call for me' – this reflexion he showed he was familiar
with. 'I've stood in her light so long – her "social" light, outside of
which everything is for Sue black darkness – that I don't really see the
410   reason she should ever want me back. That at any rate is what I'm
doing – I'm just waiting. And I didn't expect the luck of being able to
wait in your company. I couldn't suppose – that's the truth,' he added –
'that there was another, anywhere about, with the same ideas or the
same strong character. It had never seemed to be possible,' he ruminated
415   'that there could be any one like Mrs Taker.'

He was to remember afterwards how his companion had appeared
to consider this approximation. 'Another, you mean, like my Mattie?'

'Yes – like my Sue. Any one that really comes up to her. It will be,'
he declared, 'the first one I've struck.'

420   'Well,' said Mrs Vanderplank, 'my Mattie's remarkably handsome.'

'I'm sure – ! But Mrs Taker's remarkably handsome too. Oh,' he
added, both with humour and with earnestness, 'if it wasn't for that I
wouldn't trust her so! Because, for what she wants,' he developed, 'it's
a great help to be fine-looking.'

425   'Ah it's always a help for a lady!' – and Mrs Magaw's sigh fluttered
vaguely between the expert and the rueful. 'But what is it,' she asked,
'that Mrs Taker wants?'

'Well, she could tell you herself. I don't think she'd trust me to give
an account of it. Still,' he went on, 'she *has* stated it more than once
430   for my benefit, and perhaps that's what it all finally comes to. She wants
to get where she truly belongs.'

Mrs Magaw had listened with interest. 'That's just where Mattie
wants to get! And she seems to know just where it is.'

'Oh Mrs Taker knows – you can bet your life,' he laughed, 'on that.
435   It seems to be somewhere in London or in the country round, and I
dare say it's the same place as your daughter's. Once she's there, as I
understand it, she'll be all right; but she has got to get there – that is to
be seen there thoroughly fixed and photographed, and have it in all the
papers – first. After she's fixed, she says, we'll talk. We *have* talked a

440   good deal: when Mrs Taker says "We'll talk" I know what she means.
But this time we'll have it out.'
There were communities in their fate that made his friend turn pale.
'Do you mean she won't want you to come?'
'Well, for me to "come," don't you see? will be for me to come to
445   life. How can I come to life when I've been as dead as I am now?'
Mrs Vanderplank looked at him with a dim delicacy. 'But surely, sir,
I'm not conversing with the remains – !'
'You're conversing with C. P. Addard. *He* may be alive – but even
this I don't know yet; I'm just trying him,' he said: 'I'm trying him,
450   Mrs Magaw, on you. Abel Taker's in his grave, but does it strike you
that Mr Addard is at all above ground?'
He had smiled for the slightly gruesome joke of it, but she looked
away as if it made her uneasy. Then, however, as she came back to
him, 'Are you going to wait here?' she asked.
455   He held her, with some gallantry, in suspense. 'Are you?'
She postponed her answer, visibly not quite comfortable now; but
they were inevitably the next day up to their necks again in the question;
and then it was that she expressed more of her sense of her situation.
'Certainly I feel as if I must wait – as long as I *have* to wait. Mattie
460   likes this place – I mean she likes it for *me*. It seems the right *sort* of
place,' she opined with her perpetual earnest emphasis.
But it made him sound again the note. 'The right sort to pass for
dead in?'
'Oh she doesn't want me to pass for *dead*.'
465   'Then what does she want you to pass for?'
The poor lady cast about. 'Well, only for Mrs Vanderplank?'
'And who or what is Mrs Vanderplank?'
Mrs Magaw considered this personage, but didn't get far. 'She isn't
any one in particular, I guess.'
470   'That means,' Abel returned, 'that she isn't alive.'
'She isn't more than *half* alive,' Mrs Magaw conceded. 'But it isn't
what I *am* – it's what I'm passing for. Or rather' – she worked it out –
'what I'm just not. I'm not passing – I don't, can't here, where it doesn't
matter, you see – for her mother.'
475   Abel quite fell in. 'Certainly – she doesn't want to have any mother.'
'She doesn't want to have *me*. She wants me to lay low. If I lay low,
she says –'
'Oh I know what she says' – Abel took it straight up. 'It's the very
same as what Mrs Taker says. If you lie low she can fly high.'
480   It kept disconcerting her in a manner, as well as steadying, his free
possession of their case. 'I don't feel as if I *was* lying – I mean as low
as she wants – when I talk to you so.' She broke it off thus, and again
and again, anxiously, responsibly; her sense of responsibility making

Taker feel, with his braver projection of humour, quite ironic and
485   sardonic; but as for a week, for a fortnight, for many days more, they
kept frequently and intimately meeting, it was natural that the so
extraordinary fact of their being, as he put it, in the same sort of box,
and of their boxes having so even more remarkably bumped together
under Madame Massin's *tilleuls* [limetrees], shouldn't only make them
490   reach out to each other across their queer coil of communications, cut
so sharp off in other quarters, but should prevent their pretending to
any real consciousness but that of their ordeal. It was Abel's idea,
promptly enough expressed to Mrs Magaw, that they ought to get
something out of it; but when he had said that a few times over (the
495   first time she had met it in silence), she finally replied, and in a manner
that he thought quite sublime: 'Well, we *shall* – if they do all they want.
We shall feel we've helped. And it isn't so *very* much to do.'
       'You think it isn't so very much to do – to lie down and die for
them?'
500   'Well, if I don't hate it any worse when I'm really dead – !' She took
herself up, however as if she had skirted the profane. 'I don't say that
if I didn't *believe* in Mat – ! But I do believe, you see. That's where she
has me.'
       'Oh I see more or less. That's where Sue has *me*.'
505   Mrs Magaw fixed him with a milder solemnity. 'But what has Mrs
Taker against you?'
       'It's sweet of you to ask,' he smiled; while it really came to him that
he was living with her under ever so much less strain than what he had
been feeling for ever so long before from Sue. Wouldn't he have liked
510   it to go on and on – wouldn't that have suited C. P. Addard? He seemed
to be finding out who C. P. Addard was – so that it came back again
to the way Sue fixed things. She had fixed them so that C. P. Addard
could become quite interested in Mrs Vanderplank and quite soothed
by her – and so that Mrs Vanderplank as well, wonderful to say, had
515   lost her impatience for Mattie's summons a good deal more, he was
sure, than she confessed. It was from this moment none the less that he
began, with a strange but distinct little pang, to see that he couldn't be
sure of her. Her question had produced in him a vibration of the
sensibility that even the long series of mortifications, of publicly proved
520   inaptitudes, springing originally from his lack of business talent, but
owing an aggravation of aspect to an absence of nameable 'type' of
which he hadn't been left unaware, wasn't to have wholly toughened.
Yet it struck him positively as the prettiest word ever spoken to him,
so straight a surprise at his wife's dissatisfaction; and he was verily so
525   unused to tributes to his adequacy that this one lingered in the air a
moment and seemed almost to create a possibility. He wondered,
honestly, what she could see in him, in whom Sue now at last saw

really less than nothing; and his fingers instinctively moved to his
moustache, a corner of which he twiddled up again, also wondering if
530   it were perhaps only *that* – though Sue had as good as told him that
the undue flourish of this feature but brought out to her view the
insignificance of all the rest of him. Just to hang in the iridescent ether
with Mrs Vanderplank, to whom he wasn't insignificant, just for them
to sit on there together, protected indeed positively ennobled, by their
535   loss of identity, struck him as the foretaste of a kind of felicity that he
hadn't in the past known enough about really to miss it. He appeared
to have become aware that he should miss it quite sharply, that he
would find how he had already learned to, if she should go; and the
very sadness of his apprehension quickened his vision of what would
540   work with her. She would want, with all the roundness of her kind,
plain eyes, to see Mattie fixed – whereas he'd be hanged if he wasn't
willing, on his side, to take Sue's elevation quite on trust. For the
instant, however, he said nothing of that; he only followed up a little
his acknowledgement of her having touched him. 'What you ask me,
545   you know, is just what I myself was going to ask. What has Miss
Magaw got against *you?*'
'Well, if you were to see her I guess you'd know.'
'Why I should think she'd like to show you,' said Abel Taker.
'She doesn't so much mind their *seeing* me – when once she has had
550   a look at me first. But she doesn't like them to hear me – though I don't
talk so very much. Mattie speaks in the real English style,' Mrs Magaw
explained.
'But ain't the real English style not to speak at all?'
'Well, she's having the best kind of time, she writes me – so I presume
555   there must be some talk in which she can shine.'
'Oh I've no doubt at all Miss Magaw *talks!*' – and Abel, in his
contemplative way, seemed to have it before him.
'Well, don't you go and believe she talks too much,' his companion
rejoined with spirit; and this it was that brought to a head his prevision
560   of his own fate.
'I see what's going to happen. You only want to go to her. You want
to get your share, after all. You'll leave me without a pang.'
Mrs Magaw stared. 'But won't you be going too? When Mrs Taker
sends for you?'
565   He shook, as by a rare chance, a competent head. 'Mrs Taker won't
send for me. I don't make out the use Mrs Taker can ever have for me
again.'
Mrs Magaw looked grave. 'But not to enjoy your seeing – ?'
'My seeing where she has come out? Oh that won't be necessary to
570   *her* enjoyment of it. It would be well enough perhaps if I could see
without being seen; but the trouble with me – for I'm worse than you,'

Abel said – 'is that it doesn't do for me either to be heard *or* seen. I haven't got *any* side – !' But it dropped; it was too old a story.

'Not any possible side at all?' his friend, in her candour, doubtingly
575   echoed. 'Why what do they want over there?'

It made him give a comic pathetic wail. 'Ah to know a person who says such things as that to me, and to have to give her up – !'

She appeared to consider with a certain alarm what this might portend, and she really fell back before it. 'Would you think I'd be able
580   to give up Mattie?'

'Why not – if she's successful? The thing you wouldn't like – *you* wouldn't, I'm sure – would be to give her up if she should find, or if you should find, she wasn't.'

'Well, I guess Mattie will be successful,' said Mrs Magaw.
585   'Ah you're a worshipper of success!' he groaned. 'I'd give Mrs Taker up, definitely, just to remain C. P. Addard with you.'

She allowed it her thought; but, as he felt, superficially. 'She's your wife, sir, you know, whatever you do.'

' "Mine" ? Ah but whose? She isn't C. P. Addard's.'
590   She rose at this as if they were going too far; yet she showed him, he seemed to see, the first little concession – which was indeed to be the only one – of her inner timidity; something that suggested how she must have preserved as a token, laid away among spotless properties, the visiting-card he had originally handed her. 'Well, I guess the one I
595   feel for is Abel F. Taker!'

This, in the end, however, made no difference; since one of the things that inevitably came up between them was that if Mattie had a quarrel with her name her most workable idea would be to get somebody to give her a better. That, he easily made out, was fundamentally what
600   she was after, and, though, delicately and discreetly, as he felt, he didn't reduce Mrs Vanderplank to so stating the case he finally found himself believing in Miss Magaw with just as few reserves as those with which he believed in Sue. If it was a question of her 'shining' she would indubitably shine; she was evidently, like the wife by whom he had
605   been, in the early time, too provincially, too primitively accepted, of the great radiating substance, and there were times, here at Madame Massin's, while he strolled to and fro and smoked, when Mrs Taker's distant lustre fairly peeped at him over the opposite mountaintops, fringing their silhouettes as with the little hard bright rim of a coming
610   day. It was clear that Mattie's mother couldn't be expected not to want to see her married; the shade of doubt bore only on the stage of the business at which Mrs Magaw might safely be let out of the box. Was she to emerge abruptly *as* Mrs Magaw? – or was the lid simply to be tipped back so that, for a good look, she might sit up a little straighter?
615   She had got news at any rate, he inferred, which suggested to her that

the term of her suppression was in sight; and she even let it out to him that, yes, certainly, for Mattie to be ready for her – and she did look as if she were going to be ready – she must be right down sure. They had had further lights by this time moreover, lights much more vivid always in Mattie's bulletins than in Sue's; which latter, as Abel insistently imaged it, were really each time, on Mrs Taker's part, as limited as a peep into a death-chamber. The death-chamber was Madame Massin's terrace; and – he completed the image – how could Sue *not* want to know how things were looking for the funeral, which was in any case to be thoroughly 'quiet'? *The* vivid thing seemed to pass before Abel's eyes the day he heard of the bright compatriot, just the person to go round with, a charming handsome witty widow, whom Miss Magaw had met at Fordham Castle, whose ideas were, on all important points, just the same as her own, whose means also (so that they could join forces on an equality) matched beautifully, and whose name in fine was Mrs Sherrington Reeve. 'Mattie has felt the want,' Mrs Magaw explained, 'of some lady, some real lady like that, to go round with: she says she sometimes doesn't find it very pleasant going round alone.'

Abel Taker had listened with interest – this information left him staring. 'By Gosh then, she has struck Sue!'

' "Struck" Mrs Taker – ?'

'She isn't Mrs Taker now – she's Mrs Sherrington Reeve.' It had come to him with all its force – as if the glare of her genius were at a bound, high over the summits. 'Mrs Taker's dead: I thought, you know, all the while, she must be, and this makes me sure. She died at Fordham Castle. So we're both dead.'

His friend, however, with her large blank face, lagged behind. 'At Fordham Castle too – died there!'

'Why she has been as good as *living* there!' Abel Taker emphasised. ' "Address Fordham Castle" - that's about all she has written me. But perhaps she died before she went' – he had it before him, he made it out. 'Yes, she must have gone as Mrs Sherrington Reeve. She had to die to go – as it would be for her like going to heaven. Marriages, sometimes, they say, are made up there; and so, sometimes then, apparently, are friendships – that, you see for instance, of our two shining ones.'

Mrs Magaw's understanding was still in the shade. 'But are you sure – ?'

'Why Fordham Castle settles it. If she wanted to get where she truly belongs she has got *there*. She belongs at Fordham Castle.'

The noble mass of this structure seemed to rise at his words, and his companion's grave eyes, he could see, to rest on its towers. 'But how has she become Mrs Sherrington Reeve?'

'By my death. And also after that by her own. I had to die first, you

660   see, for *her* to be able to – that is for her to be sure. It's what she has
been looking for, as I told you – to *be* sure. But oh – she was sure from
the first. She knew I'd die off, when she had made it all right for me –
so she felt no risk. She simply became, the day I became C. P. Addard,
something as different as possible from the thing she had always so
665   hated to be. She's what she always would have liked to be – so why
shouldn't we rejoice for her? Her baser part, her vulgar part, has ceased
to be, and she lives only as an angel.' It affected his friend, this
elucidation, almost with awe; she took it at least, as she took everything,
stolidly. 'Do you call Mrs Taker an angel?'
670   Abel had turned about, as he rose to the high vision, moving, with
his hands in his pockets, to and fro. But at Mrs Magaw's question he
stopped short – he considered with his head in the air. 'Yes – now!'
'But do you mean it's her idea to marry?'
He thought again. 'Why for all I know she is married.'
675   'With you, Abel Taker, living?'
'But I ain't living. That's just the point.'
'Oh you're too dreadful' – and she gathered herself up. 'And I won't,'
she said as she broke off, 'help to bury you!'
This office, none the less, as she practically had herself to acknowledge,
680   was in a manner, and before many days, forced upon her by further
important information from her daughter, in the light of the true
inevitability of which they had, for that matter, been living. She was
there before him with her telegram, which she simply held out to him
as from a heart too full for words. 'Am engaged to Lord Dunderton,
685   and Sue thinks you can come.'
Deep emotion sometimes confounds the mind – and Mrs Magaw
quite flamed with excitement. But on the other hand it sometimes
illumines, and she could see, it appeared, what Sue meant. 'It's because
he's so much in love.'
690   'So far gone that she's safe?' Abel frankly asked.
'So far gone that she's safe?'
'Well,' he said, 'if Sue feels it – !' He had so much, he showed, to go
by. 'Sue *knows*.'
Mrs Magaw visibly yearned, but she could look at all sides. 'I'm
695   bound to say, since you speak of it, that I've an idea Sue has helped.
She'll like to have her there.'
'Mattie will like to have Sue?'
'No, Sue will like to have Mattie.' Elation raised to such a point was
in fact already so clarifying that Mrs Magaw could come all the way.
700   'As Lady Dunderton.'
'Well,' Abel smiled, 'one good turn deserves another!' If he meant it,
however, in any such sense as that Mattie might be able in due course
to render an equivalent of aid, this notion clearly had to reckon with

his companion's sense of its strangeness, exhibited in her now at last
705 upheaved countenance. 'Yes,' he accordingly insisted, 'it will work
round to that – you see if it doesn't. If that's where they were to come
out, and they *have* come – by which I mean if Sue has realised it for
Mattie and acted as she acts when she does realise, then she can't
neglect it in her own case: she'll just *have* to realise it for herself. And,
710 for that matter, you'll help her too. You'll be able to tell her, you know,
that you've seen the last of me.' And on the morrow, when, starting
for London, she had taken her place in the train, to which he had
accompanied her, he stood by the door of her compartment and repeated
this idea. 'Remember, for Mrs Taker, that you've seen the last – !'
715   'Oh but I hope I haven't, sir.'
'Then you'll come back to me? If you only will, you know, Sue will
be delighted to fix it.'
'To fix it – how?'
'Well, she'll tell you how. You've seen how she can fix things, and
720 that will be the way, as I say, you'll help her.'
She stared at him from her corner, and he could see she was sorry
for him; but it was as if she had taken refuge behind her large high-
shouldered reticule, which she held in her lap, presenting it almost as a
bulwark. 'Mr Taker,' she launched at him over it, 'I'm afraid of you.'
725   'Because I'm dead?'
'Oh sir!' she pleaded, hugging her morocco defence. But even through
this alarm her finer thought came out. 'Do you suppose I shall go to
Fordham Castle?'
'Well, I guess that's what they're discussing now. You'll know soon
730 enough.'
'If I write you from there,' she asked, 'won't you come?'
'I'll come as the ghost. Don't old castles always have one?'
She looked at him darkly; the train had begun to move. 'I *shall* fear
you!' she said.
735   'Then there you are.' And he moved an instant beside the door.
'You'll be glad, when you get there, to be able to say – ' But she got
out of hearing, and, turning away, he felt as abandoned as he had
known he should – felt left, in his solitude, to the sense of his extinction.
He faced it completely now, and to himself at least could express it
740 without fear of protest. 'Why certainly I'm dead.'

1904   1905

George Bernard Shaw
1856–1950

George Bernard Shaw was born in Dublin where he attended Wesley College, a day-school, until he was fifteen; he moved to London in 1876. He worked as a journalist, reviewing art, music and plays, and became a public speaker, a well-known wit and a polemicist for the Fabians. His first play, *Widowers' Houses*, was performed in 1892; his seventh, *John Bull's Other Island*, was his first London success, in 1907. He wrote more than fifty plays. *Major Barbara*, first performed in London in 1905, *Androcles and the Lion*, in Hamburg in 1913, *Pygmalion*, in Vienna in 1913, *Heartbreak House*, in New York in 1920, *Saint Joan*, in New York in 1923, and *The Apple Cart*, in Warsaw in 1929, are among the best. The following scene from *Major Barbara*, which presents a conflict between the spiritual faith of Barbara, a Major in the Salvation Army, and the secular shrewdness of her millionaire father, shows Shaw's ability to dramatise ideas with theatrical flair and liveliness; he had little interest in character. He published his plays with long explanatory prefaces. *Collected Plays, with their Prefaces* was issued in seven volumes between 1970 and 1974.

From MAJOR BARBARA
[Proper Names]

BARBARA UNDERSHAFT. Oh, there you are, Mr Shirley! [*Between them*] This is my father: I told you he was a Secularist,[†] didnt I? Perhaps youll[†] be able to comfort one another.

　　ANDREW UNDERSHAFT. [*startled*] A Secularist! Not the least in the world: on the contrary, a confirmed mystic.

5

　　BARBARA. Sorry, I'm sure. By the way, papa, what is your religion? in case I have to introduce you again.

Secularist G. J. Holyoake advocated a 'Secularist' system of social ethics independent of religion

youll Shaw, a spelling-reformer, thought such forms as *you'll* irrational

UNDERSHAFT. My religion? Well, my dear, I am a Millionaire. That is my religion.

10   BARBARA. Then I'm afraid you and Mr Shirley wont be able to comfort one another after all. Youre not a Millionaire, are you, Peter?

PETER SHIRLEY. No; and proud of it.

UNDERSHAFT [*gravely*] Poverty, my friend, is not a thing to be proud of.

15   SHIRLEY [*angrily*] Who made your millions for you? Me and my like. Whats kep us poor? Keepin you rich. I wouldnt have your conscience, not for all your income.

UNDERSHAFT. I wouldnt have your income, not for all your conscience, Mr Shirley. [*He goes to the penthouse*[†] *and sits down on a form*].

20   BARBARA [*stopping Shirley adroitly as he is about to retort*] You wouldnt think he was my father, would you, Peter? Will you go into the shelter and lend the lasses a hand for a while: we're worked off our feet.

SHIRLEY [*bitterly*] Yes: I'm in their debt for a meal, aint I?

25   BARBARA. Oh, not because youre in their debt, but for love of them, Peter, for love of them. [*He cannot understand, and is rather scandalized*] There! dont start at me. In with you; and give that conscience of yours a holiday [*bustling him into the shelter*].

SHIRLEY [*as he goes in*] Ah! it's a pity you never was trained to use
30   your reason, miss. Youd have been a very taking lecturer on Secularism.

Barbara turns to her father.

UNDERSHAFT. Never mind me, my dear. Go about your work; and let me watch it for a while.

BARBARA. All right.

UNDERSHAFT. For instance, whats the matter with that out-patient over
35   there?

BARBARA [*looking at Bill, whose attitude has never changed, and whose expression of brooding wrath has deepened*] Oh, we shall cure him in no time. Just watch. [*She goes over to Bill and waits. He glances up at her and casts his eyes down again, uneasy, but grimmer than ever*]. It
40   would be nice to just stamp on Mog Habbijam's face, wouldnt it, Bill?

BILL WALKER. [*starting up from the trough in consternation*] It's a loy:[†] Aw never said so. [*She shakes her head*]. Oo taold you wot was in moy mawnd?[†]

BARBARA. Only your new friend.

45   BILL. Wot new friend?

BARBARA. The devil, Bill. When he gets round people they get miserable, just like you.

---

penthouse   a shed or lean-to   *Oo taold . . . mawnd*   Who told you what was
loy   lie. The spelling indicates London dialect   in my mind?

BILL [*with a heartbreaking attempt at devil-may-care cheerfulness*] Aw
aint† miserable. [*He sits down again, and stretches his legs in an attempt
to seem indifferent*].

BARBARA. Well, if youre happy, why dont you look happy, as we do?

BILL [*his legs curling back in spite of him*] Aw'm eppy enaff, Aw tell
you. Woy cawnt you lea me alown? Wot ev I dan to you? Aw aint
smashed your fice, ev Aw?†

BARBARA [*softly: wooing his soul*] It's not me thats getting at you, Bill.

BILL. Oo† else is it?

BARBARA. Somebody that doesnt intend you to smash women's faces,
I suppose. Somebody or something that wants to make a man of you.

BILL [*blustering*] Mike a menn† o me! Aint Aw a menn? eh? Oo sez
Aw'm not a menn?

BARBARA. Theres a man in you somewhere, I suppose. But why did he
let you hit poor little Jenny Hill? That wasnt very manly of him, was
it?

BILL [*tormented*] Ev dan wiv it, Aw tell you. Chack it.† Aw'm sick o
your Jenny Ill and er silly little fice.

BARBARA. Then why do you keep thinking about it? Why does it keep
coming up against you in your mind? Youre not getting converted, are
you?

BILL [*with conviction*] Not ME. Not lawkly.†

BARBARA. Thats right, Bill. Hold out against it. Put out your strength.
Dont lets get you cheap. Todger Fairmile said he wrestled for three
nights against his salvation harder than he ever wrestled with the Jap
at the music hall. He gave in to the Jap when his arm was going to
break. But he didnt give in to his salvation until his heart was going to
break. Perhaps youll escape that. You havnt any heart, have you?

BILL. Wot d'ye mean? Woy† aint Aw got a awt the sime as ennybody
else?†

BARBARA. A man with a heart wouldnt have bashed poor little Jenny's
face, would he?

BILL [*almost crying*] Ow, will you lea me alown? Ev Aw ever offered
to meddle with you, that you cam neggin† and provowkin me lawk
this? [*He writhes convulsively from his eyes to his toes*].

BARBARA [*with a steady soothing hand on his arm and a gentle voice
that never lets him go*] It's your soul thats hurting you, Bill, and not
me. Weve been through it all ourselves. Come with us, Bill [*He looks*

Aw aint I'm not
Aw'm eppy . . . Aw I'm happy enough, I tell
 you. Why can't you leave me alone? I haven't
 smashed your face, have I?
Oo Who
Mike a menn Make a man

Ev dan . . . it Have done with it, I tell you.
 Chuck it
lawkly likely
Woy . . . else Why haven't I got a heart the
 same as anybody else?
neggin nagging

wildly round]. To brave manhood on earth and eternal glory in heaven.
[*He is on the point of breaking down*]. Come. [*A drum is heard in the
shelter; and Bill, with a gasp, escapes from the spell as Barbara turns
quickly. Adolphus enters from the shelter with a big drum*]. Oh! there
90 you are, Dolly. Let me introduce a new friend of mine, Mr Bill Walker.
This is my bloke, Bill: Mr Cusins. [*Cusins salutes with his drumstick*].

BILL. Gowin to merry[†] im?

BARBARA. Yes.

BILL [*fervently*] Gawd elp im! Gaw-aw-aw-awd elp im!

95 BARBARA. Why? Do you think he wont be happy with me?

BILL. Awve aony[†] ed to stend it for a mawnin: e'll ev to stend it for a
lawftawm.[†]

ADOLPHUS CUSINS. That is a frightful reflection, Mr Walker. But I cant
tear myself away from her.

100 BILL. Well, Aw ken. [*To Barbara*] Eah! do you knaow where Aw'm
gowin to, and wot Aw'm gowin to do?

BARBARA. Yes: youre going to heaven; and youre coming back here
before the week's out to tell me so.

BILL. You loy. Aw'm gowin to Kennintahn,[†] to spit in Todger
105 Fairmawl's eye. Aw beshed Jenny Ill's fice; an nar Aw'll git me aown
fice beshed[†] and cam beck and shaow it to er. Ee'll itt me ardern Aw
itt her. Thatll mike us square. [*To Adolphus*] Is thet fair or is it not?
Youre a genlmn: you oughter knaow.

BARBARA. Two black eyes wont make one white one, Bill.

110 BILL. Aw didnt awst[†] you. Cawnt you never keep your mahth shat?
Oy awst the genlmn.

CUSINS [*reflectively*] Yes: I think youre right, Mr Walker. Yes: I should
do it. It's curious; it's exactly what an ancient Greek[†] would have done.

BARBARA. But what good will it do?

115 CUSINS. Well, it will give Mr Fairmile some exercise; and it will satisfy
Mr Walker's soul.

BILL. Rot! there aint nao such a thing as a saoul. Ah kin you tell
wevver Awve a saoul or not? You never seen it.

BARBARA. Ive seen it hurting you when you went against it.

120 BILL [*with compressed aggravation*] If you was maw gel and took the
word aht o me mahth lawk thet, Aw'd give you sathink youd feel urtin,
Aw would. [*To Adolphus*] You tike maw tip, mite. Stop er jawr; or
youll doy afoah your tawm [*With intense expression*] Wore aht: thets

---

Gowin to merry Going to marry
Awve aony . . . lawftawm I've only had to
  stand it for a morning: he'll have to stand it
  for a lifetime
Kennintahn Canning Town, a poor district
  in East London

beshed bashed
awst asked
an ancient Greek Cusins is a portrait of
  Professor Gilbert Murray (1866–1957), the
  Greek scholar and translator

wot youll be: wore aht. [*He goes away through the gate*].

125   CUSINS [*looking after him*] I wonder!

BARBARA. Dolly!† [*indignant, in her mother's manner*].

CUSINS. Yes, my dear, it's very wearing to be in love with you. If it lasts, I quite think I shall die young.

BARBARA. Should you mind?

130   CUSINS. Not at all. [*He is suddenly softened, and kisses her over the drum, evidently not for the first time, as people cannot kiss over a big drum without practice. Undershaft coughs*].

BARBARA. It's all right, papa, weve not forgotten you. Dolly: explain the place to papa: I havnt time [*She goes busily into the shelter*].

Undershaft and Adolphus now have the yard to themselves. Undershaft, seated on a form, and still keenly attentive, looks hard at Adolphus. Adolphus looks hard at him.

135   UNDERSHAFT. I fancy you guess something of what is in my mind, Mr Cusins. [*Cusins flourishes his drumsticks as if in the act of beating a lively rataplan,† but makes no sound*]. Exactly so. But suppose Barbara finds you out!

CUSINS. You know, I do not admit that I am imposing on Barbara. I
140   am quite genuinely interested in the views of the Salvation Army. The fact is, I am a sort of collector of religions; and the curious thing is that I find I can believe them all. By the way, have you any religion?

UNDERSHAFT. Yes.

CUSINS. Anything out of the common?

145   UNDERSHAFT. Only that there are two things necessary to Salvation.

CUSINS [*disappointed but polite*] Ah, the Church Catechism.† Charles Lomax also belongs to the Established Church.

UNDERSHAFT. The two things are —

CUSINS. Baptism and —†

150   UNDERSHAFT. No. Money and gunpowder.

CUSINS [*surprised, but interested*] That is the general opinion of our governing classes. The novelty is in hearing any man confess it.

UNDERSHAFT. Just so.

CUSINS. Excuse me: is there any place in your religion for honor,
155   justice, truth, love, mercy and so forth?

UNDERSHAFT. Yes: they are the graces and luxuries of a rich, strong, and safe life.

CUSINS. Suppose one is forced to choose between them and money or gunpowder?

Dolly   from Adolphus
rataplan   rapid drum beats
Catechism   prescribed questions and answers
     on points of Church doctrine

Baptism and —   Baptism and Communion,
     according to the Church of England
     Catechism

160   UNDERSHAFT. Choose money and gunpowder; for without enough of
both you cannot afford the others.

   CUSINS. That is your religion?

   UNDERSHAFT. Yes.

*The cadence of this reply makes a full close in the conversation. Cusins
twists his face dubiously and contemplates Undershaft. Undershaft
contemplates him.*

165   CUSINS. Barbara wont stand that. You will have to choose between
your religion and Barbara.

   UNDERSHAFT. So will you, my friend. She will find out that that drum
of yours is hollow.

   CUSINS. Father Undershaft: you are mistaken: I am a sincere Salvation-
170   ist. You do not understand the Salvation Army. It is the army of joy,
of love, of courage: it has banished the fear and remorse and despair
of the old hell-ridden evangelical sects: it marches to fight the devil with
trumpet and drum, with music and dancing, with banner and palm, as
becomes a sally from heaven by its happy garrison. It picks the waster
175   out of the public house and makes a man of him; it finds a worm
wriggling in a back kitchen, and lo! a woman! Men and women of
rank too, sons and daughters of the Highest. It takes the poor professor
of Greek, the most artificial and self-suppressed of human creatures,
from his meal of roots, and lets loose the rhapsodist† in him; reveals
180   the true worship of Dionysos† to him; sends him down the public
street drumming dithyrambs† [*he plays a thundering flourish on the
drum*].

   UNDERSHAFT. You will alarm the shelter.

   CUSINS. Oh, they are accustomed to these sudden ecstasies. However,
if the drum worries you – [*he pockets the drumsticks; unhooks the
185   drum; and stands it on the ground opposite the gateway*].

   UNDERSHAFT. Thank you.

   CUSINS. You remember what Euripides says about your money and
gunpowder?

   UNDERSHAFT. No.

190   CUSINS [*declaiming*]

           One and another†
   In money and guns may outpass his brother;
   And men in their millions float and flow
   And seethe with a million hopes as leaven;
195   And they win their will; or they miss their will;

---

rhapsodist in ancient Greece, the singer or
  reciter of epic poetry
Dionysos Greek god of wine, revelry, fertility,
  ecstasy and rebirth
dithyrambs Greek hymns in honour of

Dionysos
One and another the lines are from Gilbert
Murray's translation of the *Bacchae*, a play
in which Dionysos figures, by Euripides (480–
406 BC)

> And their hopes are dead or are pined for still;
> > But whoe'er can know
> > As the long days go
> That to live is happy, has found his heaven.

200   My translation: what do you think of it?

UNDERSHAFT. I think, my friend, that if you wish to know, as the long days go, that to live is happy, you must first acquire money enough for a decent life, and power enough to be your own master.

CUSINS. You are damnably discouraging. [*He resumes his declamation*].

205   > Is it so hard a thing to see
> > That the spirit of God — whate'er it be —
> The law that abides and changes not, ages long,
> The Eternal and Nature-born: these things be strong?
> What else is Wisdom? What of Man's endeavor,
210   > Or God's high grace so lovely and so great?
> To stand from fear set free? to breathe and wait?
> To hold a hand uplifted over Fate?
> And shall not Barbara be loved for ever?

UNDERSHAFT. Euripides mentions Barbara, does he?

215   CUSINS. It is a fair translation. The word means Loveliness.

UNDERSHAFT. May I ask — as Barbara's father — how much a year she is to be loved for ever on?

CUSINS. As Barbara's father, that is more your affair than mine. I can feed her by teaching Greek: that is about all.

220   UNDERSHAFT. Do you consider it a good match for her?

CUSINS [*with polite obstinacy*] Mr Undershaft: I am in many ways a weak, timid, ineffectual person; and my health is far from satisfactory. But whenever I feel that I must have anything, I get it, sooner or later. I feel that way about Barbara. I dont like marriage: I feel intensely
225   afraid of it; and I dont know what I shall do with Barbara or what she will do with me. But I feel that I and nobody else must marry her. Please regard that as settled. — Not that I wish to be arbitrary; but why should I waste your time in discussing what is inevitable?

UNDERSHAFT. You mean that you will stick at nothing: not even the
230   conversion of the Salvation Army to the worship of Dionysos.

CUSINS. The business of the Salvation Army is to save, not to wrangle about the name of the pathfinder. Dionysos or another: what does it matter?

UNDERSHAFT [*rising and approaching him*] Professor Cusins: you are a
235   young man after my own heart.

CUSINS. Mr Undershaft: you are, as far as I am able to gather, a most infernal old rascal; but you appeal very strongly to my sense of ironic humor.

Undershaft mutely offers his hand. They shake.

UNDERSHAFT [*suddenly concentrating himself*] And now to business.

240 CUSINS. Pardon me. We are discussing religion. Why go back to such an uninteresting and unimportant subject as business?

UNDERSHAFT. Religion is our business at present, because it is through religion alone that we can win Barbara.

CUSINS. Have you, too, fallen in love with Barbara?

245 UNDERSHAFT. Yes, with a father's love.

CUSINS. A father's love for a grown-up daughter is the most dangerous of all infatuations. I apologize for mentioning my own pale, coy, mistrustful fancy in the same breath with it.

UNDERSHAFT. Keep to the point. We have to win her; and we are neither

250 of us Methodists.

CUSINS. That doesnt matter. The power Barbara wields here – the power that wields Barbara herself – is not Calvinism, not Presbyterianism, not Methodism –

UNDERSHAFT. Not Greek Paganism either, eh?

255 CUSINS. I admit that. Barbara is quite original in her religion.

UNDERSHAFT [*triumphantly*] Aha! Barbara Undershaft would be. Her inspiration comes from within herself.

CUSINS. How do you suppose it got there?

UNDERSHAFT [*in towering excitement*] It is the Undershaft inheritance.

260 I shall hand on my torch to my daughter. She shall make my converts and preach my gospel –

CUSINS. What! Money and gunpowder!

UNDERSHAFT. Yes, money and gunpowder. Freedom and power. Command of life and command of death.

265 CUSINS [*urbanely: trying to bring him down to earth*] This is extremely interesting, Mr Undershaft. Of course you know that you are mad.

UNDERSHAFT [*with redoubled force*] And you?

CUSINS. Oh, mad as a hatter. You are welcome to my secret since I have discovered yours. But I am astonished. Can a madman make

270 cannons?

UNDERSHAFT. Would anyone else than a madman make them? And now [*with surging energy*] question for question. Can a sane man translate Euripides?

CUSINS. No.

275 UNDERSHAFT [*seizing him by the shoulder*] Can a sane woman make a man of a waster or a woman of a worm?

CUSINS [*reeling before the storm*] Father Colossus – Mammoth Millionaire –

UNDERSHAFT [*pressing him*] Are there two mad people or three in this

280 Salvation shelter today?

CUSINS. You mean Barbara is as mad as we are?

UNDERSHAFT [*pushing him lightly off and resuming his equanimity suddenly and completely*] Pooh, Professor! let us call things by their proper names. I am a millionaire; you are a poet; Barbara is a savior
285 of souls. What have we three to do with the common mob of slaves and idolaters? [*He sits down again with a shrug of contempt for the mob*].

CUSINS. Take care! Barbara is in love with the common people. So am I. Have you never felt the romance of that love?
290 UNDERSHAFT [*cold and sardonic*] Have you ever been in love with Poverty, like St Francis:† Have you ever been in love with Dirt, like St Simeon!† Have you ever been in love with disease and suffering, like our nurses and philanthropists? Such passions are not virtues, but the most unnatural of all the vices. This love of the common people may
295 please an earl's granddaughter and a university professor; but I have been a common man and a poor man; and it has no romance for me. Leave it to the poor to pretend that poverty is a blessing: leave it to the coward to make a religion of his cowardice by preaching humility: we know better than that. We three must stand together above the common
300 people: how else can we help their children to climb up beside us? Barbara must belong to us, not to the Salvation Army.

CUSINS. Well, I can only say that if you think you will get her away from the Salvation Army by talking to her as you have been talking to me, you dont know Barbara.
305 UNDERSHAFT. My friend: I never ask for what I can buy.

CUSINS [*in a white fury*] Do I understand you to imply that you can buy Barbara?

UNDERSHAFT. No; but I can buy the Salvation Army.

CUSINS. Quite impossible.
310 UNDERSHAFT. You shall see. All religious organizations exist by selling themselves to the rich.

CUSINS. Not the Army. That is the Church of the poor.

UNDERSHAFT. All the more reason for buying it.

CUSINS. I dont think you quite know what the Army does for the poor.
315 UNDERSHAFT. Oh yes I do. It draws their teeth: that is enough for me as a man of business.

CUSINS. Nonsense! It makes them sober –

UNDERSHAFT. I prefer sober workmen. The profits are larger.

CUSINS – honest –
320 UNDERSHAFT. Honest workmen are the most economical.

CUSINS – attached to their homes –

St Francis   Francis of Assisi, Giovanni
  Francesco Bernadone (?1181–1226),
  founded the Franciscan Order of Friars

devoted to the poor
St Simeon   Simeon Stylites (387–459) who
  spent years without leaving his monastic cell

UNDERSHAFT. So much the better: they will put up with anything sooner than change their shop.

CUSINS – happy –

325   UNDERSHAFT. An invaluable safeguard against revolution.

CUSINS – unselfish –

UNDERSHAFT. Indifferent to their own interests, which suits me exactly.

CUSINS – with their thoughts on heavenly things –

UNDERSHAFT [*rising*] And not on Trade Unionism nor Socialism.

330   Excellent.

CUSINS [*revolted*] You really are an infernal old racal.

UNDERSHAFT [*indicating Peter Shirley, who has just come from the shelter and strolled dejectedly down the yard between them*] And this is an honest man!

335   SHIRLEY. Yes; and what av I got by it? [*he passes on bitterly and sits on the form, in the corner of the penthouse*].

Snobby Price, beaming sanctimoniously, and Jenny Hill, with a tambourine full of coppers, come from the shelter and go to the drum, on which Jenny begins to count the money.

UNDERSHAFT [*replying to Shirley*] Oh, your employers must have got a good deal by it from first to last. [*He sits on the table, with one foot on the side form, Cusins, overwhelmed, sits down on the same form*

340   *nearer the shelter. Barbara comes from the shelter to the middle of the yard. She is excited and a little overwrought*].

BARBARA. Weve just had a splendid experience meeting at the other gate in Cripps's Lane. Ive hardly ever seen them so much moved as they were by your confession, Mr Price.

345   PRICE. I could almost be glad of my past wickedness if I could believe that it would elp to keep hathers straight.†

BARBARA. So it will, Snobby. How much, Jenny?

JENNY. Four and tenpence, Major.

BARBARA. Oh Snobby, if you had given your poor mother just one

350   more kick, we should have got the whole five shillings!

PRICE. If she heard you say that, miss, she'd be sorry I didnt. But I'm glad. Oh what a joy it will be to her when she hears I'm saved!

UNDERSHAFT. Shall I contribute the odd twopence, Barbara? The millionaire's mite,† eh? [*He takes a couple of pennies from his pocket*].

355   BARBARA. How did you make that twopence?

UNDERSHAFT. As usual. By selling cannons, torpedoes, submarines, and my new patent Grand Duke hand grenade.

BARBARA. Put it back in your pocket. You cant buy your salvation here for twopence: you must work it out.

---

hathers straight others straight   *mite* see Mark 12. 41–4

360   UNDERSHAFT. Is twopence not enough? I can afford a little more, if you
press me.

BARBARA. Two million millions would not be enough. There is bad
blood on your hands; and nothing but good blood can cleanse them.
Money is no use. Take it away. [*She turns to Cusins*]. Dolly: you must
365   write another letter for me to the papers. [*He makes a wry face*]. Yes: I
know you dont like it; but it must be done. The starvation this winter
is beating us: everybody is unemployed. The General says we must
close this shelter if we cant get more money, I force the collections at
the meetings until I am ashamed: dont I, Snobby?

370   PRICE. It's a fair treat to see you work it, miss. The way you got them
up from three-and-six to four-and-ten with that hymn, penny by penny
and verse by verse, was a caution. Not a Cheap Jack† on Mile End†
Waste could touch you at it.

BARBARA. Yes; but I wish we could do without it. I am getting at last
375   to think more of the collection than of the people's souls. And what
are those hatfuls of pence and halfpence? We want thousands! tens of
thousands! hundreds of thousands! I want to convert people, not to be
always begging for the Army in a way I'd die sooner than beg for
myself.

380   UNDERSHAFT [*in profound irony*] Genuine unselfishness is capable of
anything, my dear.

BARBARA [*unsuspectingly, as she turns away to take the money from
the drum and put it in a cash bag she carries*] Yes, isnt it? [*Undershaft
looks sardonically at Cusins*].

385   CUSINS [*aside to Undershaft*] Mephistopheles!† Machiavelli!†

1905–7   1907

Cheap Jack   auctioneer   *Machiavelli*   Niccolo Machiavelli (1469–
Mile End   an open-air market in East London   1527), Italian political theorist, argued that
Mephistopheles   a devil   effective measures may need to be unethical

Joseph Conrad
1857–1924

Teodor Josef Konrad Korzeniowski was born in the Russian-ruled Ukraine, of an aristocratic Polish family which had suffered for its patriotism; his life-long dislike of Russians appears in *The Secret Agent* and in other works. He joined the French merchant marine at the age of seventeen, and transferred to the English merchant navy in 1878 (master's certificate 1880). He became a British subject in 1886, settled in England in 1894 and published his first novel, *Almayer's Folly*, in 1895. He was helped towards his remarkable control of literary English (his third language) by Ford Madox Ford (see p. 190). Henry James also gave advice and encouragement. *The Nigger of the Narcissus* (1897) and *Lord Jim* (1900) impressed critics but failed to win a large readership; *Chance* (1913) was Conrad's first popular success. He published further novels and stories which drew on his life at sea, including *Typhoon* (1902), *Youth* (1902) and *The Shadow Line* (1917). A journey to the Belgian Congo inspired his short novel, *Heart of Darkness* (1902). *Nostromo* (1904), his masterpiece, is set in an imaginary South American country. *The Secret Agent* (1907) and *Under Western Eyes* (1911) are novels about revolutionaries. Conrad's approach to narrative technique was experimental, but his scepticism and his values (courage, work, duty, solidarity) were traditional. The high quality of his achievement has never been questioned.

From TYPHOON

[Bad Weather]

Jukes was as ready a man as any half-dozen young mates that may be caught by casting a net upon the waters; and though he had been somewhat taken aback by the startling viciousness of the first squall, he had pulled himself together on the instant, had called out the hands
5   and had rushed them along to secure such openings about the deck as had not been already battened down earlier in the evening. Shouting in his fresh, stentorian voice, 'Jump, boys, and bear a hand!' he led in the work, telling himself the while that he had 'just expected this.'

But at the same time he was growing aware that this was rather more
10   than he had expected. From the first stir of the air felt on his cheek the
gale seemed to take upon itself the accumulated impetus of an avalanche.
Heavy sprays enveloped the 'Nan-Shan' from stem to stern, and instantly
in the midst of her regular rolling she began to jerk and plunge as
though she had gone mad with fright.
15   Jukes thought, 'This is no joke.' While he was exchanging explanatory
yells with his captain, a sudden lowering of the darkness came upon
the night, falling before their vision like something palpable. It was as
if the masked lights of the world had been turned down. Jukes was
uncritically glad to have his captain at hand. It relieved him as though
20   that man had, by simply coming on deck, taken most of the gale's
weight upon his shoulders. Such is the prestige, the privilege, and the
burden of command.

Captain MacWhirr could expect no relief of that sort from any one
on earth. Such is the loneliness of command. He was trying to see, with
25   that watchful manner of a seaman who stares into the wind's eye as if
into the eye of an adversary, to penetrate the hidden intention and guess
the aim and force of the thrust. The strong wind swept at him out of a
vast obscurity; he felt under his feet the uneasiness of his ship, and he
could not even discern the shadow of her shape. He wished it were not
30   so; and very still he waited, feeling stricken by a blind man's helplessness.

To be silent was natural to him, dark or shine. Jukes, at his elbow,
made himself heard yelling cheerily in the gusts, 'We must have got the
worst of it at once, sir.' A faint burst of lightning quivered all round,
as if flashed into a cavern – into a black and secret chamber of the sea,
35   with a floor of foaming crests.

It unveiled for a sinister, fluttering moment a ragged mass of clouds
hanging low, the lurch of the long outlines of the ship, the black figures
of men caught on the bridge, heads forward, as if petrified in the act of
butting. The darkness palpitated down upon all this, and then the real
40   thing came at last.

It was something formidable and swift, like the sudden smashing of
a vial of wrath. It seemed to explode all round the ship with an
overpowering concussion and a rush of great waters, as if an immense
dam had been blown up to windward. In an instant the men lost touch
45   of each other. This is the disintegrating power of a great wind: it isolates
one from one's kind. An earthquake, a landslip, an avalanche, overtake
a man incidentally, as it were – without passion. A furious gale attacks
him like a personal enemy, tries to grasp his limbs, fastens upon his
mind, seeks to rout his very spirit out of him.
50   Jukes was driven away from his commander. He fancied himself
whirled a great distance through the air. Everything disappeared – even,
for a moment, his power of thinking; but his hand had found one of

the rail-stanchions. His distress was by no means alleviated by an inclination to disbelieve the reality of this experience. Though young, he had seen some bad weather, and had never doubted his ability to imagine the worst; but this was so much beyond his powers of fancy that it appeared incompatible with the existence of any ship whatever. He would have been incredulous about himself in the same way, perhaps, had he not been so harassed by the necessity of exerting a wrestling effort against a force trying to tear him away from his hold. Moreover, the conviction of not being utterly destroyed returned to him through the sensations of being half-drowned, bestially shaken, and partly choked.

It seemed to him he remained there precariously alone with the stanchion for a long, long time. The rain poured on him, flowed, drove in sheets. He breathed in gasps; and sometimes the water he swallowed was fresh and sometimes it was salt. For the most part he kept his eyes shut tight, as if suspecting his sight might be destroyed in the immense flurry of the elements. When he ventured to blink hastily, he derived some moral support from the green gleam on the starboard light shining feebly upon the flight of rain and sprays. He was actually looking at it when its ray fell upon the uprearing sea which put it out. He saw the head of the wave toppled over, adding the mite of its crash to the tremendous uproar raging around him, and almost at the same instant the stanchion was wrenched away from his embracing arms. After a crushing thump on his back he found himself suddenly afloat and borne upwards. His first irresistible notion was that the whole China Sea had climbed on the bridge. Then, more sanely, he concluded himself gone overboard. All the time he was being tossed, flung, and rolled in great volumes of water, he kept on repeating mentally, with the utmost precipitation, the words: 'My God! My God! My God! My God!'

All at once, in a revolt of misery and despair, he formed the crazy resolution to get out of that. And he began to thresh about with his arms and legs. But as soon as he commenced his wretched struggles he discovered that he had become somehow mixed up with a face, an oilskin coat, somebody's boots. He clawed ferociously all these things in turn, lost them, found them again, lost them once more, and finally was himself caught in the firm clasp of a pair of stout arms. He returned the embrace closely round a thick solid body. He had found his captain.

They tumbled over and over tightening their hug. Suddenly the water let them down with a brutal bang; and, stranded against the side of the wheelhouse, out of breath and bruised, they were left to stagger up in the wind and hold on where they could.

Jukes came out of it rather horrified, as though he had escaped some unparalleled outrage directed at his feelings. It weakened his faith in himself. He started shouting aimlessly to the man he could feel near

him in that fiendish blackness 'Is it you, sir? Is it you, sir?' till his
temples seemed ready to burst. And he heard in answer a voice, as if
crying far away, as if screaming to him fretfully from a very great
100   distance, the one word 'Yes!' Other seas swept again over the bridge.
He received them defencelessly right over his bare head, with both his
hands engaged in holding.

The motion of the ship was extravagant. Her lurches had an appalling
helplessness: she pitched as if taking a header into a void, and seemed
105   to find a wall to hit every time. When she rolled she fell on her side
headlong, and she would be righted back by such a demolishing blow
that Jukes felt her reeling as a clubbed man reels before he collapses.
The gale howled and scuffled about gigantically in the darkness, as
though the entire world were one black gully. At certain moments the
110   air streamed against the ship as if sucked through a tunnel with a
concentrated solid force of impact that seemed to lift her clean out of
the water and keep her up for an instant with only a quiver running
through her from end to end. And then she would begin her tumbling
again as if dropped back into a boiling cauldron. Jukes tried hard to
115   compose his mind and judge things coolly.

The sea, flattened down in the heavier gusts, would uprise and
overwhelm both ends of the 'Nan-Shan' in snowy rushes of foam,
expanding wide, beyond both rails, into the night. And on this dazzling
sheet, spread under the blackness of the clouds and emitting a bluish
120   glow, Captain MacWhirr could catch a desolate glimpse of a few tiny
specks black as ebony, the tops of the hatches, the battened companions,†
the heads of the covered winches, the foot of a mast. This was all he
could see of his ship. Her middle structure, covered by the bridge which
bore him, his mate, the closed wheelhouse where a man was steering
125   shut up with the fear of being swept overboard together with the whole
thing in one great crash – her middle structure was like a half-tide rock
awash upon a coast. It was like an outlying rock with the water boiling
up, streaming over, pouring off, beating round – like a rock in the surf
to which shipwrecked people cling before they let go – only it rose, it
130   sank, it rolled continuously, without respite and rest, like a rock that
should have miraculously struck adrift from a coast and gone wallowing
upon the sea.

The 'Nan-Shan' was being looted by the storm with a senseless,
destructive fury: trysails† torn out of the extra gaskets, double-lashed
135   awnings blown away, bridge swept clean, weather-cloths burst, rails
twisted, light-screens smashed – and two of the boats had gone already.
They had gone unheard and unseen, melting, as it were, in the shock
and smother of the wave. It was only later, when upon the white flash

---

battened companions   firmly fastened hatches   *trysails*   small sails

of another high sea hurling itself amidships, Jukes had a vision of two
140   pairs of davits† leaping black and empty out of the solid blackness,
with one overhauled fall† flying and an iron-bound block capering in
the air, that he became aware of what had happened within about three
yards of his back.

He poked his head forward, groping for the ear of his commander.
145   His lips touched it – big, fleshy, very wet. He cried in an agitated tone,
'Our boats are going now, sir.'

And again he heard that voice, forced and ringing feebly, but with a
penetrating effect of quietness in the enormous discord of noises, as if
sent out from some remote spot of peace beyond the black wastes of
150   the gale; again he heard a man's voice – the frail and indomitable sound
that can be made to carry an infinity of thought, resolution and purpose,
that shall be pronouncing confident words on the last day, when heavens
fall, and justice is done – again he heard it, and it was crying to him, as
if from very, very far – 'All right.'

155   He thought he had not managed to make himself understood. 'Our
boats – I say boats – the boats, sir! Two gone!'

The same voice, within a foot of him and yet so remote, yelled
sensibly, 'Can't be helped.'

Captain MacWhirr had never turned his face, but Jukes caught some
160   more words on the wind.

'What can – expect – when hammering through – such – Bound to
leave – something behind – stands to reason.'

Watchfully Jukes listened for more. No more came. This was all
Captain MacWhirr had to say; and Jukes could picture to himself rather
165   than see the broad squat back before him. An impenetrable obscurity
pressed down upon the ghostly glimmers of the sea. A dull conviction
seized upon Jukes that there was nothing to be done.

If the steering-gear did not give way, if the immense volumes of water
did not burst the deck in or smash one of the hatches, if the engines
170   did not give up, if way could be kept on the ship against this terrific
wind, and she did not bury herself in one of these awful seas, of whose
white crests alone, topping high above her bows, he could now and
then get a sickening glimpse – then there was a chance of her coming
out of it. Something within him seemed to turn over, bringing uppermost
175   the feeling that the 'Nan-Shan' was lost.

'She's done for,' he said to himself, with a surprising mental agitation,
as though he had discovered an unexpected meaning in this thought.
One of these things was bound to happen. Nothing could be prevented
now, and nothing could be remedied. The men on board did not count,

---

davits constructions for lowering and raising   *overhauled fall* a rope drawn too far
boats

180   and the ship could not last. This weather was too impossible.

Jukes felt an arm thrown heavily over his shoulders; and to this overture he responded with great intelligence by catching hold of his captain round the waist.

They stood clasped thus in the blind night, bracing each other against
185   the wind, cheek to cheek and lip to ear, in the manner of two hulks lashed stem to stern together.

And Jukes heard the voice of his commander hardly any louder than before, but nearer, as though, starting to march athwart the prodigious rush of the hurricane, it had approached him, bearing that strange effect
190   of quietness like the serene glow of a halo.

'D'ye know where the hands got to?' it asked, vigorous and evanescent at the same time, overcoming the strength of the wind, and swept away from Jukes instantly.

Jukes didn't know. They were all on the bridge when the real force
195   of the hurricane struck the ship. He had no idea where they had crawled to. Under the circumstances they were nowhere, for all the use that could be made of them. Somehow the Captain's wish to know distressed Jukes.

'Want the hands, sir?' he cried, apprehensively.
200   'Ought to know,' asserted Captain MacWhirr. 'Hold hard.'

They held hard. An outburst of unchained fury, a vicious rush of the wind absolutely steadied the ship; she rocked only, quick and light like a child's cradle, for a terrific moment of suspense, while the whole atmosphere, as it seemed, streamed furiously past her, roaring away
205   from the tenebrous earth.

It suffocated them, and with eyes shut they tightened their grasp. What from the magnitude of the shock might have been a column of water running upright in the dark, butted against the ship, broke short, and fell on her bridge, crushingly, from on high, with a dead burying
210   weight.

A flying fragment of that collapse, a mere splash, enveloped them in one swirl from their feet over their heads, filling violently their ears, mouths and nostrils with salt water. It knocked out their legs, wrenched in haste at their arms, seethed away swiftly under their chins; and
215   opening their eyes, they saw the piled-up masses of foam dashing to and fro amongst what looked like the fragments of a ship. She had given way as if driven straight in. Their panting hearts yielded, too, before the tremendous blow; and all at once she sprang up again to her desperate plunging, as if trying to scramble out from under the
220   ruins.

The seas in the dark seemed to rush from all sides to keep her back where she might perish. There was hate in the way she was handled, and a ferocity in the blows that fell. She was like a living creature

thrown to the rage of a mob: hustled terribly, struck at, borne up, flung
225   down, leaped upon. Captain MacWhirr and Jukes kept hold of each
other, deafened by the noise, gagged by the wind; and the great physical
tumult beating about their bodies, brought, like an unbridled display
of passion, a profound trouble to their souls. One of those wild and
appalling shrieks that are heard at times passing mysteriously overhead
230   in the steady roar of a hurricane, swooped, as if borne on wings, upon
the ship, and Jukes tried to outscream it.

'Will she live through this?'

The cry was wrenched out of his breast. It was as unintentional as
the birth of a thought in the head, and he heard nothing of it himself.
235   It all became extinct at once – thought, intention, effort – and of his
cry the inaudible vibration added to the tempest waves of the air.

He expected nothing from it. Nothing at all. For indeed what answer
could be made? But after a while he heard with amazement the frail
and resisting voice in his ear, the dwarf sound, unconquered in the
240   giant tumult.

'She may!'

It was a dull yell, more difficult to seize than a whisper. And presently
the voice returned again, half submerged in the vast crashes, like a ship
battling against the waves of an ocean.
245   'Let's hope so!' it cried – small, lonely and unmoved, a stranger to
the visions of hope or fear; and it flickered into disconnected words:
'Ship.... This.... Never – Anyhow ... for the best.' Jukes gave it
up.

Then, as if it had come suddenly upon the one thing fit to withstand
250   the power of a storm, it seemed to gain force and firmness for the last
broken shouts:

'Keep on hammering ... builders ... good men.... And chance it
... engines.... Rout ... good man.'

Captain MacWhirr removed his arm from Jukes's shoulders, and
255   thereby ceased to exist for his mate, so dark it was; Jukes, after a tense
stiffening of every muscle, would let himself go limp all over. The
gnawing of profound discomfort existed side by side with an incredible
disposition to somnolence, as though he had been buffeted and worried
into drowsiness. The wind would get hold of his head and try to shake
260   it off his shoulders; his clothes, full of water, were as heavy as lead,
cold and dripping like an armour of melting ice: he shivered – it lasted
a long time; and with his hands closed hard on his hold, he was letting
himself sink slowly into the depths of bodily misery. His mind became
concentrated upon himself in an aimless, idle way, and when something
265   pushed lightly at the back of his knees he nearly, as the saying is,
jumped out of his skin.

In the start forward he bumped the back of Captain MacWhirr, who

didn't move; and then a hand gripped his thigh. A lull had come, a
menacing lull of the wind, the holding of a stormy breath – and he felt
270   himself pawed all over. It was the boatswain. Jukes recognized these
hands, so thick and enormous that they seemed to belong to some new
species of man.

The boatswain had arrived on the bridge, crawling on all fours
against the wind, and had found the chief mate's legs with the top of
275   his head. Immediately he crouched and began to explore Jukes's person
upwards with prudent, apologetic touches, as became an inferior.

He was an ill-favoured, undersized, gruff sailor of fifty, coarsely hairy,
short-legged, long-armed, resembling an elderly ape. His strength was
immense; and in his great lumpy paws, bulging like brown boxing-
280   gloves on the end of furry forearms, the heaviest objects were handled
like playthings. Apart from the grizzled pelt on his chest, the menacing
demeanour and the hoarse voice, he had none of the classical attributes
of his rating. His good nature almost amounted to imbecility: the men
did what they liked with him, and he had not an ounce of initiative in
285   his character, which was easy-going and talkative. For these reasons
Jukes disliked him; but Captain MacWhirr, to Jukes's scornful disgust,
seemed to regard him as a first-rate petty officer.

He pulled himself up by Jukes's coat, taking that liberty with the
greatest moderation, and only so far as it was forced upon him by the
290   hurricane.

'What is it, boss'n, what is it?' yelled Jukes, impatiently. What could
that fraud of a boss'n want on the bridge? The typhoon had got on
Jukes's nerves. The husky bellowings of the other, though unintelligible,
seemed to suggest a state of lively satisfaction. There could be no
295   mistake. The old fool was pleased with something.

The boatswain's other hand had found some other body, for in a
changed tone he began to inquire: 'Is it you, sir? Is it you, sir?' The
wind strangled his howls.

'Yes!' cried Captain MacWhirr.

1900–1   1903

From THE SECRET AGENT
[England is Absurd]

Such was the house, the household, and the business Mr Verloc left
behind him on his way westward at the hour of half-past ten in the

morning. It was unusually early for him; his whole person exhaled the charm of almost dewy freshness; he wore his blue cloth overcoat
5 unbuttoned; his boots were shiny; his cheeks, freshly shaven, had a sort of gloss; and even his heavy-lidded eyes, refreshed by a night of peaceful slumber, sent out glances of comparative alertness. Through the park railings these glances beheld men and women riding in the Row,[†] couples cantering past harmoniously, others advancing sedately
10 at a walk, loitering groups of three or four, solitary horsemen looking unsociable, and solitary women followed at a long distance by a groom with a cockade to his hat and a leather belt over his tight-fitting coat. Carriages went bowling by, mostly two-horse broughams,[†] with here and there a victoria[†] with the skin of some wild beast inside and a
15 woman's face and hat emerging above the folded hood. And a peculiarly London sun – against which nothing could be said except that it looked bloodshot – glorified all this by its stare. It hung at a moderate elevation above Hyde Park Corner with an air of punctual and benign vigilance. The very pavement under Mr Verloc's feet had an old-gold tinge in that
20 diffused light, in which neither wall, nor tree, nor beast, nor man cast a shadow. Mr Verloc was going westward through a town without shadows in an atmosphere of powdered old gold. There were red, coppery gleams on the roofs of houses, on the corners of walls, on the panels of carriages, on the very coats of the horses, and on the broad
25 back of Mr Verloc's overcoat, where they produced a dull effect of rustiness. But Mr Verloc was not in the least conscious of having got rusty. He surveyed through the park railings the evidences of the town's opulence and luxury with an approving eye. All these people had to be protected. Protection is the first necessity of opulence and luxury. They
30 had to be protected; and their horses, carriages, houses, servants had to be protected; and the source of their wealth had to be protected in the heart of the city and the heart of the country; the whole social order favourable to their hygienic idleness had to be protected against the shallow enviousness of unhygienic labour. It had to – and Mr Verloc
35 would have rubbed his hands with satisfaction had he not been constitutionally averse from every superfluous exertion. His idleness was not hygienic, but it suited him very well. He was in a manner devoted to it with a sort of inert fanaticism, or perhaps rather with a fanatical inertness. Born of industrious parents for a life of toil, he had
40 embraced indolence from an impulse as profound as inexplicable and as imperious as the impulse which directs a man's preference for one particular woman in a given thousand. He was too lazy even for a mere demagogue, for a workman orator, for a leader of labour. It was too

---

the Row Rotten Row, the avenue in Hyde
Park where rich Londoners rode their horses

broughams fast carriages
victoria a light four-wheeled carriage

much trouble. He required a more perfect form of ease; or it might
45   have been that he was the victim of a philosophical unbelief in the
effectiveness of every human effort. Such a form of indolence requires,
implies, a certain amount of intelligence. Mr Verloc was not devoid of
intelligence – and at the notion of a menaced social order he would
perhaps have winked to himself if there had not been an effort to make
50   in that sign of scepticism. His big, prominent eyes were not well adapted
to winking. They were rather of the sort that closes solemnly in slumber
with majestic effect.

Undemonstrative and burly in a fat-pig style, Mr Verloc, without
either rubbing his hands with satisfaction or winking sceptically at his
55   thoughts, proceeded on his way. He trod the pavement heavily with his
shiny boots, and his general get-up was that of a well-to-do mechanic
in business for himself. He might have been anything from a picture-
frame maker to a locksmith; an employer of labour in a small way. But
there was also about him an indescribable air which no mechanic could
60   have acquired in the practice of his handicraft however dishonestly
exercised: the air common to men who live on the vices, the follies, or
the baser fears of mankind; the air of moral nihilism common to keepers
of gambling hells† and disorderly houses; to private detectives and
inquiry agents; to drink sellers and, I should say, to the sellers of
65   invigorating electric belts and to the inventors of patent medicines. But
of that last I am not sure, not having carried my investigations so far
into the depths. For all I know, the expression of these last may be
perfectly diabolic. I shouldn't be surprised. What I want to affirm is
that Mr Verloc's expression was by no means diabolic.

70   Before reaching Knightsbridge, Mr Verloc took a turn to the left out
of the busy main thoroughfare, uproarious with the traffic of swaying
omnibuses and trotting vans, in the almost silent, swift flow of hansoms.
Under his hat, worn with a slight backward tilt, his hair had been
carefully brushed into respectful sleekness; for his business was with
75   an Embassy. And Mr Verloc, steady like a rock – a soft kind of rock –
marched now along a street which could with every propriety be
described as private. In its breadth, emptiness and extent it had the
majesty of inorganic nature, of matter that never dies. The only reminder
of mortality was a doctor's brougham arrested in august solitude close
80   to the curbstone. The polished knockers of the doors gleamed as far as
the eye could reach, the clean windows shone with a dark opaque
lustre. And all was still. But a milk cart rattled noisily across the distant
perspective; a butcher boy, driving with the noble recklessness of a
charioteer at Olympic Games, dashed round the corner sitting high
85   above a pair of red wheels. A guilty-looking cat issuing from under the

---

hells   gambling houses

stones ran for a while in front of Mr Verloc then dived into another basement; and a thick police constable, looking a stranger to every emotion, as if he, too, were part of inorganic nature, surging apparently out of a lamp-post, took not the slightest notice of Mr Verloc. With a
90 turn to the left Mr Verloc pursued his way along a narrow street by the side of a yellow wall which, for some inscrutable reason, had No. 1 Chesham Square written on it in black letters. Chesham Square was at least sixty yards away, and Mr Verloc, cosmopolitan enough not to be deceived by London's topographical mysteries, held on steadily,
95 without a sign of surprise or indignation. At last, with business-like persistency, he reached the Square, and made diagonally for the number 10. This belonged to an imposing carriage gate in a high, clean wall between two houses, of which one rationally enough bore the number 9 and the other was numbered 37; but the fact that this last belonged
100 to Porthill Street, a street well known in the neighbourhood, was proclaimed by an inscription placed above the ground-floor windows by whatever highly efficient authority is charged with the duty of keeping track of London's strayed houses. Why powers are not asked of Parliament (a short act would do) for compelling those edifices
105 to return where they belong is one of the mysteries of municipal administration. Mr Verloc did not trouble his head about it, his mission in life being the protection of the social mechanism, not its perfectionment or even its criticism.
It was so early that the porter of the Embassy issued hurriedly out of
110 his lodge still struggling with the left sleeve of his livery coat. His waistcoat was red, and he wore knee-breeches, but his aspect was flustered. Mr Verloc, aware of the rush on his flank, drove it off by simply holding out an envelope stamped with the arms of the Embassy, and passed on. He produced the same talisman also to the footman
115 who opened the door, and stood back to let him enter the hall.
A clear fire burned in a tall fireplace, and an elderly man standing with his back to it, in evening dress and with a chain round his neck, glanced up from the newspaper he was holding spread out in both hands before his calm and severe face. He didn't move; but another
120 lackey, in brown trousers and clawhammer coat edged with thin yellow cord, approaching Mr Verloc listened to the murmur of his name, and turning round on his heel in silence, began to walk, without looking back once. Mr Verloc, thus led along a ground-floor passage to the left of the great carpeted staircase, was suddenly motioned to enter a quite
125 small room furnished with a heavy writing-table and a few chairs. The servant shut the door, and Mr Verloc remained alone. He did not take a seat. With his hat and stick held in one hand he glanced about, passing his other podgy hand over his uncovered sleek head.
Another door opened noiselessly, and Mr Verloc immobilizing his

130   glance in that direction saw at first only black clothes, the bald top of
a head, and a drooping dark grey whisker on each side of a pair of
wrinkled hands. The person who had entered was holding a batch of
papers before his eyes and walked up to the table with a rather mincing
step, turning the papers over the while. Privy Councillor Wurmt,
135   Chancelier d'Ambassade,[†] was rather shortsighted. This meritorious
official, laying the papers on the table, disclosed a face of pasty
complexion and of melancholy ugliness surrounded by a lot of fine,
long dark grey hairs, barred heavily by thick and bushy eyebrows. He
put on a black-framed pince-nez upon a blunt and shapeless nose,
140   and seemed struck by Mr Verloc's appearance. Under the enormous
eyebrows his weak eyes blinked pathetically through the glasses.

He made no sign of greeting; neither did Mr Verloc who certainly
knew his place; but a subtle change about the general outlines of his
shoulders and back suggested a slight bending of Mr Verloc's spine
145   under the vast surface of his overcoat. The effect was of unobtrusive
deference.

'I have here some of your reports,' said the bureaucrat in an
unexpectedly soft and weary voice, and pressing the tip of his forefinger
on the papers with force. He paused; and Mr Verloc, who had
150   recognized his own handwriting very well, waited in an almost breathless
silence. 'We are not very satisfied with the attitude of the police here,'
the other continued with every appearance of mental fatigue.

The shoulders of Mr Verloc, without actually moving, suggested a
shrug. And for the first time since he left his home that morning his
155   lips opened.

'Every country has its police,' he said, philosophically. But as the
official of the Embassy went on blinking at him steadily he felt
constrained to add: 'Allow me to observe that I have no means of
action upon the police here.'

160   'What is desired,' said the man of papers, 'is the occurrence of
something definite which should stimulate their vigilance. That is within
your province – is it not so?'

Mr Verloc made no answer except by a sigh, which escaped him
involuntarily, for instantly he tried to give his face a cheerful expression.
165   The official blinked doubtfully, as if affected by the dim light of the
room. He repeated vaguely:

'The vigilance of the police – and the severity of the magistrates. The
general leniency of the judicial procedure here, and the utter absence
of all repressive measures, are a scandal to Europe. What is wished for

---

Chancelier d'Ambassade   (French) the head of
chancery in charge of an embassy's political office

170   just now is the accentuation of the unrest – of the fermentation which undoubtedly exists –'

'Undoubtedly, undoubtedly,' broke in Mr Verloc in a deep, deferential bass of an oratorical quality, so utterly different from the tone in which he had spoken before that his interlocutor remained profoundly

175   surprised. 'It exists to a dangerous degree. My reports for the last twelve months make it sufficiently clear.'

'Your reports for the last twelve months,' State Councillor Wurmt began in his gentle and dispassionate tone, 'have been read by me. I failed to discover why you wrote them at all.'

180   A sad silence reigned for a time. Mr Verloc seemed to have swallowed his tongue, and the other gazed at the papers on the table fixedly. At last he gave them a slight push.

'The state of affairs you expose there is assumed to exist as the first condition of your employment. What is required at present is not

185   writing, but the bringing to light of a distinct, significant fact – I would almost say of an alarming fact.'

'I need not say that all my endeavours shall be directed to that end,' Mr Verloc said, with convinced modulations in his conversational husky tone. But the sense of being blinked at watchfully behind the blind

190   glitter of these eyeglasses on the other side of the table disconcerted him. He stopped short with a gesture of absolute devotion. The useful, hard-working, if obscure member of the Embassy had an air of being impressed by some newly-born thought.

'You are very corpulent,' he said.

195   This observation, really of a psychological nature, and advanced with the modest hesitation of an officeman more familiar with ink and paper than with the requirements of active life, stung Mr Verloc in the manner of a rude personal remark. He stepped back a pace.

'Eh? What were you pleased to say?' he exclaimed, with husky

200   resentment.

The Chancelier d'Ambassade, entrusted with the conduct of this interview, seemed to find it too much for him.

'I think,' he said, 'that you had better see Mr Vladimir. Yes, decidedly I think you ought to see Mr Vladimir. Be good enough to wait here,'

205   he added, and went out with mincing steps.

At once Mr Verloc passed his hand over his hair. A slight perspiration had broken out on his forehead. He let the air escape from his pursed-up lips like a man blowing at a spoonful of hot soup. But when the servant in brown appeared at the door silently, Mr Verloc had not

210   moved an inch from the place he had occupied throughout the interview. He had remained motionless, as if feeling himself surrounded by pitfalls.

He walked along a passage lighted by a lonely gasjet, then up a flight of winding stairs, and through a glazed and cheerful corridor on the first floor. The footman threw open a door, and stood aside. The feet
215 of Mr Verloc felt a thick carpet. The room was large, with three windows; and a young man with a shaven, big face, sitting in a roomy arm-chair before a vast mahogany writing-table, said in French to the Chancelier d'Ambassade, who was going out with the papers in his hand:
220 'You are quite right, mon cher. He's fat – the animal.'

Mr Vladimir, First Secretary, had a drawing-room reputation as an agreeable and entertaining man. He was something of a favourite in society. His wit consisted in discovering droll connections between incongruous ideas; and when talking in that strain he sat well forward
225 on his seat, with his left hand raised, as if exhibiting his funny demonstrations between the thumb and forefinger, while his round and clean-shaven face wore an expression of merry perplexity.

But there was no trace of merriment or perplexity in the way he looked at Mr Verloc. Lying far back in the deep arm-chair, with squarely
230 spread elbows, and throwing one leg over a thick knee, he had with his smooth and rosy countenance the air of a preternaturally thriving baby that will not stand nonsense from anybody.

'You understand French, I suppose?' he said.

Mr Verloc stated huskily that he did. His whole vast bulk had a
235 forward inclination. He stood on the carpet in the middle of the room, clutching his hat and stick in one hand; the other hung lifelessly by his side. He muttered unobtrusively somewhere deep down in his throat something about having done his military service in the French artillery. At once, with contemptuous perversity, Mr Vladimir changed the
240 language, and began to speak idiomatic English without the slightest trace of a foreign accent.

'Ah! Yes. Of course. Let's see. How much did you get for obtaining the design of the improved breech-block of their new field-gun?'

'Five years' rigorous confinement in a fortress,' Mr Verloc answered,
245 unexpectedly, but without any sign of feeling.

'You got off easily,' was Mr Vladimir's comment. 'And, anyhow, it served you right for letting yourself get caught. What made you go in for that sort of thing – eh?'

Mr Verloc's husky conversational voice was heard speaking of youth,
250 of a fatal infatuation for an unworthy –

'Aha! Cherchez la femme,† Mr Vladimir deigned to interrupt, unbending, but without affability; there was, on the contrary, a touch of

---

cherchez la femme   (French) look for the
woman [in the case and you find the answer]

grimness in his condescension. 'How long have you been employed by the Embassy here?' he asked.

255 'Ever since the time of the late Baron Stott Wartenheim,' Mr Verloc answered in subdued tones, and protruding his lips sadly, in sign of sorrow for the deceased diplomat. The First Secretary observed this play of physiognomy steadily.

'Ah! ever since. . . . Well! What have you got to say for yourself?' 260 he asked, sharply.

Mr Verloc answered with some surprise that he was not aware of having anything special to say. He had been summoned by a letter – And he plunged his hand busily into the side pocket of his overcoat, but before the mocking, cynical watchfulness of Mr Vladimir, concluded 265 to leave it there.

'Bah!' said the latter. 'What do you mean by getting out of condition like this? You haven't even got the physique of your profession. You – a member of a starving proletariat – never! You – a desperate socialist or anarchist – which is it?'

270 'Anarchist,' stated Mr Verloc in a deadened tone.

'Bosh!' went on Mr Vladimir, without raising his voice. 'You startled old Wurmt himself. You wouldn't deceive an idiot. They all are that by-the-by, but you seem to me simply impossible. So you began your connection with us by stealing the French gun designs. And you 275 got yourself caught. That must have been very disagreeable to our Government. You don't seem to be very smart.'

Mr Verloc tried to exculpate himself huskily.

'As I've had occason to observe before, a fatal infatuation for an unworthy –'

280 Mr Vladimir raised a large white, plump hand.

'Ah, yes. The unlucky attachment – of your youth. She got hold of the money, and then sold you to the police – eh?'

The doleful change in Mr Verloc's physiognomy, the momentary drooping of his whole person, confessed that such was the regrettable 285 case. Mr Vladimir's hand clasped the ankle reposing on his knee. The sock was of dark blue silk.

'You see, that was not very clever of you. Perhaps you are too susceptible.'

Mr Verloc intimated in a throaty, veiled murmur that he was no 290 longer young.

'Oh! That's a failing which age does not cure,' Mr Vladimir remarked, with sinister familiarity. 'But no! You are too fat for that. You could not have come to look like this if you had been at all susceptible. I'll tell you what I think is the matter: you are a lazy fellow. How long 295 have you been drawing pay from this Embassy?'

'Eleven years,' was the answer, after a moment of sulky hesitation.

'I've been charged with several missions to London while His Excellency Baron Stott-Wartenheim was still Ambassador in Paris. Then by his Excellency's instructions I settled down in London. I am English.'

300   'You are! Are you? Eh?'

'A natural-born British subject,' Mr Verloc said, stolidly. 'But my father was French, and so –'

'Never mind explaining,' interrupted the other. 'I daresay you could have been legally a Marshal of France and a Member of Parliament in

305   England – and then, indeed, you would have been of some use to our Embassy.'

This flight of fancy provoked something like a faint smile on Mr Verloc's face. Mr Vladimir retained an imperturbable gravity.

'But, as I've said, you are a lazy fellow; you don't use your

310   opportunities. In the time of Baron Stott-Wartenheim we had a lot of soft-headed people running this Embassy. They caused fellows of your sort to form a false conception of the nature of a secret service fund. It is my business to correct this misapprehension by telling you what the secret service is not. It is not a philanthropic institution. I've had you

315   called here on purpose to tell you this.'

Mr Vladimir observed the forced expression of bewilderment on Verloc's face, and smiled sarcastically.

'I see that you understand me perfectly. I daresay you are intelligent enough for your work. What we want now is activity – activity.'

320   On repeating this last word Mr Vladimir laid a long white forefinger on the edge of the desk. Every trace of huskiness disappeared from Verloc's voice. The nape of his gross neck became crimson above the velvet collar of his overcoat. His lips quivered before they came widely open.

325   'If you'll only be good enough to look up my record,' he boomed out in his great, clear, oratorical bass, 'you'll see I gave a warning only three months ago on the occasion of the Grand Duke Romuald's visit to Paris, which was telegraphed from here to the French police, and –'

'Tut, tut!' broke out Mr Vladimir, with a frowning grimace. 'The

330   French police had no use for your warning. Don't roar like this. What the devil do you mean?'

With a note of proud humility Mr Verloc apologized for forgetting himself. His voice, famous for years at open-air meetings and at workmen's assemblies in large halls, had contributed, he said, to his

335   reputation of a good and trustworthy comrade. It was, therefore, a part of his usefulness. It had inspired confidence in his principles. 'I was always put up to speak by the leaders at a critical moment,' Mr Verloc declared, with obvious satisfaction. There was no uproar above which he could not make himself heard, he added, and suddenly he made a

340   demonstration.

'Allow me,' he said. With lowered forehead, without looking up, swiftly and ponderously, he crossed the room to one of the French windows. As if giving way to an uncontrollable impulse, he opened it a little. Mr Vladimir, jumping up amazed from the depths of the arm-
345 chair, looked over his shoulder; and below, across the courtyard of the Embassy, well beyond the open gate, could be seen the broad back of a policeman watching idly the gorgeous perambulator of a wealthy baby being wheeled in state across the Square.

'Constable!' said Mr Verloc, with no more effort than if he were
350 whispering; and Mr Vladimir burst into a laugh on seeing the policeman spin round as if prodded by a sharp instrument. Mr Verloc shut the window quietly, and returned to the middle of the room

'With a voice like that,' he said, putting on the husky conversational pedal,† 'I was naturally trusted. And I knew what to say, too.'
355 Mr Vladimir, arranging his cravat, observed him in the glass over the mantelpiece.

'I daresay you have the social revolutionary jargon by heart well enough,' he said, contemptuously. 'Vox et. . . . You haven't ever studied Latin – have you?'
360 'No,' growled Mr Verloc. 'You did not expect me to know it. I belong to the million. Who knows Latin? Only a few hundred imbeciles who aren't fit to take care of themselves.'

For some thirty seconds longer Mr Vladimir studied in the mirror the fleshy profile, the gross bulk, of the man behind him. And at the
365 same time he had the advantage of seeing his own face, clean-shaved and round, rosy about the gills, and with the thin, sensitive lips formed exactly for the utterance of those delicate witticisms which had made him such a favourite in the very highest society. Then he turned, and advanced into the room with such determination that the very ends of his
370 quaintly old-fashioned bow necktie seemed to bristle with unspeakable menaces. The movement was so swift and fierce that Mr Verloc, casting an oblique glance, quailed inwardly.

'Aha! You dare be impudent,' Mr Vladimir began, with an amazingly guttural intonation not only utterly un-English, but absolutely un-
375 European, and startling even to Mr Verloc's experience of cosmopolitan slums. 'You dare! Well, I am going to speak plain English to you. Voice won't do. We have no use for your voice. We don't want a voice. We want facts – startling facts – damn you,' he added, with a sort of ferocious discretion, right into Mr Verloc's face.
380 'Don't you try to come over me with your Hyperborean† manners,' Mr Verloc defended himself, huskily, looking at the carpet. At this his

---

pedal tone (piano metaphor)   *Hyperborean* from the far north interlocutor, smiling mockingly above the bristling bow of his necktie, switched the conversation into French.

'You give yourself for an "agent provocateur." The proper business of an "agent provocateur" is to provoke. As far as I can judge from your record kept here, you have done nothing to earn your money for the last three years.'

'Nothing!' exclaimed Verloc, stirring not a limb, and not raising his eyes, but with the note of sincere feeling in his tone. 'I have several times prevented what might have been –'

'There is a proverb in this country which says prevention is better than cure,' interrupted Mr Vladimir, throwing himself into the armchair. 'It is stupid in a general way. There is no end or prevention. But it is characteristic. They dislike finality in this country. Don't you be too English. And in this particular instance, don't be absurd. The evil is already here. We don't want prevention – we want cure.'

He paused, turned to the desk, and turning over some papers lying there, spoke in a changed, business-like tone, without looking at Mr Verloc.

'You know, of course, of the International Conference assembled in Milan?'

Mr Verloc intimated hoarsely that he was in the habit of reading the daily papers. To a further question his answer was that, of course, he understood what he read. At this Mr Vladimir, smiling faintly at the documents he was still scanning one after another, murmured 'As long as it is not written in Latin, I suppose.'

'Or Chinese,' added Mr Verloc, stolidly.

'H'm. Some of your revolutionary friends' effusions are written in a *charabia*† every bit as incomprehensible as Chinese –' Mr Vladimir let fall disdainfully a grey sheet of printed matter. 'What are all these leaflets headed F. P., with a hammer, pen, and torch crossed? What does it mean, this F. P.?' Mr Verloc approached the imposing writing-table.

'The Future of the Proletariat. It's a society,' he explained, standing ponderously by the side of the arm-chair, 'not anarchist in principle, but open to all shades of revolutionary opinion.'

'Are you in it?'

'One of the Vice-Presidents,' Mr Verloc breathed out heavily; and the First Secretary of the Embassy raised his head to look at him.

'Then you ought to be ashamed of yourself,' he said, incisively. 'Isn't your society capable of anything else but printing this prophetic bosh in blunt type on this filthy paper – eh? Why don't you do something? Look here. I've this matter in hand now, and I tell you plainly that you

---

charabia   (French) Auvergne patois, bad French, gibberish

will have to earn your money. The good old Stott-Wartenheim times
425 are over. No work, no pay.'

Mr Verloc felt a queer sensation of faintness in his stout legs. He
stepped back one pace, and blew his nose loudly.

He was, in truth, startled and alarmed. The rusty London sunshine
struggling clear of the London mist shed a lukewarm brightness into
430 the First Secretary's private room: and in the silence Mr Verloc heard
against a window-pane the faint buzzing of a fly – his first fly of the
year – heralding better than any number of swallows the approach of
spring. The useless fussing of that tiny, energetic organism affected
unpleasantly this big man threatened in his indolence.

435 In the pause Mr Vladimir formulated in his mind a series of
disparaging remarks concerning Mr Verloc's face and figure. The fellow
was unexpectedly vulgar, heavy, and impudently unintelligent. He
looked uncommonly like a master plumber come to present his bill.
The First Secretary of the Embassy, from his occasional excursions into
440 the field of American humour, had formed a special notion of that class
of mechanic as the embodiment of fraudulent laziness and incompetency.

This was then the famous and trusty secret agent, so secret that he
was never designated otherwise but by the symbol △. in the late Baron
Stott-Wartenheim's official, semi-official, and confidential correspon-
445 dence, the celebrated agent △. whose warnings had the power to change
the schemes and the dates of royal, imperial, grand-ducal journeys, and
sometimes cause them to be put off altogether! This fellow! And Mr
Vladimir indulged mentally in an enormous and derisive fit of merriment,
partly at his own astonishment, which he judged naïve, but mostly at
450 the expense of the universally regretted Baron Stott-Wartenheim. His
late Excellency, whom the august favour of his Imperial master had
imposed as Ambassador upon several reluctant Ministers of Foreign
Affairs, had enjoyed in his lifetime a fame for an owlish, pessimistic
gullibility. His Excellency had the social revolution on the brain. He
455 imagined himself to be a diplomatist set apart by a special dispensation
to watch the end of diplomacy, and pretty nearly the end of the world,
in a horrid, democratic upheaval. His prophetic and doleful despatches
had been for years the joke of Foreign Offices. He was said to have
exclaimed on his deathbed (visited by his Imperial friend and master):
460 'Unhappy Europe! Thou shalt perish by the mortal insanity of thy
children!' He was fated to be the victim of the first humbugging rascal
that came along, thought Mr Vladimir, smiling vaguely at Mr Verloc.

'You ought to venerate the memory of Baron Stott-Wartenheim,' he
exclaimed, suddenly.

465 The lowered physiognomy of Mr Verloc expressed a sombre and
weary annoyance.

'Permit me to observe to you,' he said, 'that I came here because I

was summoned by a peremptory letter. I have been here only twice
before in the last eleven years, and certainly never at eleven in the
470   morning. It isn't very wise to call me up like this. There is just a chance
of being seen. And that would be no joke for me.'

Mr Vladimir shrugged his shoulders.

'It would destroy my usefulness,' continued the other hotly.

'That's your affair,' murmured Mr Vladimir, with soft brutality.
475   'When you cease to be useful you shall cease to be employed. Yes. Right
off. Cut short. You shall –' Mr Vladimir, frowning, paused, at a loss
for a sufficiently idiomatic expression, and instantly brightened up, with
a grin of beautifully white teeth. 'You shall be chucked,' he brought
out, ferociously.

480   Once more Mr Verloc had to react with all the force of his will
against that sensation of faintness running down one's legs which once
upon a time had inspired some poor devil with the felicitous expression:
'My heart went down into my boots.' Mr Verloc, aware of the sensation,
raised his head bravely.

485   Mr Vladimir bore the look of heavy inquiry with perfect serenity.

'What we want is to administer a tonic to the Conference in Milan,'
he said, airily. 'Its deliberations upon international action for the
suppression of political crime don't seem to get anywhere. England
lags. This country is absurd with its sentimental regard for individual
490   liberty. It's intolerable to think that all your friends have got only to
come over to –'

'In that way I have them all under my eye,' Mr Verloc interrupted,
huskily.

'It would be much more to the point to have them all under lock and
495   key. England must be brought into line. The imbecile bourgeoisie of
this country make themselves the accomplices of the very people whose
aim is to drive them out of their houses to starve in ditches. And they
have the political power still, if they only had the sense to use it for
their preservation. I suppose you agree that the middle classes are
500   stupid?'

Mr Verloc agreed hoarsely.

'They are.'

'They have no imagination. They are blinded by an idiotic vanity.
What they want just now is a jolly good scare. This is the psychological
505   moment to set your friends to work. I have had you called here to
develop to you my idea.'

And Mr Vladimir developed his idea from on high, with scorn and
condescension, displaying at the same time an amount of ignorance as
to the real aims, thoughts, and methods of the revolutionary world
510   which filled the silent Mr Verloc with inward consternation. He
confounded causes with effects more than was excusable; the most

distinguished propagandists with impulsive bomb throwers; assumed
organization where in the nature of things it could not exist; spoke of
the social revolutionary party one moment as of a perfectly disciplined
515 army, where the word of chiefs was supreme, and at another as if it
had been the loosest association of desperate brigands that ever camped
in a mountain gorge. Once Mr Verloc had opened his mouth for a
protest, but the raising of a shapely, large white hand arrested him.
Very soon he became too appalled to even try to protest. He listened in
520 a stillness of dread which resembled the immobility of profound
attention.

'A series of outrages,' Mr Vladimir continued, calmly, 'executed here
in this country; not only *planned* here – that would not do – they would
not mind. Your friends could set half the Continent on fire without
525 influencing the public opinion here in favour of a universal repressive
legislation. They will not look outside their backyard here.'

Mr Verloc cleared his throat, but his heart failed him, and he said
nothing.

'These outrages need not be especially sanguinary,' Mr Vladimir went
530 on, as if delivering a scientific lecture, 'but they must be sufficiently
startling – effective. Let them be directed against buildings, for instance.
What is the fetish of the hour that all the bourgeoisie recognize – eh,
Mr Verloc?'

Mr Verloc opened his hands and shrugged his shoulders slightly.

535 'You are too lazy to think,' was Mr Vladimir's comment upon that
gesture. 'Pay attention to what I say. The fetish of to-day is neither
royalty nor religion. Therefore the palace and the church should be left
alone. You understand what I mean, Mr Verloc?'

The dismay and the scorn of Mr Verloc found vent in an attempt at
540 levity.

'Perfectly. But what of the Embassies? A series of attacks on the
various Embassies,' he began; but he could not withstand the cold,
watchful stare of the First Secretary.

'You can be facetious, I see,' the latter observed, carelessly. 'That's
545 all right. It may enliven your oratory at socialistic congresses. But this
room is no place for it. It would be infinitely safer for you to follow
carefully what I am saying. As you are being called upon to furnish
facts instead of cock-and-bull stories, you had better try to make your
profit off what I am taking the trouble to explain to you. The sacrosanct
550 fetish of to-day is science. Why don't you get some of your friends to
go for that wooden-faced panjandrum – eh? Is it not part of these
institutions which must be swept away before the F. P. comes along?'

Mr Verloc said nothing. He was afraid to open his lips lest a groan
should escape him.

555 'This is what you should try for. An attempt upon a crowned head

or on a president is sensational enough in a way, but not so much as it used to be. It has entered into the general conception of the existence of all chiefs of state. It's almost conventional – especially since so many presidents have been assassinated. Now let us take an outrage upon –
560 say a church. Horrible enough at first sight, no doubt, and yet not so effective as a person of an ordinary mind might think. No matter how revolutionary and anarchist in inception, there would be fools enough to give such an outrage the character of a religious manifestation. And that would detract from the especial alarming significance we wish to
565 give to the act. A murderous attempt on a restaurant or a theatre would suffer in the same way from the suggestion of non-political passion; the exasperation of a hungry man, an act of social revenge. All this is used up; it is no longer instructive as an object lesson in revolutionary anarchism. Every newspaper has ready-made phrases to explain such
570 manifestations away. I am about to give you the philosophy of bomb throwing from my point of view; from the point of view you pretend to have been serving for the last eleven years. I will try not to talk above your head. The sensibilities of the class you are attacking are soon blunted. Property seems to them an indestructible thing. You can't
575 count upon their emotions either of pity or fear for very long. A bomb outrage to have any influence on public opinion now must go beyond the intention of vengeance or terrorism. It must be purely destructive. It must be that, and only that, beyond the faintest suspicion of any other object. You anarchists should make it clear that you are perfectly
580 determined to make a clean sweep of the whole social creation. But how to get that appallingly absurd notion into the heads of the middle classes so that there should be no mistake? That's the question. By directing your blows at something outside the ordinary passions of humanity is the answer. Of course, there is art. A bomb in the National
585 Gallery would make some noise. But it would not be serious enough. Art has never been their fetish. It's like breaking a few back windows in a man's house; whereas, if you want to make him really sit up, you must try at least to raise the roof. There would be some screaming of course, but from whom? Artists – art critics and such like – people of
590 no account. Nobody minds what they say. But there is learning – science. Any imbecile that has got an income believes in that. He does not know why, but he believes it matters somehow. It is the sacrosanct fetish. All the damned professors are radicals at heart. Let them know that their great panjandrum has got to go, too, to make room for the
595 Future of the Proletariat. A howl from all these intellectual idiots is bound to help forward the labours of the Milan Conference. They will be writing to the papers. Their indignation would be above suspicion, no material interests being openly at stake, and it will alarm every selfishness of the class which should be impressed. They believe that in

600   some mysterous way science is at the source of their material prosperity.
        They do. And the absurd ferocity of such a demonstration will affect
        them more profoundly than the mangling of a whole street – or theatre –
        full of their own kind. To that last they can always say: 'Oh! it's mere
        class hate.' But what is one to say to an act of destructive ferocity so
605   absurd as to be incomprehensible, inexplicable, almost unthinkable; in
        fact, mad? Madness alone is truly terrifying, inasmuch as you cannot
        placate it either by threats, persuasion, or bribes. Moreover, I am a
        civilized man. I would never dream of directing you to organize a mere
        butchery, even if I expected the best results from it. But I wouldn't
610   expect from a butchery the result I want. Murder is always with us. It
        is almost an institution. The demonstration must be against learning –
        science. But not every science will do. The attack must have all the
        shocking senselessness of gratuitous blasphemy. Since bombs are your
        means of expression, it would be really telling if one could throw a
615   bomb into pure mathematics. But that is impossible. I have been trying
        to educate you; I have expounded to you the higher philosophy of your
        usefulness, and suggested to you some serviceable arguments. The
        practical application of my teaching interests *you* mostly. But from the
        moment I have undertaken to interview you I have also given some
620   attention to the practical aspect of the question. What do you think of
        having a go at astronomy?'
           For sometime already Mr Verloc's immobility by the side of the arm-
        chair resembled a state of collapsed coma – a sort of passive insensibility
        interrupted by slight convulsive starts, such as may be observed in the
625   domestic dog having a nightmare on the hearthrug. And it was in an
        uneasy, doglike growl that he repeated the word:
           'Astronomy.'
           He had not recovered thoroughly as yet from the state of bewilderment
        brought about by the effort to follow Mr Vladimir's rapid, incisive
630   utterance. It had overcome his power of assimilation. It had made him
        angry. This anger was complicated by incredulity. And suddenly it
        dawned upon him that all this was an elaborate joke. Mr Vladimir
        exhibited his white teeth in a smile, with dimples on his round, full face
        posed with a complacent inclination above the bristling bow of his
635   necktie. The favourite of intelligent society women had assumed his
        drawing-room attitude accompanying the delivery of delicate witticisms.
        Sitting well forward, his white hand upraised, he seemed to hold
        delicately between his thumb and forefinger the subtlety of his sugges-
        tion.
640   'There could be nothing better. Such an outrage combines the greatest
        possible regard for humanity with the most alarming display of ferocious
        imbecility. I defy the ingenuity of journalists to persuade their public
        that any given member of the proletariat can have a personal grievance

against astronomy. Starvation itself could hardly be dragged in there –
645   eh? And there are other advantages. The whole civilized world has
heard of Greenwich. The very boot-blacks in the basement of Charing
Cross Station know something of it. See?'

The features of Mr Vladimir, so well known in the best society by
their humorous urbanity, beamed with cynical self-satisfaction, which
650   would have astonished the intelligent women his wit entertained so
exquisitely. 'Yes,' he continued, with a contemptuous smile, 'the blowing
up of the first meridian is bound to raise a howl of execration.'

'A difficult business,' Mr Verloc mumbled, feeling that this was the
only safe thing to say.
655   'What is the matter? Haven't you the whole gang under your hand?
The very pick of the basket? That old terrorist Yundt is here. I see him
walking about Piccadilly in his green havelock† almost every day. And
Michaelis, the ticket-of-leave† apostle† – you don't mean to say you
don't know where he is? Because if you don't, I can tell you,' Mr
660   Vladimir went on menacingly. 'If you imagine that you are the only
one on the secret fund list, you are mistaken.'

This perfectly gratuitous suggestion caused Mr Verloc to shuffle his
feet slightly.

'And the whole Lausanne lot – eh? Haven't they been flocking over
665   here at the first hint of the Milan Conference? This is an absurd
country.'

'It will cost money,' Mr Verloc said, by a sort of instinct.

'That cock won't fight,' Mr Vladimir retorted, with an amazingly
genuine English accent. 'You'll get your screw every month, and no
670   more till something happens. And if nothing happens very soon you
won't get even that. What's your ostensible occupation? What are you
supposed to live by?'

'I keep a shop,' answered Mr Verloc.

'A shop! What sort of shop?'
675   'Stationery, newspapers. My wife –'

'Your what?' interrupted Mr Vladimir in his guttural Central Asian
tones.

'My wife.' Mr Verloc raised his husky voice slightly. 'I am married.'

'That be damned for a yarn,' exclaimed the other in unfeigned
680   astonishment. 'Married! And you a professed anarchist, too! What is
this confounded nonsense? But I suppose it's merely a manner of
speaking. Anarchists don't marry. It's well known. They can't. It would
be apostasy.'

---

havelock   a military covering for a cap, with a   *ticket of leave*   parole from prison
  neckflap   *apostle*   champion in a cause

'My wife isn't one,' Mr Verloc mumbled, sulkily. 'Moreover, it's no
685 concern of yours.'

'Oh, yes, it is,' snapped Mr Vladimir. 'I am beginning to be convinced
that you are not at all the man for the work you've been employed on.
Why you must have discredited yourself completely in your own world
by your marriage. Couldn't you have managed without? This is your
690 virtuous attachment – eh? What with one sort of attachment and
another you are doing away with your usefulness.'

Mr Verloc, puffing out his cheeks, let the air escape violently, and
that was all. He had armed himself with patience. It was not to be tried
much longer. The First Secretary became suddenly very curt, detached,
695 final.

'You may go now,' he said. 'A dynamite outrage must be provoked.
I give you a month. The sittings of the Conference are suspended. Before
it reassembles again something must have happened here or your
connection with us ceases.'

700 He changed the note once more with an unprincipled versatility.

'Think over my philosophy, Mr – Mr – Verloc,' he said, with a sort
of chaffing condescension, waving his hand towards the door. 'Go for
the first meridian. You don't know the middle classes as well as I do.
Their sensibilities are jaded. The first meridian. Nothing better, and
705 nothing easier, I should think.'

He had got up, and with his thin sensitive lips twitching humorously,
watched in the glass over the mantelpiece Mr Verloc backing out of
the room heavily, hat and stick in hand. The door closed.

1905   1907

A. E. Housman

1859–1936

Alfred Edward Housman, born at Fockbury in Worcestershire, was educated in Bromsgrove and at St John's College, Oxford. Overcoming a failure in examinations at the university, he became the greatest Latin scholar of his generation (Professor at Cambridge from 1911). A *Shropshire Lad* (1896), his first book of poignant, sorrowful poems, gradually came to be widely admired. *Last Poems* (1922) was very successful. *More Poems* followed in 1936; *Collected Poems* was published in 1939.

OTHERS, I AM NOT THE FIRST

Others, I am not the first,
Have willed more mischief than they durst:
If in the breathless night I too
Shiver now, 'tis nothing new.

5　More than I, if truth were told,
Have stood and sweated hot and cold,
And through their reins* in ice and fire　　　　　loins
Fear contended with desire.

Agued once like me were they,
10　But I like them shall win my way
Lastly to the bed of mould
Where there's neither heat nor cold.

But from my grave across my brow
Plays no wind of healing now,
15　And fire and ice within me fight
Beneath the suffocating night.

1895　　　　　　　　　　　　　　1896

ON WENLOCK EDGE

On Wenlock Edge† the wood's in trouble;
 His forest fleece the Wrekin† heaves;
The gale, it plies the saplings double,
 And thick on Severn snow the leaves.

5 'Twould blow like this through holt* and hanger†   wood
 When Uricon† the city stood:
'Tis the old wind in the old anger,
 But then it threshed another wood.

Then, 'twas before my time, the Roman
10 At yonder heaving hill would stare:
The blood that warms an English yeoman,
 The thoughts that hurt him, they were there.

There, like the wind through woods in riot,
 Through him the gale of life blew high;
15 The tree of man was never quiet:
 Then 'twas the Roman, now 'tis I.

The gale, it plies the saplings double,
 It blows so hard, 'twill soon be gone:
To-day the Roman and his trouble
20 Are ashes under Uricon.

1895   1896

THE CHESTNUT CASTS HIS FLAMBEAUX

The chestnut casts his flambeaux,† and the flowers
 Stream from the hawthorn on the wind away,
The doors clap to, the pane is blind with showers.
 Pass me the can,* lad; there's an end of May.   drinking mug

---

Wenlock Edge a limestone scarp in Shropshire
Wrekin a prominent hill near Shrewsbury and
 the River Severn
hanger wood on a hillside

Uricon the Roman town Uriconium, now
 Wroxeter, in Shropshire
flambeaux torches, because chestnut blossoms
 are red

5   There's one spoilt spring to scant our mortal lot,
        One season ruined of our little store.
     May will be fine next year as like as not:
        Oh ay, but then we shall be twenty-four.

     We for a certainty are not the first
10   Have sat in taverns while the tempest hurled
     Their hopeful plans to emptiness, and cursed
        Whatever brute and blackguard made the world.

     It is in truth iniquity on high
        To cheat our sentenced souls of aught they crave,
15   And mar the merriment as you and I
        Fare on our long fool's-errand to the grave.

     Iniquity it is; but pass the can.
        My lad, no pair of kings our mothers bore;
     Our only portion is the estate of man:
20   We want the moon, but we shall get no more.

     If here to-day the cloud of thunder lours
        To-morrow it will hie on far behests;
     The flesh will grieve on other bones than ours
        Soon, and the soul will mourn in other breasts.

25   The troubles of our proud and angry dust
        Are from eternity, and shall not fail.
     Bear them we can, and if we can we must.
        Shoulder the sky, my lad, and drink your ale.

     1900–22   1922

THE ORACLES

'Tis mute, the word they went to hear on high Dodona† mountain
    When winds were in the oakenshaws† and all the cauldrons tolled,
And mute's the midland navel-stone† beside the singing fountain,
    And echoes list to silence now where gods told lies of old.

Dodona   the oracle of Zeus at Dodona, in
Epirus in northern Greece, surrounded by
oaks. It was the oldest of the Greek oracles.
Bronze cauldrons, a 'murmuring' fountain
and priests and priestesses are mentioned in
ancient accounts of the shrine
oakenshaws   small oak-woods
midland navel-stone   a stone believed to be of
divine origin, and to stand at the centre of
the world. There was another, later, at Delphi

5   I took my question to the shrine that has not ceased from speaking,
      The heart within, that tells the truth and tells it twice as plain;
    And from the cave of oracles I heard the priestess shrieking[†]
      That she and I should surely die and never live again.

    Oh priestess, what you cry is clear, and sound good sense I think it;
10   But let the screaming echoes rest, and froth your mouth no more.
    'Tis true there's better boose* than brine, but he that drowns   booze
      must drink it;
      And oh, my lass, the news is news that men have heard before.

The King with half the East at heel is marched from lands of morning;
     Their fighters drink the rivers up, their shafts benight the air.
15 *And he that stands will die for nought, and home there's no returning.*
    The Spartans[†] on the sea-wet rock[†] sat down and combed their hair.

?1904   1922

COULD MAN BE DRUNK FOR EVER

Could man be drunk for ever
    With liquor, love or fights,
Lief* should I rouse at morning   willingly
    And lief lie down of nights.

5 But men at whiles are sober
    And think by fits and starts.
And if they think, they fasten
    Their hands upon their hearts.

1904–5   1922

---

shrieking ancient priestesses, possessed by the god, spoke in a state of frenzy
Spartans the troops of King Leonidas of Sparta are said to have combed their hair before going to certain death in defence of the pass of Thermopylae against the invading army of Xerxes, King of Persia, in 480 BC. The poet Simonides (*c. 556–c.* 468 BC) immortalised them in the epitaph: 'Go stranger, and tell the Spartans that we lie here, obedient to their laws'
sea-wet rock Thermopylae is between Mt Callidromus and the Malian Gulf

THE FIRST OF MAY

The orchards half the way
   From home to Ludlow† fair
Flowered on the first of May
   In Mays when I was there;
5 And seen from stile or turning
   The plume of smoke would show
Where fires were burning
   That went out long ago.

The plum broke forth in green,
10   The pear stood high and snowed,
My friends and I between
   Would take the Ludlow road;
Dressed to the nines and drinking
   And light in heart and limb,
15 And each chap thinking
   The fair was held for him.

Between the trees in flower
   New friends at fairtime tread
The way where Ludlow tower
20   Stands planted on the dead.
Our thoughts, a long while after,
   They think, our words they say;
Theirs now's the laughter,
   The fair, the first of May.

25 Ay, yonder lads are yet
   The fools that we were then;
For oh, the sons we get
   Are still the sons of men.
The sumless tale of sorrow
30   Is all unrolled in vain:
May comes to-morrow
   And Ludlow fair again.

?1905   1922

Ludlow   a town in Shropshire dear to
Housman, who is buried there

WHEN I WOULD MUSE IN BOYHOOD

When I would muse in boyhood
  The wild green woods among,
Then nurse resolves and fancies
  Because the world was young,
5 It was not foes to conquer,
    Nor sweethearts to be kind,
But it was friends to die for
  That I would seek and find.

I sought them far and found them,
10 The sure, the straight, the brave,
The hearts I lost my own to,
  The souls I could not save.
They braced their belts about them,
  They crossed in ships the sea,
15 They sought and found six feet of ground,
  And there they died for me.

1922   1922

IN VALLEYS GREEN AND STILL

In valleys green and still
  Where lovers wander maying
They hear from over hill
  A music playing.

5 Behind the drum and fife,
  Past hawthornwood and hollow,
Through earth and out of life
  The soldiers follow.

The soldier's is the trade:
10 In any wind or weather
He steals the heart of maid
  And man together.

The lover and his lass
  Beneath the hawthorn lying

15   Have heard the soldiers pass,
          And both are sighing.

      And down the distance they
          With dying note and swelling
      Walk the resounding way
20   To the still dwelling.

      1922   1922

STARS, I HAVE SEEN THEM FALL

      Stars, I have seen them fall,
          But when they drop and die
      No star is lost at all
          From all the star-sown sky.
5   The toil of all that be
          Helps not the primal fault;
      It rains into the sea,
          And still the sea is salt.

                                    1936

PARTA QUIES†

      Good-night;† ensured release,
      Imperishable peace,
          Have these for yours.
      While sea abides, and land,
5   And earth's foundations stand,
          And heaven endures.

      When earth's foundations flee,
      Nor sky nor land nor sea
          At all is found,

Parta Quies (Latin) rest obtained (the sleep of death)

Good night . . .   These first three lines are inscribed on Housman's tomb

10   Content you, let them burn:
    It is not your concern;
       Sleep on, sleep sound.

1881   1936

W. B. Yeats
1865–1939

William Butler Yeats was born in Dublin and educated at the Godolphin School, London, the High School, Dublin, and the School of Art, Dublin. His early volumes of romantic pre-Raphaelite verse were fortified by knowledge of Irish songs and legends. In 1896 he met Lady Gregory, an Anglo-Irish widow, with whom he founded the Abbey Theatre in Dublin (1904). His love for Maud Gonne, a fervent nationalist for whom he wrote the play *The Countess Cathleen* (performed in Dublin in 1899), involved him in Irish political movements; these activities later helped to make him a Senator in the Irish Free State (1922–8). *In the Seven Woods* (1903) and *The Green Helmet* (1910) include poems celebrating Maud Gonne's beauty and his unrequited love. Yeats's verse grew more colloquial and realistic with every volume. In *The Wild Swans at Coole* (1919), *Michael Robartes and the Dancer* (1921), and *The Tower* (1928), he evolved a new kind of poetry, taut but graceful in style, enriched by images and symbols from the private, mystical 'system' he developed, encouraged by Georgie Hyde-Lees, whom he married in 1917, and set out in his prose-work *The Vision* (privately printed in 1926). He won the Nobel Prize for Literature in 1923. Later volumes include *Words for Music Perhaps* (1931), *The Winding Stair* (1933), *A Full Moon in March* (1935) and *Last Poems* (1939). His *Collected Poems* was published in 1950 and *Collected Plays* in 1952.

DOWN BY THE SALLEY GARDENS†

Down by the salley* gardens my love and I did meet;   willow
She passed the salley gardens with little snow-white feet.
She bid me take love easy, as the leaves grow on the tree;
But I, being young and foolish, with her would not agree.

Down by the Salley Gardens   the poem is
  based on a snatch of an old song Yeats heard
  in County Sligo

5 In a field by the river my love and I did stand,
And on my leaning shoulder she laid her snow-white hand.
She bid me take life easy, as the grass grows on the weirs;
But I was young and foolish, and now am full of tears.

1889

THE LAKE ISLE OF INNISFREE

I will arise† and go now, and go to Innisfree,†
And a small cabin build there, of clay and wattles made:
Nine bean-rows will I have there, a hive for the honey-bee,
And live alone in the bee-loud glade.

5 And I shall have some peace there, for peace comes dropping slow,
Dropping from the veils of the morning to where the cricket sings;
There midnight's all a glimmer, and noon a purple glow,
And evening full of the linnet's wings.

I will arise and go now, for always night and day
10 I hear lake water lapping with low sounds by the shore;
While I stand on the roadway, or on the pavements grey,
I hear it in the deep heart's core.

1890   1890

THE FIDDLER OF DOONEY

When I play on my fiddle in Dooney,
Folk dance like a wave of the sea;
My cousin is priest in Kilvarnet,
My brother in Mocharabuiee.†

5 I passed my brother and cousin:
They read in their books of prayer;

I will arise . . . Innisfree See Luke 15. 18: 'I will arise and go to my father'. Innisfree is an island in Lough Gill, County Sligo

Mocharabuiee pronounced as if spelt 'Mockrabwee'

I read in my book of songs
I bought at the Sligo fair.

10 When we come at the end of time
To Peter sitting in state,
He will smile on the three old spirits,
But call me first through the gate;

For the good are always the merry,
Save by an evil chance,
15 And the merry love the fiddle,
And the merry love to dance:

And when the folk there spy me,
They will all come up to me,
With 'Here is the fiddler of Dooney!'
20 And dance like a wave of the sea.

1892   1892

NEVER GIVE ALL THE HEART

Never give all the heart, for love
Will hardly seem worth thinking of
To passionate women if it seem
Certain, and they never dream
5 That it fades out from kiss to kiss;
For everything that's lovely is
But a brief, dreamy, kind delight.
O never give the heart outright,
For they, for all smooth lips can say,
10 Have given their hearts up to the play.
And who could play it well enough
If deaf and dumb and blind with love?
He that made this knows all the cost,
For he gave all his heart and lost.

1905

WORDS

I had this thought a while ago,
'My darling† cannot understand
What I have done, or what would do
In this blind bitter land.'

5   And I grew weary of the sun
Until my thoughts cleared up again,
Remembering that the best I have done
Was done to make it plain;

That every year I have cried, 'At length
10   My darling understands it all,
Because I have come into my strength,
And words obey my call';

That had she done so who can say
What would have shaken from the sieve?
15   I might have thrown poor words away
And been content to live.

1908   1910

NO SECOND TROY

Why should I blame her† that she filled my days
With misery, or that she would of late
Have taught to ignorant men most violent ways,
Or hurled the little streets upon the great,
5   Had they but courage equal to desire?
What could have made her peaceful with a mind
That nobleness made simple as a fire,
With beauty like a tightened bow; a kind
That is not natural in an age like this,
10   Being high and solitary and most stern?
Why, what could she have done, being what she is?
Was there another Troy† for her to burn?

1908   1910

My darling   Maud Gonne
her   Maud Gonne
another Troy   Troy was burned and sacked by
the Greeks in vengeance for the theft of

Helen, according to Greek legend the most
beautiful of women, with whom Yeats
associates Maud Gonne

A COAT

I made my song a coat
Covered with embroideries
Out of old mythologies
From heel to throat;
5   But the fools[†] caught it,
Wore it in the world's eyes
As though they'd wrought it.
Song, let them take it,
For there's more enterprise
10   In walking naked.

1912   1914

THE SCHOLARS

Bald heads forgetful of their sins,
Old learned, respectable bald heads
Edit and annotate the lines
That young men, tossing on their beds,
5   Rhymed out in love's despair
To flatter beauty's ignorant ear.

All shuffle there; all cough in ink;
All wear the carpet with their shoes;
All think what other people think;
10   All know the man their neighbour knows.
Lord, what would they say
Did their Catullus[†] walk that way?

1914–15   1915

THE FISHERMAN

Although I can see him still,
The freckled man who goes

---

the fools   imitators of Yeats's earlier verse   c. 54 BC), whose erotic (Latin) poems Yeats
Catullus   Gaius Valerius Catullus (c. 84–   has in mind

To a grey place on a hill
In grey Connemara clothes
5 At dawn to cast his flies,
It's long since I began
To call up to the eyes
This wise and simple man.
All day I'd looked in the face
10 What I had hoped 'twould be
To write for my own race
And the reality;

The living men that I hate,
The dead man that I loved,
15 The craven man in his seat,
The insolent unreproved,
And no knave brought to book
Who has won a drunken cheer,
The witty man and his joke
20 Aimed at the commonest ear,
The clever man who cries
The catch-cries of the clown,
The beating down of the wise
And great Art beaten down.

25 Maybe a twelvemonth since
Suddenly I began,
In scorn of this audience,
Imagining a man,
And his sun-freckled face,
30 And grey Connemara cloth,
Climbing up to a place
Where stone is dark under froth,
And the down-turn of his wrist
When the flies drop in the stream;
35 A man who does not exist,
A man who is but a dream;
And cried, 'Before I am old
I shall have written him one
Poem maybe as cold
40 And passionate as the dawn.'

1914–15   1916

AN IRISH AIRMAN FORESEES HIS DEATH

I know[†] that I shall meet my fate
Somewhere among the clouds above;
Those that I fight I do not hate,
Those that I guard[†] I do not love;
5   My country is Kiltartan Cross,[†]
My countrymen Kiltartan's poor,
No likely end could bring them loss
Or leave them happier than before.
Nor law, nor duty bade me fight,
10   Nor public men, nor cheering crowds,
A lonely impulse of delight
Drove to this tumult in the clouds;
I balanced all, brought all to mind,
The years to come seemed waste of breath,
15   A waste of breath the years behind
In balance with this life, this death.

1918   1919

THE SECOND COMING

Turning and turning in the widening gyre[†]
The falcon cannot hear the falconer;
Things fall apart; the centre cannot hold;
Mere anarchy is loosed upon the world,
5   The blood-dimmed tide is loosed, and everywhere
The ceremony of innocence is drowned;
The best lack all conviction, while the worst
Are full of passionate intensity.

I know the poem is a tribute to Lady Gregory's
son, Major Robert Gregory, killed in action
in 1918
those that I guard the British

Kiltartan Cross a village near the Gregory
estate at Coole Park, County Galway
gyre gyration, the falcon's circling flight

Surely some revelation is at hand;
10 Surely the Second Coming is at hand.
The Second Coming! Hardly are those words out
When a vast image out of *Spiritus Mundi*[†]
Troubles my sight: somewhere in sands of the desert
A shape[†] with lion body and the head of a man,
15 A gaze blank and pitiless as the sun,
Is moving its slow thighs, while all about it
Reel shadows of the indignant desert birds.
The darkness drops again; but now I know
That twenty centuries of stony sleep
20 Were vexed to nightmare by a rocking cradle,[†]
And what rough beast, its hour[†] come round at last,
Slouches towards Bethlehem to be born?

1919   1921

LEDA AND THE SWAN

A sudden blow: the great wings beating still
Above the staggering girl, her thighs caressed
By the dark webs, her nape caught in his bill,
He holds her helpless breast upon his breast.

5   How can those terrified vague fingers push
The feathered glory from her loosening thighs?
And how can body, laid in that white rush,
But feel the strange heart beating where it lies?

A shudder in the loins engenders there
10 The broken wall,[†] the burning roof and tower
And Agamemnon[†] dead.
                              Being so caught up,

Spiritus Mundi Yeats's term for mankind's
  collective memory
a shape Yeats associated this creature with
  destruction
cradle at Christ's birth
its hour Yeats believed that a new cycle of
  twenty centuries was about to succeed the

Christian era
the broken wall of Troy. Raped by Zeus in
  the form of a swan, Leda gave birth to Helen
Agamemnon Leda's daughter Clytemnestra
  killed her husband Agamemnon after the fall
  of Troy

So mastered by the brute blood of the air,
Did she put on his knowledge with his power
15   Before the indifferent beak could let her drop?

1923   1924

SAILING TO BYZANTIUM

I

That is no country† for old men. The young
In one another's arms, birds in the trees
– Those dying generations – at their song,
The salmon-falls, the mackerel-crowded seas.
5   Fish, flesh, or fowl, commend all summer long
Whatever is begotten, born, and dies.
Caught in that sensual music all neglect
Monuments of unageing intellect.

II

An aged man is but a paltry thing,
10   A tattered coat upon a stick, unless
Soul clap its hands and sing, and louder sing
For every tatter in its mortal dress,
Nor is there singing school but studying
Monuments of its own magnificence;
15   And therefore I have sailed the seas and come
To the holy city of Byzantium.†

III

O sages standing in God's holy fire
As in the gold mosaic of a wall,
Come from the holy fire, perne in a gyre,†
20   And be the singing-masters of my soul.
Consume my heart away; sick with desire
And fastened to a dying animal
It knows not what it is; and gather me
Into the artifice of eternity.

---

country   the country described is reminiscent
of Ireland
Byzantium   Yeats idealised the civilisation of
Byzantium (Constantinople); he had seen
Byzantine art in Italy

perne in a gyre   a pern(e) is a bobbin; to perne
is to move in a spiral or gyre. The poet asks
the sages to leave eternity and spin within his
cycle of history

IV

25 Once out of nature I shall never take
    My bodily form from any natural thing,
    But such a form as Grecian goldsmiths make
    Of hammered gold and gold enamelling
    To keep a drowsy Emperor awake;
30 Or set upon a golden bough to sing
    To lords and ladies of Byzantium
    Of what is past, or passing, or to come.

1926   1927

AMONG SCHOOL CHILDREN

I

    I walk through the long schoolroom questioning;
    A kind old nun in a white hood replies;
    The children learn to cipher and to sing,
    To study reading-books and histories,
5   To cut and sew, be neat in everything
    In the best modern way – the children's eyes
    In momentary wonder stare upon
    A sixty-year-old smiling public man.

II

    I dream of a Ledaean† body, bent
10 Above a sinking fire, a tale that she
    Told of a harsh reproof, or trivial event
    That changed some childish day to tragedy –
    Told, and it seemed that our two natures blent
    Into a sphere from youthful sympathy,
15 Or else, to alter Plato's parable,†
    Into the yolk and white of the one shell.

III

    And thinking of that fit of grief or rage
    I look upon one child or t'other there

Ledaean as beautiful as Leda's daughter
Helen. Yeats was thinking of Maud Gonne

Plato's parable In the *Symposium* Zeus is said
to have split the nature of man into two parts

And wonder if she stood so at that age –
20   For even daughters of the swan† can share
Something of every paddler's heritage –
And had that colour upon cheek or hair,
And thereupon my heart is driven wild:
She stands before me as a living child.

IV

25   Her present image floats into the mind –
Did Quattrocento finger† fashion it
Hollow of cheek as though it drank the wind
And took a mess* of shadows for its meat?   meal
And I though never of Ledaean kind
30   Had pretty plumage once – enough of that,
Better to smile on all that smile, and show
There is a comfortable kind of old scarecrow.

V

What youthful mother, a shape upon her lap
Honey of generation had betrayed,
35   And that must sleep, shriek, struggle to escape
As recollection or the drug decide,
Would think her son, did she but see that shape
With sixty or more winters on its head,
A compensation for the pang of his birth,
40   Or the uncertainty of his setting forth?

VI

Plato† thought nature but a spume that plays
Upon a ghostly paradigm of things;†
Solider† Aristotle played the taws
Upon the bottom of a king of kings;†
45   World-famous† golden-thighed Pythagoras
Fingered upon a fiddle-stick or strings
What a star sang and careless Muses heard:†
Old clothes† upon old sticks to scare a bird.

---

swan   See 'Leda and the Swan'
Quattrocento finger   that is, of an Italian artist
   of the fifteenth century
Plato . . . things   the philosopher Plato (c. 427–
   348 BC) held that the material world is only
   a reflection of real, eternal 'forms'
Solider . . . kings   Alexander the Great, when
   a boy, was tutored by Aristotle; a taws is a
   leather strap for punishment

World-famous . . . heard   One legend about
   the philosopher Pythagoras (sixth century BC)
   gave him a golden thigh. Pythagoras was
   interested in mathematical theories about
   music and the nature of things
Old clothes . . .   Yeats commented on a draft
   of these lines that 'even the greatest men are
   owls, scarecrows, by the time their fame has
   come'

VII

Both nuns and mothers worship images,
50   But those the candles light are not as those
That animate a mother's reveries,
But keep a marble or a bronze repose.
And yet they too break hearts – O Presences
That passion, piety or affection knows,
55   And that all heavenly glory symbolise –
O self-born mockers of man's enterprise;

VIII

Labour is blossoming or dancing where
The body is not bruised to pleasure soul,
Nor beauty born out of its own despair,
60   Nor blear-eyed wisdom out of midnight oil.
O chestnut-tree, great-rooted blossomer,
Are you the leaf, the blossom or the bole?
O body swayed to music, O brightening glance,
How can we know the dancer from the dance?

1926   1928

SWIFT'S EPITAPH†

Swift has sailed into his rest;
Savage indignation there
Cannot lacerate his breast.
Imitate him if you dare,
5   World-besotted traveller; he
Served human liberty.

1929–30   1931

BYZANTIUM†

The unpurged images of day recede;
The Emperor's drunken soldiery are abed;

Epitaph   The satirist Jonathan Swift (1667–1745) is a national hero in his native Ireland. This poem is an English version of Swift's Latin lines on his tomb in St Patrick's Cathedral, Dublin, of which he was Dean
Byzantium   Yeats's diary for 1930 notes: 'Describe Byzantium as it is in the system towards the end of the first Christian millenium. A walking Mummy. Flames at the street corners where the soul is purified, birds of hammered gold singing in their golden trees, in the harbour [dolphins] offering their backs to the wailing dead that they may carry them to Paradise'

Night resonance recedes, night-walkers'* song   prostitutes
After great cathedral gong;
5   A starlit or a moonlit dome† disdains
All that man is,
All mere complexities,
The fury and the mire of human veins.

Before me floats an image, man or shade,
10   Shade more than man, more image than a shade;
For Hades' bobbin bound in mummy-cloth
May unwind the winding path;
A mouth that has no moisture and no breath
Breathless mouths may summon;
15   I hail the superhuman;
I call it death-in-life and life-in-death.

Miracle, bird or golden handiwork,
More miracle than bird or handiwork,
Planted on the star-lit golden bough,
20   Can like the cocks of Hades crow,
Or, by the moon embittered, scorn aloud
In glory of changeless metal
Common bird or petal
And all complexities of mire or blood.

25   At midnight on the Emperor's pavement flit
Flames that no faggot† feeds, nor steel has lit,
Nor storm disturbs, flames begotten of flame,
Where blood-begotten spirits come
And all complexities of fury leave,
30   Dying into a dance,
An agony of trance,
An agony of flame that cannot singe a sleeve.

Astraddle on the dolphin's mire and blood,
Spirit after spirit! The smithies break the flood,
35   The golden smithies of the Emperor!
Marbles of the dancing floor
Break bitter furies of complexity,

---

dome   of the cathedral of St Sophia   *faggot*   a bundle of sticks for fuel

Those images that yet
Fresh images beget,
40   That dolphin-torn, that gong-tormented sea.

1930   1932

COOLE PARK AND BALLYLEE,† 1931

Under my window-ledge the waters race,
Otters below and moor-hens on the top,
Run for a mile undimmed in Heaven's face
Then darkening through 'dark' Raftery's 'cellar'† drop,
5   Run underground, rise in a rocky place
In Coole demesne, and there to finish up
Spread to a lake and drop into a hole.
What's water but the generated soul?

Upon the border of that lake's a wood
10   Now all dry sticks under a wintry sun,
And in a copse of beeches there I stood,
For Nature's pulled her tragic buskin on
And all the rant's a mirror of my mood:
At sudden thunder of the mounting swan
15   I turned about and looked where branches break
The glittering reaches of the flooded lake.

Another emblem there! That stormy white
But seems a concentration of the sky;
And, like the soul, it sails into the sight
20   And in the morning's gone, no man knows why;
And is so lovely that it sets to right
What knowledge or its lack had set awry,
So arrogantly pure, a child might think
It can be murdered with a spot of ink.

25   Sound of a stick upon the floor, a sound
From somebody that toils from chair to chair;

Coole Park and Ballylee Coole Park was Lady
Gregory's estate in County Galway. Yeats
bought the then ruined castle, which he called
Thorne (from the Irish *tor/tur*, a tower), at
Ballylee Co Galway for £35 in 1917
'dark' Raftery's 'cellar' the Gaelic poet
Anthony Raftery (1784–1834) was blind

Beloved books that famous hands have bound,
Old marble heads, old pictures everywhere;
Great rooms where travelled men and children found
30   Content or joy; a last inheritor
Where none has reigned that lacked a name and fame
Or out of folly into folly came.

A spot whereon the founders lived and died
Seemed once more dear than life; ancestral trees,
35   Or gardens rich in memory glorified
Marriages, alliances and families,
And every bride's ambition satisfied.
Where fashion or mere fantasy decrees
We shift about – all that great glory spent –
40   Like some poor Arab tribesman and his tent.

We were the last romantics – chose for theme
Traditional sanctity and loveliness;
Whatever's written in what poets name
The book of the people; whatever most can bless
45   The mind of man or elevate a rhyme;
But all is changed, that high horse riderless,
Though mounted in that saddle Homer rode
Where the swan drifts upon a darkening flood.

1931   1933

LAPIS LAZULI†

I have heard that hysterical women say
They are sick of the palette and fiddle-bow,
Of poets that are always gay,
For everybody knows or else should know
5   That if nothing drastic is done
Aeroplane and Zeppelin will come out,
Pitch like King Billy† bomb-balls in
Until the town lie beaten flat.

Lapis Lazuli Yeats was given a piece of this
blue, semi-precious stone, decorated with
Chinese carvings

King Billy William III defeated James II at the
Battle of the Boyne in 1690

All perform their tragic play,
10   There struts Hamlet, there is Lear,
That's Ophelia, that Cordelia;
Yet they, should the last scene be there,
The great stage curtain about to drop,
If worthy their prominent part in the play,
15   Do not break up their lines to weep.
They know that Hamlet and Lear are gay;
Gaiety transfiguring all that dread.
All men have aimed at, found and lost;
Black out; Heaven blazing into the head:
20   Tragedy wrought to its uttermost.
Though Hamlet rambles and Lear rages,
And all the drop-scenes drop at once
Upon a hundred thousand stages,
It cannot grow by an inch or an ounce.

25   On their own feet they came, or on shipboard,
Camel-back, horse-back, ass-back, mule-back,
Old civilisations put to the sword.
Then they and their wisdom went to rack:
No handiwork of Callimachus,†
30   Who handled marble as if it were bronze,
Made draperies that seemed to rise
When sea-wind swept the corner, stands:
His long lamp-chimney shaped like the stem
Of a slender palm, stood but a day;
35   All things fall and are built again,
And those that build them again are gay.

Two Chinamen, behind them a third,
Are carved in lapis lazuli,
Over them flies a long-legged bird,
40   A symbol of longevity;
The third, doubtless a serving-man,
Carries a musical instrument.

Every discoloration of the stone,
Every accidental crack or dent,
45   Seems a water-course or an avalanche,
Or lofty slope where it still snows
Though doubtless plum or cherry-branch

Callimachus   Greek sculptor (fifth century BC)

Sweetens the little half-way house
Those Chinamen climb towards, and I
50   Delight to imagine them seated there;
There, on the mountain and the sky,
On all the tragic scene they stare.
One asks for mournful melodies;
Accomplished fingers begin to play.
55   Their eyes mid many wrinkles, their eyes,
Their ancient, glittering eyes, are gay.

1936   1938

BEAUTIFUL LOFTY THINGS

Beautiful lofty things: O'Leary's noble head;†
My father upon the Abbey stage, before him a raging crowd:
'This Land of Saints,' and then as the applause died out,
'Of plaster Saints'; his beautiful mischievous head thrown
     back.
5   Standish O'Grady† supporting himself between the tables
Speaking to a drunken audience high nonsensical words;
Augusta Gregory seated at her great ormolu table,
Her eightieth winter approaching: 'Yesterday he threatened
     my life.
I told him that nightly from six to seven I sat at this table,
10   The blinds drawn up'; Maud Gonne at Howth† station waiting
     a train,
Pallas Athene† in that straight back and arrogant head:
All the Olympians; a thing never known again.

?1937   1938

WHY SHOULD NOT OLD MEN BE MAD?

Why should not old men be mad?
Some have known a likely lad

O'Leary's noble head   John O'Leary (1830–
   1907), who influenced the poet's opinions,
   was handsome in old age
Standish O'Grady   Irish historian and
   populariser of Irish legendary stories (1846–

1928)
Howth   Yeats first proposed to Maud Gonne
   here, north of Dublin
Pallas Athene   the Greek Goddess of Wisdom

That had a sound fly-fisher's wrist
Turn to a drunken journalist;
5   A girl that knew all Dante once
Live to bear children to a dunce;
A Helen of social welfare dream,
Climb on a wagonette to scream.
Some think it a matter of course that chance
10   Should starve good men and bad advance,
That if their neighbours figured plain,
As though upon a lighted screen,
No single story would they find
Of an unbroken happy mind,
15   A finish worthy of the start.
Young men know nothing of this sort,
Observant old men know it well;
And when they know what old books tell,
And that no better can be had,
20   Known why an old man should be mad.

1936   1939

THE CIRCUS AMIMALS' DESERTION

I

I sought a theme and sought for it in vain,
I sought it daily for six weeks or so.
Maybe at last, being but a broken man,
I must be satisfied with my heart, although
5   Winter and summer till old age began
My circus animals† were all on show,
Those stilted boys,† that burnished chariot,
Lion and woman and the Lord knows what.

II

What can I but enumerate old themes?
10   First that sea-rider Oisin† led by the nose

---

my circus animals   Yeats's early work
stilted boys   heroes of Irish myth
Oisin   (pronounced Usheen) a reference to

Yeats's long poem *The Wanderings of Oisin*
(1889)

Through three enchanted islands, allegorical dreams,
Vain gaiety, vain battle, vain repose,
Themes of the embittered heart, or so it seems,
That might adorn old songs or courtly shows;
15   But what cared I that set him on to ride,
I, starved for the bosom of his faery bride?

And then a counter-truth filled out its play,
The Countess Cathleen[†] was the name I gave it;
She, pity-crazed, had given her soul away,
20   But masterful Heaven had intervened to save it.
I thought my dear[†] must her own soul destroy,
So did fanaticism and hate enslave it,
And this brought forth a dream and soon enough
This dream itself had all my thought and love.

25   And when[†] the Fool and Blind Man stole the bread
Cuchulain fought the ungovernable sea;[†]
Heart-mysteries there, and yet when all is said
It was the dream itself enchanted me:
Character isolated by a deed
30   To engross the present and dominate memory.
Players[†] and painted stage took all my love,
And not those things that they were emblems of.

III

Those masterful images because complete
Grew in pure mind, but out of what began?
35   A mound of refuse or the sweepings of a street,
Old kettles, old bottles, and a broken can,
Old iron, old bones, old rags, that raving slut
Who keeps the till. Now that my ladder's gone,
I must lie down where all the ladders start,
40   In the foul rag-and-bone shop of the heart.

?1937–8   1939

The Countess Cathleen   Yeats's play was
    performed in Dublin with Maud Gonne as
    the Countess, 8 May 1899
my dear   Maud Gonne
And when . . . sea   The Irish hero Cuchulain

dies fighting the sea while the Fool and the
    Blind Man steal bread, in Yeats's play On
    Baile's Strand (1903)
Players   Yeats managed the Abbey Theatre,
    Dublin, between 1902 and 1910

UNDER BEN BULBEN[†]

I

Swear by what the sages spoke
Round the Mareotic[†] Lake
That the Witch of Atlas knew,[†]
Spoke and set the cocks a-crow.

5   Swear by those horsemen, by those women
Complexion and form prove superhuman,
That pale, long-visaged company
That air in immortality
Completeness of their passions won;
10   Now they ride the wintry dawn
Where Ben Bulben sets the scene.

Here's the gist of what they mean.

II

Many times man lives and dies
Between his two eternities,
15   That of race and that of soul,
And ancient Ireland knew it all.
Whether man die in his bed
Or the rifle knocks him dead,
A brief parting from those dear
20   Is the worst man has to fear.
Though grave-diggers' toil is long,
Sharp their spades, their muscles strong,
They but thrust their buried men
Back in the human mind again.

III

25   You that Mitchel's prayer[†] have heard,
'Send war in our time, O Lord!'
Know that when all words are said
And a man is fighting mad,
Something drops from eyes long blind,
30   He completes his partial mind,

Ben Bulben   a mountain near Sligo. Yeats is
buried close to it in Drumcliff Churchyard
Mareotic ... knew   In Shelley's poem 'The
Witch of Atlas', the witch visits this Egyptian
lake, once frequented by Neoplatonist
philosophers
Mitchel's prayer   John Mitchel (1815–75),
Irish nationalist; Yeats quotes his *Jail Journal*
(1843)

For an instant stands at ease,
Laughs aloud, his heart at peace.
Even the wisest man grows tense
With some sort of violence
35   Before he can accomplish fate,
Know his work or choose his mate.

IV

Poet and sculptor, do the work,
Nor let the modish painter shirk
What his great forefathers did,
40   Bring the soul of man to God,
Make him fill the cradles right.

Measurement began our might:
Forms a stark Egyptian thought,
Forms that gentler Phidias[†] wrought.
45   Michael Angelo left a proof
On the Sistine Chapel roof,
Where but half-awakened Adam
Can disturb globe-trotting Madam
Till her bowels are in heat,
50   Proof that there's a purpose set
Before the secret working mind:
Profane perfection of mankind.

Quattrocento put in paint
On backgrounds for a God or Saint
55   Gardens where a soul's at ease;
Where everything that meets the eye,
Flowers and grass and cloudless sky,
Resemble forms that are or seem
When sleepers wake and yet still dream,
60   And when it's vanished still declare,
With only bed and bedstead there,
That heavens had opened.

Gyres run on;
When that greater dream had gone
65   Calvert[†]and Wilson, Blake and Claude,[†]
Prepared a rest for the people of God,

Phidias   Greek sculptor (*c.* 490–432 BC)
Calvert . . . Claude   the painters Edward
Calvert (1799–1883), a follower of William

Blake, Richard Wilson (1714–82) and Claude
Lorraine (1600–82) interested Yeats

Palmer's phrase,[†] but after that
Confusion fell upon our thought.

V

Irish poets, learn your trade,
70 Sing whatever is well made,
Scorn the sort now growing up
All out of shape from toe to top,
Their unremembering hearts and heads
Base-born products of base beds.
75 Sing the peasantry, and then
Hard-riding country gentlemen,
The holiness of monks, and after
Porter-drinkers' randy laughter;
Sing the lords and ladies gay
80 That were beaten into the clay
Through seven heroic centuries;
Cast your mind on other days
That we in coming days may be
Still the indomitable Irishry.

VI

85 Under bare Ben Bulben's head
In Drumcliff churchyard Yeats is laid.
An ancestor[†] was rector there
Long years ago, a church stands near,
By the road an ancient cross.
90 No marble, no conventional phrase;
On limestone quarried near the spot
By his command these words are cut:
         Cast a cold eye
         On life, on death.
95   *Horseman, pass by!*[†]

September 4, 1938   1939

Palmer's phrase Samuel Palmer (1805–81),
  landscape painter, said of Blake that his work
  shows 'the rest which remains to the people
  of God'

an ancestor Yeats's great grandfather, the Rev
  John Yeats (1774–1848)
Cast . . . past by these words are on Yeats's
  tomb

Rudyard Kipling
1865–1936

Rudyard Kipling was born in Bombay but educated in England, at the United Services College. As a journalist in India from 1882 to 1889, he published the stories and poems collected in *Departmental Ditties* (1886), *Plain Tales from the Hills* (1888), *Soldiers Three* (1890) and *Wee Willie Winkie* (1890). He lived in England from 1889 to 1892 and, with his American wife, in Vermont from 1892 until 1896 when the Kiplings returned to England. *Barrack Room Ballads* (1892) had made him famous. *The Jungle Book* (1894), *The Second Jungle Book* (1895), *Just So Stories* (1902) and *Puck of Pook's Hill* (1906) are among the best books ever written for children. *Kim* (1901) is his masterpiece. Kipling was awarded the Nobel Prize for Literature in 1907. His wholehearted enthusiasm for the British Empire and an element of swagger in some books have clouded his achievement but his imagination and versatility are beyond dispute.

From KIM
Chapter 1
[Friend of All the World]

> O ye who tread the Narrow Way
> By Tophet-flare† to Judgment Day,
> Be gentle when 'the heathen' pray
>   To Buddha at Kamakura!
>   *Buddha at Kamakura*

He sat, in defiance of municipal orders, astride the gun Zam-Zammah on her brick platform opposite the old Ajaib-Gher – the Wonder House, as the natives call the Lahore Museum. Who hold Zam-Zammah, that 'fire-breathing dragon,' hold the Punjab; for the great green-bronze
5 piece is always first of the conqueror's loot.

Tophet hell

There was some justification for Kim, – he had kicked Lala Dinanath's boy off the trunnions,† – since the English held the Punjab and Kim was English. Though he was burned black as any native; though he spoke the vernacular by preference, and his mother-tongue in a clipped
10   uncertain sing-song; though he consorted on terms of perfect equality with the small boys of the bazar; Kim was white – a poor white of the very poorest. The half-caste woman who looked after him (she smoked opium, and pretended to keep a second-hand furniture shop by the square where the cheap cabs wait) told the missionaries that she was
15   Kim's mother's sister; but his mother had been nurse-maid in a Colonel's family and had married Kimball O'Hara, a young colour-sergeant of the Mavericks, an Irish regiment. He afterwards took a post on the Sind, Punjab, and Delhi Railway, and his Regiment went home without him. The wife died of cholera in Ferozepore, and O'Hara fell to drink
20   and loafing up and down the line with the keen-eyed three-year-old baby. Societies and chaplains, anxious for the child, tried to catch him, but O'Hara drifted away, till he came across the woman who took opium and learned the taste from her, and died as poor whites do in India. His estate at death consisted of three papers – one he called his
25   'ne varietur' [not to be altered] because those words were written below his signature thereon, and another his 'clearance-certificate.' The third was Kim's birth-certificate. Those things, he was used to say, in his glorious opium-hours, would yet make little Kimball a man. On no account was Kim to part with them, for they belonged to a great piece
30   of magic – such magic as men practised over yonder behind the Museum, in the big blue-and-white Jadoo-Gher – the Magic House, as we name the Masonic Lodge. It would, he said, all come right some day, and Kim's horn would be exalted between pillars – monstrous pillars – of beauty and strength. The Colonel himself, riding on a horse, at the head
35   of the finest Regiment in the world, would attend to Kim, – little Kim that should have been better off than his father. Nine hundred first-class devils, whose God was a Red Bull† on a green field, would attend to Kim, if they had not forgotten O'Hara – poor O'Hara that was gang-foreman on the Ferozepore line. Then he would weep bitterly in the
40   broken rush chair on the veranda. So it came about after his death that the woman sewed parchment, paper, and birth-certificate into a leather amulet-case which she strung round Kim's neck.

   'And some day,' she said, confusedly remembering O'Hara's prophecies, 'there will come for you a great Red Bull on a green field, and
45   the Colonel riding on his tall horse, yes, and' – dropping into English – 'nine hundred devils.'

   'Ah,' said Kim, 'I shall remember. A Red Bull and a Colonel on a

---

trunnions   mountings of a big gun   *a Red Bull*   on a regimental flag

horse will come, but first, my father said, will come the two men making
ready the ground for these matters. That is how my father said they
50   always did; and it is always so when men work magic.'

If the woman had sent Kim up to the local Jadoo-Gher with those
papers, he would, of course, have been taken over by the Provincial
Lodge and sent to the Masonic Orphanage in the Hills; but what she
had heard of magic she distrusted. Kim, too, held views of his own. As
55   he reached the years of indiscretion, he learned to avoid missionaries
and white men of serious aspect who asked who he was, and what he
did. For Kim did nothing with an immense success. True, he knew the
wonderful walled city of Lahore from the Delhi Gate to the outer Fort
Ditch; was hand in glove with men who led lives stranger than anything
60   Haroun al Raschid[†] dreamed of; and he lived in a life wild as that of
the Arabian Nights, but missionaries and secretaries of charitable
societies could not see the beauty of it. His nickname through the wards
was 'Little Friend of all the World'; and very often, being lithe and
inconspicuous, he executed commissions by night on the crowded house-
65   tops for sleek and shiny young men of fashion. It was intrigue, of
course, – he knew that much, as he had known all evil since he could
speak, – but what he loved was the game for its own sake – the stealthy
prowl through the dark gullies and lanes, the crawl up a water-pipe,
the sights and sounds of the women's world on the flat roofs, and the
70   headlong flight from house-top to house-top under cover of the hot
dark. Then there were holy men, ash-smeared fakirs[†] by their brick
shrines under the trees at the riverside, with whom he was quite
familiar – greeting them as they returned from begging-tours, and, when
no one was by, eating from the same dish. The woman who looked
75   after him insisted with tears that he should wear European clothes –
trousers, a shirt, and a battered hat. Kim found it easier to slip into
Hindu or Mohammedan garb when engaged on certain businesses. One
of the young men of fashion – he who was found dead at the bottom
of a well on the night of the earthquake – had once given him a complete
80   suit of Hindu kit, the costume of a low-caste street boy, and Kim stored
it in a secret place under some baulks in Nila Ram's timber-yard,
beyond the Punjab High Court, where the fragrant deodar logs lie
seasoning after they have driven down the Ravi. Where there was
business or frolic afoot, Kim would use his properties, returning at
85   dawn to the veranda, all tired out from shouting at the heels of a
marriage procession, or yelling at a Hindu festival. Sometimes there
was food in the house, more often there was not, and then Kim went
out again to eat with his native friends.

Haroun al Raschid   Haroun ar-Rasheed (763–
809), caliph of Baghdad, appears in the

Arabian Nights
fakirs religious beggars

As he drummed his heels against Zam-Zammah he turned now and
90   again from his king-of-the-castle game with little Chota Lal and Abdullah
the sweetmeat-seller's son, to make a rude remark to the native
policeman on guard over the rows of shoes at the Museum door. The
big Punjabi grinned tolerantly: he knew Kim of old. So did the water-
carrier, sluicing water on the dry road from his goat-skin bag. So did
95   Jawahir Singh, the Museum carpenter, bent over new packing-cases. So
did everybody in sight except the peasants from the country, hurrying
up to the Wonder House to view the things that men made in their
own province and elsewhere. The Museum was given up to Indian arts
and manufactures, and anybody who sought wisdom could ask the
100   Curator to explain.

'Off! Off! Let me up!' cried Abdullah, climbing up Zam-Zammah's
wheel.

'Thy father was a pastry-cook, Thy mother stole the *ghi*,'† sang Kim.
'All Mussalmans fell off Zam-Zammah long ago!'

105   'Let *me* up!' shrilled little Chota Lal in his gilt-embroidered cap. His
father was worth perhaps half a million sterling, but India is the only
democratic land in the world.

'The Hindus fell off Zam-Zammah too. The Mussalmans pushed
them off. Thy father was a pastry-cook –'

110   He stopped; for there shuffled round the corner, from the roaring
Motee Bazar, such a man as Kim, who thought he knew all castes, had
never seen. He was nearly six feet high, dressed in fold upon fold of
dingy stuff like horse-blanketing, and not one fold of it could Kim refer
to any known trade or profession. At his belt hung a long open-work
115   iron pencase and a wooden rosary such as holy men wear. On his head
was a gigantic sort of tam-o'-shanter. His face was yellow and wrinkled,
like that of Fook Shing, the Chinese bootmaker in the bazar. His eyes
turned up at the corners and looked like little slits of onyx.

'Who is that?' said Kim to his companions.

120   'Perhaps it is a man,' said Abdullah, finger in mouth, staring.

'Without doubt,' returned Kim; 'but he is no man of India that *I*
have ever seen.'

'A priest, perhaps,' said Chota Lal, spying the rosary. 'See! He goes
into the Wonder House!'

125   'Nay, nay,' said the policeman, shaking his head. 'I do not understand
your talk.' The constable spoke Punjabi. 'O friend of all the World,
what does he say?'

'Send him hither,' said Kim, dropping from Zam-Zammah, flourishing
his bare heels. 'He is a foreigner, and thou art a buffalo.'

130   The man turned helplessly and drifted towards the boys. He was old,

---

ghi   clarified butter

and his woollen gaberdine still reeked of the stinking artemisia[†] of the mountain passes.

'O Children, what is that big house?' he said in very fair Urdu.

'The Ajaib-Gher, the Wonder House!' Kim gave him no title – such
135   as Lala or Mian. He could not divine the man's creed.

'Ah! The Wonder House! Can any enter?'

'It is written above the door – all can enter.'

'Without payment?'

'I go in and out. *I* am no banker,' laughed Kim.
140   'Alas! I am an old man. I did not know.' Then, fingering his rosary, he half turned to the Museum.

'What is your caste? Where is your house? Have you come far?' Kim asked.

'I came by Kulu – from beyond the Kailas – but what know you?
145   From the Hills where' – he sighed – 'the air and water are fresh and cool.'

'Aha! Khitai [a Chinaman],' said Abdullah proudly. Fook Shing had once chased him out of his shop for spitting at the joss[†] above the boots.

150   'Pahari [a hillman],' said little Chota Lal.

'Aye, child – a hillman from hills thou'lt never see. Didst hear of Bhotiyal [Tibet]? I am no Khitai, but a Bhotiya [Tibetan], since you must know – a lama – or, say, a *guru* in your tongue.'

'A *guru* from Tibet,' said Kim. 'I have not seen such a man. They be
155   Hindus in Tibet, then?'

'We be followers of the Middle Way, living in peace on our lamasseries, and I go to see the Four Holy Places before I die. Now do you, who are children, know as much as I do who am old.' He smiled benignantly on the boys.

160   'Hast thou eaten?'

He fumbled in his bosom and drew forth a worn wooden begging-bowl. The boys nodded. All priests of their acquaintance begged.

'I do not wish to eat yet.' He turned his head like an old tortoise in the sunlight. 'Is it true that there are many images in the Wonder House
165   of Lahore?' He repeated the last words as one making sure of an address.

'That is true,' said Abdullah. 'It is full of heathen *būts*.[†] Thou also art an idolater.'

'Never mind *him*,' said Kim. 'That is the Government's house and
170   there is no idolatry in it, but only a Sahib with a white beard. Come with me and I will show.'

---

artemisia a kind of wormwood   *būts* sculptures, regarded as idols by Muslims
joss a Chinese religious image   such as Abdellah

'Strange priests eat boys,' whispered Chota Lal.

'And he is a stranger and a *būt-parast* [idolater],' said Abdullah, the Mohammedan.

175 Kim laughed. 'He is new. Run to your mothers' laps, and be safe. Come!'

Kim clicked round the self-registering turnstile; the old man followed and halted amazed. In the entrance-hall stood the larger figures of the Greco-Buddhist sculptures done, savants know how long since, by 180 forgotten workmen whose hands were feeling, and not unskilfully, for the mysteriously transmitted Grecian touch. There were hundreds of pieces, friezes of figures in relief, fragments of statues and slabs crowded with figures that had encrusted the brick walls of the Buddhist *stupas*† and *viharas*† of the North Country and now, dug up and labelled, made 185 the pride of the Museum. In open-mouthed wonder the lama turned to this and that, and finally checked in rapt attention before a large alto-relief representing a coronation or apotheosis of the Lord Buddha. The Master was represented seated on a lotus the petals of which were so deeply under-cut as to show almost detached. Round Him was an 190 adoring hierarchy of kings, elders, and old-time Buddhas. Below were lotus-covered waters with fishes and water-birds. Two butterfly-winged *dewas*† held a wreath over His head; above them another pair supported an umbrella surmounted by the jewelled headdress of the Bodhisat.

'The Lord! The Lord! It is Sakya Muni himself,' the lama half sobbed;
195 and under his breath began the wonderful Buddhist invocation: –

> 'To Him the Way, the Law, apart,
> Whom Maya† held beneath her heart,
> Ananda's† Lord, the Bodhisat.'†

'And He is here! The Most Excellent Law is here also. My pilgrimage 200 is well begun. And what work! What work!'

'Yonder is the Sahib,' said Kim, and dodged sideways among the cases of the arts and manufactures wing. A white-bearded Englishman was looking at the lama, who gravely turned and saluted him and after some fumbling drew forth a note-book and a scrap of paper.

205 'Yes, that is my name,' smiling at the clumsy, childish print.

'One of us who had made pilgrimage to the Holy Places – he is now Abbot of the Lung-Cho Monastery – gave it me,' stammered the lama. 'He spoke of these.' His lean hand moved tremulously round.

'Welcome, then, O lama from Tibet. Here be the images, and I am 210 here' – he glanced at the lama's face – 'to gather knowledge. Come to my office awhile.' The old man was trembling with excitement.

---

stupas	Buddhist monuments	*Maya*	illusion
viharas	Buddhist monasteries	*Ananda*	Buddha's cousin and disciple
dewas	gods	*the Bodhisat*	Buddha

The hut was but a little wooden cubicle partitioned off from the sculpture-lined gallery. Kim laid himself down, his ear against a crack in the heat-split cedar door, and, following his instinct, stretched out
215 to listen and watch.

Most of the talk was altogether above his head. The lama, haltingly at first, spoke to the Curator of his own lamassery, the Such-zen, opposite the Painted Rocks, four months' march away. The Curator brought out a huge book of photos and showed him that very place,
220 perched on its crag, overlooking the gigantic valley of many-hued strata.

'Ay, ay!' The lama mounted a pair of horn-rimmed spectacles of Chinese work. 'Here is the little door through which we bring wood before winter. And thou – the English know of these things? He who is now Abbot of Lung-Cho told me, but I did not believe. The Lord – the
225 Excellent One – He has honour here too? And His life is known?'

'It is all carven upon the stones. Come and see, if thou art rested.'

Out shuffled the lama to the main hall, and, the Curator beside him, went through the collection with the reverence of a devotee and the appreciative instinct of a craftsman.

230 Incident by incident in the beautiful story he identified on the blurred stone, puzzled here and there by the unfamiliar Greek convention, but delighted as a child at each new trove. Where the sequence failed, as in the Annunciation, the Curator supplied it from his mound of books French and German, with photographs and reproductions.

235 Here was the devout Asita, the pendant of Simeon in the Christian story, holding the Holy Child on his knee while mother and father listened; and here were incidents in the legend of the cousin Devadatta. Here was the wicked woman who accused the Master of impurity, all confounded; here was the teaching in the Deer-park; the miracle that
240 stunned the fire-worshippers; here was the Bodhisat in royal state as a prince; the miraculous birth, the death of Kusinagara, where the weak disciple fainted; while there were almost countless repetitions of the meditation under the Bodhi tree; and the adoration of the alms-bowl was everywhere. In a few minutes the Curator saw that his guest was
245 no mere bead-telling mendicant, but a scholar of parts. And they went at it all over again, the lama taking snuff, wiping his spectacles, and talking at railway speed in a bewildering mixture of Urdu and Tibetan. He had heard of the travels of the Chinese pilgrims, Fu-Hiouen and Hwen-Tsiang, and was anxious to know if there was any translation of
250 their record. He drew in his breath as he turned helplessly over the pages of Beal and Stanislas Julien. ''Tis all here. A treasure locked.' Then he composed himself reverently to listen to fragments hastily rendered into Urdu. For the first time he heard of the labours of European scholars, who by the help of these and a hundred other
255 documents have identified the Holy Places of Buddhism. Then he was

shown a mighty map, spotted and traced with yellow. The brown finger
followed the Curator's pencil from point to point. Here was Kapilavastu,
here the Middle Kingdom, and here Mahabodhi, the Mecca of Buddhism,
and here was Kusinagara, sad place of the Holy One's death. The old
260 man bowed his head over the sheets in silence for a while, and the
Curator lit another pipe. Kim had fallen asleep. When he waked, the
talk, still in spate, was more within his comprehension.

'And thus it was, O Fountain of Wisdom, that I decided to go to the
Holy Places which His foot had trod – to the Birthplace, even to Kapila;
265 then to Mahabodhi, which is Buddh Gaya – to the Monastery – to the
Deer-park – to the place of His death.'

The lama lowered his voice. 'And I come here alone. For five – seven –
eighteen – forty years it was in my mind that the Old Law was not well
followed; being overlaid, as thou knowest, with devildom, charms, and
270 idolatry. Even as the child outside said but now. Ay, even as the child
said, with *būt parasti*.'

'So it comes with all faiths.'

'Thinkest thou? The books of my lamassery I read, and they were dried
pith; and the later ritual with which we of the Reformed Law have
275 cumbered ourselves – that, too, had no worth to these old eyes. Even the
followers of the Excellent One are at feud on feud with one another. It is
all illusion. Ay, *maya*, illusion. But I have another desire' – the seamed
yellow face drew within three inches of the Curator, and the long forefinger-
nail tapped on the table. 'Your scholars, by these books, have followed
280 the Blessed Feet in all their wanderings; but there are things which they
have not sought out. I know nothing, – nothing do I know, – but I go to
free myself from the Wheel of Things by a broad and open road.' He
smiled with most simple triumph. 'As a pilgrim to the Holy Places I acquire
merit. But there is more. Listen to a true thing. When our gracious Lord,
285 being as yet a youth, sought a mate, men said, in His father's Court, that
He was too tender for marriage. Thou knowest?'

The Curator nodded, wondering what would come next.

'So they made the triple trial of strength against all comers. And at
the test of the Bow, our Lord first breaking that which they gave Him,
290 called for such a bow as none might bend. Thou knowest?'

'It is written. I have read.'

'And, overshooting all other marks, the arrow passed far and far
beyond sight. At the last it fell; and, where it touched earth, there broke
out a stream which presently became a River, whose nature, by our
295 Lord's beneficence, and that merit He acquired ere He freed himself, is
that whoso bathes in it washes away all taint and speckle of sin.'

'So it is written,' said the Curator sadly.

The lama drew a long breath. 'Where is that River? Fountain of
Wisdom, where fell the arrow?'

300   'Alas, my brother, I do not know,' said the Curator.

'Nay, if it pleases thee to forget – the one thing only that thou hast not told me. Surely thou must know? See, I am an old man! I ask with my head between thy feet, O Fountain of Wisdom. We *know* He drew the bow! We *know* the arrow fell! We *know* the stream gushed! Where,
305   then, is the River? My dream told me to find it. So I came. I am here. But where is the River?'

'If I knew, think you I would not cry it aloud?'

'By it one attains freedom from the Wheel of Things,' the lama went on, unheeding. 'The River of the Arrow! Think again! Some little
310   stream, maybe – dried in the heats? But the Holy One would never so cheat an old man.'

'I do not know. I do not know.'

The lama brought his thousand-wrinkled face once more a handsbreadth from the Englishman's. 'I see thou dost not know. Not being
315   of the Law, the matter is hid from thee.'

'Ay, – hidden – hidden.'

'We are both bound, thou and I, my brother. But I' – he rose with a sweep of the soft thick drapery – 'I go to cut myself free. Come also!'

'I am bound,' said the Curator. 'But whither goest thou?'

320   'First to Kashi [Benares]: where else? There I shall meet one of the pure faith in a Jain[†] temple of that city. He also is a Seeker in secret, and from him haply I may learn. Maybe he will go with me to Buddh Gaya. Thence north and west to Kapilavastu, and there will I seek for the River. Nay, I will seek everywhere as I go – for the place is not
325   known where the arrow fell.'

'And how wilt thou go? It is a fair cry to Delhi, and farther to Benares.'

'By road and the trains. From Pathânkot, having left the hills, I came hither in a *te-rain*. It goes swiftly. At first I was amazed to see those
330   tall poles by the side of the road snatching up and snatching up their threads,' – he illustrated the stoop and whirl of a telegraph-pole flashing past the train. 'But later, I was cramped and desired to walk, as I am used.'

'And thou art sure of thy road?' said the Curator.

335   'Oh, for that one but asks a question and pays money, and the appointed persons despatch all to the appointed place. That much I knew in my lamassery from sure report,' said the lama proudly.

'And when dost thou go?' The Curator smiled at the mixture of oldworld piety and modern progress that is the note of India to-day.

340   'As soon as may be. I follow the places of His life till I come to the

---

Jain   a Hindu sect akin to Buddhism

River of the Arrow. There is, moreover, a written paper of the hours of the trains that go south.'

'And for food?' Lamas, as a rule, have good store of money somewhere about them, but the Curator wished to make sure.

345 'For the journey, I take up the Master's begging-bowl. Yes. Even as He went so go I, forsaking the ease of my monastery. There was with me when I left the hills a *chela* [disciple] who begged for me as the Rule demands, but halting in Kulu awhile a fever took him and he died. I have now no *chela*, but I will take the alms-bowl and thus enable the
350 charitable to acquire merit.' He nodded his head valiantly. Learned doctors of a lamassery do not beg, but the lama was an enthusiast in this quest.

'Be it so,' said the Curator, smiling. 'Suffer me now to acquire merit. We be craftsmen together, thou and I. Here is a new book of white
355 English paper: here be sharpened pencils two and three – thick and thin, all good for a scribe. Now lend me thy spectacles.'

The Curator looked through them. They were heavily scratched, but the power was almost exactly that of his own pair, which he slid into the lama's hand, saying: 'Try these.'

360 'A feather! A very feather upon the face!' The old man turned his head delightedly and wrinkled up his nose. 'How scarcely do I feel them! How clearly do I see!'

'They be *bilaur* – crystal – and will never scratch. May they help thee to thy River, for they are thine.'

365 'I will take them and the pencils and the white note-book,' said the lama, 'as a sign of friendship between priest and priest – and now –' He fumbled at his belt, detached the openwork iron pencase, and laid it on the Curator's table. 'That is for a memory between thee and me – my pencase. It is something old – even as I am.'

370 It was a piece of ancient design, Chinese, of an iron that is not smelted these days; and the collector's heart in the Curator's bosom had gone out to it from the first. For no persuasion would the lama resume his gift.

'When I return, having found the River, I will bring thee a written
375 picture of the Padma Samthora – such as I used to make on silk at the lamassery. Yes – and of the Wheel of Life,' he chuckled, 'for we be craftsmen together, thou and I.'

The Curator would have detained him: they are few in the world who still have the secret of the conventional brush-pen Buddhist pictures
380 which are, as it were, half written and half drawn. But the lama strode out, head high in air, and pausing an instant before the great statue of a Bodhisat in meditation, brushed through the turnstiles.

Kim followed like a shadow. What he had overheard excited him wildly. This man was entirely new to all his experience, and he meant

385 to investigate further, precisely as he would have investigated a new
building or a strange festival in Lahore city. The lama was his trove,
and he purposed to take possession. Kim's mother had been Irish too.

The old man halted by Zam-Zammah and looked round till his eye
fell on Kim. The inspiration of his pilgrimage had left him for a while,
390 and he felt old, forlorn, and very empty.

'Do not sit under that gun,' said the policeman loftily.

'Huh! Owl!' was Kim's retort on the lama's behalf. 'Sit under that
gun if it please thee. When didst thou steal the milk-woman's slippers,
Dunnoo?'

395 That was an entirely unfounded charge sprung on the spur of the
moment, but it silenced Dunnoo, who knew that Kim's clear yell could
call up legions of bad bazar boys if need arose.

'And whom didst thou worship within?' said Kim affably, squatting
in the shade beside the lama.

400 'I worshipped none, child. I bowed before the Excellent Law.'

Kim accepted this new God without emotion. He knew already a few
score.

'And what dost thou do?'

'I beg. I remember now it is long since I have eaten or drunk. What
405 is the custom of charity in this town? In silence, as we do of Tibet, or
speaking aloud?'

'Those who beg in silence starve in silence,' said Kim, quoting a
native proverb. The lama tried to rise, but sank back again, sighing for
his disciple, dead in far-away Kulu. Kim watched – head to one side,
410 considering and interested.

'Give me the bowl. I know the people of this city – all who are
charitable. Give, and I will bring it back filled.'

Simply as a child the old man handed him the bowl.

'Rest, thou. *I* know the people.'

415 He trotted off to the open shop of a *kunjri*, a low-caste vegetable-
seller, which lay opposite the belt-tramway line down the Motee Bazar.
She knew Kim of old.

'Oho, hast thou turned *yogi* with thy begging-bowl?' she cried.

'Nay,' said Kim proudly. 'There is a new priest in the city – a man
420 such as I have never seen.'

'Old priest – young tiger,' said the woman angrily. 'I am tired of new
priests! They settle on our wares like flies. Is the father of my son a
well of charity to give to all who ask!'

'No,' said Kim. 'Thy man is rather *yagi* [bad-tempered] than *yogi* [a
425 holy man]. But this priest is new. The Sahib in the Wonder House has
talked to him like a brother. O my mother, fill me this bowl. He waits.'

'That bowl indeed! That cow-bellied basket! Thou hast as much
grace as the holy bull of Shiv. He has taken the best of a basket of

onions already, this morn; and forsooth, I must fill thy bowl. He comes
430   here again.'

The huge, mouse-coloured Brahmini bull of the ward was shouldering
his way through the many-coloured crowd, a stolen plantain hanging
out of his mouth. He headed straight for the shop, well knowing his
privileges as a sacred beast, lowered his head, and puffed heavily along
435   the line of baskets ere making his choice. Up flew Kim's hard little heel
and caught him on his moist blue nose. He snorted indignantly, and
walked away across the tram-rails, his hump quivering with rage.

'See! I have saved more than the bowl will cost thrice over. Now,
mother, a little rice and some dried fish atop – yes, and some vegetable
440   curry.'

A growl came out of the back of the shop, where a man lay.

'He drove away the bull,' said the woman in an undertone. 'It is good
to give to the poor.' She took the bowl and returned it full of hot rice.

'But my *yogi* is not a cow,' said Kim gravely, making a hole with his
445   fingers in the top of the mound. 'A little curry is good, and a fried cake,
and a morsel of conserve would please him, I think.'

'It is a hole as big as thy head,' said the woman fretfully. But she
filled it, none the less, with good, steaming vegetable curry, clapped a
fried cake atop, and a morsel of clarified butter on the cake, dabbed a
450   lump of sour tamarind conserve at the side; and Kim looked at the load
lovingly.

'That is good. When I am in the bazar the bull shall not come to this
house. He is a bold beggar-man.'

'And thou?' laughed the woman. 'But speak well of bulls. Has thou
455   not told me that some day a Red Bull will come out of a field to help
thee? Now hold all straight and ask for the holy man's blessing upon
me. Perhaps, too, he knows a cure for my daughter's sore eyes. Ask
him that also, O thou Little Friend of all the World.'

But Kim had danced off ere the end of the sentence, dodging pariah
460   dogs and hungry acquaintances.

'Thus do we beg who know the way of it,' said he proudly to the
lama, who opened his eyes at the contents of the bowl. 'Eat now and –
I will eat with thee. Ohé, *bhisti!*' he called to the water-carrier, sluicing
the crotons by the Museum. 'Give water here. We men are thirsty.'

465   'We men!' said the *bhisti*, laughing. 'Is one skinful enough for such a
pair? Drink, then, in the name of the Compassionate.'[†]

He loosed a thin stream into Kim's hands, who drank native-fashion;
but the lama must needs pull out a cup from his inexhaustible upper
draperies and drink ceremonially.

---

the Compassionate   Allah

470   '*Pardesi* [a foreigner],' Kim explained, as the old man delivered in an unknown tongue what was evidently a blessing.

They ate together in great content, clearing the begging-bowl. Then the lama took snuff from a portentous wooden snuff-gourd, fingered his rosary awhile, and so dropped into the easy sleep of age, as the
475   shadow of Zam-Zammah grew long.

Kim loafed over to the nearest tobacco-seller, a rather lively young Mohammedan woman, and begged a rank cigar of the brand that they sell to students of the Punjab University who copy English customs. Then he smoked and thought, knees to chin, under the belly of the gun,
480   and the outcome of his thoughts was a sudden and stealthy departure in the direction of Nila Ram's timber-yard.

The lama did not wake till the evening life of the city had begun with lamp-lighting and the return of white-robed clerks and subordinates from the Government offices. He stared dizzily in all directions, but
485   none looked at him save a Hindu urchin in a dirty turban and Isabella-coloured clothes. Suddenly he bowed his head on his knees and wailed.

'What is this?' said the boy, standing before him. 'Hast thou been robbed?'

'It is my new *chela* [disciple] that is gone away from me, and I know
490   not where he is.'

'And what like of man was thy disciple?'

'It was a boy who came to me in place of him who died, on account of the merit which I had gained when I bowed before the Law within there.' He pointed towards the Museum. 'He came upon me to show
495   me a road which I had lost. He led me into the Wonder House, and by his talk emboldened me to speak to the Keeper of the Images, so that I was cheered and made strong. And when I was faint with hunger he begged for me, as would a *chela* for his teacher. Suddenly was he sent. Suddenly has he gone away. It was in my mind to have taught him the
500   Law upon the road to Benares.'

Kim stood amazed at this, because he had overheard the talk in the Museum, and knew that the old man was speaking the truth, which is a thing a native on the road seldom presents to a stranger.

'But I see now that he was but sent for a purpose. By this I know
505   that I shall find a certain River for which I seek.'

'The River of the Arrow?' said Kim, with a superior smile.

'Is this yet another Sending?' cried the lama. 'To none have I spoken of my search, save to the Priest of the Images. Who art thou?'

'Thy *chela*,' said Kim simply, sitting on his heels. 'I have never seen
510   any one like to thee in all this my life. I go with thee to Benares. And, too, I think that so old a man as thou, speaking the truth to chance-met people at dusk is in great need of a disciple.'

'But the River – the River of the Arrow?'

'Oh, that I heard when thou wast speaking to the Englishman. I lay
against the door.'

The lama sighed. 'I thought thou hadst been a guide permitted. Such
things fall sometimes – but I am not worthy. Thou dost not, then, know
the River?'

'Not I.' Kim laughed uneasily. 'I go to look for – for a bull – a Red
Bull on a green field who shall help me.' Boylike, if an acquaintance
had a scheme, Kim was quite ready with one of his own; and, boylike,
he had really thought for as much as twenty minutes at a time of his
father's prophecy.

'To what, child?' said the lama.

'God knows, but so my father told me. I heard thy talk in the Wonder
House of all those new strange places in the Hills, and if one so old
and so little – so used to truth-telling – may go out for the small matter
of a river, it seemed to me that I too must go a-travelling. If it is our
fate to find those things we shall find them – thou, thy River; and I,
my Bull, and the Strong Pillars and some other matters that I forget.'

'It is not pillars but a Wheel from which I would be free,' said the
lama.

'That is all one. Perhaps they will make me a king,' said Kim, serenely
prepared for anything.

'I will teach thee other and better desires upon the road,' the lama
replied in the voice of authority. 'Let us go to Benares.'

'Not by night. Thieves are abroad. Wait till the day.'

'But there is no place to sleep.' The old man was used to the order of
his monastery, and though he slept on the ground, as the Rule decrees,
preferred a decency in these things.

'We shall get good lodging at the Kashmir Serai,' said Kim, laughing
at his perplexity. 'I have a friend there. Come!'

The hot and crowded bazars blazed with light as they made their
way through the press of all the races in Upper India, and the lama
mooned through it like a man in a dream. It was his first experience of
a large manufacturing city, and the crowded tram-car with its continually
squealing brakes frightened him. Half pushed, half towed, he arrived
at the high gate of the Kashmir Serai: that huge open square over
against the railway station, surrounded with arched cloisters, where the
camel and horse caravans put up on their return from Central Asia.
Here were all manner of Northern folk, tending tethered ponies and
kneeling camels; loading and unloading bales and bundles; drawing
water for the evening meal at the creaking well-windlasses; piling grass
before the shrieking, wild-eyed stallions; cuffing the surly caravan dogs;
paying off camel-drivers; taking on new grooms; swearing, shouting,
arguing, and chaffering in the packed square. The cloisters, reached by
three or four masonry steps, made a haven of refuge around this

turbulent sea. Most of them were rented to traders, as we rent the arches of a viaduct; the space between pillar and pillar being bricked
560 or boarded off into rooms, which were guarded by heavy wooden doors and cumbrous native padlocks. Locked doors showed that the owner was away, and a few rude – sometimes very rude – chalk or paint scratches told where he had gone. Thus: 'Lutuf Ullah is gone to Kurdistan.' Below, in coarse verse: 'O Allah, who sufferest lice to live
565 on the coat of a Kabuli, why hast thou allowed this louse Lutuf to live so long?'

Kim, fending the lama between excited men and excited beasts, sidled along the cloisters to the far end, nearest the railway station, where Mahbub Ali, the horse-trader, lived when he came in from that
570 mysterious land beyond the Passes of the North.

Kim had had many dealings with Mahbub in his little life, – especially between his tenth and his thirteenth year, – and the big burly Afghan, his beard dyed scarlet with lime (for he was elderly and did not wish his grey hairs to show), knew the boy's value as a gossip. Sometimes he
575 would tell Kim to watch a man who had nothing whatever to do with horses: to follow him for one whole day and report every soul with whom he talked. Kim would deliver himself of this tale at evening, and Mahbub would listen without a word or gesture. It was intrigue of some kind, Kim knew; but its worth lay in saying nothing whatever to
580 any one except Mahbub, who gave him beautiful meals all hot from the cookshop at the head of the serai,† and once as much as eight annas in money.

'He is here,' said Kim, hitting a bad-tempered camel on the nose. 'Ohé, Mahbub Ali!' He halted at a dark arch and slipped behind the
585 bewildered lama.

The horse-trader, his deep, embroidered Bokhariot belt unloosened, was lying on a pair of silk carpet saddle bags, pulling lazily at an immense silver hookah. He turned his head very slightly at the cry; and seeing only the tall silent figure, chuckled in his deep chest.
590 'Allah! A lama! A Red Lama! It is far from Lahore to the Passes. What dost thou do here?'

The lama held out the begging-bowl mechanically.

'God's curse on all unbelievers!' said Mahbub. 'I do not give to a lousy Tibetan; but ask my Baltis over yonder behind the camels. They
595 may value your blessings. Oh, horseboys, here is a countryman of yours. See if he be hungry.'

A shaven, crouching Balti, who had come down with the horses, and who was nominally some sort of degraded Buddhist, fawned upon the

serai   an inn

priest, and in thick gutturals besought the Holy One to sit at the
600   horseboys' fire.

'Go!' said Kim, pushing him lightly, and the lama strode away,
leaving Kim at the edge of the cloister.

'Go!' said Mahbub Ali, returning to his hookah. 'Little Hindu, run
away. God's curse on all unbelievers! Beg from those of my tail who
605   are of thy faith.'

'Maharaj,' whined Kim, using the Hindu form of address, and
thoroughly enjoying the situation; 'my father is dead – my mother is
dead – my stomach is empty.'

'Beg from my men among the horses, I say. There must be some
610   Hindus in my tail.'

'Oh, Mahbub Ali, but am *I* a Hindu?' said Kim in English.

The trader gave no sign of astonishment, but looked under shaggy
eyebrows.

'Little Friend of all the World,' said he, 'what is this?'

615   'Nothing. I am now that holy man's disciple; and we go a pilgrimage
together – to Benares, he says. He is quite mad, and I am tired of Lahore
city. I wish new air and water.'

'But for whom dost thou work? Why come to me?' The voice was
harsh with suspicion.

620   'To whom else should I come? I have no money. It is not good to go
about without money. Thou wilt sell many horses to the officers. They
are very fine horses, these new ones: I have seen them. Give me a rupee,
Mahbub Ali, and when I come to my wealth I will give thee a bond
and pay.'

625   'Um!' said Mahbub Ali, thinking swiftly. 'Thou hast never before
lied to me. Call that lama – stand back in the dark.'

'Oh, our tales will agree,' said Kim, laughing.

'We go to Benares,' said the lama, as soon as he understood the drift
of Mahbub Ali's questions. 'The boy and I. I go to seek for a certain
630   River.'

'Maybe – but the boy?'

'He is my disciple. He was sent, I think, to guide me to that River.
Sitting under a gun was I when he came suddenly. Such things have
befallen the fortunate to whom guidance was allowed. But I remember
635   now, he said he was of this world – a Hindu.'

'And his name?'

'That I did not ask. Is he not my disciple?'

'His country – his race – his village? Mussalman – Sikh – Hindu –
Jain – low caste or high?'

640   'Why should I ask? There is neither high nor low in the Middle Way. If
he is my *chela* – does – will – can any one take him from me? for, look you,
without him I shall not find my River.' He wagged his head solemnly.

'None shall take him from thee. Go, sit among my Baltis,' said
Mahbub Ali, and the lama drifted off, soothed by the promise.

645 'Is he not quite mad?' said Kim coming forward to the light again.
'Why should I lie to thee, Hajji?'†

Mahbub puffed his hookah in silence. Then he began, almost
whispering: 'Umballa is on the road to Benares – if indeed ye two go
there.'

650 'Tck! Tck! I tell thee he does not know how to lie – as we two know.'

'And if thou wilt carry a message for me as far as Umballa, I will
give thee money. It concerns a horse – a white stallion which I have
sold to an officer upon the last time I returned from the Passes. But
then – stand nearer and hold up hands as begging – the pedigree of the

655 white stallion was not fully established, and that officer, who is now at
Umballa, bade me make it clear.' (Mahbub here described the house
and the appearance of the officer.) 'So the message to that officer will
be: "The pedigree of the white stallion is fully established." By this will
be known that thou comest from me. He will then say "What proof

660 has thou?" and thou wilt answer: "Mahbub Ali has given me the
proof."'

'And all for the sake of a white stallion,' said Kim, with a giggle, his
eyes aflame.

'That pedigree I will give thee now – in my own fashion – and some

665 hard words as well.' A shadow passed behind Kim, and a feeding camel.
Mahbub Ali raised his voice.

'Allah! Art thou the only beggar in the city? Thy mother is dead.
Thy father is dead. So is it with all of them. Well, well –' He turned as
feeling on the floor beside him and tossed a flap of soft, greasy

670 Mussalman bread to the boy. 'Go and lie down among my horse-boys
for to-night – thou and the lama. To-morrow I may give thee service.'

Kim slunk away, his teeth in the bread, and, as he expected, he found
a small wad of folded tissue-paper wrapped in oilskin, with three silver
rupees – enormous largesse. He smiled and thrust money and paper

675 into his leather amulet-case. The lama, sumptuously fed by Mahbub's
Baltis, was already asleep in a corner of one of the stalls. Kim lay down
beside him and laughed. He knew he had rendered a service to Mahbub
Ali, and not for one little minute did he believe the tale of the stallion's
pedigree.

680 But Kim did not suspect that Mahbub Ali, known as one of the best
horse-dealers in the Punjab, a wealthy and enterprising trader, whose
caravans penetrated far and far into the Back of Beyond, was registered
in one of the locked books of the Indian Survey Department as C.25.1B.
Twice or thrice yearly C.25 would send in a little story, badly told but

---

Hajji   Islamic title for one who has made the pilgrimage to Mecca

685 most interesting and generally – it was checked by the statements of
     R.17 and M.4 – quite true. It concerned all manner of out-of-the-way
     mountain principalities, explorers of nationalities other than English,
     and the gun-trade – was, in brief, a small portion of that vast mass of
     'information received' on which the Indian Government acts. But,
690 recently, five confederated Kings, who had no business to confederate,
     had been informed by a kindly Northern Power that there was a leakage
     of news from their territories into British India. So those Kings' Prime
     Ministers were seriously annoyed and took steps, after the Oriental
     fashion. They suspected, among many others, the bullying, red-bearded
695 horse-dealer whose caravans ploughed through their fastnesses belly-
     deep in snow. At least, his caravan that season had been ambushed and
     shot at twice on the way down, when Mahbub's men accounted for
     three strange ruffians who might, or might not, have been hired for the
     job. Therefore Mahbub had avoided halting at the insalubrious city of
700 Peshawur, and had come through without stop to Lahore, where,
     knowing his country-people, he anticipated curious developments.
        And there was that on Mahbub Ali which he did not wish to keep
     an hour longer than was necessary – a wad of closely folded tissue-
     paper, wrapped in oilskin – an impersonal, unaddressed statement, with
705 five microscopic pin-holes in one corner, that most scandalously betrayed
     the five confederated Kings, the sympathetic Northern Power, a Hindu
     banker in Peshawur, a firm of gun-makers in Belgium, and an important,
     semi-independent Mohammedan ruler to the south. This last was R.17's
     work, which Mahbub had picked up beyond the Dora Pass and was
710 carrying in for R.17, who, owing to circumstances over which he had
     no control, could not leave his post of observation. Dynamite was milky
     and innocuous beside that report of C.25; and even an Oriental, with
     an Oriental's views of the value of time, could see that the sooner it
     was in the proper hands the better. Mahbub had no particular desire
715 to die by violence, because two or three family blood-feuds across the
     Border hung unfinished on his hands, and when these scores were
     cleared he intended to settle down as a more or less virtuous citizen.
     He had never passed the serai gate since his arrival two days ago, but
     had been ostentatious in sending telegrams to Bombay, where he banked
720 some of his money; to Delhi, where a sub-partner of his own clan was
     selling horses to the agent of a Rajputana state; and to Umballa, where
     an Englishman was excitedly demanding the pedigree of a white
     stallion. The public letter-writer, who knew English, composed excellent
     telegrams, such as:- '*Creighton, Laurel Bank, Umballa. – Horse is
725 Arabian as already advised. Sorrowful delayed pedigree which am
     translating.*' And later to the same address; '*Much sorrowful delay.
     Will forward pedigree.*' To his sub-partner at Delhi he wired: '*Lutuf
     Ullah. – Have wired two thousand rupees your credit Luchman Norain's*

bank.' This was entirely in the way of trade, but every one of those
730   telegrams was discussed and re-discussed, by parties who conceived
themselves to be interested, before they went over to the railway station
in charge of a foolish Balti, who allowed all sorts of people to read
them on the road.

When, in Mahbub's own picturesque language, he had muddied the
735   wells of inquiry with the stick of precaution, Kim had dropped on him,
sent from Heaven; and, being as prompt as he was unscrupulous,
Mahbub Ali, used to taking all sorts of gusty chances, pressed him into
service on the spot.

A wandering lama with a low-caste boy-servant might attract a
740   moment's interest as they wandered about India, the land of pilgrims;
but no one would suspect them or, what was more to the point, rob.

He called for a new light-ball to his hookah, and considered the case.
If the worst came to the worst, and the boy came to harm, the paper
would incriminate nobody. And he would go up to Umballa leisurely
745   and – at a certain risk of exciting fresh suspicion – repeat his tale by
word of mouth to the people concerned.

But R.17's report was the kernel of the whole affair, and it would be
distinctly inconvenient if that failed to come to hand. However, God
was great, and Mahbub Ali felt he had done all he could for the time
750   being. Kim was the one soul in the world who had never told him a lie.
That would have been a fatal blot on Kim's character if Mahbub had
not known that to others, for his own ends or Mahbub's business, Kim
could lie like an Oriental.

Then Mahbub Ali rolled across the serai to the Gate of the Harpies
755   who paint their eyes and trap the stranger, and was at some pains to
call on the one girl who, he had reason to believe, was a particular
friend of a smooth-faced Kashmiri pundit[†] who had waylaid his simple
Balti in the matter of the telegrams. It was an utterly foolish thing to
do; because they fell to drinking perfumed brandy against the Law of
760   the Prophet, and Mahbub grew wonderfully drunk, and the gates of
his mouth were loosened, and he pursued the Flower of Delight with
the feet of intoxication till he fell flat among the cushions, where the
Flower of Delight, aided by a smooth-faced Kashmiri pundit, searched
him from head to foot most thoroughly.

765   About the same hour Kim heard soft feet in Mahbub's deserted stall.
The horse-trader, curiously enough, had left his door unlocked, and his
men were busy celebrating their return to India with a whole sheep of
Mahbub's bounty. A sleek young gentleman from Delhi, armed with a
bunch of keys which the Flower had unshackled from the senseless
770   one's belt, went through every single box, bundle, mat, and saddle-bag

pundit   a teacher

in Mahbub's possession even more systematically than the Flower and the pundit were searching the owner.

'And I think,' said the Flower scornfully an hour later, one rounded elbow on the snoring carcass, 'that he is no more than a pig of an
775 Afghan horse-dealer, with no thought except women and horses. Moreover, he may have sent it away by now – if ever there were such a thing.'

'Nay – in a matter touching Five Kings it would be next his black heart,' said the pundit. 'Was there nothing?'
780 The Delhi man laughed and resettled his turban as he entered. 'I searched between the soles of his slippers as the Flower searched his clothes. This is not the man but another. I leave little unseen.'

'They did not say he was the very man,' said the pundit, thoughtfully. 'They said, "Look if he be the man, since our counsels are troubled."'
785 'That North country is full of horse-dealers as an old coat of lice. There is Sikander Khan, Nur Ali Beg, and Farrukh Shah – all heads of kafilas [caravans] – who deal there,' said the Flower.

'They have not yet come in,' said the pundit. 'Thou must ensnare them later.'
790 'Phew!' said the Flower with deep disgust, rolling Mahbub's head from her lap. 'I earn my money. Farrukh Shah is a bear, Ali Beg a swashbuckler, and old Sikander Khan – yaie! Go! I sleep now. This swine will not stir till dawn.'

When Mahbub woke, the Flower talked to him severely on the sin
795 of drunkenness. Asiatics do not wink when they have outmanoeuvred an enemy, but as Mahbub Ali cleared his throat, tightened his belt, and staggered forth under the early morning stars, he came very near to it.

'What a colt's trick!' said he to himself. 'As if every girl in Peshawur did not use it! But 'twas prettily done. Now God He knows how many
800 more there be upon the Road who have orders to test me – perhaps with his knife. So it stands that the boy must go to Umballa – and by rail – for the writing is something urgent. I abide here, following the Flower and drinking wine as an Afghan coper should.'

He halted at the stall next but one to his own. His men lay there
805 heavy with sleep. There was no sign of Kim or the lama.

'Up!' He stirred a sleeper. 'Whither went those who lay here last even – the lama and the boy? Is aught missing?'

'Nay,' grunted the man, 'the old madman rose at second cockcrow saying he would go to Benares, and the young one led him away.'
810 'The curse of Allah on all unbelievers!' said Mahbub heartily, and climbed into his own stall, growling in his beard.

But it was Kim who wakened the lama – Kim with one eye laid against a knot-hole in the planking, who had seen the Delhi man's search through the boxes. This was no common thief that turned over

815   letters, bills, and saddles – no mere burglar who ran a little knife
sideways into the soles of Mahbub's slippers, or picked the seams of
the saddle-bags so deftly. At first Kim had been minded to give the
alarm – the long-drawn *cho-or – choor!* [thief! thief!] that sets the serai
ablaze of nights; but he looked more carefully, and, hand on amulet,
820   drew his own conclusions.

'It must be the pedigree of that made-up horse-lie,' said he, 'the thing
that I carry to Umballa. Better that we go now. Those who search bags
with knives may presently search bellies with knives. Surely there is a
woman behind this. Hai! Hai!' in a whisper to the light-sleeping old
825   man. 'Come. It is time – time to go to Benares.'

The lama rose obediently, and they passed out of the serai like
shadows.

1895/1900   1901

THE SONG OF THE LITTLE HUNTER

Ere Mor the Peacock flutters, ere the Monkey People cry,
  Ere Chil the Kite swoops down a furlong sheer,
Through the Jungle very softly flits a shadow and a sigh –
  He is Fear, O Little Hunter, he is Fear!
5   Very softly down the glade runs a waiting, watching shade,
  And the whisper spreads and widens far and near.
And the sweat is on thy brow, for he passes even now –
  He is Fear, O Little Hunter, he is Fear!

Ere the moon has climbed the mountain, ere the rocks are ribbed with
    light,
10   When the downward-dipping trails are dank and drear,
Comes a breathing hard behind thee – *snuffle-snuffle* through the night –
  It is Fear, O Little Hunter, it is Fear!
On thy knees and draw the bow; bid the shrilling arrow go;
  In the empty, mocking thicket plunge the spear!
15   But thy hands are loosed and weak, and the blood has left thy cheek –
  It is Fear, O Little Hunter, it is Fear!

When the heat-cloud sucks the tempest, when the slivered pine-trees
    fall,
  When the blinding, blaring rain-squalls lash and veer,
Through the war-gongs of the thunder rings a voice more loud than
    all –
20   It is Fear, O Little Hunter, it is Fear!

Now the spates† are banked and deep; now the footless boulders leap –
  Now the lightning shows each littlest leaf-rib clear –
But thy throat is shut and dried, and thy heart against thy side
  Hammers: Fear, O Little Hunter – this is Fear!

1895

RECESSIONAL

God of our fathers, known of old,
  Lord of our far-flung battle-line,
Beneath whose awful Hand we hold
  Dominion over palm and pine –
5 Lord God of Hosts, be with us yet,
  Lest we forget – lest we forget!

The tumult and the shouting dies;
  The Captains and the Kings depart:
Still stands Thine ancient sacrifice,
10 An humble and a contrite heart.
Lord God of Hosts, be with us yet,
Lest we forget – lest we forget!

Far-called, our navies melt away;
  On dune and headland sinks the fire:
15 Lo, all our pomp of yesterday
  Is one with Nineveh and Tyre!†
Judge of the Nations, spare us yet,
Lest we forget – less we forget!

If, drunk with sight of power, we loose
20 Wild tongues that have not Thee in awe,
Such boastings as the Gentiles† use,
  Or lesser breeds† without the Law† –
Lord God of Hosts, be with us yet,
Lest we forget – lest we forget!

---

spates flood waters
Nineveh and Tyre ancient imperial cities
Gentiles European peoples other than the
  British, whom Kipling presents as the Chosen
  People

lesser breeds other races
the Law British civilisation

25   For heathen heart that puts her trust
    In reeking tube and iron shard,[†]
All valiant dust that builds on dust,
    And guarding, calls not Thee to guard,
For frantic boast and foolish word –
30   Thy mercy on Thy People, Lord!

1897   1897

SUSSEX

God gave all men all earth to love,
    But, since our hearts are small,
Ordained for each one spot should prove
    Belovèd over all;
5   That, as He watched Creation's birth,
    So we, in godlike mood,
Many of our love create our earth
    And see that it is good.

So one shall Baltic pines content,
10   As one some Surrey glade,
Or one the palm-grove's droned lament
    Before Levuka's Trade.[†]
Each to his choice, and I rejoice
    The lot has fallen to me
15   In a fair ground – in a fair ground –
    Yea, Sussex by the sea!

No tender-hearted garden crowns,
    No bosomed woods adorn
Our blunt, bow-headed, whale-backed Downs,
20   But gnarled and writhen thorn –
Bare slopes where chasing shadows skim,
    And, through the gaps revealed,
Belt upon belt, the wooded, dim,
    Blue goodness of the Weald.

25   Clean of officious fence or hedge,
    Half-wild and wholly tame,

---

reeking tube and iron shard   guns and swords,   *Levuka's Trade*   Levuka is a sea-port of the
  the words imply, of inferior quality   Fiji islands; Trade refers to the wind.

The wise turf cloaks the white cliff-edge
   As when the Romans came.
What sign of those that fought and died
30   At shift of sword and sword?
The barrow and the camp abide,
   The sunlight and the sward.

Here leaps ashore the full Sou'west
   All heavy-winged with brine,
35 Here lies above the folded crest
   The Channel's leaden line;
And here the sea-fogs lap and cling,
   And here, each warning each,
The sheep-bells and the ship-bells ring
40   Along the hidden beach.

We have no waters to delight
   Our broad and brookless vales –
Only the dewpond on the height
   Unfed, that never fails –
45 Whereby no tattered herbage tells
   Which way the season flies –
Only our close-bit thyme that smells
   Like dawn in Paradise.

Here through the strong and shadeless days
50   The tinkling silence thrills;
Or little, lost, Down churches praise
   The Lord who made the hills:
But there the Old Gods guard their round,
   And, in her secret heart,
55 The heathen kingdom Wilfrid[†] found
   Dreams, as she dwells, apart.

Though all the rest were all my share,
   With equal soul I'd see
Here nine-and-thirty sisters[†] fair,
60   Yet none more fair than she.
Choose ye your need from Thames to Tweed,
   And I will choose instead

Wilfrid (c. 634–709) Archbishop of York,   *sisters* the English counties
who converted the people of the South Saxon
kingdom

Such lands as lie 'twixt Rake and Rye,
    Black Down and Beachy Head.

65   I will go out against the sun
        Where the rolled scarp retires,
    And the Long Man[†] of Wilmington
        Looks naked toward the shires;
    And east till doubling Rother crawls
70   To find the fickle tide,
    By dry and sea-forgotten walls,
        Our ports of stranded pride.

    I will go north about the shaws
        And the deep ghylls that breed
75   Huge oaks and old, the which we hold
        No more than Sussex weed;
    Or south where windy Piddinghoe's
        Begilded dolphin veers,
    And red beside wide-bankèd Ouse
80   Lie down our Sussex steers.

    So to the land our hearts we give
        Till the sure magic strike,
    And Memory, Use, and Love make live
        Us and our fields alike –
85   That deeper than our speech and thought,
        Beyond our reason's sway,
    Clay of the pit whence we were wrought
        Yearns to its fellow-clay.

    God gives all men all earth to love,
90   *But, since man's heart is small,*
    Ordains for each one spot shall prove
        Beloved over all.
    Each to his choice, and I rejoice
        The lot has fallen to me
95   *In a fair ground – in a fair ground –*
        Yea, Sussex by the sea!

1902   1903

Long Man   a figure cut into a chalk escarpment

HARP SONG OF THE DANE WOMEN

What is a woman that you forsake her,
And the hearth-fire and the home-acre,
To go with the old grey Widow-maker?

5   She has no house to lay a guest in –
But one chill bed for all to rest in,
That the pale suns and the stray bergs nest in.

She has no strong white arms to fold you,
But the ten-times-fingering weed to hold you –
Out on the rocks where the tide has rolled you.

10   You, when the signs of summer thicken,
And the ice breaks, and the birch-buds quicken,
Yearly you turn from our side, and sicken –

Sicken again for the shouts and the slaughters.
You steal away to the lapping waters,
15   And look at your ship in her winter-quarters.

You forget our mirth, and talk at the tables,
The kine in the shed and the horse in the stables –
To pitch her sides and go over her cables.

Then you drive out where the storm-clouds swallow,
20   And the sound of your oar-blades, falling hollow,
Is all we have left through the months to follow.

Ah, what is Woman that you forsake her,
And the hearth-fire and the home-acre,
To go with the old grey Widow-maker?

1906

CITIES AND THRONES AND POWERS

Cities and Thrones and Powers
   Stand in Time's eye,
Almost as long as flowers,

Which daily die:
5   But, as new buds put forth
        To glad new men,
    Out of the spent and unconsidered Earth
        The Cities rise again.

    This season's Daffodil,
10   She never hears
    What change, what chance, what chill,
        Cut down last year's;
    But with bold countenance,
        And knowledge small,
15 Esteems her seven days' continuance
        To be perpetual.

    So Time that is o'er-kind
        To all that be,
    Ordains us e'en as blind,
20   As bold as she:
    That in our very death,
        And burial sure,
    Shadow to shadow, well persuaded, saith,
        'See how our works endure!'

                                    1906

IF . . .

    If you can keep your head when all about you
        Are losing theirs and blaming it on you,
    If you can trust yourself when all men doubt you,
        But make allowance for their doubting too;
5   If you can wait and not be tired by waiting,
        Or being lied about, don't deal in lies,
    Or being hated, don't give way to hating,
        And yet don't look too good, nor talk too wise:

    If you can dream – and not make dreams your master;
10   If you can think – and not make thoughts your aim;
    If you can meet with Triumph and Disaster
        And treat those two impostors just the same;

If you can bear to hear the truth you've spoken
    Twisted by knaves to make a trap for fools,
15 Or watch the things you gave your life to, broken,
    And stoop and build 'em up with worn-out tools:

If you can make one heap of all your winnings
    And risk it on one turn of pitch-and-toss,
And lose, and start again at your beginnings
20   And never breathe a word about your loss;
If you can force your heart and nerve and sinew
    To serve your turn long after they are gone,
And so hold on when there is nothing in you
    Except the Will which says to them: "Hold on!"

25 If you can talk with crowds and keep your virtue,
    Or walk with Kings – nor lose the common touch,
If neither foes nor loving friends can hurt you,
    If all men count with you, but none too much;
If you can fill the unforgiving minute
30   With sixty seconds' worth of distance run,
Yours is the Earth and everything that's in it,
    And – which is more – you'll be a Man, my son!

1909   1910

THE LAND

When Julius Fabricius, Sub-Prefect[†] of the Weald,[†]
In the days of Diocletian[†] owned our Lower River-field,
He called to him Hobdenius – a Briton of the Clay,
Saying: 'What about that River-piece for layin' in to hay?'

5 And the aged Hobden answered: 'I remember as a lad
My father told your father that she wanted dreenin' bad.
An' the more that you neeglect her the less you'll get her clean.
Have it jest as you've a mind to, but, if I was you, I'd dreen.'

Sub-Prefect an administrator in Roman Britain   between the North and South Downs
the Weald wooded area of South-East England   *Diocletian* Roman emperor (284–305)

So they drained it long and crossways in the lavish Roman style –
10   Still we find among the river-drift their flakes of ancient tile,
And in drouthy middle August, when the bones of meadows show;
We can trace the lines they followed sixteen hundred years ago.

Then Julius Fabricius died as even Prefects do,
And after certain centuries, Imperial Rome died too.
15   Then did robbers enter Britain from across the Northern main
And our Lower River-field was won by Ogier the Dane.

Well could Ogier work his war-boat – well could Ogier wield his
        brand –
Much he knew of foaming waters – not so much of farming land.
So he called to him a Hobden of the old unaltered blood,
20   Saying: 'What about that River-piece; she doesn't look so good?'

And that aged Hobden answered: "Tain't for *me* to interfere,
But I've known that bit o' meadow now for five and fifty year.
Have it *jest* as you've a mind to, but I've proved it time on time,
If you want to change her nature you have *got* to give her lime!'

25   Ogier sent his wains to Lewes,[†] twenty hours' solemn walk,
And drew back great abundance of the cool, grey, healing chalk.
And old Hobden spread it broadcast, never heeding what was in't. –
Which is why in cleaning ditches, now and then we find a flint.

Ogier died. His sons grew English – Anglo-Saxon was their name –
30   Till out of blossomed Normandy another pirate[†] came;
For Duke William conquered England and divided with his men,
And our Lower River-field he gave to William of Warenne.

But the Brook (you know her habit) rose one rainy autumn night
And tore down sodden flitches of the bank to left and right.
35   So, said William to his Bailiff as they rode their dripping rounds:
'Hob, what about that River-bit – the Brook's got up no bounds?'

And that aged Hobden answered: "Tain't my business to advise,
But ye might ha' known 'twould happen from the way the valley lies.
Where ye can't hold back the water you must try and save the sile.
40   Hev it jest as you've a *mind* to, but, if I was you, I'd spile!'[†]

---

wains to Lewes   waggons to the Sussex market   *pirate*   William the Conqueror (1066–87)
town of Lewes   *spile*   plug holes

They spiled along the water-course with trunks of willow-trees,
And planks of elms behind 'em and immortal oaken knees.
And when the spates of Autumn whirl the gravel-beds away
You can see their faithful fragments, iron-hard in iron clay.

45   *Georgii Quinti Anno Sexto*,[†] I, who own the River-field,
Am fortified with title-deeds, attested, signed and sealed,
Guaranteeing me, my assigns, my executors and heirs
All sorts of powers and profits which – are neither mine nor theirs.

I have rights of chase and warren, as my dignity requires.
50   I can fish – but Hobden tickles.[†] I can shoot – but Hobden wires.
I repair, but he reopens, certain gaps which, men allege,
Have been used by every Hobden since a Hobden swapped[†] a hedge.

Shall I dog his morning progress o'er the track-betraying dew?
Demand his dinner-basket into which my pheasant flew?
55   Confiscate his evening faggot under which my conies ran,
And summons him to judgment? I would sooner summons Pan.[†]

His dead are in the churchyard – thirty generations laid.
Their names were old in history when Domesday Book[†] was made;
And the passion and the piety and prowess of his line
60   Have seeded, rooted, fruited in some land the Law calls mine.

Not for any beast that burrows, not for any bird that flies,
Would I lose his large sound counsel, miss his keen amending eyes.
He is bailiff, woodman, wheelwright, field-surveyor, engineer,
And if flagrantly a poacher – 'tain't for me to interfere.

65   'Hob, what about that River-bit?' I turn to him again,
With Fabricius and Ogier and William of Warenne.
'Hev it jest as you've a mind to, *but*' – and here he takes command.
For whoever pays the taxes old Mus' Hobden owns the land.

1916   1917

Georgii . . . Sexto   (Latin) George V in the
   sixth year of his reign (1916)
tickles   a quiet way to catch fish in the fingers
swapped   trimmed
Pan   There was a literary cult of this ancient

god of the countryside in Edwardian England
Domesday Book   'the Book of the day of
   assessment', a survey of England ordered by
   William the Conqueror in 1086

GETHSEMANE

1914–18

The Garden called Gethsemane†
  In Picardy it was,
And there the people came to see
  The English soldiers pass.
5 We used to pass – we used to pass
  Or halt, as it might be,
And ship our masks in case of gas
  Beyond Gethsemane.

The Garden called Gethsemane,
10   It held a pretty lass,
But all the time she talked to me
  I prayed my cup might pass.
The officer sat on the chair,
  The men lay on the grass,
15 And all the time we halted there
  I prayed my cup might pass.

It didn't pass – it didn't pass –
  It didn't pass from me.
I drank it when we met the gas
20   Beyond Gethsemane!

1919

Gethsemane the scene of Christ's agony in the
garden. Matthew 26. 36

H. G. Wells
1866–1946

Herbert George Wells was born in Bromley, Kent, and educated at
the Normal School of Science, in Kensington. He was a schoolteacher
and journalist for a while; he published *A Textbook of Biology* in
1893. *The Time Machine* (1895) was the first of a series of works of
science fiction. *Kipps* (1905) and *The History of Mr Polly* (1910) are
classic novels of lower-middle-class life and *Tono-Bungay* (1909) is a
shrewd social comedy. Wells wrote prolifically. His *Outline of History*
(1920) and *The Shape of Things to Come* (1933) were widely popular,
educational books. A Fabian Socialist, Wells believed in social reform
and in science, but his last books, including *The Fate of Homo Sapiens*
(1939) and *Mind at the End of Its Tether* (1945), are very pessimistic.
He was quick to see the dangers of science.

THE NEW ACCELERATOR

Certainly, if ever a man found a guinea when he was looking for a pin
it is my good friend Professor Gibberne. I have heard before of
investigators overshooting the mark, but never quite to the extent that
he had done. He has really, this time at any rate, without any touch of
5   exaggeration in the phrase, found something to revolutionize human
life. And that when he was simply seeking an all-round nervous stimulant
to bring languid people up to the stresses of these pushful days. I have
tasted the stuff now several times, and I cannot do better than describe
the effect the thing had on me. That there are astonishing experiences
10   in store for all in search of new sensations will become apparent enough.

Professor Gibberne, as many people know, is my neighbour in
Folkestone. Unless my memory plays me a trick, his portrait at various
ages has already appeared in *The Strand Magazine* – I think late in
1899; but I am unable to look it up because I have lent that volume to
15   someone who has never sent it back. The reader may, perhaps, recall
the high forehead and the singularly long black eye-brows that give
such a Mephistophelian touch to his face. He occupies one of those
pleasant detached houses in the mixed style, that make the western end
of the Upper Sandgate Road so interesting. His is the one with the
20   Flemish gables and the Moorish portico, and it is in the room with the

mullioned bay window that he works when he is down here, and in which of an evening we have so often smoked and talked together. He is a mighty jester, but, besides, he likes to talk to me about his work; he is one of those men who find a help and stimulus in talking, and so
25 I have been able to follow the conception of the New Accelerator right up from a very early stage. Of course, the greater portion of his experimental work is not done in Folkestone, but in Gower Street, in the fine new laboratory next to the hospital that he has been the first to use.
30 As everyone knows, or at least as all intelligent people know, the special department in which Gibberne has gained so great and deserved a reputation among physiologists is the action of drugs upon the nervous system. Upon soporifics, sedatives, and anaesthetics he is, I am told, unequalled. He is also a chemist of considerable eminence, and I suppose
35 in the subtle and complex jungle of riddles that centre about the ganglion cell and the axis fibre there are little cleared places of his making, glades of illumination, that, until he sees fit to publish his results, are inaccessible to every other living man. And in the last few years he has been particularly assiduous upon this question of nervous
40 stimulants, and already, before the discovery of the New Accelerator, very successful with them. Medical science has to thank him for at least three distinct and absolutely safe invigorators of unrivalled value to practising men. In cases of exhaustion the preparation known as Gibberne's B Syrup has, I suppose, saved more lives already than any
45 lifeboat round the coast.
'But none of these things begin to satisfy me yet,' he told me nearly a year ago. 'Either they increase the central energy without affecting the nerves or they simply increase the available energy by lowering the nervous conductivity; and all of them are unequal and local in their
50 operation. One wakes up the heart and viscera and leaves the brain stupefied, one gets at the brain champagne fashion and does nothing good for the solar plexus, and what I want – and what, if it's an earthly possibility, I mean to have – is a stimulant that stimulates all round, that wakes you up for a time from the crown of your head to the tip of
55 your great toe, and makes you go two – or even three to everybody else's one. Eh? That's the thing I'm after.'
'It would tire a man,' I said.
'Not a doubt of it. And you'd eat double or treble – and all that. But just think what the thing would mean. Imagine yourself with a little
60 phial like this' – he held up a bottle of green glass and marked his points with it – 'and in this precious phial is the power to think twice as fast, move twice as quickly, do twice as much work in a given time as you could otherwise do.'
'But is such a thing possible?'

65　'I believe so. If it isn't, I've wasted my time for a year. These various preparations of the hypophosphites, for example, seem to show that something of the sort. . . . Even if it was only one and a half times as fast it would do.'

'It *would* do,' I said.

70　'If you were a statesman in a corner, for example, time rushing up against you, something urgent to be done, eh?'

'He could dose his private secretary,' I said.

'And gain – double time. And think if *you*, for example, wanted to finish a book.'

75　'Usually,' I said, 'I wish I'd never begun 'em.'

'Or a doctor, driven to death, wants to sit down and think out a case. Or a barrister – or a man cramming for an examination.'

'Worth a guinea a drop,' said I, 'and more – to men like that.'

'And in a duel again,' said Gibberne, 'where it all depends on your
80　quickness in pulling the trigger.'

'Or in fencing,' I echoed.

'You see,' said Gibberne, 'if I get it as an all-round thing it will really do you no harm at all – except perhaps to an infinitesimal degree it brings you nearer old age. You will just have lived twice to other
85　people's once –'

'I suppose,' I meditated, 'in a duel – it would be fair?'

'That's a question for the seconds,' said Gibberne.

I harked back farther. 'And you really think such a thing *is* possible?' I said.

90　'As possible,' said Gibberne, and glanced at something that went throbbing by the window, 'as a motor-bus. As a matter of fact –'

He paused and smiled at me deeply, and tapped slowly on the edge of his desk with the green phial. 'I think I know the stuff. . . . Already I've got something coming.' The nervous smile upon his face betrayed
95　the gravity of his revelation. He rarely talked of his actual experimental work unless things were very near the end. 'And it may be, it may be – I shouldn't be surprised – it may even do the thing at a greater rate than twice.'

'It will be rather a big thing,' I hazarded.
100　'It will be, I think, rather a big thing.'

But I don't think he quite knew what a big thing it was to be, for all that.

I remember we had several subsequent talks about the stuff, 'The New Accelerator' he called it, and his tone about it grew more confident
105　on each occasion. Sometimes he talked nervously of unexpected physiological results its use might have, and then he would get a bit unhappy; at others he was frankly mercenary, and we debated long and anxiously how the preparation might be turned to commercial account. 'It's a

good thing,' said Gibberne, 'a tremendous thing. I know I'm giving the
110 world something, and I think it only reasonable we should expect the
world to pay. The dignity of science is all very well, but I think somehow
I must have the monopoly of the stuff for, say, ten years. I don't see
why all the fun in life should go to the dealers in ham.'

My own interest in the coming drug certainly did not wane in the
115 time. I have always had a queer twist towards metaphysics in my
mind. I have always been given to paradoxes about space and time,
and it seemed to me that Gibberne was really preparing no less than
the absolute acceleration of life. Suppose a man repeatedly dosed
with such a preparation: he would live an active and record life
120 indeed, but he would be an adult at eleven, middle-aged at twenty-
five, and by thirty well on the road to senile decay. It seemed to me
that so far Gibberne was only going to do for anyone who took this
drug exactly what Nature has done for the Jews and Orientals, who
are men in their teens and aged by fifty, and quicker in thought and
125 act than we are all the time. The marvel of drugs has always been
great to my mind; you can madden a man, calm a man, make him
incredibly strong and alert or a helpless log, quicken his passion and
allay that, all by means of drugs, and here was a new miracle to be
added to this strange armoury of phials the doctors use! But Gibberne
130 was far too eager upon his technical points to enter very keenly into
my aspect of the question.

It was the 7th or 8th of August when he told me the distillation that
would decide his failure or success for a time was going forward as we
talked, and it was on the 10th that he told me the thing was done and
135 the New Accelerator a tangible reality in the world. I met him as I was
going up the Sandgate Hill towards Folkestone – I think I was going to
get my hair cut; and he came hurrying down to meet me – I suppose
he was coming to my house to tell me at once of his success. I remember
that his eyes were unusually bright and his face flushed, and I noted
140 even then the swift alacrity of his step.

'It's done,' he cried, and gripped my hand, speaking very fast; 'it's
more than done. Come up to my house and see.'

'Really?'

'Really!' he shouted. 'Incredibly! Come up and see.'

145 'And it goes – twice?'

'It does more, much more. It scares me. Come up and see the stuff.
Taste it! Try it! It's the most amazing stuff on earth.' He gripped my
arm and, walking at such a pace that he forced me into a trot, went
shouting with me up the hill. A whole charabancful of people turned
150 and stared at us in unison after the manner of people in charabancs. It
was one of those hot, clear days that Folkestone sees so much of, every
colour incredibly bright and every outline hard. There was a breeze, of

course, but not so much breeze as sufficed under these conditions to
keep me cool and dry. I panted for mercy.

155 'I'm not walking fast, am I?' cried Gibberne, and slackened his pace
to a quick march.

'You've been taking some of this stuff,' I puffed.

'No,' he said. 'At the utmost a drop of water that stood in a beaker
from which I had washed out the last traces of the stuff. I took some
160 last night, you know. But that is ancient history, now.'

'And it goes twice?' I said, nearing his doorway in a grateful
perspiration.

'It goes a thousand times, many thousand times!' cried Gibberne,
with a dramatic gesture, flinging open his Early English carved oak
165 gate.

'Phew!' said I, and followed him to the door.

'I don't know how many times it goes,' he said, with his latch-key in
his hand.

'And you –'

170 'It throws all sorts of light on nervous physiology, it kicks the theory
of vision into a perfectly new shape! . . . Heaven knows how many
thousand times. We'll try all that after – The thing is to try the stuff
now.'

'Try the stuff?' I said, as we went along the passage.

175 'Rather,' said Gibberne, turning on me in his study. 'There it is in
that little green phial there! Unless you happen to be afraid?'

I am a careful man by nature, and only theoretically adventurous. I
was afraid. But on the other hand there is pride.

'Well,' I haggled. 'You say you've tried it?'

180 'I've tried it,' he said, 'and I don't look hurt by it, do I? I don't even
look livery and I *feel* –'

I sat down. 'Give me the potion,' I said. 'If the worst comes to the
worst it will save having my hair cut, and that I think is one of the
most hateful duties of a civilised man. How do you take the mixture?'

185 'With water,' said Gibberne, whacking down a carafe.

He stood up in front of his desk and regarded me in his easy chair;
his manner was suddenly reflected by a touch of the Harley Street
specialist. 'It's rum stuff, you know,' he said.

I made a gesture with my hand.

190 'I must warn you in the first place as soon as you've got it down to
shut your eyes, and open them very cautiously in a minute or so's time.
One still sees. The sense of vision is a question of length of vibration,
and not of multitude of impacts; but there's a kind of shock to the
retina, a nasty giddy confusion just at the time if the eyes are open.
195 Keep 'em shut.'

'Shut,' I said. 'Good!'

'And the next thing is, keep still. Don't begin to whack about. You may fetch something a nasty rap if you do. Remember you will be going several thousand times faster than you ever did before, heart, lungs, muscles, brain – everything – and you will hit hard without knowing it. You won't know it, you know. You'll feel just as you do now. Only everything in the world will seem to be going ever so many thousand times slower than it ever went before. That's what makes it so deuced queer.'

'Lor',' I said. 'And you mean –'

'You'll see,' said he, and took up a measure. He glanced at the material on his desk. 'Glasses,' he said, 'water. All here. Mustn't take too much for the first attempt.'

The little phial glucked out its precious contents. 'Don't forget what I told you,' he said, turning the contents of the measure into a glass in the manner of an Italian waiter measuring whisky. 'Sit with your eyes tightly shut and in absolute stillness for two minutes,' he said. 'Then you will hear me speak.'

He added an inch or so of water to the dose in each glass.

'By-the-by,' he said, 'don't put your glass down. Keep it in your hand and rest your hand on your knee. Yes – so. And now –'

He raised his glass.

'The New Accelerator,' I said.

'The New Accelerator,' he answered, and we touched glasses and drank, and instantly I closed my eyes.

You know that blank non-existence into which one drops when one has taken 'gas'. For an indefinite interval it was like that. Then I heard Gibberne telling me to wake up, and I stirred and opened my eyes. There he stood as he had been standing, glass still in hand. It was empty, that was all the difference.

'Well?' said I.

'Nothing out of the way?'

'Nothing. A slight feeling of exhilaration, perhaps. Nothing more.'

'Sounds?'

'Things are still,' I said. 'By Jove! yes! They *are* still. Except the sort of faint pat, patter, like rain falling on different things. What is it?'

'Analysed sounds,' I think he said, but I am not sure. He glanced at the window. 'Have you ever seen a curtain before a window fixed in that way before?'

I followed his eyes, and there was the end of the curtain, frozen, as it were, corner high, in the act of flapping briskly in the breeze.

'No,' said I; 'that's odd.'

'And here,' he said, and opened the hand that held the glass. Naturally I winced, expected the glass to smash. But so far from smashing it did not even seem to stir; it hung in mid-air – motionless. 'Roughly speaking,' said Gibberne, 'an object in these latitudes falls sixteen feet in the first second. This glass is falling sixteen feet in a second now. Only, you see, it hasn't been falling yet for the hundredth part of a second. That gives you some idea of the pace of my Accelerator.' And he waved his hand round and round, over and over the slowly sinking glass. Finally he took it by the bottom, pulled it down and placed it very carefully on the table. 'Eh?' he said to me, and laughed.

'That seems all right,' I said, and began very gingerly to raise myself from my chair. I felt perfectly well, very light and comfortable, and quite confident in my mind. I was going fast all over. My heart, for example, was beating a thousand times a second, but it caused me no discomfort at all. I looked out of the window. An immovable cyclist, head down and with a frozen puff of dust behind his driving-wheel, scorched to overtake a galloping charabanc that did not stir. I gaped in amazement at this incredible spectacle. 'Gibberne,' I cried, 'how long will this confounded stuff last?'

'Heaven knows!' he answered. 'Last time I took it I went to bed and slept it off. I tell you, I was frightened. It must have lasted some minutes, I think – it seemed like hours. But after a bit it slows down rather suddenly, I believe.'

I was proud to observe that I did not feel frightened – I suppose because there were two of us. 'Why shouldn't we go out?' I asked.

'Why not?'

'They'll see us.'

'Not they. Goodness, no! Why, we shall be going a thousand times faster than the quickest conjuring trick that was ever done. Come along! Which way shall we go? Window, or door?'

And out by the window we went.

Assuredly of all the strange experiences that I have ever had, or imagined, or read of other people having or imagining, that little raid I made with Gibberne on the Folkestone Leas, under the influence of the New Accelerator, was the strangest and maddest of all. We went out by his gate into the road, and there we made a minute examination of the statuesque passing traffic. The tops of the wheels and some of the legs of the horses of this charabanc, the end of the whip-lash and the lower jaw of the conductor – who was just beginning to yawn – were perceptibly in motion, but all the rest of the lumbering conveyance seemed still. And quite noiseless except for a faint rattling that came from one man's throat! And as parts of this frozen edifice there were a driver, you know, and a conductor, and eleven people! The effect as we walked about the thing began by being madly queer and ended by being – disagreeable. There they were, people like ourselves and yet not like ourselves, frozen in careless attitudes, caught in mid-gesture. A girl and a man smiled at one another, a leering smile that threatened to last

285 for evermore; a woman in a floppy capelline rested her arm on the rail and stared at Gibberne's house with the unwinking stare of eternity; a man stroked his moustache like a figure of wax, and another stretched a tiresome stiff hand with extended fingers towards his loosened hat. We stared at them, we laughed at them, we made faces at them, and
290 then a sort of disgust of them came upon us, and we turned away and walked round in front of the cyclist towards the Leas.

'Goodness!' cried Gibberne, suddenly; 'look there!'

He pointed, and there at the tip of his finger and sliding down the air with wings flapping slowly and at the speed of an exceptionally
295 languid snail – was a bee.

And so we came out upon the Leas. There the thing seemed madder than ever. The band was playing in the upper stand, though all the sound it made for us was a low-pitched, wheezy rattle, a sort of prolonged last sigh that passed at times into a sound like the slow
300 muffled ticking of some monstrous clock. Frozen people stood erect; strange, silent, self-conscious-looking dummies hung unstably in mid-stride, promenading upon the grass. I passed close to a poodle dog suspended in the act of leaping, and watched the slow movement of his legs as he sank to earth. 'Lord, look *here*! cried Gibberne, and we halted
305 for a moment before a magnificent person in white faint-striped flannels, white shoes, and a Panama hat, who turned back to wink at two gaily dressed ladies he had passed. A wink, studied with such leisurely deliberation as we could afford, is an unattractive thing. It loses any quality of alert gaiety, and one remarks that the winking eye does not
310 completely close, that under its drooping lid appears the lower edge of an eyeball and a line of white. 'Heaven give me memory,' said I, 'and I will never wink again.'

'Or smile,' said Gibberne, with his eye on the ladies' answering teeth.

'It's infernally hot, somehow,' said I. 'Let's go slower.'
315 'Oh, come along!' said Gibberne.

We picked our way among the bath-chairs in the path. Many of the people sitting in the chairs seemed almost natural in their passive poses, but the contorted scarlet of the bandsmen was not a restful thing to see. A purple-faced gentleman was frozen in the midst of a violent
320 struggle to refold his newspaper against the wind; there were many evidences that all these people in their sluggish way were exposed to a considerable breeze, a breeze that had no existence so far as our sensations went. We came out and walked a little way from the crowd, and turned and regarded it. To see all that multitude changed to a
325 picture, smitten rigid, as it were, into the semblance of realistic wax, was impossibly wonderful. It was absurd, of course; but it filled me with an irrational, an exultant sense of superior advantage. Consider the wonder of it! All that I had said and thought and done since the

stuff had begun to work in my veins had happened, so far as those
people, so far as the world in general went, in the twinkling of an eye.
'The New Accelerator –' I began, but Gibberne interrupted me.

'There's that infernal old woman,' he said.

'What old woman?'

'Lives next door to me,' said Gibberne. 'Has a lapdog that yaps.
Gods! The temptation is strong!'

There is something very boyish and impulsive about Gibberne at
times. Before I could expostulate with him he had dashed forward,
snatched the unfortunate animal out of visible existence, and was
running violently with it towards the cliff of the Leas. It was the most
extraordinary sight. The little brute, you know, didn't bark or wriggle
or make the slightest sign of vitality. It kept quite stiffly in an attitude
of somnolent repose, and Gibberne held it by the neck. It was like
running about with a dog of wood. 'Gibberne,' I cried, 'put it down!'
Then I said something else. 'If you run like that, Gibberne,' I cried,
'you'll set your clothes on fire. Your linen trousers are going brown as
it is!'

He clapped his hand on his thigh and stood hesitating on the verge.
'Gibberne,' I cried, coming up, 'put it down. This heat is too much! It's
our running so! Two or three miles a second! Friction of the air!'

'What?' he said, glancing at the dog.

'Friction of the air,' I shouted. 'Friction of the air. Going too fast.
Like meteorites and things. Too hot. And, Gibberne! Gibberne! I'm all
over pricking and a sort of perspiration. You can see people stirring
slightly. I believe the stuff's working off! Put that dog down.'

'Eh?' he said.

'It's working off,' I repeated. 'We're too hot and the stuff's working
off! I'm wet through.'

He stared at me. Then at the band, the wheezy rattle of whose
performance was certainly going faster. Then with a tremendous sweep
of the arm he hurled the dog away from him and it went spinning
upward, still inanimate, and hung at last over the grouped parasols of
a knot of chattering people. Gibberne was gripping my elbow. 'By
Jove!' he cried. 'I believe it is! A sort of hot pricking and – yes. That
man's moving his pocket-handkerchief! Perceptibly. We must get out
of this sharp.'

But we could not get out of it sharply enough. Luckily perhaps! For
we might have run, and if we had run we should, I believe, have burst
into flames. Almost certainly we should have burst into flames! You
know we had neither of us thought of that. . . . But before we could
even begin to run the action of the drug had ceased. It was the business
of a minute fraction of a second. The effect of the New Accelerator
passed like the drawing of a curtain, vanished in the movement of a

hand. I heard Gibberne's voice in infinite alarm. 'Sit down,' he said, and flop, down upon the turf at the edge of the Leas I sat – scorching
375   as I sat. There is a patch of grass burnt there still where I sat down. The whole stagnation seemed to wake up as I did so, the disarticulated vibration of the band rushed together into a blast of music, the promenaders put their feet down and walked their ways, the papers and flags began flapping, smiles passed into words, the winker finished
380   his wink and went on his way complacently, and all the seated people moved and spoke.

The whole world had come alive again, was going as fast as we were, or rather we were going no faster than the rest of the world. It was like slowing down as one comes into a railway station. Everything seemed
385   to spin round for a second or two, I had the most transient feeling of nausea, and that was all. And the little dog which had seemed to hang for a moment when the force of Gibberne's arm was expended fell with a swift acceleration clean through a lady's parasol.

That was the saving of us. Unless it was for one corpulent old
390   gentleman in a bath-chair, who certainly did start at the sight of us and afterwards regarded us at intervals with a darkly suspicious eye, and finally, I believe, said something to his nurse about us, I doubt if a solitary person remarked our sudden appearance among them. Plop! We must have appeared abruptly. We ceased to smoulder almost at
395   once, though the turf beneath me was uncomfortably hot. The attention of everyone – including even the Amusements Association band, which on this occasion, for the only time in its history, got out of tune – was arrested by the amazing fact, and the still more amazing yapping and uproar caused by the fact, that a respectable, over-fed lapdog sleeping
400   quietly to the east of the bandstand should suddenly fall through the parasol of a lady on the west – in a slightly singed condition due to the extreme velocity of its movements through the air. In these absurd days, too, when we are all trying to be as psychic and silly and superstitious as possible! People got up and trod on other people, chairs were
405   overturned, the Leas policeman ran. How the matter settled itself I do not know – we were much too anxious to disentangle ourselves from the affair and get out of range of the eye of the old gentleman in the bath-chair to make minute inquiries. As soon as we were sufficiently cool and sufficiently recovered from our giddiness and nausea and
410   confusion of mind to do so we stood up and, skirting the crowd, directed our steps back along the road below the Metropole towards Gibberne's house. But amidst the din I heard very distinctly the gentleman who had been sitting beside the lady of the ruptured sunshade using quite unjustifiable threats and language to one of those chair-
415   attendants who have 'Inspector' written on their caps. 'If you didn't throw the dog,' he said, 'who *did*?'

The sudden return of movement and familiar noises, and our natural anxiety about ourselves (our clothes were still dreadfully hot, and the fronts of the thighs of Gibberne's white trousers were scorched a drabbish brown), prevented the minute observations I should have liked to make on all these things. Indeed, I really made no observations of any scientific value on that return. The bee, of course, had gone. I looked for that cyclist, but he was already out of sight as we came into the Upper Sandgate Road or hidden from us by traffic; the charabanc, however, with its people now all alive and stirring, was clattering along at a spanking pace almost abreast of the nearer church.

We noted, however, that the window-sill on which we had stepped in getting out of the house was slightly singed, and that the impressions of our feet on the gravel of the path were unusually deep.

So it was I had my first experience of the New Accelerator. Practically we had been running about and saying and doing all sorts of things in the space of a second or so of time. We had lived half an hour while the band had played, perhaps, two bars. But the effect it had upon us was that the whole world had stopped for our convenient inspection. Considering all things, and particularly considering our rashness in venturing out of the house, the experience might certainly have been much more disagreeable than it was. It showed, no doubt, that Gibberne has still much to learn before his preparation is a manageable convenience, but its practicability is certainly demonstrated beyond all cavil.

Since that adventure he has been steadily bringing its use under control, and I have several times, and without the slightest bad result, taken measured doses under his direction; though I must confess I have not yet ventured abroad again while under its influence. I may mention, for example, that this story has been written at one sitting and without interruption, except for the nibbling of some chocolate, by its means. I began at 6.25, and my watch is now very nearly at the minute past the half-hour. The convenience of securing a long, uninterrupted spell of work in the midst of a day full of engagements cannot be exaggerated. Gibberne is now working at the quantitative handling of his preparation, with especial reference to its distinctive effects upon different types of constitution. He then hopes to find a Retarder with which to dilute its present rather excessive potency. The Retarder will, of course, have the reverse effect to the Accelerator; used alone, it should enable the patient to spread a few seconds over many hours of ordinary time, and so to maintain an apathetic inaction, a glacierlike absence of alacrity, amidst the most animated or irritating surroundings. The two things together must necessarily work an entire revolution to civilized existence. It is the beginning

of our escape from that Time Garment of which Carlyle[†] speaks.
460 While this Accelerator will enable us to concentrate ourselves with
tremendous impact upon any moment or occasion that demands our
utmost sense and vigour, the Retarder will enable us to pass in
passive tranquillity through infinite hardship and tedium. Perhaps I
am a little optimistic about the Retarder, which has indeed still to
465 be discovered, but about the Accelerator there is no possible sort of
doubt whatever. Its appearance upon the market in a convenient,
controllable, and assimilable form is a matter of the next few months.
It will be obtainable of all chemists and druggists, in small green
bottles, at a high but, considering its extraordinary qualities, by no
470 means excessive price. Gibberne's Nervous Accelerator it will be
called, and he hopes to be able to supply it in three strengths: one in
200, one in 900, and one in 2000, distinguished by yellow, pink,
and white labels respectively.

No doubt its use renders a great number of very extraordinary things
475 possible; for, of course, the most remarkable and, possibly, even
criminal proceedings may be effected with impunity by thus dodging,
as it were, into the interstices of time. Like all potent preparations it
will be liable to abuse. We have, however, discussed this aspect of the
question very thoroughly, and we have decided that this is purely a
480 matter of medical jurisprudence and altogether outside our province.
We shall manufacture and sell the Accelerator, and, as for the
consequences – we shall see.

1901   1903

Carlyle   Thomas Carlyle (1795–1851) in   which is the Time-vesture of God, and reveals
  Sartor Resartus (1833–4): 'But Nature,   Him to the wise, hides Him from the foolish'

Arnold Bennett

1867–1931

Enoch Arnold Bennett was born at Hanley in Staffordshire, the son of a solicitor, and was educated in Burslem and Newcastle-under-Lyme. He started work in his father's office and at the age of twenty-one became a solicitor's clerk in London. He was a versatile and prolific journalist and writer on many topics, but his great achievement is in the novels, realistic and sensitive about ordinary people in the 'Five Towns' of the Potteries (now the City of Stoke-on-Trent) where he grew up: *Anna of the Five Towns* (1902), *The Old Wives' Tale* (1908), *Clayhanger* (1910), and its sequels *Hilda Lessways* (1911) and *These Twain* (1915). *The Card* (1911) has admirers, and *Riceyman Steps* (1923) is agreed to be the best novel of his last period.

Bennett's theme in *The Old Wives' Tale* – the tragi-comedy of youth and age – is illustrated when the father of Sophie, one of the heroines, unkindly dies, during a rare moment of neglect, while his daughter is being charmed by a commercial traveller.

From THE OLD WIVES' TALE

Elephant

I

'Sophia, will you come and see the elephant? Do come!' Constance entered the drawing-room with this request on her eager lips.

'No,' said Sophia, with a touch of condescension. 'I'm far too busy for elephants.'

5   Only two years had passed; but both girls were grown up now; long sleeves, long skirts, hair that had settled down in life; and a demeanour immensely serious, as though existence were terrific in its responsibilities; yet sometimes childhood surprisingly broke through the crust of gravity, as now in Constance, aroused by such things as elephants, and

10   proclaimed with vivacious gestures that it was not dead after all. The sisters were sharply differentiated. Constance wore the black alpaca apron and the scissors at the end of long black elastic, which indicated her vocation in the shop. She was proving a considerable success in the

millinery department. She had learnt how to talk to people, and was,
in her modest way, very self-possessed. She was getting a little stouter.
Everybody liked her. Sophia had developed into the student. Time had
accentuated her reserve. Her sole friend was Miss Chetwynd, with
whom she was, having regard to the disparity of their ages, very
intimate. At home she spoke little. She lacked amiability; as her mother
said, she was 'touchy'. She required diplomacy from others, but did not
render it again. Her attitude, indeed, was one of half-hidden disdain,
now gentle, now coldly bitter. She would not wear an apron, in an age
when aprons were almost essential to decency. No! She would *not* wear
an apron, and there was an end of it. She was not so tidy as Constance,
and if Constance's hands had taken on the coarse texture which comes
from commerce with needles, pins, artificial flowers, and stuffs, Sophia's
fine hands were seldom innocent of ink. But Sophia was splendidly
beautiful. And even her mother and Constance had an instinctive idea
that that face was, at any rate, a partial excuse for her asperity.

'Well,' said Constance, 'if you won't, I do believe I shall ask mother
if she will.'

Sophia, bending over her books, made no answer. But the top of her
head said: 'This has no interest for me whatever.'

Constance left the room, and in a moment returned with her mother.

'Sophia,' said her mother, with gay excitement, 'you might go and
sit with your father for a bit while Constance and I just run up to the
playground to see the elephant. You can work just as well in there as
here. Your father's asleep.'

'Oh, very well!' Sophia agreed haughtily. 'Whatever is all this fuss
about an elephant? Anyhow, it'll be quieter in your room. The noise
here is splitting.' She gave a supercilious glance into the Square as she
languidly rose.

It was the morning of the third day of Bursley Wakes;[†] not the
modern finicking and respectable, but an orgiastic carnival, gross in all
its manifestations of joy. The whole centre of the town was given over
to the furious pleasures of the people. Most of the Square was occupied
by Wombwell's Menagerie, in a vast oblong tent, whose raging beasts
roared and growled all day and night. And spreading away from this
supreme attraction, right up through the market-place past the Town
Hall to Duck Bank, Duck Square and the waste land called the
'playground' were hundreds of booths with banners displaying all the
delights of the horrible. You could see the atrocities of the French
Revolution, and of the Fiji Islands, and the ravages of unspeakable
diseases, and the living flesh of a nearly nude human female guaranteed

---

Bursley Wakes   Bursley corresponds to
Burslem, one of the Pottery towns which are
now the city of Stoke-on-Trent; the Wakes
was a holiday for a fair

55   to turn the scale at twenty-two stone, and the skeletons of the mysterious phantoscope,[†] and the bloody contests of champions naked to the waist (with the chance of picking up a red tooth as a relic). You could try your strength by hitting an image of a fellow-creature in the stomach, and test your aim by knocking off the heads of other images with a

60   wooden ball. You could also shoot with rifles at various targets. All the streets were lined with stalls loaded with food in heaps, chiefly dried fish, the entrails of animals and gingerbread. All the public-houses were crammed and frenzied jolly drunkards, men and women, lounged along the pavements everywhere, their shouts vying with the trumpets, horns,

65   and drums of the booths, and the shrieking, rattling toys that the children carried.

It was a glorious spectacle, but not a spectacle for the leading families. Miss Chetwynd's school was closed, so that the daughters of leading families might remain in seclusion till the worst was over. The Baineses

70   ignored the Wakes in every possible way, choosing the week to have a show of mourning goods in the left-hand window, and refusing to let Maggie outside on any pretext. Therefore the dazzling social success of the elephant, which was quite easily drawing Mrs Baines into the vortex, cannot imaginably be overestimated.

75   On the previous night one of the three Wombwell elephants had suddenly knelt on a man in the tent; he had then walked out of the tent and picked up another man at haphazard from the crowd which was staring at the great pictures in front, and tried to put this second man into his mouth. Being stopped by his Indian attendant with a

80   pitchfork, he placed the man on the ground, and stuck his tusk through an artery of the victim's arm. He then, amid unexampled excitement, suffered himself to be led away. He was conducted to the rear of the tent, just in front of Baines's shuttered windows, and by means of stakes, pulleys, and ropes forced to his knees. His head was whitewashed,

85   and six men of the Rifle Corps were engaged to shoot at him at a distance of five yards, while constables kept the crowd off with truncheons. He died instantly, rolling over with a soft thud. The crowd cheered, and intoxicated by their importance, the Volunteers fired three more volleys into the carcase, and were then borne off as heroes to

90   different inns. The elephant, by the help of his two companions, was got on to a railway lorry[†] and disappeared into the night. Such was the greatest sensation that has ever occurred, or perhaps will ever occur, in Bursley. The excitement about the repeal of the Corn Laws,[†] or about Inkerman,[†] was feeble compared to that excitement. Mr Critchlow,

---

phantoscope   picture-show
railway lorry   a flat car
Corn Laws   protectionist legislation (1815),

unpopular because it kept the price of bread high, repealed, after much debate, in 1846
Inkerman   a battle in the Crimean War (1854)

95   who had been called on to put a hasty tourniquet round the arm of the
     second victim, had popped in afterwards to tell John Baines all about
     it. Mr Baines's interest, however, had been slight. Mr Critchlow
     succeeded better with the ladies, who, though they had witnessed the
     shooting from the drawing-room, were thirsty for the most trifling
100 details.
         The next day it was known that the elephant lay near the playground,
     pending the decision of the Chief Bailiff and the Medical Officer as to
     his burial. And everybody had to visit the corpse. No social exclusiveness
     could withstand the seduction of that dead elephant. Pilgrims travelled
105 from all the Five Towns to see him.
         'We're going now,' said Mrs Baines, after she had assumed her bonnet
     and shawl.
         'All right,' said Sophia, pretending to be absorbed in study, as she
     sat on the sofa at the foot of her father's bed.
110   And Constance, having put her head in at the door, drew her mother
     after her like a magnet.
         Then Sophia heard a remarkable conversation in the passage.
         'Are you going up to see the elephant, Mrs Baines?' asked the voice
     of Mr Povey.
115   'Yes. Why?'
         'I think I had better come with you. The crowd is sure to be very
     rough.' Mr Povey's tone was firm; he had a position.
         'But the shop?'
         'We shall not be long,' said Mr Povey.
120   'Oh yes, mother,' Constance added appealingly.
         Sophia felt the house thrill as the side-door banged. She sprang up
     and watched the three cross King Street diagonally, and so plunge into
     the Wakes. This triple departure was surely the crowning tribute to the
     dead elephant! It was simply astonishing. It caused Sophia to perceive
125 that she had miscalculated the importance of the elephant. It made her
     regret her scorn of the elephant as an attraction. She was left behind;
     and the joy of life was calling her. She could see down into the Vaults[†]
     on the opposite side of the street, where working men – potters and
     colliers – in their best clothes, some with high hats, were drinking,
130 gesticulating, and laughing in a row at a long counter.
         She noticed, while she was thus at the bedroom window, a young
     man ascending King Street, followed by a porter trundling a flat barrow
     of luggage. He passed slowly under the very window. She flushed. She
     had evidently been startled by the sight of this young man into no
135 ordinary state of commotion. She glanced at the books on the sofa, and
     then at her father. Mr Baines, thin and gaunt, and acutely pitiable, still

---

the Vaults   a public-house, as is the Tiger

slept. His brain had almost ceased to be active now; he had to be fed and tended like a bearded baby, and he would sleep for hours at a stretch even in the daytime. Sophia left the room. A moment later she
140 ran into the shop, an apparition that amazed the three young lady assistants. At the corner near the window on the fancy side a little nook had been formed by screening off a portion of the counter with large flower-boxes placed end-up. This corner had come to be known as 'Miss Baines's corner'. Sophia hastened to it, squeezing past a young
145 lady assistant in the narrow space between the back of the counter and the shelf-lined wall. She sat down in Constance's chair and pretended to look for something. She had examined herself in the cheval-glass in the showroom, on her way from the sick-chamber. When she heard a voice near the door of the shop asking first for Mr Povey and then for
150 Mrs Baines, she rose, and seizing the object nearest to her, which happened to be a pair of scissors, she hurried towards the showroom stairs as though the scissors had been a grail, passionately sought and to be jealously hidden away. She wanted to stop and turn round, but something prevented her. She was at the end of the counter, under the
155 curving stairs, when one of the assistants said:

'I suppose you don't know when Mr Povey or your mother are likely to be back, Miss Sophia? Here's –'

It was a divine release for Sophia.

'They're – I –' she stammered, turning round abruptly. Luckily she
160 was still sheltered behind the counter.

The young man whom she had seen in the street came boldly forward.

'Good morning, Miss Sophia,' said he, hat in hand. 'It is a long time since I had the pleasure of seeing you.'

Never had she blushed as she blushed then. She scarcely knew what
165 she was doing as she moved slowly towards her sister's corner again, the young man following her on the customers' side of the counter.

II

She knew that he was a traveller for the most renowned and gigantic of all Manchester wholesale firms – Birkinshaws. But she did not know his name, which was Gerald Scales. He was a rather short, but extremely
170 well-proportioned man of thirty, with fair hair, and a distinguished appearance, as became a representative of Birkinshaw's. His broad, tight necktie, with an edge of white collar showing above it, was particularly elegant. He had been on the road for Birkinshaw's for several years; but Sophia had only seen him once before in her life,
175 when she was a little girl, three years ago. The relations between the travellers of the great firms and their solid, sure clients in small towns were in those days often cordially intimate. The traveller came with the lustre of a historic reputation around him; there was no need to fawn

for orders; and the client's immense and immaculate respectability
180   made him the equal of no matter what ambassador. It was a case of
mutual esteem, and of that confidence-generating phenomenon, 'an old
account'. The tone in which a commercial traveller of middle age would
utter the phrase 'an old account' revealed in a flash all that was
romantic, prim, and stately in mid-Victorian commerce. In the days of
185   Baines, after one of the elaborately engraved advice-circulars had arrived
('Our Mr —— will have the pleasure of waiting upon you on – day
next, the – inst.') John might in certain cases be expected to say, on the
morning of – day, 'Missis, what have ye gotten for supper tonight?'

Mr Gerald Scales had never been asked to supper; he had never even
190   seen John Baines; but, as the youthful successor of an aged traveller
who had had the pleasure of St Luke's Square, on behalf of Birkinshaws,
since before railways, Mrs Baines had treated him with a faint agreeable
touch of maternal familiarity; and, both her daughters being once in
the shop during his visit, she had on that occasion commanded the
195   gawky girls to shake hands with him.

Sophia had never forgotten that glimpse. The young man without a
name had lived in her mind, brightly glowing, as the very symbol and
incarnation of the masculine and the elegant.

The renewed sight of him seemed to have wakened her out of a sleep.
200   Assuredly she was not the same Sophia. As she sat in her sister's chair
in the corner, entrenched behind the perpendicular boxes, playing
nervously with the scissors, her beautiful face was transfigured into the
ravishingly angelic. It would have been impossible for Mr Gerald Scales,
or anybody else, to credit, as he gazed at those lovely, sensitive,
205   vivacious, responsive features, that Sophia was not a character of
heavenly sweetness and perfection. She did not know what she was
doing; she was nothing but the exquisite expression of a deep instinct
to attract and charm. Her soul itself emanated from her in an atmosphere
of allurement and acquiescence. Could those laughing lips hang in a
210   heavy pout? Could that delicate and mild voice be harsh? Could those
burning eyes be coldly inimical? Never? The idea was inconceivable!
And Mr Gerald Scales, with his head over the top of the boxes, yielded
to the spell. Remarkable that Mr Gerald Scales, with all his experience,
should have had to come to Bursley to find the pearl, the paragon, the
215   ideal! But so it was. They met in an equal abandonment; the only
difference between them was that Mr Scales, by force of habit, kept his
head.

'I see it's your wakes here,' said he.

He was polite to the wakes but now, with the least inflection in the
220   world, he put the wakes at its proper level in the scheme of things as a
local unimportance! She adored him for this; she was thirst for sympathy
in the task of scorning everything local.

'I expect you didn't know,' she said, implying that there was every reason why a man of his mundane interests should not know.

225 'I should have remembered if I had thought,' said he. 'But I didn't think. What's this about an elephant?'

'Oh!' she exclaimed. 'Have you heard of that?'

'My porter was full of it.'

'Well,' she said, 'of course it's a very big thing in Bursley.'

230 As she smiled in gentle pity of poor Bursley, he naturally did the same. And he thought how much more advanced and broad the younger generation was than the old! He would never have dared express his real feelings about Bursley to Mrs Baines, or even to Mr Povey (who was, however, of no generation); yet there was a young woman actually

235 sharing them.

She told him all the history of the elephant.

'Must have been very exciting,' he commented, despite himself.

'Do you know,' she replied, 'it *was*.'

After all, Bursley was climbing in their opinion.

240 'And mother and my sister and Mr Povey have all gone to see it. That's why they're not here.'

That the elephant should have caused both Mr Povey and Mrs Baines to forget that the representative of Birkinshaws was due to call was indeed a final victory for the elephant.

245 'But not you!' he exclaimed.

'No,' she said. 'Not me.'

'Why didn't you go too?' He continued his flattering investigations with a generous smile.

'I simply didn't care to,' said she, proudly nonchalant.

250 'And I suppose you are in charge here?'

'No,' she answered. 'I just happened to have run down here for these scissors. That's all.'

'I often see your sister,' said he. ' "Often" do I say? – that is, generally, when I come; but never you.'

255 'I'm never in the shop,' she said. 'It's just an accident today.'

'Oh! So you leave the shop to your sister?'

'Yes.' She said nothing of her teaching.

Then there was a silence. Sophia was very thankful to be hidden from the curiosity of the shop. The shop could see nothing of her, and only

260 the back of the young man; and the conversation had been conducted in low voices. She tapped her foot, stared at the worn, polished surface of the counter, with the brass yard-measure nailed along its edge, and then she uneasily turned her gaze to the left and seemed to be examining the backs of the black bonnets which were perched on high stands in

265 the great window. Then her eyes caught his for an important moment.

'Yes,' she breathed. Somebody had to say something. If the shop missed the murmur of their voices the shop would wonder what had happened to them.

Mr Scales looked at his watch. 'I dare say if I come in again about
270   two –' he began.

'Oh yes, they're *sure* to be in then,' she burst out before he could finish his sentence.

He left abruptly, queerly, without shaking hands (but then it would have been difficult – she argued – for him to have put his arm over the
275   boxes), and without expressing the hope of seeing her again. She peeped through the black bonnets, and saw the porter put the leather strap over his shoulders, raise the rear of the barrow, and trundle off; but she did not see Mr Scales. She was drunk; thoughts were tumbling about in her brain like cargo loose in a rolling ship. Her entire conception
280   of herself was being altered; her attitude towards life was being altered. The thought which knocked hardest against its fellows was, 'Only in these moments have I begun to live!'

And as she flitted upstairs to resume watch over her father she sought to devise an innocent-looking method by which she might see Mr Scales
285   when he next called. And she speculated as to what his name was.

III

When Sophia arrived in the bedroom, she was startled because her father's head and beard were not in their accustomed place on the pillow. She could only make out something vaguely unusual sloping off the side of the bed. A few seconds passed – not to be measured in
290   time – and she saw that the upper part of his body had slipped down, and his head was hanging, inverted, near the floor between the bed and the ottoman. His face, neck, and hands were dark and congested; his mouth was open, and the tongue protruded between the black, swollen, mucous lips; his eyes were prominent and coldly staring. The fact was
295   that Mr Baines had wakened up, and, being restless, had slid out partially from his bed and died of asphyxia. After having been unceasingly watched for fourteen years, he had, with an invalid's natural perverseness, taken advantage of Sophia's brief dereliction to expire. Say what you will, amid Sophia's horror, and her terrible grief and
300   shame, she had visitings of the idea: he did it on purpose!

She ran out of the room, knowing by intuition that he was dead, and shrieked out, 'Maggie', at the top of her voice; the house echoed.

'Yes, miss,' said Maggie, quite close, coming out of Mr Povey's chamber with a slop-pail.
305   'Fetch Mr Critchlow at once. Be quick. Just as you are. It's father –'

Maggie, perceiving darkly that disaster was in the air, and instantly filled with importance and a sort of black joy, dropped her pail in the exact middle of the passage, and almost fell down the crooked stairs.

One of Maggie's deepest instincts, always held in check by the stern
dominance of Mrs Baines, was to leave pails prominent on the main
routes of the house; and now, divining what was at hand, it flamed
into insurrection.

No sleepless night had ever been so long to Sophia as the three
minutes which elapsed before Mr Critchlow came. As she stood on the
mat outside the bedroom door she tried to draw her mother and
Constance and Mr Povey by magnetic force out of the wakes into the
house, and her muscles were contracted in the strange effort. She felt
that it was impossible to continue living if the secret of the bedroom
remained unknown one instant longer, so intense was her torture, and
yet that the torture which could not be borne must be borne. Not a
sound in the house! Not a sound from the shop! Only the distant
murmur of the wakes!

'Why did I forget father?' she asked herself with awe. 'I only meant
to tell *him* that they were all out, and run back. Why did I forget
father?' She would never be able to persuade anybody that she had
literally forgotten her father's existence for quite ten minutes; but it
was true, though shocking.

Then there were noises downstairs.

'Bless us! Bless us!' came the unpleasant voice of Mr Critchlow as
he bounded up the stairs on his long legs; he strode over the pail.
'What's amiss?' He was wearing his white apron, and he carried his
spectacles in his bony hand.

'It's father – he's –' Sophia faltered.

She stood away so that he should enter the room first. He glanced at
her keenly, and as it were resentfully, and went in. She followed, timidly,
remaining near the door while Mr Critchlow inspected her handiwork.
He put on his spectacles with strange deliberation, and then, bending
his knee outwards, thus lowered his body so that he could examine
John Baines point-blank. He remained staring like this, his hands on
his sharp apron-covered knees, for a little space; and then he seized the
inert mass and restored it to the bed, and wiped those clotted lips with
his apron.

Sophia head a loud breathing behind her. It was Maggie. She heard
a huge, snorting sob; Maggie was showing her emotion.

'Go fetch doctor!' Mr Critchlow rasped. 'And don't stand gaping
there!'

'Run for the doctor, Maggie,' said Sophia.

'How came ye to let him fall?' Mr Critchlow demanded.

'I was out of the room. I just ran down into the shop –'

'Gallivanting with that young Scales!' said Mr Critchlow, with
devilish ferocity. 'Well, you've killed your father; that's all!'

He must have been at his shop door and seen the entry of the traveller!

And it was precisely characteristic of Mr Critchlow to jump in the dark at a horrible conclusion, and to be right after all. For Sophia Mr Critchlow had always been the personification of malignity and malevolence, and now these qualities in him made him, to her, almost obscene. Her pride brought up tremendous reinforcements, and she approached the bed.

'Is he dead?' she asked in a quiet tone. (Somewhere within a voice was whispering, 'So his name is Scales.')

'Don't I tell you he's dead?'

'Pail on the stairs!'

This mild exclamation came from the passage. Mrs Baines, misliking the crowds abroad, had returned alone; she had left Constance in charge of Mr Povey. Coming into her house by the shop and showroom, she had first noted the phenomenon of the pail – proof of her theory of Maggie's incurable untidiness.

'Been to see the elephant, I reckon!' said Mr Critchlow, in fierce sarcasm, as he recognised Mrs Baines's voice.

Sophia leaped towards the door, as though to bar her mother's entrance. But Mrs Baines was already opening the door.

'Well, my pet –' she was beginning cheerfully.

Mr Critchlow confronted her. And he had no more pity for the wife than for the daughter. He was furiously angry because his precious property had been irretrievably damaged by the momentary carelessness of a silly girl. Yes, John Baines was his property, his dearest toy! He was convinced that he alone had kept John Baines alive for fourteen years, that he alone had fully understood the case and sympathised with the sufferer, that none but he had been capable of displaying ordinary common sense in the sick-room. He had learned to regard John Baines as, in some sort, his creation. And now, with their stupidity, their neglect, their elephants, between them they had done for John Baines. He had always known it would come to that, and it had come to that.

'She let him fall out o'bed, and ye're a widow now, missus!' he announced with a virulence hardly conceivable. His angular features and dark eyes expressed a murderous hate for every woman named Baines.

'Mother!' cried Sophia, 'I only ran down into the shop to – to –'

She seized her mother's arm in frenzied agony.

'My child!' said Mrs Baines, rising miraculously to the situation with a calm benevolence of tone and gesture that remained for ever sublime in the stormy heart of Sophia, 'do not hold me.' With infinite gentleness she loosed herself from these clasping hands. 'Have you sent for the doctor?' she questioned Mr Critchlow.

The fate of her husband presented no mysteries to Mrs Baines. Everybody had been warned a thousand times of the danger of leaving the paralytic, whose life depended on his position, and whose fidgetiness was thereby a constant menace of death to him. For five thousand nights she had wakened infallibly every time he stirred, and rearranged him by the flicker of a little oil lamp. But Sophia, unhappy creature, had merely left him. That was all.

Mr Critchlow and the widow gazed, helplessly waiting, at the pitiable corpse, of which the salient part was the white beard. They knew not that they were gazing at a vanished era. John Baines had belonged to the past, to the age when men really did think of their souls, when orators by phrases could move crowds to fury or to pity, when no one had learnt to hurry, when Demos was only turning in his sleep, when the sole beauty of life resided in its inflexible and slow dignity, when hell really had no bottom, and a gilt-clasped Bible really was the secret of England's greatness. Mid-Victorian England lay on the mahogany bed. Ideals had passed away with John Baines. It is thus that ideals die; not in the conventional pageantry of honoured death, but sorrily, ignobly, while one's head is turned –

And Mr Povey and Constance, very self-conscious, went and saw the dead elephant, and came back; and at the corner of King Street, Constance exclaimed brightly –

'Why! who's gone out and left the side-door open?'

For the doctor had at length arrived, and Maggie, in showing him upstairs with pious haste, had forgotten to shut the door.

And they took advantage of the side-door, rather guiltily, to avoid the eyes of the shop. They feared that in the parlour they would be the centre of a curiosity half ironical and half reproving; for had they not accomplished an escapade? So they walked slowly.

The real murderer was having his dinner in the commercial room up at the Tiger, opposite the Town Hall.

IV

Several shutters were put up in the windows of the shop, to indicate a death, and the news instantly became known in trading circles through-out the town. Many people simultaneously remarked upon the coinci-dence that Mr Baines should have died while there was a show of mourning goods in his establishment. This coincidence was regarded as extremely sinister, and it was apparently felt that, for the sake of the mind's peace, one ought not to inquire into such things too closely. From the moment of putting up the prescribed shutters, John Baines and his funeral began to acquire importance in Bursley, and their importance grew rapidly almost from hour to hour. The wakes continued as usual, except that the Chief Constable, upon representations being made to him by Mr Critchlow and other citizens, descended upon St Luke's Square and forbade the activities of Wombwell's orchestra.

Wombwell and the Chief Constable differed as to the justice of the
440   decree, but every well-minded person praised the Chief Constable, and
he himself considered that he had enhanced the town's reputation for a
decent propriety. It was noticed, too, not without a shiver of the
uncanny, that that night the lions and tigers behaved like lambs, whereas
on the previous night they had roared the whole Square out of its sleep.
445   The Chief Constable was not the only individual enlisted by Mr
Critchlow in the service of his friend's fame. Mr Critchlow spent hours
in recalling the principal citizens to a due sense of John Baines's past
greatness. He was determined that his treasured toy should vanish
underground with due pomp, and he left nothing undone to that end.
450   He went over to Hanbridge on the still wonderful horse-car, and saw
the editor-proprietor of the *Staffordshire Signal* (then a two-penny
weekly with no thought of Football editions), and on the very day of
the funeral the *Signal* came out with a long and eloquent biography of
John Baines. This biography, giving details of his public life, definitely
455   restored him to his legitimate position in the civic memory as an ex-
chief bailiff, an ex-chairman of the Burial Board, and of the Five Towns
Association for the Advancement of Useful Knowledge, and also as a
'prime mover' in the local Turnpike† Act, in the negotiations for the
new Town Hall, and in the Corinthian façade of the Wesleyan Chapel;
460   it narrated the anecdote of his courageous speech from the portico of
the Shambles during the riots of 1848, and it did not omit a eulogy of
his steady adherence to the wise old English maxims of commerce and
his avoidance of dangerous modern methods. Even in the sixties the
modern had reared its shameless head. The panegyric closed with an
465   appreciation of the dead man's fortitude in the terrible affliction with
which a divine providence had seen fit to try him; and finally the *Signal*
uttered its absolute conviction that his native town would raise a
cenotaph to his honour. Mr Critchlow, being unfamiliar with the word
'cenotaph', consulted Worcester's Dictionary, and when he found that
470   it meant 'a sepulchral monument to one who is buried elsewhere', he
was as pleased with the *Signal's* language as with the idea, and decided
that a cenotaph should come to pass.
      The house and shop were transformed into a hive of preparation for
the funeral. All was changed. Mr Povey kindly slept for three nights on
475   the parlour sofa, in order that Mrs Baines might have his room. The
funeral grew into an obsession, for multitudinous things had to be
performed and done sumptuously and in strict accordance with prece-
dent. There were the family mourning, the funeral repast, the choice of
the text on the memorial card, the composition of the legend on the
480   coffin, the legal arrangements, the letters to relations, the selection of

Turnpike   toll-gate

guests, and the questions of bell-ringing, hearse, plumes, number of horses, and grave-digging. Nobody had leisure for the indulgence of grief except Aunt Maria, who, after she had helped in the laying-out, simply sat down and bemoaned unceasingly for hours her absence on
485 the fatal morning. 'If I hadn't been so fixed on polishing my candlesticks,' she weepingly repeated, 'he mit ha' been alive and well now.' Not that Aunt Maria had been informed of the precise circumstances of the death; she was not clearly aware that Mr Baines had died through a piece of neglect. But, like Mr Critchlow, she was convinced that there
490 had been only one person in the world truly capable of nursing Mr Baines. Beyond the family, no one save Mr Critchlow and Dr Harrop knew just how the martyr had finished his career. Dr Harrop, having been asked bluntly if an inquest would be necessary, had reflected a moment and had then replied: 'No.' And he added, 'Least said soonest
495 mended – mark me!' They had marked him. He was common sense in breeches.

As for Aunt Maria, she was sent about her snivelling business by Aunt Harriet. The arrival in the house of this genuine aunt from Axe, of this majestic and enormous widow whom even the imperial Mrs
500 Baines regarded with a certain awe, set a seal of ultimate solemnity on the whole event. In Mr Povey's bedroom Mrs Baines fell like a child into Aunt Harriet's arms and sobbed:

'If it had been anything else but that elephant!'

Such was Mrs Baines's sole weakness from first to last.

505 Aunt Harriet was an exhaustless fountain of authority upon every detail concerning interments. And, to a series of questions ending with the word 'sister', and answers ending with the word 'sister', the prodigious travail incident to the funeral was gradually and successfully accomplished. Dress and the repast exceeded all other matters in
510 complexity and difficulty. But on the morning of the funeral Aunt Harriet had the satisfaction of beholding her younger sister the centre of a tremendous cocoon of crape, whose slightest pleat was perfect. Aunt Harriet seemed to welcome her then, like a veteran, formally into the august army of relicts. As they stood side by side surveying the
515 special table which was being laid in the showroom for the repast, it appeared inconceivable that they had reposed together in Mr Povey's limited bed. They descended from the showroom to the kitchen where the last delicate dishes were inspected. The shop was, of course, closed for the day, but Mr Povey was busy there, and in Aunt Harriet's all-
520 seeing glance he came next after the dishes. She rose from the kitchen to speak with him.

'You've got your boxes of gloves all ready?' she questioned him.

'Yes, Mrs Maddack.'

'You'll not forget to have a measure handy?'

525   'No, Mrs Maddack.'
'You'll find you'll want more of seven-and-three-quarters and eights than anything.'
'Yes. I have allowed for that.'
'If you place yourself behind the side-door and put your boxes on
530   the harmonium, you'll be able to catch every one as they come in.'
'That is what I had thought of, Mrs Maddack.'
She went upstairs. Mrs Baines had reached the showroom again, and was smoothing out creases in the white damask cloth and arranging glass dishes of jam at equal distances from each other.
535   'Come, sister,' said Mrs Maddack. 'A last look.'
And they passed into the mortuary bedroom to gaze at Mr Baines before he should be everlastingly nailed down. In death he had recovered some of his earlier dignity; but even so he was a startling sight. The two widows bent over him, one on either side, and gravely stared at
540   that twisted, worn white face all neatly tucked up in linen.
'I shall fetch Constance and Sophia,' said Mrs Maddack, with tears in her voice. 'Do you go into the drawing-room, sister.'
But Mrs Maddack only succeeded in fetching Constance.
Then there was the sound of wheels in King Street. The long rite of
545   the funeral was about to begin. Every guest, after having been measured and presented with a pair of the finest black kid gloves by Mr Povey, had to mount the crooked stairs and gaze upon the carcase of John Baines, going afterwards to the drawing-room to condole briefly with the widow. And every guest, while conscious of the enormity of so
550   thinking, thought what an excellent thing it was that John Baines should be at last dead and gone. The tramping on the stairs was continual, and finally Mr Baines himself went downstairs, bumping against corners, and led a *cortège* of twenty vehicles.
The funeral tea was not over at seven o'clock, five hours after the
555   commencement of the rite. It was a gigantic and faultless meal, worthy of John Baines's distant past. Only two persons were absent from it – John Baines and Sophia. The emptiness of Sophia's chair was much noticed; Mrs Maddack explained that Sophia was very high-strung and could not trust herself. Great efforts were put forth by the company to
560   be lugubrious and inconsolable, but the secret relief resulting from the death would not be entirely hidden. The vast pretence of acute sorrow could not stand intact against that secret relief and the lavish richness of the food.
To the offending of sundry important relatives from a distance, Mr
565   Critchlow informally presided over that assemblage of grave men in high stocks and crinolined women. He had closed his shop, which had never before been closed on a weekday, and he had a great deal to say about this extraordinary closure. It was due as much to the elephant as

to the funeral. The elephant had become a victim to the craze of
souvenirs. Already in the night his tusks had been stolen; then his feet
disappeared for umbrella-stands, and most of his flesh had departed in
little hunks. Everybody in Bursley had resolved to participate in the
elephant. One consequence was that all the chemists' shops in the town
were assaulted by strings of boys. 'Please a peenorth o'alum to tak'
smell out o' a bit o' elephant.' Mr Critchlow hated boys.

'"I'll alum ye!" says I, and I did. I alummed him out o' my shop
with a pestle. If there'd been one there'd been twenty between opening
and nine o'clock. "George," I says to my apprentice, "shut shop up.
My old friend John Baines is going to his long home today, and I'll
close. I've had enough o' alum for one day."'

The elephant fed the conversation until after the second relay of hot
muffins. When Mr Critchlow had eaten to his capacity, he took the
Signal importantly from his pocket, posed his spectacles, and read the
obituary all through in slow, impressive accents. Before he reached the
end Mrs Baines began to perceive that familiarity had blinded her to
the heroic qualities of her late husband. The fourteen years of ceaseless
care were quite genuinely forgotten, and she saw him in his strength
and in his glory. When Mr Critchlow arrived at the eulogy of the
husband and father, Mrs Baines rose and left the showroom. The guests
looked at each other in sympathy for her. Mr Critchlow shot a glance
at her over his spectacles and continued steadily reading. After he had
finished he approached the question of the cenotaph.

Mrs Baines, driven from the banquet by her feelings, went into the
drawing-room. Sophia was there, and Sophia, seeing tears in her
mother's eyes, gave a sob, and flung herself bodily against her mother,
clutching her, and hiding her face in that broad crape, which abraded
her soft skin.

'Mother,' she wept passionately, 'I want to leave the school now. I
want to please you. I'll do anything in the world to please you. I'll go
into the shop if you'd like me to!' Her voice lost itself in tears.

'Calm yourself, my pet,' said Mrs Baines, tenderly, caressing her. It
was a triumph for the mother in the very hour when she needed a
triumph.

1908

John Galsworthy
1867–1933

John Galsworthy was born at Coombe in Surrey and educated at Harrow and New College, Oxford. He was called to the Bar in 1890; he travelled in the Far East (where he met Conrad); his short stories in *From the Four Winds* (1897) were the start of a very successful writing career. Three novels, *A Man of Property* (1906), *In Chancery* (1920) and *To Let* (1921), were issued together as *The Forsyte Saga* in 1922; more Forsyte novels followed. More than thirty of Galsworthy's plays were staged in London, and it is for the dramatic craft and the concern for justice shown in such plays as *The Silver Box* (1906) and *Strife* (1909) that he is most admired today.

In this extract, from the third and final act of *Strife*, directors of a Tin Plate Works on the Welsh border hold a meeting with representatives of the workers who have been on strike all winter. Protagonists are John Anthony, Chairman of the Board, and David Roberts, leader of the men. Other characters are recognisable as directors or workmen.

From STRIFE
[Breaking the Men]

WANKLIN. Really, Chairman, it's no use soothing ourselves with a sense of false security. If this strike's not brought to an end before the General Meeting, the shareholders will certainly haul us over the coals.

SCANTLEBURY. [*Stirring*] What – what's that?

5 WANKLIN. I know it for a fact.

ANTHONY. Let them!

WILDER. And get turned out?

WANKLIN. [*To* ANTHONY] I don't mind martyrdom for a policy in which I believe, but I object to being burnt for someone else's principles.

10 SCANTLEBURY. Very reasonable – you must see that, Chairman.

ANTHONY. We owe it to other employers to stand firm.

WANKLIN. There's a limit to that.

ANTHONY. You were all full of fight at the start.

SCANTLEBURY. [*With a sort of groan*] We thought the men would give
15 in, but they – haven't!

ANTHONY. They will!

WILDER. [*Rising and pacing up and down*] I can't have my reputation as a man of business destroyed for the satisfaction of starving the men out. [*Almost in tears.*] I can't have it! How can we meet the shareholders
20 with things in the state they are?

SCANTLEBURY. Hear, hear – hear, hear!

WILDER. [*Lashing himself*] If anyone expects me to say to them I've lost you fifty thousand pounds and sooner than put my pride in my pocket I'll lose you another – [*Glancing at* ANTHONY.] It's – it's unnatural!
25 *I don't want to* go against you, sir –

WANKLIN. [*Persuasively*] Come, Chairman, we're *not* free agents. We're part of a machine. Our only business is to see the Company earns as much profit as it safely can. If you blame me for want of principle: I say that we're Trustees. Reason tells us we shall never get
30 back in the saving of wages what we shall lose if we continue this struggle – really, Chairman, we *must* bring it to an end, on the best terms we can make.

ANTHONY. No!   [*There is a pause of general dismay.*]

WILDER. It's a deadlock them. [*Letting his hands drop with a sort of
35 despair.*] Now I shall never get off to Spain!

WANKLIN. [*Retaining a trace of irony*] You hear the consequences of your victory, Chairman?

WILDER. [*With a burst of feeling*] My wife's *ill*!

SCANTLEBURY. Dear, dear! You don't say so!

40 WILDER. If I don't get her out of this cold, I won't answer for the consequences.

[*Through the double doors* EDGAR *comes in looking very grave.*]

EDGAR. [*To his Father*] Have you heard this, sir? Mrs Roberts is dead!

[*Everyone stares at him, as if trying to gauge the importance of this news.*]

Enid saw her this afternoon, she had no coals, or food, or anything. It's enough!

[*There is a silence, everyone avoiding the other's eyes, except* ANTHONY, *who stares hard at his son.*]

45 SCANTLEBURY. You don't suggest that we could have helped the poor thing?

WILDER. [*Flustered*] The woman was in bad health. Nobody can say there's any responsibility on us. At least – not on me.

EDGAR. [*Hotly*] I say that we *are* responsible.

50 ANTHONY. War is war!

EDGAR. Not on women!

WANKLIN. It not infrequently happens that women are the greatest sufferers.

EDGAR. If we knew that, all the more responsibility rests on us.

55   ANTHONY. This is no matter for amateurs.

EDGAR. Call me what you like, sir. It's sickened me. We had no right to carry things to such a length.

WILDER. I don't like this business a bit – that Radical rag will twist it to their own ends; see if they don't! They'll get up some cock-and-bull
60   story about the poor woman's dying from starvation. I wash my hands of it.

EDGAR. You can't. None of us can.

SCANTLEBURY. [*Striking his fist on the arm of his chair*] But I protest against this –

65   EDGAR. Protest as you like, Mr Scantlebury, it won't alter facts.

ANTHONY. That's enough.

EDGAR. [*Facing him angrily*] No, sir. I tell you exactly what I think. If we pretend the men are not suffering, it's humbug; and if they're suffering, we know enough of human nature to know the women are
70   suffering more, and as to the children – well – it's damnable!

[SCANTLEBURY *rises from his chair.*]

I don't say that we meant to be cruel, I don't say anything of the sort; but I do say it's criminal to shut our eyes to the facts. We employ these men, and we can't get out of it. I don't care so much about the men, but I'd sooner resign my position on the Board than go on starving
75   women in this way.

[*All except* ANTHONY *are now upon their feet,* ANTHONY *sits grasping the arms of his chair and staring at his son.*]

SCANTLEBURY. I don't – I don't like the way you're putting it, young sir.

WANKLIN. You're rather overshooting the mark.

WILDER. I should think so indeed!

80   EDGAR. [*Losing control*] It's no use blinking things! if *you* want to have the death of women on your hands – *I* don't!

SCANTLEBURY. Now, now, young man!

WILDER. On *our* hands? Not on *mine*, I won't have it!

EDGAR. We are five members of this Board; if we were four against
85   it, why did we let it drift till it came to this? You know perfectly well why – because we hoped we should starve the men out. Well, all we've done is to starve one woman out!

SCANTLEBURY. [*Almost hysterically*] I protest, I protest! I'm a humane man – we're all humane men!

90   EDGAR. [*Scornfully*] There's nothing wrong with our *humanity*. It's our imaginations, Mr Scantlebury.

WILDER. Nonsense! My imagination's as good as yours.

EDGAR. If so, it isn't good enough.

WILDER. I foresaw this!

95   EDGAR. Then why didn't you put your foot down?

WILDER. Much good that would have done.

[*He looks at* ANTHONY.]

EDGAR. If you, and I, and each one of us here who say that our imaginations are so good –

SCANTLEBURY. [*Flurried*] I never said so.

100 EDGAR. [*Paying no attention*] – had put our feet down, the thing would have been ended long ago, and this poor woman's life wouldn't have been crushed out of her like this. For all we can tell there may be a dozen other starving women.

SCANTLEBURY. For God's sake, sir, don't use that word at a – at a

105 Board meeting; it's – it's monstrous.

EDGAR. I *will* use it, Mr Scantlebury.

SCANTLEBURY. Then I shall not listen to you. I shall not listen! It's painful to me. [*He covers his ears.*]

WANKLIN. None of us are opposed to a settlement, except your Father.

110 EDGAR. I'm certain that if the shareholders knew –

WANKLIN. I don't think you'll find their imaginations are any better than ours. Because a woman happens to have a weak heart –

EDGAR. A struggle like this finds out the weak spots in everybody. Any child knows that. If it hadn't been for this cut-throat policy, she

115 needn't have died like this; and there wouldn't be all this misery that anyone who isn't a fool can see is going on.

[*Throughout the foregoing* ANTHONY *has eyed his son; he now moves as though to rise, but stops as* EDGAR *speaks again.*]

I don't defend the men, or myself, or anybody.

WANKLIN. You may have to! A coroner's jury of disinterested sympathizers may say some very nasty things. We mustn't lose sight of our position.

120 SCANTLEBURY. [*Without uncovering his ears*] Coroner's jury! No, no, it's not a case for that?

EDGAR. I've had enough of cowardice.

WANKLIN. Cowardice is an unpleasant word, Mr Edgar Anthony. It will look very like cowardice if we suddenly concede the men's demands

125 when a thing like this happens; we must be careful!

WILDER. Of course we must. We've no knowledge of this matter, except a rumour. The proper course is to put the whole thing into the hands of Harness to settle for us; that's natural, that's what we *should* have come to any way.

130 SCANTLEBURY. [*With dignity*] Exactly! [*Turning to* EDGAR.] And as to you, young sir, I can't sufficiently express my – my distaste for the way you've treated the whole matter. You ought to withdraw! Talking of starvation, talking of cowardice! Considering what our views are! Except your own Father – we're all agreed the only policy is – is one of

135 goodwill – it's most irregular, it's most improper, and all I can say is it's – it's given me pain –

[*He places his hand on the centre of his scheme.*]

EDGAR. [*Stubbornly*] I withdraw nothing.

[*He is about to say more when* SCANTLEBURY *once more covers up his ears.* TENCH *suddenly makes a demonstration with the minute-book. A sense of having been engaged in the unusual comes over all of them, and one by one they resume their seats.* EDGAR *alone remains on his feet.*]

WILDER. [*With an air of trying to wipe something out*] I pay no attention to what young Mr Anthony has said. Coroner's Jury! The
140   idea's proposterous. I – I move this amendment to the Chairman's Motion: That the dispute be placed at once in the hands of Mr Simon Harness for settlement on the lines indicated by him this morning. Anyone second that?   [TENCH *writes in the book.*]

WANKLIN. I do.

145   WILDER. Very well, then; I ask the Chairman to put it to the Board.

ANTHONY. [*With a great sigh – slowly*] We have been made the subject of an attack. [*Looking round at* WILDER *and* SCANTLEBURY *with ironical contempt.*] I take it on *my* shoulders. I am seventy-six years old. I have been Chairman of this Company since its inception two-and-thirty years
150   ago. I have seen it pass through good and evil report. My connection with it began in the year that this young man was born.

[EDGAR *bows his head.* ANTHONY, *gripping his chair, goes on.*] I have had to do with 'men' for fifty years; I've always stood up to them; I have never been beaten yet. I have fought the men of this Company four times, and four times I have beaten them. It has been
155   said that I am not the man I was. [*He looks at* WILDER.] However that may be, I am man enough to stand to my guns.

[*His voice grows stronger. The double doors are opened.* ENID *slips in, followed by* UNDERWOOD, *who restrains her.*]

The men have been treated justly, they have had fair wages, we have always been ready to listen to complaints. It has been said that times have changed; if they have, I have not changed with them. Neither will
160   I. It has been said that masters and men are equal! Cant! There can only be one master in a house! Where two men meet the better man will rule. It has been said that Capital and Labour have the same interests. Cant! Their interests are as wide asunder as the poles. It has been said that the Board is only part of a machine. Cant! We *are* the
165   machine; its brains and sinews; it is for us to lead and to determine what is to be done, and to do it without fear or favour. Fear of the men! Fear of the shareholders! Fear of our own shadows! Before I am like that, I hope to die.

[*He pauses, and meeting his son's eyes, goes on.*]

There is only one way of treating 'men' – with *the iron hand*. This half-
170   and-half business, the half-and-half manners of this generation has

brought all this upon us. Sentiment and softness, and what this young man, no doubt, would call his social policy. You can't eat cake and have it! This middle-class sentiment, or socialism, or whatever it may be, is rotten. Masters are masters, men are men! Yield one demand, and they
175 will make it six. They are [*he smiles grimly*] like Oliver Twist, asking for more. If I were in *their* place I should be the same. But I am not in their place. Mark my words: one fine morning, when you have given way here, and given way there – you will find you have parted with the ground beneath your feet, and are deep in the bog of bankruptcy; and with you,
180 floundering in that bog, will be the very men you have given way to. I have been accused of being a domineering tyrant, thinking only of my pride – I am thinking of the future of this country, threatened with the black waters of confusion, threatened with mob government, threatened with what I cannot see. If by any conduct of mine I help to bring this on
185 us, I shall be ashamed to look my fellows in the face.

> [ANTHONY *stares before him, at what he cannot see, and there is perfect stillness.* FROST *comes in from the hall, and all but* ANTHONY *look round at him uneasily.*]

FROST. [*To his master*] The men are here, sir.

> [ANTHONY *makes a gesture of dismissal.*]

Shall I bring them in, sir?

ANTHONY. Wait!

> [FROST *goes out,* ANTHONY *turns to face his son.*]

I come to the attack that has been made upon me.

> [EDGAR, *with a gesture of deprecation, remains motionless with his head a little bowed.*]

190 A woman has died. I am told that her blood is on my hands; I am told that on my hands is the starvation and the suffering of other women and of children.

EDGAR. I said 'on *our* hands,' sir.

ANTHONY. It is the same. [*His voice grows stronger and stronger, his*
195 *feeling is more and more made manifest.*] I am not aware that if my adversary suffer in a fair fight not sought by me, it is *my* fault. If I fall under *his* feet – as fall I may – I shall not complain. That will be *my* look-out – and this is – his. I cannot separate, as I would, these men from their women and children. A fair fight is a fair fight! Let them
200 learn to think before they pick a quarrel!

EDGAR. [*In a low voice*] But is it a fair fight, Father? Look at them, and look at us! They've only this one weapon!

ANTHONY. [*Grimly*] And you're weak-kneed enough to teach them how to use it! It seems the fashion nowadays for men to take their
205 enemy's side. I have not learnt that art. Is it my fault that they quarrelled with their Union too?

EDGAR. There is such a thing as Mercy.

ANTHONY. And Justice comes before it.

EDGAR. What seems just to one man, sir, is injustice to another.

210   ANTHONY. [*With suppressed passion*] You accuse me of injustice – of what amounts to inhumanity – of cruelty –

> [EDGAR *makes a gesture of horror – a general frightened movement.*]

WANKLIN. Come, come, Chairman!

ANTHONY. [*In a grim voice*] These are the words of my own son. They are the words of a generation that I don't understand; the words of a

215   soft breed.

> [*A general murmur. With a violent effort* ANTHONY *recovers his control.*]

EDGAR. [*Quietly*] I said it of *myself*, too, Father.

> [*A long look is exchanged between them, and* ANTHONY *puts out his hand with a gesture as if to sweep the personalities away; then places it against his brow, swaying as though from giddiness. There is a movement towards him. He waves them back.*]

ANTHONY. Before I put this amendment to the Board, I have one more word to say. [*He looks from face to face.*] If it is carried, it means that we shall fail in what we set ourselves to do. It means that we shall fail

220   in the duty that we owe to all Capital. It means that we shall fail in the duty that we owe ourselves. It means that we shall be open to constant attack to which we as constantly shall have to yield. Be under no misapprehension – run this time, and you will never make a stand again! You will have to fly like curs before the whips of your own men.

225   If that is the lot you wish for, you will vote for this amendment.

> [*He looks again from face to face, finally resting his gaze on* EDGAR; *all sit with their eyes on the ground.* ANTHONY *makes a gesture, and* TENCH *hands him the book. He reads.*]

'Moved by Mr Wilder, and seconded by Mr Wanklin: That the men's demands be placed at once in the hands of Mr Simon Harness for settlement on the lines indicated by him this morning.' [*With sudden vigour.*] Those in favour: Signify the same in the usual way!

> [*For a minute no one moves; then hastily, just as* ANTHONY *is about to speak,* WILDER'S *hand and* WANKLIN'S *are held up, then* SCANTLEBURY'S, *and last* EDGAR'S, *who does not lift his head.*]

230   Contrary?   [ANTHONY *lifts his own hand.*]

[*In a clear voice.*] The amendment is carried. I resign my position on this Board.

> [ENID *gasps, and there is dead silence.* ANTHONY *sits motionless, his head slowly drooping; suddenly he heaves as though the whole of his life had risen up within him.*]

Fifty years! You have disgraced me, gentlemen. Bring in the men!

[*He sits motionless, staring before him. The board draws hurriedly together, and forms a group.* TENCH *in a frightened manner speaks into the hall.* UNDERWOOD *almost forces* ENID *from the room.*]

WILDER. [*Hurriedly*] What's to be said to them? Why isn't Harness
235 here? Ought we to see the men before he comes? I don't —

TENCH. Will you come in, please?

[*Enter* THOMAS, GREEN, BULGIN *and* ROUS, *who file up in a row past the little table.* TENCH *sits down and writes. All eyes are fixed on* ANTHONY, *who makes no sign.*]

WANKLIN. [*Stepping up to the little table, with nervous cordiality*] Well, Thomas, how's it to be? What's the result of your meeting?

ROUS. Sim Harness has our answer. He'll tell you what it is. We're
240 waiting for him. He'll speak for us.

WANKLIN. Is that so, Thomas?

THOMAS. [*Sullenly*] Yes. Roberts will not be coming, his wife is dead.

SCANTLEBURY. Yes, yes! Poor woman! Yes! Yes!

FROST. [*Entering from the hall*] Mr Harness, sir!

[*As* HARNESS *enters he retires.*]

[HARNESS *has a piece of paper in his hand, he bows to the Directors, nods towards the men, and takes his stand behind the little table in the very centre of the room.*]

245 HARNESS. Good evening, gentlemen.

[TENCH, *with the paper he has been writing, joins him, they speak together in low tones.*]

WILDER. We've been waiting for you, Harness. Hope we shall come to some —

FROST. [*Entering from the hall*] Roberts. [*He goes.*]

[ROBERTS *comes hastily in, and stands staring at* ANTHONY. *His face is drawn and old.*]

ROBERTS. Mr Anthony, I am afraid I am a little late. I would have
250 been here in time but for something that — has happened. [*To the men.*] Has anything been said?

THOMAS. No! But, man, what made ye come?

ROBERTS. Ye told us this morning, gentlemen, to go away and reconsider our position. We have reconsidered it; we are here to bring
255 you the men's answer. [*To* ANTHONY.] Go ye back to London. We have nothing for you. By no jot or tittle do we abate our demands, nor will we until the whole of those demands are yielded.

[ANTHONY *looks at him but does not speak. There is a movement amongst the men as though they were bewildered.*]

HARNESS. Roberts!

ROBERTS. [*Glancing fiercely at him, and back to* ANTHONY] Is that clear

260 enough for ye? Is it short enough and to the point? Ye made a mistake to think that we would come to heel. Ye may break the body, but ye cannot break the spirit. Get back to London, the men have nothing for ye.

> [*Pausing uneasily he takes a step towards the unmoving* ANTHONY.]

EDGAR. We're all sorry for you, Roberts, but –

265 ROBERTS. Keep your sorrow, young man. Let your Father speak!

HARNESS. [*With the sheet of paper in his hand, speaking from behind the little table*] Roberts!

ROBERTS. [*To* ANTHONY, *with passionate intensity*] Why don't ye answer?

270 HARNESS. Roberts!

ROBERTS. [*Turning sharply*] What is it?

HARNESS. [*Gravely*] You're talking without the book; things have travelled past you.

> [*He makes a sign to* TENCH, *who beckons the Directors. They quickly sign his copy of the terms.*]

Look at this, man!   [*Holding up his sheet of paper.*]

275 'Demands conceded, *with the exception of those relating to the engineers and furnace men*. Double wages for Saturday's overtime. Night-shifts as they are.' These terms have been agreed. The men go back to work again to-morrow. The strike is at an end.

ROBERTS. [*Reading the paper, and turning on the men. They shrink

280 back from him, all but* ROUS, *who stands his ground. With deadly stillness*] Ye have gone back on me? I stood by ye to the death; ye waited for *that* to throw me over!

> [*The men answer, all speaking together.*]

ROUS. It's a lie!

THOMAS. Ye were past endurance, man.

285 GREEN. If ye'd listen to me –

BULGIN. [*Under his breath*] Hold your jaw!

ROBERTS. Ye waited for *that*!

HARNESS. [*Taking the Directors' copy of the terms, and handing his own to* TENCH] That's enough, men. You had better go.

> [*The men shuffle slowly, awkwardly away.*]

290 WILDER. [*In a low, nervous voice*] There's nothing to stay for now, I suppose. [*He follows to the door.*] I shall have a try for that train! Coming, Scantlebury?

SCANTLEBURY. [*Following with* WANKLIN] Yes, yes; wait for me.

> [*He stops as* ROBERTS *speaks.*]

ROBERTS. [*To* ANTHONY] But *ye* have not signed them terms! They

295 can't make terms without their Chairman! Ye would never sign them terms!   [ANTHONY *looks at him without speaking.*]

Don't tell me ye have! for the love o' God! [*With passionate appeal.*] I
reckoned on ye!

300   HARNESS. [*Holding out the Directors' copy of the terms*] The Board
has signed!

> [ROBERTS *looks dully at the signatures – dashes the paper from
> him, and covers up his eyes.*]

SCANTLEBURY. [*Behind his hand to* TENCH] Look after the Chairman! He's
not well; he's not well – he had no lunch. If there's any fund started for
the women and children, put me down for – for twenty pounds.

> [*He goes out into the hall, in cumbrous haste; and* WANKLIN,
> *who has been staring at* ROBERTS *and* ANTHONY *with twitch-
> ings of his face, follows.* EDGAR *remains seated on the sofa,
> looking at the ground;* TENCH, *returning to the bureau,
> writes in his minute-book.* HARNESS *stands by the little table,
> gravely watching* ROBERTS.]

ROBERTS. Then you're no longer Chairman of this Company! [*Breaking
305   into half-mad laughter.*] Ah! ha – ah, ha, ha! They've thrown ye over –
thrown over their Chairman: Ah – ha – ha! [*With a sudden dreadful
calm.*] So – they've done us both down, Mr Anthony?

> [ENID, *hurrying through the double doors, comes quickly to her
> father and bends over him.*]

HARNESS. [*Coming down and laying his hands on* ROBERTS' *sleeve*] For
shame, Roberts! Go home quietly, man; go home!

310   ROBERTS. [*Tearing his arm away*] Home? [*Shrinking together – in a
whisper.*] Home!

ENID. [*Quietly to her father*] Come away, dear! Come to your room!

> [ANTHONY *rises with an effort. He turns to* ROBERTS, *who looks
> at him. They stand several seconds, gazing at each other
> fixedly;* ANTHONY *lifts his hand, as though to salute, but lets
> it fall. The expression of* ROBERTS' *face changes from hostility
> to wonder. They bend their heads in token of respect.*
> ANTHONY *turns, and slowly walks towards the curtained
> door. Suddenly he sways as though about to fall, recovers
> himself and is assisted out by* ENID *and* EDGAR, *who has
> hurried across the room.* ROBERTS *remains motionless for
> several seconds, staring intently after* ANTHONY, *then goes
> out into the hall.*]

TENCH. [*Approaching* HARNESS] It's a great weight off my mind, Mr
Harness! But what a painful scene, sir!   [*He wipes his brow.*]

315   > [HARNESS, *pale and resolute, regards with a grim half-smile the
> quavering* TENCH.]

It's all been so violent! What did he mean by: 'Done us both down?' If
he has lost his wife, poor fellow, he oughtn't to have spoken to the
Chairman like that!

320   HARNESS. A woman dead; and the two best men both broken!

[UNDERWOOD *enters suddenly.*]

TENCH. [*Staring at* HARNESS – *suddenly excited*] D'you know, sir – these terms, they're the *very same* we drew up together, you and I, and put to both sides before the fight began ? All this – all this – and – and what for?

325   HARNESS. [*In a slow grim voice*] That's where the fun comes in!

[UNDERWOOD *without turning from the door makes a gesture of assent.*]

[*The curtain falls.*]

1905   1909

'Saki': H. H. Munro

1870–1916

Hugh Hector Munro was born in Burma, and was brought up by aunts in Devonshire. He was educated in Exmouth and at Bedford Grammar School. After a brief spell in the Burma police he settled in London in 1896 as a journalist. His political satires written for *The Westminster Gazette* were collected as *The Westminster Alice* in 1902. He was in Eastern Europe and Russia and in Paris as a foreign correspondent between 1902 and 1908. He made his name as a writer of cruel wit in stories for magazines, collected under the pseudonym 'Saki' in *Reginald* (1904), *Reginald in Russia* (1910), *The Chronicles of Clovis* (1911), *Beasts and Superbeasts* (1914), *The Toys of Peace* (1919) and *The Square Eagle* (1924). *The Unbearable Bassington* (1912) is an accomplished short novel. The best stories, which often involve wild animals and soft, over-civilised Edwardian people, are small masterpieces. Munro enlisted in the Royal Fusiliers in 1914 and was killed on the Western Front.

SREDNI VASHTAR

Conradin was ten years old, and the doctor had pronounced his professional opinion that the boy would not live another five years. The doctor was silky and effete, and counted for little, but his opinion was endorsed by Mrs De Ropp, who counted for nearly everything. Mrs De
5 Ropp was Conradin's cousin and guardian, and in his eyes she represented those three-fifths of the world that are necessary and disagreeable and real; the other two-fifths, in perpetual antagonism to the foregoing, were summed up in himself and his imagination. One of these days Conradin supposed he would succumb to the mastering
10 pressure of wearisome necessary things – such as illnesses and coddling restrictions and drawnout dulness. Without his imagination, which was rampant under the spur of loneliness, he would have succumbed long ago.

Mrs De Ropp would never, in her honestest moments, have confessed
15 to herself that she disliked Conradin, though she might have been dimly aware that thwarting him 'for his good' was a duty which she did not

find particularly irksome. Conradin hated her with a desperate sincerity which he was perfectly able to mask. Such few pleasures as he could contrive for himself gained an added relish from the likelihood that
20   they would be displeasing to his guardian, and from the realm of his imagination she was locked out – an unclean thing, which should find no entrance.

In the dull, cheerless garden, overlooked by so many windows that were ready to open with a message not to do this or that, or a reminder
25   that medicines were due, he found little attraction. The few fruit-trees that it contained were set jealously apart from his plucking, as though they were rare specimens of their kind blooming in an arid waste; it would probably have been difficult to find a market-gardener who would have offered ten shillings for their entire yearly produce. In a
30   forgotten corner, however, almost hidden behind a dismal shrubbery, was a disused tool-shed of respectable proportions, and within its walls Conradin found a haven, something that took on the varying aspects of a playroom and a cathedral. He had peopled it with a legion of familiar phantoms, evoked partly from fragments of history and partly
35   from his own brain, but it also boasted two inmates of flesh and blood. In one corner lived a ragged-plumaged Houdan hen, on which the boy lavished an affection that had scarcely another outlet. Further back in the gloom stood a large hutch, divided into two compartments, one of which was fronted with close iron bars. This was the abode of a large
40   polecat-ferret, which a friendly butcher-boy had once smuggled, cage and all, into its present quarters, in exchange for a long-secreted hoard of small silver. Conradin was dreadfully afraid of the lithe, sharp-fanged beast, but it was his most treasured possession. Its very presence in the tool-shed was a secret and fearful joy, to be kept scrupulously from the
45   knowledge of the Woman, as he privately dubbed his cousin. And one day, out of Heaven knows what material, he spun the beast a wonderful name, and from that moment it grew into a god and a religion. The Woman indulged in religion once a week at a church near by, and took Conradin with her, but to him the church service was an alien rite in
50   the House of Rimmon.† Every Thursday, in the dim and musty silence of the tool-shed, he worshipped with mystic and elaborate ceremonial before the wooden hutch where dwelt Sredni Vashtar, the great ferret. Red flowers in their season and scarlet berries in the winter-time were offered at this shrine, for he was a god who laid some special stress on
55   the fierce impatient side of things, as opposed to the Woman's religion, which, as far as Conradin could observe, went to great lengths in the contrary direction. And on great festivals powdered nutmeg was strewn in front of his hutch, an important feature of the offering being that

---

House of Rimmon   See II Kings 5. 18

the nutmeg had to be stolen. These festivals were of irregular occurrence, and were chiefly appointed to celebrate some passing event. On one occasion, when Mrs De Ropp suffered from acute toothache for three days, Conradin kept up the festival during the entire three days, and almost succeeded in persuading himself that Sredni Vashtar was personally responsible for the toothache. If the malady had lasted for another day the supply of nutmeg would have given out.

The Houdan hen was never drawn into the cult of Sredni Vashtar. Conradin had long ago settled that she was an Anabaptist. He did not pretend to have the remotest knowledge as to what an Anabaptist was, but he privately hoped that it was dashing and not very respectable. Mrs De Ropp was the ground plan on which he based and detested all respectability.

After a while Conradin's absorption in the tool-shed began to attract the notice of his guardian. 'It is not good for him to be pottering down there in all weathers,' she promptly decided, and at breakfast one morning she announced that the Houdan hen had been sold and taken away overnight. With her short-sighted eyes she peered at Conradin, waiting for an outbreak of rage and sorrow, which she was ready to rebuke with a flow of excellent precepts and reasoning. But Conradin said nothing: there was nothing to be said. Something perhaps in his white set face gave her a momentary qualm, for at tea that afternoon there was toast on the table, a delicacy which she usually banned on the ground that it was bad for him; also because the making of it 'gave trouble,' a deadly offence in the middle-class feminine eye.

'I thought you liked toast,' she exclaimed, with an injured air, observing that he did not touch it.

'Sometimes,' said Conradin.

In the shed that evening there was an innovation in the worship of the hutch-god. Conradin had been wont to chant his praises, to-night he asked a boon.

'Do one thing for me, Sredni Vashtar.'

The thing was not specified. As Sredni Vashtar was a god he must be supposed to know. And choking back a sob as he looked at that other empty corner, Conradin went back to the world he so hated.

And every night, in the welcome darkness of his bedroom, and every evening in the dusk of the tool-shed, Conradin's bitter litany went up: 'Do one thing for me, Sredni Vashtar.'

Mrs De Ropp noticed that the visits to the shed did not cease, and one day she made a further journey of inspection.

'What are you keeping in that locked hutch?' she asked. 'I believe it's guinea-pigs. I'll have them all cleared away.'

Conradin shut his lips tight, but the Woman ransacked his bedroom till she found the carefully hidden key, and forthwith marched down

to the shed to complete her discovery. It was a cold afternoon, and
Conradin had been bidden to keep to the house. From the furthest
105 window of the dining-room the door of the shed could just be seen
beyond the corner of the shrubbery, and there Conradin stationed
himself. He saw the Woman enter, and then he imagined her opening
the door of the sacred hutch and peering down with her short-sighted
eyes into the thick straw bed where his god lay hidden. Perhaps she
110 would prod at the straw in her clumsy impatience. And Conradin
fervently breathed his prayer for the last time. But he knew as he prayed
that he did not believe. He knew that the Woman would come out
presently with that pursed smile he loathed so well on her face, and
that in an hour or two the gardener would carry away his wonderful
115 god, a god no longer, but a simple brown ferret in a hutch. And he
knew that the Woman would triumph always as she triumphed now,
and that he would grow ever more sickly under her pestering and
domineering and superior wisdom, till one day nothing would matter
much more with him, and the doctor would be proved right. And in
120 the sting and misery of his defeat, he began to chant loudly and defiantly
the hymn of his threatened idol:

Sredni Vashtar went forth,
His thoughts were red thoughts and his teeth were white.
His enemies called for peace, but he brought them death.
125 Sredni Vashtar the Beautiful.

And then of a sudden he stopped his chanting and drew closer to the
window-pane. The door of the shed still stood ajar as it had been left,
and the minutes were slipping by. They were long minutes, but they
slipped by nevertheless. He watched the starlings running and flying in
130 little parties across the lawn; he counted them over and over again,
with one eye always on that swinging door. A sour-faced maid came in
to lay the table for tea, and still Conradin stood and waited and
watched. Hope had crept by inches into his heart, and now a look of
triumph began to blaze in his eyes that had only known the wistful
135 patience of defeat. Under his breath, with a furtive exultation, he began
once again the pæan of victory and devastation. And presently his eyes
were rewarded: out through that doorway came a long, low, yellow-
and-brown beast, with eyes a-blink at the waning daylight, and dark
wet stains around the fur of jaws and throat. Conradin dropped on his
140 knees. The great polecat-ferret made its way down to a small brook at
the foot of the garden, drank for a moment, then crossed a little plank
bridge and was lost to sight in the bushes. Such was the passing of
Sredni Vashtar.

'Tea is ready,' said the sour-faced maid; 'where is the mistress?'
145 'She went down to the shed some time ago,' said Conradin.

And while the maid went to summon her mistress to tea, Conradin fished a toasting-fork out of the sideboard drawer and proceeded to toast himself a piece of bread. And during the toasting of it and the buttering of it with much butter and the slow enjoyment of eating it,
150 Conradin listened to the noises and silences which fell in quick spasms beyond the dining-room door. The loud foolish screaming of the maid, the answering chorus of wondering ejaculations from the kitchen region, the scuttering footsteps and hurried embassies for outside help, and then, after a lull, the scared sobbings and the shuffling tread of those
155 who bore a heavy burden into the house.

'Whoever will break it to the poor child? I couldn't for the life of me!' exclaimed a shrill voice. And while they debated the matter among themselves, Conradin made himself another piece of toast.

1910   1911

Hilaire Belloc

1870–1953

Joseph Hilary Pierre Belloc was born in France, but educated at the Oratory School, Birmingham, and Balliol College, Oxford. He became a British subject in 1902 and was Liberal MP for Salford, from 1906 to 1909, and again in 1910, after which he abandoned politics. He was a prolific and popular writer, associated in readers' minds with his friend and fellow-Catholic, G. K. Chesterton. Belloc wrote novels and books of history, travel – *The Path to Rome* (1902) – essays and verse. He is best known today for his 'cautionary tales' – whimsical verses which parody nineteenth-century 'moral' poems for children. He was also a gifted writer of epigrams. His *Collected Verse* was published in 1958.

LORD LUNDY

WHO WAS TOO FREELY MOVED TO TEARS,

AND THEREBY RUINED HIS

POLITICAL CAREER

Lord Lundy from his earliest years
Was far too freely moved to Tears.
For instance, if his Mother said,
'Lundy! It's time to go to Bed!'
5   He bellowed like a Little Turk.
Or if his father, Lord Dunquerque,
Said, 'Hi!' in a Commanding Tone,
'Hi, Lundy! Leave the Cat alone!'
Lord Lundy! letting go its tail,
10   Would raise so terrible a wail
As moved his Grandpapa the Duke
To utter the severe rebuke:
'When I, Sir! was a little Boy,
An Animal was not a Toy!'

15   His father's Elder Sister, who
Was married to a Parvenoo,

Confided to Her Husband, 'Drat!
The Miserable, Peevish Brat!
Why don't they drown the Little Beast?'
20 Suggestions which, to say the least,
Are not what we expect to hear
From Daughters of an English Peer.
His grandmamma, His Mother's Mother,
Who had some dignity or other,
25 The Garter,† or no matter what,
I can't remember all the Lot!
Said, 'Oh! that I were Brisk and Spry
To give him that for which to cry!'
(An empty wish, alas! for she
30 Was Blind and nearly ninety-three).

The Dear Old Butler thought – but there!
I really neither know nor care
For what the Dear Old Butler thought!
In my opinion, Butlers ought
35 To know their place, and not to play
The Old Retainer night and day.
I'm getting tired and so are you,
Let's cut the Poem into two!

.   .   .

LORD LUNDY
(*Second Canto*)

It happened to Lord Lundy then,
40 As happens to so many men:
Towards the age of twenty-six,
They shoved him into politics;
In which profession he commanded
The income that his rank demanded
45 In turn as Secretary for
India, the Colonies, and War.
But very soon his friends began
To doubt if he were quite the man:
Thus, if a member rose to say
50 (As members do from day to day),
'Arising out of that reply. . . !'
Lord Lundy would begin to cry.
A Hint at harmless little jobs†

The Garter   the Most Noble Order of the
   Garter, the highest British order of chivalry

jobs   the improper bestowal of office, honours
   or public money to win political support

Would shake him with convulsive sobs.

55   While as for Revelations, these
      Would simply bring him to his knees,
      And leave him whimpering like a child.
      It drove his Colleagues raving wild!
      They let him sink from Post to Post,
60   From fifteen hundred at the most
      To eight, and barely six – and then
      To be Curator of Big Ben! . . .
      And finally there came a Threat
      To oust him from the Cabinet!

65   The Duke – his aged grand-sire – bore
      The shame till he could bear no more.
      He rallied his declining powers,
      Summoned the youth to Brackley Towers,
      And bitterly addressed him thus –
70   'Sir! you have disappointed us!
      We had intended you to be
      The next Prime Minister but three:
      The stocks were sold; the Press was squared;
      The Middle Class was quite prepared.
75   But as it is! . . . My language fails!
      Go out and govern New South Wales!'

                    .   .   .

      The Aged Patriot groaned and died:
      And gracious! how Lord Lundy cried!

                                        1907

From EPIGRAMS

On Lady Poltagrue, a Public Peril

The Devil, having nothing else to do,
Went off to tempt My Lady Poltagrue.
My Lady, tempted by a private whim,
To his extreme annoyance, tempted him.

The Statue

When we are dead, some Hunting-boy will pass
And find a stone half-hidden in tall grass
And grey with age: but having seen that stone
(Which was your image), ride more slowly on.

On Mundane Acquaintances

Good morning, Algernon: Good morning, Percy.
Good morning, Mrs Roebeck. Christ have mercy!

On a General Election

The accursed power which stands on Privilege
(And goes with Women, and Champagne and Bridge)
Broke – and Democracy resumed her reign:
(Which goes with Bridge, and Women and Champagne).

On a Sleeping Friend

Lady, when your lovely head
Droops to sink among the Dead,
And the quiet places keep
You that so divinely sleep;
5   Then the dead shall blessèd be
With a new solemnity,
For such Beauty, so descending,
Pledges them that Death is ending.
Sleep your fill – but when you wake
10 Dawn shall over Lethe† break.

1923

Lethe   in Greek mythology, a river in Hades
   where the dead drink the waters of
   forgetfulness

Walter de la Mare
1873–1956

Walter de la Mare was born at Charlton in Kent and educated at St Paul's Choir School in London. He became a distinguished man of letters. A gifted writer for children, he also wrote very mature short stories, and some magical poems. He was made a Companion of Honour in 1948 and awarded the Order of Merit in 1953. W. H. Auden edited *A Choice of de la Mare's Verse* (1963).

AUTUMN

There is a wind where the rose was;
Cold rain where sweet grass was;
  And clouds like sheep
  Stream o'er the steep
5 Grey skies where the lark was.

Nought gold where your hair was;
Nought warm where your hand was;
  But phantom, forlorn,
  Beneath the thorn,
10 Your ghost where your face was.

Sad winds where your voice was;
Tears, tears where my heart was;
  And ever with me,
  Child, ever with me,
15 Silence where hope was.

1906

ALL THAT'S PAST

Very old are the woods;
  And the buds that break
Out of the brier's boughs,
  When March winds wake,

5 So old with their beauty are –
  Oh, no man knows
 Through what wild centuries
  Roves back the rose.

 Very old are the brooks;
10 And the rills that rise
 Where snow sleeps cold beneath
  The azure skies
 Sing such a history
  Of come and gone,
15 Their every drop is as wise
  As Solomon.

 Very old are we men;
  Our dreams are tales
 Told in dim Eden
20 By Eve's nightingales;
 We wake and whisper awhile,
  But, the day gone by,
 Silence and sleep like fields
  Of amaranth† lie.

1912

THE GHOST

'Who knocks?' 'I, who was beautiful,
 Beyond all dreams to restore,
I, from the roots of the dark thorn am hither.
 And knock on the door.'

5 'Who speaks?' 'I – once was my speech
 Sweet as the bird's on the air,
When echo lurks by the waters to heed;
 'Tis I speak thee fair.'

---

amaranth an unfading red flower, believed to symbol of immortality
grow in Paradise and, since ancient times, a

'Dark is the hour!' 'Ay, and cold.'
10   'Lone is my house.' 'Ah, but mine?'
'Sight, touch, lips, eyes yearned in vain.'
        'Long dead these to thine . . .'

Silence. Still faint on the porch
    Brake the flames of the stars.
15 In gloom groped a hope-wearied hand
    Over keys, bolts, and bars.

A face peered. All the grey night
    In chaos of vacancy shone;
Nought but vast sorrow was there –
20   The sweet cheat gone.

                              1918

Ford Madox Ford
1873–1939

Ford Madox Ford, born Ford Hermann Hueffer, the son of Francis Hueffer, a *Times* music critic, and the grandson of the Pre-Raphaelite painter Ford Madox Brown, grew up in a Bohemian milieu, in London. Except for two years (1915–17) in the army in France and allowing for his complicated, emotional, often unhappy relations with women, his life was devoted to literature. He collaborated with Conrad, with whom he wrote the novels *The Inheritors* (1901) and *Romance* (1903). He settled in Paris in 1922 and there set up and edited the *Transatlantic Review* which accepted work by Joyce and other modernist writers whom Ford did much to encourage. He wrote so copiously, and in so many genres, that his achievement as a novelist has been somewhat obscured, although his fellow-Catholic Graham Greene has helped to spread recognition of his work and especially of his masterpiece, the novel *The Good Soldier* (1915). His series of four novels, *Some Do Not* (1924), *No More Parades* (1925), *A Man Could Stand Up* (1926) and *Last Post* (1928), is known as *Parade's End* or 'The Tietjens Tetralogy'.

The Good Soldier is subtitled 'A Tale of Passion'. In this extract the narrator, a wealthy American with an ailing and unfaithful wife, describes his meeting with an Englishman and his wife. They appear 'a model couple', decent county folk, but the husband's passion for women and his wife's reactions will lead to death, suicide, insanity and 'two ruined lives'.

From THE GOOD SOLDIER
[The Ashburnhams]

It was a very hot summer, in August, 1904; and Florence had already been taking the baths for a month. I don't know how it feels to be a patient at one of those places. I never was a patient anywhere. I daresay the patients get a home feeling and some sort of anchorage in the spot.
5   They seem to like the bath attendants, with their cheerful faces, their

air of authority, their white linen. But, for myself, to be at Nauheim†
gave me a sense – what shall I say? – a sense almost of nakedness – the
nakedness that one feels on the sea-shore or in any great open space. I
had no attachments, no accumulations. In one's own home it is as if
10   little, innate sympathies draw one to particular chairs that seem to
enfold one in an embrace, or take one along particular streets that seem
friendly when others may be hostile. And, believe me, that feeling is a
very important part of life. I know it well, that have been for so long a
wanderer upon the face of public resorts. And one is too polished up.
15   Heaven knows I was never an untidy man. But the feeling that I had
when, whilst poor Florence was taking her morning bath, I stood upon
the carefully swept steps of the Englischer Hof,† looking at the carefully
arranged trees in tubs upon the carefully arranged gravel whilst carefully
arranged people walked past in carefully calculated gaiety, at the
20   carefully calculated hour, the tall trees of the public gardens, going up
to the right; the reddish stone of the baths – or were they white half-
timber châlets? Upon my word I have forgotten, I who was there so
often. That will give you the measure of how much I was in the
landscape. I could find my way blindfolded to the hot rooms, to the
25   douche rooms, to the fountain in the centre of the quadrangle where
the rusty water gushes out. Yes, I could find my way blindfolded. I
know the exact distances. From the Hotel Regina you took one hundred
and eighty-seven paces, then, turning sharp, lefthanded, four hundred
and twenty took you straight down to the fountain. From the Englischer
30   Hof, starting on the sidewalk, it was ninety-seven paces and the same
four hundred and twenty, but turning lefthanded this time.

And now you understand that, having nothing in the world to do –
but nothing whatever! I fell into the habit of counting my footsteps. I
would walk with Florence to the baths. And, of course, she entertained
35   me with her conversation. It was, as I have said, wonderful what she
could make conversation out of. She walked very lightly, and her hair
was very nicely done, and she dressed beautifully and very expensively.
Of course she had money of her own, but I shouldn't have minded.
And yet you know I can't remember a single one of her dresses. Or I
40   can remember just one, a very simple one of blue figured silk – a Chinese
pattern – very full in the skirts and broadening out over the shoulders.
And her hair was copper-coloured, and the heels of her shoes were
exceedingly high, so that she tripped upon the points of her toes. And
when she came to the door of the bathing place, and when it opened to
45   receive her, she would look back at me with a little coquettish smile so
that her cheek appeared to be caressing her shoulder.

Nauheim   town and spa in north Germany,   *Englischer Hof*   (German) English hotel
   noted for the medicinal quality of its waters

I seem to remember that, with that dress, she wore an immensely broad Leghorn hat[†] – like the Chapeau de Paille[†] of Rubens,[†] only very white. The hat would be tied with a lightly knotted scarf of the same
50   stuff as her dress. She knew how to give value to her blue eyes. And round her neck would be some simple pink, coral beads. And her complexion had a perfect clearness, a perfect smoothness . . .

Yes, that is how I most exactly remember her, in that dress, in that hat, looking over her shoulder at me so that the eyes flashed very blue –
55   dark pebble blue . . .

And, what the devil! For whose benefit did she do it? For that of the bath attendant? of the passers-by? I don't know. Anyhow, it can't have been for me, for never, in all the years of her life, never on any possible occasion, or in any other place did she so smile to me, mockingly,
60   invitingly. Ah, she was a riddle; but then, all other women are riddles. And it occurs to me that some way back I began a sentence that I have never finished . . . It was about the feeling that I had when I stood on the steps of my hotel every morning before starting out to fetch Florence back from the bath. Natty, precise, well-brushed, conscious of being
65   rather small amongst the long English, the lank Americans, the rotund Germans, and the obese Russian Jewesses, I should stand there, tapping a cigarette on the outside of my case, surveying for a moment the world in the sunlight. But a day was to come when I was never to do it again alone. You can imagine, therefore, what the coming of the Ashburnhams
70   meant for me.

I have forgotten the aspect of many things but I shall never forget the aspect of the dining-room of the Hotel Excelsior on that evening – and on so many other evenings. Whole castles have vanished from my memory, whole cities that I have never visited again, but that white
75   room, festooned with papier-maché fruits and flowers; the tall windows; the many tables; the black screen round the door with three golden cranes flying upward on each panel; the palm-tree in the centre of the room; the swish of the waiter's feet; the cold expensive elegance; the mien of the diners as they came in every evening – their air of earnestness
80   as if they must go through a meal prescribed by the Kur[†] authorities and their air of sobriety as if they must seek not by any means to enjoy their meals – those things I shall not easily forget. And then, one evening, in the twilight, I saw Edward Ashburnham lounge round the screen into the room. The head waiter, a man with a face all grey – in
85   what subterranean nooks or corners do people cultivate those absolutely grey complexions? – went with the timorous patronage of these creatures

---

Leghorn hat   a hat of fine straw, named after
  Leghorn, the English for Livorno, in Italy
Chapeau de Paille   (French) Straw Hat (*c.* 1625
  National Gallery London)

Rubens   Peter Paul Rubens (1577–1640)
  Flemish painter; his flamboyant use of colour
  has influenced generations of artists
Kur   (German) health-cure

towards him and held out a grey ear to be whispered into. It was
generally a disagreeable ordeal for newcomers but Edward Ashburnham
bore it like an Englishman and a gentleman. I could see his lips form a
90   word of three syllables – remember I had nothing in the world to do
but to notice these niceties – and immediately I knew that he must
be Edward Ashburnham, Captain, Fourteenth Hussars, of Branshaw
House, Branshaw Teleragh. I knew it because every evening just before
dinner, whilst I waited in the hall, I used, by the courtesy of Monsieur
95   Schontz, the proprietor, to inspect the little police reports that each
guest was expected to sign upon taking a room.

The head waiter piloted him immediately to a vacant table, three
away from my own – the table that the Grenfalls of Falls River, N.J.,
had just vacated. It struck me that that was not a very nice table for
100   the newcomers, since the sunlight, low though it was, shone straight
down upon it, and the same idea seemed to come at the same moment
into Captain Ashburnham's head. His face hitherto had, in the wonderful
English fashion, expressed nothing whatever. Nothing. There was in it
neither joy nor despair; neither hope nor fear; neither boredom nor
105   satisfaction. He seemed to perceive no soul in that crowded room; he
might have been walking in a jungle. I never came across such a perfect
expression before and I never shall again. It was insolence and
not insolence; it was modesty and not modesty. His hair was fair,
extraordinarily ordered in a wave, running from the left temple to the
110   right; his face was a light brick-red, perfectly uniform in tint up to the
roots of the hair itself; his yellow moustache was as stiff as a toothbrush
and I verily believe that he had his black smoking jacket thickened a
little over the shoulder-blades so as to give himself the air of the slightest
possible stoop. It would be like him to do that; that was the sort of
115   thing he thought about. Martingales, Chiffney bits,† boots; where you
got the best soap, the best brandy, the name of the chap who rode a
plater down the Khyber cliffs; the spreading power of number three
shot before a charge of number four powder . . . by heavens, I hardly
ever heard him talk of anything else. Not in all the years that I knew
120   him did I hear him talk of anything but these subjects. Oh, yes, once
he told me that I could buy my special shade of blue ties cheaper from
a firm in Burlington Arcade† than from my own people in New York.
And I have bought my ties from that firm ever since. Otherwise I should
not remember the name of the Burlington Arcade. I wonder what it
125   looks like. I have never seen it. I imagine it to be two immense rows of
pillars, like those of the Forum at Rome, with Edward Ashburnham
striding down between them. But it probably isn't – the least like that.

Martingales etc.   restraints for horses
Burlington Arcade   covered shopping area in London

Once also he advised me to buy Caledonian Deferred, since they were due to rise. And I did buy them and they did rise. But of how he got the knowledge I haven't the faintest idea. It seemed to drop out of the blue sky.

And that was absolutely all that I knew of him until a month ago – that and the profusion of his cases, all of pigskin and stamped with his initials, E. F. A. There were guncases, and collar cases, and shirt cases, and letter cases and cases each containing four bottles of medicine; and hat cases and helmet cases. It must have needed a whole herd of the Gadarene swine† to make up his outfit. And, if I ever penetrated into his private room it would be to see him standing, with his coat and waistcoat off and the immensely long line of his perfectly elegant trousers from waist to boot heel. And he would have a slightly reflective air and he would be just opening one kind of case and just closing another.

Good God, what did they all see in him? for I swear there was all there was of him, inside and out; though they said he was a good soldier. Yet, Leonora adored him with a passion that was like an agony, and hated him with an agony that was as bitter as the sea. How could he arouse anything like a sentiment, in anybody?

What did he even talk to them about – when they were under four eyes? – Ah, well, suddenly, as if by a flash of inspiration, I know. For all good soldiers are sentimentalists – all good soldiers of that type. Their profession, for one thing, is full of the big words, courage, loyalty, honour, constancy. And I have given a wrong impression of Edward Ashburnham if I have made you think that literally never in the course of our nine years of intimacy did he discuss what he would have called 'the graver things.' Even before his final outburst to me, at times, very late at night, say, he has blurted out something that gave an insight into the sentimental view of the cosmos that was his. He would say how much the society of a good woman could do towards redeeming you, and he would say that constancy was the finest of the virtues. He said it very stiffly, of course, but still as if the statement admitted of no doubt.

Constancy! Isn't that the queer thought? And yet, I must add that poor dear Edward was a great reader – he would pass hours lost in novels of a sentimental type – novels in which typewriter girls married Marquises and governesses Earls. And in his books, as a rule, the course of true love ran as smooth as buttered honey. And he was fond of poetry, of a certain type – and he could even read a perfectly sad love story. I have seen his eyes filled with tears at reading of a hopeless

---

Gadarene swine   See Mark 5. 1

parting. And he loved, with a sentimental yearning, all children, puppies
170   and the feeble generally . . .

So, you see, he would have plenty to gurgle about to a woman – with
that and his sound common sense about martingales and his – still
sentimental – experiences as a county magistrate; and with his intense,
optimistic belief that the woman he was making love to at the moment
175   was the one he was destined, at last, to be eternally constant to . . .
Well, I fancy he could put up a pretty good deal of talk when there
was no man around to make him feel shy. And I was quite astonished,
during his final burst out to me – at the very end of things, when the
poor girl was on her way to that fatal Brindisi and he was trying to
180   persuade himself and me that he had never really cared for her – I was
quite astonished to observe how literary and how just his expressions
were. He talked like quite a good book – a book not in the least cheaply
sentimental. You see, I suppose he regarded me not so much as a man.
I had to be regarded as a woman or a solicitor. Anyhow, it burst out
185   of him on that horrible night. And then, next morning, he took me over
to the Assizes and I saw how, in a perfectly calm and business-like way,
he set to work to secure a verdict of not guilty for a poor girl, the
daughter of one of his tenants, who had been accused of murdering her
baby. He spent two hundred pounds on her defence . . . Well, that was
190   Edward Ashburnham.

I had forgotten about his eyes. They were as blue as the sides of a
certain type of box of matches. When you looked at them carefully you
saw that they were perfectly honest, perfectly straightforward, perfectly,
perfectly stupid. But the brick pink of his complexion, running perfectly
195   level to the brick pink of his inner eyelids, gave them a curious, sinister
expression – like a mosaic of blue porcelain set in pink china. And that
chap, coming into a room, snapped up the gaze of every woman in it,
as dexterously as a conjurer pockets billiard balls. It was most amazing.
You know the man on the stage who throws up sixteen balls at once
200   and they all drop into pockets all over his person, on his shoulders, on
his heels, on the inner side of his sleeves; and he stands perfectly still
and does nothing. Well, it was like that. He had rather a rough, hoarse
voice.

And, there he was, standing by the table. I was looking at him, with
205   my back to the screen. And, suddenly, I saw two distinct expressions
flicker across his immobile eyes. How the deuce did they do it, those
unflinching blue eyes with the direct gaze? For the eyes themselves never
moved, gazing over my shoulder towards the screen. And the gaze was
perfectly level and perfectly direct and perfectly unchanging. I suppose
210   that the lids really must have rounded themselves a little and perhaps
the lips moved a little too, as if he should be saying: – 'There you are,
my dear.' At any rate, the expression was that of pride, of satisfaction,

of the possessor. I saw him once afterwards, for a moment, gaze upon the sunny fields of Branshaw and say: – 'All this is my land!'

215 And then again, the gaze was perhaps more direct, harder if possible – hardy too. It was a measuring look; a challenging look. Once when we were at Wiesbaden[†] watching him play in a polo match against the Bonner Hussaren I saw the same look come into his eyes, balancing the possibilities, looking over the ground. The German Captain, Count

220 Baron Idigon von Lelöffel, was right up by their goal posts, coming with the ball in an easy canter in that tricky German fashion. The rest of the field were just anywhere. It was only a scratch sort of affair. Ashburnham was quite close to the rails not five yards from us and I heard him saying to himself: – 'Might just be done!' And he did it.

225 Goodness! he swung that pony round with all its four legs spread out, like a cat dropping off a roof. . . .

Well, it was just that look that I noticed in his eyes:– 'It might,' I seem even now to hear him muttering to himself, 'just be done.'

I looked round over my shoulder and saw, tall, smiling brilliantly

230 and buoyant – Leonora. And, little and fair, and as radiant as the track of sunlight along the sea – my wife.

That poor wretch! to think that he was at that moment in a perfect devil of a fix, and there he was, saying at the back of his mind: – 'It might just be done.' It was like a chap in the middle of the eruption of

235 a volcano, saying that he might just manage to bolt into the tumult and set fire to a haystack. Madness? Predestination? Who the devil knows?

Mrs Ashburnham exhibited at that moment more gaiety than I have ever since known her to show. There are certain classes of English people – the nicer ones when they have been to many spas, who seem

240 to make a point of becoming much more than usually animated when they are introduced to my compatriots. I have noticed this often. Of course, they must first have accepted the Americans. But that once done, they seem to say to themselves: 'Hallo, these women are so bright. We aren't going to be outdone in brightness.' And for the time being

245 they certainly aren't. But it wears off. So it was with Leonora – at least until she noticed me. She began, Leonora did – and perhaps it was that that gave me the idea of a touch of insolence in her character, for she never afterwards did any one single thing like it – she began by saying in quite a loud voice and from quite a distance;

250 'Don't stop over by that stuffy old table, Teddy. Come and sit by these nice people!'

And that was an extraordinary thing to say. Quite extraordinary. I couldn't for the life of me refer to total strangers as nice people. But, of course, she was taking a line of her own in which I at any rate – and

---

Wiesbaden   another north German spa (30 hot springs)

255 no one else in the room, for she too had taken the trouble to read through the list of guests – counted any more than so many clean, bull terriers. And she sat down rather brilliantly at a vacant table, beside ours – one that was reserved for the Guggenheimers. And she just sat absolutely deaf to the remonstrances of the head waiter with his face
260 like a grey ram's. That poor chap was doing his steadfast duty too. He knew that the Guggenheimers of Chicago, after they had stayed there a month and had worried the poor life out of him, would give him two dollars fifty and grumble at the tipping system. And he knew that Teddy Ashburnham and his wife would give him no trouble whatever except
265 what the smiles of Leonora might cause in his apparently unimpressionable bosom – though you never can tell what may go on behind even a not quite spotless plastron! – And every week Edward Ashburnham would give him a solid, sound, golden English sovereign. Yet this stout fellow was intent on saving that table for the Guggenheimers of Chicago.
270 It ended in Florence saying:

'Why shouldn't we all eat out of the same trough? – that's a nasty New York saying. But I'm sure we're all nice quiet people and there can be four seats at our table. It's round.'

Then came, as it were, an appreciative gurgle from the Captain and I
275 was perfectly aware of a slight hesitation – a quick sharp motion in Mrs Ashburnham, as if her horse had checked. But she put it at the fence all right, rising from the seat she had taken and sitting down opposite me, as it were, all in one motion.

I never thought that Leonora looked her best in evening dress. She
280 seemed to get it too clearly cut, there was no ruffling. She always affected black and her shoulders were too classical. She seemed to stand out of her corsage as a white marble bust might out of a black Wedgwood vase. I don't know.

I loved Leonora always and, to-day, I would very cheerfully lay down
285 my life, what is left of it, in her service. But I am sure I never had the beginnings of a trace of what is called the sex instinct towards her. And I suppose – no I am certain that she never had it towards me. As far as I am concerned I think it was those white shoulders that did it. I seemed to feel when I looked at them that, if ever I should press my lips upon
290 them that they would be slightly cold – not icily, not without a touch of human heat, but, as they say of baths, with the chill off. I seemed to feel chilled at the end of my lips when I looked at her . . .

No, Leonora always appeared to me at her best in a blue tailor-made. Then her glorious hair wasn't deadened by her white shoulders. Certain
295 women's lines guide your eyes to their necks, their eyelashes, their lips, their breasts. But Leonora's seemed to conduct your gaze always to her wrist. And the wrist was at its best in a black or a dog-skin glove and there was always a gold circlet with a little chain supporting a very

small golden key to a dispatch box. Perhaps it was that in which she
300 locked up her heart and her feelings.

Anyhow, she sat down opposite me and then, for the first time, she
paid any attention to my existence. She gave me, suddenly, yet
deliberately, one long stare. Her eyes too were blue and dark and the
eyelids were so arched that they gave you the whole round of the irises.
305 And it was a most remarkable, a most moving glance, as if for a moment
a lighthouse had looked at me. I seemed to perceive the swift questions
chasing each other through the brain that was behind them. I seemed
to hear the brain ask and the eyes answer with all the simpleness of a
woman who was a good hand at taking in qualities of a horse – as
310 indeed she was. 'Stands well; has plenty of room for his oats behind
the girth. Not so much in the way of shoulders,' and so on. And so her
eyes asked: 'Is this man trustworthy in money matters; is he likely to
try to play the lover; is he likely to let his women be troublesome? Is
he, above all, likely to babble about my affairs?'
315 And, suddenly, into those cold, slightly defiant, almost defensive
china blue orbs, there came a warmth, a tenderness, a friendly
recognition . . . oh, it was very charming and very touching – and quite
mortifying. It was the look of a mother to her son, of a sister to her
brother. It implied trust; it implied the want of any necessity for barriers.
320 By God, she looked at me as if I were an invalid – as any kind woman
may look at a poor chap in a bath chair. And, yes, from that day
forward she always treated me and not Florence as if I were the invalid.
Why, she would run after me with a rug upon chilly days. I suppose,
therefore that her eyes had made a favourable answer. Or, perhaps, it
325 wasn't a favourable answer. And then Florence said: 'And so the whole
round table is begun.' Again Edward Ashburnham gurgled slightly in
his throat; but Leonora shivered a little, as if a goose[†] had walked over
her grave. And I was passing her the nickel-silver basket of rolls.
Avanti! . . .

1913/14   1915

---

goose   alternatively, 'ghost' – a sign of
  impending disaster

G. K. Chesterton
1874–1936

Gilbert Keith Chesterton was born in London and educated there at St Paul's School. Like his friend and fellow campaigner Hilaire Belloc (1870–1953), he was a prolific journalist, a novelist, a writer on many topics, a gifted versifier and, from 1922, a Roman Catholic and a polemicist for his religion. In his journalism and in his fantasy novels *The Napoleon of Notting Hill* (1904) and *The Man Who Was Thursday: A Nightmare* (1908), he celebrated traditional Englishness and denigrated capitalism and bureaucracy. His 'Father Brown' detective stories which began with *The Innocence of Father Brown* (1911) are classics. Chesterton loved paradox, and his writing conveys the exuberant pleasure he found in the incongruities of life. He was a brilliant parodist.

THE PRAISE OF DUST

'What of vile dust?' the preacher said.
    Methought the whole world woke,
The dead stone lived beneath my foot,
    And my whole body spoke.

5 'You, that played tyrant to the dust,
    And stamp its wrinkled face,
This patient star that flings you not
    Far into homeless space.

'Come down out of your dusty shrine
10   The living dust to see,
The flowers that at your sermon's end
    Stand blazing silently.

'Rich white and blood-red blossom; stones,
    Lichens like fire encrust;
15 A gleam of blue, a glare of gold,
    The vision of the dust.

'Pass them all by: till, as you come
   Where, at the city's edge,
Under a tree – I know it well –
20   Under a lattice ledge,

'The sunshine falls on one brown head.
   You, too, O cold of clay,
Eater of stones, may haply hear
   The trumpets of that day.

25 'When God to all his paladins
   By his own splendour swore
To make a fairer face than heaven.
   Of dust and nothing more.'

                                    1900

THE SECRET PEOPLE

Smile at us, pay us, pass us; but do not quite forget;
For we are the people of England, that never have spoken yet.
There is many a fat farmer that drinks less cheerfully,
There is many a free French peasant who is richer and sadder than we.
5   There are no folk in the whole world so helpless or so wise.
There is hunger in our bellies, there is laughter in our eyes;
You laugh at us and love us, both mugs and eyes are wet:
Only you do not know us. For we have not spoken yet.

The fine French kings[†] came over in a flutter of flags and dames.
10   We liked their smiles and battles, but we never could say their names.
The blood ran red to Bosworth[†] and the high French lords went down;
There was naught but a naked people under a naked crown.

And the eyes of the King's Servants turned terribly every way,
And the gold of the King's Servants rose higher every day.
15   They burnt the homes of the shaven men,[†] that had been quaint and
         kind,
Till there was no bed in a monk's house, nor food that man could find.

French kings   after the Norman Conquest in   ended the English civil wars of the later
   1066   Middle Ages
Bosworth   the Battle of Bosworth in 1485   shaven men   monks

The inns of God[†] where no man paid, that were the wall of the weak,
The King's Servants[†] ate them all. And still we did not speak.

And the face of the King's Servants grew greater than the King:
20   He tricked them, and they trapped him, and stood round him in a ring.
The new grave lords closed round him, that had eaten the abbey's fruits,
And the men of the new religion,[†] with their bibles in their boots,
We saw their shoulders moving, to menace or discuss,
And some were pure and some were vile; but none took heed of us.
25   We saw the King[†] as they killed him, and his face was proud and pale;
And a few men talked of freedom, while England talked of ale.

A war[†] that we understood not came over the world and woke
Americans, Frenchmen, Irish; but we know not the things they spoke.
They talked about rights and nature and peace and the people's reign:
30   And the squires, our masters, bade us fight; and scorned us never again.
Weak if we be for ever, could none condemn us then;
Men called us serfs and drudges; men knew that we were men.
In foam and flame at Trafalgar,[†] on Albuera[†] plains,
We did and died like lions, to keep ourselves in chains,
35   We lay in living ruins; firing and fearing not
The strange fierce face of the Frenchmen who knew for what they
      fought,
And the man who seemed to be more than man we strained against
      and broke;
And we broke our own rights with him. And still we never spoke.

Our patch of glory ended; we never heard guns again.
40   But the squire seemed struck in the saddle; he was foolish, as if in pain.
He leaned on a staggering lawyer,[†] he clutched a cringing Jew,
He was stricken; it may be, after all, he was stricken at Waterloo.
Or perhaps the shades of the shaven men, whose spoil is in his house,
Come back in shining shapes at last to spoil his last carouse:
45   We only know the last sad squires ride slowly towards the sea,
And a new people takes the land: and still it is not we.

---

inns of God   monasteries
King's Servants   Henry VIII dissolved the
   English monasteries between 1536 and 1540
new religion   Protestantism
the King   Charles I was executed in 1649
war   the French Revolution and the wars which
   followed
Trafalgar ... Albuera   Nelson defeated a
French and Spanish naval force off Cape
Trafalgar in 1805; Albuera, near the Spanish
border with Portugal, was the scene of a very
bloody battle in 1811
lawyer   the lawyer and the Jew (as money-
   lender) represent Chesterton's distaste for
   nineteenth-century capitalism

They have given us into the hand of new unhappy lords,
Lords without anger and honour, who dare not carry their swords.
They fight by shuffling papers; they have bright dead alien eyes;
50 They look at our labour and laughter as a tired man looks at flies.
And the load of their loveless pity is worse than the ancient wrongs,
Theirs doors are shut in the evening; and they know no songs.

We hear men speaking for us of new laws strong and sweet,
Yet is there no man speaketh as we speak in the street.
55 It may be we shall rise the last as Frenchman rose the first,
Our wrath come after Russia's wrath and our wrath be the worst.
It may be we are meant to mark with our riot and our rest
God's scorn for all men governing. It may be beer is best.
But we are the people of England; and we have not spoken yet.
60 Smile at us, pay us, pass us. But do not quite forget.

1915

THE HOUSE OF CHRISTMAS

There fared a mother driven forth
Out of an inn to roam;
In the place where she was homeless
All men are at home.
5 The crazy stable close at hand,
With shaking timber and shifting sand,
Grew a stronger thing to abide and stand
Than the square stones of Rome.

For men are homesick in their homes,
10 And strangers under the sun,
And they lay their heads in a foreign land
Whenever the day is done.
Here we have battle and blazing eyes,
And chance and honour and high surprise,
15 But our homes are under miraculous skies
Where the yule tale was begun.

A Child in a foul stable,
Where the beasts feed and foam;
Only where He was homeless
20 Are you and I at home;

We have hands that fashion and heads that know,
But our hearts we lost – how long ago!
In a place no chart nor ship can show
Under the sky's dome.

25   This world is wild as an old wives' tale,
And strange the plain things are,
The earth is enough and the air is enough
For our wonder and our war;
But our rest is as far as the fire-drake swings
30   And our peace is put in impossible things
Where clashed and thundered unthinkable wings
Round an incredible star.

To an open house in the evening
Home shall men come,
35   To an older place than Eden
And a taller town than Rome.
To the end of the way of the wandering star,
To the things that cannot be and that are,
To the place where God was homeless
40   And all men are at home.

                                        1915

VARIATIONS OF AN AIR

Composed on Having to Appear in a Pageant
as Old King Cole

Old King Cole was a merry old soul,
And a merry old soul was he;
He called for his pipe,
He called for his bowl,
5   And he called for his fiddlers three.

After Lord Tennyson

Cole, that unwearied prince of Colchester,
Growing more gay with age and with long days
Deeper in laughter and desire of life,
As that Virginian climber on our walls
5   Flames scarlet with the fading of the year;

Called for his wassail and that other weed
Virginian also, from the western woods
Where English Raleigh checked the boast of Spain,
And lighting joy with joy, and piling up
10   Pleasure as crown for pleasure, bade men bring
Those three, the minstrels whose emblazoned coats
Shone with the oyster-shells of Colchester;
And these three played, and playing grew more fain
Of mirth and music; till the heathen came,
15   And the King slept beside the northern sea.

After W. B. Yeats

Of an old King in a story
   From the grey sea-folk I have heard,
Whose heart was no more broken
   Than the wings of a bird.

5   As soon as the moon was silver
   And the thin stars began,
He took his pipe and his tankard,
   Like an old peasant man.

And three tall shadows were with him
10   And came at his command;
And played before him for ever
   The fiddles of fairyland.

And he died in the young summer
   Of the world's desire;
15   Before our hearts were broken
   Like sticks in a fire.

After Robert Browning

Who smoke-snorts toasts o' My Lady Nicotine,
Kick stuffing out of Pussyfoot, bids his trio
Strike up their Stradivarii (that's the plural)
Or near enough, my fatheads; *nimium*
5   *Vicina Cremonae*[†] (that's a bit too near).
Is there some stockfish fails to understand?
Catch hold o' the notion, bellow and blurt back 'Cole'?
Must I bawl lessons from a horn-book, howl,
Cat-call the cat-gut "fiddles"? Fiddlesticks!

---

nimium . . . Cremonae   (Latin) too near Cremona, a town known for its violins

After Walt Whitman

Me clairvoyant,
Me conscious of you, old camarado,
Needing no telescope, lorgnette, field-glass, opera-glass, myopic pince-
    nez,
Me piercing two thousand years with eye naked and not ashamed;
5   The crown cannot hide you from me;
Musty old feudal-heraldic trappings cannot hide you from me,
I perceive that you drink.
(I am drinking with you. I am as drunk as you are.)
I see you are inhaling tobacco, puffing, smoking, spitting
10 (I do not object to your spitting),
You prophetic of American largeness,
You anticipating the broad masculine manners of these States;
I see in you also there are movements, tremors, tears, desire for the
    melodious,
I salute your three violinists, endlessly making vibrations,
15 Rigid, relentless, capable of going on for ever;
They play my accompaniment; but I shall take no notice of any
    accompaniment;
I myself am a complete orchestra.
So long.

After Swinburne

In the time of old sin without sadness
    And golden with wastage of gold
Like the gods that grow old in their gladness
    Was the king that was glad, growing old;
5   And with sound of loud lyres from his palace
    The voice of his oracles spoke,
And the lips that were red from his chalice
    Were splendid with smoke.
When the weed was as flame for a token
10   And the wine was as blood for a sign;
And upheld in his hands and unbroken
    The fountains of fire and of wine.
And a song without speech, without singer,
    Stung the soul of a thousand in three
15 As the flesh of the earth has to sting her,
    The soul of the sea.

1933

Winston Churchill
1874–1965

Sir Winston Spencer Churchill was born at Blenheim Palace, the eldest
son of Lord Randolph Churchill and grandson of the seventh Duke
of Marlborough. He was educated at Harrow and the Royal Military
College, Sandhurst. He recounted his military adventures in *My Early
Life* (1903). Early books about army campaigns were followed by
Lord Randolph Churchill (1906), *Liberalism and the Social Problem*
(1909), *The World Crisis* (4 vols, 1923–9), and *Marlborough: his Life
and Times* (1933–8), among many other publications. The extent of
his writing is extraordinary, given the demands of political life and
office. *War Speeches 1940–45* (1946) was followed by *The Second
World War* (6 vols, 1948–54), and *A History of the English-Speaking
Peoples* (4 vols, 1956–8). As an historian and as an orator, he revived
the grand style of English prose. He was too grandiloquent for some;
but W. W. Robson has rightly said of his speeches as Prime Minister
in the early 1940s that 'he used English literature as a weapon of
war'. Churchill was awarded the Nobel Prize for Literature in 1953.

A SPEECH TO THE HOUSE OF COMMONS, 13 May 1940

On Friday evening last I received His Majesty's commission to form a
new administration. It was the evident wish and will of Parliament and
the nation that this should be conceived on the broadest possible basis
and that it should include all parties, both those who supported the
5   late Government and also the parties of the Opposition. I have completed
the most important part of this task. A War Cabinet has been formed
of five Members, representing, with the Opposition Liberals, the unity
of the nation. The three party leaders have agreed to serve, either in
the War Cabinet or in high executive office. The three fighting services
10   have been filled. It was necessary that this should be done in one single
day, on account of the extreme urgency and rigour of events. A number
of other key positions were filled yesterday, and I am submitting a
further list to His Majesty tonight. I hope to complete the appointment
of the principal Ministers during tomorrow. The appointment of the

15   other Ministers usually takes a little longer, but I trust that, when
      Parliament meets again, this part of my task will be completed, and
      that the administration will be complete in all respects.

      I considered it in the public interest to suggest that the House should
      be summoned to meet today. Mr Speaker agreed, and took the necessary
20   steps, in accordance with the powers conferred upon him by the
      Resolution of the House. At the end of the proceedings today, the
      adjournment of the House will be proposed until Tuesday, May 21,
      with, of course, provision for earlier meeting if need be. The business
      to be considered during that week will be notified to Members at the
25   earliest opportunity. I now invite the House, by the Resolution which
      stands in my name, to record its approval of the steps taken and to
      declare its confidence in the new Government.

      To form an administration of this scale and complexity is a serious
      undertaking in itself, but it must be remembered that we are in the
30   preliminary stage of one of the greatest battles in history, that we are
      in action at many points in Norway and in Holland, that we have to
      be prepared in the Mediterranean, that the air battle is continuous and
      that many preparations have to be made here at home. In this crisis I
      hope I may be pardoned if I do not address the House at any length
35   today. I hope that any of my friends and colleagues, or former colleagues,
      who are affected by the political reconstruction, will make all allowance
      for any lack of ceremony with which it has been necessary to act. I
      would say to the House, as I said to those who have joined this
      Government: 'I have nothing to offer but blood, toil, tears and sweat.'
40   We have before us an ordeal of the most grievous kind. We have
      before us many, many long months of struggle and of suffering. You
      ask what is our policy? I will say: It is to wage war, by sea, land and
      air, with all our might and with all the strength that God can give us:
      to wage war against a monstrous tyranny, never surpassed in the dark,
45   lamentable catalogue of human crime. That is our policy. You ask,
      What is our aim? I can answer in one word: Victory – victory at all
      costs, victory in spite of all terror, victory, however long and hard the
      road may be; for without victory, there is no survival. Let that be
      realized; no survival for the British Empire; no survival for all that the
50   British Empire has stood for, no survival for the urge and impulse of
      the ages, that mankind will move forward towards its goal. But I take
      up my task with buoyancy and hope. I feel sure that our cause will not
      be suffered to fail among men. At this time I feel entitled to claim the
      aid of all, and I say, 'Come, then, let us go forward together with our
55   united strength.'

1940   1941

THE DUNKIRK EVACUATION, 4 June 1940

Turning once again, and this time more generally, to the question of invasion, I would observe that there has never been a period in all these long centuries of which we boast when an absolute guarantee against invasion, still less against serious raids, could have been given to our
5   people. In the days of Napoleon the same wind which would have carried his transports across the Channel might have driven away the blockading fleet. There was always the chance, and it is that chance which has excited and befooled the imaginations of many Continental tyrants. Many are the tales that are told. We are assured that novel methods will be adopted,
10 and when we see the originality of malice, the ingenuity of aggression, which our enemy displays, we may certainly prepare ourselves for every kind of novel stratagem and every kind of brutal and treacherous manoeuvre. I think that no idea is so outlandish that it should not be considered and viewed with a searching, but at the same time, I hope,
15 with a steady eye. We must never forget the solid assurances of sea-power and those which belong to air-power if it can be locally exercised.

    I have, myself, full confidence that if all do their duty, if nothing is neglected, and if the best arrangements are made, as they are being made, we shall prove ourselves once again able to defend our island home, to ride
20 out the storm of war, and to outlive the menace of tyranny, if necessary for years, if necessary alone. At any rate, that is what we are going to try to do. That is the resolve of His Majesty's Government – every man of them. That is the will of Parliament and the nation. The British Empire and the French Republic, linked together in their cause and in their need, will defend to the
25 death their native soil, aiding each other like good comrades to the utmost of their strength. Even though large tracts of Europe and many old and famous States have fallen or may fall into the grip of the Gestapo and all the odious apparatus of Nazi rule, we shall not flag or fail. We shall go on to the end, we shall fight in France, we shall fight on the seas and oceans, we
30 shall fight with growing confidence and growing strength in the air, we shall defend our island, whatever the cost may be, we shall fight on the beaches, we shall fight on the landing grounds, we shall fight in the fields and in the streets, we shall fight in the hills; we shall never surrender, and even if, which I do not for a moment believe, this island or a large part of it were subjugated
35 and starving, then our Empire beyond the seas, armed and guarded by the British Fleet, would carry on the struggle, until, in God's good time, the new world, with all its power and might, steps forth to the rescue and the liberation of the old.

THE FINEST HOUR, 18 June 1940

During the first four years of the last war the Allies experienced nothing but disaster and disappointment. That was our constant fear: one blow after another, terrible losses, frightful dangers. Everything miscarried. And yet at the end of those four years the morale of the Allies was
5 higher than that of the Germans, who had moved from one aggressive triumph to another, and who stood everywhere triumphant invaders of the lands into which they had broken. During that war we repeatedly asked ourselves the question: How are we going to win? and no one was able ever to answer it with much precision, until at the end, quite
10 suddenly, quite unexpectedly, our terrible foe collapsed before us, and we were so glutted with victory that in our folly we threw it away.

    We do not yet know what will happen in France or whether the French resistance will be prolonged, both in France and in the French Empire overseas. The French Government will be throwing away great
15 opportunities and casting adrift their future if they do not continue the war in accordance with their treaty obligations, from which we have not felt able to release them. The House will have read the historic declaration in which, at the desire of many Frenchmen – and of our own hearts – we have proclaimed our willingness at the darkest hour
20 in French history to conclude a union of common citizenship in this struggle. However matters may go in France or with the French Government, or other French Governments, we in this island and in the British Empire will never lose our sense of comradeship with the French people. If we are now called upon to endure what they have
25 been suffering, we shall emulate their courage, and if final victory rewards our toils they shall share the gains, aye, and freedom shall be restored to all. We abate nothing of our just demands; not one jot or tittle do we recede. Czechs, Poles, Norwegians, Dutch, Belgians have joined their causes to our own. All these shall be restored.
30   What General Weygand[†] called the Battle of France is over. I expect that the battle of Britain is about to begin. Upon this battle depends the survival of Christian civilization. Upon it depends our own British life, and the long continuity of our institutions and our Empire. The whole fury and might of the enemy must very soon be turned on us.
35 Hitler knows that he will have to break us in this island or lose the war. If we can stand up to him, all Europe may be free and the life of the world may move forward into broad, sunlit uplands. But if we fail, then the whole world, including the United States, including all that we

---

General Weygand Maxime Weygand (1867–1965) commanded French forces in the last days of the Battle of France, in 1940. After the armistice, he advised that Britain would 'have her neck wrung like a chicken's in three weeks'

have known and cared for, will sink into the abyss of a new dark age
40   made more sinister, and perhaps more protracted, by the lights of
perverted science. Let us therefore brace ourselves to our duties, and so
bear ourselves that, if the British Empire and its Commonwealth last
for a thousand years, men will still say, 'This was their finest hour.'

1940   1941

A BROADCAST SPEECH, 11 September 1940

When I said in the House of Commons the other day that I thought it
improbable that the enemy's air attack in September could be more
than three times as great as it was in August, I was not, of course,
referring to barbarous attacks upon the civil population, but to the
5   great air battle which is being fought out between our fighters and the
German Air Force.

You will understand that whenever the weather is favourable waves
of German bombers, protected by fighters often 300 or 400 at a time,
surge over this island, especially the promontory of Kent, in the hope
10   of attacking military and other objectives by daylight. However, they
are met by our fighter squadrons and nearly always broken up; and
their losses average three to one in machines and six to one in pilots.

This effort of the Germans to secure daylight mastery of the air over
England is, of course, the crux of the whole war. So far it has failed
15   conspicuously. It has cost them very dear, and we have felt stronger
and actually are relatively a good deal stronger, than when the hard
fighting began in July. There is no doubt that Herr Hitler is using up
his fighter force at a very high rate, and that if he goes on for many
more weeks he will wear down and ruin this vital part of his Air Force.
20   That will give us a very great advantage.

On the other hand, for him to try to invade this country without having
secured mastery of the air would be a very hazardous undertaking.
Nevertheless, all his preparations for invasion on a great scale are
steadily going forward. Several hundreds of self-propelled barges are
25   moving down the coasts of Europe, from the German and Dutch
harbours to the ports of northern France; from Dunkirk to Brest; and
beyond Brest to the French harbours in the Bay of Biscay.

Besides this, convoys of merchant ships in tens of dozens are being moved
through the Straits of Dover into the Channel, dodging along from port to
30   port under the protection of the new batteries which the Germans have built

on the French shore. There are now considerable gatherings of shipping in the German, Dutch, Belgian and French harbours – all the way from Hamburg to Brest. Finally, there are some preparations made of ships to carry an invading force from the Norwegian harbours.

35 Behind these clusters of ships or barges, there stand very large numbers of German troops, awaiting the order to go on board and set out on their very dangerous and uncertain voyage across the seas. We cannot tell when they will try to come; we cannot be sure that in fact they will try at all; but no one should blind himself to the fact that a
40 heavy, full-scale invasion of this island is being prepared with all the usual German thoroughness and method, and that it may be launched now – upon England, upon Scotland, or upon Ireland, or upon all three.

If this invasion is going to be tried at all, it does not seem that it can be long delayed. The weather may break at any time. Besides this, it is
45 difficult for the enemy to keep these gatherings of ships waiting about indefinitely, while they are bombed every night by our bombers, and very often shelled by our warships which are waiting for them outside.

Therefore, we must regard the next week or so as a very important period in our history. It ranks with the days when the Spanish Armada
50 was approaching the Channel, and Drake was finishing his game of bowls; or when Nelson stood between us and Napoleon's Grand Army at Boulogne. We have read all about this in the history books; but what is happening now is on a far greater scale and of far more consequence to the life and future of the world and its civilization than these brave
55 old days of the past.

Every man and woman will therefore prepare himself to do his duty, whatever it may be, with special pride and care. Our fleets and flotillas are very powerful and numerous; our Air Force is at the highest strength it has ever reached, and it is conscious of its proved superiority, not
60 indeed in numbers, but in men and machines. Our shores are well fortified and strongly manned, and behind them, ready to attack the invaders, we have a far larger and better-equipped mobile Army than we have ever had before.

Besides this, we have more than a million and a half men of the
65 Home Guard, who are just as much soldiers of the Regular Army as the Grenadier Guards, and who are determined to fight for every inch of the ground in every village and in every street.

It is with devout but sure confidence that I say: Let God defend the Right.

70 These cruel, wanton, indiscriminate bombings of London are, of course, a part of Hitler's invasion plans. He hopes, by killing large numbers of civilians, and women and children, that he will terrorize and cow the people of this mighty imperial city, and make them a burden and an anxiety to the Government and thus distract our attention

75 unduly from the ferocious onslaught he is preparing. Little does he
know the spirit of the British nation, or the tough fibre of the
Londoners, whose forebears played a leading part in the establishment of
Parliamentary institutions and who have been bred to value freedom
far above their lives. This wicked man, the repository and embodiment
80 of many forms of soul-destroying hatred, this monstrous product of
former wrongs and shame, has now resolved to try to break our famous
island race by a process of indiscriminate slaughter and destruction.
What he has done is to kindle a fire in British hearts, here and all over
the world, which will glow long after all traces of the conflagration he
85 has caused in London have been removed. He has lighted a fire which
will burn with a steady and consuming flame until the last vestiges of
Nazi tyranny have been burnt out of Europe, and until the Old World –
and the New – can join hands to rebuild the temples of man's freedom
and man's honour, upon foundations which will not soon or easily be
90 overthrown.

This is a time for everyone to stand together, and hold firm, as they
are doing. I express my admiration for the exemplary manner in which
all the Air Raid Precautions services of London are being discharged,
especially the Fire Brigade, whose work has been so heavy and also
95 dangerous. All the world that is still free marvels at the composure and
fortitude with which the citizens of London are facing and surmounting
the great ordeal to which they are subjected, the end of which or the
severity of which cannot yet be foreseen.

It is a message of good cheer to our fighting forces on the seas, in the
100 air, and to our waiting armies in all their posts and stations, that we
send them from this capital city. They know that they have behind
them a people who will not flinch or weary of the struggle – hard and
protracted though it will be; but that we shall rather draw from the
heart of suffering itself the means of inspiration and survival, and of a
105 victory won not only for our own time, but for the long and better
days that are to come.

1940   1941

John Masefield
1878–1967

John Edward Masefield was born in Herefordshire and trained while still a boy, after school in Warwick, for the Merchant Navy. After a very brief period at sea he became, for a time, a tramp and odd-job man in the United States. On his return to England he began his career, with *Salt Water Ballads* (1902), as a prolific and very successful poet, novelist and playwright. He was also one of the century's most gifted writers of stories for children (notably *The Midnight Folk*, 1927). He became Poet Laureate in 1930 and received the Order of Merit in 1935.

SEA-FEVER

I must go down to the seas again, to the lonely sea and the sky,
And all I ask is a tall ship and a star to steer her by,
And the wheel's kick and the wind's song and the white sail's shaking,
And a grey mist on the sea's face and a grey dawn breaking.

5   I must go down to the seas again, for the call of the running tide
Is a wild call and a clear call that may not be denied;
And all I ask is a windy day with the white clouds flying,
And the flung spray and the blown spume, and the sea-gulls crying.

I must go down to the seas again, to the vagrant gypsy life,
10   To the gull's way and the whale's way where the wind's like a whetted
      knife;
And all I ask is a merry yarn from a laughing fellow-rover,
And quiet sleep and a sweet dream when the long trick's† over.

1902

---

trick   a seaman's spell of duty

CARGOES

Quinquireme[†] of Nineveh[†] from distant Ophir[†]
Rowing home to haven in sunny Palestine,
With a cargo of ivory,
And apes and peacocks,
5   Sandalwood, cedarwood, and sweet white wine.

Stately Spanish galleon coming from the Isthmus,[†]
Dipping through the Tropics by the palm-green shores,
With a cargo of diamonds,
Emeralds, amethysts,
10   Topazes, and cinnamon, and gold moidores.[†]

Dirty British coaster with a salt-caked smoke stack
Butting through the Channel in the mad March days,
With a cargo of Tyne coal,
Road-rail, pig-lead,
15   Firewood, iron-ware, and cheap tin trays.

                                        1903

Quinquireme a quinquereme was an ancient
  ship with five banks of oars
Nineveh the capital of ancient Assyria
Ophir a region of fabulous wealth; see I Kings
  9. 26–8

Isthmus that of Panama
moidores old Portuguese gold coins

Edward Thomas
1878–1917

Philip Edward Thomas was born in London and educated at St Paul's School and Lincoln College, Oxford. He was a journalist and a biographer; books such as *The Heart of England* express his love of nature. The American poet Robert Frost (1874–1963), whom he met in 1912, encouraged him to write poetry. He joined the army in 1915. *Poems* was published shortly after he was killed at Arras, in 1917. Walter de la Mare, in his Foreword to the *Collected Poems* of 1920, commended his 'grave and sensitive mind'. New editions of his poems appeared in 1928, 1949 and 1978.

ADLESTROP

Yes, I remember Adlestrop† –
The name, because one afternoon
Of heat the express-train drew up there
Unwontedly. It was late June.

5   The steam hissed. Someone cleared his throat.
No one left and no one came
On the bare platform. What I saw
Was Adlestrop – only the name

And willows, willow-herb, and grass,
10   And meadowsweet, and haycocks dry,
No whit less still and lonely fair
Than the high cloudlets in the sky.

And for that minute a blackbird sang
Close by, and round him, mistier,
15   Farther and farther, all the birds
Of Oxfordshire and Gloucestershire.

1915   1917

Adlestrop   a village in Gloucestershire

SWEDES

They have taken the gable from the roof of clay
On the long swede pile. They have let in the sun
To the white and gold and purple of curled fronds
Unsunned. It is a sight more tender-gorgeous
5   At the wood-corner where Winter moans and drips
Than when, in the Valley of the Tombs of Kings,
A boy crawls down into a Pharaoh's tomb
And, first of Christian men, beholds the mummy,
God and monkey, chariot and throne and vase,
10   Blue pottery, alabaster, and gold.

But dreamless long-dead Amen-hotep† lies.
This is a dream of Winter, sweet as Spring.

1915   1917

THE OWL

Downhill I came, hungry, and yet not starved;
Cold, yet had heat within me that was proof
Against the North wind; tired, yet so that rest
Had seemed the sweetest thing under a roof.

5   Then at the inn I had food, fire, and rest,
Knowing how hungry, cold, and tired was I.
All of the night was quite barred out except
An owl's cry, a most melancholy cry

Shaken out long and clear upon the hill,
10   No merry note, nor cause of merriment,
But one telling me plain what I escaped
And others could not, that night, as in I went.

And salted was my food, and my repose,
Salted and sobered, too, by the bird's voice

Amen-hotep Pharaoh Amenhotep IV (reigned 1375–57 BC)

15   Speaking for all who lay under the stars,
     Soldiers and poor, unable to rejoice.

1915   1917

AS THE TEAM'S HEAD BRASS

As the team's head brass† flashed out on the turn
The lovers disappeared into the wood.
I sat among the boughs of the fallen elm
That strewed an angle of the fallow, and
5   Watched the plough narrowing a yellow square
Of charlock. Every time the horses turned
Instead of treading me down, the ploughman leaned
Upon the handles to say or ask a word,
About the weather, next about the war.
10   Scraping the share he faced towards the wood,
And screwed along the furrow till the brass flashed
Once more.
              The blizzard felled the elm whose crest
I sat in, by a woodpecker's round hole,
The ploughman said. 'When will they take it away?'
15   'When the war's over.' So the talk began –
One minute and an interval of ten,
A minute more and the same interval.
'Have you been out?' 'No.' 'And don't want to, perhaps?'
'If I could only come back again, I should.
20   I could spare an arm. I shouldn't want to lose
A leg. If I should lose my head, why, so,
I should want nothing more. . . . Have many gone
From here?' 'Yes.' 'Many lost?' 'Yes, a good few.
Only two teams work on the farm this year.
25   One of my mates is dead. The second day
In France they killed him. It was back in March,
The very night of the blizzard, too. Now if
He had stayed here we should have moved the tree.'
'And I should not have sat here. Everything
30   Would have been different. For it would have been
Another world.' 'Ay, and a better, though

brass on the harness of the team of plough-horses

If we could see all all might seem good.' Then
The lovers came out of the wood again:
The horses started and for the last time
35   I watched the clods crumble and topple over
After the ploughshare and the stumbling team.

1916   1917

LIGHTS OUT

I have come to the borders of sleep,
The unfathomable deep
Forest, where all must lose
Their way, however straight
5   Or winding, soon or late;
They can not choose.

Many a road and track
That since the dawn's first crack
Up to the forest brink
10   Deceived the travellers,
Suddenly now blurs,
And in they sink.

Here love ends –
Despair, ambition ends;
15   All pleasure and all trouble,
Although most sweet or bitter,
Here ends, in sleep that is sweeter
Than tasks most noble.

There is not any book
20   Or face of dearest look
That I would not turn from now
To go into the unknown
I must enter, and leave, alone,
I know not how.

25   The tall forest towers:
Its cloudy foliage lowers
Ahead, shelf above shelf:

Its silence I hear and obey
That I may lose my way
30 And myself.

1916   1917

HOME

Not the end: but there's nothing more.
Sweet Summer and Winter rude
I have loved, and friendship and love,
The crowd and solitude:

5   But I know them: I weary not;
But all that they mean I know.
I would go back again home
Now. Yet how should I go?

This is my grief. That land,
10 My home, I have never seen;
No traveller tells of it,
However far he has been.

And could I discover it,
I fear my happiness there,
15 Or my pain, might be dreams of return
Here, to these things that were.

Remembering ills, though slight
Yet irremediable,
Brings a worse, an impurer pang
20 Than remembering what was well.

No: I cannot go back,
And would not if I could.
Until blindness come, I must wait
And blink at what is not good.

1915   1918

GOOD-NIGHT

The skylarks are far behind that sang over the down;
I can hear no more those suburb nightingales;
Thrushes and blackbirds sing in the gardens of the town
In vain: the noise of man, beast, and machine prevails.

5　But the call of children in the unfamiliar streets
That echo with a familiar twilight echoing,
Sweet as the voice of nightingale or lark, completes
A magic of strange welcome, so that I seem a king

Among man, beast, machine, bird, child, and the ghost
10　That in the echo lives and with the echo dies.
The friendless town is friendly; homeless, I am not lost;
Though I know none of these doors, and meet but strangers' eyes.

Never again, perhaps, after tomorrow, shall
I see these homely streets, these church windows alight,
15　Not a man or woman or child among them all:
But it is All Friends' Night, a traveller's good night.

1915   1918

Harold Monro
1879–1932

Harold Edward Monro was born in Brussels and was educated at Radley College and at Cambridge. At his poetry bookshop, opened in Bloomsbury in 1913, he published the five volumes of *Georgian Poetry*, edited by Edward Marsh between 1912 and 1922; and he offered encouragement and financial assistance to many poets. His own *Collected Poems* (1933) had an introduction by T. S. Eliot.

GREAT CITY

When I returned at sunset,
The serving-maid was singing softly
Under the dark stairs, and in the house
Twilight had entered like a moonray.
5   Time was so dead I could not understand
The meaning of midday or of midnight,
But like falling waters, falling, hissing, falling,
Silence seemed an everlasting sound.

I sat in my dark room,
10 And watched sunset,
And saw starlight.
I heard the tramp of homing men,
And the last call of the last child;
Then a lone bird twittered,
15 And suddenly, beyond the housetops,

I imagined dew in the country,
In the hay, on the buttercups;
The rising moon,
The scent of early night,
20 The songs, the echoes,
Dogs barking,
Day closing,
Gradual slumber,
Sweet rest.

25   When all the lamps were lighted in the town
     I passed into the streetways, and I watched,
     Wakeful, almost happy,
     And half the night I wandered in the street.

1912   1914

STREET FIGHT

From prehistoric distance, beyond clocks,
Fear radiates to life
And thrills into the elbows of two men.
Fear drives imagination to renew
5   Their prehistoric interrupted throttle.

The street turns out and runs about,
And windows rise, and women scream;
Their husbands grunt, or scratch and hunt
Their heads, but cannot trace the dream.

10 Meanwhile those:
    They rush, they close:
    flick, flap, bang, bang, blood, sweat, stars, moon,
    push, roar, rush, hold, part, bang, grind, swoon,
    O slow, O swift, O now – But soon,

15 How soon the heavy policeman rolls in sight,
    And barges slowly through that little crowd,
    And lays his large hands calmly on those shoulders.
    Now all will be exactly as it should be,
    And everybody quietly go to bed.

20 Occasional spectator,
    Do not you think it was very entertaining?
    You, standing behind your vast round belly,
    With your truss, your operation scar,
    Your hairless head, your horn-rimmed eyes,
25 Your varicose veins,
    Neuritis, neurasthenia, rheumatism,
    Flat-foot walking, awkward straining of sinews,
    Over the whole of your body

The slowly advancing pains of approaching death,
30   What comes into your mind when two men fight?

                                              1928

LIVING

Slow bleak awakening from the morning dream
Brings me in contact with the sudden day.
I am alive – this I.
I let my fingers move along my body.
5   Realisation warns them, and my nerves
Prepare their rapid messages and signals.
While Memory begins recording, coding,
Repeating; all the time Imagination
Mutters: You'll only die.

10   Here's a new day. O Pendulum move slowly!
My usual clothes are waiting on their peg.
I am alive – this I.
And in a moment Habit, like a crane,
Will bow its neck and dip its pulleyed cable,
15   Gathering me, my body, and our garment,
And swing me forth, oblivious of my question,
Into the daylight – why?

I think of all the others who awaken,
And wonder if they go to meet the morning
20   More valiantly than I;
Nor asking of this Day they will be living:
What have I done that I should be alive?
O, can I not forget that I am living?
How shall I reconcile the two conditions:
25   Living, and yet – to die?

Between the curtains the autumnal sunlight
With lean and yellow finger points me out;
The clock moans: Why? Why? Why?
But suddenly, as if without a reason,
30   Heart, Brain and Body, and Imagination
All gather in tumultuous joy together,

Running like children down the path of morning
To fields where they can play without a quarrel:
A country I'd forgotten, but remember,
35   And welcome with a cry.

O cool glad pasture; living tree, tall corn,
Great cliff, or languid sloping sand, cold sea,
Waves; rivers curving: you, eternal flowers,
Give me content, while I can think of you:
40   Give me your living breath!
Back to your rampart, Death.

1924   1928

E. M. Forster

1879–1970

Edward Morgan Forster was born in London and educated at Tonbridge School, which he hated, and at King's College, Cambridge, which he loved. He became a Fellow of King's in 1946 and made the college his home. Travels in Italy provided the background for his first novel *Where Angels Fear To Tread* (1905). He published three more novels in quick succession: *The Longest Journey* (1907), *A Room with a View* (1908) and *Howard's End* (1910). *The Celestial Omnibus* (1911) was a collection of short stories. Forster travelled in India in 1912 and 1913, and again in 1921. *A Passage to India* (1924), one of the best books ever written by an Englishman about India, consolidated his reputation. *Aspects of the Novel* (1927) is a pleasantly informal introduction to its subject. *Abinger Harvest* (1936) and *Two Cheers for Democracy* (1951) are collections of essays and radio broadcasts in which Forster asserts the thoughtful, humane liberalism he championed throughout his life. He was awarded the Order of Merit in 1969.

In the following chapter Miss Lucy Honeychurch, a young lady newly engaged, comes across the unconventional George Emerson, a meeting with whom on a recent holiday in Italy caused her some disturbing emotions. She finds him in the company of her brother and the rector of her parish.

From A ROOM WITH A VIEW

[Not Truly Refined]

It was a Saturday afternoon, gay and brilliant after abundant rains, and the spirit of youth dwelt in it, though the season was now autumn. All that was gracious triumphed. As the motor-cars passed through Summer Street they raised only a little dust, and their stench was soon dispersed
5 by the wind and replaced by the scent of the wet birches or of the pines. Mr Beebe, at leisure for life's amenities, leant over his rectory gate. Freddy leant by him, smoking a pendant pipe.

'Suppose we go and hinder those new people opposite for a little.'

'M'm.'

10   'They might amuse you.'

Freddy, whom his fellow-creatures never amused, suggested that the new people might be feeling a bit busy, and so on, since they had only just moved in.

'I suggested we should hinder them,' said Mr Beebe. 'They are worth
15   it.' Unlatching the gate, he sauntered over the triangular green to Cissie Villa. 'Hullo!' he called, shouting in at the open door, through which much squalor was visible.

A grave voice replied, 'Hullo!'

'I've brought someone to see you.'

20   'I'll be down in a minute.'

The passage was blocked by a wardrobe, which the removal men had failed to carry up the stairs. Mr Beebe edged round it with difficulty. The sitting-room itself was blocked with books.

'Are these people great readers?' Freddy whispered. 'Are they that
25   sort?'

'I fancy they know how to read – a rare accomplishment. What have they got? Byron.[†] Exactly. "A Shropshire Lad".[†] Never heard of it. "The Way of All Flesh".[†] Never heard of it. Gibbon.[†] Hullo! dear George reads German. Um – um – Schopenhauer,[†] Nietzsche,[†] and so
30   we go on. Well, I suppose your generation knows its own business, Honeychurch.'

'Mr Beebe, look at that,' said Freddy in awestruck tones.

On the cornice of the wardrobe the hand of an amateur had painted this inscription: 'Mistrust all enterprises that require new clothes.'

35   'I know. Isn't it jolly? I like that. I'm certain that's the old man's doing.'

'How very odd of him!'

'Surely you agree?'

But Freddy was his mother's son, and felt that one ought not to go
40   spoiling the furniture.

'Pictures!' the clergyman continued, scrambling about the room. 'Giotto[†] – they got that at Florence, I'll be bound.'

'The same as Lucy's got.'

'Oh, by the by, did Miss Honeychurch enjoy London?'

45   'She came back yesterday.'

'I suppose she had a good time?'

Byron   George Gordon, sixth baron (1788–
   1814), Romantic poet and dramatist
A Shropshire Lad   collection of poems by
   A. E. Housman (q.v.)
The Way of All Flesh   a novel by Samuel Butler
   (1835–1902)
Gibbon   Edward (1737–94), historian of the
fall of the Roman Empire
Schopenhauer   Arthur (1788–1860),
   pessimistic German philosopher
Nietzsche   Friedrich Wilhelm (1844–1900),
   German philosopher and poet
Giotto   (c. 1267–1337) celebrated Italian
   painter

'Yes, very,' said Freddy, taking up a book. 'She and Cecil are thicker than ever.'

'That's good hearing.'

50 'I wish I wasn't such a fool, Mr Beebe.'

Mr Beebe ignored the remark.

'Lucy used to be nearly as stupid as I am, but it'll be very different now, mother thinks. She will read all kinds of books.'

'So will you.'

55 'Only medical books. Not books that you can talk about afterwards. Cecil is teaching Lucy Italian, and he says her playing is wonderful. There are all kinds of things in it that we have never noticed. Cecil says –'

'What on earth are those people doing upstairs? Emerson – we think
60 we'll come another time.'

George ran downstairs and pushed them into the room without speaking.

'Let me introduce Mr Honeychurch, a neighbour.'

Then Freddy hurled one of the thunderbolts of youth. Perhaps he
65 was shy, perhaps he was friendly, or perhaps he thought that George's face wanted washing. At all events, he greeted him with, 'How d'ye do? Come and have a bathe.'

'Oh, all right,' said George, impassive.

Mr Beebe was highly entertained.

70 ' "How d'ye do? how d'ye do? Come and have a bathe," ' he chuckled. 'That's the best conversational opening I've ever heard. But I'm afraid it will only act between men. Can you picture a lady who has been introduced to another lady by a third lady opening civilities with "How do you do? Come and have a bathe"? And yet you will tell me that the
75 sexes are equal.'

'I tell you that they shall be,' said Mr Emerson, who had been slowly descending the stairs. 'Good afternoon, Mr Beebe. I tell you they shall be comrades, and George thinks the same.'

'We are to raise ladies to our level?' the clergyman inquired.

80 'The Garden of Eden,' pursued Mr Emerson, still descending, 'which you place in the past, is really yet to come. We shall enter it when we no longer despise our bodies.'

Mr Beebe disclaimed placing the Garden of Eden anywhere.

'In this – not in other things – we men are ahead. We despise the
85 body less than women do. But not until we are comrades shall we enter the garden.'

'I say, what about this bathe?' murmured Freddy, appalled at the mass of philosophy that was approaching him.

'I believed in a return to Nature once. But how can we return to
90 Nature when we have never been with her? Today, I believe that we

must discover Nature. After many conquests we shall attain simplicity. It is our heritage.'

'Let me introduce Mr Honeychurch, whose sister you will remember at Florence.'

95 'How do you do? Very glad to see you, and that you are taking George for a bathe. Very glad to hear that your sister is going to marry. Marriage is a duty. I am sure that she will be happy, for we know Mr Vyse, too. He has been most kind. He met us by chance in the National Gallery, and arranged everything about this delightful house. Though I
100 hope I have not vexed Sir Harry Otway. I have met so few Liberal landowners, and I was anxious to compare his attitude towards the game laws with the Conservative attitude. Ah, this wind! You do well to bathe. Yours is a glorious country, Honeychurch!'

'Not a bit!' mumbled Freddy. 'I must – that is to say, I have to –
105 have the pleasure of calling on you later on, my mother says, I hope.'

'*Call*, my lad? Who taught us that drawing-room twaddle? Call on your grandmother! Listen to the wind among the pines! Yours is a glorious country.'

Mr Beebe came to the rescue.

110 'Mr Emerson, he will call, I shall call; you or your son will return our calls before ten days have elapsed. I trust that you have realized about the ten days' interval. It does not count that I helped you with the stair-eyes yesterday. It does not count that they are going to bathe this afternoon.'

115 'Yes, go and bathe, George. Why do you dawdle talking? Bring them back to tea. Bring back some milk, cakes, honey. The change will do you good. George has been working very hard at his office. I can't believe he's well.'

George bowed his head, dusty and sombre, exhaling the peculiar
120 smell of one who has handled furniture.

'Do you really want this bathe?' Freddy asked him. 'It is only a pond, don't you know. I dare say you are used to something much better.'

'Yes – I have said "Yes" already.'

Mr Beebe felt bound to assist his young friend, and led the way out
125 of the house and into the pine-woods. How glorious it was! For a little time the voice of old Mr Emerson pursued them, dispensing good wishes and philosophy. It ceased, and they only heard the fair wind blowing the bracken and the trees.

Mr Beebe, who could be silent, but who could not bear silence, was
130 compelled to chatter, since the expedition looked like a failure, and neither of his companions would utter a word. He spoke of Florence. George attended gravely, assenting or dissenting with slight but determined gestures that were as inexplicable as the motions of the tree-tops above their heads.

135   'And what a coincidence that you should meet Mr Vyse! Did you
realize that you would find all the Pension Bertolini† down here?'

'I did not. Miss Lavish told me.'

'When I was a young man I always meant to write a "History of
Coincidence".'

140   No enthusiasm.

'Though, as a matter of fact, coincidences are much rarer than we
suppose. For example, it isn't pure coincidentality that you are here
now, when one comes to reflect.'

To his relief, George began to talk.

145   'It is. I have reflected. It is Fate. Everything is Fate. We are flung
together by Fate, drawn apart by Fate – flung together, drawn apart.
The twelve winds blow us – we settle nothing –'

'You have not reflected at all,' rapped the clergyman. 'Let me give
you a useful tip, Emerson: attribute nothing to Fate. Don't say, "I

150   didn't do this," for you did it, ten to one. Now I'll cross-question you.
Where did you first meet Miss Honeychurch and myself?'

'Italy.'

'And where did you meet Mr Vyse, who is going to marry Miss
Honeychurch?'

155   'National Gallery.'

'Looking at Italian art. There you are, and yet you talk of coincidence
and Fate! You naturally seek out things Italian, and so do we and our
friends. This narrows the field immeasurably, and we meet again in it.'

'It is Fate that I am here,' persisted George. 'But you can call it Italy

160   if it makes you less unhappy.'

Mr Beebe slid away from such heavy treatment of the subject. But
he was infinitely tolerant of the young, and had no desire to snub
George.

'And so for this and for other reasons my "History of Coincidence"

165   is still to write.'

Silence.

Wishing to round off the episode, he added:

'We are all so glad that you have come.'

Silence.

170   'Here we are!' called Freddy.

'Oh, good!' exclaimed Mr Beebe, mopping his brow.

'In there's the pond. I wish it was bigger,' he added apologetically.

They climbed down a slippery bank of pine-needles. There lay the
pond set in its little alp of green – only a pond, but large enough to

175   contain the human body, and pure enough to reflect the sky. On account
of the rains, the waters had flooded the surrounding grass, which

---

Pension Bertolini   the private hotel in Florence where Lucy met George

showed like a beautiful emerald path, tempting the feet towards the central pond.

'It's distinctly successful, as ponds go,' said Mr Beebe.

180 'No apologies are necessary for the pond.'

George sat down where the ground was dry, and drearily unlaced his boots.

'Aren't those masses of willow-herb splendid? I love willow-herb in seed. What's the name of this aromatic plant?'

185 No one knew, or seemed to care.

'These abrupt changes of vegetation – this little spongeous tract of water-plants, and on either side of it all the growths are tough or brittle – heather, bracken, hurts, pines. Very charming, very charming.'

'Mr Beebe, aren't you bathing?' called Freddy, as he stripped himself.

190 Mr Beebe thought he was not.

'Water's wonderful!' cried Freddy, prancing in.

'Water's water,' murmured George. Wetting his hair first – a sure sign of apathy – he followed Freddy into the divine, as indifferent as if he were a statue and the pond a pail of soapsuds. It was necessary to

195 use his muscles. It was necessary to keep clean. Mr Beebe watched them, and watched the seed of the willow-herb dance chorically above their heads.

'Apooshoo, apooshoo, apooshoo,' went Freddy, swimming for two strokes in either direction, and then becoming involved in reeds or mud.

200 'Is it worth it?' asked the other, Michelangelesque[†] on the flooded margin.

The bank broke away, and he fell into the pool before he had weighed the question properly.

'Hee – poof – I've swallowed a polly-wog.[†] Mr Beebe, water's

205 wonderful, water's simply ripping.'

'Water's not so bad,' said George, reappearing from his plunge, and spluttering at the sun.

'Water's wonderful. Mr Beebe, do.'

'Apooshoo, kouf.'

210 Mr Beebe, who was hot, and who always acquiesced where possible, looked around him. He could detect no parishioners except the pine-trees, rising up steeply on all sides, and gesturing to each other against the blue. How glorious it was! The world of motor-cars and Rural Deans[†] receded illimitably. Water, sky, evergreens, a wind – these things

215 not even the seasons can touch, and surely they lie beyond the intrusion of man?

Michelangelesque Michelangelo Buonarrotti (1475–1564), Florentine artist noted for his portrayal of the male nude figure

polly-wog tadpole
Rural Dean church dignitary senior to a rector

'I may as well wash too'; and soon his garments made a third little pile on the sward, and he too asserted the wonder of the water.

It was ordinary water, nor was there very much of it, and, as Freddy
220 said, it reminded one of swimming in a salad. The three gentlemen rotated in the pool breast high, after the fashion of the nymphs in Götterdämmerung.† But either because the rains had given a freshness, or because the sun was shedding the most glorious heat, or because two of the gentlemen were young in years and the third young in the
225 spirit – for some reason or other a change came over them, and they forgot Italy and Botany and Fate. They began to play. Mr Beebe and Freddy splashed each other. A little deferentially, they splashed George. He was quiet: they feared they had offended him. Then all the forces of youth burst out. He smiled, flung himself at them, splashed them,
230 ducked them, kicked them, muddied them, and drove them out of the pool.

'Race you round it, then,' cried Freddy, and they raced in the sunshine, and George took a short cut and dirtied his shins, and had to bathe a second time. Then Mr Beebe consented to run – a memorable sight.
235 They ran to get dry, they bathed to get cool, they played at being Indians in the willow-herbs and in the bracken, they bathed to get clean. And all the time three little bundles lay discreetly on the sward, proclaiming:

'No. We are what matters. Without us shall no enterprise begin. To
240 us shall all flesh turn in the end.'

'A try! A try!' yelled Freddy, snatching up George's bundle and placing it beside an imaginary goal-post.

'Socker rules,' George retorted, scattering Freddy's bundle with a kick.
245 'Goal!'
'Goal!'
'Pass!'
'Take care my watch!' cried Mr Beebe.
Clothes flew in all directions.
250 'Take care my hat! No, that's enough, Freddy. Dress now. No, I say!'
But the two young men were delirious. Away they twinkled into the trees, Freddy with a clerical waistcoat under his arm, George with a wide-awake hat on his dripping hair.

'That'll do!' shouted Mr Beebe, remembering that after all he was in
255 his own parish. Then his voice changed as if every pine-tree was a Rural Dean. 'Hi! Steady on! I see people coming, you fellows!'

Yells and widening circles over the dappled earth.

Götterdämmerung (German) 'The Twilight of
  the Gods', an opera by Richard Wagner (1813–83)

'Hi! Hi! *Ladies!*'

Neither George nor Freddy was truly refined. Still, they did not hear
Mr Beebe's last warning or they would have avoided Mrs Honeychurch,
Cecil and Lucy, who were walking down to call on old Mrs Butterworth.
Freddy dropped the waistcoat at their feet, and dashed into some
bracken. George whooped in their faces, turned, and scudded away
down the path to the pond, still clad in Mr Beebe's hat.

'Gracious alive!' cried Mrs Honeychurch. 'Whoever are those unfortunate people? Oh, dears, look away! And poor Mr Beebe, too! Whatever
has happened?'

'Come this way immediately,' commanded Cecil, who always felt
that he must lead women, though he knew not whither, and protect
them, though he knew not against what. He led them now towards the
bracken where Freddy sat concealed.

'Oh, poor Mr Beebe! Was that his waistcoat we left in the path?
Cecil, Mr Beebe's waistcoat –'

'No business of ours,' said Cecil, glancing at Lucy, who was all
parasol and evidently 'minded'.

'I fancy Mr Beebe jumped back into the pond.'

'This way, please, Mrs Honeychurch, this way.'

They followed him up the bank, attempting the tense yet nonchalant
expression that is suitable for ladies on such occasions.

'Well, *I* can't help it,' said a voice close ahead, and Freddy reared a
freckled face and a pair of snowy shoulders out of the fronds. 'I can't
be trodden on, can I?'

'Good gracious me, dear; so it's you! What miserable management!
Why not have a comfortable bath at home, with hot and cold laid on?'

'Look here, mother: a fellow must wash, and a fellow's got tto dry,
and if another fellow –'

'Dear, no doubt you're right as usual, but you are in no position to
argue. Come, Lucy.' They turned. 'Oh, look – don't look! Oh, poor
Mr Beebe! How unfortunate again –'

For Mr Beebe was just crawling out of the pond, on whose surface
garments of an intimate nature did float; while George, the world-
weary George, shouted to Freddy that he had hooked a fish.

'And me, I've swallowed one,' answered he of the bracken. 'I've
swallowed a polly-wog. It wriggleth in my tummy. I shall die – Emerson,
you beast, you've got on my bags.'

'Hush, dears,' said Mrs Honeychurch, who found it impossible to
remain shocked. 'And do be sure you dry yourselves thoroughly first.
All these colds come of not drying thoroughly.'

'Mother, do come away,' said Lucy. 'Oh, for goodness' sake, do
come.'

'Hullo!' cried George, so that again the ladies stopped.

He regarded himself as dressed. Barefoot, bare-chested, radiant and personable against the shadowy woods, he called:

'Hullo, Miss Honeychurch! Hullo!'

305 'Bow, Lucy; better bow. Whoever is it? I shall bow.'

Miss Honeychurch bowed.

That evening and all that night the water ran away. On the morrow the pool had shrunk to its old size and lost its glory. It had been a call to the blood and to the relaxed will, a passing benediction whose

310 influences did not pass, a holiness, a spell, a momentary chalice for youth.

1908

Lytton Strachey
1880–1932

Giles Lytton Strachey, born in London, was educated at Leamington College, Liverpool University, and Trinity College, Cambridge. With his friends Virginia Woolf, E. M. Forster and the economist John Maynard Keynes (1883–1946), he was one of a set of friends known later as the 'Bloomsbury Group' of anti-Victorian, avant-garde writers, painters and intellectuals. His elegant, concise *Landmarks in French Literature* appeared in 1912 but he made his name after the First World War (in which, as a conscientious objector, he took no part) with *Eminent Victorians* (1918). The book's four biographical essays, on Cardinal Manning, Florence Nightingale, Thomas Arnold and General Gordon, shocked and excited their first readers. *Queen Victoria* (1921) and *Elizabeth and Essex* (1928) confirmed Strachey's reputation as a new type of biographer, caustic in irony and disrespectful of eminence.

From EMINENT VICTORIANS
Dr Arnold

In the actual sphere of teaching, Dr Arnold's[†] reforms were tentative and few. He introduced modern history, modern languages, and mathematics into the school curriculum; but the results were not encouraging. He devoted to the teaching of history one hour a week;

5 yet though he took care to inculcate in these lessons a wholesome hatred of moral evil, and to point out from time to time the indications of the providential government of the world, his pupils never seemed to make much progress in the subject. Could it have been that the time allotted to it was insufficient? Dr Arnold had some suspicions that this might

10 be the case. With modern languages there was the same difficulty. Here his hopes were certainly not excessive. 'I assume it,' he wrote, 'as the foundation of all my view of the case, that boys at a public school never will learn to speak or pronounce French well, under any circumstance.'

Dr Arnold Thomas Arnold (1795–1842) became headmaster of Rugby School in 1828

It would be enough if they could 'learn it grammatically as a dead
15 language'. But even this they very seldom managed to do. 'I know too
well,' he was obliged to confess, 'that most of the boys would pass a
very poor examination even in French grammar. But so it is with their
mathematics; and so it will be with any branch of knowledge that is
taught but seldom, and is felt to be quite subordinate to the boys' main
20 study.'

The boys' main study remained the dead languages of Greece and
Rome. That the classics should form the basis of all teaching was an
axiom with Dr Arnold. 'The study of language,' he said, 'seems to me
as if it was given for the very purpose of forming the human mind in
25 youth; and the Greek and Latin languages seem the very instruments
by which this is to be effected.' Certainly, there was something
providential about it – from the point of view of the teacher as well as
of the taught. If Greek and Latin had not been 'given' in that convenient
manner, Dr Arnold, who had spent his life in acquiring those languages,
30 might have discovered that he had acquired them in vain. As it was, he
could set the noses of his pupils to the grindstone of syntax and prosody
with a clear conscience. Latin verses and Greek prepositions divided
between them the labours of the week. As time went on, he became, he
declared, 'increasingly convinced that it is not knowledge, but the means
35 of gaining knowledge which I have to teach'. The reading of the school
was devoted almost entirely to selected passages from the prose writers
of antiquity. 'Boys,' he remarked, 'do not like poetry.' Perhaps his own
poetical taste was a little dubious; at any rate, it is certain that he
considered the Greek Tragedians greatly overrated, and that he ranked
40 Propertius as 'an indifferent poet'. As for Aristophanes, owing to his
strong moral disapprobation, he could not bring himself to read him
until he was forty, when, it is true, he was much struck by the 'Clouds'.
But Juvenal the Doctor could never bring himself to read at all.

Physical science was not taught at Rugby. Since, in Dr Arnold's
45 opinion, it was 'too great a subject to be studied ἐν παρέργῳ' [in
passing], obviously only two alternatives were possible: it must either
take the chief place in the school curriculum, or it must be left out
altogether. Before such a choice, Dr Arnold did not hesitate for a
moment. 'Rather than have physical science the principal thing in my
50 son's mind,' he exclaimed in a letter to a friend, 'I would gladly have
him think that the sun went round the earth, and that the stars were so
many spangles set in the bright blue firmament. Surely the one thing
needful for a Christian and an Englishman to study is Christian and
moral and political philosophy.'

55 A Christian and an Englishman! After all, it was not in the class-room,
nor in the boarding-house, that the essential elements of instruction could
be imparted which should qualify the youthful neophyte to deserve

those names. The final, the fundamental lesson could only be taught in
the school chapel; in the school chapel the centre of Dr Arnold's system
60   of education was inevitably fixed. There, too, the Doctor himself
appeared in the plentitude of his dignity and his enthusiasm. There,
with the morning sun shining on the freshly scrubbed faces of his 300
pupils, or, in the dusk of evening, through a glimmer of candles, his
stately form, rapt in devotion or vibrant with exhortation, would
65   dominate the scene. Every phase of the Church service seemed to receive
its supreme expression in his voice, his attitude, his look. During the
Te Deum laudamus [Thee, God, we praise] his whole countenance
would light up; and he read the Psalms with such conviction that boys
would often declare, after hearing him, that they understood them now
70   for the first time. It was his opinion that the creeds in public worship
ought to be used as triumphant hymns of thanksgiving, and, in
accordance with this view, although unfortunately he possessed no
natural gift for music, he regularly joined in the chanting of the Nicene
Creed[†] with a visible animation and a peculiar fervour, which it was
75   impossible to forget. The Communion service he regarded as a direct and
special counterpoise to that false communion and false companionship,
which, as he often observed, was a great source of mischief in the
school; and he bent himself down with glistening eyes, and trembling
voice, and looks of paternal solicitude, in the administration of the
80   elements. Nor was it only the different sections of the liturgy, but the
very divisions of the ecclesiastical year that reflected themselves in his
demeanour; the most careless observer, we are told, 'could not fail to
be struck by the triumphant exultation of his whole manner on Easter
Sunday'; though it needed a more familiar eye to discern the subtleties
85   in his bearing which were produced by the approach of Advent, and
the solemn thoughts which it awakened of the advance of human life,
the progress of the human race, and the condition of the Church of
England.
    At the end of the evening service the culminating moment of the week
90   had come: the Doctor delivered his sermon. It was not until then, as
all who had known him agreed, it was not until one had heard and
seen him in the pulpit, that one could fully realize what it was to be
face to face with Dr Arnold. The whole character of the man – so we
are assured – stood at last revealed. His congregation sat in fixed
95   attention (with the exception of the younger boys, whose thoughts
occasionally wandered), while he propounded the general principles
both of his own conduct and that of the Almighty, or indicated the
bearing of the incidents of Jewish history in the sixth century BC upon
the conduct of English schoolboys in 1830. Then, more than ever, his

---

Nicene Creed   Summary of Christian Faith formulated by the Council of Nicaea in 325

100   deep consciousness of the invisible world became evident; then, more
than ever, he seemed to be battling with the wicked one. For his sermons
ran on the eternal themes of the darkness of evil, the craft of the tempter,
the punishment of obliquity, and he justified the persistence with which
he dwelt upon these painful subjects by an appeal to a general principle:
105   'The spirit of Elijah,' he said, 'must ever precede the spirit of Christ.' The
impression produced upon the boys was remarkable. It was noticed that
even the most careless would sometimes, during the course of the week,
refer almost involuntarily to the sermon of the past Sunday, as a
condemnation of what they were doing. Others were heard to wonder
110   how it was that the Doctor's preaching, to which they had attended at the
time so assiduously, seemed, after all, to have such a small effect upon
what they did. An old gentleman, recalling those vanished hours, tried to
recapture in words his state of mind as he sat in the darkened chapel,
while Dr Arnold's sermons, with their high-toned exhortations, their grave
115   and sombre messages of incalculable import, clothed, like Dr Arnold's
body in its gown and bands, in the traditional stiffness of a formal
phraseology, reverberated through his adolescent ears. 'I used,' he said, 'to
listen to those sermons from first to last with a kind of awe.'

His success was not limited to his pupils and immediate auditors.
120   The sermons were collected into five large volumes; they were the first
of their kind; and they were received with admiration by a wide circle
of pious readers. Queen Victoria herself possessed a copy, in which
several passages were marked in pencil, by the Royal hand.

Dr Arnold's energies were by no means exhausted by his duties at
125   Rugby. He became known, not merely as a headmaster, but as a public
man. He held decided opinions upon a large number of topics; and he
enunciated them – based as they were almost invariably upon general
principles – in pamphlets, in prefaces, and in magazine articles, with
an impressive self-confidence. He was, as he constantly declared, a
130   Liberal. In his opinion, by the very constitution of human nature, the
principles of progress and reform had been those of wisdom and justice
in every age of the world – except one: that which had preceded the
fall of man from Paradise. Had he lived then, Dr Arnold would have
been a Conservative. As it was, his Liberalism was tempered by an
135   'abhorrence of the spirit of 1789, of the American War, of the French
Economistes, and of the English Whigs of the latter part of the
seventeenth century'; and he always entertained a profound respect for
the hereditary peerage. It might almost be said, in fact, that he was an
orthodox Liberal. He believed in toleration, too, within limits; that is
140   to say, in the toleration of those with whom he agreed. 'I would give
James Mill† as much opportunity for advocating his opinion,' he said,

James Mill   (1773–1836) liberal philosopher, father of J. S. Mill

'as is consistent with a voyage to Botany Bay.' He had become convinced
of the duty of sympathizing with the lower orders since he had made a
serious study of the Epistle of St James; but he perceived clearly that
145 the lower orders fell into two classes, that it was necessary to distinguish
between them. There were the 'good poor' – and there were the others.
'I am glad that you have made acquaintance with some of the good
poor,' he wrote to a Cambridge undergraduate; 'I quite agree with you
that it is most instructive to visit them.' Dr Arnold himself occasionally
150 visited them, in Rugby; and the condescension with which he shook
hands with old men and women of the working classes was long
remarked in the neighbourhood. As for the others, he regarded them
with horror and alarm. 'The disorders in our social state,' he wrote to
the Chevalier Bunsen[†] in 1834, 'appear to me to continue unabated.
155 You have heard, I doubt not, of the Trades Unions; a fearful engine of
mischief, ready to riot or to assassinate; and I see no counteracting
power.'
On the whole, his view of the condition of England was a gloomy
one. He recommended a correspondent to read 'Isaiah iii, v, xxii;
160 Jeremiah v, xxii, xxx; Amos iv; and Habakkuk ii', adding, 'you will be
struck, I think, with the close resemblance of our own state with that
of the Jews before the second destruction of Jerusalem'. When he was
told that the gift of tongues had descended on the Irvingites[†] at Glasgow,
he was not surprised. 'I should take it,' he said, 'merely as a sign of the
165 coming of the day of the Lord.' And he was convinced that the day of
the Lord was coming – 'the termination of one of the great αἰῶνες
[ages] of the human race.' Of that he had no doubt whatever; wherever
he looked he saw 'calamities, wars, tumults, pestilences, earthquakes,
etc., all marking the time of one of God's peculiar seasons of visitation'.
170 His only uncertainty was whether this termination of an αἰών [age]
would turn out to be the absolutely final one; but that he believed 'no
created being knows or can know'. In any case he had 'not the slightest
expectation of what is commonly meant by the Millennium.'[†] And his
only consolation was that he preferred the present Ministry, inefficient
175 as it was, to the Tories.
He had planned a great work on Church and State, in which he
intended to lay bare the causes and to point out the remedies of the
evils which afflicted society. Its theme was to be, not the alliance or
union, but the absolute identity of the Church and the State; and he
180 felt sure that if only this fundamental truth were fully realized by the
public, a general reformation would follow. Unfortunately, however,

---

Bunsen   Baron Christian (1791–1860)   (1792–1834) who believed in the gift of
    Prussian diplomat and theologian)   tongues
Irvingites   followers of the Rev Edward Irving   Millennium   the coming of a golden age

as time went on, the public seemed to realize it less and less. In spite of his protests, not only were Jews admitted to Parliament, but a Jew was actually appointed a governor of Christ's Hospital;[†] and Scripture was
185   not made an obligatory subject at the London University.

There was one point in his theory which was not quite plain to Dr Arnold. If Church and State were absolutely identical, it became important to decide precisely which classes of persons were to be excluded, owing to their beliefs, from the community. Jews, for instance,
190   were decidedly outside the pale; while Dissenters – so Dr Arnold argued – were as decidedly within it. But what was the position of the Unitarians?[†] Were they, or were they not, Members of the Church of Christ? This was one of those puzzling questions which deepened the frown upon the Doctor's forehead and intensified the pursing of his
195   lips. He thought long and earnestly upon the subject; he wrote elaborate letters on it to various correspondents; but his conclusions remained indefinite. 'My great objection to Unitarianism,' he wrote, 'in its present form in England, is that it makes Christ virtually dead.' Yet he expressed 'a fervent hope that if we could get rid of the Athanasian Creed[†] many
200   good Unitarians would join their fellow Christians in bowing the knee to Him who is Lord both of the dead and the living'. Amid these perplexities, it was disquieting to learn that 'Unitarianism is becoming very prevalent in Boston'. He inquired anxiously as to its 'complexion' there; but received no very illuminating answer. The whole matter
205   continued to be wrapped in a painful obscurity: there were, he believed, Unitarians and Unitarians; and he could say no more.

In the meantime, pending the completion of his great work, he occupied himself with putting forward various suggestions of a practical kind. He advocated the restoration of the Order of Deacons, which, he
210   observed, had long been '*quoad*' [to the extent of] the reality, dead'; for he believed that 'some plan of this sort might be the small end of the wedge, by which Antichrist[†] might hereafter be burst asunder like the Dragon of Bel's temple.'[†] But the Order of Deacons was never restored, and Dr Arnold turned his attention elsewhere, urging in a
215   weighty pamphlet the desirability of authorizing military officers, in congregations where it was impossible to procure the presence of clergy, to administer the Eucharist, as well as Baptism. It was with the object of laying such views as these before the public – 'to tell them plainly', as he said, 'the evils that exist, and lead them, if I can, to their causes

---

Christ's Hospital   the distinguished 'Blue-Coat' school for boys

Unitarians   the Unitarian Society of Christians who rejected the doctrine of the Trinity was founded in 1791

Athanasian Creed   attributed to St Athanasius (*c.* 296–373), the Creed places less emphasis

than the Nicene Creed on belief in the Trinity in the Anglican Church Service

Antichrist   supposed by some to precede Christ's second coming

Dragon of Bel's temple   the story is an Apocryphal addition to Daniel

220 and remedies' – that he started, in 1831, a weekly newspaper, *The Englishman's Register*. The paper was not a success, in spite of the fact that it set out to improve its readers morally and that it preserved, in every article, an avowedly Christian tone. After a few weeks, and after he had spent upon it more than £200, it came to an end.

225 Altogether, the prospect was decidedly discouraging. After all his efforts, the absolute identity of Church and State remained as unrecognized as ever. 'So deeply,' he was at last obliged to confess, 'is the distinction between the Church and the State seated in our laws, our language, and our very notions, that nothing less than a miraculous
230 interposition of God's Providence seems capable of eradicating it.' Dr Arnold waited in vain.

But he did not wait in idleness. He attacked the same question from another side: he explored the writings of the Christian Fathers, and began to compose a commentary on the New Testament. In his view,
235 the Scriptures were as fit a subject as any other book for free inquiry and the exercise of the individual judgement, and it was in this spirit that he set about the interpretation of them. He was not afraid of facing apparent difficulties of admitting inconsistencies, or even errors, in the sacred text. Thus he observed that 'in Chronicles xi, 20, and xiii, 2,
240 there is a decided difference in the parentage of Abijah's mother'; – 'which', he added, 'is curious on any supposition'. And at one time he had serious doubts as to the authorship of the Epistle to the Hebrews. But he was able, on various problematical points, to suggest interesting solutions. At first, for instance, he could not but be startled by the
245 cessation of miracles in the early Church; but on consideration he came to the conclusion that this phenomenon might be 'truly accounted for by the supposition that none but the Apostles ever conferred miraculous powers, and that therefore they ceased of course after one generation'. Nor did he fail to base his exegesis, whenever possible, upon an appeal
250 to general principles. One of his admirers points out how Dr Arnold 'vindicated God's command to Abraham to sacrifice his son, and to the Jews to exterminate the nations of Canaan, by explaining the principles on which these commands were given, and their reference to the moral state of those to whom they were addressed; thereby educing light out
255 of darkness, unravelling the thread of God's religious education of the human race, and holding up God's marvellous counsels to the devout wonder and meditation of the thoughtful believer.'

There was one of his friends, however, who did not share this admiration for the Doctor's methods of Scriptural interpretation. W. G.
260 Ward,[†] while still a young man at Oxford, had come under his influence,

---

W. G. *Ward* (1812–82) 'Ideal Ward', a fellow of Balliol College, Oxford, until the   university condemned him for heresy

and had been for some time one of his most enthusiastic disciples. But the star of Newman[†] was rising at the University; Ward soon felt the attraction of that magnetic power; and his belief in his old teacher began to waver. It was, in particular, Dr Arnold's treatment of the
265 Scriptures which filled Ward's argumentative mind, at first with distrust, and at last with positive antagonism. To subject the Bible to free inquiry, to exercise upon it the criticism of the individual judgement – where might not such methods lead? Who could say that they would not end in Socinianism?[†] – nay, in Atheism itself? If the text of Scripture was
270 to be submitted to the searchings of human reason, how could the question of its inspiration escape the same tribunal? And the proofs of revelation, and even of the existence of God? What human faculty was capable of deciding upon such enormous questions? And would not the logical result be a condition of universal doubt? 'On a very moderate
275 computation,' Ward argued, 'five times the amount of a man's natural life might qualify a person endowed with extraordinary genius to have some faint notion (though even this we doubt) on which side truth lies.' It was not that he had the slightest doubt of Dr Arnold's orthodoxy – Dr Arnold, whose piety was universally recognized – Dr Arnold, who
280 had held up to scorn and execration Strauss's *Leben Jesu*[†] without reading it. What Ward complained of was the Doctor's lack of logic, not his lack of faith. Could he not see that if he really carried out his own principles to a logical conclusion he would eventually find himself, precisely, in the arms of Strauss? The young man, whose personal
285 friendship remained unshaken, determined upon an interview, and went down to Rugby primed with first principles, syllogisms, and dilemmas. Finding that the headmaster was busy in school, he spent the afternoon reading novels on the sofa in the drawing-room. When at last, late in the evening, the Doctor returned, tired out with his day's work, Ward
290 fell upon him with all his vigour. The contest was long and furious; it was also entirely inconclusive. When it was over, Ward, with none of his brilliant arguments disposed of, and none of his probing questions satisfactorily answered, returned to the University, to plunge headlong into the vortex of the Oxford Movement;[†] and Dr Arnold, worried,
295 perplexed, and exhausted, went to bed, where he remained for the next thirty-six hours.

The Commentary on the New Testament was never finished, and the

---

Newman John Henry Newman (1809–90; Cardinal, 1879), leader of Anglo-Catholic opinion in Oxford; his defection to the Roman Catholic Church, in 1845, caused a national furore
Socinianism a sixteenth-century Italian system of belief which denied Christ's divinity
Strauss's Leben Jesu *Das Leben Jesu Kritisch*

Bearbeitet (1835–6) by David Friedrich Strauss (1808–74) was an historical critique of the gospel accounts of the life of Jesus
Oxford Movement Newman and others at Oxford led a movement to reassert the divine authority of the Church of England; many Anglicans feared that they were not 'good Protestants'

great work of Church and State itself remained a fragment. Dr Arnold's
active mind was diverted from political and theological speculations to
300 the study of philology and to historical composition. His Roman
History, which he regarded as 'the chief monument of his historical
fame', was based partly upon the researches of Niebuhr,[†] and partly
upon an aversion to Gibbon. 'My highest ambition,' he wrote, 'is to
make my history the very reverse of Gibbon – in this respect, that
305 whereas the whole spirit of his work, from its low morality, is hostile
to religion, without speaking directly against it, so my greatest desire
would be, in my History, by its high morals and its general tone, to be
of use to the cause without actually bringing it forward.' These efforts
were rewarded, in 1841, by the Professorship of Modern History at
310 Oxford. Meanwhile, he was engaged in the study of the Sanskrit and
Slavonic languages, bringing out an elaborate edition of Thucydides,[†]
and carrying on a voluminous correspondence upon a multitude of
topics with a large circle of men of learning. At his death, his published
works, composed during such intervals as he could spare from the
315 management of a great public school, filled, besides a large number of
pamphlets and articles, no less than seventeen volumes. It was no
wonder that Carlyle,[†] after a visit to Rugby, should have characterized
Dr Arnold as a man of 'unhasting, unresting diligence'.

Mrs Arnold, too, no doubt agreed with Carlyle. During the first eight
320 years of their married life, she bore him six children; and four more
were to follow. In this large and growing domestic circle his hours of
relaxation were spent. There those who had only known him in his
professional capacity were surprised to find him displaying the tenderness and jocosity of a parent. The dignified and stern headmaster was
325 actually seen to dandle infants and to caracole[†] upon the hearthrug on
all fours. Yet, we are told, 'the sense of his authority as a father was
never lost in his playfulness as a companion'. On more serious occasions,
the voice of the spiritual teacher sometimes made itself heard. An
intimate friend described how 'on a comparison having been made in
330 his family circle, which seemed to place St Paul above St John,' the
tears rushed to the Doctor's eyes and how, repeating one of the verses
from St John, he begged that the comparison might never again be
made. The longer holidays were spent in Westmorland, where, rambling
with his offspring among the mountains, gathering wild flowers, and
335 pointing out the beauties of Nature, Dr Arnold enjoyed, as he himself
would often say, 'an almost awful happiness'. Music he did not
appreciate, though he occasionally desired his eldest boy, Matthew, to

---

Niebuhr Barthold Georg (1776–1831)
  German historian
Thucydides Greek historian, *c.* 460–400 BC

Carlyle Thomas Carlyle (1795–1881),
  historian and theorist, visited Rugby in 1842
caracole prance

sing him the Confirmation Hymn of Dr Hinds,[†] to which he had become
endeared, owing to its use in Rugby Chapel. But his lack of ear was, he
340   considered, amply recompensed by his love of flowers; 'they are my
music', he declared. Yet, in such a matter, he was careful to refrain
from an excess of feeling, such as, in his opinion, marked the famous
lines[†] of Wordsworth:

345
> To me the meanest flower that blows can give
> Thoughts that do often lie too deep for tears.

He found the sentiment morbid. 'Life,' he said, 'is not long enough to
take such intense interest in objects in themselves so little.' As for the
animal world, his feelings toward it were of a very different cast. 'The
whole subject,' he said, 'of the brute creation is to me one of such
350   painful mystery, that I dare not approach it.' The Unitarians themselves
were a less distressing thought.

Once or twice he found time to visit the Continent, and the letters
and journals recording in minute detail his reflections and impressions
in France or Italy show us that Dr Arnold preserved, in spite of the
355   distractions of foreign scenes and foreign manners, his accustomed
habits of mind. Taking very little interest in works of art, he was
occasionally moved by the beauty of natural objects; but his principal
preoccupation remained with the moral aspects of things. From this
point of view, he found much to reprehend in the conduct of his own
360   countrymen. 'I fear,' he wrote, 'that our countrymen who live abroad
are not in the best possible moral state, however much they may do in
science or literature.' And this was unfortunate, because 'a thorough
English gentleman – Christian, manly, and enlightened – is more, I
believe, than Guizot[†] or Sismondi[†] could comprehend; it is a finer
365   specimen of human nature than any other country, I believe, could
furnish'. Nevertheless, our travellers would imitate foreign customs
without discrimination, 'as in the absurd habit of not eating fish with a
knife, borrowed from the French, who do it because they have no knives
fit for use'. Places, no less than people, aroused similar reflections. By
370   Pompeii, Dr Arnold was not particularly impressed. 'There is only,' he
observed, 'the same sort of interest with which one would see the ruins
of Sodom and Gomorrah, but indeed there is less. One is not authorized
to ascribe so solemn a character to the destruction of Pompeii.'
The lake of Como moved him profoundly. As he gazed upon the
375   overwhelming beauty around him, he thought of 'moral evil', and was
appalled by the contrast. 'May the sense of moral evil', he prayed, 'be

---

Dr Hinds   Samuel Hinds (1793–1872), author
of the hymn 'Lord, Shall thy children come'
lines   the closing lines of the ode 'Intimations
of Immortality'

Guizot   F. P. G. Guizot (1787–1874) French
historian and politician
Sismondi   L. S. Sismondi (1773–1842) French
historian

as strong in me as my delight in external beauty, for in a deep sense of moral evil, more perhaps than in anything else, abides a saving knowledge of God!'

380   His prayer was answered: Dr Arnold was never in any danger of losing his sense of moral evil. If the landscapes of Italy only served to remind him of it, how could he forget it among the boys at Rugby School? The daily sight of so many young creatures in the hands of the Evil One filled him with agitated grief. 'When the spring and activity
385   of youth,' he wrote, 'is altogether unsanctified by anything pure and elevated in its desires, it becomes a spectacle that is as dizzying and almost more morally distressing than the shouts and gambols of a set of lunatics.' One thing struck him as particularly strange: 'It is very startling,' he said, 'to see so much of sin combined with so little sorrow.'
390   The naughtiest boys positively seemed to enjoy themselves most. There were moments when he almost lost faith in his whole system of education, when he began to doubt whether some far more radical reforms than any he had attempted might not be necessary, before the multitude of children under his charge – shouting and gambolling, and
395   yet plunged all the while in moral evil – could ever be transformed into a set of Christian gentlemen. But then he remembered his general principles, the conduct of Jehovah with the Chosen People, and the childhood of the human race. No, it was for him to make himself, as one of his pupils afterwards described him, in the words of Bacon,†
400   'kin to God in spirit'; he would rule the school majestically from on high. He would deliver a series of sermons analysing 'the six vices' by which 'great schools were corrupted, and changed from the likeness of God's temple to that of a den of thieves'. He would exhort, he would denounce, he would sweep through the corridors, he would turn the
405   pages of Facciolati's Lexicon† more imposingly than ever; and the rest he would leave to the Praepostors† in the Sixth Form.

Upon the boys in the Sixth Form, indeed, a strange burden would seem to have fallen. Dr Arnold himself was very well aware of this. 'I cannot deny,' he told them in a sermon, 'that you have an anxious
410   duty – a duty which some might suppose was too heavy for your years'; and every term he pointed out to them, in a short address, the responsibilities of their position, and impressed upon them 'the enormous influence' they possessed 'for good or for evil'. Nevertheless most youths of seventeen, in spite of the warnings of the elders, have a
415   singular trick of carrying moral burdens lightly. The Doctor might

---

Bacon   Francis Bacon, viscount St Albans
(1561–1626), in his essay 'Of Atheism'
Facciolati's Lexicon   Latin dictionary

composed by Jacopo Facciolati (1682–1769)
Praepostors   senior boys with responsibility
for discipline

preach and look grave; but young Brooke† was ready enough to preside at a fight behind the Chapel, though he was in the Sixth, and knew that fighting was against the rules. At their best, it may be supposed that the Praepostors administered a kind of barbaric justice; but they were not always at their best, and the pages of *Tom Brown's Schooldays* show us what was no doubt the normal condition of affairs under Dr Arnold, when the boys in the Sixth Form were weak or brutal, and the blackguard Flashman, in the intervals of swigging brandy-punch with his boon companions, amused himself by roasting fags† before the fire.

1918

Brooke a senior boy in the novel about Rugby, *Tom Brown's Schooldays* (1857), by Thomas Hughes (1822–96)

fags junior boys. The bully Flashman 'roasts' the young Tom Brown

P. G. Wodehouse
1881–1975

Sir Pelham Grenville 'Plum' Wodehouse (pronounced Woodhouse) was born in Guildford and educated at Dulwich College. He worked for two years in a London bank but left in 1903 to write for a living. In his school-stories for the boys' magazine *The Captain* he began to create the idealised comic world he was later to evolve in the course of dozens of novels and books of stories. Jeeves, the perfect manservant, his 'mentally negligible' employer Bertie Wooster and, in another series of books, the absent-minded Lord Emsworth of Blandings Castle, head Wodehouse's huge cast of vivid, lovable figures of farce. T. S. Eliot and Evelyn Waugh were among the earliest critical admirers of his skills as a stylist. Wodehouse emigrated to America in 1909 and spent most of the rest of his life there. He was knighted just before his death.

From THE INIMITABLE JEEVES
The Great Sermon Handicap

After Goodwood's[†] over, I generally find that I get a bit restless. I'm not much of a lad for the birds and the trees and the great open spaces as a rule, but there's no doubt that London's not at its best in August, and rather tends to give me the pip and make me think of popping
5 down into the country till things have bucked up a trifle. London, about a couple of weeks after that spectacular finish of young Bingo's which I've just been telling you about, was empty and smelled of burning asphalt. All my pals were away, most of the theatres were shut, and they were taking up Piccadilly in large spadefuls.
10   It was most infernally hot. As I sat in the old flat one night trying to muster up energy enough to go to bed, I felt I couldn't stand it much longer: and when Jeeves came in with tissue-restorers on a tray I put the thing to him squarely.
     'Jeeves,' I said, wiping the brow and gasping like a stranded goldfish,
15 'it's beastly hot.'

Goodwood   a racecourse in Sussex; the races are held at the end of July

'The weather *is* oppressive, sir.'

'Not all the soda, Jeeves.'

'No, sir.'

20 'I think we've had about enough of the metrop. for the time being, and require a change. Shift-ho, I think, Jeeves, what?'

'Just as you say, sir. There is a letter on the tray, sir.'

'By Jove, Jeeves, that was practically poetry. Rhymed, did you notice?'
I opened the letter. 'I say, this is rather extraordinary.'

'Sir?'

25 'You know Twing Hall?'

'Yes, sir.'

'Well, Mr Little is there.'

'Indeed, sir?'

'Absolutely in the flesh. He's had to take another of those tutoring
30 jobs.'

After that fearful mix-up at Goodwood, when young Bingo Little, a broken man, had touched me for a tenner and whizzed silently off into the unknown, I had been all over the place, asking mutual friends if they had heard anything of him, but nobody had. And all the time he
35 had been at Twing Hall. Rummy. And I'll tell you why it was rummy. Twing Hall belongs to old Lord Wickhammersley, a great pal of my guv'nor's when he was alive, and I have a standing invitation to pop down there when I like. I generally put in a week or two some time in the summer, and I was thinking of going there before I read the letter.

40 'And, what's more, Jeeves, my cousin Claude, and my cousin Eustace – you remember them?'

'Very vividly, sir.'

'Well, they're down there, too, reading for some exam. or other with the vicar. I used to read with him myself at one time. He's known far
45 and wide as a pretty hot coach for those of fairly feeble intellect. Well, when I tell you he got *me* through Smalls,[†] you'll gather that he's a bit of a hummer. I call this most extraordinary.'

I read the letter again. It was from Eustace. Claude and Eustace are twins, and more or less generally admitted to be the curse of the human
50 race.

> The Vicarage,
> Twing, Glos.
>
> *Dear Bertie – Do you want to make a bit of money? I hear*
55 > *you had a bad Goodwood, so you probably do. Well, come*
> *down here quick and get in on the biggest sporting event*

Smalls   examinations at Oxford

of the season. I'll explain when I see you, but you can take it from me it's all right.

Claude and I are with a reading-party at old Heppenstall's. There are nine of us, not counting your pal Bingo Little, who is tutoring the kid up at the Hall.

Don't miss this golden opportunity, which may never occur again. Come and join us.

Yours,

Eustace

I handed this to Jeeves. He studied it thoughtfully.

'What do you make of it? A rummy communication, what?'

'Very high-spirited young gentlemen, sir, Mr Claude and Mr Eustace. Up to some game, I should be disposed to imagine.'

'Yes. But what game, do you think?'

'It is impossible to say, sir. Did you observe that the letter continues over the page?'

'Eh, what?' I grabbed the thing. This was what was on the other side of the last page:

SERMON HANDICAP
RUNNERS AND BETTING
PROBABLE STARTERS

Rev. Joseph Tucker (Badgwick), scratch.
Rev. Leonard Starkie (Stapleton), scratch.
Rev. Alexander Jones (Upper Bingley), receives three minutes.
Rev. W. Dix (Little Clickton-in-the-Wold), receives five minutes.
Rev. Francis Heppenstall (Twing), receives eight minutes.
Rev. Cuthbert Dibble (Boustead Parva), receives nine minutes.
Rev. Orlo Hough (Boustead Magna), receives nine minutes.
Rev. J. J. Roberts (Fale-by-the-Water), receives ten minutes.
Rev. G. Hayward (Lower Bingley), receives twelve minutes.
Rev. James Bates (Gandle-by-the-Hill), receives fifteen minutes.
(The above have arrived)
PRICES. – *5–2, Tucker, Starkie; 3–1, Jones; 9–2, Dix; 6–1, Heppenstall, Dibble, Hough; 100–8 any other.*

It baffled me.

'Do you understand it, Jeeves?'

'No, sir.'

'Well, I think we ought to have a look into it, anyway, what?'

'Undoubtedly, sir.'

'Right-o, then. Pack our spare dickey† and a toothbrush in a neat

---

dickey   usually a detachable, stiff, white shirt-front; here, facetiously, an evening-dress shirt

brown-paper parcel, send a wire to Lord Wickhammersley to say we're coming, and buy two tickets on the five-ten at Paddington to-morrow.'

*

100 The five-ten was late as usual, and everybody was dressing for dinner when I arrived at the Hall. It was only by getting into my evening things in record time and taking the stairs to the dining-room in a couple of bounds that I managed to dead-heat with the soup. I slid into the vacant chair, and found that I was sitting next to old Wickhammersley's youngest daughter, Cynthia.

105 'Oh, hallo, old thing,' I said.

Great pals we've always been. In fact, there was a time when I had an idea I was in love with Cynthia. However it blew over. A dashed pretty and lively and attractive girl, mind you, but full of ideals and all that. I may be wronging her, but I have an idea that she's the sort of

110 girl who would want a fellow to carve out a career and what not. I know I've heard her speak favourably of Napoleon. So what with one thing and another the jolly old frenzy sort of petered out, and now we're just pals. I think she's a topper, and she thinks me next door to a looney, so everything's nice and matey.

115 'Well, Bertie, so you've arrived?'

'Oh, yes, I've arrived. Yes, here I am. I say, I seem to have plunged into the middle of quite a young dinner-party. Who are all these coves?'

'Oh, just people from round about. You know most of them. You remember Colonel Willis, and the Spencers –'

120 'Of course, yes. And there's old Heppenstall. Who's the other clergyman next to Mrs Spencer?'

'Mr Hayward, from Lower Bingley.'

'What an amazing lot of clergymen there are round here. Why, there's another, next to Mrs Willis.'

125 'That's Mr Bates, Mr Heppenstall's nephew. He's an assistant-master at Eton. He's down here during the summer holidays, acting as *locum tenens* [substitute] for Mr Spettigue, the rector of Gandle-by-the-Hill.'

'I thought I knew his face. He was in his fourth year at Oxford when I was a fresher. Rather a blood.[†] Got his rowing-blue[†] and all that.' I

130 took another look round the table, and spotted young Bingo. 'Ah, there he is,' I said. 'There's the old egg.'

'There's who?'

'Young Bingo Little. Great pal of mine. He's tutoring your brother, you know.'

135 'Good gracious! Is he a friend of yours?'

---

blood . . . blue a blood is good at sports; a
blue rows for the university against Cambridge

'Rather! Known him all my life.'

'Then tell me, Bertie, is he at all weak in the head?'

'Weak in the head?'

'I don't mean simply because he's a friend of yours. But he's so
strange in his manner.'

'How do you mean?'

'Well, he keeps looking at me so oddly.'

'Oddly? How? Give an imitation.'

'I can't in front of all these people.'

'Yes, you can. I'll hold my napkin up.'

'All right, then. Quick, There!'

Considering that she had only about a second and a half to do it
in, I must say it was a jolly fine exhibition. She opened her mouth
and eyes pretty wide and let her jaw drop sideways, and managed
to look so like a dyspeptic calf that I recognized the symptoms
immediately.

'Oh, that's all right,' I said. 'No need to be alarmed. He's simply in
love with you.'

'In love with me. Don't be absurd.'

'My dear old thing, you don't know young Bingo. He can fall in love
with *anybody*.'

'Thank you!'

'Oh, I didn't mean it that way, you know. I don't wonder at his
taking to you. Why, I was in love with you myself once.'

'Once? Ah! And all that remains now are the cold ashes. This isn't
one of your tactful evenings, Bertie.'

'Well, my dear sweet thing, dash it all, considering that you gave me
the bird and nearly laughed yourself into a permanent state of hiccoughs
when I asked you –'

'Oh, I'm not reproaching you. No doubt there were faults on both
sides. He's very good-looking, isn't he?'

'Good-looking? Bingo? Bingo good-looking? No, I say, come now,
really!'

'I mean, compared with some people,' said Cynthia.

Some time after this, Lady Wickhammersley gave the signal for the
females of the species to leg it, and they duly stampeded. I didn't get a
chance of talking to young Bingo when they'd gone, and later, in the
drawing-room, he didn't show up. I found him eventually in his room,
lying on the bed with his feet on the rail, smoking a toofah. There was
a notebook on the counterpane beside him.

'Hallo, old scream,' I said.

'Hallo, Bertie,' he replied, in what seemed to me rather a moody,
distrait sort of manner.

'Rummy finding you down here. I take it your uncle cut off your

180   allowance after that Goodwood binge and you had to take this tutoring
       job to keep the wolf from the door?'
       'Correct,' said young Bingo tersely.
       'Well, you might have let your pals know where you were.'
       He frowned darkly.
185   'I didn't want them to know where I was. I wanted to creep away
       and hide myself. I've been through a bad time, Bertie, these last weeks.
       The sun ceased to shine –'
       'That's curious. We've had gorgeous weather in London.'
       'The birds ceased to sing –'
190   'What birds?'
       'What the devil does it matter what birds?' said young Bingo, with
       some asperity. 'Any birds. The birds round about here. You don't
       expect me to specify them by their pet names, do you? I tell you, Bertie,
       it hit me hard at first, very hard.'
195   'What hit you?' I simply couldn't follow the blighter.
       'Charlotte's calculated callousness.'
       'Oh, ah!' I've seen poor old Bingo through so many unsuccessful
       love-affairs that I'd almost forgotten there was a girl mixed up with
       that Goodwood business. Of course! Charlotte Corday Rowbotham.
200   And she had given him the raspberry, I remembered, and gone off with
       Comrade Butt.
       'I went through torments. Recently, however, I've – er – bucked up a
       bit. Tell me, Bertie, what are you doing down here? I didn't know you
       knew these people.'
205   'Me? Why, I've known them since I was a kid.'
       Young Bingo put his feet down with a thud.
       'Do you mean to say you've known Lady Cynthia all that time?'
       'Rather! She can't have been seven when I met her first.'
       'Good Lord!' said young Bingo. He looked at me for the first time as
210   though I amounted to something, and swallowed a mouthful of smoke
       the wrong way. 'I love that girl, Bertie,' he went on, when he'd finished
       coughing.
       'Yes. Nice girl, of course.'
       He eyed me with pretty deep loathing.
215   'Don't speak of her in that horrible casual way. She's an angel. An
       angel! Was she talking about me at all at dinner, Bertie?'
       'Oh, yes.'
       'What did she say?'
       'I remember one thing. She said she thought you good-looking.'
220   Young Bingo closed his eyes in a sort of ecstasy. Then he picked up
       the notebook.
       'Pop off now, old man, there's a good chap,' he said, in a hushed,
       far-away voice. 'I've got a bit of writing to do.'

'Writing?'

225 'Poetry, if you must know. I wish the dickens,' said young Bingo, not without some bitterness, 'she had been christened something except Cynthia. There isn't a dam' word in the language it rhymes with. Ye gods, how I could have spread myself if she had only been called Jane!'

Bright and early next morning, as I lay in bed blinking at the sunlight on 230 the dressing-table and wondering when Jeeves was going to show up with a cup of tea, a heavy weight descended on my toes, and the voice of young Bingo polluted the air. The blighter had apparently risen with the lark.

'Leave me,' I said, 'I would be alone. I can't see anybody till I've had my tea.'

235 'When Cynthia smiles,' said young Bingo, 'the skies are blue; the world takes on a roseate hue: birds in the garden trill and sing, and Joy is king of everything, when Cynthia smiles.' He coughed, changing gears. 'When Cynthia frowns –'

'What the devil are you talking about?'

240 'I'm reading you my poem. The one I wrote to Cynthia last night. I'll go on, shall I?'

'No!'

'No?'

'No. I haven't had my tea.'

245 At this moment Jeeves came in with the good old beverage, and I sprang on it with a glad cry. After a couple of sips things looked a bit brighter. Even young Bingo didn't offend the eye to quite such an extent. By the time I'd finished the first cup I was a new man, so much so that I not only permitted but encouraged the poor fish to read the 250 rest of the bally thing, and even went so far as to criticize the scansion of the fourth line of the fifth verse. We were still arguing the point when the door burst open and in blew Claude and Eustace. One of the things which discourage me about rural life is the frightful earliness with which events begin to break loose. I've stayed at places in the 255 country where they've jerked me out of the dreamless at about six-thirty to go for a jolly swim in the lake. At Twing, thank heaven, they know me, and let me breakfast in bed.

The twins seemed pleased to see me.

'Good old Bertie!' said Claude.

260 'Stout fellow!' said Eustace. 'The Rev. told us you had arrived. I thought that letter of mine would fetch you.'

'You can always bank on Bertie,' said Claude. 'A sportsman to the finger-tips. Well, has Bingo told you about it?'

'Not a word. He's been –'

265 'We've been talking,' said Bingo hastily, 'of other matters.'

Claude pinched the last slice of thin bread-and-butter, and Eustace poured himself out a cup of tea.

'It's like this, Bertie,' said Eustace, settling down cosily. 'As I told
you in my letter, there are nine of us marooned in this desert spot,
reading with old Heppenstall. Well, of course, nothing is jollier than
sweating up the Classics when it's a hundred in the shade, but there
does come a time when you begin to feel the need of a little relaxation;
and, by Jove, there are absolutely no facilities for relaxation in this
place whatever. And then Steggles got this idea. Steggles is one of our
reading-party, and, between ourselves, rather a worm as a general thing.
Still you have to give him credit for getting this idea.'

'What idea?'

'Well, you know how many parsons there are round about here.
There are about a dozen hamlets within a radius of six miles, and each
hamlet has a church and each church has a parson and each parson
preaches a sermon every Sunday. To-morrow week – Sunday the twenty-
third – we're running off the great Sermon Handicap. Steggles is making
the book. Each parson is to be clocked by a reliable steward of the
course, and the one that preaches the longest sermon wins. Did you
study the race-card I sent you?'

'I couldn't understand what it was all about.'

'Why, you chump, it gives the handicaps and the current odds on
each starter. I've got another one here, in case you've lost yours. Take
a careful look at it. It gives you the thing in a nutshell. Jeeves, old son,
do you want a sporting flutter?'

'Sir?' said Jeeves, who had just meandered in with my breakfast.

Claude explained the scheme. Amazing the way Jeeves grasped it
right off. But he merely smiled in a paternal sort of way.

'Thank you, sir, I think not.'

'Well, you're with us, Bertie, aren't you?' said Claude, sneaking a
roll and a slice of bacon. 'Have you studied that card? Well, tell me,
does anything strike you about it?'

Of course it did. It had struck me the moment I looked at it.

'Why, it's a sitter for old Heppenstall,' I said. 'He's got the event
sewed up in a parcel. There isn't a parson in the land who could give
him eight minutes. Your pal Steggles must be an ass, giving him a
handicap like that. Why, in the days when I was with him, old
Heppenstall never used to preach under half an hour, and there was
one sermon of his on Brotherly Love which lasted forty-five minutes if
it lasted a second. Has he lost his vim lately, or what is it?'

'Not a bit of it,' said Eustace. 'Tell him what happened, Claude.'

'Why', said Claude, 'the first Sunday we were here, we all went to
Twing church, and old Heppenstall preached a sermon that was well
under twenty minutes. This is what happened. Steggles didn't notice it,
and the Rev. didn't notice it himself, but Eustace and I both spotted
that he had dropped a chunk of at least half a dozen pages out of his

sermon-case as he was walking up to the pulpit. He sort of flickered when he got to the gap in the manuscript, but carried on all right, and Steggles went away with the impression that twenty minutes or a bit
315 under was his usual form. The next Sunday we heard Tucker and Starkie, and they both went well over the thirty-five minutes, so Steggles arranged the handicapping as you see on the card. You must come into this, Bertie. You see, the trouble is that I haven't a bean, and Eustace hasn't a bean, and Bingo Little hasn't a bean, so you'll have to finance
320 the syndicate. Don't weaken! It's just putting money in all our pockets. Well, we'll have to be getting back now. Think the thing over, and phone me later in the day. And, if you let us down, Bertie, may a cousin's curse — Come on, Claude, old thing.'

The more I studied the scheme, the better it looked.
325 'How about it, Jeeves?' I said.

Jeeves smiled gently, and drifted out.

'Jeeves has no sporting blood,' said Bingo.

'Well, I have. I'm coming into this. Claude's quite right. It's like finding money by the wayside.'
330 'Good man!' said Bingo. 'Now I can see daylight. Say I have a tenner on Heppenstall, and cop; that'll give me a bit in hand to back Pink Pill with in the two o'clock at Gatwick the week after next: cop on that, put the pile on Musk-Rat for the one-thirty at Lewes, and there I am with a nice little sum to take to Alexandra Park on September the tenth,
335 when I've got a tip straight from the stable.'

It sounded like a bit out of *Smiles's Self-Help*.[†]

'And then,' said young Bingo, 'I'll be in a position to go to my uncle and beard him in his lair somewhat. He's quite a bit of a snob, you know, and when he hears that I'm going to marry the daughter of an
340 earl —'

'I say, old man,' I couldn't help saying, 'aren't you looking ahead rather far?'

'Oh, that's all right. It's true nothing's actually settled yet, but she practically told me the other day she was fond of me.'
345 'What!'

'Well, she said that the sort of man she liked was the self-reliant, manly man with strength, good looks, character, ambition, and initiative.'

'Leave me, laddie,' I said. 'Leave me to my fried egg.'

*

Directly I'd got up I went to the phone, snatched Eustace away from
350 his morning's work, and instructed him to put a tenner on the Twing

---

Smiles's Self-Help   *Self-Help* (1859) by Samuel
Smiles (1812–1904), urged hard work and
thrift; it was a best-seller in the nineteenth
century

flier at current odds for each of the syndicate; and after lunch Eustace
rang me up to say that he had done business at a snappy seven-to-one,
the odds having lengthened owing to a rumour in knowledgeable circles
that the Rev. was subject to hay-fever, and was taking big chances
355   strolling in the paddock behind the Vicarage in the early mornings. And
it was dashed lucky, I thought next day, that we had managed to get
the money on in time, for on the Sunday morning old Heppenstall fairly
took the bit between his teeth, and gave us thirty-six solid minutes on
Certain Popular Superstitions. I was sitting next to Steggles in the pew,
360   and I saw him blench visibly. He was a little, rat-faced fellow, with
shifty eyes and a suspicious nature. The first thing he did when we
emerged into the open air was to announce, formally, that anyone who
fancied the Rev. could now be accommodated at fifteen-to-eight on,
and he added in a rather nasty manner, that if he had his way, this sort
365   of in-and-out running would be brought to the attention of the Jockey
Club, but that he supposed that there was nothing to be done about it.
This ruinous price checked the punters at once, and there was little
money in sight. And so matters stood till just after lunch on Tuesday
afternoon, when, as I was strolling up and down in front of the house
370   with a cigarette, Claude and Eustace came bursting up the drive on
bicycles, dripping with momentous news.

'Bertie,' said Claude, deeply agitated 'unless we take immediate action
and do a bit of quick thinking, we're in the cart.'

'What's the matter?'

375   'G. Hayward's the matter,' said Eustace morosely. 'The Lower Bingley
starter.'

'We never even considered him,' said Claude. 'Somehow or other, he
got overlooked. It's always the way. Steggles overlooked him. We all
overlooked him. But Eustace and I happened by the merest fluke to be
380   riding through Lower Bingley this morning, and there was a wedding
on at the church, and it suddenly struck us that it wouldn't be a bad
move to get a line on G. Hayward's form, in case he might be a dark
horse.'

'And it was jolly lucky we did,' said Eustace. 'He delivered an address
385   of twenty-six minutes by Claude's stopwatch. At a village wedding,
mark you! What'll he do when he really extends himself!'

'There's only one thing to be done, Bertie,' said Claude. 'You must
spring some more funds, so that we can hedge on Hayward and save
ourselves.'

390   'But —'

'Well, it's the only way out.'

'But I say, you know, I hate the idea of all that money we put on
Heppenstall being chucked away.'

'What else can you suggest? You don't suppose the Rev. can give

395 this absolute marvel a handicap and win, do you?'

'I've got it!' I said.

'What?'

'I see a way by which we can make it safe for our nominee. I'll pop over this afternoon, and ask him as personal favour to preach that
400 sermon of his on Brotherly Love on Sunday.'

Claude and Eustace looked at each other, like those chappies in the poem, with a wild surmise.

'It's a scheme,' said Claude.

'A jolly brainy scheme,' said Eustace. 'I didn't think you had it in
405 you, Bertie.'

'But even so,' said Claude, 'fizzer as that sermon no doubt is, will it be good enough in the face of a four-minute handicap?'

'Rather!' I said. 'When I told you it lasted forty-five minutes, I was probably understating it. I should call it – from my recollection of the
410 thing – nearly fifty.'

'Then carry on,' said Claude.

I toddled over in the evening and fixed the thing up. Old Heppenstall was most decent about the whole affair. He seemed pleased and touched that I should have remembered the sermon all these years, and said he
415 had once or twice had an idea of preaching it again, only it had seemed to him, on reflection, that it was perhaps a trifle long for a rustic congregation.

'And in these restless times my dear Wooster,' he said, 'I fear that brevity in the pulpit is becoming more and more desiderated by even
420 the bucolic churchgoer, who one might have supposed would be less afflicted with the spirit of hurry and impatience than his metropolitan brother. I have had many arguments on the subject with my nephew, young Bates, who is taking my old friend Spettigue's cure over at Gandle-by-the-Hill. His view is that a sermon nowadays should be a
425 bright, brisk, straight-from-the-shoulder address, never lasting more than ten or twelve minutes.'

'Long?' I said. 'Why, my goodness! you don't call that Brotherly Love sermon of yours *long*, do you?'

'It takes fully fifty minutes to deliver.'
430 'Surely not?'

'Your incredulity, my dear Wooster, is extremely flattering – far more flattering, of course, than I deserve. Nevertheless, the facts are as I have stated. You are sure that I would not be well advised to make certain excisions and eliminations? You do not think it would be a good thing
435 to cut, to prune? I might, for example, delete the rather exhaustive excursus into the family life of the early Assyrians?'

'Don't touch a word of it, or you'll spoil the whole thing.' I said earnestly.

'I am delighted to hear you say so, and I shall preach the sermon
440   without fail next Sunday morning.'

*

What I have always said, and what I always shall say is, that this ante-
post† betting is a mistake, an error, and a mug's game. You never can
tell what's going to happen. If fellows would only stick to the good old
S.P.,† there would be fewer young men go wrong. I'd hardly finished
445   my breakfast on the Saturday morning, when Eustace came to my bedside
to say that Eustace wanted me on the telephone.
    'Good Lord, Jeeves, what's the matter, do you think?'
    I'm bound to say I was beginning to get a bit jumpy by this time.
    'Mr Eustace did not confide in me, sir.'
450   'Has he got the wind up?'
    'Somewhat vertically, sir, to judge by his voice.'
    'Do you know what I think, Jeeves? Something's gone wrong with
the favourite.'
    'Which is the favourite, sir?'
455   'Mr Heppenstall. He's gone to odds on. He was intending to preach
a sermon on Brotherly Love which would have brought him home by
lengths. I wonder if anything's happened to him.'
    'You could ascertain, sir, by speaking to Mr Eustace on the telephone.
He is holding the wire.'
460   'By Jove, yes!'
    I shoved on a dressing-gown, and flew downstairs like a mighty,
rushing wind. The moment I heard Eustace's voice I knew we were for
it. It had a croak of agony in it.
    'Bertie?'
465   'Here I am.'
    'Deuce of a time you've been. Bertie, we're sunk. The favourite's
blown up.'
    'No!'
    'Yes. Coughing in his stable all last night.'
470   'What!'
    'Absolutely! Hay-fever.'
    'Oh, my sainted aunt!'
    'The doctor is with him now, and it's only a question of minutes
before he's officially scratched. That means the curate will show up at
475   the post instead, and he's no good at all. He is being offered at a
hundred-to-six, but no takers. What shall we do?'
    I had to grapple with the thing for a moment in silence.
    'Eustace.'

---

ante-post   before the start of the race   *S.P.*   starting-price

'Hallo?'

480 'What can you get on G. Hayward?'

'Only four-to-one now. I think there's been a leak, and Steggles has heard something. The odds shortened late last night in a significant manner.'

'Well, four-to-one will clear us. Put another fiver all round on G.
485 Hayward for the syndicate. That'll bring us out on the right side of the ledger.'

'If he wins.'

'What do you mean? I thought you considered him a cert, bar Heppenstall.'

490 'I'm beginning to wonder,' said Eustace gloomily, 'if there's such a thing as a cert. in this world. I'm told the Rev. Joseph Tucker did an extraordinarily fine trial gallop at a mothers' meeting over at Badgwick yesterday. However, it seems our only chance. So-long.'

Not being one of the official stewards, I had my choice of churches
495 next morning, and naturally I didn't hesitate. The only drawback to going to Lower Bingley was that it was ten miles away, which meant an early start, but I borrowed a bicycle from one of the grooms and tooled off. I had only Eustace's word for it that G. Hayward was such a stayer, and it might have been that he had showed too flattering form
500 at that wedding where the twins had heard him preach; but any misgivings I may have had disappeared the moment he got into the pulpit. Eustace had been right. The man was a trier. He was a tall, rangy-looking greybeard, and he went off from the start with a nice, easy action, pausing and clearing his throat at the end of each sentence,
505 and it wasn't five minutes before I realized that here was the winner. His habit of stopping dead and looking round the church at intervals was worth minutes to us, and in the home stretch we gained no little advantage owing to his dropping his pince-nez and having to grope for them. At the twenty-minute mark he had merely settled down. Twenty-
510 five minutes saw him going strong. And when he finally finished with a good burst, the clock showed thirty-five minutes fourteen seconds. With the handicap which he had been given, this seemed to me to make the event easy for him, and it was with much bonhomie and goodwill to all men that I hopped on to the old bike and started back to the Hall
515 for lunch.

Bingo was talking on the phone when I arrived.

'Fine! Splendid! Topping!' he was saying. 'Eh? Oh, we needn't worry about him. Right-o, I'll tell Bertie.' He hung up the receiver and caught sight of me. 'Oh, hallo, Bertie; I was just talking to Eustace. It's all
520 right, old man. The report from Lower Bingley has just got in. G. Hayward romps home.'

'I knew he would. I've just come from there.'

'Oh, were you there? I went to Badgwick. Tucker ran a splendid race, but the handicap was too much for him. Starkie had a sore throat
525 and was nowhere. Roberts, of Fale-by-the-Water, ran third. Good old G. Hayward!' said Bingo affectionately, and we strolled out on to the terrace.

'Are all the returns in, then?' I asked.

'All except Gandle-by-the-Hill. But we needn't worry about Bates.
530 He never had a chance. By the way, poor old Jeeves loses his tenner. Silly ass!'

'Jeeves? How do you mean?'

'He came to me this morning, just after you had left, and asked me to put a tenner on Bates for him. I told him he was a chump and begged
535 him not to throw his money away, but he would do it.'

'I beg your pardon, sir. This note arrived for you just after you had left the house this morning.'

Jeeves had materialized from nowhere, and was standing at my elbow.

'Eh? What? Note?'
540 'The Reverend Mr Heppenstall's butler brought it over from the Vicarage, sir. It came too late to be delivered to you at the moment.'

Young Bingo was talking to Jeeves like a father on the subject of betting against the form-book. The yell I gave made him bite his tongue in the middle of a sentence.
545 'What the dickens is the matter?' he asked, not a little peeved.

'We're dished! Listen to this!'

I read him the note:

>   *The Vicarage,*
550 >   *Twing, Glos.*
>
> *My Dear Wooster, – As you may have heard, circumstances over which I have no control will prevent my preaching the sermon on Brotherly Love for which you made such a flattering request. I am unwilling, however, that you shall*
555 > *be disappointed, so, if you will attend divine service at Gandle-by-the-Hill this morning, you will hear my sermon preached by young Bates, my nephew. I have lent him the manuscript at his urgent desire, for, between our selves, there are wheels within wheels. My nephew is one of the*
560 > *candidates for the headmastership of a well-known public school, and the choice has narrowed down between him and one rival.*
>
> *Late yesterday evening James received private infor-mation that the head of the Board of Governors of the*
565 > *school proposed to sit under him this Sunday in order to*

> judge of the merits of his preaching, a most important item
> in swaying the Board's choice. I acceded to his plea that I
> lend him my sermon on Brotherly Love, of which, like you,
> he apparently retains a vivid recollection. It would have
> been too late for him to compose a sermon of suitable
> length in place of the brief address which – mistakenly, in
> my opinion – he had designed to deliver to his rustic flock,
> and I wished to help the boy.
>
> Trusting that his preaching of the sermon will supply
> you with as pleasant memories as you say you have of
> mine, I remain,
>
> > Cordially yours,
> > F. Heppenstall
>
> P.S. – The hay-fever has rendered my eyes unpleasantly
> weak for the time being, so I am dictating this letter to my
> butler, Brookfield, who will convey it to you.

I don't know when I've experienced a more massive silence than the
one that followed my reading of this cheery epistle. Young Bingo gulped
once or twice, and practically every known emotion came and went on
his face. Jeeves coughed one soft, low, gentle cough like a sheep with a
blade of grass stuck in its throat, and then stood gazing serenely at the
landscape. Finally young Bingo spoke.

'Great Scott!' he whispered hoarsely. 'An S.P. job!'

'I believe that is the technical term, sir,' said Jeeves.

'So you had inside information, dash it!' said young Bingo.

'Why, yes, sir,' said Jeeves. 'Brookfield happened to mention the
contents of the note to me when he brought it. We are old friends.'

Bingo registered grief, anguish, rage, despair and resentment.

'Well, all I can say,' he cried, 'is that it's a bit thick! Preaching another
man's sermon! Do you call that honest? Do you call that playing the
game?'

'Well, my dear old thing,' I said, 'be fair. It's quite within the rules.
Clergymen do it all the time. They aren't expected always to make up
the sermons they preach.'

Jeeves coughed again, and fixed me with an expressionless eye.

'And in the present case, sir, if I may be permitted to take the liberty
of making the observation, I think we should make allowances. We
should remember that the securing of this headmastership meant
everything to the young couple.'

'Young couple! What young couple?'

'The Reverend James Bates, sir, and Lady Cynthia. I am informed by
her ladyship's maid that they have been engaged to be married for some
weeks – provisionally, so to speak; and his lordship made his consent

conditional on Mr Bates securing a really important and remunerative
610   position.'

Young Bingo turned a light green.

'Engaged to be married!'

'Yes, sir.'

There was a silence.

615   'I think I'll go for a walk,' said Bingo.

'But, my dear old thing,' I said, 'it's just lunch-time. The gong will
be going any minute now.'

'I don't want any lunch!' said Bingo.

1923

Virginia Woolf
1882–1941

Adeline Virginia Woolf was born in London, daughter of the critic
and biographer Sir Leslie Stephen (1832–1904). She was educated at
home. With her sister Vanessa (1879–1961), who married the art critic
Clive Bell in 1907, she was a leading figure in the avant-garde circle
which came to be known as the 'Bloomsbury Group' because the
Stephen sisters' home was in Bloomsbury. With her husband, the
novelist and political theorist Leonard Woolf (1880–1969), she founded the Hogarth Press in 1917. Virginia Woolf's first two novels, *The
Voyage Out* (1915) and *Night and Day* (1919) followed usual story-
telling conventions, but *Jacob's Room* (1922), *Mrs Dalloway* (1925),
To the Lighthouse (1927), *Orlando* (1928), *The Waves* (1931) and
Between the Acts (1941) are experiments with fictional technique,
most impressive in their prose poetry. The two volumes of *The
Common Reader* (1925, 1932) are collections of critical essays. *A
Room of One's Own* (1929) is a discussion of feminist themes. Virginia
Woolf was a brilliant letter-writer and diarist.

Near the end of *To the Lighthouse* James Ramsay is steering his
father and his sister Cam out to the lighthouse, making a voyage for
which he longed in vain when a child ten years earlier.

From TO THE LIGHTHOUSE
[Loneliness]

Mr Ramsay had almost done reading. One hand hovered over the page
as if to be in readiness to turn it the very instant he had finished it.
He sat there bareheaded with the wind blowing his hair about,
extraordinarily exposed to everything. He looked very old. He looked,
5   James thought, getting his head now against the Lighthouse, now
against the waste of waters running away into the open, like some old
stone lying on the sand; he looked as if he had become physically what
was always at the back of both of their minds – that loneliness which
was for both of them the truth about things.
10   He was reading very quickly, as if he were eager to get to the end.

Indeed they were very close to the Lighthouse now. There it loomed up, stark and straight, glaring white and black, and one could see the waves breaking in white splinters like smashed glass upon the rocks. One could see lines and creases in the rocks. One could see the windows clearly; a dab of white on one of them, and a little tuft of green on the rock. A man had come out and looked at them through a glass and gone in again. So it was like that, James thought, the Lighthouse one had seen across the bay all these years; it was a stark tower on a bare rock. It satisfied him. It confirmed some obscure feeling of his about his own character. The old ladies, he thought, thinking of the garden at home, went dragging their chairs about on the lawn. Old Mrs Beckwith, for example, was always saying how nice it was and how sweet it was and how they ought to be so proud and they ought to be so happy, but as a matter-of-fact James thought, looking at the Lighthouse stood there on its rock, it's like that. He looked at his father reading fiercely with his legs curled tight. They shared that knowledge. 'We are driving before a gale – we must sink,' he began saying to himself, half aloud exactly as his father said it.

Nobody seemed to have spoken for an age. Cam was tired of looking at the sea. Little bits of black cork had floated past; the fish were dead in the bottom of the boat. Still her father read, and James looked at him and she looked at him, and they vowed that they would fight tyranny to the death, and he went on reading quite unconscious of what they thought. It was thus that he escaped, she thought. Yes, with his great forehead and his great nose, holding his little mottled book firmly in front of him, he escaped. You might try to lay hands on him, but then like a bird, he spread his wings, he floated off to settle out of reach somewhere far away on some desolate stump. She gazed at the immense expanse of the sea. The island had grown so small that it scarcely looked like a leaf any longer. It looked like the top of a rock which some big wave would cover. Yet in its frailty were all those paths, those terraces, those bedrooms – all those innumerable things. But as, just before sleep, things simplify themselves so that only one of all the myriad details has power to assert itself, so, she felt, looking drowsily at the island, all those paths and terraces and bedrooms were fading and disappearing, and nothing was left but a pale blue censer swinging rhythmically this way and that across her mind. It was a hanging garden; it was a valley, full of birds, and flowers, and antelopes. . . . She was falling asleep.

'Come now,' said Mr Ramsay, suddenly shutting his book.

Come where? To what extraordinary adventure? She woke with a start. To land somewhere, to climb somewhere? Where was he leading them? For after his immense silence the words startled them. But it was absurd. He was hungry, he said. It was time for lunch. Besides, look, he said. There's the Lighthouse. 'We're almost there.'

55   'He's doing very well,' said Macalister, praising James, 'He's keeping
her very steady.'

But his father never praised him, James thought grimly.

Mr Ramsay opened the parcel and shared out the sandwiches among
them. Now he was happy, eating bread and cheese with these fishermen.
60 He would have liked to live in a cottage and lounge about in the
harbour spitting with the other old men, James thought, watching him
slice his cheese into thin yellow sheets with his penknife.

This is right, this is it, Cam kept feeling, as she peeled her hard-boiled
egg. Now she felt as she did in the study when the old men were reading
65 *The Times*. Now I can go on thinking whatever I like, and I shan't fall
over a precipice or be drowned, for there he is, keeping his eye on me,
she thought.

At the same time they were sailing so fast along by the rocks that it
was very exciting – it seemed as if they were doing two things at once;
70 they were eating their lunch here in the sun and they were also making
for safety in a great storm after a shipwreck. Would the water last?
Would the provisions last? she asked herself, telling herself a story but
knowing at the same time what was the truth.

They would soon be out of it, Mr Ramsay was saying to old
75 Macalister; but their children would see some strange things. Macalister
said he was seventy-five last March; Mr Ramsay was seventy-one.
Macalister said he had never seen a doctor; he had never lost a tooth.
And that's the way I'd like my children to live – Cam was sure that her
father was thinking that, for he stopped her throwing a sandwich into
80 the sea and told her, as if he were thinking of the fishermen and how
they live, that if she did not want it she should put it back in the parcel.
She should not waste it. He said it so wisely, as if he knew so well all
the things that happened in the world, that she put it back at once, and
then he gave her, from his own parcel, a gingerbread nut, as if he were
85 a great Spanish gentleman, she thought, handing a flower to a lady at a
window (so courteous his manner was). But he was shabby, and simple,
eating bread and cheese; and yet he was leading them on a great
expedition where, for all she knew, they would be drowned.

'That was where she sunk,' said Macalister's boy suddenly.
90   'Three men were drowned where we are now,' said the old man. He
had seen them clinging to the mast himself. And Mr Ramsay taking a
look at the spot was about, James and Cam were afraid, to burst out:

But I beneath a rougher sea,[†]

and if he did, they could not bear it; they would shriek aloud; they

---

But I beneath . . . sea W. Cowper (1731–   are 'We perished, each alone'
1800), 'The Castaway'; the preceding words

95   could not endure another explosion of the passion that boiled in him;
      but to their surprise all he said was 'Ah' as if he thought to himself,
      But why make a fuss about that? Naturally men are drowned in a
      storm, but it is a perfectly straightforward affair, and the depths of the
      sea (he sprinkled the crumbs from his sandwich paper over them) are
100   only water after all. Then having lighted his pipe he took out his watch.
      He looked at it attentively; he made, perhaps, some mathematical
      calculation. At last he said, triumphantly:
      'Well done!' James had steered them like a born sailor.
      There! Cam thought, addressing herself silently to James. You've got
105   it at last. For she knew that this was what James had been wanting,
      and she knew that now he had got it he was so pleased that he would
      not look at her or at his father or at any one. There he sat with his
      hand on the tiller sitting bolt upright, looking rather sulky and frowning
      slightly. He was so pleased that he was not going to let anybody take a
110   grain of his pleasure. His father had praised him. They must think that
      he was perfectly indifferent. But you've got it now, Cam thought.
      They had tacked, and they were sailing swiftly, buoyantly on long
      rocking waves which handed them on from one to another with an
      extraordinary lilt and exhilaration beside the reef. On the left a row of
115   rocks showed brown through the water which thinned and became
      greener and on one, a higher rock, a wave incessantly broke and spurted
      a little column of drops which fell down in a shower. One could hear
      the slap of the water and the patter of falling drops and a kind of
      hushing and hissing sound from the waves rolling and gambolling and
120   slapping the rocks as if they were wild creatures who were perfectly
      free and tossed and tumbled and sported like this for ever.
      Now they could see two men on the Lighthouse, watching them and
      making ready to meet them.
      Mr Ramsay buttoned his coat, and turned up his trousers. He took a
125   large, badly packed, brown paper parcel which Nancy had got ready and
      sat with it on his knee. Thus in complete readiness to land he sat looking
      back at the island. With his long-sighted eyes perhaps he could see the
      dwindled leaf-like shape standing on end on a plate of gold quite clearly.
      What could he see? Cam wondered. It was all a blur to her. What was he
130   thinking now? she wondered. What was it he sought, so fixedly, so intently,
      so silently? They watched him, both of them, sitting bareheaded with his
      parcel on his knee staring and staring at the frail blue shape which seemed
      like the vapour of something that had burnt itself away. What do you
      want? they both wanted to ask. They both wanted to say, Ask us anything
135   and we will give it you. But he did not ask them anything. He sat and
      looked at the island and he might be thinking, We perished, each alone,
      or he might be thinking, I have reached it. I have found it, but he said
      nothing.

Then he put on his hat.

140 'Bring those parcels,' he said, nodding his head at the things Nancy had done up for them to take to the Lighthouse. 'The parcels for the Lighthouse men,' he said. He rose and stood in the bow of the boat, very straight and tall, for all the world, James thought, as if he were saying, 'There is no God,' and Cam thought, as if he were leaping into

145 space, and they both rose to follow him as he sprang, lightly like a young man, holding his parcel, on to the rock.

13

'He must have reached it,' said Lily Briscoe aloud, feeling suddenly completely tired out. For the Lighthouse had become almost invisible, had melted away into a blue haze, and the effort of looking at it and

150 the effort of thinking of him landing there, which both seemed to be one and the same effort, had stretched her body and mind to the utmost. Ah, but she was relieved. Whatever she had wanted to give him, when he left her that morning, she had given him at last.

'He has landed,' she said aloud. 'It is finished.' Then, surging up,

155 puffing slightly, old Mr Carmichael stood beside her, looking like an old pagan God, shaggy, with weeds in his hair and the trident (it was only a French novel) in his hand. He stood by her on the edge of the lawn, swaying a little in his bulk, and said, shading his eyes with his hand: 'They will have landed,' and she felt that she had been right.

160 They had not needed to speak. They had been thinking the same things and he had answered her without her asking him anything. He stood there spreading his eyes with his hand: 'They will have landed,' and she felt that she had been right. They had not needed to speak. They had been thinking the same things and he had answered her without

165 her asking him anything. He stood there spreading his hands over all the weakness and suffering of mankind; she thought he was surveying, tolerantly, compassionately, their final destiny. Now he has crowned the occasion, she thought, when his hand slowly fell, as if she had seen him let fall from his great height a wreath of violets and asphodels

170 which, fluttering slowly, lay at length upon the earth.

Quickly, as if she were recalled by something over there, she turned to her canvas. There it was – her picture. Yes, with all its green and blues, its lines running up and across, its attempt at something. It would be hung in the attics, she thought; it would be destroyed. But what did

175 that matter? she asked herself, taking up her brush again. She looked at the steps; they were empty; she looked at her canvas; it was blurred. With a sudden intensity, as if she saw it clear for a second, she drew a line there, in the centre. It was done; it was finished. Yes, she thought,

Gerald Brenan   traveller and man of letters (1894–), met the Woolfs in 1922

laying down her brush in extreme fatigue, I have had my vision.

1925/6   1927

LETTERS
To Gerald Brenan†

Monk's House, Rodmell,
Near Lewes, Sussex

Christmas Day 1922

Dear Gerald,

Very stupidly I came away without your letter, though I have been putting off writing till Christmas, hoping to have time and some calmness. It interested me, very much, and now I can't take it up and
5   answer it as I had meant. But no doubt this is as well. What one wants from a letter is not an answer. So I shall ramble on, until the cook goes off to tea with Mrs Dedman, when I must scramble the eggs.

First however, we certainly hope to come to you about the end of March, or beginning of April. This depends on things that can't be
10   settled now; so may we leave it, and write definitely later? Apart from talking to you, as we want to do, at leisure, fully, at night, at dawn, about people, books, life, and so on and so on, my eyes are entirely grey with England – nothing but England for 10 years; and you can't imagine how much of a physical desire it becomes to feed them on
15   colour and crags – something violent and broken and dry – not perpetually sloping and sloppy like the country here. (This is a very wet Christmas day).

I have been thinking a great deal about what you say of writing novels. One must renounce, you say. I can do better than write novels,
20   you say. I don't altogether understand. I don't see how to write a book without people in it. Perhaps you mean that one ought not to attempt a 'view of life'? – one ought to limit oneself to one's own sensations – at a quartet for instance; one ought to be lyrical, descriptive: but not set people in motion, and attempt to enter them, and give them impact
25   and volume? Ah, but I'm doomed! As a matter of fact, I think that we all are. It is not possible now, and never will be, to say I renounce. Nor would it be a good thing for literature were it possible. This generation must break its neck in order that the next may have smooth going. For I agree with you that nothing is going to be achieved by us. Fragments –
30   paragraphs – a page perhaps: but no more. Joyce to me seems strewn

---

Hugh Walpole   Sir Hugh (1884–1941), a very popular novelist

with disaster. I can't even see, as you see, his triumphs. A gallant
approach, that is all that is obvious to me: then the usual smash and
splinters (I have only read him, partly, once). The human soul, it seems
to me, orientates itself afresh every now and then. It is doing so now.
35 No one can see it whole, therefore. The best of us catch a glimpse of a
nose, a shoulder, something turning away, always in movement. Still,
it seems better to me to catch this glimpse, than to sit down with Hugh
Walpole,† Wells, etc. etc. and make large oil paintings of fabulous fleshy
monsters complete from top to toe. Of course, being under 30, this
40 does not apply to you. To you, something more complete may be
vouchsafed. If so, it will be partly because I, and some others, have
made our attempts first. I have wandered from the point. Never mind.
I am only scribbling, more to amuse myself than you, who may never
read, or understand: for I am doubtful whether people, the best disposed
45 towards each other, are capable of more than an intermittent signal as
they forge past – sentimental metaphor, leading obviously to ships, and
night and storm and reefs and rocks, and the obscured, uncompassionate
moon. I wish I had your letter for I could then go ahead; without so
many jerks.
50   You said you were very wretched, didn't you? You described your
liver rotting, and how you read all night, about the early fathers; and
then walked, and saw the dawn. But were wretched, and tore up all
you wrote, and felt you could never never write – and compared this
state of yours with mine, which you imagine to be secure, rooted,
55 benevolent, industrious – you did not say dull – but somehow unattain-
able, and I daresay, unreal. But you must reflect that I am 40: further,
every 10 years, at 20, again at 30, such agony of different sorts possessed
me that not content with rambling and reading I did most emphatically
attempt to end it all; and should have been often thankful, if by stepping
60 on one flagstone rather than another I could have been annihilated
where I stood. I say this partly in vanity that you may not think me
insipid; partly as a token (one of those flying signals out of the night
and so on) that so we live, all of us who feel and reflect, with recurring
cataclysms of horror: starting up in the night in agony: Every ten years
65 brings, I suppose, one of those private orientations which match the
vast one which is, to my mind, general now in the race. I mean, life has
to be sloughed: has to be faced: to be rejected; then accepted on new
terms with rapture. And so on, and so on; till you are 40, when the
only problem is how to grasp it tighter and tighter to you, so quick it
70 seems to slip, and so infinitely desirable is it.
    As for writing, at 30 I was still writing, reading; tearing up
industriously. I had not published a word (save reviews). I despaired.

Perhaps at that age one is really most a writer. Then one cannot write,
not for lack of skill, but because the object is too near, too vast. I think
75   perhaps it must recede before one can take a pen to it. At any rate, at
20, 30, 40, and I've no doubt 50, 60, and 70, that to me is the task;
not particularly noble or heroic, as I see it in my own case, for all my
inclinations are to write; but the object of adoration to me, when there
comes along someone capable of achieving – if only the page or
80   paragraph; for there are no teachers, saints, prophets, good people, but
the artists – as you said – But the last sentence is hopelessly unintelligible.
Indeed, I am getting to the end of my letter writing capacity. I have
many more things to say; but they cower under their coverlets, and
nothing remains but to stare at the fire, and finger some book till the
85   ideas freshen within me, or they once more become impartible.
        I think, too, there is a great deal of excitement and fun and pure
pleasure and brilliance in one's fellow creatures. I'm not sure that you
shouldn't desert your mountain, take your chance, and adventure with
your human faculties – friendships, conversations, relations, the mere
90   daily intercourse. Why do young men hold books up before their eyes
so long? French literature falls like a blue tint over the landscape.
        But I am not saying what I mean, and had better stop. Only you
must write to me again – anything that occurs to you – And what about
something for the Hogarth Press?
95   Leonard adds his wishes to mine for the future.

Yours
Virginia Woolf

1922   1976

To V. Sackville-West†

52 Tavistock Square, London, W.C.1

16th March 1926
        I have been meaning every day to write something – such millions of
things strike me to write to you about – and never did, and now have
only scraps and splinters of time, damn it all – We are rather rushed –
But, dearest Vita, why not take quinine, and sleep under mosquitoe
5   nets? I could have told you about fever: do tell me if you are all right
again (a vain question: time has spun a whole circle since you had fever
off the Coast of Baluchistan). Much to my relief, Lady Sackville† wrote
and told me you had arrived: also she asks me to go and see her, to

---

V. Sackville-West Hon. Victoria Mary 'Vita'   Lady Sackville (1862–1936), Victoria's
Sackville-West (1892–1962), poet and   mother, a lively eccentric
novelist

talk about you, I suppose. 'I know you are very fond of Vita'; but I
10 haven't the courage, without you.

Last Saturday night I found a letter from you in the box: then
another: What luck! I thought; then a third; incredible!, I thought;
then a fourth: But Vita is having a joke, I thought, profoundly distrusting
you – Yet they were all genuine letters. I have spelt them out every
15 word, four times, I daresay. They do yield more on suction; they are
very curious in that way. Is it that I am, as Ly Sackville says, very fond
of you: are you, like a good writer, a very careful picker of words? (Oh
look here: your book of travels.[†] May we have it? Please say yes, for
the autumn.) I like your letters I was saying, when overcome by the
20 usual Hogarth Press spasm. And I would write a draft if I could, of my
letters; and so tidy them and compact them; and ten years ago I did
write drafts, when I was in my letter writing days, but now, never.
Indeed, these are the first letters I have written since I was married. As
for the *mot juste*, you are quite wrong. Style is a very simple matter; it
25 is all rhythm. Once you get that, you can't use the wrong words. But
on the other hand here am I sitting after half the morning, crammed
with ideas, and visions, and so on, and can't dislodge them, for lack of
the right rhythm. Now this is very profound, what rhythm is, and goes
far deeper than words. A sight, an emotion, creates this wave in the
30 mind, long before it makes words to fit it; and in writing (such is my
present belief) one has to recapture this, and set this working (which
has nothing apparently to do with words) and then, as it breaks and
tumbles in the mind, it makes words to fit it: But no doubt I shall think
differently next year. Then there's my character (you see how egotistic
35 I am, for I answer only questions that are about myself) I agree about
the lack of jolly vulgarity. But then think how I was brought up! No
school; mooning about alone among my father's books; never any
chance to pick up all that goes on in schools – throwing balls; ragging:
slang; vulgarity; scenes; jealousies – only rages with my half brothers,
40 and being walked off my legs round the Serpentine by my father. This
is an excuse: I am often conscious of the lack of jolly vulgarity but did
Proust[†] pass that way? Did you? Can you chaff a table of officers?

Do tell me scraps of the Loraine's[†] talk: or what the woman says
who has read Oscar Wilde. Then about the expeditions you make to
45 find flowers. I must go and lunch. We have had lunch, off roast beef
and Yorkshire pudding. Also a romantic pudding in which you find
almonds lodged in cream. It is bitter cold; a black wind is blowing and
scraping old newspapers along the street – a sound I connect with
March in London.

---

book of travels   the Hogarth Press published
  Passage to Teheran in November 1926
Proust   She thinks the fiction of Marcel Proust

(1871–1922) the far extreme from vulgarity
Loraine   Sir Percy Loraine, Ambassador at
  Teheran 1921–6

50   But I was going to talk about Ottoline:† and the ghastliness of that
party at Ethels. It was a blizzard, thunder and snow; and Dadie fetched
me, and we had to cross London to Chelsea. Well, by the time I got
there, my poor old hat (I never bought a new one) was like a cabmans
cape: and a piece of fur, hurriedly attached by a safety pin, flapping.
55   And those damned people sitting smug round their urn, their fire their
tea table, thought O Lord, why cant Virginia look more of a lady:
which so infuriated me, through vanity I own, and the consciousness
of being better than them, with all their pearl necklaces and orange
coloured clothes, that I could only arch my back like an infuriated tom
60   cat. As for Ottoline, she is peeling off powder like flakes on a house;
yet her skirts are above her knees: I cant describe the mingling of
decrepitude and finery: and all the talk had to be brought back to her.
There was Percy Lubbock.† We were egged on to discuss the passions.
He mumbled like an old nurse that *he* never had such nasty things:
65   whereupon, in the vilest taste, I contradicted him, never thinking of
Lady Sybil,† and he bubbled and sizzled on his seat with discomfort,
and said, please Mrs Woolf leave *me* alone. And I felt inclined to leave
them all alone, for ever and ever, these tea parties, these Ottolines,
these mumbling sodomitical old maids (Leigh Ashton was there too.)
70   Talk of the romance, the experience and upset and devastation of
Persia! Come with me further and remoter (I doubt that this is English,
though it may be the *mot juste*) to the living, unconcerned, contented,
indifferent middle classes of England. I've lived in Persia half my life;
but never been among the stockbrokers, till this spring. Last week it
75   was Lord Rothschilds agent – that is another brother of Leonards
[Philip Woolf], – at Waddesdon. There again I fell in love – But Eddy
says this is snobbery: a belief in some glamour which is unreal. They
are again, entirely direct, on the top of every object without a single
inhibition or hesitation – When my sister in law showed me her hunter
80   (for hunting is the passion of her life) I had the thrill in the thighs which,
they say, is the sign of a work of art. Then she was so worn to the bone
with living. Seven miles from a village: no servant will stay; weekend
parties at the Great House; Princess Mary playing cross word puzzles
after lunch, my sister in law stripping her one pair of shoes and skirt to
85   ribbons hunting rabbits in the bushes by way of amusing Princess Mary;
two babies; and so on. Well, I felt, nothing that I shall ever do all my
life equals a single day of this. But Eddy says he knows about it: it is
my snobbery. I like Eddy: I like the sharpness of his spine: his odd
individualities, and angles. But the young are dangerous. They mind so

---

Ottoline Lady Ottoline Morrell (1873–1938),
    the literary hostess
Percy Lubbock (1879–1965) biographer and

critic, author of *The Craft of Fiction* (1921)
Sybil Lady Sybil Scott: Sybil on line 96 is Lady
Sybil Colefax

90   much what one thinks of them. One has to be very careful what one
      says. That buzzing bluebottle Clive[†] almost involved us in a row: but
      it is past; and I am dining with Clive tomorrow, to meet some mysterious
      admirer, for Clive thinks me so vain I must always meet admirers, and
      drink the usual champagne.
95   Sure enough – here is Clive ringing up to ask us to lunch to meet
      Sybil – yes, Sybil's back: here's a note to remind you of Sybil. Then I
      met Rose Macaulay[†] and George Moore[†] (d'you remember scolding
      me – one of your scoldings – for not meeting writers?) What I say about
      writers is that they are the salt of the earth (even if to say it I must
100   unsay something of my rapture for the middle classes – the huntresses
      the stock brokers) With both of these people, Rose and George, one
      can tell the truth – a great advantage. Never did anyone talk such
      nonsense as George. 'Do not tell me you admire Hardy, Mrs Woolf.
      My good friend, tell me if he has written a single sentence well? Not
105   one. Is there a single scene in all those novels one remembers?' Whatever
      I said he poohpoohed; till at last (this was at Mary's with Jack in plum
      coloured velvet, like a tea cosy) I said 'Mr Moore, when one is Mr
      Moore that is enough'. And we floated off to waterclosets and Paris;
      and he attacked Conrad and Henry James and Anatole France.[†] but I
110   cant tell you how urbane and sprightly the old poll parrot was; and,
      (this is what I think using the brain does for one) not a pocket, not a
      crevice, of pomp, humbug, respectability in him: he was fresh as a
      daisy.
           Devil, you have never sent me your photograph. Angel, you wish to
115   know about Grizzle: she has eczema, and a cough. Someimes we peer
      into her throat and Leonard moves a bone.
           The publishing season trembles: not a review of us so far. I have
      done up 19 parcels to China, via Siberia; which as you know, must not
      weigh over 4 lbs: each; and be open ended. Also, folded a myriad of
120   these leaflets. Also rejected [Doris] Daglish on Pope. Also accepted
      Mary's stories.[†] And today began a new writing book, having filled the
      old, and written close on 40,000 words in 2 months – my record. Birds
      flap and fluster at my panes; but mostly the common sparrow, the
      domestic hen. Never mind. In the intervals of being leaden with despair,
125   I am very excited. I say, *when* do you get back? *When* shall I stop
      writing to you? All our plans about holidays are in the fire again; God
      know when we shall get off: but I dont want to be poking about in
      Provence when you're here.

Clive   Clive Bell (1881–1962), art critic
Rose Macaulay   Dame Emilie Rose Macaulay
   (1881–1958), novelist and essayist
George Moore   George Augustus Moore
   (1852–1933), Anglo-Irish novelist

Anatole France   the pseudonym of Jacques-
   Anatole-François Thibault (1844–1922),
   French novelist
Mary's stories   *Fugitive Pieces* (1927) by Mary
   Hutchinson (1889–1977)

Yes, dearest Vita: I do miss you; I think of you: I have a million
130   things, not so much to say, as to sink into you.
Tell me how you are *and be very careful*.

Yr VW

1926   1976

James Joyce
1882–1941

James Augustine Aloysius Joyce was born in Dublin and educated at Clongowes Wood College, Belvedere College, Dublin, and University College, Dublin. He visited Paris in 1902 and soon afterwards finding Ireland's Catholicism narrow and intolerant he left, to spend the rest of his life abroad. Ireland, none the less, was to be the inspiration of all his writings. He taught English in Trieste, living with Nora Barnacle, the mother of his son and daughter. They moved to Zurich in 1915 and lived in Paris after the war, struggling with poverty and illness. Joyce published a volume of verse, *Chamber Music*, in 1907 and *Dubliners*, a collection of stories, in 1914. A play *Exiles* was performed in Munich in 1918. *A Portrait of the Artist as a Young Man*, an autobiographical novel about a Catholic upbringing, appeared as a serial, 1914–15. Joyce outraged the Church, the Law and much of the literary world with his second novel *Ulysses*, published in Paris in 1922 and confiscated by the British Customs in 1923. (It was not legally available in Britain until 1933.) This strange masterpiece is unusual in its structure, which depends on correspondences with Homer's *Odyssey*, and in its style, which records the minds of its characters during one Dublin day, in a 'stream of consciousness', full of puns, allusions, fantasy, parody and unfastidious realism. The novel treats the plight of modern man, lacking religious faith, and socially alienated. In the passage below we share the funeral thoughts – irreligious, vulgar, sensual, but lively and appealingly human – of Leopold Bloom, who is one of the three protagonists (with his faithless wife Molly, and Stephen Dedalus). Joyce took the principle of experiment with prose and with the English language to a further extreme in *Finnegans Wake*. His influence on modern literature has been incalculable.

From A PORTRAIT OF THE ARTIST AS A YOUNG MAN

[Mortal Beauty]

He[†] could wait no longer.

From the door of Byron's public-house to the gate of Clontarf Chapel, from the gate of Clontarf Chapel to the door of Byron's public-house and then back again to the chapel and then back again to the public-house he had paced slowly at first, planting his steps scrupulously in the spaces of the patchwork of the footpath, then timing their fall to the fall of verses. A full hour had passed since his father had gone in with Dan Crosby, the tutor, to find out for him something about the university. For a full hour he had paced up and down, waiting: but he could wait no longer.

He set off abruptly for the Bull, walking rapidly lest his father's shrill whistle might call him back; and in a few moments he had rounded the curve at the police barrack and was safe.

Yes, his mother was hostile to the idea, as he had read from her listless silence. Yet her mistrust pricked him more keenly than his father's pride and he thought coldly how he had watched the faith which was fading down in his soul ageing and strengthening in her eyes. A dim antagonism gathered force within him and darkened his mind as a cloud against her disloyalty and when it passed, cloud-like, leaving his mind serene and dutiful towards her again, he was made aware dimly and without regret of a first noiseless sundering of their lives.

The university! So he had passed beyond the challenge of the sentries who had stood as guardians of his boyhood and had sought to keep him among them that he might be subject to them and serve their ends. Pride after satisfaction uplifted him like long slow waves. The end he had been born to serve yet did not see had led him to escape by an unseen path and now it beckoned to him once more and a new adventure was about to be opened to him. It seemed to him that he heard notes of fitful music leaping upwards a tone and downwards a diminished fourth, upwards a tone and downwards a major third, like triple-branching flames leaping fitfully, flame after flame, out of a midnight wood. It was an elfin prelude, endless and formless; and, as it grew wilder and faster, the flames leaping out of time, he seemed to hear from under the boughs and grasses wild creatures racing, their feet pattering like rain upon the leaves. Their feet passed in pattering tumult

---

He   Stephen Dedalus, the Young Man

over his mind, the feet of hares and rabbits, the feet of harts and hinds
and antelopes, until he heard them no more and remembered only a
proud cadence from Newman:

40 — Whose feet are as the feet of harts and underneath the everlasting
arms.[†]

The pride of that dim image brought back to his mind the dignity of
the office[†] he had refused. All through his boyhood he had mused upon
that which he had so often thought to be his destiny and when the
45 moment had come for him to obey the call he had turned aside, obeying
a wayward instinct. Now time lay between: the oils of ordination would
never anoint his body. He had refused. Why?

He turned seaward from the road at Dollymount and as he passed
on to the thin wooden bridge he felt the planks shaking with the tramp
50 of heavily shod feet. A squad of christian brothers was on its way back
from the Bull and had begun to pass, two by two, across the bridge.
Soon the whole bridge was trembling and resounding. The uncouth
faces passed him two by two, stained yellow or red or livid by the sea,
and, as he strove to look at them with ease and indifference, a faint
55 stain of personal shame and commiseration rose to his own face. Angry
with himself he tried to hide his face from their eyes by gazing down
sideways into the shallow swirling water under the bridge but he still
saw a reflection therein of their topheavy silk hats and humble tape-
like collars[†] and loosely-hanging clerical clothes.

60 — Brother Hickey.
Brother Quaid.
Brother MacArdle.
Brother Keogh. —

Their piety would be like their names, like their faces, like their
65 clothes, and it was idle for him to tell himself that their humble and
contrite hearts, it might be, paid a far richer tribute of devotion than
his had ever been, a gift tenfold more acceptable than his elaborate
adoration. It was idle for him to move himself to be generous towards
them, to tell himself that if he ever came to their gates, stripped of his
70 pride, beaten and in beggar's weeds, that they would be generous
towards him, loving him as themselves. Idle and embittering, finally, to
argue, against his own dispassionate certitude, that the commandment
of love bade us not to love our neighbour as ourselves with the same
amount and intensity of love but to love him as ourselves with the same
75 kind of love.

Whose feet . . . arms from *The Idea of a University* by John Henry Newman (1809–90)
the office of a priest. Stephen, educated by Jesuits, has recently been musing romantically on the appeal of the Catholic priesthood
tape-like collars the order of Christian Brothers wear narrow clerical collars

He drew forth a phrase from his treasure and spoke it softly to himself:

– A day of dappled seaborne clouds.

The phrase and the day and the scene harmonized in a chord. Words.
80 Was it their colours? He allowed them to glow and fade, hue after hue: sunrise gold, the russet and green of apple orchards, azure of waves, the grey-fringed fleece of clouds. No, it was not their colours: it was the poise and balance of the period itself. Did he then love the rhythmic rise and fall of words better than their associations of legend and
85 colour? Or was it that, being as weak of sight as he was shy of mind, he drew less pleasure from the reflection of the glowing sensible world through the prism of a language many-coloured and richly storied than from the contemplation of an inner world of individual emotions mirrored perfectly in a lucid supple periodic prose?

90 He passed from the trembling bridge on to firm land again. At that instant, as it seemed to him, the air was chilled and, looking askance towards the water, he saw a flying squall darkening and crisping suddenly the tide. A faint click at his heart, a faint throb in his throat told him once more of how his flesh dreaded the cold infrahuman odour
95 of the sea; yet he did not strike across the downs on his left but held straight on along the spine of rocks that pointed against the river's mouth.

A veiled sunlight lit up faintly the grey sheet of water where the river was embayed. In the distance along the course of the slow-flowing
100 Liffey slender masts flecked the sky and, more distant still, the dim fabric of the city lay prone in haze. Like a scene on some vague arras, old as man's weariness, the image of the seventh city† of christendom was visible to him across the timeless air, no older nor more weary nor less patient of subjection than in the days of the thingmote.†
105 Disheartened, he raised his eyes towards the slow-drifting clouds, dappled and seaborne. They were voyaging across the deserts of the sky, a host of nomads on the march, voyaging high over Ireland, westward bound. The Europe they had come from lay out there beyond the Irish Sea, Europe of strange tongues and valleyed and woodbegirt
110 and citadelled and of entrenched and marshalled races. He heard a confused music within him as of memories and names which he was almost conscious of but could not capture even for an instant; then the music seemed to recede, to recede, to recede, and from each receding trail of nebulous music there fell always one long-drawn calling note,
115 piercing like a star the dusk of silence. Again! Again! Again! A voice from beyond the world was calling.

---

seventh city Dublin   the period of Danish occupation
thingmote the council which ruled Dublin in

    – Hello, Stephanos!

    – Here comes The Dedalus!

    – Ao! . . . Eh, give it over, Dwyer, I'm telling you, or I'll give you a

120   stuff in the kisser for yourself. . . . Ao!

    – Good man, Towser! Duck him!

    – Come along, Dedalus! Bous Stephanoumenos! Bous Stephaneforos!†

    – Duck him! Guzzle him now, Towser!

    – Help! Help! . . . Ao!

125   He recognized their speech collectively before he distinguished their faces. The mere sight of that medley of wet nakedness chilled him to the bone. Their bodies, corpse-white or suffused with a pallid golden light or rawly tanned by the sun, gleamed with the wet of the sea. Their diving-stone, poised on its rude supports and rocking under their

130   plunges, and the rough-hewn stones of the sloping breakwater over which they scrambled in their horseplay gleamed with cold wet lustre. The towels with which they smacked their bodies were heavy with cold seawater; and drenched with cold brine was their matted hair.

    He stood still in deference to their calls and parried their banter with

135   easy words. How characterless they looked: Shuley without his deep unbuttoned collar, Ennis without his scarlet belt with the snaky clasp, and Connolly without his Norfolk coat with the flapless side-pockets! It was a pain to see them, and a sword-like pain to see the signs of adolescence that made repellent their pitiable nakedness. Perhaps they

140   had taken refuge in number and noise from the secret dread in their souls. But he, apart from them and in silence, remembered in what dread he stood of the mystery of his own body.

    – Stephanos Dedalos! Bous Stephanoumenos! Bous Stephaneforos!

    Their banter was not new to him and now it flattered his mild proud

145   sovereignty. Now, as never before, his strange name seemed to him a prophecy. So timeless seemed the grey warm air, so fluid and impersonal his own mood, that all ages were as one to him. A moment before the ghost of the ancient kingdom of the Danes had looked forth through the vesture of the haze-wrapped city. Now, at the name of the fabulous

150   artificer,† he seemed to hear the noise of dim waves and to see a winged form† flying above the waves and slowly climbing the air. What did it mean? Was it a quaint device opening a page of some medieval book of prophecies and symbols, a hawk-like man flying sunward above the sea, a prophecy of the end he had been born to serve and had been

155   following through the mists of childhood and boyhood, a symbol of the artist forging anew in his workshop out of the sluggish matter of

---

Bous . . . Stephaneforos in Greek, an ox garlanded (for sacrifice), an ox bearing garlands
artificer . . . form Daedalus, the craftsman of

Greek legend, escaped from King Minos of Crete on artificial wings (although his son Icarus perished, flying too near the sun)

the earth a new soaring impalpable imperishable being?

His heart trembled; his breath came faster and a wild spirit passed
over his limbs as though he was soaring sunward. His heart trembled
160   in an ecstasy of fear and his soul was in flight. His soul was soaring in
an air beyond the world and the body he knew was purified in a breath
and delivered of incertitude and made radiant and commingled with
the element of the spirit. An ecstasy of flight made radiant his eyes and
wild his breath and tremulous and wild and radiant his windswept
165   limbs.

– One! Two! . . . Look out!

– Oh, Cripes, I'm drownded!

– One! Two! Three and away!

– The next! The next!

170   – One! . . . Uk!

– Stephaneforos!

His throat ached with a desire to cry aloud, the cry of a hawk or
eagle on high, to cry piercingly of his deliverance to the winds. This
was the call of life to his soul not the dull gross voice of the world of
175   duties and despair, not the inhuman voice that had called him to the
pale service of the altar. An instant of wild flight had delivered him and
the cry of triumph which his lips withheld cleft his brain.

– Stephaneforos!

What were they now but cerements shaken from the body of death –
180   the fear he had walked in night and day, the incertitude that had ringed
him round, the shame that had abased him within and without –
cerements, the linens of the grave?

His soul had arisen from the grave of boyhood, spurning her grave-
clothes. Yes! Yes! Yes! He would create proudly out of the freedom
185   and power of his soul, as the great artificer whose name he bore, a
living thing, new and soaring and beautiful, impalpable, imperishable.

He stared up nervously from the stone-block for he could no longer
quench the flame in his blood. He felt his cheeks aflame and his throat
throbbing with song. There was a lust of wandering in his feet that
190   burned to set out for the ends of the earth. On! On! his heart seemed
to cry. Evening would deepen above the sea, night fall upon the plains,
dawn glimmer before the wanderer and show him strange fields and
hills and faces. Where?

He looked northward towards Howth.† The sea had fallen below the
195   line of seawrack on the shallow side of the breakwater and already the
tide was running out fast along the foreshore. Already one long oval
bank of sand lay warm and dry amid the wavelets. Here and there
warm isles of sand gleamed above the shallow tide and about the isles

---

Howth   north of Dublin

and around the long bank and amid the shallow currents of the beach
200 were light-clad figures, wading and delving.

In a few moments he was barefoot, his stockings folded in his pockets
and his canvas shoes dangling by their knotted laces over his shoulders
and, picking a pointed salt-eaten stick out of the jetsam among the
rocks, he clambered down the slope of the breakwater.

205 There was a long rivulet in the strand and, as he waded slowly up its
course, he wondered at the endless drift of seaweed. Emerald and black
and russet and olive, it moved beneath the current, swaying and turning.
The water of the rivulet was dark with endless drift and mirrored the
high-drifting clouds. The clouds were drifting above him silently and
210 silently the sea-tangle was drifting below him and the grey warm air
was still and a new wild life was singing in his veins.

Where was his boyhood now? Where was the soul that had hung
back from her destiny, to brood alone upon the shame of her wounds
and in her house of squalor and subterfuge to queen it in faded cerements
215 and in wreaths that withered at the touch? Or where was he?

He was alone. He was unheeded, happy and near to the wild heart
of life. He was alone and young and wilful and wild-hearted, alone
amid a waste of wild air and brackish waters and the sea-harvest of
shells and tangle and veiled grey sunlight and gayclad lightclad figures
220 of children and girls and voices childish and girlish in the air.

A girl stood before him in midstream, alone and still, gazing out to
sea. She seemed like one whom magic had changed into the likeness of
a strange and beautiful seabird. Her long slender bare legs were delicate
as a crane's and pure save where an emerald trail of seaweed had
225 fashioned itself as a sign upon the flesh. Her thighs, fuller and soft-hued
as ivory, were bared almost to the hips, where the white fringes of her
drawers were like feathering of soft white down. Her slate-blue skirts
were kilted boldly about her waist and dovetailed behind her. Her
bosom was as a bird's, soft and slight, slight and soft as the breast of
230 some dark-plumaged dove. But her long fair hair was girlish: and girlish,
and touched with the wonder of mortal beauty, her face.

She was alone and still, gazing out to sea; and when she felt his
presence and the worship of his eyes her eyes turned to him in quiet
sufferance of his gaze, without shame or wantonness. Long, long she
235 suffered his gaze and then quietly withdrew her eyes from his and bent
them towards the stream, gently stirring the water with her foot hither
and thither. The first faint noise of gently moving water broke the
silence, low and faint and whispering, faint as the bells of sleep; hither
and thither, hither and thither; and a faint flame trembled on her cheek.
240 – Heavenly God! cried Stephen's soul, in an outburst of profane joy.

He turned away from her suddenly and set off across the strand. His
cheeks were aflame; his body was aglow; his limbs were trembling. On

and on and on and on he strode, far out over the sands, singing wildly to the sea, crying to greet the advent of the life that had cried to him.

245 Her image had passed into his soul for ever and no word had broken the holy silence of his ecstasy. Her eyes had called him and his soul had leaped at the call. To live, to err, to fall, to triumph, to recreate life out of life! A wild angel had appeared to him, the angel of mortal youth and beauty, an envoy from the fair courts of life, to throw open before 250 him in an instant of ecstasy the gates of all the ways of error and glory. On and on and on and on!

He halted suddenly and heard his heart in the silence. How far had he walked? What hour was it?

There was no human figure near him nor any sound borne to him 255 over the air. But the tide was near the turn and already the day was on the wane. He turned landward and ran towards the shore and, running up the sloping beach, reckless of the sharp shingle, found a sandy nook amid a ring of tufted sandknolls and lay down there that the peace and silence of the evening might still the riot of his blood.

260 He felt above him the vast indifferent dome and the calm processes of the heavenly bodies; and the earth beneath him, the earth that had borne him, had taken him to her breast.

He closed his eyes in the languor of sleep. His eyelids trembled as if they felt the vast cyclic movement of the earth and her watchers, 265 trembled as if they felt the strange light of some new world. His soul was swooning into some new world, fantastic, dim, uncertain as under sea, traversed by cloudy shapes and beings. A world, a glimmer or a flower? Glimmering and trembling, trembling and unfolding, a breaking light, an opening flower, it spread in endless succession to itself, breaking 270 in full crimson and unfolding and fading to palest rose, leaf by leaf and wave of light by wave of light, flooding all the heavens with its soft flushes, every flush deeper than the other.

Evening had fallen when he woke and the sand and arid grasses of his bed glowed no longer. He rose slowly and, recalling the rapture of 275 his sleep, sighed at its joy.

He climbed to the crest of the sandhill and gazed about him. Evening had fallen. A rim of the young moon cleft the pale waste of skyline, the rim of a silver hoop embedded in grey sand; and the tide was flowing in fast to the land with a low whisper of her waves, islanding a few 280 last figures in distant pools.

1914/15   1916

From ULYSSES

[Hades]

Paltry funeral:† coach and three carriages. It's all the same. Pall-
bearers, gold reins, requiem mass, firing a volley. Pomp of death. Beyond
the hind carriage a hawker stood by his barrow of cakes and fruit.
Simnel cakes those are, stuck together: cakes for the dead. Dogbiscuits.
5   Who ate them? Mourners coming out.

He followed his companions. Mr Kernan and Ned Lambert followed,
Hynes walking after them. Corny Kelleher stood by the opened hearse
and took out the two wreaths. He handed one to the boy.

Where is that child's funeral disappeared to?

10   A team of horses passed from Finglas with toiling plodding tread,
dragging through the funereal silence a creaking waggon on which lay
a granite block. The waggoner marching at their head saluted.

Coffin now. Got here before us, dead as he is. Horse looking round
at it with his plume skeowways. Dull eye: collar tight on his neck,
15   pressing on a bloodvessel or something. Do they know what they cart
out here every day? Must be twenty or thirty funerals every day.
Then Mount Jerome for the protestants. Funerals all over the world
everywhere every minute. Shovelling them under by the cartload
doublequick. Thousands every hour. Too many in the world.

20   Mourners came out through the gates: woman and a girl. Lean-jawed
harpy, hard woman at a bargain, her bonnet awry. Girl's face stained
with dirt and tears, holding the woman's arm looking up at her for a
sign to cry. Fish's face, bloodless and livid.

The mutes shouldered the coffin and bore it in through the gates. So
25   much dead weight. Felt heavier myself stepping out of that bath. First
the stiff: then the friends of the stiff. Corny Kelleher and the boy
followed with their wreaths. Who is that beside them? Ah, the brother-
in-law.

All walked after.

30   Martin Cunningham whispered:

—I was in mortal agony with you talking of suicide before Bloom.

—What? Mr Power whispered. How so?

—His father poisoned himself, Martin Cunningham whispered. Had
the Queen's hotel in Ennis. You heard him say he was going to Clare.
35   Anniversary.

—O God! Mr Power whispered. First I heard of it. Poisoned himself!

Paltry funeral Leopold Bloom, a Jewish
advertising salesman, is attending the Roman
Catholic funeral of Paddy Dignam at
Glasnevin Cemetery in Dublin, in the
espisode which corresponds to Ulysses's
descent into Hades in the *Odyssey*. With him
are cronies, including Simon Dedalus, father
of the hero of *Portrait*

He glanced behind him to where a face with dark thinking eyes followed towards the cardinal's mausoleum. Speaking.

—Was he insured? Mr Bloom asked.

40 —I believe so, Mr Kernan answered, but the policy was heavily mortgaged. Martin is trying to get the youngster into Artane.

—How many children did he leave?

—Five. Ned Lambert says he'll try to get one of the girls into Todd's.

—A sad case, Mr Bloom said gently. Five young children.

45 —A great blow to the poor wife, Mr Kernan added.

—Indeed yes, Mr Bloom agreed.

Has the laugh at him now.

He looked down at the boots he had blacked and polished. She had outlived him, lost her husband. More dead for her than for me. One
50 must outlive the other. Wise men say. There are more women than men in the world. Condole with her. Your terrible loss. I hope you'll soon follow him. For Hindu widows† only. She would marry another. Him? No. Yet who knows after? Widowhood not the thing since the old queen† died. Drawn on a guncarriage. Victoria and Albert. Frogmore†
55 memorial mourning. But in the end she put a few violets in her bonnet. Vain in her heart of hearts. All for a shadow. Consort† not even a king. Her son was the substance. Something new to hope for not like the past she wanted back, waiting. It never comes. One must go first: alone under the ground: and lie no more in her warm bed.

60 —How are you, Simon? Ned Lambert said softly, clasping hands. Haven't seen you for a month of Sundays.

—Never better. How are all in Cork's own town?

—I was down there for the Cork park races on Easter Monday, Ned Lambert said. Same old six and eightpence. Stopped with Dick Tivy.

65 —And how is Dick, the solid man?

—Nothing between himself and heaven, Ned Lambert answered.

—By the holy Paul! Mr Dedalus said in subdued wonder. Dick Tivy bald?

—Martin is going to get up a whip† for the youngsters, Ned Lambert
70 said, pointing ahead. A few bob a skull. Just to keep them going till the insurance is cleared up.

—Yes, yes, Mr Dedalus said dubiously. Is that the eldest boy in front?

—Yes, Ned Lambert said, with the wife's brother. John Henry Menton is behind. He put down his name for a quid.

75 —I'll engage he did, Mr Dedalus said. I often told poor Paddy he

---

Hindu widows in the rite of suttee, they were burned alive at their husbands' funerals
the old queen Victoria (reigned 1837–1901) was long dedicated to mournful widowhood
Frogmore Royal residence in Windsor Park, where Victoria was buried in 1901
Consort Albert, Victoria's husband, Prince Consort (1840–61), also buried at Frogmore
a whip a collection of money

ought to mind that job. John Henry is not the worst in the world.

—How did he lose it? Ned Lambert asked. Liquor, what?

—Many a good man's fault, Mr Dedalus said with a sigh.

They halted about the door of the mortuary chapel. Mr Bloom stood
80 behind the boy with the wreath, looking down at his sleek combed hair
and the slender furrowed neck inside his brandnew collar. Poor boy!
Was he there when the father? Both unconscious. Lighten up at the last
moment and recognise for the last time. All he might have done. I owe
three shillings to O'Grady. Would he understand? The mutes bore the
85 coffin into the chapel. Which end is his head?

After a moment he followed the others in, blinking in the screened
light. The coffin lay on its bier before the chancel, four tall yellow
candles at its corners. Always in front of us. Corny Kelleher, laying a
wreath at each fore corner, beckoned to the boy to kneel. The mourners
90 knelt here and there in praying desks. Mr Bloom stood behind near the
font and, when all had knelt dropped carefully his unfolded newspaper
from his pocket and knelt his right knee upon it. He fitted his black
hat gently on his left knee and, holding its brim, bent over piously.

A server, bearing a brass bucket with something in it, came out
95 through a door. The whitesmocked priest came after him tidying his
stole with one hand, balancing with the other a little book against his
toad's belly. Who'll read the book? I, said the rook.

They halted by the bier and the priest began to read out of his book
with a fluent croak.

100 Father Coffey. I knew his name was like a coffin. *Domine-namine.*[†]
Bully about the muzzle he looks. Bosses the show. Muscular christian.
Woe betide anyone that looks crooked at him: priest. Thou art Peter.[†]
Burst sideways like a sheep in clover Dedalus says he will. With a belly
on him like a poisoned pup. Most amusing expressions that man finds.
105 Hhhn: burst sideways.

—*Non intres in judicium cum servo tuo, Domine.*[†]

Makes them feel more important to be prayed over in Latin. Requiem
mass. Crape weepers. Blackedged notepaper. Your name on the altarlist.
Chilly place this. Want to feed well, sitting in there all the morning in
110 the gloom kicking his heels waiting for the next please. Eyes of a toad
too. What swells him up that way? Molly gets swelled after cabbage.
Air of the place maybe. Looks full up of bad gas. Must be an infernal
lot of bad gas round the place. Butchers for instance: they get like raw
beefsteaks. Who was telling me? Mervyn Brown. Down in the vaults

---

Domine-namine a jumbling of the words for
 'the name of the Lord' in the Latin funeral
 service
Thou art Peter Christ's words (Matthew 16.
 18) are held by Roman Catholics to have

bestowed divine authority on the Church
Non intres . . . Domine (Latin) Enter not in
 judgment with thy servant O Lord. Psalms
 143. 2

115 of saint Werburgh's lovely old organ hundred and fifty they have to
bore a hole in the coffins sometimes to let out the bad gas and burn it.
Out it rushes: blue. One whiff of that and you're a goner.
My kneecap is hurting me. Ow. That's better.
The priest took a stick with a knob at the end of it out of the boy's
120 bucket and shook it over the coffin. Then he walked to the other end
and shook it again. Then he came back and put it back in the bucket.
As you were before you rested. It's all written down: he has to do it.
—*Et ne nos inducas in tentationem.*†
The server piped the answers in the treble. I often thought it would
125 be better to have boy servants. Up to fifteen or so. After that of
course . . .
Holy water that was, I expect. Shaking sleep out of it. He must be
fed up with that job, shaking that thing over all the corpses they trot
up. What harm if he could see what he was shaking it over. Every
130 mortal day a fresh batch: middleaged men, old women, children,
women dead in childbirth, men with beards, baldheaded business men,
consumptive girls with little sparrow's breasts. All the year round he
prayed the same thing over them all and shook water on top of them:
sleep. On Dignam now.
135 —*In paradisum.*
Said he was going to paradise or is in paradise. Says that over
everybody. Tiresome kind of a job. But he has to say something.
The priest closed his book and went off, followed by the server.
Corny Kelleher opened the sidedoors and the gravediggers came in,
140 hoisted the coffin again, carried it out and shoved it on their cart. Corny
Kelleher gave one wreath to the boy and one to the brother-in-law. All
followed them out of the sidedoors into the mild grey air. Mr Bloom
came last, folding his paper again into his pocket. He gazed gravely at
the ground till the coffincart wheeled off to the left. The metal wheels
145 ground the gravel with a sharp grating cry and the pack of blunt boots
followed the barrow along a lane of sepulchres.
The ree the ra the ree the ra the roo. Lord, I mustn't lilt here.
—The O'Connell circle, Mr Dedalus said about him.
Mr Power's soft eyes went up to the apex of the lofty cone.
150 —He's at rest, he said, in the middle of his people, old Dan O'.† But
his heart is buried in Rome. How many broken hearts are buried here,
Simon!
—Her grave is over there, Jack, Mr Dedalus said. I'll soon be stretched
beside her. Let Him take me whenever He likes.

Et . . . tentationem   (Latin) 'And lead us not
   into temptation' Mark 6. 13

old Dan O   Daniel O'Connell (1775–1847),
   'the Liberator'

155 Breaking down, he began to weep to himself quietly, stumbling a little in his walk. Mr Power took his arm.

–She's better where she is, he said kindly.

–I suppose so, Mr Dedalus said with a weak gasp. I suppose she is in heaven if there is a heaven.

160 Corny Kelleher stepped aside from his rank and allowed the mourners to plod by.

–Sad occasions, Mr Kernan began politely.

Mr Bloom closed his eyes and sadly twice bowed his head.

–The others are putting on their hats, Mr Kernan said. I suppose we
165 can do so too. We are the last. This cemetery is a treacherous place.

They covered their heads.

–The reverend gentleman read the service too quickly, don't you think? Mr Kernan said with reproof.

Mr Bloom nodded gravely, looking in the quick bloodshot eyes.
170 Secret eyes, secret searching eyes. Mason, I think: not sure. Beside him again. We are the last. In the same boat. Hope he'll say something else.

Mr Kernan added:

–The service of the Irish church,† used in Mount Jerome, is simpler, more impressive, I must say.

175 Mr Bloom gave prudent assent. The language of course was another thing.

Mr Kernan said with solemnity:

–*I am the resurrection and the life.*† That touches a man's inmost heart.

180 –It does, Mr Bloom said.

Your heart perhaps but what price the fellow in the six feet by two with his toes to the daises? No touching that. Seat of the affections. Broken heart. A pump after all, pumping thousands of gallons of blood every day. One fine day it gets bunged up and there you are. Lots of
185 them lying around here: lungs, hearts, livers. Old rusty pumps: damn the thing else. The resurrection and the life. Once you are dead you are dead. That last day idea. Knocking them all up out of their graves. Come forth, Lazarus!† And he came fifth and lost the job. Get up! Last day! Then every fellow mousing around for his liver and his lights and
190 the rest of his traps. Find damn all of himself that morning. Pennyweight of powder in a skull. Twelve grammes one pennyweight. Troy measure.

Corny Kelleher fell into step at their side.

–Everything went off A1, he said. What?

He looked on them from his drawling eye. Policeman's shoulders.
195 With your tooraloom tooraloom.

---

the Irish Church the Protestant Church of Ireland

I am . . . life John 11. 25

Lazarus John 11 relates how Christ raised him from the dead

–As it should be, Mr Kernan said.

–What? Eh? Corny Kelleher said.

Mr Kernan assured him.

–Who is that chap behind with Tom Kernan? John Henry Menton asked. I know his face.

Ned Lambert glanced back.

–Bloom, he said, Madam Marion Tweedy that was, is, I mean, the soprano. She's his wife.

–O, to be sure, John Henry Menton said. I haven't seen her for some time. She was a finelooking woman. I danced with her, wait, fifteen seventeen golden years ago, at Mat Dillon's, in Roundtown. And a good armful she was.

He looked behind through the others.

–What is he? he asked. What does he do? Wasn't he in the stationery line? I fell foul of him one evening, I remember, at bowls.

Ned Lambert smiled.

–Yes, he was, he said, in Wisdom Hely's. A traveller for blotting-paper.

–In God's name, John Henry Menton said, what did she marry a coon like that for? She had plenty of game in her then.

–Has still, Ned Lambert said. He does some canvassing for ads.

John Henry Menton's large eyes stared ahead.

The barrow turned into a side lane. A portly man, ambushed among the grasses, raised his hat in homage. The gravediggers touched their caps.

–John O'Connell, Mr Power said, pleased. He never forgets a friend.

Mr O'Connell shook all their hands in silence. Mr Dedalus said:

–I am come to pay you another visit.

–My dear Simon, the caretaker answered in a low voice. I don't want your custom at all.

Saluting Ned Lambert and John Henry Menton he walked on at Martin Cunningham's side, puzzling two keys at his back.

–Did you hear that one, he asked them, about Mulcahy from the Coombe?

–I did not, Martin Cunningham said.

They bent their silks hats in concert and Hynes inclined his ear. The caretaker hung his thumbs in the loops of his gold watch chain and spoke in a discreet tone to their vacant smiles.

–They tell the story, he said, that two drunks came out here one foggy evening to look for the grave of a friend of theirs. They asked for Mulcahy from the Coombe and were told where he was buried. After traipsing about in the fog they found the grave, sure enough. One of the drunks spelt out the name; Terence Mulcahy. The other drunk was blinking up at a statue of our Savour the widow had got put up.

240   The caretaker blinked up at one of the sepulchres they passed. He resumed:

    —And, after blinking up the sacred figure, *Not a bloody bit like the man*, says he. *That's not Mulcahy*, says he, *who ever done it.*

    Rewarded by smiles he fell back and spoke with Corny Kelleher,
245 accepting the dockets given him, turning them over and scanning them as he walked.

    —That's all done with a purpose, Martin Cunningham explained to Hynes.

    —I know, Hynes said, I know that.

250   —To cheer a fellow up, Martin Cunningham said. It's pure good-heartedness: damn the thing else.

    Mr Bloom admired the caretaker's prosperous bulk. All want to be on good terms with him. Decent fellow, John O'Connell, real good sort. Keys: like Keyes's ad: no fear of anyone getting out, no passout
255 checks. *Habeat corpus.* [He may keep the body] I must see about that ad after the funeral. Did I write Ballsbridge on the envelope I took to cover when she disturbed me writing to Martha? Hope it's not chucked in the dead letter office. Be the better of a shave. Grey sprouting beard. That's the first sign when the hairs come out grey and temper getting
260 cross. Silver threads among the grey. Fancy being his wife. Wonder how he had the gumption to propose to any girl. Come out and live in the graveyard. Dangle that before her. It might thrill her first. Courting death . . . Shades of night hovering here with all the dead stretched about. The shadows of the tombs when churchyards yawn and Daniel
265 O'Connell must be a descendant I suppose who is this used to say he was a queer breedy man great catholic all the same like a big giant in the dark. Will o' the wisp. Gas of graves. Want to keep her mind off it to conceive at all. Women especially are so touchy. Tell her a ghost story in bed to make her sleep. Have you ever seen a ghost? Well, I
270 have. It was a pitchdark night. The clock was on the stroke of twelve. Still they'd kiss all right if properly keyed up. Whores in Turkish graveyards. Learn anything if taken young. You might pick up a young widow here. Men like that. Love among the tombstones. Romeo. Spice of pleasure. In the midst of death we are in life. Both ends meet.
275 Tantalising for the poor dead. Smell of frilled beefsteaks to the starving gnawing their vitals. Desire to grig people. Molly[†] wanting to do it at the window. Eight children he has anyway.

    He has seen a fair share go under in his time, lying around him field after field. Holy fields. More room if they buried them standing. Sitting
280 or kneeling you couldn't. Standing? His head might come up some day above ground in a landslip with his hand pointing. All honeycombed

---

Molly Bloom's wife

the ground must be: oblong cells. And very neat he keeps it too, trim grass and edgings. His garden Major Gamble calls Mount Jerome. Well so it is. Ought to be flowers of sleep. Chinese cemeteries with giant poppies
285 growing produce the best opium Mastiansky told me. The Botanic Gardens are just over there. It's the blood sinking in the earth gives new life. Same idea those jews they said killed the christian boy.[†] Every man his price. Well preserved fat corpse gentleman, epicure, invaluable for fruit garden. A bargain. By carcass of William Wilkinson, auditor and accountant, lately
290 deceased, three pounds thirteen and six. With thanks.

I daresay the soil would be quite fat with corpse manure, bones, flesh, nails, charnelhouses. Dreadful. Turning green and pink, decomposing. Rot quick in damp earth. The lean old ones tougher. Then a kind of a tallowy kind of a cheesy. Then begin to get black, treacle oozing out of
295 them. Then dried up. Deathmoths. Of course the cells or whatever they are go on living. Changing about. Live for ever practically. Nothing to feed on feed on themselves.

But they must breed a devil of a lot of maggots. Soil must be simply swirling with them. Your head it simply swurls. Those pretty little
300 seaside gurls. He looks cheerful enough over it. Gives him a sense of power seeing all the others go under first. Wónder how he looks at life. Cracking his jokes too: warms the cockles of his heart. The one about the bulletin. Spurgeon went to heaven 4 a.m. this morning. 11 p.m. (closing time). Not arrived yet. Peter. The dead themselves the men
305 anyhow would like to hear an odd joke or the women to know what's in fashion. A juicy pear or ladies' punch, hot, strong and sweet. Keep out the damp. You must laugh sometimes so better do it that way. Gravediggers in *Hamlet*. Shows the profound knowledge of the human heart. Daren't joke about the dead for two years at least. *De mortuis*
310 *nil nisi prius*.[†] Go out of mourning first. Hard to imagine his funeral. Seems a sort of a joke. Read your own obituary notice they say you live longer. Gives you second wind. New lease of life.

–How many have you for tomorrow? the caretaker asked.

–Two, Corny Kelleher said. Half ten and eleven.
315 The caretaker put the papers in his pocket. The barrow had ceased to trundle. The mourners split and moved to each side of the hole, stepping with care round the graves. The gravediggers bore the coffin and set its nose on the brink, looping the bands round it.

Burying him. We come to bury Cæsar. His ides of March or June.[†]
320 He doesn't know who is here nor care.

---

those jews . . . christian boy   such stories began to be told in the Middle Ages
De Mortuis nil nisi prius   (Latin) 'Concerning the dead [say] nothing unless before . . .'.
'. . . unless good' (*nisi bonum*) is the usual tag

We come . . . June   See Shakespeare's *Julius Caesar* III.2.75; I.1.18. The action of the novel takes place 16 June 1904

Now who is that lankylooking galoot over there in the macintosh?[†]
Now who is he I'd like to know? Now, I'd give a trifle to know who
he is. Always someone turns up you never dreamt of. A fellow could
live on his lonesome all his life. Yes, he could. Still he'd have to get
325 someone to sod him after he died though he could dig his own grave.
We all do. Only man buries. No ants too. First thing strikes anybody.
Bury the dead. Say Robinson Crusoe was true to life. Well then Friday
buried him. Every Friday buries a Thursday if you come to look at it.

> *O, poor Robinson Crusoe,*
330 > *How could you possibly do so?*

Poor Dignam! His last lie on the earth in his box. When you think
of them all it does seem a waste of wood. All gnawed through. They
could invent a handsome bier with a kind of panel sliding let it down
that way. Ay but they might object to be buried out of another fellow's.
335 They're so particular. Lay me in my native earth. Bit of clay from the
holy land. Only a mother and deadborn child ever buried in the one
coffin. I see what it means. I see. To protect him as long as possible
even in the earth. The Irishman's house is his coffin. Enbalming in
catacombs, mummies, the same idea.
340 Mr Bloom stood far back, his hat in his hand, counting the bared
heads. Twelve. I'm thirteen. No. The chap in the macintosh is thirteen.
Death's number. Where the deuce did he pop out of? He wasn't in the
chapel, that I'll swear. Silly superstition that about thirteen.
Nice soft tweed Ned Lambert has in that suit. Tinge of purple. I had
345 one like that when we lived in Lombard street west. Dressy fellow he
was once. Used to change three suits in the day. Must get that grey suit
of mine turned by Mesias. Hello. It's dyed. His wife I forgot he's not
married or his landlady ought to have picked out those threads for him.
The coffin dived out of sight, eased down by the men straddled on
350 the gravetrestles. They struggled up and out: and all uncovered. Twenty.
Pause.
If we were all suddenly somebody else.
Far away a donkey brayed. Rain. No such ass. Never see a dead one,
they say. Shame of death. They hide. Also poor papa went away.
355 Gentle sweet air blew round the bared heads in a whisper. Whisper.
The boy by the gravehead held his wreath with both hands staring
quietly in the black open space. Mr Bloom moved behind the portly
kindly caretaker. Well cut frockcoat. Weighing them up perhaps to see
which will go next. Well it is a long rest. Feel no more. It's the moment
360 you feel. Must be damned unpleasant. Can't believe it at first. Mistake
must be: someone else. Try the house opposite. Wait, I wanted to. I

---

galoot . . . in the macintosh   a mysterious clumsy fellow ('galoot') throughout the novel

haven't yet. Then darkened deathchamber. Light they want. Whispering around you. Would you like to see a priest? Then rambling and wandering. Delirium all you hid all your life. The death struggle. His
365 sleep is not natural. Press his lower eyelid. Watching is his nose pointed is his jaw sinking are the sole of his feet yellow. Pull the pillow away and finish it off on the floor since he's doomed. Devil in that picture of sinner's death showing him a woman. Dying to embrace her in his shirt. Last act of *Lucia*.[†] *Shall I nevermore behold thee?* Bam! expires. Gone
370 at last. People talk about you a bit: forget you. Don't forget to pray for him. Remember him in your prayers. Even Parnell. Ivy day[†] dying out. Then they follow: dropping into a hole one after the other.

We are praying now for the repose of his soul. Hoping you're well and not in hell. Nice change of air. Out of the fryingpan of life into the
375 fire of purgatory.

Does he ever think of the hole waiting for himself? They say you do when you shiver in the sun. Someone walking over it. Callboy's warning. Near you. Mine over there towards Finglas, the plot I bought. Mamma poor mamma, and little Ruddy.[†]
380 The gravediggers took up their spades and flung heavy clods of clay in on the coffin. Mr Bloom turned his face. And if he was alive all the time? Whew! By Jingo, that would be awful! No, no: he is dead, of course. Of course he is dead. Monday he died. They ought to have some law to pierce the heart and make sure or an electric clock or a
385 telephone in the coffin and some kind of a canvas airhole. Flag of distress. Three days. Rather long to keep them in summer. Just as well to get shut of them as soon as you are sure there's no.

The clay fell softer. Begin to be forgotten. Out of sight, out of mind.

The caretaker moved away a few paces and put on his hat. Had
390 enough of it. The mourners took heart of grace, one by one, covering themselves without show. Mr Bloom put on his hat and saw the portly figure make its way deftly through the maze of graves. Quietly, sure of his ground, he traversed the dismal fields.[†]

Hynes jotting down something in his notebook. Ah, the names. But
395 he knows them all. No: coming to me.

—I am just taking the names, Hynes said below his breath. What is your christian name? I'm not sure.

—L, Mr Bloom said. Leopold. And you might put down M'Coy's name too. He asked me to.

---

last act of Lucia in the Italian opera *Lucia di Lammermoor* (1835) by Gaetano Donizetti (1797–1848)
Parnell. Ivy Day ivy was worn on 6 October, the day of the death of Charles Stewart Parnell (1846–91), the controversial

champion of Home Rule
little Ruddy Rudy, Bloom's son who died in infancy
he traversed the dismal fields the language suggests Ulysses in Hades

400   —Charley, Hynes said writing. I know. He was on the *Freeman* once.
So he was before he got the job in the morgue under Louis Byrne.
Good idea a postmortem for doctors. Find out what they imagine they
know. He died of a Tuesday. Got the run. Levanted with the cash of a
few ads. Charley, you're my darling. That was why he asked me to. O
405   well, does no harm. I saw to that, M'Coy. Thanks, old chap: much
obliged. Leave him under an obligation: costs nothing.
        —And tell us, Hynes said, do you know that fellow in the, fellow was
over there in the . . .
        He looked around.
410   —Macintosh. Yes, I saw him, Mr Bloom said. Where is he now?
        —McIntosh, Hynes said, scribbling, I don't know who he is. Is that
his name?
        He moved away, looking about him.
        —No, Mr Bloom began, turning and stopping. I say, Hynes!
415   Didn't hear. What? Where has he disappeared to? Not a sign. Well
of all the. Has anybody here seen? Kay ee double ell. Become invisible.
Good Lord, what became of him?
        A seventh gravedigger came beside Mr Bloom to take up an idle
spade.
420   —O, excuse me!
        He stepped aside nimbly.
        Clay, brown, damp, began to be seen in the hole. It rose. Nearly
over. A mound of damp clods rose more, rose, and the gravediggers
rested their spades. All uncovered again for a few instants. The boy
425   propped his wreath against a corner: the brother-in-law his on a lump.
The gravediggers put on their caps and carried their earthly spades
towards the barrow. Then knocked the blades lightly on the turf: clean.
One bent to pluck from the haft a long tuft of grass. One, leaving his
mates, walked slowly on with shouldered weapon, its blade blueglancing.
430   Silently at the gravehead another coiled the coffinband. His navelcord.
The brother-in-law, turning away, placed something in his free hand.
Thanks in silence. Sorry, sir: trouble. Headshake. I know that. For
yourselves just.
        The mourners moved away slowly, without aim, by devious paths,
435   staying awhile to read a name on a tomb.
        —Let us go round by the chief's grave,† Hynes said. We have time.
        —Let us, Mr Power said.
        They turned to the right, following their slow thoughts. With awe
Mr Power's blank voice spoke:
440   —Some say he is not in that grave at all. That the coffin was filled
with stones. That one day he will come again.

the chief's grave   Parnell's

Hynes shook his head.

–Parnell will never come again, he said. He's there, all that was mortal of him. Peace to his ashes.

445   Mr Bloom walked unheeded along his grove by saddened angels, crosses, broken pillars, family vaults, stone hopes praying with upcast eyes, old Ireland's hearts and hands. More sensible to spend the money on some charity for the living. Pray for the repose of the soul of. Does anybody really? Plant him and have done with him. Like down a
450   coalshoot. Then lump them together to save time. All souls' day. Twentyseventh I'll be at his grave. Ten shillings for the gardener. He keeps it free of weeds. Old man himself. Bent down double with his shears clipping. Near death's door. Who passed away. Who departed this life. As if they did it of their own accord. Got the shove, all of
455   them. Who kicked the bucket. More interesting if they told you what they were. So and so, wheelwright. I travelled for cork lino. I paid five shillings in the pound. Or a woman's with her saucepan. I cooked good Irish stew. Eulogy† in a country churchyard it ought to be that poem of whose is it Wordsworth or Thomas Campbell.† Entered into rest the
460   protestants put it. Old Dr Murren's. The great physician called him home. Well it's God's acre for them. Nice country residence. Newly plastered and painted. Ideal spot to have a quiet smoke and read the *Church Times*. Marriage ads they never try to beautify. Rusty wreaths hung on knobs, garlands of bronzefoil. Better value that for the money.
465   Still, the flowers are more poetical. The other gets rather tiresome, never withering. Expresses nothing. Immortelles.†

A bird sat tamely perched on a poplar branch. Like stuffed. Like the wedding present alderman Hooper gave us. Hu! Not a budge out of him. Knows there are no catapults to let fly at him. Dead animal even
470   sadder. Silly-Milly† burying the little dead bird in the kitchen matchbox, a daisychain and bits of broken chainies on the grave.

The Sacred Heart that is: showing it. Heart on his sleeve. Ought to be sideways and red it should be painted like a real heart. Ireland was dedicated to it or whatever that. Seems anything but pleased. Why this
475   infliction? Would birds come then and peck like the boy with the basket of fruit but he said no because they ought to have been afraid of the boy. Apollo that was.

How many! All these here once walked round Dublin. Faithful departed. As you are now so once were we.
480   Besides how could you remember everybody? Eyes, walk, voice. Well, the voice, yes: gramophone. Have a gramophone in every grave or

---

Eulogy Bloom is thinking of the 'Elegy Written in a Country-Churchyard' (1751) by Thomas Gray (1716–71), not by Thomas Campbell (1774–1844)

Immortelles papery flowers so called in French ('Everlastings'), placed on graves
Silly Milly Molly Bloom

keep it in the house. After dinner on a Sunday. Put on poor old greatgrandfather Kraahraark! Hellohellohello amawfullyglad kraark awfullygladaseeragain hellohello amarawf kopthsth. Remind you of the
485　voice like the photograph reminds you of the face. Otherwise you couldn't remember the face after fifteen years, say. For instance who? For instance some fellow that died when I was in Wisdom Hely's.

Rtststr! A rattle of pebbles. Wait. Stop.

He looked down intently into a stone crypt. Some animal. Wait.
490　There he goes.

An obese grey rat toddled along the side of the crypt, moving the pebbles. An old stager: greatgrandfather: he knows the ropes. The grey alive crushed itself in under the plinth, wriggled itself in under it. Good hidingplace for treasure.
495　Who lives there? Are laid the remains of Robert Emery. Robert Emmet was buried here by torchlight, wasn't he? Making his rounds.

Tail gone now.

One of those chaps would make short work of a fellow. Pick the bones clean no matter who it was. Ordinary meat for them. A corpse
500　is meat gone bad. Well and what's cheese? Corpse of milk. I read in that *Voyages in China* that the Chinese say a white man smells like a corpse. Cremation better. Priests dead against it. Devilling for the other firm. Wholesale burners and Dutch oven dealers. Time of the plague. Quicklime fever pits to eat them. Lethal chamber. Ashes to ashes. Or
505　bury at sea. Where is that Parsee tower of silence?† Eaten by birds. Earth, fire, water. Drowning they say is the pleasantest. See your whole life in a flash. But being brought back to life no. Can't bury in the air however. Out of a flying machine. Wonder does the news go about whenever a fresh one is let down. Underground communication. We
510　learned that from them. Wouldn't be surprised. Regular square feed for them. Flies come before he's well dead. Got wind of Dignam. They wouldn't care about the smell of it. Saltwhite crumbling mush of corpse: smell, taste like raw white turnips.

The gates glimmered in front: still open. Back to the world again.
515　Enough of this place. Brings you a bit nearer every time. Last time I was here was Mrs Sinico's funeral. Poor papa too. The love that kills. And even scraping up the earth at night with a lantern like that case I read of to get at fresh buried females or even putrefied with running gravesores. Give you the creeps after a bit. I will appear to you after
520　death. You will see my ghost after death. My ghost will haunt you after death. There is another world after death named hell. I do not like that other world she wrote. No more do I. Plenty to see and hear and feel

---

Parsee tower of silence　Parsees, in the
Zoroastrian religion, exposed their dead on towers

yet. Feel live warm beings near you. Let them sleep in their maggoty
beds. They are not going to get me this innings. Warm beds: warm
525   fullblooded life.

Martin Cunningham emerged from a sidepath, talking gravely.

Solicitor, I think. I know his face. Menton. John Henry, solicitor,
commissioner for oaths and affidavits. Dignam used to be in his office.
Mat Dillon's long ago. Jolly Mat convivial evenings. Cold fowl, cigars,
530   the Tantalus glasses. Heart of gold really. Yes, Menton. Got his rag
out that evening on the bowling green because I sailed inside him. Pure
fluke of mine: the bias. Why he took such a rooted dislike to me. Hate
at first sight. Molly and Floey Dillon linked under the lilactree, laughing.
Fellow always like that, mortified if women are by.

535   Got a dinge in the side of his hat. Carriage probably.

–Excuse me, sir, Mr Bloom said beside them.

They stopped.

–Your hat is a little crushed, Mr Bloom said, pointing.

John Henry Menton stared at him for an instant without moving.

540   –There, Martin Cunningham helped, pointing also.

John Henry Menton took off his hat, bulged out the dinge and
smoothed the nap with care on his coatsleeve. He clapped the hat on
his head again.

–It's all right now, Martin Cunningham said.

545   John Henry Menton jerked his head down in acknowledgment.

–Thank you, he said shortly.

They walked on towards the gates. Mr Bloom, chapfallen, drew
behind a few paces so as not to overhear. Martin laying down the law.
Martin could wind a sappyhead like that round his little finger without
550   his seeing it.

Oyster eyes. Never mind. Be sorry after perhaps when it dawns on
him. Get the pull over him that way.

Thank you. How grand we are this morning.

1906/20   1922

James Elroy Flecker
1884–1915

James Herman Elroy Flecker was born in London and educated at Uppingham and Trinity College, Oxford. He was in the Consular Service at Constantinople and Beirut, but tuberculosis forced him to retire to Switzerland, where he died. He published several books of verse, including *The Golden Journey to Samarkand* (1913). His exotic verse-drama *Hassan*, staged and first published in 1922, was then widely considered a masterpiece; it remains a curiosity of literature.

THE PARROT

The old professor of Zoology
Shook his long beard and spake these words to me:
'Compare the Parrot with the Dove. They are
In shape the same: in hue dissimilar.
5   The Indian bird, which may be sometimes seen
In red or black, is generally green.
His beak is very hard: it has been known
To crack thick nuts and penetrate a stone.
Alas that when you teach him how to speak
10   You find his head is harder than his beak.
The passionless Malay can safely drub
The pates of parrots with an iron club:
The ingenious fowls, like boys they beat at school,
Soon learn to recognize a Despot's rule.
15   Now if you'd train a parrot, catch him young
While soft the mouth and tractable the tongue.
Old birds are fools: they dodder in their speech,
More eager to forget than you to teach;
They swear one curse, then gaze at you askance,
20   And all oblivion thickens in their glance.
    Thrice blest whose parrot of his own accord
Invents new phrases to delight his Lord,
Who spurns the dull quotidian task and tries
Selected words that prove him good and wise.

25   Ah, once it was my privilege to know
     A bird like this . . .
                         But that was long ago!'

1909   1916

TO A POET A THOUSAND YEARS HENCE

I who am dead a thousand years,
    And wrote this sweet archaic song,
Send you my words for messengers
    The way I shall not pass along.

5   I care not if you bridge the seas,
        Or ride secure the cruel sky,
    Or build consummate palaces
        Of metal or of masonry.

    But have you wine and music still,
10   And statues and a bright-eyed love,
    And foolish thoughts of good and ill,
        And prayers to them who sit above?

    How shall we conquer? Like a wind
        That falls at eve our fancies blow,
15 And old Mæonides* the blind   Homer
        Said it three thousand years ago.

    O friend unseen, unborn, unknown,
        Student of our sweet English tongue,
    Read out my words at night, alone:
20   I was a poet, I was young.

    Since I can never see your face,
        And never shake you by the hand,
    I send my soul through time and space
        To greet you. You will understand.

1907   1911

THE OLD SHIPS

I have seen old ships sail like swans asleep
Beyond the village which men still call Tyre,
With leaden age o'ercargoed, dipping deep
For Famagusta[†] and the hidden sun
5   That rings black Cyprus with a lake of fire;
And all those ships were certainly so old
Who knows how oft with squat and noisy gun,
Questing brown slaves or Syrian oranges,
The pirates Genoese
10 Hell-raked them till they rolled
Blood, water, fruit and corpses up the hold.
But now through friendly seas they softly run,
Painted the mid-sea blue or shore-sea green,
Still patterned with the vine and grapes in gold.

15 But I have seen,
Pointing her shapely shadows from the dawn
And image tumbled on a rose-swept bay,
A drowsy ship of some yet older day;
And, wonder's breath indrawn,
20 Thought I – who knows – who knows – but in that same
(Fished up beyond Æa,[†] patched up new
– Stern painted brighter blue –)
That talkative, bald-headed seaman* came   Odysseus
(Twelve patient comrades sweating at the oar)
25 From Troy's doom-crimson shore,
And with great lies about his wooden horse
Set the crew laughing, and forgot his course.

It was so old a ship – who knows, who knows?
– And yet so beautiful, I watched in vain
30 To see the mast burst open with a rose,
And the whole deck put on its leaves again.

1913   1915

Famagusta   a port in the east of Cyprus   *Æaea*   the island of Circe in the *Odyssey*

D. H. Lawrence

1885–1930

David Herbert Richards Lawrence was born in Eastwood, Nottinghamshire, the son of a coal-miner. *Sons and Lovers* (1913), Lawrence's third novel, reflects his early experience of a divided home and a possessive mother. He was educated at Nottingham High School and Nottingham University College, and he worked for a time as a schoolmaster. His first novel, *The White Peacock* (1911), was immature but impressive, and he gradually found recognition and friends in literary London. He planned a new novel, to be original in method and approach to character: provisionally called 'The Sisters', this developed into two books, *The Rainbow* (1915) and *Women in Love* (written in 1916). The first edition of *The Rainbow*, considered obscene by most reviewers, was destroyed by court-order. Undeterred, Lawrence wrote and rewrote *Women in Love* (1921), the most original and effective expression of his ideas of truth to one's own manhood or womanhood. With his German wife Frieda, he travelled abroad after the war, moving from Florence and Sicily to Ceylon, Australia and New Mexico. In later novels such as *The Plumed Serpent* (1926) and *Lady Chatterley's Lover*, not published unexpurgated in England until 1960, he continued to write with a passionate confidence in his personal vision of life. Books of poems included *Look! We Have Come Through!* (1917), *Birds, Beasts and Flowers* (1923) and *Pansies* (1929). He published over fifty books, including essays, tracts, criticism, travelogues and polemic. He died in France, of tuberculosis.

In the third chapter of *Women in Love*, Ursula Brangwen, dissatisfied with her job in a midland school, receives a visit from Rupert Birkin, an inspector of schools; they are joined by Birkin's aristocratic mistress, Hermione Roddice.

From WOMEN IN LOVE

Classroom

A school-day was drawing to a close. In the class-room the last lesson was in progress, peaceful and still. It was elementary botany. The desks were littered with catkins, hazel and willow, which the children had been sketching. But the sky had come over dark, as the end of the afternoon approached: there was scarcely light to draw any more. Ursula stood in front of the class, leading the children by questions to understand the structure and the meaning of the catkins.

A heavy, copper-coloured beam of light came in at the west window, gilding the outlines of the children's heads with red gold, and falling on the wall opposite in a rich, ruddy illumination. Ursula, however, was scarcely conscious of it. She was busy, the end of the day was here, the work went on as a peaceful tide that is at flood, hushed to retire.

This day had gone by like so many more, in an activity that was like a trance. At the end there was a little haste, to finish what was in hand. She was pressing the children with questions, so that they should know all they were to know, by the time the gong went. She stood in shadow in front of the class, with catkins in her hand, and she leaned towards the children, absorbed in the passion of instruction.

She heard, but did not notice the click of the door. Suddenly she started. She saw, in the shaft of ruddy, copper-coloured light near her, the face of a man. It was gleaming like fire, watching her, waiting for her to be aware. It startled her terribly. She thought she was going to faint. All her suppressed, subconscious fear sprang into being, with anguish.

'Did I startle you?' said Birkin, shaking hands with her. 'I thought you had heard me come in.'

'No,' she faltered, scarcely able to speak. He laughed, saying he was sorry. She wondered why it amused him.

'It is so dark,' he said. 'Shall we have the light?'

And moving aside, he switched on the strong electric lights. The classroom was distinct and hard, a strange place after the soft dim magic that filled it before he came. Birkin turned curiously to look at Ursula. Her eyes were round and wondering, bewildered, her mouth quivered slightly. She looked like one who is suddenly wakened. There was a living, tender beauty, like a tender light of dawn shining from her face. He looked at her with a new pleasure, feeling gay in his heart, irresponsible.

'You are doing catkins?' he asked, picking up a piece of hazel from a scholar's desk in front of him. 'Are they as far out as this? I hadn't noticed them this year.'

He looked absorbedly at the tassel of hazel in his hand.

'The red ones too!' he said, looking at the flickers of crimson that came from the female bud.

Then he went in among the desks, to see the scholars' books. Ursula watched his intent progress. There was a stillness in his motion that

hushed the activities of her heart. She seemed to be standing aside in
arrested silence, watching him move in another concentrated world.
His presence was so quiet, almost like a vacancy in the corporate air.

Suddenly he lifted his face to her, and her heart quickened at the
50   flicker of his voice.

'Give them some crayons, won't you?' he said, 'so that they can make
the gynaecious flowers red, and the androgynous yellow. I'd chalk them
in plain, chalk in nothing else, merely the red and the yellow. Outlines
scarcely matter in this case. There is just the one fact to emphasise.'

55   'I haven't any crayons,' said Ursula.

'There will be some somewhere – red and yellow, that's all you want.'
Ursula sent out a boy on a quest.

'It will make the books untidy,' she said to Birkin, flushing deeply.

'Not very,' he said. 'You must mark in these things obviously. It's
60   the fact you want to emphasise, not the subjective impression to record.
What's the fact? – red little spiky stigmas of the female flower, dangling
yellow male catkin, yellow pollen flying from one to the other. Make a
pictorial record of the fact, as a child does when drawing a face – two
eyes, one nose, mouth with teeth – so –' And he drew a figure on the
65   blackboard.

At that moment another vision was seen through the glass panels of
the door. It was Hermoine Roddice. Birkin went and opened to her.

'I saw your car,' she said to him. 'Do you mind my coming to find
you? I wanted to see you when you were on duty.'

70   She looked at him for a long time, intimate and playful, then she
gave a short, little laugh. And then only she turned to Ursula, who,
with all the class, had been watching the little scene between the lovers.

'How do you do, Miss Brangwen,' sang Hermione, in her low, odd,
singing fashion, that sounded almost as if she were poking fun. 'Do
75   you mind my coming in?'

Her grey, almost sardonic eyes rested all the while on Ursula, as if
summing her up.

'Oh no,' said Ursula.

'Are you *sure*?' repeated Hermione, with complete sang froid, and
80   an odd, half-bullying effrontery.

'Oh no, I like it awfully,' laughed Ursula, a little bit excited and
bewildered, because Hermione seemed to be compelling her, coming
very close to her, as if intimate with her; and yet, how could she be
intimate?

85   This was the answer Hermione wanted. She turned satisfied to Birkin.

'What are you doing?' she sang, in her casual, inquisitive fashion.

'Catkins,' he replied.

'Really!' she said. 'And what do you learn about them?' She spoke
all the while in a mocking, half teasing fashion, as if making game of

90　the whole business. She picked up a twig of the catkin, piqued by
Birkin's attention to it.

She was a strange figure in the class-room, wearing a large, old cloak
of greenish cloth, on which was a raised pattern of dull gold. The high
collar, and the inside of the cloak, was lined with dark fur. Beneath she
95　had a dress of fine lavender-coloured cloth, trimmed with fur, and her
hat was close-fitting, made of fur and of the dull, green-and-gold figured
stuff. She was tall and strange, she looked as if she had come out of
some new, bizarre picture.

'Do you know the little red ovary flowers, that produce the nuts?
100　Have you ever noticed them?' he asked her. And he came close and
pointed them out to her, on the sprig she held.

'No,' she replied. 'What are they?'

'Those are the little seed-producing flowers, and the long catkins,
they only produce pollen, to fertilise them.'

105　'Do they, do they!' repeated Hermione, looking closely.

'From those little red bits, the nuts come; if they receive pollen from
the long danglers.'

'Little red flames, little red flames,' murmured Hermione to herself.
And she remained for some moments looking only at the small buds
110　out of which the red flickers of the stigma issued.

'Aren't they beautiful? I think they're so beautiful,' she said, moving
close to Birkin, and pointing to the red filaments with her long, white
finger.

'Had you never noticed them before?' he asked.

115　'No, never before,' she replied.

'And now you will always see them,' he said.

'Now I shall always see them,' she repeated. 'Thank you so much for
showing me. I think they're so beautiful – little red flames –'

Her absorption was strange, almost rhapsodic. Both Birkin and
120　Ursula were suspended. The little red pistillate flowers had some strange,
almost mystic-passionate attraction for her.

The lesson was finished, the books were put away, at last the class
was dismissed. And still Hermione sat at the table, with her chin in her
hand, her elbow on the table, her long white face pushed up, not
125　attending to anything. Birkin had gone to the window, and was looking
from the brilliantly-lighted room to the grey, colourless outside, where
rain was noiselessly falling. Ursula put away her things in the cupboard.

At length Hermione rose and came near to her.

'Your sister has come home?' she said.

130　'Yes,' said Ursula.

'And does she like being back in Beldover?'

'No,' said Ursula.

'No, I wonder she can bear it. It takes all my strength, to bear the

ugliness of this district, when I stay here. Won't you come and see me?
135   Won't you come with your sister to stay at Breadalby for a few days? –
do –'

'Thank you very much,' said Ursula.

'Then I will write to you,' said Hermione. 'You think your sister will
come? I should be so glad. I think she is wonderful. I think some of
140   her work is really wonderful. I have two water-wagtails, carved in
wood, and painted – perhaps you have seen it?'

'No,' said Ursula.

'I think it is perfectly wonderful – like a flash of instinct –'

'Her little carvings *are* strange,' said Ursula.

145   'Perfectly beautiful – full of primitive passion –'

'Isn't it queer that she always likes little things? – she must always
work small things, that one can put between one's hands, birds and
tiny animals. She likes to look through the wrong end of the opera-
glasses, and see the world that way – why is it, do you think?'

150   Hermione looked down at Ursula with that long, detached scrutinising
gaze that excited the younger woman.

'Yes,' said Hermione at length. 'It is curious. The little things seem
to be more subtle to her –'

'But they aren't, are they? A mouse isn't any more subtle than a lion,
155   is it?'

Again Hermione looked down at Ursula with that long scrutiny, as
if she were following some train of thought of her own, and barely
attending to the other's speech.

'I don't know,' she replied.

160   'Rupert, Rupert,' she sang mildly, calling him to her. He approached
in silence.

'Are little things more subtle than big things?' she asked, with the
odd grunt of laughter in her voice, as if she were making a game of
him in the question.

165   'Dunno,' he said.

'I hate subtleties,' said Ursula.

Hermione looked at her slowly.

'Do you?' she said.

'I always think they are a sign of weakness,' said Ursula, up in arms,
170   as if her prestige were threatened.

Hermione took no notice. Suddenly her face puckered, her brow was
knit with thought, she seemed twisted in troublesome effort for
utterance.

'Do you really think, Rupert,' she asked, as if Ursula were not present,
175   'do you really think it is worth while? Do you really think the children
are better for being roused to consciousness?'

A dark flash went over his face, a silent fury. He was hollow-

cheeked and pale, almost unearthly. And the woman, with her serious,
conscience-harrowing question tortured him on the quick.

180 'They are not roused to consciousness,' he said. 'Consciousness comes
to them, willy-nilly.'

'But do you think they are better for having it quickened, stimulated?
Isn't it better that they should remain unconscious of the hazel, isn't it
better that they should see as a whole, without all this pulling to pieces,
185 all this knowledge?'

'Would you rather, for yourself, know or not know, that the little
red flowers are there, putting out for pollen?' he asked harshly. His
voice was brutal, scornful, cruel.

Hermione remained with her face lifted up, abstracted. He hung
190 silent in irritation.

'I don't know,' she replied, balancing mildly. 'I don't know.'

'But knowing is everything to you, it is all your life,' he broke out.
She slowly looked at him.

'Is it?' she said.

195 'To know, that is your all, that is your life – you have only this, this
knowledge,' he cried. 'There is only one tree, there is only one fruit, in
your mouth.'

Again she was some time silent.

'Is there?' she said at last, with the same untouched calm. And then
200 in a tone of whimsical inquisitiveness: 'What fruit, Rupert?'

'The eternal apple,' he replied in exasperation, hating his own
metaphors.

'Yes,' she said. There was a look of exhaustion about her. For some
moments there was silence. Then, pulling herself together with a
205 convulsed movement, Hermione resumed, in a sing-song, casual voice.

'But leaving me apart, Rupert; do you think the children are better,
richer, happier, for all this knowledge; do you really think they are?
Or is it better to leave them untouched, spontaneous. Hadn't they better
be animals, simple animals, crude, violent, *anything*, rather than this
210 self-consciousness, this incapacity to be spontaneous.'

They thought she had finished. But with a queer rumbling in her
throat she resumed. 'Hadn't they better be anything than grow up
crippled, crippled in their souls, crippled in their feelings – so thrown
back – so turned back on themselves – incapable –' Hermione clenched
215 her fist like one in a trance – 'of any spontaneous action, always
deliberate, always burdened with choice, never carried away.'

Again they thought she had finished. But just as he was going to
reply, she resumed her queer rhapsody – 'never carried away, out of
themselves, always conscious, always self-conscious, always aware of
220 themselves. Isn't *anything* better than this? Better be animals, mere
animals with no mind at all, than this, this *nothingness* –'

'But do you think it is knowledge that makes us unliving and self-conscious?' he asked irritably.

She opened her eyes and looked at him slowly.

225   'Yes,' she said. She paused, watching him all the while, her eyes vague. Then she wiped her fingers across her brow, with a vague weariness. It irritated him bitterly. 'It is the mind,' she said, 'and that is death.' She raised her eyes slowly to him: 'Isn't the mind –' she said, with the convulsed movement of her body, 'isn't it our death? Doesn't

230   it destroy all our spontaneity, all our instincts? Are not the young people growing up to-day, really dead before they have a chance to live?'

'Not because they have too much mind, but too little,' he said brutally.

235   'Are you *sure*?' she cried. 'It seems to me the reverse. They are over-conscious, burdened to death with consciousness.'

'Imprisoned within a limited, false set of concepts,' he cried.

But she took no notice of this, only went on with her own rhapsodic interrogation.

240   'When we have knowledge, don't we lose everything but knowledge?' she asked pathetically. 'If I know about the flower, don't I lose the flower and have only the knowledge? Aren't we exchanging the substance for the shadow, aren't we forfeiting life for this dead quality of knowledge? And what does it mean to me after all? What does all

245   this knowing mean to me? It means nothing.'

'You are merely making words,' he said; 'knowledge means everything to you. Even your animalism, you want it in your head. You don't want to *be* an animal, you want to observe your own animal functions, to get a mental thrill out of them. It is all purely secondary – and more

250   decadent than the most hide-bound intellectualism. What is it but the worst and last form of intellectualism, this love of yours for passion and the animal instincts? Passion and the instincts – you want them hard enough, but through your head, in your consciousness. It all takes place in your head, under that skull of yours. Only you won't be

255   conscious of what *actually* is: you want the lie that will match the rest of your furniture.'

Hermione set hard and poisonous against this attack. Ursula stood covered with wonder and shame. It frightened her, to see how they hated each other.

260   'It's all that Lady of Shalott† business,' he said, in his strong abstract voice. He seemed to be charging her before the unseeing air. 'You've got that mirror, your own fixed will, your immortal understanding,

---

Lady of Shalott she sees the world through a   1842) by Alfred, Lord Tennyson (1809–92)
mirror in the poem of this title (1832 rev.

your own tight conscious world, and there is nothing beyond it. There, in the mirror, you must have everything. But now you have come to all
265 your conclusions, you want to go back and be like a savage, without knowledge. You want a life of pure sensation and "passion".'

He quoted the last word satirically against her. She sat convulsed with fury and violation, speechless, like a stricken pythoness of the Greek oracle.†
270 'But your passion is a lie,' he went on violently. 'It isn't passion at all, it is your *will*. It's your bullying will. You want to clutch things and have them in your power. You want to have things in your power. And why? Because you haven't got any real body, any dark sensual body of life. You have no sensuality. You have only your will and your
275 conceit of consciousness, and your lust for power, to *know*.'

He looked at her in mingled hate and contempt, also in pain because she suffered, and in shame because he knew he tortured her. He had an impulse to kneel and plead for forgiveness. But a bitterer red anger burned up to fury in him. He became unconscious of her, he was only
280 a passionate voice speaking.

'Spontaneous!' he cried. 'You and spontaneity! You, the most deliberate thing that ever walked or crawled! You'd be verily deliberately spontaneous – that's you. Because you want to have everything in your own volition, your deliberate voluntary consciousness. You want it all
285 in that loathsome little skull of yours, that ought to be cracked like a nut. For you'll be the same till it *is* cracked, like an insect in its skin. If one cracked your skull perhaps one might get a spontaneous, passionate woman out of you, with real sensuality. As it is, what you want is pornography – looking at yourself in mirrors, watching your naked
290 animal actions in mirrors, so that you can have it all in your consciousness, make it all mental.'

There was a sense of violation in the air, as if too much was said, the unforgivable. Yet Ursula was concerned now only with solving her own problems, in the light of his words. She was pale and abstracted.
295 'But do you really *want* sensuality?' she asked puzzled.

Birkin looked at her, and became intent in his explanation.

'Yes,' he said, 'that and nothing else, at this point. It is a fulfilment – the great dark knowledge you can't have in your head – the dark involuntary being. It is death to one's self – but it is the coming into
300 being of another.'

'But how? How can you have knowledge not in your head?' she asked, quite unable to interpret his phrases.

'In the blood,' he answered; 'when the mind and the known world is

---

pythoness ... oracle the priestess of Apollo   was called the Pythia
(who slew a python) at the oracle of Delphi

drowned in darkness – everything must go – there must be the deluge.
305   Then you find yourself in a palpable body of darkness, a demon –'

'But why should I be a demon –?' she asked.

' *"Woman wailing for her demon lover"*† –' he quoted – 'why, I don't
know.'

Hermione roused herself as from a death – annihilation.

310   'He is such a *dreadful* satanist, isn't he?' she drawled to Ursula, in a
queer resonant voice, that ended in a shrill little laugh of pure ridicule.
The two women were jeering at him, jeering him into nothingness. The
laugh of the shrill, triumphant female sounded from Hermione, jeering
him as if he were a neuter.

315   'No,' he said. 'You are the real devil who won't let life exist.'

She looked at him with a long, slow look, malevolent, supercilious.

'You know all about it, don't you?' she said, with slow, cold, cunning
mockery.

'Enough,' he replied, his face fixing fine and clear like steel. A horrible
320   despair, and at the same time a sense of release, liberation, came over
Hermione. She turned with a pleasant intimacy to Ursula.

'You are sure you will come to Breadalby?' she said, urging.

'Yes, I should like to very much,' replied Ursula.

Hermione looked down at her, gratified, reflecting, and strangely
325   absent, as if possessed, as if not quite there.

'I'm so glad,' she said, pulling herself together. 'Some time in about
a fortnight. Yes? I will write to you here, at the school, shall I? Yes.
And you'll be sure to come? Yes. I shall be so glad. Good-bye! Good-
bye!'

330   Hermione held out her hand and looked into the eyes of the other
woman. She knew Ursula as an immediate rival, and the knowledge
strangely exhilarated her. Also she was taking leave. It always gave her
a sense of strength, advantage, to be departing and leaving the other
behind. Moreover she was taking the man with her, if only in hate.

335   Birkin stood aside, fixed and unreal. But now, when it was his turn
to bid good-bye, he began to speak again.

'There's the whole difference in the world,' he said, 'between the
actual sensual being and the vicious mental-deliberate profligacy our
lot goes in for. In our night-time, there's always the electricity switched
340   on, we watch ourselves, we get it all in the head, really. You've got to
lapse out before you can know what sensual reality is, lapse into
unknowingness, and give up your volition. You've got to do it. You've
got to learn not-to-be, before you can come into being.

'But we have got such a conceit of ourselves – that's where it is. We
345   are so conceited, and so unproud. We've got no pride, we're all conceit,

---

woman wailing . . . demon lover   from the poem 'Kubla Khan' (1797) by S. T. Coleridge

so conceited in our own papier-mâché realised selves. We'd rather die than give up our little self-righteous self-opinionated self-will.'

There was silence in the room. Both women were hostile and resentful. He sounded as if he were addressing a meeting. Hermione merely paid no attention, stood with her shoulders tight in a shrug of dislike.

Ursula was watching him as if furtively, not really aware of what she was seeing. There was a great physical attractiveness in him – a curious hidden richness, that came through his thinness and his pallor like another voice, conveying another knowledge of him. It was in the curves of his brows and his chin, rich, fine, exquisite curves, the powerful beauty of life itself. She could not say what it was. But there was a sense of richness and of liberty.

'But we are sensual enough, without making ourselves so, aren't we?' she asked, turning to him with a certain golden laughter flickering under her greenish eyes, like a challenge. And immediately the queer, careless, terribly attractive smile came over his eyes and brows, though his mouth did not relax.

'No,' he said, 'we aren't. We're too full of ourselves.'

'Surely it isn't a matter of conceit,' she cried.

'That and nothing else.'

She was frankly puzzled.

'Don't you think that people are most conceited of all about their sensual powers?' she asked.

'That's why they aren't sensual – only sensuous — which is another matter. They're *always* aware of themselves – and they're so conceited, that rather than release themselves, and live in another world, from another centre, they'd –'

'You want your tea, don't you,' said Hermione, turning to Ursula with a gracious kindliness. 'You've worked all day –'

Birkin stopped short. A spasm of anger and chagrin went over Ursula. His face set. And he bade good-bye, as if he had ceased to notice her.

They were gone. Ursula stood looking at the door for some moments. Then she put out the lights. And having done so, she sat down again in her chair, absorbed and lost. And then she began to cry, bitterly, bitterly weeping: but whether for misery or joy, she never knew.

1916   1921

THE BRIDE

My love looks like a girl tonight,
      But she is old.
The plaits that lie along her pillow
      Are not gold,
5   But threaded with filigree silver,
      And uncanny cold.

She looks like a young maiden, since her brow
      Is smooth and fair;
Her cheeks are very smooth, her eyes are closed,
10   She sleeps a rare,
Still, winsome sleep, so still, and so composed.

Nay, but she sleeps like a bride, and dreams her dreams
      Of perfect things.
She lies at last, the darling, in the shape of her dream,
15   And her dead mouth sings
By its shape, like thrushes in clear evenings.

1916   1918

SNAKE

A snake came to my water-trough
On a hot, hot day, and I in pyjamas for the heat,
To drink there.

In the deep, strange-scented shade of the great dark carob-tree
5   I came down the steps with my pitcher
And must wait, must stand and wait, for there he was at the trough
      before me.

He reached down from a fissure in the earth-wall in the gloom
And trailed his yellow-brown slackness soft-bellied down, over the edge
      of the stone trough
And rested his throat upon the stone bottom,
10 And where the water had dripped from the tap, in a small clearness,
He sipped with his straight mouth,
Softly drank through his straight gums, into his slack long body,
Silently.

Someone was before me at my water-trough,
15   And I, like a second comer, waiting.

He lifted his head from his drinking, as cattle do,
And looked at me vaguely, as drinking cattle do,
And flickered his two-forked tongue from his lips, and mused a moment,
And stooped and drank a little more,
20   Being earth-brown, earth-golden from the burning bowels of the earth
On the day of Sicilian July, with Etna smoking.
The voice of my education said to me
He must be killed,
For in Sicily the black, black snakes are innocent, the gold are venomous.

25   And voices in me said, If you were a man
You would take a stick and break him now, and finish him off.

But must I confess how I liked him,
How glad I was he had come like a guest in quiet, to drink at my water-
     trough
And depart peaceful, pacified, and thankless,
30   Into the burning bowels of this earth?

Was it cowardice, that I dared not kill him?
Was it perversity, that I longed to talk to him?
Was it humility, to feel so honoured?
I felt so honoured.

35   And yet those voices:
If you were not afraid, you would kill him!
And truly I was afraid, I was most afraid,
But even so, honoured still more
That he should seek my hospitality
40   From out the dark door of the secret earth.

He drank enough
And lifted his head, dreamily, as one who has drunken,
And flickered his tongue like a forked night on the air, so black;
Seeming to lick his lips,
45   And looked around like a god, unseeing, into the air,
And slowly turned his head,
And slowly, very slowly, as if thrice adream,
Proceeded to draw his slow length curving round
And climb again the broken bank of my wall-face.

50   And as he put his head into that dreadful hole,
    And as he slowly drew up, snake-easing his shoulders, and entered
        farther,
    A sort of horror, a sort of protest against his withdrawing into that
        horrid black hole,
    Deliberately going into the blackness, and slowly drawing himself after,
    Overcame me now his back was turned.

55   I looked round, I put down my pitcher,
    I picked up a clumsy log
    And threw it at the water-trough with a clatter.

    I think it did not hit him,
    But suddenly that part of him that was left behind convulsed in
        undignified haste,
60   Writhed like lightning, and was gone
    Into the black hole, the earth-lipped fissure in the wall-front,
    At which, in the intense still noon, I stared with fascination.

    And immediately I regretted it.
    I thought how paltry, how vulgar, what a mean act!
65   I despised myself and the voices of my accursed human education.

    And I thought of the albatross,[†]
    And I wished he would come back, my snake.

    For he seemed to me again like a king,
    Like a king in exile, uncrowned in the underworld,
70   Now due to be crowned again.

    And so, I missed my chance with one of the lords
    Of life.
    And I have something to expiate;
    A pettiness.

                   Taormina.

1920   1921

---

albatross   see 'The Rime of the Ancient Mariner' by S. T. Coleridge (1772–1834)

THE MOSQUITO

When did you start your tricks,
Monsieur?

What do you stand on such high legs for?
Why this length of shredded shank,
5   You exaltation?

Is it so that you shall lift your centre of gravity upwards
And weigh no more than air as you alight upon me,
Stand upon me weightless, you phantom?

I heard a woman call you the Winged Victory†
10   In sluggish Venice.
You turn your head towards your tail, and smile.

How can you put so much devilry
Into that translucent phantom shred
Of a frail corpus?

15   Queer, with your thin wings and your streaming legs,
How you sail like a heron, or a dull clot of air,
A nothingness.

Yet what an aura surrounds you;
Your evil little aura, prowling, and casting numbness on my mind.
20   That is your trick, your bit of filthy magic:
Invisibility, and the anæsthetic power
To deaden my attention in your direction.

But I know your game now, streaky sorcerer.
Queer, how you stalk and prowl the air
25   In circles and evasions, enveloping me,
Ghoul on wings
Winged Victory.

Settle, and stand on long thin shanks
Eyeing me sideways, and cunningly conscious that I am aware,
30   You speck.

Winged Victory the Winged Victory of
  Samothrace, although headless and armless,
is a magnificent Hellenistic sculpture,
representing Nike, goddess of victory

I hate the way you lurch off sideways into the air
Having read my thoughts against you.

Come then, let us play at unawares,
And see who wins in this sly game of bluff.
35   Man or mosquito.

You don't know that I exist, and I don't know that you exist.
Now then!

It is your trump,
It is your hateful little trump,
40   You pointed fiend,
Which shakes my sudden blood to hatred of you:
It is your small, high, hateful bugle in my ear.

Why do you do it?
Surely it is bad policy.
45   They say you can't help it.

If that is so, then I believe a little in Providence protecting the innocent.
But it sounds so amazingly like a slogan,
A yell of triumph as you snatch my scalp.

Blood, red blood
50   Super-magical
Forbidden liquor.

I behold you stand
For a second enspasmed in oblivion,
Obscenely ecstasied
55   Sucking live blood,
My blood.

Such silence, such suspended transport,
Such gorging,
Such obscenity of trespass.

60   You stagger
As well as you may.
Only your accursed hairy frailty,
Your own imponderable weightlessness
Saves you, wafts you away on the very draught my anger makes in its snatching.

65 Away with a pæan of derision,
You winged blood-drop.

Can I not overtake you?
Are you one too many for me,
Winged Victory?
70 Am I not mosquito enough to out-mosquito you?

Queer what a big stain my sucked blood makes
Beside the infinitesimal faint smear of you!
Queer, what a dim dark smudge you have disappeared into!

Siracusa.

1921   1923

KANGAROO

In the northern hemisphere
Life seems to leap at the air, or skim under the wind
Like stags on rocky ground, or pawing horses, or springy scut-tailed
    rabbits.

Or else rush horizontal to charge at the sky's horizon,
5 Like bulls or bisons or wild pigs.

Or slip like water slippery towards its ends,
As foxes, stoats, and wolves, and prairie dogs.

Only mice, and moles, and rats, and badgers, and beavers, and perhaps
    bears
Seem belly-plumbed to the earth's mid-navel.
10 Or frogs that when they leap come flop, and flop to the centre of the
    earth.

But the yellow antipodal Kangaroo, when she sits up,
Who can unseat her, like a liquid drop that is heavy, and just touches
    earth.
The downward drip
The down-urge.
15 So much denser than cold-blooded frogs.

Delicate mother Kangaroo
Sitting up there rabbit-wise, but huge, plumb-weighted,
And lifting her beautiful slender face, oh! so much more gently and
    finely lined than a rabbit's, or than a hare's,

Lifting her face to nibble at a round white peppermint drop which she
loves, sensitive mother Kangaroo.

20   Her sensitive, long, pure-bred face.
Her full antipodal eyes, so dark,
So big and quiet and remote, having watched so many empty dawns in
silent Australia.

Her little loose hands, and drooping Victorian shoulders.
And then her great weight below the waist, her vast pale belly
25   With a thin young yellow little paw hanging out, and straggle of a long
thin ear, like ribbon,
Like a funny trimming to the middle of her belly, thin little dangle of
an immature paw, and one thin ear.

Her belly, her big haunches
And, in addition, the great muscular python-stretch of her tail.

There, she shan't have any more peppermint drops.
30   So she wistfully, sensitively sniffs the air, and then turns, goes off in
slow sad leaps.

On the long flat skis of her legs,
Steered and propelled by that steel-strong snake of a tail.

Stops again, half turns, inquisitive to look back.
While something stirs quickly in her belly, and a lean little face comes
out, as from a window,
35   Peaked and a bit dismayed,
Only to disappear again quickly away from the sight of the world, to
snuggle down in the warmth,
Leaving the trail of a different paw hanging out.

Still she watches with eternal, cocked wistfulness!
How full her eyes are, like the full, fathomless, shining eyes of an
Australian black-boy
40   Who has been lost so many centuries on the margins of existence!

She watches with insatiable wistfulness.
Untold centuries of watching for something to come,
For a new signal from life, in that silent lost land of the South.

Where nothing bites but insects and snakes and the sun, small life.
45   Where no bull roared, no cow ever lowed, no stag cried, no leopard
screeched, no lion coughed, no dog barked,

But all was silent save for parrots occasionally, in the haunted blue
    bush.

Wistfully watching, with wonderful liquid eyes.
And all her weight, all her blood, dripping sack-wise down towards the
    earth's centre,
And the live little-one taking in its paw at the door of her belly.

50 Leap then, and come down on the line that draws to the earth's deep,
    heavy centre.

                                                        Sydney.

1922   1923

INNOCENT ENGLAND

Oh what a pity, Oh! don't you agree
that figs aren't found in the land of the free!

Fig-trees don't grow in my native land;
there's never a fig-leaf near at hand

5   when you want one; so I did without;
and that is what the row's about.

Virginal, pure policemen came
and hid their faces for very shame,

while they carried the shameless things away
10 to gaol, to be hid from the light of day.

And Mr Mead,† that old, old lily
said: 'Gross! coarse! hideous!' – and I, like a silly,

thought he meant the faces of the police-court officials,
and how right he was, and I signed my initials

15 to confirm what he said; but alas, he meant
my pictures, and on the proceedings went.

Mr Mead Frederick Mead was the magistrate
who, at the age of eighty-two, presided in
the case against Lawrence (whose paintings
had been seized by police, 5 July 1929) at
the Marlborough Street Police Court, 8
August 1929

The upshot was, my picture must burn
that English artists might finally learn

when they painted a nude, to put a *cache sexe* on,
20   a cache sexe, a cache sexe, or else begone!

A fig-leaf; or, if you cannot find it
a wreath of mist, with nothing behind it.

A wreath of mist is the usual thing
in the north, to hide where the turtles* sing.   doves

25   Though they never sing, they never sing,
don't you dare to suggest such a thing

or Mr Mead will be after you.
– But what a pity I never knew

A wreath of English mist would do
30   as a cache sexe! I'd have put a whole fog.

But once and forever barks the old dog,
so my pictures are in prison, instead of in the Zoo.

1929   1930

THE SHIP OF DEATH

I

Now it is autumn and the falling fruit
and the long journey towards oblivion.

The apples falling like great drops of dew
to bruise themselves an exit from themselves.

5   And it is time to go, to bid farewell
to one's own self, and find an exit
from the fallen self.

II

Have you built your ship of death, O have you?
O build your ship of death, for you will need it.

10   The grim frost is at hand, when the apples will fall
     thick, almost thundrous, on the hardened earth.

     And death is on the air like a smell of ashes!
     Ah! can't you smell it?

     And in the bruised body, the frightened soul
15   finds itself shrinking, wincing from the cold
     that blows upon it through the orifices.

III

     And can a man his own quietus make
     with a bare bodkin?†

     With daggers, bodkins, bullets, man can make
20   a bruise or break of exit for his life;
     but is that a quietus, O tell me, is it quietus?

     Surely not so! for how could murder, even self-murder
     ever a quietus make?

IV

     O let us talk of quiet that we know,
25   that we can know, the deep and lovely quiet
     of a strong heart at peace!

     How can we this, our own quietus, make?

V

     Build then the ship of death, for you must take
     the longest journey, to oblivion.
30   And die the death, the long and painful death
     that lies between the old self and the new.

     Already our bodies are fallen, bruised, badly bruised,
     already our souls are oozing through the exit
     of the cruel bruise.

35   Already the dark and endless ocean of the end
     is washing in through the breaches of our wounds,
     already the flood is upon us.

---

quietus . . . bodkin See *Hamlet* III. 1. 75–6

Oh build your ship of death, your little ark
and furnish it with food, with little cakes, and wine
40   for the dark flight down oblivion.

VI

Piecemeal the body dies, and the timid soul
has her footing washed away, as the dark flood rises.

We are dying, we are dying, we are all of us dying
and nothing will stay the death-flood rising within us
45   and soon it will rise on the world, on the outside world.

We are dying, we are dying, piecemeal our bodies are dying
and our strength leaves us,
and our soul cowers naked in the dark rain over the flood,
cowering in the last branches of the tree of our life.

VII

50   We are dying, we are dying, so all we can do
is now to be willing to die, and to build the ship
of death to carry the soul on the longest journey.

A little ship, with oars and food
and little dishes, and all accoutrements
55   fitting and ready for the departing soul.
Now launch the small ship, now as the body dies
and life departs, launch out, the fragile soul
in the fragile ship of courage, the ark of faith
with its store of food and little cooking pans
60   and change of clothes,
upon the flood's black waste
upon the waters of the end
upon the sea of death, where still we sail
darkly, for we cannot steer, and have no port.

65   There is no port, there is nowhere to go
only the deepening black darkening still
blacker upon the soundless, ungurgling flood
darkness at one with darkness, up and down
and sideways utterly dark, so there is no direction any more.
70   And the little ship is there; yet she is gone.
She is not seen, for there is nothing to see her by.

She is gone! gone! and yet
somewhere she is there.
Nowhere!

VIII

75 And everything is gone, the body is gone
completely under, gone, entirely gone.
The upper darkness is heavy on the lower,
between them the little ship
is gone
80 she is gone.

It is the end, it is oblivion.

IX

And yet out of eternity, a thread
separates itself on the blackness,
a horizontal thread
85 that fumes a little with pallor upon the dark.
Is it illusion? or does the pallor fume
A little higher?
Ah wait, wait, for there's the dawn,
the cruel dawn of coming back to life
90 out of oblivion.

Wait, wait, the little ship
drifting, beneath the deathly ashy grey
of a flood-dawn.

Wait, wait! even so, a flush of yellow
95 and strangely, O chilled wan soul, a flush of rose.

A flush of rose, and the whole thing starts again.

X

The flood subsides, and the body, like a worn sea-shell
emerges strange and lovely.
And the little ship wings home, faltering and lapsing
100 on the pink flood,
and the frail soul steps out, into her house again
filling the heart with peace.

Swings the heart renewed with peace
even of oblivion.

105   Oh build your ship of death, oh build it!
        for you will need it.
        For the voyage of oblivion awaits you.

      1929   1932

BAVARIAN GENTIANS

Not every man has gentians in his house
in Soft September, at slow, sad Michaelmas.*   29 September

    Bavarian gentians, big and dark, only dark
    darkening the day-time, torch-like with the smoking blueness of Pluto's
        gloom,†
5   ribbed and torch-like, with their blaze of darkness spread blue
    down flattening into points, flattened under the sweep of white day
    torch-flower of the blue-smoking darkness, Pluto's dark-blue daze,
    black lamps from the halls of Dis,* burning dark blue,   Pluto
    giving off darkness, blue darkness, as Demeter's† pale lamps give off
        light,
10 lead me then, lead the way.

    Reach me a gentian, give me a torch!
    let me guide myself with the blue, forked torch of this flower
    down the darker and darker stairs, where blue is darkened on blueness
    even where Persephone† goes, just now, from the frosted September
15 to the sightless realm where darkness is awake upon the dark

    and Persephone herself is but a voice
    or a darkness invisible enfolded in the deeper dark
    of the arms Plutonic, and pierced with the passion of dense gloom,
    among the splendour of torches of darkness, shedding darkness on the
        lost bride and her groom.

      1932   1932

Pluto's gloom Pluto was god of the
    underworld
Demeter goddess of harvest
Persephone the daughter of Demeter, she was
carried off by Pluto. Demeter persuaded Zeus
to grant Persephone six months of each year
in this world. She spent the remaining
(winter) months in the underworld

Siegfried Sassoon
1886–1967

Siegfried Lorraine Sassoon was born in London and educated at Marlborough College and Clare College, Cambridge. His early enthusiasms were for sports, especially hunting, and for poetry. He joined the army in 1914 and won the MC, but later tried unsuccessfully to organise public opposition to the war. The anti-war poems of *The Old Huntsman* (1917) and *Counterattack* (1918), for which he is best known today, were followed by volumes of religious verse including *Vigils* (1935) and *Sequences* (1956). Sassoon also wrote several charming semi-autobiographical prose-works beginning with *Memoirs of a Foxhunting Man* (1928).

THE GENERAL

'Good-morning; good-morning!' the General said
When we met him last week on our way to the line.
Now the soldiers he smiled at are most of 'em dead,
And we're cursing his staff for incompetent swine.
5 'He's a cheery old card,' grunted Harry to Jack
As they slogged up to Arras[†] with rifle and pack.

．　　．　　．　　．

But he did for them both by his plan of attack.

1917

TO ANY DEAD OFFICER

Well, how are things in Heaven? I wish you'd say,
Because I'd like to know that you're all right.

Arras There was heavy fighting around this
northern French town throughout the First World War

Tell me, have you found everlasting day,
    Or been sucked in by everlasting night?
5 For when I shut my eyes your face shows plain;
    I hear you make some cheery old remark –
I can rebuild you in my brain,
    Though you've gone out patrolling in the dark.

You hated tours of trenches; you were proud
10   Of nothing more than having good years to spend;
Longed to get home and join the careless crowd
    Of chaps who work in peace with Time for friend.
That's all washed out now. You're beyond the wire:
    No earthly chance can send you crawling back;
15 You've finished with machine-gun fire –
    Knocked over in a hopeless dud-attack.

Somehow I always thought you'd get done in,
    Because you were so desperate keen to live:
You were all out to try and save your skin,
20   Well knowing how much the world had got to give.
You joked at shells and talked the usual 'shop,'
    Stuck to your dirty job and did it fine:
With 'Jesus Christ! when *will* it stop?
    Three years . . . It's hell unless we break their line.'

25 So when they told me you'd been left for dead
    I wouldn't believe them, feeling it *must* be true.
Next week the bloody Roll of Honour said
    'Wounded and missing' – (That's the thing to do
When lads are left in shell-holes dying slow,
30   With nothing but blank sky and wounds that ache,
Moaning for water till they know
    It's night, and then it's not worth while to wake!)

          .   .   .   .

Good-bye, old lad! Remember me to God,
    And tell Him that our Politicians swear
35 They won't give in till Prussian Rule's been trod
    Under the Heel of England . . . Are you there? . . .
Yes . . . and the War won't end for at least two years;
    But we've got stacks of men . . . I'm blind with tears,
    Staring into the dark. Cheero!
40 I wish they'd killed you in a decent show.

1917   1918

EVERYONE SANG

Everyone suddenly burst out singing;
And I was filled with such delight
As prisoned birds must find in freedom,
Winging wildly across the white
5   Orchards and dark-green fields; on – on – and out of sight.

Everyone's voice was suddenly lifted;
And beauty came like the setting sun:
My heart was shaken with tears; and horror
Drifted away . . . O, but Everyone
10 Was a bird; and the song was wordless; the singing will never be done.

1918   1918

Rupert Brooke

1887–1915

Rupert Chawner Brooke was born at Rugby, the son of a master at Rugby School. He was educated at Rugby and King's College, Cambridge. When he became a Fellow of King's in 1912 he was already well known for *Poems 1911* and for the verses contributed to the first volume (1912) of the series *Georgian Poetry*. In 1913 he travelled through North America to Tahiti. The five 'War Sonnets' published in *New Numbers* in 1915 when he was with the Royal Naval Volunteer Reserve gave him a fame which grew after his death, from blood-poisoning, at Scyros, although men in the trenches found their tone false. *Collected Poems* (1918) was followed by *Poetical Works* (1946), which contains additional pieces.

HEAVEN

Fish (fly-replete, in depth of June,
Dawdling away their wat'ry noon)
Ponder deep wisdom, dark or clear,
Each secret fishy hope or fear.
5   Fish say, they have their Stream and Pond;
But is there anything Beyond?
This life cannot be All, they swear,
For how unpleasant, if it were!
One may not doubt that, somehow, Good
10 Shall come of Water and of Mud;
And, sure, the reverent eye must see
A Purpose of Liquidity.
We darkly know, by Faith we cry,
The future is not Wholly Dry.
15 Mud unto mud! – Death eddies near –
Not here the appointed End, not here!
But somewhere, beyond Space and Time,
Is wetter water, slimier slime!
And there (they trust) there swimmeth One
20 Who swam ere rivers were begun,
Immense, of fishy form and mind,

Squamous, omnipotent, and kind;
And under that Almighty Fin,
The littlest fish may enter in.
25   Oh! never fly conceals a hook,
Fish say, in the Eternal Brook,
But more than mundane weeds are there,
And mud, celestially fair;
Fat caterpillars drift around,
30   And Paradisal grubs are found;
Unfading moths, immortal flies,
And the worm that never dies.
And in that Heaven of all their wish,
There shall be no more land, say fish.

1913   1915

CLOUDS

Down the blue night the unending columns press
   In noiseless tumult, break and wave and flow,
   Now tread the far South, or lift rounds of snow
Up to the white moon's hidden loveliness.
5   Some pause in their grave wandering comradeless,
      And turn with profound gesture vague and slow,
      As who would pray good for the world, but know
Their benediction empty as they bless.

They say that the Dead die not, but remain
10   Near to the rich heirs of their grief and mirth.
         I think they ride the calm mid-heaven, as these,
In wise majestic melancholy train,
         And watch the moon, and the still-raging seas,
         And men, coming and going on the earth.

The Pacific, October 1913   1915

PEACE

Now, God be thanked Who has matched us with His hour,
   And caught our youth, and wakened us from sleeping,
With hand made sure, clear eye, and sharpened power,
   To turn, as swimmers into cleanness leaping,
5   Glad from a world grown old and cold and weary,
   Leave the sick hearts that honour could not move,
And half-men, and their dirty songs and dreary,
   And all the little emptiness of love!

Oh! we, who have known shame, we have found release there,
10 Where there's no ill, no grief, but sleep has mending,
     Naught broken save this body, lost but breath;
Nothing to shake the laughing heart's long peace there
   But only agony, and that has ending;
     And the worst friend and enemy is but Death.

1914   1915

THE DEAD

These hearts were woven of human joys and cares,
   Washed marvellously with sorrow, swift to mirth.
The years had given them kindness. Dawn was theirs,
   And sunset, and the colours of the earth.
5   These had seen movement, and heard music; known
   Slumber and waking; loved; gone proudly friended;
Felt the quick stir of wonder; sat alone;
   Touched flowers and furs and cheeks. All this is ended.

There are waters blown by changing winds to laughter
10 And lit by the rich skies, all day. And after,
   Frost, with a gesture, stays the waves that dance
And wandering loveliness. He leaves a white
   Unbroken glory, a gathered radiance,
A width, a shining peace, under the night.

1914   1915

THE SOLDIER

If I should die, think only this of me:
   That there's some corner of a foreign field
That is for ever England. There shall be
   In that rich earth a richer dust concealed;
5 A dust whom England bore, shaped, made aware,
   Gave, once, her flowers to love, her ways to roam,
A body of England's, breathing English air,
   Washed by the rivers, blest by suns of home.

And think, this heart, all evil shed away,
10 A pulse in the eternal mind, no less
   Gives somewhere back the thoughts by England given;
Her sights and sounds; dreams happy as her day;
   And laughter, learnt of friends; and gentleness,
   In hearts at peace, under an English heaven.

November–December 1914   1915

Edwin Muir
1887–1959

Edwin Muir, novelist, essayist and critic, was born and educated on Orkney. With his wife he translated Kafka and other writers in German, but his poetry is little influenced by modernist trends. T. S. Eliot wrote the Preface to his *Collected Poems 1921–58* (1960).

THE COVENANT

The covenant of god and animal,
The frieze of fabulous creatures winged and crowned,
And in the midst the woman and the man –

Lost long ago in fields beyond the Fall –
5   Keep faith in sleep-walled night and there are found
On our long journey back where we began.

Then the heraldic crest of nature lost
Shines out again until the weariless wave
Roofs with its sliding horror all that realm.

10   What jealousy, what rage could overwhelm
The golden lion and lamb and vault a grave
For innocence, innocence past defence or cost?

1946

THE LABYRINTH

Since I emerged that day from the labyrinth,
Dazed with the tall and echoing passages,
The swift recoils, so many I almost feared
I'd meet myself returning at some smooth corner,
5   Myself or my ghost, for all there was unreal

After the straw ceased rustling and the bull[†]
Lay dead upon the straw and I remained,
Blood-splashed, if dead or alive I could not tell
In the twilight nothingness (I might have been
10   A spirit seeking his body through the roads
Of intricate Hades) – ever since I came out
To the world, the still fields swift with flowers, the trees
All bright with blossom, the little green hills, the sea,
The sky and all in movement under it,
15   Shepherds and flocks and birds and the young and old,
(I stared in wonder at the young and the old,
For in the maze time had not been with me;
I had strayed, it seemed, past sun and season and change,
Past rest and motion, for I could not tell
20   At last if I moved or stayed; the maze itself
Revolved around me on its hidden axis
And swept me smoothly to its enemy,
The lovely world) – since I came out that day,
There have been times when I have heard my footsteps
25   Still echoing in the maze, and all the roads
That run through the noisy world, deceiving streets
That meet and part and meet, and rooms that open
Into each other – and never a final room –
Stairways and corridors and antechambers
30   That vacantly wait for some great audience,
The smooth sea-tracks that open and close again,
Tracks undiscoverable, indecipherable,
Paths on the earth and tunnels underground,
And birds-tracks in the air – all seemed a part
35   Of the great labyrinth. And then I'd stumble
In sudden blindness, hasten, almost run,
As if the maze itself were after me
And soon must catch me up. But taking thought,
I'd tell myself, 'You need not hurry. This
40   Is the firm good earth. All roads lie free before you.'
But my bad spirit would sneer, 'No, do not hurry.
No need to hurry. Haste and delay are equal
In this one world, for there's no exit, none,
No place to come to, and you'll end where you are,
45   Deep in the centre of the endless maze.'

---

the bull   the Minotaur, a man-bull monster,
    was killed by Theseus in the labyrinth on Crete

I could not live if this were not illusion.
It is a world, perhaps; but there's another.
For once in a dream or trance I saw the gods
Each sitting on the top of his mountain-isle,
50 While down below the little ships sailed by,
Toy multitudes swarmed in the harbours, shepherds drove
Their tiny flocks to the pastures, marriage feasts
Went on below, small birthdays and holidays,
Ploughing and harvesting and life and death,
55 And all permissible, all acceptable,
Clear and secure as in a limpid dream.
But they, the gods, as large and bright as clouds,
Conversed across the sounds in tranquil voices
High in the sky above the untroubled sea,
60 And their eternal dialogue was peace
Where all these things were woven, and this our life
Was as a chord deep in that dialogue,
As easy utterance of harmonious words,
Spontaneous syllables bodying forth a world.

65 That was the real world; I have touched it once,
And now shall know it always. But the lie,
The maze, the wild-wood waste of falsehood, roads
That run and run and never reach an end,
Embowered in error – I'd be prisoned there
70 But that my soul has birdwings to fly free.

Oh these deceits are strong almost as life.
Last night I dreamt I was in the labyrinth,
And woke far on. I did not know the place.

1949

THE HORSES

Barely a twelvemonth after
The seven days war that put the world to sleep,
Late in the evening the strange horses came.
By then we had made our covenant with silence,
5 But in the first few days it was so still
We listened to our breathing and were afraid.
On the second day

The radios failed; we turned the knobs; no answer.
On the third day a warship passed us, heading north,
10   Dead bodies piled on the deck. On the sixth day
A plane plunged over us into the sea. Thereafter
Nothing. The radios dumb;
And still they stand in corners of our kitchens,
And stand, perhaps, turned on, in a million rooms
15   All over the world. But now if they should speak,
If on a sudden they should speak again,
If on the stroke of noon a voice should speak,
We would not listen, we would not let it bring
That old bad world that swallowed its children quick
20   At one great gulp. We would not have it again.
Sometimes we think of the nations lying asleep,
Curled blindly in impenetrable sorrow,
And then the thought confounds us with its strangeness.
The tractors lie about our fields; at evening
25   They look like dank sea-monsters couched and waiting.
We leave them where they are and let them rust:
'They'll moulder away and be like other loam'.
We make our oxen drag our rusty ploughs,
Long laid aside. We have gone back
30   Far past our fathers' land.
                                        And then, that evening
Late in the summer the strange horses came.
We heard a distant tapping on the road,
A deepening drumming; it stopped, went on again
35   And at the corner changed to hollow thunder.
We saw the heads
Like a wild wave charging and were afraid.
We had sold our horses in our fathers' time
To buy new tractors. Now they were strange to us
40   As fabulous steeds set on an ancient shield
Or illustrations in a book of knights.
We did not dare go near them. Yet they waited,
Stubborn and shy, as if they had been sent
By an old command to find our whereabouts
45   And that long-lost archaic companionship.
In the first moment we had never a thought
That they were creatures to be owned and used.
Among them were some half-a-dozen colts
Dropped in some wilderness of the broken world,
50   Yet new as if they had come from their own Eden.
Since then they have pulled our ploughs and borne our loads,

But that free servitude still can pierce our hearts.
Our life is changed; their coming our beginning.

1956

Edith Sitwell

1887–1964

Dame Edith Louise Sitwell, born at Scarborough, the daughter of Sir George Sitwell, grew up and was educated at home at Renishaw Hall, Derbyshire, in trying circumstances described by her brother, Sir Osbert (1892–1969), in his autobiography. Dame Edith was a journalist, critic, biographer and broadcaster, and a distinguished, although eccentric, public figure. She published poetry for nearly fifty years. Her early work was praised by Yeats, and her wartime poems of the London blitz were widely admired; her last collection *Music and Ceremonies* was published in 1963.

STILL FALLS THE RAIN

The Raids, 1940. Night and Dawn

Still falls the Rain –
Dark as the world of man, black as our loss –
Blind as the nineteen hundred and forty nails
Upon the Cross.

5 Still falls the Rain
With a sound like the pulse of the heart that is changed to the hammer-
    beat
In the Potter's Field,† and the sound of the impious feet

On the Tomb:
        Still falls the Rain
10 In the Field of Blood where the small hopes breed and the human brain
Nurtures its greed, that worm with the brow of Cain.

Still falls the Rain
At the feet of the Starved Man hung upon the Cross.
Christ that each day, each night, nails there, have mercy on us –
15 On Dives and on Lazarus:†
Under the Rain the sore and the gold are as one.

---

the Potter's Field   a cemetery near Jerusalem   *Dives . . . Lazarus*   See Luke 16. 19–31
  bought with Judas's blood-money

Still falls the Rain –
Still falls the Blood from the Starved Man's wounded Side:
He bears in His Heart all wounds, – those of the light that died,

20   The last faint spark
In the self-murdered heart, the wounds of the sad uncomprehending dark,
The wounds of the baited bear, –
The blind and weeping bear whom the keepers beat
On his helpless flesh . . . the tears of the hunted hare.

25   Still falls the Rain –
Then – O Ile† leape up to my God: who pulles me doune –
See, see where Christ's blood streames in the firmament:†
It flows from the Brow we nailed upon the tree
Deep to the dying, to the thirsting heart
30   That holds the fires of the world, – dark-smirched with pain
As Caesar's laurel crown.

Then sounds the voice of One who like the heart of man
Was once a child who among beasts has lain –
'Still do I love, still shed my innocent light, my Blood, for thee.'

1940   1942

O Ile . . . firmament   the words of the damned
Faustus at the close of the play Doctor

Faustus (?1592) by Christopher Marlowe
(1564–93)

T. E. Lawrence

1888–1935

Thomas Edward Lawrence, born in Tremadoc, the illegitimate son of Sir Robert Chapman, was educated at Oxford High School and Jesus College, Oxford. He went to Syria in 1909 and was an archaeologist there from 1910 until he joined British Intelligence in 1914. He was sent in 1916 to assist the Arab revolt against the Turks; he was with the Arab army which entered Damascus in 1918. As 'Lawrence of Arabia' he became a public hero in England. *Seven Pillars of Wisdom: A Triumph*, Lawrence's romantic account of these events, was written in three drafts (the first lost at Reading railway station). Edited by G. B. Shaw and Mrs Shaw, it was published privately in 1926 (trade edition, 1935). There has been much discussion of Lawrence's complicated, unusual personality, and of his years, from 1922 onwards, as an aircraftsman (under the assumed name of J. H. Ross) and as a private soldier (having changed his name, by deed poll, to T. E. Shaw). *The Mint*, which describes his service life, was published in New York in 1936 and in England in 1955.

From SEVEN PILLARS OF WISDOM

[Death Was Cheap]

Such news† shook us into quick life. We threw our baggage across our camels on the instant and set out over the rolling downs of this end of the tableland of Syria. Our hot bread was in our hands, and, as we ate, there mingled with it the taste of the dust of our large force crossing
5 the valley bottoms, and some taint of the strange keen smell of the wormwood which overgrew the slopes. In the breathless air of these evenings in the hills, after the long days of summer, everything struck very acutely on the senses: and when marching in a great column, as we were, the front camels kicked up the aromatic dust-laden branches
10 of the shrubs, whose scent-particles rose into the air and hung in a long mist, making fragrant the road of those behind.

Such news   that the Turks threatened to block the approach to Akaba

The slopes were clean with the sharpness of wormwood, and the hollows oppressive with the richness of their stronger, more luxuriant growths. Our night-passage might have been through a planted garden,
15 and these varieties part of the unseen beauty of successive banks of flowers. The noises too were very clear. Auda[†] broke out singing, away in front, and the men joined in from time to time, with the greatness, the catch at heart, of an army moving into battle.

We rode all night, and when dawn came were dismounting on the
20 crest of the hills between Batra and Aba el Lissan, with a wonderful view westwards over the green and gold Guweira plain, and beyond it to the ruddy mountains hiding Akaba and the sea. Gasim abu Dumeik, head of the Dhumaniyeh, was waiting anxiously for us, surrounded by his hard-bitten tribesmen, their grey strained faces flecked with the
25 blood of the fighting yesterday. There was a deep greeting for Auda and Nasir.[†] We made hurried plans, and scattered to the work, knowing we could not go forward to Akaba with this battalion in possession of the pass. Unless we dislodged it, our two months' hazard and effort would fail before yielding even first-fruits.

30 Fortunately the poor handling of the enemy gave us an unearned advantage. They slept on, in the valley, while we crowned the hills in wide circle about them unobserved. We began to snipe them steadily in their positions under the slopes and rock-faces by the water, hoping to provoke them out and up the hill in a charge against us. Meanwhile,
35 Zaal[†] rode away with our horsemen and cut the Maan telegraph and telephone in the plain.

This went on all day. It was terribly hot – hotter than ever before I had felt it in Arabia – and the anxiety and constant moving made it hard for us. Some even of the tough tribesmen broke down under the
40 cruelty of the sun, and crawled or had to be thrown under the rocks to recover in their shade. We ran up and down to supply our lack of numbers by mobility, ever looking over the long ranges of hill for a new spot from which to counter this or that Turkish effort. The hillsides were steep, and exhausted our breath, and the grasses twined like little
45 hands about our ankles as we ran, and plucked us back. The sharp reefs of limestone which cropped out over the ridges tore our feet, and long before evening the more energetic men were leaving a rusty print upon the ground with every stride.

Our rifles grew so hot with sun and shooting that they seared our
50 hands; and we had to be grudging of our rounds, considering every shot and spending great pains to make it sure. The rocks on which we flung ourselves for aim were burning, so that they scorched our breasts

---

Auda Chief of the Howeitat, a Beduin tribe of   *Nasir* Sherif of Medina
        northern Arabia   *Zaal* Auda's nephew

and arms, from which later the skin drew off in ragged sheets. The present smart made us thirst. Yet even water was rare with us; we
55 could not afford men to fetch enough from Batra, and if all could not drink, it was better that none should.

We consoled ourselves with knowledge that the enemy's enclosed valley would be hotter than our open hills: also that they were Turks, men of white meat, little apt for warm weather. So we clung to them,
60 and did not let them move or mass or sortie out against us cheaply. They could do nothing valid in return. We were no targets for their rifles, since we moved with speed, eccentrically. Also we were able to laugh at the little mountain guns which they fired up at us. The shells passed over our heads, to burst behind us in the air; and yet, of course,
65 for all that they could see from their hollow place, fairly amongst us above the hostile summits of the hill.

Just after noon I had a heat-stroke, or so pretended, for I was dead weary of it all, and cared no longer how it went. So I crept into a hollow where there was a trickle of thick water in a muddy cup of the
70 hills, to suck some moisture off its dirt through the filter of my sleeve. Nasir joined me, panting like a winded animal, with his cracked and bleeding lips shrunk apart in his distress: and old Auda appeared, striding powerfully, his eyes bloodshot and staring, his knotty face working with excitement.

75 He grinned with malice when he saw us lying there, spread out to find coolness under the bank, and croaked at me harshly, 'Well, how is it with the Howeitat? All talk and no work?' 'By God, indeed,' spat I back again, for I was angry with everyone and with myself, 'they shoot a lot and hit a little.' Auda, almost pale with rage, and trembling, tore
80 his head-cloth off and threw it on the ground beside me. Then he ran back up the hill like a madman, shouting to the men in his dreadful strained and rustling voice.

They came together to him, and after a moment scattered away downhill. I feared things were going wrong, and struggled to where he
85 stood alone on the hill-top, glaring at the enemy: but all he would say to me was, 'Get your camel if you want to see the old man's work'. Nasir called for his camel and we mounted.

The Arabs passed before us into a little sunken place, which rose to a low crest; and we knew that the hill beyond went down in a facile
90 slope to the main valley of Aba el Lissan, somewhat below the spring. All our four hundred camel men were here tightly collected, just out of sight of the enemy. We rode to their head, and asked the Shimt what it was and where the horsemen had gone.

He pointed over the ridge to the next valley above us, and said, 'With
95 Auda there': and as he spoke yells and shots poured up in a sudden torrent from beyond the crest. We kicked our camels furiously to the

edge, to see our fifty horsemen coming down the last slope into the main valley like a run-away, at full gallop, shooting from the saddle. As we watched, two or three went down, but the rest thundered forward at marvellous speed, and the Turkish infantry, huddled together under the cliff ready to cut their desperate way out towards Maan, in the first dusk began to sway in and out, and finally broke before the rush, adding their flight to Auda's charge.

Nasir screamed at me, 'Come on', with his bloody mouth; and we plunged our camels madly over the hill, and down towards the head of the fleeing enemy. The slope was not too steep for a camel-gallop, but steep enough to make their pace terrific, and their course uncontrollable: yet the Arabs were able to extend to right and left and to shoot into the Turkish brown. The Turks had been too bound up in the terror of Auda's furious charge against their rear to notice us as we came over the eastward slope: so we also took them by surprise and in the flank; and a charge of ridden camels going nearly thirty miles an hour was irresistible.

My camel, the Sherari racer, Naama, stretched herself out, and hurled downhill with such might that we soon out-distanced the others. The Turks fired a few shots, but mostly only shrieked and turned to run: the bullets they did send at us were not very harmful, for it took much to bring a charging camel down in a dead heap.

I had got among the first of them, and was shooting, with a pistol of course, for only an expert could use a rifle from such plunging beasts; when suddenly my camel tripped and went down emptily upon her face, as though pole-axed. I was torn completely from the saddle, sailed grandly through the air for a great distance, and landed with a crash which seemed to drive all the power and feeling out of me. I lay there, passively waiting for the Turks to kill me, continuing to hum over the verses of a half-forgotten poem, whose rhythm something, perhaps the prolonged stride of the camel, had brought back to my memory as we leaped down the hill-side:

For Lord I was free of all Thy flowers, but I chose the world's sad roses,
And that is why my feet are torn and mine eyes are blind with sweat.

While another part of my mind thought what a squashed thing I should look when all that cataract of men and camels had poured over.

After a long time I finished my poem, and no Turks came, and no camel trod on me: a curtain seemed taken from my ears: there was a great noise in front. I sat up and saw the battle over, and our men driving together and cutting down the last remnants of the enemy. My camel's body had laid behind me like a rock and divided the charge

into two streams: and in the back of its skull was the heavy bullet of
140   the fifth shot I fired.

Mohammed brought Obeyd, my spare camel, and Nasir came back
leading the Turkish commander, whom he had rescued, wounded, from
Mohammed el Dheilan's[†] wrath. The silly man had refused to surrender,
and was trying to restore the day for his side with a pocket pistol. The
145   Howeitat were very fierce, for the slaughter of their women on the day
before had been a new and horrible side of warfare suddenly revealed
to them. So there were only a hundred and sixty prisoners, many of
them wounded; and three hundred dead and dying were scattered over
the open valleys.

150   A few of the enemy got away, the gunners on their teams, and some
mounted men and officers with their Jazi guides. Mohammed el Dheilan
chased them for three miles into Mreigha, hurling insults as he rode,
that they might know him and keep out of his way. The feud of Auda
and his cousins had never applied to Mohammed, the political-minded,
155   who showed friendship to all men of his tribe when he was alone to do
so. Among the fugitives was Dhaif-Allah, who had done us the good
turn about the King's Well at Jefer.

Auda came swinging up on foot, his eyes glazed over with the rapture
of battle, and the words bubbling with incoherent speed from his mouth.
160   'Work, work, where are words, work, bullets, Abu Tayi' . . . and he
held up his shattered field-glasses, his pierced pistol-holster, and his
leather sword-scabbard cut to ribbons. He had been the target of a
volley which had killed his mare under him, but the six bullets through
his clothes had left him scatheless.

165   He told me later, in strict confidence, that thirteen years before he
had bought an amulet Koran for one hundred and twenty pounds and
had not since been wounded. Indeed, Death had avoided his face, and
gone scurvily about killing brothers, sons and followers. The book was
a Glasgow reproduction, costing eighteen pence; but Auda's deadliness
170   did not let people laugh at his superstition.

He was wildly pleased with the fight, most of all because he had
confounded me and shown what his tribe could do. Mohammed was
wroth with us for a pair of fools, calling me worse than Auda, since I
had insulted him by words like flung stones to provoke the folly which
175   had nearly killed us all: though it had killed only two of us, one Rueili
and one Sherari.

It was, of course, a pity to lose any one of our men, but time was of
importance to us, and so imperative was the need of dominating Maan,
to shock the little Turkish garrisons between us and the sea into
180   surrender, that I would have willingly lost much more than two. On

---

Mohammed el Dheilan   Auda's cousin

occasions like this Death justified himself and was cheap.

I questioned the prisoners about themselves, and the troops in Maan; but the nerve crisis had been too severe for them. Some gaped at me and some gabbled, while others, with helpless weepings, embraced my
185   knees, protesting at every word from us that they were fellow Moslems and my brothers in the faith.

Finally I got angry and took one of them aside and was rough to him, shocking him by new pain into a half-understanding, when he answered well enough, and reassuringly, that their battalion was the
190   only reinforcement, and it merely a reserve battalion; the two companies in Maan would not suffice to defend its perimeter.

This meant we could take it easily, and the Howeitat clamoured to be led there, lured by the dream of unmeasured loot, though what we had taken here was a rich prize. However, Nasir, and afterwards Auda,
195   helped me stay them. We had no supports, no regulars, no guns, no base nearer than Wejh, no communications, no money even, for our gold was exhausted, and we were issuing our own notes, promises to pay 'when Akaba is taken', for daily expenses. Besides, a strategic scheme was not changed to follow up a tactical success. We must push
200   to the coast, and re-open sea-contact with Suez.

Yet it would be good to alarm Maan further: so we sent mounted men to Mreigha and took it; and to Waheida and took it. News of this advance, of the loss of the camels on the Shobek road, of the demolition of El Haj, and of the massacre of their relieving battalion all came to
205   Maan together, and caused a very proper panic. The military head-quarters wired for help, the civil authorities loaded their official archive into trucks, and left, hot-speed, for Damascus.

1922   1926

T. S. Eliot
1888–1965

Thomas Stearns Eliot was born in St Louis, Missouri, and educated at Harvard, the Sorbonne, and Merton College, Oxford. He lived in England from 1915 and became a British subject (and member of the Church of England) in 1927. He taught at Highgate School during the First World War and worked for Lloyds Bank from 1917 until 1925, when he became a director of the publishing firm of Faber and Gwyer. His first volumes of verse, *Prufrock and Other Observations* (1917), followed by *Poems* (1919) and *The Waste Land* (1922), made him a leader of the literary avant-garde. From an awareness of the fragmented, rootless nature of modern culture, expressed in the poems of this period, Eliot moved towards the High Anglican faith reflected in 'Journey of the Magi' (1927), 'Ash Wednesday' (1930), and *Four Quartets* ('Burnt Norton', 1936, 'East Coker', 1940, 'The Dry Salvages', 1941, 'Little Gidding', 1942, published together in New York, 1943). Of his verse plays, *Murder in the Cathedral* (1935), which dramatised the martyrdom of St Thomas Becket and was written to be performed in Canterbury Cathedral, is the most successful. As a critic Eliot helped to revive appreciation of seventeenth-century poetry. *The Sacred Wood: Essays on Poetry and Criticism* (1920) and *Notes Towards the Definition of Culture* (1948) were especially influential in the teaching of English literature, despite the conservatism behind Eliot's emphasis on literary tradition. *Old Possum's Book of Practical Cats* (1939) is a children's classic. Eliot was awarded the Nobel Prize in 1948 and the Order of Merit in the same year.

It had been planned to include here one section from *The Waste Land*, but it was the poet's wish that the work should not appear except in its entirety.

THE LOVE SONG OF J. ALFRED PRUFROCK

S'io credessi che mia risposta fosse
a persona che mai tornasse al mondo,

questa fiamma staria senza più scosse.
Ma per ciò che giammai di questo fondo
non tornò vivo alcun, s'i'odo il vero,
senza tema d'infamia ti rispondo.†

Let us go then, you and I,
When the evening is spread out against the sky
Like a patient etherised upon a table;
Let us go, through certain half-deserted streets,
5   The muttering retreats
Of restless nights in one-night cheap hotels
And sawdust restaurants with oyster-shells:
Streets that follow like a tedious argument
Of insidious intent
10   To lead you to an overwhelming question . . .
Oh, do not ask, 'What is it?'
Let us go and make our visit.

In the room the women come and go
Talking of Michelangelo.

15   The yellow fog that rubs its back upon the window-panes,
The yellow smoke that rubs its muzzle on the window-panes,
Licked its tongue into the corners of the evening,
Lingered upon the pools that stand in drains,
Let fall upon its back the soot that falls from chimneys,
20   Slipped by the terrace, made a sudden leap,
And seeing that it was a soft October night,
Curled once about the house, and fell asleep.
And indeed there will be time
For the yellow smoke that slides along the street
25   Rubbing its back upon the window-panes;
There will be time, there will be time
To prepare a face to meet the faces that you meet;
There will be time to murder and create,
And time for all the works and days† of hands
30   That lift and drop a question on your plate;
Time for you and time for me,
And time yet for a hundred indecisions,

S'io credessi . . . rispondo Guido de Montefeltro is speaking in the eighth circle of hell, in the *Inferno* (xxvii 61–66) of Dante Alighieri (1265–1321): 'If I thought that I were speaking to someone who would ever return to the world of the living, this flame [in which I am imprisoned] would remain undisturbed [by my speech]; but since nobody has ever returned alive from these depths, I can reply to you without fear of infamy'
works and days the English title of a poem by the Greek poet Hesiod (eighth century BC)

And for a hundred visions and revisions,
Before the taking of a toast and tea.

35   In the room the women come and go
Talking of Michelangelo.

    And indeed there will be time
To wonder, 'Do I dare?' and, 'Do I dare?'
Time to turn back and descend the stair,
40   With a bald spot in the middle of my hair –
(They will say: 'How his hair is growing thin!')
My morning coat, my collar mounting firmly to the chin,
My necktie rich and modest, but asserted by a simple pin –
(They will say: 'But how his arms and legs are thin!')
45   Do I dare
Disturb the universe?
In a minute there is time
For decisions and revisions which a minute will reverse.

    For I have known them all already, known them all –
50   Have known the evenings, mornings, afternoons,
I have measured out my life with coffee spoons;
I know the voices dying with a dying fall†
Beneath the music from a farther room.
    So how should I presume?

55   And I have known the eyes already, known them all –
The eyes that fix you in a formulated phrase,
And when I am formulated, sprawling on a pin,
When I am pinned and wriggling on the wall,
Then how should I begin
60   To spit out all the butt-ends of my days and ways?
    And how should I presume?

    And I have known the arms already, known them all –
Arms that are braceleted and white and bare
(But in the lamplight, downed with light brown hair!)
65   Is it perfume from a dress
That makes me so digress?
Arms that lie along a table, or wrap about a shawl.
    And should I then presume?
    And how should I begin?

---

dying fall   see *Twelfth Night* I.1.4

70   Shall I say, I have gone at dusk through narrow streets
        And watched the smoke that rises from the pipes
        Of lonely men in shirt-sleeves, leaning out of windows? . . .

            I should have been a pair of ragged claws
            Scuttling across the floors of silent seas.

75   And the afternoon, the evening, sleeps so peacefully!
        Smoothed by long fingers,
        Asleep . . . tired . . . or it malingers,
        Stretched on the floor, here beside you and me.
        Should I, after tea and cakes and ices,
80   Have the strength to force the moment to its crisis?
        But though I have wept and fasted, wept and prayed,
        Though I have seen my head (grown slightly bald)
                brought in upon a platter,†
        I am no prophet† – and here's no great matter;
        I have seen the moment of my greatness flicker,
85   And I have seen the eternal Footman hold my coat, and
                snicker,
        And in short, I was afraid.

            And would it have been worth it, after all,
        After the cups, the marmalade, the tea,
        Among the porcelain, among some talk of you and me,
90   Would it have been worth while,
        To have bitten off the matter with a smile,
        To have squeezed the universe into a ball
        To roll† it towards some overwhelming question,
        To say: 'I am Lazarus,† come from the dead,
95   Come back to tell you all, I shall tell you all' –
        If one, settling a pillow by her head,
            Should say: 'That is not what I meant at all.
            That is not it, at all.'

            And would it have been worth it, after all,
100   Would it have been worth while,
        After the sunsets and the dooryards and the sprinkled
                streets,
        After the novels, after the teacups, after the skirts that

---

a platter . . . prophet an allusion to the death
of John the Baptist. See Mark 6 and Matthew
17
squeezed . . . roll an echo of 'To His Coy

Mistress' by Andrew Marvell (1621–78): 'Let
us roll all our strength and all / Our sweetness
up into one ball'
Lazarus See John 11

trail along the floor –
And this, and so much more? –
It is impossible to say just what I mean!
105   But as if a magic lantern threw the nerves in patterns on a
       screen:
Would it have been worth while
If one, settling a pillow or throwing off a shawl,
And turning toward the window, should say:
   'That is not it at all,
110   That is not what I meant, at all.'

   No! I am not Prince Hamlet, nor was meant to be;
Am an attendant lord, one that will do
To swell a progress, start a scene or two,
Advise the prince; no doubt, an easy tool,
115   Deferential, glad to be of use,
Politic,† cautious, and meticulous;
Full of high sentence,† but a bit obtuse;
At times, indeed, almost ridiculous –
Almost, at times, the Fool.†

120   I grow old . . . I grow old . . .
I shall wear the bottoms of my trousers rolled.

   Shall I part my hair behind? Do I dare to eat a peach?
I shall wear white flannel trousers, and walk upon the beach.
I have heard the mermaids singing, each to each.

125   I do not think that they will sing to me.

I have seen them riding seaward on the waves
Combing the white hair of the waves blown back
When the wind blows the water white and black.

We have lingered in the chambers of the sea
130   By sea-girls wreathed with seaweed red and brown
Till human voices wake us, and we drown.

1910/11   1915

Politic   this line suggests Polonius in *Hamlet*   *the Fool*   another Shakespearean role
high sentence   solemn opinions

SWEENEY AMONG THE NIGHTINGALES

ὦμοι, πέπληγμαι καιρίαν πληγὴν ἔσω.
['Alas, I have been struck a fatal blow' – Aeschylus, *Agememnon*)

Apeneck Sweeney spreads his knees
Letting his arms hang down to laugh,
The zebra stripes along his jaw
Swelling to maculate* giraffe.   spotted

5   The circles of the stormy moon
Slide westward toward the River Plate,†
Death and the Raven† drift above
And Sweeney guards the hornèd gate.†

Gloomy Orion and the Dog†
10   Are veiled; and hushed the shrunken seas;
The person in the Spanish cape
Tries to sit on Sweeney's knees

Slips and pulls the table cloth
Overturns a coffee-cup,
15   Reorganised upon the floor
She yawns and draws a stocking up;

The silent man in mocha brown
Sprawls at the window-sill and gapes;
The waiter brings in oranges
20   Bananas figs and hothouse grapes;

The silent vertebrate in brown
Contracts and concentrates, withdraws;
Rachel *née* Rabinovitch
Tears at the grapes with murderous paws;

25   She and the lady in the cape
Are suspect, thought to be in league;
Therefore the man with heavy eyes
Declines the gambit, shows fatigue,

River Plate   in South America
the Raven   the constellation
horned gate   the gate of the underworld by

which dreams pass
Orion . . . Dog   the constellations of the hunter
Orion and the dog Canis major

Leaves the room and reappears
30 Outside the window, leaning in,
Branches of wistaria
Circumscribe a golden grin;

The host with someone indistinct
Converses at the door apart,
35 The nightingales are singing near
The Convent of the Sacred Heart,

And sang within the bloody wood[†]
When Agamemnon cried aloud
And let their liquid siftings fall
40 To stain the stiff dishonoured shroud.

1918   1919

From FOUR QUARTETS

Little Gidding[†]

I

Midwinter spring is its own season
Sempiternal though sodden towards sundown,
Suspended in time, between pole and tropic.
When the short day is brightest, with frost and fire,
5 The brief sun flames the ice, on pond and ditches,
In windless cold that is the heart's heat,
Reflecting in a watery mirror
A glare that is blindness in the early afternoon.
And glow more intense than blaze of branch, or brazier,
10 Stirs the dumb spirit: no wind, but pentecostal fire[†]
In the dark time of the year. Between melting and freezing
The soul's sap quivers. There is no earth smell
Or smell of living thing. This is the spring time
But not in time's covenant. Now the hedgerow

---

the bloody wood Eliot had in mind the wood
where, in Greek mythology, Orpheus was
torn apart by Thracian women, as well as
Agamemnon's murder by his wife
Clytemnestra

Little Gidding A manor near Huntingdon
where a religious community lived between
1625 and 1646
pentecostal fire See Acts 2. 3

15   Is blanched for an hour with transitory blossom
      Of snow, a bloom more sudden
      Than that of summer, neither budding nor fading,
      Not in the scheme of generation.
      Where is the summer, the unimaginable
20   Zero summer?

                    If you came this way,
      Taking the route you would be likely to take
      From the place you would be likely to come from,
      If you came this way in may time, you would find the hedges
25   White again, in May, with voluptuary sweetness.
      It would be the same at the end of the journey,
      If you came at night like a broken king,†
      If you came by day not knowing what you came for,
      It would be the same, when you leave the rough road
30   And turn behind the pig-sty to the dull façade
      And the tombstone. And what you thought you came for
      Is only a shell, a husk, of meaning
      From which the purpose breaks only when it is fulfilled
      If at all. Either you had no purpose
35   Or the purpose is beyond the end you figured
      And is altered in fulfilment. There are other places
      Which also are the world's end, some at the sea jaws,
      Or over a dark lake, in a desert or a city –
      But this is the nearest, in place and time,
40   Now and in England.

                    If you came this way,
      Taking any route, starting from anywhere,
      At any time or at any season,
      It would always be the same: you would have to put off
45   Sense and notion. You are not here to verify,
      Instruct yourself, or inform curiosity
      Or carry report. You are here to kneel
      Where prayer has been valid. And prayer is more
      Than an order of words, the conscious occupation
50   Of the praying mind, or the sound of the voice praying.
      And what the dead had no speech for, when living,
      They can tell you, being dead: the communication
      Of the dead is tongued with fire† beyond the language of the living.

---

a broken king   Charles I visited Little Gidding   *tongued with fire*   see Acts 2. 4
      after his defeat at Naseby in 1645

Here, the intersection of the timeless moment
55   Is England and nowhere. Never and always.

II

Ash on an old man's sleeve
Is all the ash the burnt roses leave.
Dust in the air[†] suspended
Marks the place where a story ended.
60   Dust inbreathed was a house –
The wail, the wainscot and the mouse.
The death of hope and despair,
      This is the death of air.

There are flood and drouth
65   Over the eyes and in the mouth,
Dead water and dead sand
Contending for the upper hand.
The parched eviscerate soil
Gapes at the vanity of toil,
70   Laughs without mirth.
      This is the death of earth.

Water and fire succeed
The town, the pasture and the weed.
Water and fire deride
75   The sacrifice that we denied.
Water and fire shall rot
The marred foundations we forgot,
Of sanctuary and choir.
      This is the death of water and fire.

80   In the uncertain hour before the morning
      Near the ending of interminable night
      At the recurrent end of the unending
After the dark dove with the flickering tongue
      Has passed below the horizon of his homing
85   While the dead leaves still rattled on like tin
Over the asphalt where no other sound was
      Between three districts whence the smoke arose
      I met one walking, loitering and hurried
As if blown towards me like the metal leaves
90   Before the urban dawn wind unresisting.

Dust in the air   Eliot was a 'fire-watcher' in the London Blitz

---

And as I fixed upon the down-turned face
That pointed scrutiny with which we challenge
  The first-met stranger in the waning dusk
  I caught the sudden look of some dead master
95 Whom I had known, forgotten, half recalled
  Both one and many; in the brown baked features
  The eyes of a familiar compound ghost
Both intimate and unidentifiable.
  So I assumed a double part, and cried
100 And heard another's voice cry: 'What! are *you* here?'
Although we were not. I was still the same,
  Knowing myself yet being someone other –
  And he a face still forming; yet the words sufficed
To compel the recognition they preceded.
105 And so, compliant to the common wind,
  Too strange to each other for misunderstanding,
In concord at this intersection time
  Of meeting nowhere, no before and after,
  We trod the pavement in a dead patrol.
110 I said: 'The wonder that I feel is easy,
  Yet ease is cause of wonder. Therefore speak:
  I may not comprehend, may not remember.'
And he: 'I am not eager to rehearse
  My thoughts and theory which you have forgotten.
115 These things have served their purpose: let them be.
So with your own, and pray they be forgiven
  By others, as I pray you to forgive
  Both bad and good. Last season's fruit is eaten
And the fullfed beast shall kick the empty pail.
120 For last year's words belong to last year's language
  And next year's words await another voice.
But, as the passage now presents no hindrance
  To the spirit unappeased and peregrine[†]
  Between two worlds become much like each other,
125 So I find words I never thought to speak
  In streets I never thought I should revisit
  When I left my body on a distant shore.
Since our concern was speech, and speech impelled us
  To purify the dialect of the tribe[†]
130 And urge the mind to aftersight and foresight,

---

peregrine   in flight
To purify . . . tribe   Translates a line in 'Le
 Tombeau d'Edgar Poe' by the French poet

Stéphane Mallarmé (1842–98): '*Donner un
sens plus pur aux mots de la tribu*'

Let me disclose the gifts reserved for age
    To set a crown upon your lifetime's effort.
    First, the cold friction of expiring sense
Without enchantment, offering no promise
135   But bitter tastelessness of shadow fruit
    As body and soul begin to fall asunder.
Second, the conscious impotence of rage
    At human folly, and the laceration
    Of laughter at what ceases to amuse.
140 And last, the rending pain of re-enactment
    Of all that you have done, and been; the shame
    Of motives late revealed, and the awareness
Of things ill done and done to others' harm
    Which once you took for exercise of virtue.
145   Then fools' approval stings, and honour stains.
From wrong to wrong the exasperated spirit
    Proceeds, unless restored by that refining fire
    Where you must move in measure, like a dancer.'
The day was breaking. In the disfigured street
150 He left me, with a kind of valediction,
    And faded on the blowing of the horn.

III

There are three conditions which often look alike
Yet differ completely, flourish in the same hedgerow:
Attachment to self and to things and to persons, detachment
155 From self and from things and from persons; and, growing between
      them, indifference
Which resembles the others as death resembles life,
Being between two lives – unflowering, between
The live and the dead nettle. This is the use of memory:
For liberation – not less of love but expanding
160 Of love beyond desire, and so liberation
From the future as well as the past. Thus, love of a country
Begins as attachment to our own field of action
And comes to find that action of little importance
Though never indifferent. History may be servitude,
165 History may be freedom. See, now they vanish,
The faces and places, with the self which, as it could, loved them,
To become renewed, transfigured, in another pattern.
Sin is Behovely,[†] but

Sin is behovely . . . well A quotation from
   Sixteen Revelations of Divine Love by the

mystic Dame Julian of Norwich (?1342–
?1416)

All shall be well, and
170   All manner of thing shall be well.
      If I think, again, of this place,
      And of people, not wholly commendable,
      Of no immediate kin or kindness,
      But some of peculiar genius,
175   All touched by a common genius,
      United in the strife which divided them;
      If I think of a king† at nightfall,
      Of three men,† and more, on the scaffold
      And a few† who died forgotten
180   In other places, here and abroad,
      And of one who died† blind and quiet,
      Why should we celebrate
      These dead men more than the dying?
      It is not to ring the bell backward
185   Nor is it an incantation
      To summon the spectre of a Rose.
      We cannot revive old factions
      We cannot restore old policies
      Or follow an antique drum.
190   These men, and those who opposed them
      And those whom they opposed
      Accept the constitution of silence
      And are folded in a single party.
      Whatever we inherit from the fortunate
195   We have taken from the defeated
      What they had to leave us – a symbol:
      A symbol perfected in death.
      And all shall be well and
      All manner of thing shall be well
200   By the purification of the motive
      In the ground of our beseeching.
      Is a step to the block, to the fire, down the sea's throat
      Or to an illegible stone: and that is where we start.
      We die with the dying:
205   See, they depart, and we go with them.
      We are born with the dead:
      See, they return, and bring us with them.

---

a king   Charles I, but also, allegorically, Christ
three men   We may think of Thomas (first earl of) Strafford (1593–1641), Archbishop William Laud (1573–1645) and King Charles I (1600–49) – all beheaded – or of Christ and the two thieves crucified beside him
a few   other Christian martyrs
one who died   John Milton (1608–74), who advocated King Charles's execution; also St John the Divine

The moment of the rose and the moment of the yew-tree
Are of equal duration. A people without history
210   Is not redeemed from time, for history is a pattern
Of timeless moments. So, while the light fails
On a winter's afternoon, in a secluded chapel
History is now and England.

With the drawing of this Love and the voice of this Calling†

215   We shall not cease from exploration
And the end of all our exploring
Will be to arrive where we started
And know the place for the first time.
Through the unknown, remembered gate
220   When the last of earth left to discover
Is that which was the beginning;
At the source of the longest river
The voice of the hidden waterfall
And the children in the apple-tree
225   Not known, because not looked for
But heard, half-heard, in the stillness
Between two waves of the sea.
Quick now, here, now, always –
A condition of complete simplicity
230   (Costing not less than everything)
And all shall be well and
All manner of thing shall be well
When the tongues of flame are in-folded
Into the crowned knot of fire
235   And the fire and the rose are one.

1942   1943

With the drawing . . . Calling   a quotation from   fourteenth century, *The Cloud of Unknowing*
the anonymous mystical work of the

Isaac Rosenberg
1890–1918

Isaac Rosenberg was born in Bristol, the son of a Jewish immigrant from Russia, and was brought up in the East End of London where he went to school. He then attended the Slade School of Art, published two books of verse, *Night and Day* (1912) and *Youth* (1915), and enlisted in the ranks in 1915. He was killed in action. The quality of his war poems was not widely recognised until his *Collected Works* appeared in 1937.

GOD MADE BLIND

It were a proud God-guiling, to allure
And flatter, by some cheat of ill, our Fate
To hold back the perfect crookedness, its hate
Devised, and keep it poor,
5   And ignorant of our joy —
Masked in a giant wrong of cruel annoy,
That stands as some bleak hut to frost and night,
While hidden in bed is warmth and mad delight.

For all Love's heady valour and loved pain
10   Towers in our sinews that may not suppress
(Shut to God's eye) Love's springing eagerness,
And mind to advance his gain
Of gleeful secrecy
Through dolorous clay, which his eternity
15   Has pierced, in light that pushes out to meet
Eternity without us, heaven's heat.

And then, when Love's power hath increased so
That we must burst or grow to give it room,
And we can no more cheat our God with gloom,
20   We'll cheat Him with our joy.
For say? what can God do

To us, to Love, whom we have grown into?
Love! the poured rays of God's Eternity!
We are grown God – and shall His self-hate be?

1914   1915

BREAK OF DAY IN THE TRENCHES

The darkness crumbles away.
It is the same old druid Time as ever,
Only a live thing leaps my hand,
A queer sardonic rat,
5 As I pull the parapet's poppy
To stick behind my ear.
Droll rat, they would shoot you if they knew
Your cosmopolitan sympathies.
Now you have touched this English hand
10 You will do the same to a German
Soon, no doubt, if it be your pleasure
To cross the sleeping green between.
It seems you inwardly grin as you pass
Strong eyes, fine limbs, haughty athletes,
15 Less chanced than you for life,
Bonds to the whims of murder,
Sprawled in the bowels of the earth,
The torn fields of France.
What do you see in our eyes
20 At the shrieking iron and flame
Hurled through still heavens?
What quaver – what heart aghast?
Poppies whose roots are in man's veins
Drop, and are ever dropping;
25 But mine in my ear is safe –
Just a little white with the dust.

June 1916   1922

LOUSE HUNTING

Nudes – stark and glistening,
Yelling in lurid glee. Grinning faces
And raging limbs
Whirl over the floor one fire.
5   For a shirt verminously busy
Yon soldier tore from his throat, with oaths
Godhead might shrink at, but not the lice.
And soon the shirt was aflare
Over the candle he'd lit while we lay.

10 Then we all sprang up and stript
To hunt the verminous brood.
Soon like a demons' pantomime
The place was raging.
See the silhouettes agape,
15 See the gibbering shadows
Mixed with the battled arms on the wall.
See gargantuan hooked fingers
Pluck in supreme flesh
To smutch supreme littleness.
20 See the merry limbs in hot Highland fling
Because some wizard vermin
Charmed from the quiet this revel
When our ears were half lulled
By the dark music
25 Blown from Sleep's trumpet.

1917   1922

RETURNING, WE HEAR THE LARKS

Sombre the night is.
And though we have our lives, we know
What sinister threat lurks there.

Dragging these anguished limbs, we only know
5 This poison-blasted track opens on our camp –
On a little safe sleep.

But hark! joy – joy – strange joy.
Lo! heights of night ringing with unseen larks.
Music showering our upturned list'ning faces.

10 Death could drop from the dark
As easily as song –
But song only dropped,
Like a blind man's dreams on the sand
By dangerous tides,
15 Like a girl's dark hair for she dreams no ruin lies there,
Or her kisses where a serpent hides.

1917   1922

DEAD MAN'S DUMP

The plunging limbers over the shattered track
Racketed with their rusty freight,
Stuck out like many crowns of thorns,
And the rusty stakes like sceptres old
5 To stay the flood of brutish men
Upon our brothers dear.

The wheels lurched over sprawled dead
But pained them not, though their bones crunched,
Their shut mouths made no moan,
10 They lie there huddled, friend and foeman,
Man born of man, and born of woman,
And shells go crying over them
From night till night and now.

Earth has waited for them
15 All the time of their growth
Fretting for their decay:
Now she has them at last!
In the strength of their strength
Suspended – stopped and held.

20 What fierce imaginings their dark souls lit
Earth! have they gone into you?
Somewhere they must have gone,
And flung on your hard back

Is their souls' sack,
25   Emptied of God-ancestralled essences.
Who hurled them out? Who hurled?

None saw their spirits' shadow shake the grass,
Or stood aside for the half used life to pass
Out of those doomed nostrils and the doomed mouth,
30   When the swift iron burning bee
Drained the wild honey of their youth.

What of us, who flung on the shrieking pyre,
Walk, our usual thoughts untouched,
Our lucky limbs as on ichor fed,
35   Immortal seeming ever?
Perhaps when the flames beat loud on us,
A fear may choke in our veins
And the startled blood may stop.

The air is loud with death,
40   The dark air spurts with fire
The explosions ceaseless are.
Timelessly now, some minutes past,
These dead strode time with vigorous life,
Till the shrapnel called 'an end!'
45   But not to all. In bleeding pangs
Some borne on stretchers dreamed of home,
Dear things, war-blotted from their hearts.

A man's brains splattered on
A stretcher-bearer's face;
50   His shook shoulders slipped their load,
But when they bent to look again
The drowning soul was sunk too deep
For human tenderness.
They left this dead with the older dead,
55   Stretched at the cross roads.

Burnt black by strange decay,
Their sinister faces lie
The lid over each eye,
The grass and coloured clay
60   More motion have than they,
Joined to the great sunk silences.

Here is one not long dead;
His dark hearing caught our far wheels,
And the choked soul stretched weak hands
65 To reach the living word the far wheels said,
The blood-dazed intelligence beating for light,
Crying through the suspense of the far torturing wheels
Swift for the end to break,
Or the wheels to break,
70 Cried as the tide of the world broke over his sight.

Will they come? Will they ever come?
Even as the mixed hoofs of the mules,
The quivering-bellied mules,
And the rushing wheels all mixed
75 With his tortured upturned sight,
So we crashed round the bend,
We heard his weak scream,
We heard his very last sound,
And our wheels grazed his dead face.

1917   1922

Ivy Compton-Burnett
1892–1969

Dame Ivy Compton-Burnett was born in London and educated privately and at Royal Holloway College, London University. *Pastors and Masters* (1925) inaugurated a long series of novels, composed mostly of dialogue, set in large households of country gentry at the end of the nineteenth century, remarkable for their blend of humour and savagery. *A House and its Head* (1935), *A Family and a Fortune* (1939), and *Manservant and Maidservant* (1947) are among the best.

The family headed by Duncan Grant experiences, with a calmness that is both chilling and absurd, a series of shocking events. Here a simple matter of the widower's departure on a visit reveals a degree of detachment in his daughters and nephew which reflects his own macabre lack of feeling.

From A HOUSE AND ITS HEAD

[Father]

'Here is a letter from my invalid sister, your Aunt Maria,' said Duncan, in an incidental tone. 'She wishes me to pay her a visit; and it may be my duty; I even fear it is. I must not become so sunk in myself, that I am careless of her need. I have made the excuse of reluctance to
5   leave your mother: I cannot make it now.'

'Yes, do go to see her, Father. It will do you good,' said Sibyl.

'Do me good? Do her good, you mean? There would be little point in the visit, if my good were its object.' Duncan gave a little laugh. 'That need not be taken into account.'

10   There was a pause.

'I suppose this is one of those silences that speak,' murmured Grant. 'I hope it does not really.'

'Your mother was not easy about your aunt's isolation. I must try to recall her words. How clearly they come back to me!'

15   'She would hardly wish you to go just now, if it goes against the grain.'

'Would she not, Nance?' said Duncan, almost gently. 'I am afraid I cannot tell myself that: I happen to know, you see, what her wishes would be.'

20 'It would anyhow be a change, Father.'

'It would not be that, Sibyl. The past is outside the sphere of change; and my life is in the past. There is one thing of which I can assure myself. It cannot be worse with me.'

'Is Aunt Maria's life in the present?' said Nance. 'Though she is a
25 widow, and has lost her children? We hear of the differences in families.'

'She is a widow, Nance, and has lost her children. And I am a widower; and, I sometimes think, have lost my children. It seems meet we should be together.'

'I believe he inclines to the trip,' muttered Grant.

30 'Yes, Grant, I expect you do believe it,' said Duncan, whose hearing maintained its inconsistence. 'Yes, you would believe that.'

'Would you want me to do anything, while you were away, Uncle?'

'What you would want to do, yourself,' said Duncan in his own tone. 'You know you should get a grip of the workings of the place. It is for
35 your own sake and your own future. You may stop putting it all on to me. Miss Jekyll, will you very kindly give directions about my packing?'

'You should ask me to do that, Father.'

'Yes, Nance, I should. Ask yourself why I do not.'

'You are not going at once, Father?' said Sibyl.

40 'To-morrow,' said Duncan, in a faintly weary tone. 'If I put it off, my resolution will fail: I almost feel it failing.'

'Is Aunt Maria expecting you?'

'My poor sister!' said Duncan, almost with a laugh. 'She has long been expecting me. I reproach myself when I think of it; I hear your
45 mother's reproaches. We will telegraph, and end her suspense, and incidentally bind me to my project.'

'He hears Mother's reproaches!' murmured Nance. 'How different Mother is getting!'

'She is, Nance,' said Duncan, in almost pleasant tone. 'With every
50 day I realise more, what were the workings of her mind; and how our two minds bore upon each other.'

'It would be a shame to disappoint Aunt Maria,' said Sibyl.

'Oh, I don't know. Would it? She is very used to it. I admit I am still dallying with the idea. It may get the better of me.'

55 'The silence spoke,' murmured Grant.

'I never can make out whether Father's hearing is below the average or above it,' said Nance.

'You have made up your mind for some time,' said Duncan. 'It would have to be very much below, to prevent my realising that.'

60 'What time does the train go, if you decide to take it?' said Cassie.

'My sister has kept me informed of the trains. The one she always recommends, is at a quarter past eleven.'

'And you want to catch that?'

65 'I do not want to,' said Duncan, leaning back. 'But if we assume I am going to, it will dispose of this shilly-shallying, which needs to be apparent, as well as real.'

'Do you want anything done for you, before you go?' said Nance.

'If there is anything to be done, see that it is done,' said her father, going to the door. 'We don't want question and answer over what goes 70 without saying.'

'What goes without saying! Does it really?' said Grant. 'I shall hold my breath until it comes to pass.'

'You may hold it too long,' said Nance: 'I can't think it can happen.'

'Well, I believe that would kill me, anyhow.'

75 The next day Duncan appeared submissive to fate, and simply acquiescent in arrangements; but as the morning advanced, there was a change.

'Grant!' he called from his bedroom landing, 'fetch my writing case from my desk; and put in some pens and stamps, and bring it up here! 80 I have been calling until I am hoarse; I thought you were all stone deaf.'

'It was odd to continue calling,' said Grant, as he hastened on the quest.

'Grant! Grant! Don't you hear me? Can't you answer me, boy?'

'I am getting the things, Uncle! I will be up in a minute.'

85 'But can't you answer me? Can't you open your mouth to reply, when I stand and shout myself hoarse? Are you dumb as well as deaf?'

'I thought you would know I was getting the case, Uncle.'

'How was I to know, when I shouted and got no response? How was I to guess at what moment I should pierce your senses? How was I 90 to know you had any senses, when there was no evidence of it?'

Grant ran upstairs and offered the case, Sibyl on his heels with its supplies. Something in the zeal attending these offices, caused Duncan to meet them with deliberation.

'Pens; stamps; yes. Paper? Do I want paper? Will not your aunt have 95 that, Sibyl? That is' – he gave his little laugh – 'if I get there, and need it.'

'Of course she will, Father. How stupid of me! I will take it back, and look round to see if there is anything else.'

'There is no reason for hurry: I don't want the final look round made 100 yet. We may never get to it. Who knows?' Duncan raised his arms with a yawn and a sigh. 'So many things came in the way of really getting off, more than the business is worth.'

He broke off, and looked up and down a newspaper from a trunk, smiling to himself at its reminders.

105 Grant and Sibyl went downstairs.

  'Nance, we betrayed an eagerness to get Uncle off. I can hardly believe in our foolishness.'

  'What about putting some obstacles in his path?'

  'There will be enough in it,' said Cassie. 'You had better avoid his
110 path.'

  'There he is, calling again!' said Sibyl.

  'He has soon begun to miss us.'

  'Has anyone seen my old gloves, that I wear in the grounds? Those that are kept in the drawer in the hall, or should be kept there? I know
115 people are always disturbing that drawer.'

  'They are not there, Father!' called Sibyl, after a swift search.

  'Of course they are not there!' said Duncan, coming to the stairs. 'If they were there, should I ask you if you had seen them? I should simply tell you to fetch them.' This was accepted as true.

120 'I thought you wanted them fetched, Father.'

  'Of course I wanted them fetched,' said Duncan, moving from foot to foot. 'If I did not, should I have asked about them? I should not expect them to walk to me, should I? Or to fly to my hand?'

  'If they don't fly to his hand, I don't know what we are to do,' said
125 Cassie.

  "Why, you have them in your hand, Father, waving them about!' said Sibyl, with an easy laugh that laid no stress on the mistake.

  Duncan glanced at the gloves, and continued to wave them.

  'Fetch me the scarf from the drawer, that I wear with the gloves,' he
130 said, giving a quick glance behind him, as though arrested by something.

  'I believe the gloves did fly to his hand,' said Grant.

  'There he is again!' said Sibyl, running with the scarf.

  Duncan stood still, his hand outstretched, until his daughter had mounted the stairs and put the scarf into it.

135 'The fire in my room is smoking again,' he observed, tossing up the scarf and catching it.

  'We shall never get him off in time,' said Nance, 'if the things in one drawer prove such an obstacle. So far he is equipped with one scarf and a pair of gloves, and neither of them suitable for general wear.'

140 'We had better resign ourselves to frustration,' said Grant. 'The hope has been very sweet.'

  Duncan entered the drawing-room, with a bag and rug, using these objects to wave from his path Bethia, with some offer of assistance. He put his burdens down, and taking a chair picked up the paper.

145 'I should not have left the paper lying idle, when I was your age,' he said, smiling. 'You have very little curiosity about the nation's affairs.'

  'True, when they are swamped by an acute private anxiety,' said Grant.

'You don't think this election business will follow that course—'

150   'No, Uncle, I scarcely think it will.'

Duncan continued his perusal with an air of alertness and interest, pausing to comment or quote.

'Father, it is a quarter to eleven,' said Sibyl.

'A quarter to eleven?' said Duncan, taking out his watch. 'A shade
155   past the quarter. My watch is absolutely right, exactly to the second. A quarter of a minute past the quarter.' He smiled at the coincidence of the words, and resumed the journal.

'You like half an hour between leaving the house and catching the train,' said Nance. 'The cob is at the door.'

160   Duncan glanced out of the window, and back to the page.

'He stamps and paws, that little brute,' he observed, his tone preoccupied. 'It will do him good to learn patience.'

'Too hard a lesson for a dumb beast,' muttered Grant.

'Horses are said to know the moods of human beings,' said Nance.
165   'I hope we shall not render this one unfit to take Father to the train.'

'Father, Williams is looking through the window,' said Sibyl. 'He cannot get down because of the horse.'

Duncan lifted his eyes, and catching the signs of the groom, rose from his seat.

170   'My umbrella, my rug!' he said in a quick, curt tone, turning rapidly about. 'I suppose you can hand me the things before your eyes. Grant, you know by which end to hand an umbrella! You do not comfortably take the handle yourself, and offer the point! Nance, here is a list of the things I want remembered. It is clearly written. You can read it, I suppose?'

175   'Certainly, in that case, Father.'

'My purse!' said Duncan, pausing with a jerk. 'Will somebody give me my purse? Can I do without it? Shall I have to pay for my ticket, for my luncheon, for my porter? Sibyl, will you fetch it? You seem the least phlegmatic of the three.'

180   Sibyl made a dart in a vague direction, and glanced back at her father.

'I can't see it, Father; I shall find it in a second; I shall be sure to sight it?'

Duncan stood still, his eyes on her movements, and suddenly let his possessions fall, and sat down on the hall bench.

185   'Well, bring the paper then,' he called to his daughter, as though making provision for a period.

'Did you put the purse in your pocket, Father?'

Duncan put his hand to his waistcoat, and withdrew it, picked up his belongings, and walked to the door, in one smooth, unglancing
190   movement.

Sibyl sprang back; Nance gathered up the rug; Grant ran out to the door of the trap.

'Good-bye, Father! Good-bye, Uncle! Good-bye, Father!'

'Good-bye, Miss Jekyll,' said Duncan, turning to Cassie with deliberate
195 courtesy. 'I fear some of my responsibilities will devolve on you. And
good-bye, Nance; good-bye, Sibyl. Grant, don't block the way out of
the house. I may miss the train yet; though if I do, I shall be back in
ample time for luncheon. Let me hear from one of you twice a week,
and go to church on Sunday mornings. In the evenings do as you please.'
200 'Good-bye, Father. Good-bye, Uncle. Good-bye, Father. Take care of
yourself. You will let us hear when you arrive?'

'If I stay more than a day or two,' said Duncan, pausing with his
foot on the step of the trap. 'If I do not, one letter will serve a double
purpose. Have you any messages for your aunt? I shall be able to deliver
205 them anyhow.'

'The messages usual between people who do not meet,' said Nance,
'and would not know each other, if they did.'

'So no message. Good-bye, all of you,' said Duncan, mounting the
steps.
210 Sibyl waved in the porch, and her father looked back and raised his hat.

'How you have the spirit to wave, when the train may yet be missed!'
said Grant.

'If I had not had the spirit for a good deal, the train would not have
been aimed at at all.'
215 'The train will not be missed,' said Cassie.

'Nance, we are to go to church on Sunday mornings,' said Grant.
'Does that mean he will be away for weeks?

'What should I be, if I did not prick up my ears at that? Not Father's
daughter.'
220 'The trap is coming back!' said Sibyl.

'The trap? With Uncle in it?'

'Of course with him in it. They could not have got to the station and
back.'

'He might have been thrown out and killed. I see that his death would
225 be the only thing.'

'The trap might have headed the sad procession,' said Nance.

'It could hardly be sadder,' said her cousin.

The trap came up the drive, with Duncan leaning forward over the
horse.
230 'Hold back, Williams! Do you want to destroy the beast? A horse
for the sake of a train! What a muddle of values! Now pull up gently,
and quiet him. Grant, come to his head, and see if harm is done.
Williams, you may keep your seat, in case we want to start again.'

'None at all, Uncle. He is hardly in a heat. He is fresh, and wants to
235 get along.'

'No harm done!' said Nance.

Duncan sat waiting to be asked to explain his return, and as no one put the enquiry, took out his purse and went through his change, and then leaned back and crossed his legs.

240 Bethia hurried out with his dressing bag, and he made a quick movement towards it, but checked himself and signed to his nephew.

'That bag is rather heavy for a woman,' he said in a tone almost of interest, his eyes on the bag. 'You should keep your wits about you. Well, good-bye again, if only for the moment. It will be a matter of

245 minutes or weeks, I suppose; and it does not much matter which it is.'

1935

Wilfred Owen
1893–1918

Wilfred Owen was born in Oswestry in Shropshire, where his father was a railway worker, and educated at Shrewsbury Technical College. His pre-war verses, influenced by Keats, are undistinguished. He served as an officer in France from 1915. Siegfried Sassoon, whom he met in hospital in Edinburgh, encouraged him to persevere with poems in which he sought to express 'the pity of war'. Owen returned to France in 1918, won the MC, and was killed, a few days before the Armistice, on the Sambre Canal. Sassoon brought out Owen's *Collected Poems* in 1920. There have been revised editions by Edmund Blunden (1931) and C. Day-Lewis (1963). Benjamin Britten set some of the poems to music in his *War Requiem* of 1962.

ANTHEM FOR DOOMED YOUTH

What passing-bells for these who die as cattle?
   Only the monstrous anger of the guns.
   Only the stuttering rifles' rapid rattle
Can patter out their hasty orisons.
5 No mockeries now for them; no prayers nor bells,
   Nor any voice of mourning save the choirs, –
The shrill, demented choirs of wailing shells;
   And bugles calling for them from sad shires.

What candles may be held to speed them all?
10   Not in the hands of boys, but in their eyes
Shall shine the holy glimmers of good-byes.
   The pallor of girls' brows shall be their pall;
The flowers the tenderness of patient minds;
And each slow dusk a drawing-down of blinds.

1917   1920

DULCE ET DECORUM EST

Bent double, like old beggars under sacks,
Knock-kneed, coughing like hags, we cursed through sludge,
Till on the haunting flares we turned our backs
And towards our distant rest began to trudge.
5   Men marched asleep. Many had lost their boots
But limped on, blood-shod. All went lame; all blind;
Drunk with fatigue; deaf even to the hoots
Of tired, outstripped Five-Nines that dropped behind.

Gas! Gas! Quick, boys! – An ecstasy of fumbling,
10   Fitting the clumsy helmets just in time;
But someone still was yelling out and stumbling
And flound'ring like a man in fire or lime . . .
Dim, through the misty panes and thick green light,
As under a green sea, I saw him drowning.

15   In all my dreams, before my helpless sight,
He plunges at me, guttering, choking, drowning.

If in some smothering dreams you too could pace
Behind the wagon that we flung him in,
And watch the white eyes writhing in his face,
20   His hanging face, like a devil's sick of sin;
If you could hear, at every jolt, the blood
Come gargling from the froth-corrupted lungs,
Obscene as cancer, bitter as the cud
Of vile, incurable sores on innocent tongues, –
25   My friend, you would not tell with such high zest
To children ardent for some desperate glory,
The old lie: Dulce et decorum est
Pro patria mori.†

1917   1920

Dulce . . mori   'It is sweet and fitting to die   verse schoolboys learned in Latin lessons
for one's country' (Horace, Odes, III, ii), a

STRANGE MEETING

It seemed that out of battle I escaped
Down some profound dull tunnel, long since scooped
Through granites which titanic wars had groined.
Yet also there encumbered sleepers groaned,
5   Too fast in thought or death to be bestirred.
Then, as I probed them, one sprang up, and stared
With piteous recognition in fixed eyes,
Lifting distressful hands as if to bless.
And by his smile, I knew that sullen hall,
10   By his dead smile I knew we stood in Hell.
With a thousand pains that vision's face was grained;
Yet no blood reached there from the upper ground,
And no guns thumped, or down the flues made moan.
'Strange friend,' I said, 'here is no cause to mourn.'
15   'None,' said that other, 'save the undone years,
The hopelessness. Whatever hope is yours,
Was my life also; I went hunting wild
After the wildest beauty in the world,
Which lies not calm in eyes, or braided hair,
20   But mocks the steady running of the hour,
And if it grieves, grieves richlier than here.
For of my glee might many men have laughed,
And of my weeping something had been left,
Which must die now. I mean the truth untold,
25   The pity of war, the pity war distilled.
Now men will go content with what we spoiled,
Or, discontent, boil bloody, and be spilled.
They will be swift with swiftness of the tigress.
None will break ranks, though nations trek from progress.
30   Courage was mine, and I had mystery,
Wisdom was mine, and I had mastery:
To miss the march of this retreating world
Into vain citadels that are not walled.
Then, when much blood had clogged their chariot-wheels,
35   I would go up and wash them from sweet wells,
Even with truths that lie too deep for taint.
I would have poured my spirit without stint
But not through wounds; not on the cess of war.
Foreheads of men have bled where no wounds were.
40   I am the enemy you killed, my friend.
I knew you in this dark: for so you frowned

Yesterday through me as you jabbed and killed.
I parried; but my hands were loath and cold.
Let us sleep now . . .'

1918   1920

Aldous Huxley

1894–1963

Aldous Leonard Huxley, grandson of T. H. Huxley (1825–95) the
champion of Darwinism, and brother of the biologist Sir Julian Huxley
(1887–1975), was born at Godalming and educated at Eton and Balliol
College, Oxford. Seriously impaired eyesight thwarted his medical
training. His satire *Crome Yellow* (1921) confirmed his reputation as
a brilliant, cynical young man. He lived in Italy and France between
the wars. His novels *Point Counter Point* (1928) and *Eyeless in Gaza*
(1936) are very readable 'novels of ideas', and his satirical fantasy
Brave New World (1932) has always been popular. When he went to
California in 1937 he became interested in mysticism and paranormal
states of mind; such later writings as *The Doors of Perception* (1954)
appeal to a narrower readership.

From BRAVE NEW WORLD

[Suggestions from the State]

Mr Foster was left in the Decanting Room. The D.H.C.[†] and his students
stepped into the nearest lift and were carried up to the fifth floor.

INFANT NURSERIES. NEO-PAVLOVIAN[†] CONDITIONING ROOMS, announced the
notice board.

5   The Director opened a door. They were in a large bare room, very
bright and sunny; for the whole of the southern wall was a single
window. Half a dozen nurses, trousered and jacketed in the regulation
white viscose-linen uniform, their hair aseptically hidden under white
caps, were engaged in setting out bowls of roses in a long row across
10   the floor. Big bowls, packed tight with blossom. Thousands of petals,
ripe-blown and silkily smooth, like the cheeks of innumerable little
cherubs, but of cherubs, in that bright light, not exclusively pink and
Aryan, but also luminously Chinese, also Mexican, also apoplectic with

---

D.H.C.   Director of Hatcheries and
Conditioning
NEO-PAVLOVIAN   Ivan Petrovich Pavlov (1849–
1936), the Russian scientist whose
experiments with dogs led him to the theory

of 'conditioned reflexes' which led to the
doctrine known as behaviourism. Presumably
'NEO' indicates that further advances have
been made

too much blowing of celestial trumpets, also pale as death, pale with
15 the posthumous whiteness of marble.

The nurses stiffened to attention as the D.H.C. came in.

'Set out the books,' he said curtly.

In silence the nurses obeyed his command. Between the rose bowls
the books were duly set out – a row of nursery quartos opened invitingly
20 each at some gaily coloured image of beast or fish or bird.

'Now bring in the children.'

They hurried out of the room and returned in a minute or two, each
pushing a kind of tall dumb-waiter laden, on all its four wire-netted
shelves, with eight-month-old babies, all exactly alike (a Bokanovsky
25 Group, it was evident) and all (since their caste was Delta) dressed in
khaki.

'Put them down on the floor.'

The infants were unloaded.

'Now turn them so that they can see the flowers and books.'

30 Turned, the babies at once fell silent, then began to crawl towards
those clusters of sleek colours, those shapes so gay and brilliant on the
white pages. As they approached, the sun came out of a momentary
eclipse behind a cloud. The roses flamed up as though with a sudden
passion from within; a new and profound significance seemed to suffuse
35 the shining pages of the books. From the ranks of the crawling babies
came little squeals of excitement, gurgles and twitterings of pleasure.

The Director rubbed his hands. 'Excellent!' he said. 'It might almost
have been done on purpose.'

The swiftest crawlers were already at their goal. Small hands reached
40 out uncertainly, touched, grasped, unpetaling the transfigured roses,
crumpling the illuminated pages of the books. The Director waited until
all were happily busy. Then, 'Watch carefully,' he said. And, lifting his
hand, he gave the signal.

The Head Nurse, who was standing by a switchboard at the other
45 end of the room, pressed down a little lever.

There was a violent explosion. Shriller and ever shriller, a siren
shrieked. Alarm bells maddeningly sounded.

The children started, screamed; their faces were distorted with terror.

'And now,' the Director shouted (for the noise was deafening), 'now
50 we proceed to rub in the lesson with a mild electric shock.'

He waved his hand again, and the Head Nurse pressed a second
lever. The screaming of the babies suddenly changed its tone. There
was something desperate, almost insane, about the sharp spasmodic
yelps to which they now gave utterance. Their little bodies twitched
55 and stiffened; their limbs moved jerkily as if to the tug of unseen wires.

'We can electrify that whole strip of floor,' bawled the Director in
explanation. 'But that's enough,' he signalled to the nurse.

The explosions ceased, the bells stopped ringing, the shriek of the siren died down from tone to tone into silence. The stiffly twitching bodies relaxed, and what had become the sob and yelp of infant maniacs broadened out once more into a normal howl of ordinary terror.

'Offer them the flowers and the books again.'

The nurses obeyed; but at the approach of the roses, at the mere sight of those gaily-coloured images of pussy and cock-a-doodle-doo and baa-baa black sheep, the infants shrank away in horror; the volume of their howling suddenly increased.

'Observe,' said the Director triumphantly, 'observe.'

Books and loud noises, flowers and electric shocks – already in the infant mind these couples were compromisingly linked; and after two hundred repetitions of the same or a similar lesson would be wedded indissolubly. What man has joined, nature is powerless to put asunder.

'They'll grow up with what the psychologists used to call an "instinctive" hatred of books and flowers. Reflexes unalterably conditioned. They'll be safe from books and botany all their lives.' The Director turned to his nurses. 'Take them away again.'

Still yelling, the khaki babies were loaded on to their dumb-waiters and wheeled out, leaving behind them the smell of sour milk and a most welcome silence.

One of the students held up his hand; and though he could see quite well why you couldn't have lower-caste people wasting the Community's time over books, and that there was always the risk of their reading something which might undesirably decondition one of their reflexes, yet ... well, he couldn't understand about the flowers. Why go to the trouble of making it psychologically impossible for Deltas to like flowers?

Patiently the D.H.C. explained. If the children were made to scream at the sight of a rose, that was on grounds of high economic policy. Not so very long ago (a century or thereabouts), Gammas, Deltas, even Epsilons, had been conditioned to like flowers – flowers in particular and wild nature in general. The idea was to make them want to be going out into the country at every available opportunity, and so compel them to consume transport.

'And didn't they consume transport?' asked the student.

'Quite a lot,' the D.H.C. replied. 'But nothing else.'

Primroses and landscapes, he pointed out, have one grave defect: they are gratuitous. A love of nature keeps no factories busy. It was decided to abolish the love of nature, at any rate among the lower classes; to abolish the love of nature, but *not* the tendency to consume transport. For of course it was essential that they should keep on going to the country, even though they hated it. The problem was to find an economically sounder reason for consuming transport than a mere affection for primroses and landscapes. It was duly found.

'We condition the masses to hate the country,' concluded the Director.
'But simultaneously we condition them to love all country sports. At
105   the same time, we see to it that all country sports shall entail the use of
elaborate apparatus. So that they consume manufactured articles as
well as transport. Hence those electric shocks.'

'I see,' said the student, and was silent, lost in admiration.

There was a silence; then, clearing his throat, 'Once upon a time,'
110   the Director began, 'while Our Ford† was still on earth, there was a
little boy called Reuben Rabinovitch. Reuben was the child of Polish-
speaking parents.' The Director interrupted himself. 'You know what
Polish is, I suppose?'

'A dead language.'

115   'Like French and German,' added another student, officiously showing
off his learning.

'And "parent"?' questioned the D.H.C.

There was an uneasy silence. Several of the boys blushed. They had
not yet learned to draw the significant but often very fine distinction
120   between smut and pure science. One, at last, had the courage to raise a
hand.

'Human beings used to be . . .' he hesitated; the blood rushed to his
cheeks. 'Well, they used to be viviparous.'

'Quite right.' The Director nodded approvingly.

125   'And when the babies were decanted . . .'

' "Born," ' came the correction.

'Well, then they were the parents – I means, not the babies, of course;
the other ones.' The poor boy was overwhelmed with confusion.

'In brief,' the Director summed up, 'the parents were the father and
130   the mother.' The smut that was really science fell with a crash into the
boys' eye-avoiding silence. 'Mother,' he repeated loudly, rubbing in the
science, and, leaning back in his chair, 'There,' he said gravely, 'are
unpleasant facts; I know it. But, then, most historical facts *are*
unpleasant.'

135   He returned to Little Reuben – to Little Reuben, in whose room, one
evening, by an oversight, his father and mother (crash, crash!) happened
to leave the radio turned on.

('For you must remember that in those days of gross viviparous
reproduction, children were always brought up by their parents and
140   not in State Conditioning Centres.')

While the child was asleep, a broadcast programme from London
suddenly started to come through; and the next morning, to the

---

Our Ford Henry Ford (1863–1947) American   line, mass-production methods
car-manufacturer, introduced new assembly-

astonishment of his crash and crash (the more daring of the boys
ventured to grin at one another), Little Reuben woke up repeating word
145 for word a long lecture by the curious old writer ('one of the very few
whose works have been permitted to come down to us'), George Bernard
Shaw, who was speaking, according to a well-authenticated tradition,
about his own genius. To Little Reuben's wink and snigger, this lecture
was, of course, perfectly incomprehensible and, imagining that their
150 child had suddenly gone mad, they sent for a doctor. He, fortunately,
understood English, recognized the discourse as that which Shaw had
broadcasted the previous evening, realized the significance of what had
happened, and sent a letter to the medical press about it.

'The principle of sleep-teaching, or hypnopædia, had been discovered.'
155 The D.H.C. made an impressive pause.

The principle had been discovered; but many, many years were to
elapse before that principle was usefully applied.

'The case of Little Reuben occurred only twenty-three years after Our
Ford's first T-Model was put on the market.' (Here the Director made
160 a sign of the T on his stomach and all the students reverently followed
suit.) 'And yet . . .'

Furiously the students scribbled. '*Hypnopædia, first used officially in
A.F. 214. Why not before? Two reasons. (a) . . .*'

'These early experimenters,' the D.H.C. was saying, 'were on the
165 wrong track. They thought that hypnopædia could be made an
instrument of intellectual education . . .'

(A small boy asleep on his right side, the right arm stuck out, the
right hand hanging limply over the edge of the bed. Through a round
grating in the side of a box a voice speaks softly.

170 'The Nile is the longest river in Africa and the second in length of all
the rivers of the globe. Although falling short of the length of the
Mississippi–Missouri, the Nile is at the head of all rivers as regards the
length of its basin, which extends through 35 degrees of latitude . . .'

At breakfast the next morning, 'Tommy,' some one says, 'do you
175 know which is the longest river in Africa?' A shaking of the head. 'But
don't you remember something that begins: The Nile is the . . .'

'The-Nile-is-the-longest-river-in-Africa-and-the-second-in-length-of-
all-the-rivers-of-the-globe . . .' The words come rushing out. 'Although-
falling-short-of . . .'

180 'Well now, which is the longest river in Africa?'
The eyes are blank. 'I don't know.'
'But the Nile, Tommy.'
'The-Nile-is-the-longest-river-in-Africa-and-second. . .'
'Then which river is the longest, Tommy?'

185 Tommy bursts into tears. 'I don't know,' he howls.)
That howl, the Director made it plain, discouraged the earliest

investigators. The experiments were abandoned. No further attempt was made to teach children the length of the Nile in their sleep. Quite rightly. You can't learn a science unless you know what it's all about.

190 'Whereas, if they'd only started on *moral* education,' said the Director, leading the way towards the door. The students followed him, desperately scribbling as they walked and all the way up in the lift. 'Moral education, which ought never, in any circumstances, to be rational.'

195 'Silence, silence,' whispered a loud-speaker as they stepped out at the fourteenth floor, and 'Silence, silence,' the trumpet mouths indefatigably repeated at intervals down every corridor. The students and even the Director himself rose automatically to the tips of their toes. They were Alphas, of course; but even Alphas have been well conditioned. 'Silence,

200 silence.' All the air of the fourteenth floor was sibilant with the categorical imperative.

Fifty yards of tiptoeing brought them to a door which the Director cautiously opened. They stepped over the threshold into the twilight of a shuttered dormitory. Eighty cots stood in a row against the wall.

205 There was a sound of light regular breathing and a continuous murmur, as of very faint voices remotely whispering.

A nurse rose as they entered and came to attention before the Director. 'What's the lesson this afternoon?' he asked.

'We had Elementary Sex for the first forty minutes,' she answered.

210 'But now it's switched over to Elementary Class Consciousness.'

The Director walked slowly down the long line of cots. Rosy and relaxed with sleep, eighty little boys and girls lay softly breathing. There was a whisper under every pillow. The D.H.C. halted and, bending over one of the little beds, listened attentively.

215 'Elementary Class Consciousness, did you say? Let's have it repeated a little louder by the trumpet.'

At the end of the room a loud-speaker projected from the wall. The Director walked up to it and pressed a switch.

'. . . all wear green,' said a soft but very distinct voice, beginning in

220 the middle of a sentence, 'and Delta children wear khaki. Oh no, I don't want to play with Delta children. And Epsilons are still worse. They're too stupid to be able to read or write. Besides, they wear black, which is such a beastly colour. I'm *so* glad I'm a Beta.'

There was a pause; then the voice began again.

225 'Alpha children wear grey. They work much harder than we do, because they're so frightfully clever. I'm really awfully glad I'm a Beta, because I don't work so hard. And then we are much better than the Gammas and Deltas. Gammas are stupid. They all wear green, and Delta children wear khaki. Oh no, I *don't* want to play with Delta children. And Epsilons are

230 still worse. They're too stupid to be able . . .'

The Director pushed back the switch. The voice was silent. Only its thin ghost continued to mutter from beneath the eighty pillows.

'They'll have that repeated forty or fifty times more before they wake; then again on Thursday, and again on Saturday. A hundred and twenty
235 times three times a week for thirty months. After which they go on to a more advanced lesson.'

Roses and electric shocks, the khaki of Deltas and a whiff of asafœtida – wedded indissolubly before the child can speak. But wordless conditioning is crude and wholesale; cannot bring home
240 the finer distinctions, cannot inculcate the more complex courses of behaviour. For that there must be words, but words without reason. In brief, hypnopædia.

'The greatest moralizing and socializing force of all time.'

The students took it down in their little books. Straight from the
245 horse's mouth.

Once more the Director touched the switch.

'... so frightfully clever,' the soft, insinuating, indefatigable voice was saying. 'I'm really awfully glad I'm a Beta, because ...'

Not so much like drops of water, though water, it is true, can wear
250 holes in the hardest granite; rather, drops of liquid sealing-wax, drops that adhere, incrust, incorporate themselves with what they fall on, till finally the rock is all one scarlet blob.

'Till at last the child's mind *is* these suggestions, and the sum of the suggestions *is* the child's mind. And not the child's mind only. The
255 adult's mind too – all his life long. The mind that judges and desires and decides – made up of these suggestions. But all these suggestions are *our* suggestions!' The Director almost shouted in his triumph. 'Suggestions from the State.' He banged the nearest table. 'It therefore follows ...'

260 A noise made him turn round.

'Oh, Ford!' he said in another tone, 'I've gone and woken the children.'

1932

Robert Graves
1895–1986

Robert von Ranke Graves, son of the Irish writer A. P. Graves (1846–1931) and Amalia von Ranke, was born in Wimbledon and educated at Charterhouse and, later, at St John's College, Oxford; he joined the army straight from school, in 1914. Apart from one year spent teaching in Egypt (1926) he lived by writing, publishing more than a hundred books; and except for the years of the Second World War, he lived abroad – in Majorca from 1946. He is best known for the autobiography of his early life *Goodbye to All That* (1929), for historical novels including *I Claudius* and *Claudius the God* in 1934, for *The White Goddess* (1948) which assigns poetry to the province of a goddess-muse, *The Greek Myths* (a handbook, 1955), and for his versatile, lucid poetry which belongs to no 'movement'. *Collected Poems* (1955) was enlarged in 1975. Graves was Oxford Professor of Poetry (while still resident in Majorca) from 1961 to 1966.

THE COOL WEB

Children are dumb to say how hot the day is,
How hot the scent is of the summer rose,
How dreadful the black wastes of evening sky,
How dreadful the tall soldiers drumming by.

5   But we have speech, to chill the angry day,
And speech, to dull the rose's cruel scent.
We spell away the overhanging night,
We spell away the soldiers and the fright.

There's a cool web of language winds us in,
10   Retreat from too much joy or too much fear:
We grow sea-green at last and coldly die
In brininess and volubility.

But if we let our tongues lose self-possession,
Throwing off language and its watery clasp

15 Before our death, instead of when death comes,
  Facing the wide glare of the children's day,
  Facing the rose, the dark sky and the drums,
  We shall go mad no doubt and die that way.

  1925/6   1927

SICK LOVE

  O Love, be fed with apples while you may,
  And feel the sun and go in royal array,
  A smiling innocent on the heavenly causeway.

  Though in what listening horror for the cry
5 That soars in outer blackness dismally,
  The dumb blind beast, the paranoiac fury:

  Be warm, enjoy the season, lift your head,
  Exquisite in the pulse of tainted blood,
  That shivering glory not to be despised.

10 Take your delight in momentariness,
  Walk between dark and dark – a shining space
  With the grave's narrowness, though not its peace.

                1938

WELSH INCIDENT

  'But that was nothing to what things came out
  From the sea-caves of Criccieth yonder.'
  'What were they? Mermaids? dragons? ghosts?'
  'Nothing at all of any things like that.'
5 'What were they, then?'
          'All sorts of queer things,
  Things never seen or heard or written about,
  Very strange, un-Welsh, utterly peculiar
  Things. Oh, solid enough they seemed to touch,

10   Had anyone dared it. Marvellous creation,
       All various shapes and sizes, and no sizes,
       All new, each perfectly unlike his neighbour,
       Though all came moving slowly out together.'
       'Describe just one of them.'

15   'I am unable.'
       'What were their colours?'
                               'Mostly nameless colours,
       Colours you'd like to see; but one was puce
       Or perhaps more like crimson, but not purplish.

20   Some had no colour.'
                        'Tell me, had they legs?'
       'Not a leg nor foot among them that I saw.'
       'But did these things come out in any order?
       What o'clock was it? What was the day of the week?

25   Who else was present? How was the weather?'
       'I was coming to that. It was half-past three
       On Easter Tuesday last. The sun was shining.
       The Harlech Silver Band played *Marchog Jesu*
       On thirty-seven shimmering instruments,

30   Collecting for Caernarvon's (Fever) Hospital Fund.
       The populations of Pwillheli, Criccieth,
       Portmadoc, Borth, Tremadoc, Penrhyndeudraeth,
       Were all assembled. Criccieth's major addressed them
       First in good Welsh and then in fluent English,

35   Twisting his fingers in his chain of office,
       Welcoming the things. They came out on the sand,
       Not keeping time to the band, moving seaward
       Silently at a snail's pace. But at last
       The most odd, indescribable thing of all,

40   Which hardly one man there could see for wonder,
       Did something recognizably a something.'
       'Well, what?'
                    'It made a noise.'
                               'A frightening noise?'

45   'No, no.'
               'A musical noise? A noise of scuffling?'
       'No, but a very loud, respectable noise –
       Like groaning to oneself on Sunday morning
       In Chapel, close before the second psalm.'

50   'What did the mayor do?'
                         'I was coming to that.'

                                1938

Charles Sorley
1895–1915

Charles Hamilton Sorley was born in Aberdeen and educated at Marlborough. He joined the army in 1914 and was killed near Loos. He left thirty-seven complete poems. *Marlborough and Other Poems* (1916) was successful in the 1920s but afterwards neglected. Robert Graves and Edmund Blunden judged him one of the best poets of the First World War.

TO GERMANY

You are blind like us. Your hurt no man designed,
And no man claimed the conquest of your land.
But gropers both through fields of thought confined
We stumble and we do not understand.
5   You only saw your future bigly planned,
And we, the tapering paths of our own mind,
And in each other's dearest ways we stand,
And hiss and hate. And the blind fight the blind.

When it is peace, then we may view again
10 With new-won eyes each other's truer form
And wonder. Grown more loving-kind and warm
We'll grasp firm hands and laugh at the old pain,
When it is peace. But until peace, the storm,
The darkness and the thunder and the rain.

1914   1916

WHEN YOU SEE MILLIONS OF THE MOUTHLESS DEAD

When you see millions of the mouthless dead
Across your dreams in pale battalions go,

Say not soft things as other men have said,
That you'll remember. For you need not so.
5   Give them not praise. For, deaf, how should they know
It is not curses heaped on each gashed head?
Nor tears. Their blind eyes see not your tears flow.
Nor honour. It is easy to be dead.
Say only this. 'They are dead.' Then add thereto,
10   'Yet many a better one has died before.'
Then, scanning all the o'ercrowded mass, should you
Perceive one face that you loved heretofore,
It is a spook. None wears the face you knew.
Great death has made all his for evermore.

1915   1916

Edmund Blunden
1896–1974

Edmund Charles Blunden was born in London and educated at Christ's
Hospital and The Queen's College, Oxford. He served in the army in
the First World War; later poems and his prose *Undertones of War*
(1928) drew on that experience. Most of his best verse appeared in
The Poems of Edmund Blunden (1930), although there were later
collections, including *Poems of Many Years* (1957). Blunden was a
critic, teacher (Oxford Professor of Poetry from 1966 to 1969), and
editor – notably of poems by John Clare.

THE PIKE

From shadows of rich oaks outpeer
The moss-green bastions of the weir,
Where the quick dipper forages
In elver-peopled crevices.
5   And a small runlet trickling down the sluice
Gossamer music tires not to unloose.

Else round the broad pool's hush
    Nothing stirs.
Unless sometime a straggling heifer crush
10   Through the thronged spinney whence the pheasant whirs;
    Or martins in a flash
Come with wild mirth to dip their magical wings,
While in the shallow some doomed bulrush swings
    At whose hid root the diver vole's teeth gnash.
15   And nigh this toppling reed, still as the dead
    The great pike lies, the murderous patriarch,
    Watching the waterpit shelving and dark
Where through the plash his lithe bright vassals thread.

The rose-finned roach and bluish bream
20   And staring ruffe steal up the stream
    Hard by their glutted tyrant, now
    Still as a sunken bough.

He on the sandbank lies,
 Sunning himself long hours
25 With stony gorgon eyes:
 Westward the hot sun lowers.

Sudden the gray pike changes, and quivering poises for slaughter;
 Intense terror wakens around him, the shoals scud awry, but there
  chances
30 A chub unsuspecting; the prowling fins quicken, in fury he lances;
And the miller that opens the hatch stands amazed at the whirl in the
  water.

1919   1920

FOREFATHERS

Here they went with smock and crook,
 Toiled in the sun, lolled in the shade,
Here they mudded out the brook
 And here their hatchet cleared the glade:
5 Harvest-supper woke their wit,
 Huntsman's moon their wooings lit.

From this church they led their brides,
 From this church themselves were led
Shoulder-high; on these waysides
10 Sat to take their beer and bread.
Names are gone – what men they were
These their cottages declare.

Names are vanished save the few
 In the old brown Bible scrawled;
15 These were men of pith and thew,
 Whom the city never called;
Scarce could read or hold a quill,
Built the barn, the forge, the mill.

On the green they watched their sons
20 Playing till too dark to see,
As their fathers watched them once,
 As my father once watched me;

While the bat and beetle flew
On the warm air webbed with dew.

25 Unrecorded, unrenowned,
    Men from whom my ways begin,
Here I know you by your ground
    But I know you not within –
There is silence, there survives
30 Not a moment of your lives.

Like the bee that now is blown
    Honey-heavy on my hand,
From his toppling tansy-throne
    In the green tempestuous land –
35 I'm in clover now, nor know
Who made honey long ago.

                              1922

THE MIDNIGHT SKATERS

The hop-poles stand in cones,
    The icy pond lurks under,
The pole-tops steeple to the thrones
    Of stars, sound gulfs of wonder;
5 But not the tallest there, 'tis said,
Could fathom to this pond's black bed.

Then is not death at watch
    Within those secret waters?
What wants he but to catch
10   Earth's heedless sons and daughters?
With but a crystal parapet
Between, he has his engines set.

Then on, blood shouts, on, on,
    Twirl, wheel and whip above him,
15 Dance on this ball-floor thin and wan,

Use him as though you love him;
Court him, elude him, reel and pass,
And let him hate you through the glass.

1925   1926

OCTOBER COMES

I heard the graybird bathing in the rill,
And fluttering his wings dry within thorn boughs
Which all embowered the rill; with tiny bill
The robin on red-berried spray bade rouse
5   One whom I could not see, a field away;
I heard the passing girl to her young man say,
'O look, there's a buttercup'; for Autumn brought them still.

Upon my hand the fly so small that sight
Hardly could shape him settled, quested, flew;
10   Above me crowns of cloud and thrones of light
Moved with the minutes, and the season's blue,
    Autumn's soft raiment, veiled some forms of dream
    Which I yet reverence; once more to my stream
The clear forget-me-not drew my eyes; the vole watched too.

15   He watched, and ate his chosen leaf; well-furred,
Well-fed he felt for water, winter, all.
Whoever else came by, midge, moth or bird,
The time was easy, nor did one leaf fall
    From willow or elm that hour, though millions glowed
20   With such wild flame as evening shot abroad
To warn that even this calm was not perpetual.

1944

Basil Bunting
1900–85

Basil Bunting was born in Scotswood-on-Tyne and educated at Leighton Park School and the London School of Economics. A Quaker, he was in prison as a Conscientious Objector during the First World War. He worked in Paris on the *Transatlantic Review*, lived in Italy and America, was Persian correspondent for *The Times*, and taught at universities in America and England. His verse was better known in America than in England until *Briggflatts*, a long poem whose background is the Northumberland of his childhood, was published in 1966, followed by *Collected Poems* (1968).

ON THE FLY-LEAF OF POUND'S CANTOS†

There are the Alps. What is there to say about them?
They don't make sense. Fatal glaciers, crags cranks climb,
jumbled boulder and weed, pasture and boulder, scree,†
et l'on entend, maybe, *le refrain joyeux et leger.*†
5 Who knows what the ice will have scraped on the rock it is smoothing?

There they are, you will have to go a long way round
if you want to avoid them.
It takes some getting used to. There are the Alps,
fools! Sit down and wait for them to crumble!

1949   1965

Pound's Cantos   The Cantos of the American
poet Ezra Pound (1885–1972)
scree   rocky debris

et l'on . . . leger   (French) and one hears the
joyous, light refrain

[A thrush in the syringa sings]

A thrush in the syringa sings.

'Hunger ruffles my wings, fear,
lust, familiar things.

Death thrusts hard. My sons
5   by hawk's beak, by stones,
trusting weak wings
by cat and weasel, die.

Thunder smothers the sky.
From a shaken bush I
10   list familiar things,
fear, hunger, lust.'

O gay thrush!

1964   1965

[Three Michaelmas daisies]

Three Michaelmas daisies
on an ashtray;
one abets love;
one droops and woos;

5   one stiffens her petals
remembering
the root, the sap
and the bees' play.

1965   1966

[Gone to hunt]

Gone to hunt; and my brothers,
but the hut is clean, said the girl.
I have curds, besides whey.

Pomegranates, traveller;
5   butter, if you need it,
in a bundle of cress.

Soft, so soft, my bed.
Few come this road.
I am not married: —— yet

10   today I am fourteen years old.

1965   1966

[You idiot!]

You idiot! What makes you think decay will
never stink from your skin? Your warts sicken
typists, girls in the tube avoid you. Must they
also stop their ears to your tomcat
5   wailing, a promise your body cannot keep?

A lame stag, limping after the hinds, with tines[†]
shivered by impact and scarred neck – but
look! Spittle fills his mouth, overflows,
snuffing their sweet scent. His feet lift lightly
10   with mere memory of gentler seasons. Lungs
full of the drug, antlers rake back, he
halts the herd, his voice filled with
custom of combat and unslaked lust.

Did the girl[†] shrink from David? Did she hug his
15   ribs, death shaking them, and milk dry
the slack teat from which Judah had sucked life?

1965   1968

---

tines the points of antlers
the girl the fair young virgin required to warm

the body of the aged David, King of Judah;
see 1 Kings 1. 1–5

Stevie Smith
1902–71

Florence Margaret Smith was born in Hull and brought up in London. *Novel on Yellow Paper* (1936) was followed by two other novels, *Over the Frontier* (1938) and *The Holiday* (1949). Her poems, of which there were several volumes, including *A Good Time Was Had by All* (1937) and *Not Waving but Drowning* (1957), are clever and unusual. *Collected Poems* was published in 1975.

THE SINGING CAT

It was a little captive cat
  Upon a crowded train
His mistress takes him from his box
  To ease his fretful pain.

5 She holds him tight upon her knee
  The graceful animal
And all the people look at him
  He is so beautiful.

But oh he pricks and oh he prods
10 And turns upon her knee
Then lifteth up his innocent voice
  In plaintive melody.

He lifteth up his innocent voice
  He lifteth up, he singeth
15 And to each human countenance
  A smile of grace he bringeth.

He lifteth up his innocent paw
  Upon her breast he clingeth
And everybody cries, Behold
20 The cat, the cat that singeth.

He lifteth up his innocent voice
  He lifteth up, he singeth
And all the people warm themselves
  In the love his beauty bringeth.

1957

NOT WAVING BUT DROWNING

Nobody heard him, the dead man,
  But still he lay moaning:
I was much further out than you thought
  And not waving but drowning.

5   Poor chap, he always loved larking
  And now he's dead
It must have been too cold for him his heart gave way,
  They said.

Oh, no no no, it was too cold always
10 (Still the dead one lay moaning)
I was much too far out all my life
  And not waving but drowning.

1957

Evelyn Waugh

1903–66

Evelyn Arthur St John Waugh was born in Hampstead, son of the critic and publisher Arthur Waugh (1866–1943). He was educated at Lancing and Hertford College, Oxford. He studied art for a while and taught in private schools. His first novels, *Decline and Fall* (1928) and *Vile Bodies* (1930) established his reputation as a very amusing satirist of fashionable upper-class English society. *Black Mischief* (1932) is an unkind comic treatment of Abyssinia, which Waugh visited in 1930. *A Handful of Dust* (1934), a bitter, only intermittently funny novel, was followed by *When the Going Was Good* (1946), a collection of Waugh's travel books of the 1930s, and *Scoop: A Novel about Journalists* (1938). Waugh had become a Roman Catholic in 1930. His religious convictions first became conspicuous in *Brideshead Revisited* (1945). *The Loved One* (1950), a satire on the luxurious vulgarity of cemeteries in California, increased Waugh's reputation and so did the three entertaining volumes of *Sword of Honour* (1952, 1955, 1961); based on Waugh's army service, they follow the fortunes of an old-fashioned Catholic gentleman in the Second World War. Among his later books, *The Ordeal of Gilbert Pinfold* (1957), in which he satirised himself as a pedantic author sheltering in the role of a crusty country squire, is the most attractive. The posthumous publication of his *Journals* (1973) and *Letters* (1980) has added to his stature as a comic observer and an artist in prose.

From THE ORDEAL OF GILBERT PINFOLD

Portrait of the Artist in Middle-age

It may happen in the next hundred years that the English novelists of the present day will come to be valued as we now value the artists and craftsmen of the late eighteenth century. The originators, the exuberant men, are extinct and in their place subsists and modestly flourishes a
5 generation notable for elegance and variety of contrivance. It may well

happen that there are lean years ahead in which our posterity will look back hungrily to this period, when there was so much will and so much ability to please.

Among these novelists Mr Gilbert Pinfold stood quite high. At the time of his adventure, at the age of fifty, he had written a dozen books all of which were still bought and read. They were translated into most languages and in the United States of America enjoyed intermittent but lucrative seasons of favour. Foreign students often chose them as the subject for theses, but those who sought to detect cosmic significance in Mr Pinfold's work, to relate it to fashions in philosophy, social predicaments or psychological tensions, were baffled by his frank, curt replies to their questionnaires; their fellows in the English Literature School, who chose more egotistical writers, often found their theses more than half composed for them. Mr Pinfold gave nothing away. Not that he was secretive or grudging by nature; he had nothing to give these students. He regarded his books as objects which he had made, things quite external to himself to be used and judged by others. He thought them well made, better than many reputed works of genius, but he was not vain of his accomplishment, still less of his reputation. He had no wish to obliterate anything he had written, but he would dearly have liked to revise it, envying painters, who are allowed to return to the same theme time and time again, clarifying and enriching until they have done all they can with it. A novelist is condemned to produce a succession of novelties, new names for characters, new incidents for his plots, new scenery; but, Mr Pinfold maintained, most men harbour the germs of one or two books only; all else is professional trickery of which the most daemonic of the masters – Dickens and Balzac even – were flagrantly guilty.

At the beginning of this fifty-first year of his life Mr Pinfold presented to the world most of the attributes of wellbeing. Affectionate, high-spirited and busy in childhood; dissipated and often despairing in youth; sturdy and prosperous in early manhood; he had in middle-age degenerated less than many of his contemporaries. He attributed this superiority to his long, lonely, tranquil days at Lychpole, a secluded village some hundred miles from London.

He was devoted to a wife many years younger than himself, who actively farmed the small property. Their children were numerous, healthy, good-looking and good-mannered, and his income just sufficed for their education. Once he had travelled widely; now he spent most of the year in the shabby old house which, over the years, he had filled with pictures and books and furniture of the kind he relished. As a soldier he had sustained, in good heart, much discomfort and some danger. Since the end of the war his life had been strictly private. In his own village he took very lightly the duties which he might have thought

50   incumbent on him. He contributed adequate sums to local causes but he had no interest in sport or in local government, no ambition to lead or to command. He had never voted in a parliamentary election, maintaining an idiosyncratic toryism which was quite unrepresented in the political parties of his time and was regarded by his neighbours as
55   being almost as sinister as socialism.

    These neighbours were typical of the English countryside of the period. A few rich men farmed commercially on a large scale; a few had business elsewhere and came home merely to hunt; the majority were elderly and in reduced circumstances; people who, when the
60   Pinfolds settled at Lychpole, lived comfortably with servants and horses, and now lived in much smaller houses and met at the fishmonger's. Many of these were related to one another and formed a compact little clan. Colonel and Mrs Bagnold, Mr and Mrs Graves, Mrs and Miss Fawdle, Colonel and Miss Garbett, Lady Fawdle-Upton and Miss
65   Clarissa Bagnold all lived in a radius of ten miles from Lychpole. All were in some way related. In the first years of their marriage Mr and Mrs Pinfold had dined in all these households and had entertained them in return. But after the war the decline of fortune, less sharp in the Pinfold's case than their neighbours', made their meetings less frequent.
70   The Pinfolds were addicted to nicknames and each of these surrounding families had its own private, unsuspected appellation at Lychpole, not malicious but mildly derisive, taking its origin in most cases from some half forgotten incident in the past. The nearest neighbour whom they saw most often was Reginald Graves-Upton, an uncle of the Graves-
75   Uptons ten miles distant at Upper Mewling; a gentle, bee-keeping old bachelor who inhabited a thatched cottage up the lane less than a mile from the Manor. It was his habit on Sunday mornings to walk to church across the Pinfolds' fields and leave his Cairn terrier in the Pinfolds' stables while he attended Matins. He called for quarter of an hour
80   when he came to fetch his dog, drank a small glass of sherry and described the wireless programmes he had heard during the preceding week. This refined, fastidious old gentleman went by the recondite name of 'the Bruiser', sometimes varied to 'Pug', 'Basher', and 'Old Fisticuffs', all of which sobriquets derived from 'Boxer'; for in recent years he had
85   added to his interests an object which he reverently referred to as 'The Box'.

    This Box was one of many operating in various parts of the country. It was installed, under the sceptical noses of Reginald Graves-Upton's nephew and niece, at Upper Mewling. Mrs Pinfold, who had been taken
90   to see it, said it looked like a makeshift wireless-set. According to the Bruiser and other devotees, The Box exercised diagnostic and therapeutic powers. Some part of a sick man or animal – a hair, a drop of blood preferably – was brought to The Box, whose guardian would then 'tune

in' to the 'life-waves' of the patient, discern the origin of the malady
95 and prescribe treatment.

Mr Pinfold was as sceptical as the younger Graves-Uptons. Mrs
Pinfold thought there must be something in it, because it had been
tried, without her knowledge, on Lady Fawdle-Upton's nettle-rash and
immediate relief had followed.

100 'It's all suggestion,' said young Mrs Graves-Upton.

'It can't be suggestion, if she didn't know it was being done,' said
Mr Pinfold.

'No. It's simply a matter of measuring the Life-Waves,' said Mrs
Pinfold.

105 'An extremely dangerous device in the wrong hands,' said Mr Pinfold.

'No, no. That is the beauty of it. It can't do any harm. You see it
only transmits *Life* Forces. Fanny Graves tried it on her spaniel for
worms, but they simply grew enormous with all the Life Force going
into them. Like serpents, Fanny said.'

110 'I should have thought this Box counted as sorcery,' Mr Pinfold said
to his wife when they were alone. 'You ought to confess it.'

'D'you really think so?'

'No, not really. It's just a lot of harmless nonsense.'

The Pinfolds' religion made a slight but perceptible barrier between
115 them and these neighbours, a large part of whose activities centred
round their parish churches. The Pinfolds were Roman Catholic, Mrs
Pinfold by upbringing, Mr Pinfold by a later development. He had been
received into the Church – 'conversion' suggests an event more sudden
and emotional than his calm acceptance of the propositions of his faith –
120 in early manhood, at the time when many Englishmen of humane
education were falling into communism. Unlike them Mr Pinfold
remained steadfast. But he was reputed bigoted rather than pious. His
trade by its nature is liable to the condemnation of the clergy as, at the
best, frivolous; at the worst, corrupting. Moreover by the narrow
125 standards of the age his habits of life were self-indulgent and his
utterances lacked prudence. And at the very time when the leaders of
his Church were exhorting their people to emerge from the catacombs
into the forum, to make their influence felt in democratic politics and
to regard worship as a corporate rather than a private act, Mr Pinfold
130 burrowed ever deeper into the rock. Away from his parish he sought
the least frequented Mass; at home he held aloof from the multifarious
organizations which have sprung into being at the summons of the
hierarchy to redeem the times.

But Mr Pinfold was far from friendless and he set great store by his
135 friends. They were the men and women who were growing old with
him, whom in the 1920s and '30s he had seen constantly; who in the

diaspora of the '40s and '50s kept more tenuous touch with one another, the men at Bellamy's Club, the women at the half-dozen poky, pretty houses of Westminster and Belgravia to which had descended the larger
140   hospitality of a happier age.

He had made no new friends in late years. Sometimes he thought he detected a slight coldness among his old cronies. It was always he, it seemed to him, who proposed a meeting. It was always they who first rose to leave. In particular there was one, Roger Stillingfleet, who had
145   once been an intimate but now seemed to avoid him. Roger Stillingfleet was a writer, one of the few Mr Pinfold really liked. He knew of no reason for their estrangement and, enquiring, was told that Roger had grown very odd lately. He never came to Bellamy's now, it was said, except to collect his letters or to entertain a visiting American.

150   It sometimes occurred to Mr Pinfold that he must be growing into a bore. His opinions certainly were easily predictable.

His strongest tastes were negative. He abhorred plastics, Picasso, sunbathing and jazz – everything in fact that had happened in his own lifetime. The tiny kindling of charity which came to him through his
155   religion, sufficed only to temper his disgust and change it to boredom. There was a phrase in the '30s: 'It is later than you think', which was designed to cause uneasiness. It was never later than Mr Pinfold thought. At intervals during the day and night he would look at his watch and learn always with disappointment how little of his life was past, how
160   much there was still ahead of him. He wished no one ill, but he looked at the world *sub specie aeternitatis* [in the light of eternity] and he found it flat as a map; except when, rather often, personal annoyance intruded. Then he would come tumbling from his exalted point of observation. Shocked by a bad bottle of wine, an impertinent stranger,
165   or a fault in syntax, his mind like a cinema camera trucked furiously forward to confront the offending object close-up with glaring lens; with the eyes of a drill sergeant inspecting an awkward squad, bulging with wrath that was half-facetious, and with half-simulated incredulity; like a drill sergeant he was absurd to many but to some rather
170   formidable.

Once upon a time all this had been thought diverting. People quoted his pungent judgments and invented anecdotes of his audacity, which were recounted as 'typical Pinfolds'. Now, he realized, his singularity had lost some of its attraction for others, but he was too old a dog to
175   learn new tricks.

As a boy, at the age of puberty when most of his schoolfellows coarsened, he had been as fastidious as the Bruiser and in his early years of success diffidence had lent him charm. Prolonged prosperity had wrought the change. He had seen sensitive men make themselves a
180   protective disguise against the rebuffs and injustices of manhood. Mr

Pinfold had suffered little in these ways; he had been tenderly reared and, as a writer, welcomed, and over-rewarded early. It was his modesty which needed protection and for this purpose, but without design, he gradually assumed this character of burlesque. He was neither a scholar nor a regular soldier; the part for which he cast himself was a combination of eccentric don and testy colonel and he acted it strenuously, before his children at Lychpole and his cronies in London, until it came to dominate his whole outward personality. When he ceased to be alone, when he swung into his club or stumped up the nursery stairs, he left half of himself behind and the other half swelled to fill its place. He offered the world a front of pomposity mitigated by indiscretion, that was as hard, bright and antiquated as a cuirass.

Mr Pinfold's nanny used to say: 'Don't care went to the gallows'; also: 'Sticks and stones can break my bones, but words can never hurt me.' Mr Pinfold did not care what the village or his neighbours said of him. As a little boy he had been acutely sensitive to ridicule. His adult shell seemed impervious. He had long held himself inaccessible to interviewers and the young men and women who were employed to write 'profiles' collected material where they could. Every week his press-cutting agents brought to his breakfast-table two or three rather offensive allusions. He accepted without much resentment the world's estimate of himself. It was part of the price he paid for privacy. There were also letters from strangers, some abusive, some adulatory. Mr Pinfold was unable to discover any particular superiority of taste or expression in the writers of either sort. To both he sent printed acknowledgments.

His days passed in writing, reading and managing his own small affairs. He had never employed a secretary and for the last two years he had been without a manservant. But Mr Pinfold did not repine. He was perfectly competent to answer his own letters, pay his bills, tie his parcels and fold his clothes. At night his most frequent recurring dream was of doing *The Times* cross-word puzzle; his most disagreeable that he was reading a tedious book aloud to his family.

Physically, in his late forties, he had become lazy. Time was, he rode to hounds, went for long walks, dug his garden, felled small trees. Now he spent most of the day in an armchair. He ate less, drank more, and grew corpulent. He was very seldom so ill as to spend a day in bed. He suffered intermittently from various twinges and brief bouts of pain in his joints and muscles – arthritis, gout, rheumatism, fibrositis; they were not dignified by any scientific name. Mr Pinfold seldom consulted his doctor. When he did so it was as a 'private patient'. His children availed themselves of the National Health Act but Mr Pinfold was reluctant to disturb a relationship which had been formed in his first years at Lychpole. Dr Drake, Mr Pinfold's medical attendant, had

225   inherited the practice from his father and had been there before the Pinfolds came to Lychpole. Lean, horsy and weather-beaten in appearance, he had deep roots and wide ramifications in the countryside, being brother of the local auctioneer, brother-in-law of the solicitor, and cousin of three neighbouring rectors. His recreations were sporting.
230   He was not a man of high technical pretentions but he suited Mr Pinfold well. He too suffered, more sharply, from Mr Pinfold's troubles and when consulted remarked that Mr Pinfold must expect these things at his age; that the whole district was afflicted in this way and that Lychpole was notoriously the worst spot in it.

235   Mr Pinfold also slept badly. It was a trouble of long standing. For twenty-five years he had used various sedatives, for the last ten years a single specific, chloral and bromide which, unknown to Dr Drake, he bought on an old prescription in London. There were periods of literary composition when he would find the sentences he had written during
240   the day running in his head, the words shifting and changing colour kaleidoscopically, so that he would again and again climb out of bed, pad down to the library, make a minute correction, return to his room, lie in the dark dazzled by the pattern of vocables until obliged once more to descend to the manuscript. But those days and nights of obsession, of what
245   might without vainglory be called 'creative' work, were a small part of his year. On most nights he was neither fretful nor apprehensive. He was merely bored. After even the idlest day he demanded six or seven hours of insensibility. With them behind him, with them to look forward to, he could face another idle day with something approaching jauntiness; and
250   these his doses unfailingly provided.

At about the time of his fiftieth birthday there occurred two events which seemed trivial at the time but grew to importance in his later adventures.

The first of these primarily concerned Mrs Pinfold. During the war
255   Lychpole was let, the house to a convent, the fields to a grazier. This man, Hill, had collected parcels of grass-land in and around the parish and on them kept a nondescript herd of 'unattested' dairy-cattle. The pasture was rank, the fences dilapidated. When the Pinfolds came home in 1945 and wanted their fields back, the War Agricultural Committee, normally
260   predisposed towards the sitting tenant, were in no doubt of their decision in Mrs Pinfold's favour. Had she acted at once, Hill would have been out, with his compensation, at Michaelmas, but Mrs Pinfold was tender-hearted and Hill was adroit. First he pleaded, then having established new rights, asserted them. Lady Day succeeded Michaelmas;[†] Michaelmas, Lady Day

---

Lady Day . . . Michaelmas   25 March and 29
September, Quarter-days, for payment of rent, in England

265 for four full years. Hill retreated meadow by meadow. The committee, still popularly known as 'the War Ag.', returned, walked the property anew, again found for Mrs Pinfold. Hill, who now had a lawyer, appealed. So it went on. Mr Pinfold held aloof from it all, merely noting with sorrow the anxiety of his wife. At length at Michaelmas 1949 Hill finally moved.
270 He boasted in the village inn of his cleverness, and left for the other side of the country with a comfortable profit.

The second event occurred soon after. Mr Pinfold received an invitation from the B.B.C. to record an 'interview'. In the previous twenty years there had been many such proposals and he had always
275 refused them. This time the fee was more liberal and the conditions softer. He would not have to go to the offices in London. Electricians would come to him with their apparatus. No script had to be submitted; no preparation of any kind was required; the whole thing would take an hour. In an idle moment Mr Pinfold agreed and at once regretted it.
280 The day came towards the end of the summer holidays. Soon after breakfast there arrived a motor-car, and a van of the sort used in the army by the more important kinds of signaller, which immediately absorbed the attention of the younger children. Out of the car there came three youngish men, thin of hair, with horn-rimmed elliptical
285 glasses, cord trousers and tweed coats; exactly what Mr Pinfold was expecting. Their leader was named Angel. He emphasized his primacy by means of a neat, thick beard. He and his colleagues, he explained, had slept in the district, where he had an aunt. They would have to leave before luncheon. They would get through their business in the
290 morning. The signallers began rapidly uncoiling wires and setting up their microphone in the library, while Mr Pinfold drew the attention of Angel and his party to the more noticeable of his collection of works of art. They did not commit themselves to an opinion, merely remarking that the last house they visited had a gouache by Rouault.[†]
295 'I didn't know he ever painted in gouache,' said Mr Pinfold. 'Anyway he's a dreadful painter.'

'Ah!' said Angel. 'That's very nice. Very nice indeed. We must try and work that into the broadcast.'

When the electricians had made their arrangements Mr Pinfold sat
300 at his table with the three strangers, a microphone in their midst. They were attempting to emulate a series that had been cleverly done in Paris with various French celebrities, in which informal, spontaneous discussion had seduced the objects of inquiry into self-revelation.

They questioned Mr Pinfold in turn about his tastes and habits. Angel
305 led and it was at him that Mr Pinfold looked. The commonplace face

---

Rouault Georges Rouault (1871–1958), a French expressionist painter, admired by people more sympathetic than Mr Pinfold is (or affects to be) to modern art

above the beard became slightly sinister, the accentless, but insidiously plebeian voice, menacing. The questions were civil enough in form but Mr Pinfold thought he could detect an underlying malice. Angel seemed to believe that anyone sufficiently eminent to be interviewed by him
310 must have something to hide, must be an imposter whom it was his business to trap and expose, and to direct his questions from some basic, previous knowledge of something discreditable. There was the hint of the under-dog's snarl which Mr Pinfold recognized from his press-cuttings.

315 He was well equipped to deal with insolence, real or imagined, and answered succinctly and shrewdly, disconcerting his adversaries, if adversaries they were, point by point. When it was over Mr Pinfold offered his visitors sherry. Tension relaxed. He asked politely who was their next subject.

320 'We're going on to Stratford,' said Angel, 'to interview Cedric Thorne.'

'You evidently have not seen this morning's paper,' said Mr Pinfold.

'No, we left before it came.'

'Cedric Thorne has escaped you. He hanged himself yesterday
325 afternoon in his dressing-room.'

'Good heavens, are you sure?'

'It's in *The Times*.'

'May I see?'

Angel was shaken from his professional calm. Mr Pinfold brought
330 the paper and he read the paragraph with emotion.

'Yes, yes. That's him. I half expected this. He was a personal friend. I must get on to his wife. May I phone?'

Mr Pinfold apologized for the levity with which he had broken the news and led Angel to the business-room. He refilled the sherry glasses
335 and attempted to appear genial. Angel returned shortly to say: 'I couldn't get through. I'll have to try again later.'

Mr Pinfold repeated his regrets.

'Yes, it is a terrible thing – not wholly unexpected though.'

A macabre note had been added to the discords of the morning.
340 Then hands were shaken; the vehicles turned on the gravel and drove away.

When they were out of sight down the turn of the drive, one of the children who had been listening to the conversation in the van said: 'You didn't like those people much, did you, papa?'

345 He had definitely not liked them and they left an unpleasant memory which grew sharper in the weeks before the recording was broadcast. He brooded. It seemed to him that an attempt had been made against his privacy and he was not sure how effectively he had defended it. He strained to remember his precise words and his memory supplied various

350 distorted versions. Finally the evening came when the performance was made public. Mr Pinfold had the cook's wireless carried into the drawing-room. He and Mrs Pinfold listened together. His voice came to him strangely old and fruity, but what he said gave him no regret. 'They tried to make an ass of me,' he said. 'I don't believe they
355 succeeded.'

Mr Pinfold for the time forgot Angel.

Boredom alone and some stiffness in the joints disturbed that sunny autumn. Despite his age and dangerous trade Mr Pinfold seemed to himself and to others unusually free of the fashionable agonies of *angst*.

1955   1957

George Orwell
1903–1950

George Orwell was the pseudonym of Eric Arthur Blair who was born in Bengal but grew up in England and was educated at Eton. His experiences as a colonial police-officer in Burma (1922–7) are recounted in his book of essays *Shooting an Elephant* (1950) and in his first novel *Burmese Days* (1934). Burma left him with a lifelong distaste for power. He turned to menial jobs. *Down and Out in Paris and London* (1933) and *The Road to Wigan Pier* (1937) are accounts of his life among the poor. He fought for the Republicans in the Spanish Civil War and published *Homage to Catalonia* in 1939. He was an outstanding essayist and journalist, writing in the 1940s, in *Tribune* and elsewhere, from a liberal socialist point of view. His political satires, *Animal Farm* (1945) and *Nineteen Eighty-Four* (1949), made him famous. Their influence, even in Eastern Europe where they are banned but widely read, has been considerable.

From NINETEEN EIGHTY-FOUR
[The Principles of Newspeak]

Newspeak was the official language of Oceania and had been devised to meet the ideological needs of Ingsoc, or English Socialism. In the year 1984, there was not as yet anyone who used Newspeak as his sole means of communication, either in speech or writing. The leading
5 articles in the *Times* were written in it, but this was a *tour de force* which could only be carried out by a specialist. It was expected that Newspeak would have finally superseded Oldspeak (or Standard English, as we should call it) by about the year 2050. Meanwhile it gained ground steadily, all Party members tending to use Newspeak words and
10 grammatical constructions more and more in their everyday speech. The version in use in 1984, and embodied in the Ninth and Tenth Editions of the Newspeak Dictionary, was a provisional one, and contained many superfluous words and archaic formations which were due to be suppressed later. It is with the final, perfected version, as
15 embodied in the Eleventh Edition of the Dictionary, that we are concerned here.

The purpose of Newspeak was not only to provide a medium of expression for the world-view and mental habits proper to the devotees of Ingsoc, but to make all other modes of thought impossible. It was intended that when Newspeak had been adopted once and for all and Oldspeak forgotten, a heretical thought – that is, a thought diverging from the principles of Ingsoc – should be literally unthinkable, at least so far as thought is dependent on words. Its vocabulary was so constructed as to give exact and often very subtle expression to every meaning that a Party member could properly wish to express, while excluding all other meanings and also the possibility of arriving at them by indirect methods. This was done partly by the invention of new words, but chiefly by eliminating undesirable words and by stripping such words as remained of unorthodox meanings, and so far as possible of all secondary meanings whatever. To give a single example. The word *free* still existed in Newspeak, but it could only be used in such statements as 'This dog is free from lice' or 'This field is free from weeds'. It could not be used in its old sense of 'politically free' or 'intellectually free', since political and intellectual freedom no longer existed even as concepts, and were therefore of necessity nameless. Quite apart from the suppression of definitely heretical words, reduction of vocabulary was regarded as an end in itself, and no word that could be dispensed with was allowed to survive. Newspeak was designed not to extend but to *diminish* the range of thought, and this purpose was indirectly assisted by cutting the choice of words down to a minimum.

Newspeak was founded on the English language as we now know it, though many Newspeak sentences, even when not containing newly-created words, would be barely intelligible to an English-speaker of our own day. Newspeak words were divided into three distinct classes, known as the A vocabulary, the B vocabulary (also called compound words), and the C vocabulary. It will be simpler to discuss each class separately, but the grammatical peculiarities of the language can be dealt with in the section devoted to the A vocabulary, since the same rules held good for all three categories.

The A vocabulary. The A vocabulary consisted of the words needed for the business of everyday life – for such things as eating, drinking, working, putting on one's clothes, going up and down stairs, riding in vehicles, gardening, cooking, and the like. It was composed almost entirely of words that we already possess – words like *hit*, *run*, *dog*, *tree*, *sugar*, *house*, *field* – but in comparison with the present-day English vocabulary their number was extremely small, while their meanings were far more rigidly defined. All ambiguities and shades of meaning had been purged out of them. So far as it could be achieved, a Newspeak word of this class was simply a staccato sound expressing *one* clearly

60   understood concept. It would have been quite impossible to use the A
vocabulary for literary purposes or for political or philosophical
discussion. It was intended only to express simple, purposive thoughts,
usually involving concrete objects or physical actions.

The grammar of Newspeak had two outstanding peculiarities. The
65   first of these was an almost complete interchangeability between
different parts of speech. Any word in the language (in principle this
applied even to very abstract words such as *if* or *when*) could be used
either as verb, noun, adjective or adverb. Between the verb and the
noun form, when they were of the same root, there was never any
70   variation, this rule of itself involving the destruction of many archaic
forms. The word *thought*, for example, did not exist in Newspeak. Its
place was taken by *think*, which did duty for both noun and verb. No
etymological principle was followed here: in some cases it was the
original noun that was chosen for retention, in other cases the verb.
75   Even where a noun and verb of kindred meaning were not etymologically
connected, one or other of them was frequently suppressed. There was,
for example, no such word as *cut*, its meaning being sufficiently covered
by the noun-verb *knife*. Adjectives were formed by adding the suffix
-ful to the noun-verb, and adverbs by adding *-wise*. Thus, for example,
80   *speedful* meant 'rapid' and *speedwise* meant 'quickly'. Certain of our
present-day adjectives, such as *good, strong, big, black, soft*, were
retained, but their total number was very small. There was little need
for them, since almost any adjectival meaning could be arrived at by
adding *-ful* to a noun-verb. None of the now-existing adverbs was
85   retained, except for a very few already ending in *-wise*: the *-wise*
termination was invariable. The word *well*, for example, was replaced
by *goodwise*.

In addition, any word – this again applied in principle to every word
in the language – could be negatived by adding the affix *un-*, or could
90   be strengthened by the affix *plus-*, or, for still greater emphasis,
doubleplus-. Thus, for example, *uncold* meant 'warm', while *plus-cold*
and *doublepluscold* meant, respectively 'very cold' and 'superlatively
cold'. It was also possible, as in present-day English, to modify the
meaning of almost any word by prepositional affixes such as *ante-*,
95   *post-, up-, down-*, etc. By such methods it was found possible to bring
about an enormous diminution of vocabulary. Given, for instance, the
word *good*, there was no need for such a word as *bad*, since the required
meaning was equally well – indeed, better – expressed by *ungood*. All
that was necessary, in any case where two words formed a natural pair
100 of opposites, was to decide which of them to suppress. *Dark*, for
example, could be replaced by *unlight*, or *light* by *undark*, according
to preference.

The second distinguishing mark of Newspeak grammar was its

regularity. Subject to a few exceptions which are mentioned below, all inflections followed the same rules. Thus, in all verbs the preterite and the past participle were the same and ended in -*ed*. The preterite of *steal* was *stealed*, the preterite of *think* was *thinked*, and so on throughout the language, all such forms as *swam, gave, brought, spoke, taken*, etc., being abolished. All plurals were made by adding -*s* or -*es* as the case might be. The plurals of *man, ox, life*, were *mans, oxes, lifes*. Comparison of adjectives was invariably made by adding -*er*, -*est* (*good, gooder, goodest*), irregular forms and the *more, most* formation being suppressed.

The only classes of words that were still allowed to inflect irregularly were the pronouns, the relatives, the demonstrative adjectives and the auxiliary verbs. All of these followed their ancient usage, except that *whom* had been scrapped as unnecessary, and the *shall, should* tenses had been dropped, all their uses being covered by *will* and *would*. There were also certain irregularities in word-formation arising out of the need for rapid and easy speech. A word which was difficult to utter, or was liable to be incorrectly heard, was held to be *ipso facto* a bad word: occasionally therefore, for the sake of euphony, extra letters were inserted into a word or an archaic formation was retained. But this need made itself felt chiefly in connection with the B vocabulary. *Why* so great an importance was attached to ease of pronunciation will be made clear later in this essay.

The B vocabulary. The B vocabulary consisted of words which had been deliberately constructed for political purposes: words, that is, to say, which not only had in every case a political implication, but were intended to impose a desirable mental attitude upon the person using them. Without a full understanding of the principles of Ingsoc it was difficult to use these words correctly. In some cases they could be translated into Oldspeak, or even into words taken from the A vocabulary, but this usually demanded a long paraphrase and always involved the loss of certain overtones. The B words were a sort of verbal shorthand, often packing whole ranges of ideas into a few syllables, and at the same time more accurate and forcible than ordinary language.

The B words were in all cases compound words. They consisted of two or more words, or portions of words, welded together in an easily pronounceable form. The resulting amalgam was always a noun-verb, and inflected according to the ordinary rules. To take a single example: the word *goodthink*, meaning, very roughly, 'orthodoxy', or, if one chose to regard it as a verb, 'to think in an orthodox manner'. This inflected as follows: noun-verb, *goodthink*; past tense and past participle, *goodthinked*; present participle, *goodthinking*; adjective, *goodthinkful*; adverb, *goodthinkwise*; verbal noun, *goodthinker*.

The B words were not constructed on any etymological plan. The words of which they were made up could be any parts of speech, and could be placed in any order and mutilated in any way which made
150   them easy to pronounce while indicating their derivation. In the word *crimethink* (thoughtcrime), for instance, the *think* came second, whereas in *thinkpol* (Thought Police) it came first, and in the latter word *police* had lost its second syllable. Because of the greater difficulty in securing euphony, irregular formations were commoner in the B vocabulary than
155   in the A vocabulary. For example, the adjective forms of *Minitrue*, *Minipax* and *Miniluv* were, respectively, *Minitruthful*, *Minipeaceful* and *Minilovely*, simply because *-trueful*, *-paxful* and *-loveful* were slightly awkward to pronounce. In principle, however, all B words could inflect, and all inflected in exactly the same way.
160   Some of the B words had highly subtilized meanings, barely intelligible to anyone who had not mastered the language as a whole. Consider, for example, such a typical sentence from a *Times* leading article as *Oldthinkers unbellyfeel Ingsoc*. The shortest rendering that one could make of this in Oldspeak would be: 'Those whose ideas were formed
165   before the Revolution cannot have a full emotional understanding of the principles of English Socialism.' But this is not an adequate translation. To begin with, in order to grasp the full meaning of the Newspeak sentence quoted above, one would have to have a clear idea of what is meant by *Ingsoc*. And in addition, only a person thoroughly
170   grounded in Ingsoc could appreciate the full force of the word *bellyfeel*, which implied a blind, enthusiastic acceptance difficult to imagine to-day; or of the word *oldthink*, which was inextricably mixed up with the idea of wickedness and decadence. But the special function of certain Newspeak words, of which *oldthink* was one, was not so much to
175   express meanings as to destroy them. These words, necessarily few in number, had had their meanings extended until they contained within themselves whole batteries of words which, as they were sufficiently covered by a single comprehensive term, could now be scrapped and forgotten. The greatest difficulty facing the compilers of the Newspeak
180   Dictionary was not to invent new words, but, having invented them, to make sure what they meant: to make sure, that is to say, what ranges of words they cancelled by their existence.
As we have already seen in the case of the word *free*, words which had once borne a heretical meaning were sometimes retained for the
185   sake of convenience, but only with the undesirable meanings purged out of them. Countless other words such as *honour*, *justice*, *morality*, *internationalism*, *democracy*, *science* and *religion* had simply ceased to exist. A few blanket words covered them, and, in covering them, abolished them. All words grouping themselves round the concepts of
190   liberty and equality, for instance, were contained in the single word

crimethink, while all words grouping themselves round the concepts of objectivity and rationalism were contained in the single word *oldthink*. Greater precision would have been dangerous. What was required in a Party member was an outlook similar to that of the ancient Hebrew
195 who knew, without knowing much else, that all nations other than his own worshipped 'false gods'. He did not need to know that these gods were called Baal, Osiris, Moloch, Ashtaroth and the like: probably the less he knew about them the better for his orthodoxy. He knew Jehovah and the commandments of Jehovah: he knew, therefore, that all gods
200 with other names or other attributes were false gods. In somewhat the same way, the Party member knew what constituted right conduct, and in exceedingly vague, generalized terms he knew what kinds of departure from it were possible. His sexual life, for example, was entirely regulated by the two Newspeak words *sexcrime* (sexual immorality) and *goodsex*
205 (chastity). *Sexcrime* covered all sexual misdeeds whatever. It covered fornication, adultery, homosexuality and other perversions, and, in addition, normal intercourse practised for its own sake. There was no need to enumerate them separately, since they were all equally culpable, and, in principle, all punishable by death. In the C vocabulary, which
210 consisted of scientific and technical words, it might be necessary to give specialized names to certain sexual aberrations, but the ordinary citizen had no need of them. He knew what was meant by *goodsex* – that is to say, normal intercourse between man and wife, for the sole purpose of begetting children, and without physical pleasure on the part of the
215 woman: all else was *sexcrime*. In Newspeak it was seldom possible to follow a heretical thought further than the perception that it *was* heretical: beyond that point the necessary words were non-existent.

No word in the B vocabulary was ideologically neutral. A great many were euphemisms. Such words, for instance, as *joycamp* (forced-labour
220 camp) or *Minipax* (Ministry of Peace, i.e. Ministry of War) meant almost the exact opposite of what they appeared to mean. Some words, on the other hand, displayed a frank and contemptuous understanding of the real nature of Oceanic society. An example was *prolefeed*, meaning the rubbishy entertainment and spurious news which the Party
225 handed out to the masses. Other words, again, were ambivalent, having the connotation 'good' when applied to the Party and 'bad' when applied to its enemies. But in addition there were great numbers of words which at first sight appeared to be mere abbreviations and which derived their ideological colour not from their meaning but from their
230 structure.

So far as it could be contrived, everything that had or might have political significance of any kind was fitted into the B vocabulary. The name of every organization, or body of people, or doctrine, or country, or institution, or public building, was invariably cut down into the

235   familiar shape; that is, a single easily pronounced word with the smallest number of syllables that would preserve the original derivation. In the Ministry of Truth, for example, the Records Department, in which Winston Smith worked, was called *Recdep*, the Fiction Department was called *Ficdep*, the Tele-programmes Department was called *Teledep*,
240   and so on. This was not done solely with the object of saving time. Even in the early decades of the twentieth century, telescoped words and phrases had been one of the characteristic features of political language; and it had been noticed that the tendency to use abbreviations of this kind was most marked in totalitarian countries and totalitarian
245   organizations. Examples were such words as *Nazi, Gestapo, Comintern*,[†] *Inprecorr*,[†] *Agitprop*.[†] In the beginning the practice had been adopted as it were instinctively, but in Newspeak it was used with a conscious purpose. It was perceived that in thus abbreviating a name one narrowed and subtly altered its meaning, by cutting out most of
250   the associations that would otherwise cling to it. The words *Communist International*, for instance, call up a composite picture of universal human brotherhood, red flags, barricades, Karl Marx and the Paris Commune. The word *Comintern*, on the other hand, suggests merely a tightly-knit organization and a well-defined body of doctrine. It refers
255   to something almost as easily recognized, and as limited in purpose, as a chair or a table. *Comintern* is a word that can be uttered almost without taking thought, whereas *Communist International* is a phrase over which one is obliged to linger at least momentarily. In the same way, the associations called up by a word like *Minitrue* are fewer and
260   more controllable than those called up by *Ministry of Truth*. This accounted not only for the habit of abbreviating whenever possible, but also for the almost exaggerated care that was taken to make every word easily pronounceable.

In Newspeak, euphony outweighed every consideration other than
265   exactitude of meaning. Regularity of grammar was always sacrificed to it when it seemed necessary. And rightly so, since what was required, above all for political purposes, was short clipped words of unmistakable meaning which could be uttered rapidly and which roused the minimum of echoes in the speaker's mind. The words of the B vocabulary even
270   gained in force from the fact that nearly all of them were very much alike. Almost invariably these words – *goodthink, Minipax, prolefeed, sexcrime, joycamp, Ingsoc, bellyfeel, thinkpol* and countless others – were words of two or three syllables, with the stress distributed equally between the first syllable and the last. The use of them encouraged a
275   gabbling style of speech, at once staccato and monotonous. And this

---

Comintern   the Third (or Communist) International (1919–43)

Inprecorr   International Press Correspondence
Agitprop   Communist propaganda

was exactly what was aimed at. The intention was to make speech, and especially speech on any subject not ideologically neutral, as nearly as possible independent of consciousness. For the purposes of everyday life it was no doubt necessary, or sometimes necessary, to reflect before speaking, but a Party member called upon to make a political or ethical judgment should be able to spray forth the correct opinions as automatically as a machine gun spraying forth bullets. His training fitted him to do this, the language gave him an almost foolproof instrument, and the texture of the words, with their harsh sound and a certain wilful ugliness which was in accord with the spirit of Ingsoc, assisted the process still further.

So did the fact of having very few words to choose from. Relative to our own, the Newspeak vocabulary was tiny, and new ways of reducing it were constantly being devised. Newspeak, indeed, differed from almost all other languages in that its vocabulary grew smaller instead of larger every year. Each reduction was a gain, since the smaller the area of choice, the smaller the temptation to take thought. Ultimately it was hoped to make articulate speech issue from the larynx without involving the higher brain centres at all. This aim was frankly admitted in the Newspeak word *duckspeak*, meaning 'to quack like a duck'. Like various other words in the B vocabulary, *duckspeak* was ambivalent in meaning. Provided that the opinions which were quacked out were orthodox ones, it implied nothing but praise, and when the *Times* referred to one of the orators of the Party as a *doubleplusgood duckspeaker* it was paying a warm and valued compliment.

The C vocabulary. The C vocabulary was supplementary to the others and consisted entirely of scientific and technical terms. These resembled the scientific terms in use to-day, and were constructed from the same roots, but the usual care was taken to define them rigidly and strip them of undesirable meanings. They followed the same grammatical rules as the words in the other two vocabularies. Very few of the C words had any currency either in everyday speech or in political speech. Any scientific worker or technician could find all the words he needed in the list devoted to his own speciality, but he seldom had more than a smattering of the words occurring in the other lists. Only a very few words were common to all lists, and there was no vocabulary expressing the function of Science as a habit of mind, or a method of thought, irrespective of its particular branches. There was, indeed, no word for 'Science', any meaning that it could possibly bear being already sufficiently covered by the word *Ingsoc*.

From the foregoing account it will be seen that in Newspeak the expression of unorthodox opinions, above a very low level, was well-

nigh impossible. It was of course possible to utter heresies of a very crude kind, a species of blasphemy. It would have been possible, for
320   example, to say *Big Brother is ungood*. But this statement, which to an orthodox ear merely conveyed a self-evident absurdity, could not have been sustained by reasoned argument, because the necessary words were not available. Ideas inimical to Ingsoc could only be entertained in a vague wordless form, and could only be named in very broad terms
325   which lumped together and condemned whole groups of heresies without defining them in doing so. One could, in fact, only use Newspeak for unorthodox purposes by illegitimately translating some of the words back into Oldspeak. For example, *All mans are equal* was a possible Newspeak sentence, but only in the same sense in which *All*
330   *men are redhaired* is a possible Oldspeak sentence. It did not contain a grammatical error, but it expressed a palpable untruth – i.e. that all men are of equal size, weight or strength. The concept of political equality no longer existed, and this secondary meaning had accordingly been purged out of the word *equal*. In 1984, when Oldspeak was still
335   the normal means of communication, the danger theoretically existed that in using Newspeak words one might remember their original meanings. In practice it was not difficult for any person well grounded in *doublethink* to avoid doing this, but within a couple of generations even the possibility of such a lapse would have vanished. A person
340   growing up with Newspeak as his sole language would no more know that *equal* had once had the secondary meaning of 'politically equal', or that *free* had once meant 'intellectually free', than, for instance, a person who had never heard of chess would be aware of the secondary meanings attaching to *queen* and *rook*. There would be many crimes
345   and errors which it would be beyond his power to commit, simply because they were nameless and therefore unimaginable. And it was to be foreseen that with the passage of time the distinguishing characteristics of Newspeak would become more and more pronounced – its words growing fewer and fewer, their meanings more and more rigid, and the
350   chance of putting them to improper uses always diminishing.

When Oldspeak had been once and for all superseded, the last link with the past would have been severed. History had already been rewritten, but fragments of the literature of the past survived here and there, imperfectly censored, and so long as one retained one's knowledge
355   of Oldspeak it was possible to read them. In the future such fragments, even if they chanced to survive, would be unintelligible and untranslatable. It was impossible to translate any passage of Oldspeak into Newspeak unless it either referred to some technical process or some very simple everyday action, or was already orthodox (*goodthinkful*
360   would be the Newspeak expression) in tendency. In practice this meant that no book written before approximately 1960 could be translated

as a whole. Pre-revolutionary literature could only be subjected to ideological translation – that is, alteration in sense as well as language. Take for example the well-known passage from the Declaration of Independence:

> *We hold these truths to be self-evident, that all men are created equal, that they are endowed by their creator with certain inalienable rights, that among these are life, liberty and the pursuit of happiness. That to secure these rights, Governments are instituted among men, deriving their powers from the consent of the governed. That whenever any form of Government becomes destructive of those ends, it is the right of the People to alter or abolish it, and to institute new Government. . . .*

It would have been quite impossible to render this into Newspeak while keeping to the sense of the original. The nearest one could come to doing so would be to swallow the whole passage up in the single word *crimethink*. A full translation could only be an ideological translation, whereby Jefferson's words[†] would be changed into a panegyric on absolute government.

A good deal of the literature of the past was, indeed, already being transformed in this way. Considerations of prestige made it desirable to preserve the memory of certain historical figures, while at the same time bringing their achievements into line with the philosophy of Ingsoc. Various writers, such as Shakespeare, Milton, Swift, Byron, Dickens and some others were therefore in process of translation: when the task had been completed, their original writings, with all else that survived of the literature of the past, would be destroyed. These translations were a slow and difficult business, and it was not expected that they would be finished before the first or second decade of the twenty-first century. There were also large quantities of merely utilitarian literature – indispensable technical manuals, and the like – that had to be treated in the same way. It was chiefly in order to allow time for the preliminary work of translation that the final adoption of Newspeak had been fixed for so late a date as 2050.

1948   1949

Jefferson's words Thomas Jefferson (1743–1826), third President of the United States and author of the Declaration of Independence

Graham Greene
1904–

Henry Graham Greene was born at Berkhamsted and was educated at Berkhamsted School and Balliol College, Oxford. He joined *The Times* as a subeditor in 1926, but became a freelance writer after the success of his first novel, *The Man Within* (1929). *Stamboul Train* (1932) and *Brighton Rock* (1938) established his reputation as a writer of thrillers which are far more than just entertainments. After wartime service in West Africa, Greene travelled tirelessly as a foreign correspondent. His visits to Vietnam in the early 1950s provided the background for *The Quiet American* (1955); *A Burnt-Out Case* (1961) followed research in the Belgian Congo; *The Comedians* (1966), which shows conditions in Haiti under 'Papa Doc' Duvalier, was a result of his visit there in 1963. Greene had become a Roman Catholic in 1926. *The Power and the Glory* (1940), *The Heart of the Matter* (1948) and *The End of the Affair* (1951), made him appear 'a Catholic novelist' – a term he rejected. Subsequent novels with Catholic characters tend to explore religious doubts and loss of faith rather than to assert Catholic doctrine. Greene's gift for dark comedy is most apparent in later work, including *The Honorary Consul* (1973), his favourite. He has also written plays and short stories, criticism, film reviews, travel books, essays, and stories for children.

From THE HONORARY CONSUL
[The Hostage]

Charley Fortnum woke with the worst head he could ever remember having. His eyes were aching and his vision was blurred. He whispered, 'Clara,' putting out his hand to touch her side, but all he touched was a mud wall. Then an image came to his mind of Doctor Plarr standing
5 over him during the night with an electric torch. The doctor had told him some implausible story of an accident.

It was daylight now. The sunlight seeped across the floor under the door of the next room, and he could tell, even through his bruised eyes, that this was no hospital. Nor was the hard box on which he lay a

10   hospital bed. He swung his legs over the side and tried to stand up. He
was giddy and nearly fell. Clutching the side of the box, he saw that he
had been lying all night upon a coffin. It gave him, as he would have
put it, a nasty turn.

'Ted?' he called. He didn't associate Doctor Plarr with practical jokes,
15   but there had to be some sort of explanation, and he was anxious to
be back with Clara. Clara would be frightened, Clara wouldn't know
what to do. Why, she was afraid even to use the telephone. 'Ted?' he
called again in a dry croak. Whisky had never treated him like this
before, not even the local brand. Whom the bloody hell had he been
20   drinking with and where? Mason,[†] he told himself, you've got to pull
yourself together. It was always to Mason he attributed his worst errors
and his worst failings. In his boyhood when he still practised confession
it was always Mason who knelt in the box and muttered abstract
phrases concerning sins against purity, though it was Charley Fortnum
25   who would leave the box, his face ashine with beneficence after Mason's
absolution. 'Mason, Mason,' he whispered now, 'you snotty little beast,
Mason, what were you up to last night?' He knew that when he
exceeded the proper measure he was apt to forget things, but never
before had he forgotten to quite this extent . . . He took a stumbling
30   step towards the door and for the third time called out to Doctor Plarr.

The door was pushed open and a stranger stood there waving a sub-
machine gun at him. He had the narrow eyes and jet black hair of an
Indian and he shouted at Fortnum in Guaraní.[†] Fortnum, in spite of
his father's angry insistence, had never learnt more than a few words
35   of Guaraní, but it was clear enough that the man was telling him to get
back onto the so-called bed. 'All right, all right,' Fortnum said, speaking
English so that the man would no more understand him than he
understood Guaraní. 'Keep your shirt on, old man.' He sat down on
the coffin and said, 'Piss off,' with a sense of relief.

40   Another stranger in blue jeans, naked to the waist, came in and
ordered the Indian away. He carried a cup of coffee. The coffee smelt
like home, and Charley Fortnum was a little comforted. The man had
protruding ears and for a moment Charley was reminded of a boy at
school whom Mason had unmercifully teased, though Fortnum repented
45   afterwards and shared a bar of chocolate with the victim. This memory
gave him a sense of reassurance. He asked, 'Where am I?'

'You do not need to worry,' the man replied. He held out the coffee.

'I have to go home. My wife will be anxious.'

'Tomorrow. I hope you will be able to go tomorrow.'
50   'Who was that man with a gun?'

Mason Fortnum and Mason's is a London   *Guaraní* the language of the Guarani, a group
      store   of South American tribes

'Miguel. A good man. Drink your coffee, please. You will feel much better then.'

'What's your name?' Charley Fortnum asked.

'León,' the man said.

55 'I mean your family name?'

'None of us here have familes,' the man said, 'so we are nameless.'

Charley Fortnum turned this statement over in his mind like a difficult phrase in a book; it made no more sense to him at the second reading.

'Doctor Plarr was here last night,' he said.

60 'Plarr? Plarr? I do not think I know anyone called Plarr.'

'He told me I had been in an accident.'

'It was I who told you that,' the man said.

'It was not you. I saw him. He carried an electric torch.'

'You dreamt him. You have had a shock . . . Your car was badly 65 damaged. Please drink your coffee. You will remember things better perhaps afterwards.'

Charley Fortnum obeyed. It was very strong coffee, and it was true that his head began to clear. He asked, 'Where is the Ambassador?'

'I do not know of any Ambassador.'

70 'I left him in the ruins. I wanted to see my wife before dinner. I wanted to see that she was all right. I don't like leaving her for long. She is expecting a baby.'

'Yes? That must make you very happy. It is a fine thing to be the father of a child.'

75 'I remember now. There was a car across the road. I had to stop. There was no accident. I'm quite sure there was no accident. And why the gun?' His hand shook a little as he drank his coffee. He said, 'I want to go home now.'

'It is much too far to walk from here,' the man said. 'You are not fit 80 yet. And the way – you do not know the way.'

'I will find a road. I can stop a car.'

'Better to rest today. After the shock. Tomorrow perhaps we can find you some transport. Today it is not possible.'

Fortnum threw what was left of his coffee in the man's face and 85 charged into the outer room. Then he stopped. The Indian stood twelve feet away in front of the outer door, pointing his gun at Charley Fortnum's stomach. His dark eyes shone with pleasure, as he moved the gun a little this way, a little that, as though he were deciding his target, between the navel and the appendix. He said something which 90 amused him in Guaraní.

The man called León came from the inner room. He said, 'You see. I told you. You cannot go today.' One cheek was flushed red from the hot coffee, but he spoke gently, without anger. He had the patience of someone who was more used to enduring pain than inflicting it. He

95   said, 'You must be hungry, Señor Fortnum. If you would like some
eggs . . .'

'You know who I am?'

'Yes, yes, of course. You are the British Consul.'

'What are you going to do with me?'

100   'You will have to stay with us for a little while. Believe me, we are
not your enemies, Señor Fortnum. You will be helping us to save
innocent men from imprisonment and torture. By this time our man in
Rosario[†] will have telephoned to the *Nación*[†] to tell them you are in
our care.'

105   Charley Fortnum began to understand. 'You got the wrong man, is
that it? You were after the American Ambassador?'

'Yes, it was an unfortunate mistake.'

'A very bad mistake. No one is going to bother about Charley
Fortnum. What will you do then?'

110   The man said, 'I am sure you are wrong. You will see. Everything
will be arranged. The British Ambassador will talk to the President.
The President will speak to the General.[†] He is here in Argentina on a
holiday. The American Ambassador will intervene too. We are only
asking the General to release a few men. Everything would have been

115   quite easy if one of our men had not made a mistake.'

'You were not very well informed, were you? The Ambassador had
two police officers with him. And his secretary. That was why there
was no room for me in his car.'

'We could have dealt with them.'

120   'All right. Give me your eggs,' Charley Fortnum said, 'but tell that
man Miguel to put away his gun. It spoils my appetite.'

The man called León knelt before a small spirit stove on the earth
floor and busied himself with matches, a frying pan, a bit of lard.

'I could do with some whisky if you have it.'

125   'I am sorry. We have no spirits.'

The lard began to bubble in the pan.

'You name is León, eh?'

'Yes,' The man broke two eggs one after the other on the edge of the
pan. As he held two half shells over the pan there was something in the

130   position of the fingers which reminded Fortnum of that moment at the
altar when a priest breaks the Host over the chalice.

'What will you do if they refuse?'

'I pray they will accept,' the kneeling man said, 'I am sure they will
accept.'

Rosario   the second city of Argentina   *the General*   General Stroessner (1912–), head
Nación   the *Nation*, a newspaper   of state in Paraguay

135   'Then I hope to God God hears you,' Charley Fortnum said. 'Don't fry the eggs too hard.'

It was not until the afternoon that Charley Fortnum heard the official news about himself. The man León turned on a pocket radio at noon, but the battery failed in the middle of some Guaraní music and he had
140   no spares. The young man with a beard whom León called Aquino went into town to buy more batteries. He was a long time gone. A woman came in from the market with food and cooked their lunch, a vegetable soup with a few scraps of meat. She made a great show too of cleaning the hut, raising the dust in one part so that it settled in
145   another. She had a lot of untidy black hair and a wart on her face and she treated León with a mixture of possessiveness and servility. He called her Marta.

Once Charley Fortnum, with embarrassment because of the woman's presence, said he wanted to use a lavatory. León gave an order to the
150   Indian who led him to a cabin in the yard at the back of the hut. The door had lost one of its hinges and wouldn't close, and inside there was only a deep hole dug in the earth with a couple of boards across it. When he came out the Guaraní was sitting a few feet away playing with his gun, sighting it on a tree, a bird flying past, at a stray mongrel
155   dog. Through the trees Charley Fortnum could see another hut, even poorer than the one to which he was returning. He thought of running to it for help, but he felt sure the Indian would welcome the chance to try his gun. When he got back he said to León, 'If you can get a couple of bottles of whisky I'll pay you for them.' No one had stolen his wallet,
160   he had noticed that, and he took out the necessary notes.

León gave the money to Marta. He said, 'You will have to be patient, Señor Fortnum. Aquino is not back. No one can go till he returns. And it is a long walk into the town.'

'I will pay for a taxi.'
165   'I am afraid that is not possible. There are no taxis here.'

The Indian squatted down again by the door. Charley Fortnum said, 'I'm going off to sleep a bit. That drug you gave me was pretty strong.' He went back into the inner room and stretched out on the coffin. He tried to sleep, but he was kept awake by his thoughts. He wondered
170   how Clara was managing in his absence. He had never left her alone for a whole night before. He knew nothing about childbirth, but he had an idea that shock or anxiety could affect the unborn child. He had even tried to cut down his drinking after he married Clara – except for that first married night of whisky and champagne when for the first
175   time they made love properly, without impediment, in the Hotel Italia in Rosario – an old-fashioned hotel which smelt agreeably of undisturbed dust like an ancient library.

They had gone there because he thought she would be a little scared

of the Riviera Hotel which was new, expensive and air-conditioned.
180 There were papers he had to collect at the Consulate at Santa Fe 939
(he remembered the number because it represented the month and year
of his first marriage), the papers which if inquiries were made would
show that there was no impediment to his second marriage – it had
taken weeks to get a copy of Evelyn's death certificate from a small
185 town in Idaho. He was able at the same time to leave his will in a sealed
envelope in the Consulate safe. The Consul was a pleasant middle-aged
man. He and Charley Fortnum had hit it off right away when for some
reason the subject of horses came up. He invited them back after the
civil and religious ceremonies and opened a bottle of genuine French
190 champagne. That little drinking ceremony among the file boxes compared very favourably with the reception in Idaho after his first marriage.
He remembered with horror the white cake and the relations-in-law
who wore dark suits and even hard collars, although it was a civil
marriage which was not acceptable in Argentina. They had been prudent
195 and not spoken of it when they returned. His wife had refused a Catholic
marriage – it was against her conscience as she had become a Christian
Scientist. Of course the civil marriage made her inheritance unsafe –
which was also an indignity. He wanted very much to arrange things
more safely for Clara; to ensure there were no cracks in the walls of
200 this second marriage. He intended to leave her, when he came to die,
in a security which was impregnable.

After a while he slid into a deep dreamless sleep; he was only woken
when the radio in the next room began to repeat his own name – Señor
Carlos Fortnum. The police – the announcer said – believed he might
205 have been brought to Rosario because the telephone call to the *Nación*
had been traced to that city. A city of more than half a million
inhabitants couldn't be searched very thoroughly, and the authorities
had been given only four days in which to agree to the kidnappers'
terms. One of these four days had already passed. Charley Fortnum
210 thought: Clara will be listening to the broadcast, and he thanked God
Ted would be around to reassure her. Ted would know what had
happened. Ted would go to see her. Ted would do something to keep
her calm. Ted would tell her that, even if they killed him, she would be
all right. She had so much fear of the past – he could tell that from the
215 way she never spoke of it. It was one of his reasons for marrying her,
to prove she would never under any circumstances have to return to
Mother Sanchez. He took exaggerated care of her happiness like a
clumsy man entrusted with something of great fragility which didn't
belong to him. He was always afraid of dropping her happiness.
220 Someone was talking now about the Argentine football team which
was touring Europe. He called, 'León!'

The small head with the bat-ears and the attentive eyes of a good servant peered round the door. León said, 'You have slept a long time, Señor Fortnum. That is good.'

225 'I heard the radio, León.'

'Ah yes.' León was carrying a glass in one hand and a bottle of whisky was tucked under each arm. He said, 'My wife has brought two bottles from the town.' He showed the whisky proudly (it was an Argentine brand) and counted out the change with care. 'You must not

230 worry. Everything will be over in a few days.'

'Everything will be over with me, you mean? Give me that whisky.' He poured out a third of a glass and drank it down.

'I am sure tonight we shall hear them announce that they have accepted our terms. And then by tomorrow evening you can go home.'

235 Charley Fortnum poured out another dose.

'You are drinking too much,' the man called León said with friendly anxiety.

'No, no. I know the right measure. And it's the measure that counts. What's your other name, León?'

240 'I told you I have no other name.'

'But you have a title, haven't you? Tell me what you are doing in this set-up, Father León.'

He could almost believe the ears twitched, like a dog's, at a familiar intonation – 'Father' taking the place of 'walk' or perhaps 'cat'.

245 'You are mistaken. You saw my wife just now. Marta. She brought you the whisky.'

'But once a priest always a priest, Father. I spotted you when you broke those eggs over the dish. I could see you at the altar, Father.'

'You are imagining things, Señor Fortnum.'

250 'And what are *you* imagining? You might have made a good bargain for the Ambassador, but you can't get anything in return for me. I'm not worth a peso to a human soul – except my wife. It seems an odd thing for a priest to become a murderer, but I suppose you'll get someone else to do the thing.'

255 'No,' the other said with great seriousness, 'if it should ever come to that, which God forbid, I will be the one. I do not want to shift the guilt.'

'Then I'd better leave you some of this whisky. You'll need a swig of it – in how many days did they say – three was it?'

260 The other man's eyes shifted. He had a frightened air. He shuffled two steps towards the door as though he were leaving the altar and was afraid of treading on the skirt of a soutane which was too long for him.

'You might stay and talk a bit,' Charley Fortnum said. 'I feel more scared when I'm alone. I don't mind telling *you* that. If one can't talk

265 to a priest who can one talk to? That Indian now . . . he sits there and stares at me and smiles. He *wants* to kill.'

'You are wrong, Señor Fortnum. Miguel is a good man. He has no Spanish, that is all, and so he smiles just to show he is a friend. Try to sleep again.'

270 'I've had enough sleep. I want to talk to you.'

The man made a gesture with his hands, and Charley Fortnum could imagine him in church, making his formal passes. 'I have so many things to do.'

'I can always keep you here if I try.'

275 'No, no. I *must* go.'

'I can keep you here easily. I know the way.'

'I will come back presently, I promise.'

'All I have to say to keep you is – Father, please hear my confession.'

The man stayed stuck in the doorway with his back turned. His
280 protruding ears stood out like little hands raised over an offering.

'Since my last confession, Father ...'

The man swung round and said angrily, 'You must not joke about things like that. I will not listen to you if you joke ...'

'But that's no joke, Father. I'm not in a position to joke about
285 anything at all. Surely every man has a lot to confess when it comes to dying.'

'My faculties have been taken away,' the other said in a stubborn voice. 'You must know what that means if you are really a Catholic.'

'I seem to know the rules better than you, Father. You do not need
290 faculties, not in an emergency – if there is no other priest available ... there isn't, is there? Your men would never let you bring one here ...'

'There is no emergency – not yet.'

'All the same time is short ... if I ask ...'

The man reminded him again of a dog, a dog who has been reproved
295 for a fault which he does not clearly understand. He began to plead, 'Señor Fortnum, I assure you there never will be an emergency ... it will never be necessary ...'

'"I am sorry and beg pardon" – that's how I begin, isn't it? It's been the hell of a long time ... I've been once to church in the last forty
300 years ... a while ago when I got married. I was damned if I'd go to confession though. It would have taken too long and I couldn't keep the lady waiting.'

'Please Señor Fortnum, do not mock me.'

'I'm not mocking *you*, Father. Perhaps I'm mocking myself a bit. I
305 can do that as long as the whisky lasts.' He added, 'It really is a funny thing when you come to think of it. "I ask forgiveness of God through you, Father." That *is* the formula, isn't it – and all the time you'll have the gun ready. Don't you think we ought to begin now? Before the gun is loaded. There are plenty of things I have on my mind.'

310 'I will not listen to you.' He made the gesture of putting his hands

against the protruding ears. They flattened and sprang back.

Charley Fortnum said, 'Oh, don't worry, forget it. I was only half serious. What difference does it make anyway?'

'What do you mean?'

315   'I don't believe a thing, Father. I would never have bothered to marry in a church if the law hadn't forced me to. There was the question of money. For my wife, I mean. What was your intention, Father, when *you* married?' He added quickly, 'Forgive me. I had no business to ask that.'

320   But the little man, it seemed, was not angry. The question even appeared to have an attraction for him. He came slowly across the floor with his mouth ajar, as though he were a starving man drawn irresistibly by the offer of bread. A little saliva hung at the corner of his mouth. He came and crouched down on the floor beside the coffin. He said in
325   a low voice (he might have been kneeling in the confessional box himself), 'I think it was anger and loneliness, Señor Fortnum. I never meant any harm to her, poor woman.'

'I can understand the loneliness,' Charley Fortnum said, 'I've suffered from that too. But why the anger? Who were you angry with?'

330   'The Church,' the man said and added with irony, 'my Mother the Church.'

'I used to be angry with my father. He didn't understand me, I thought, or care a nickel about me. I hated him. All the same I was bloody lonely when he died. And now –' he lifted his glass – 'I even
335   imitate him. Though he drank more than I do. All the same a father's a father – I don't see how you can be angry with a Mother Church. I could never get angry with a fucking institution.'

'She is a sort of person too,' the man said, 'they claim she is Christ on earth – I still half believe it even now. Someone like you – *un Inglés* [an
340   Englishman] – you are not able to understand how ashamed I felt of the things they made me read to people. I was a priest in the poor part of Asunción near the river. Have you noticed how the poor always cling close to the river? They do it here too, as though they plan one day to swim away, but they have no idea how to swim and there is nowhere to swim to for any
345   of them. On Sunday I had to read to them out of the Gospels.'

Charley Fortnum listened with a little sympathy and a good deal of cunning. His life depended on this man, and it was vitally important for him to know what moved him. There might be some chord he could touch of fellow feeling. The man was speaking immoderately as a thirsty
350   man drinks. Perhaps he had been unable to speak freely for a long time: perhaps this was the only way he could unburden himself to a man who was safely dying and would remember no more what he said than a priest in the confessional. Charley Fortnum asked, 'What's wrong with the Gospels, Father?'

355 'They make no sense,' the ex-priest said, 'anyway not in Paraguay. "Sell all and give to the poor"[†] – I had to read that out to them while the old Archbishop we had in those days was eating a fine fish from Iguazú and drinking a French wine with the General. Of course the people were not actually starving – you can keep them from starving
360 on mandioca, and malnutrition is much safer for the rich than starvation. Starvation makes a man desperate. Malnutrition makes him too tired to raise a fist. The Americans understand that well – the aid they give us makes just that amount of difference. Our people do not starve – they wilt. The words used to stick on my lips – "Suffer little children",[†]
365 and there the children sat in the front rows with their pot bellies and their navels sticking out like door knobs. "It were better that a millstone were hung around his neck", "He who gives to one of the least of these". Gives what? gives mandioca? and then I distributed the Host – it's not so nourishing as a good *chipá*[†] – and then I drank the wine.
370 Wine! Which of these poor souls have ever tasted wine? Why could we not use water in the sacrament? He used it at Cana. Wasn't there a beaker of water at the Last Supper He could have used instead?' To Charley Fortnum's astonishment the dog-like eyes were swollen with unshed tears.
375 The man said, 'Oh, you must not think we are all of us bad Christians as I am. The Jesuits do what they can. But they are watched by the police. Their telephones are tapped. If anyone seems dangerous he is quickly pushed across the river. They do not kill him. The Yankees would not like a priest to be killed, and anyway we are not dangerous
380 enough. I spoke in a sermon once about Father Torres who was shot with the guerrillas in Columbia. I only said that unlike Sodom[†] the Church did sometimes produce one just man, so perhaps she would not be destroyed like Sodom. The police reported me to the Archbishop and the Archbishop forbade me to preach any more. Oh well, poor
385 man, he was very old and the General liked him, and he thought he was doing right, rendering to Caesar[†] . . .'
'These things are a bit above my head, Father,' Charley Fortnum said, lying propped on his elbow on the coffin and looking down at the dark head which still showed the faint trace of a tonsure through the
390 hair, like a prehistoric camp in a field seen from a plane. He interjected "Father" as often as he could: it was somehow reassuring. A father didn't usually kill his son, although of course it had been a near miss in the case of Abraham. 'I am not to blame, Father.'
'I am not blaming you, Señor Fortnum, God forbid.'

Sell . . . poor Matthew 19. 21   *unlike Sodom* see Genesis 18–19
Suffer . . . children Mark 10. 14   *rendering to Caesar* Matthew 22. 21
chipá manioc or corn-cake

395 'I can see how the American Ambassador from your point of view –
well, he was a legitimate objective. But me – I'm not even a proper
Consul and the English are not in *this* fight, Father.'

The priest muttered a cliché absent-mindedly, 'They say one man has
to die for the people.'[†]

400 'But that was what the crucifiers said, not the Christians.'

The priest looked up. 'Yes, you are right,' he said, 'I was not thinking
when I spoke. You know your Testament.'

'I have not read it since I was a boy. But that's the kind of scene
which sticks in the mind. Like Struwwelpeter.'[†]

405 'Struwwelpeter?'

'He had his thumbs cut off.'

'I never heard of him. Is he one of your martyrs?'

'No, no, it's a nursery story, Father.'

'Have you children?' the priest asked sharply.

410 'No, but I told you. In a few months there should be one around. He
kicks hard already.'

'Yes, I remember now.' He added, 'Don't worry, you will be home
soon.' It was as though the sentence were framed in question marks
and he wanted the prisoner to reassure him by agreeing, "Yes, of course.

415 It goes without saying," but Charley Fortnum refused to play that
game.

'Why this coffin, Father? It seems a bit morbid to me.'

'The earth is too damp for sleeping on, even with a cloth under you.
We did not want you to catch rheumatism.'

420 'Well, that was a kindly thought, Father.'

'We are not barbarians. There is a man near here in the *barrio*[†] who
makes coffins. We bought one from him. It was much safer than buying
a bed . . . There is a greater demand in the *barrio* for coffins than beds.
Nobody asks questions about a coffin.'

425 'And I suppose you thought it might be handy later on for stowing
away a body.'

'That was not in our minds, I swear. To ask for a bed would have
been dangerous.'

'Oh well, I think I *will* have another whisky, Father. Have one with

430 me.'

'No. You see – I am on duty. I have to guard you.' He gave a timid
smile.

'You would not be difficult to overpower, would you? Even for an
old man like me.'

---

one man . . . people John 18. 14   Hoffman (1809–74)
Struwwelpeter 'Shock-headed Peter', the   *barrio* shanty town
    children's classic (1847) by Heinrich

435   'There are always two of us on duty,' the priest said. 'Miguel is out
there now with his gun. These are El Tigre's orders. There is another
reason for that too. One man might be talked around. Or even bribed.
We are all of us human beings. This is not the sort of life any of us
would have chosen.'

440   'The Indian does not speak Spanish?'
'Yes, that too is a good thing.'
'Do you mind if I stretch my legs a little?'
'Of course you may.'
Charley Fortnum went to the doorway and checked the truth of what

445   the priest had said. The Indian was squatting by the door with the gun
on his lap. He smiled at Fortnum confidentially, as though they shared
a secret joke. Almost imperceptibly he moved the position of his gun.
'You speak Guaraní, Father?'
'Yes. I used to preach in Guaraní once.'

450   A few minutes ago there had been a moment of closeness, of sympathy,
even of friendship between them, but that moment had passed. When
a Confession is finished, the priest and the penitent are each alone.
They pretend not to recognize each other if they pass in the church. It
was as though it were the penitent who stood now by the coffin looking

455   at his watch. Charley Fortnum thought: he is checking to see now many
hours are left.
'Change your mind and have a whisky with me, Father.'
'No. No thank you. One day perhaps when all this is over.' He
added, 'He is late. I should have been gone long before now.'

460   'Who is late?'
The priest answered angrily, 'I have told you before that people like
us have no names.'

1973

Anthony Powell

1905–

Anthony Dymoke Powell (pronounced to rhyme with Noel) was born in London and educated at Eton and Balliol College, Oxford. He worked for the publishing firm of Duckworth, and then as a scriptwriter for Warner Brothers. During the Second World War he served at first in the Welch Regiment and later in the Intelligence Corps as a liaison officer working with Polish, Belgian and Czech military establishments in London. Literary Editor of *Punch* 1952–8, he has long been a reviewer for *The Times Literary Supplement* and other papers. He published five novels before the war, but his reputation rests on the twelve books, published between 1951 and 1975, which make up one novel, *A Dance to the Music of Time*. Their narrator Nicholas Jenkins recalls his life, from childhood in 1914 to the early 1970s, and the lives of friends and acquaintances in various overlapping upper-class, literary, bohemian, military and political circles. The novels are full of amusing anecdotes and gossip but they are carefully planned and the whole work offers a complex and mature appraisal of modern England. Powell has also published *John Aubrey and his Friends* (1948), two plays, *The Garden God* and *The Rest I'll Whistle* (1971), and an autobiography in four volumes, *To Keep the Ball Rolling* (1976–82).

In the following extract, set in the mid 1930s, the narrator, a novelist and writer for the cinema, is about twenty-nine years old, the general about eighty. Widmerpool, a character of monstrous egoism, has perplexed the narrator since they were at school.

From AT LADY MOLLY'S

[*General Conyers*]

We talked together for a minute or two. Then Jeavons wandered off among the guests. By then General and Mrs Conyers had arrived. I went across the room to speak to them. They had come up from the country the day before. After making the conventional remarks about
5   my engagement, Mrs Conyers was removed by Molly to be introduced

to some new acquaintance of hers. I was left with the General. He seemed in excellent form, although at the same time giving the impression that he was restless about something: had a problem on his mind. All at once he took me by the arm. 'I want a word with you, Nicholas,' he
10   said, in his deep, though always unexpectedly mild, voice. 'Can't we get out of this damned, milling crowd of people for a minute or two?'

The Jeavonses' guests habitually flowed into every room in the house, so that to retire to talk, for example in Molly's bedroom, or Jeavons's dressing-room, would be considered not at all unusual. We moved, in
15   fact, a short way up the stairs into a kind of boudoir of Molly's, constricted in space and likely to attract only people who wanted to enjoy a heart-to-heart talk together: a place chiefly given over to cats, two or three of which sat in an ill-humoured group at angles to one another, stirring with disapproval at this invasion of their privacy. I
20   had no idea what the General could wish to say, even speculating for an instant as to whether he was about to offer some piece of advice – too confidential and esoteric to risk being overheard – regarding the conduct of married life. The period of engagement is one when you are at the mercy of all who wish to proffer counsel, and experience already
25   prepared me for the worst. The truth turned out to be more surprising.

As soon as we were alone together, the General sat down on a chair in front of the writing-table, straightening out his leg painfully. It still seemed to be giving him trouble. Alone with him, I became aware of that terrible separateness which difference of age imposes between
30   individuals. Perhaps feeling something of this burden himself, he began at first to speak of his own advancing years.

'I'm beginning to find all this standing about at Buck House† a bit of a strain,' he said. 'Not so young as I was. Dropped my eyeglass not so long ago in one of the anterooms at St James's† and had to get a fellow who
35   was standing beside me to pick it up for me. Secretary from the Soviet Embassy. Perfectly civil. Just couldn't get down that far myself. Afraid I'd drop my axe too, if I tried. Still, although I'm getting on in life, I've had a good run for my money. Seen some odd things at one time or another.'

He moved his leg again, and groaned a bit. I always had the impression
40   that he liked talking about his appearances at Court.

'I'm a great believer in people knowing the truth,' he said. 'Always have been.'

Without seeing at all clearly where this maxim would lead us, I agreed that truth was best.

45   'Something happened the other day,' said the General, 'that struck me as interesting. Damned interesting. Got on my mind a bit, especially

---

Buck House   Buckingham Palace
St James's   George V held his levées at St James's Palace, Pall Mall

as I had been reading about that kind of thing. Odd coincidence, I
mean. The fact is, you are the only fellow I can tell.'

By that time I began to feel even a little uneasy, having no idea at all
50 what might be coming next.

'When you came to tea with us not so long ago, I told you I had
been reading about this business of psychoanalysis. Don't tie myself
down to Freud. Jung has got some interesting stuff too. No point in an
amateur like myself being dogmatic about something he knows little or
55 nothing about. Just make a fool of yourself. Don't you agree?'

'Absolutely.'

'Well, a rather interesting illustration of some of the points I'd been
reading about happened to come my way the other day. Care to hear
about it?'

60 'I should like to very much indeed.'

'In ccconnexion with this fellow you say you were at school with – this
fellow Widmerpool – who wanted to marry my sister-in-law, Mildred.'

'I hear the engagement is off.'

'You knew that already?'

65 'I was told so the other day.'

'Common knowledge, is it?'

'Yes.'

'Know why it's off?'

'No. But I wasn't altogether surprised.'

70 'Nor was I, but it is an odd story. Not to be repeated, of course.
Happened during their stay at Dogdene. Perhaps you've heard about
that too?'

'I knew they were going to Dogdene.'

'Ever stopped there yourself?'

75 'No. I've never met either of the Sleafords.'

'I was once able to do Geoffrey Sleaford a good turn in South Africa,'
said the General. 'He was A.D.C. to the Divisional Commander, and a
more bone-headed fellow I never came across. Sleaford – or Fines, as
he was then – had landed in a mess over some mislaid papers. I got
80 him out of it. He is a stupid fellow, but always grateful. Made a point
of trying out our poodle dogs at his shoots. Then Bertha knew Alice
Sleaford as a girl. Went to the same dancing class. Bertha never much
cared for her. Still, they get on all right now. Long and the short of it
is that we stop at Dogdene from time to time. Uncomfortable place
85 nowadays. Those parterres are very fine, of course. Alice Sleaford takes
an interest in the garden. Wonderful fruit in the hot-houses. Then there
is the Veronese.[†] Geoffrey Sleaford has been advised to have it cleaned,

---

Veronese Paolo Caliari (c. 1528–88), born at
Verona, a luxurious colourist of the Venetian school

but won't hear of it. Young fellow called Smethyck told him. Smethyck
saw our Van Troost[†] and said it was certainly genuine. Nice things at
90 Dogdene, some of them, but I could name half a dozen houses in
England I'd rather stop at.'

None of this seemed to be getting us much further so far as
Widmerpool was concerned. I waited for development. General Conyers
did not intend to be hurried. I suspected that he might regard this
95 narrative he was unfolding in so leisurely a manner as the last good
story of his life; one that he did not propose to squander in the telling.
That was reasonable enough.

'I was not best pleased,' he said, 'when Bertha told me we had been
asked to Dogdene at the same time as Mildred and her young man. I
100 know the Sleafords don't have many people to stop. All the same it
would have been quite easy to have invited some of their veterans. Even
had us there by ourselves. Just like Alice Sleaford to arrange something
like that. Hasn't much tact. All the same, I thought it would be a chance
to get to know something about Widmerpool. After all, he was going
105 to be my brother-in-law. Got to put up with your relations. Far better
know the form from the beginning.'

'I've been seeing Widmerpool on and off for ages,' I said, hoping to
encourage the General's flow of comment. 'I really know him quite
well.'

110 'You do?'

'Yes.'

'Now, look here,' he said. 'Have you ever noticed at all how
Widmerpool gets on with women?'

'He never seemed to find them at all easy to deal with. I was surprised
115 that he should be prepared to take on someone like Mrs Haycock.'

We had plunged into an intimacy of discussion that I had never
supposed possible with an older man of the General's sort.

'You were?'

'Yes.'

120 'So was I,' he said. 'So was I. Very surprised. And I did not take long
to see that they were getting on each other's nerves when they arrived
at Dogdene. She was being very crisp with him. Very crisp. Nothing
much in that, of course. Engaged couples bound to have their differences.
Now I know Mildred pretty well by this time, and, although I did not
125 much take to Widmerpool when I first met him, I thought she might
do worse at her age. What?'

'So I should imagine.'

'Not every man would want to take her on. Couple of step-children
into the bargain.'

Van Troost Cornelius Troost (1697–1750), Dutch painter and printmaker

130   'No.'

'All the same Widmerpool seemed to me rather a trying fellow. Half
the time he was being obsequious, behaving as if he was applying for
the job as footman, the other half, he was telling Geoffrey Sleaford and
myself how to run our own affairs. It was then I began to mark down
135   his psychological type. I had brought the book with me.'

'How did he get on with Lord Sleaford?'

'Pretty well,' said the General. 'Pretty well. Better than you might
think. You know, Widmerpool talks sense about business matters. No
doubt of it. Made some suggestions about developing the home farm
140   at Dogdene which were quite shrewd. It was with Mildred there was
some awkwardness. Mildred is not a woman to hang about with. If he
wanted to marry her, he ought to have got down to matters and have
done it. No good delaying in things of that sort.'

'He has been having jaundice.'

145   'I knew he'd been ill. He made several references to the fact. Seemed
rather too fond of talking about his health. Another sign of his type.
Anyway, his illness was beside the point. The fact was, Mildred did not
think he was paying her enough attention. That was plain as a pikestaff.
Mildred is a woman who expects a good deal of fuss to be made over
150   her. I could see he was in for trouble.'

'What form did it take?'

'First of all, as I told you, she was a bit short with him. Then she
fairly told him off to his face. That was on Saturday afternoon. Thought
there was going to be a real row between them. Alice Sleaford never
155   noticed a thing. In the evening they seemed to have made it up. In fact,
after dinner, they were more like an engaged couple than I'd ever seen
'em. Now, look here, where would you put his type? Psychologically, I
mean.'

'Rather hard to say in a word – I know him so well –'

160   'It seems to me,' said the General, 'that he is a typical intuitive
extrovert – classical case, almost. Cold-blooded. Keen on a thing for a
moment, but never satisfied. Wants to get on to something else. Don't
really know about these things, but Widmerpool seems to fit into the
classification. That's the category in which I'd place him, just as if a
165   recruit turns up with a good knowledge of carpentry and you draft him
into the Sappers. You are going to say you are a hard-bitten Freudian,
and won't hear of Jung and his ideas. Very well, I'll open another field
of fire.'

'But –'

170   'You haven't heard the rest of the story yet. I came down to breakfast
early on Sunday morning. I thought I'd have a stroll in the garden, and
have another look at those hot-houses. What do you think I found?
Widmerpool in the hall, making preparations to leave the house. Some

story about a telephone call, and being summoned back to London.
175   Fellow looked like death. Shaking like a jelly and the colour of wax.
Told me he'd slept very badly. Hardly closed his eyes. I'm quite prepared
to believe that. Alice Sleaford won't use the best bedrooms for some
reason. Never know where you are going to be put.'

'And did he go back to London?'

180   'Drove off, there and then, under my eyes. Whole house had been
turned upside down to get him away at that hour on Sunday morning.
Left a message for the host and hostess to say how sorry he was, neither
of them having come down yet. Never saw a man more disgruntled
than the Sleafords' chauffeur.'

185   'But what had happened? Had there really been a telephone call? I
don't understand.'

'There had been some telephoning that morning, but the butler said
it had been Widmerpool putting the call through. Only heard the true
story that afternoon from Mildred when we were walking together in
190   the Dutch garden. She didn't make any bones about it. Widmerpool
had been in her room the night before. Things hadn't gone at all well.
Made up her mind he wasn't going to be any use as a husband. Mildred
can be pretty outspoken when she is cross.'

The General said these things in a manner entirely free from any of
195   those implied comments which might be thought inseparable from such
a chronicle of events. That is to say he was neither shocked, facetious,
nor caustic. It was evident that the situation interested, rather than
surprised him. He was complete master of himself in allowing no trace
of ribaldry or ill nature to colour his narrative. For my own part, I felt
200   a twinge of compassion for Widmerpool in his disaster, even though I
was unable to rise to the General's heights of scientific detachment. I
had known Widmerpool too long.

'Mildred told me in so many words. Doesn't care what she says,
Mildred. That's what young people are like nowadays. Of course, I
205   don't expect Mildred appears young to you, but I always think of her
as a young woman.'

I did not know what comment to make. However, General Conyers
did not require comment. He wished to elaborate his own conception
of what had happened.

210   'Widmerpool's trouble is not as uncommon as you might think,' he
said. 'I've known several cases. Last fellows in the world you'd expect.
I don't expect the name Peploe-Gordon means anything to you?'

'No.'

'Dead now. Had a heart attack in the Lebanon. I remember it
215   happened in the same week Queen Draga† was murdered in Belgrade.

Queen Draga   unsuitable wife of the King of Serbia, brutally murdered in 1903

At Sandhurst[†] with me. Splendid rider. First-class shot. Led an expedition into Tibet. Married one of the prettiest girls I've ever seen. Used to see her out with the Quorn.[†] He had the same trouble. Marriage annulled. Wife married again and had a string of children. This is the point I
220   want to make. I saw Peploe-Gordon about eighteen months after at the yearling sales at Newmarket with another damned pretty girl on his arm. Do you know, he looked as pleased as Punch. Didn't give a damn. Still, you don't know what neuroses weren't at work under the surface. That is what you have got to remember. Looking back in the light of
225   what I have been reading, I can see the fellow had a touch of exaggerated narcissism. Is that Widmerpool's trouble?'

'It wouldn't surprise me. As I said before I've only dipped into these things.'

'I don't set up as an expert myself. Last thing in the world I'd pretend
230   to do. But look here, something I want to ask – do you know anything of Widmerpool's mother?'

'I've met her.'

'What is she like?'

I felt as usual some difficulty in answering directly the General's
235   enquiry, put in his most pragmatical manner.

'Rather a trying woman, I thought.'

'Domineering?'

'In her way.'

'Father?'
240   'Dead.'

'What did he do?'

'Manufactured artificial manure, I believe.'

'Did he . . .' said the General. 'Did he . . .'

There was a pause while he thought over this information. It was
245   undeniable that he had been setting the pace. I felt that I must look to my psycho-analytical laurels, if I was not to be left far behind.

'Do you think it was fear of castration?' I asked.

The General shook his head slowly.

'Possibly, possibly,' he said. 'Got to be cautious about that. You see
250   this is how I should approach the business, with the greatest humility – with the *greatest* humility. Widmerpool strikes me as giving himself away all the time by his – well, to quote the text-book – purely objective orientation. If you are familiar with tactics, you know you can be up against just that sort of fellow in a battle. Always trying to get a move
255   on, and bring off something definite. Quite right too, in a battle. But in ordinary life a fellow like that may be doing himself no good so far as

---

Sandhurst   the Royal Military College (now   *Quorn*   the Leicestershire hunt
Academy) for the training of officers

his own subjective emotions are concerned. No good at all. Quite the
reverse. Always leads to trouble. No use denying subjective emotions.
Just as well to face the fact. All of us got a lot of egoism and infantilism
260 to work off. I'd be the last to deny it. I can see now that was some of
Peploe-Gordon's trouble, when I look back.'

'I'm sure Widmerpool thought a lot about this particular matter.
Indeed, I know he did. He spoke to me about it quite soon after he
became engaged to Mrs Haycock.'

265 'Probably thought about it a great deal too much. Doesn't do to
think about anything like that too much. Need a bit of relaxation from
time to time. Everlastingly talks about his work too. Hasn't he any
hobbies?'

'He used to knock golf balls into a net at Barnes.† But he told me he
270 had given that up.'

'Pity, pity. Not surprised, though,' said the General, 'Nothing disturbs
feeling so much as thinking. I'm only repeating what the book says,
but I didn't spend thirty odd years in the army without discovering that
for myself. Got to have a plan, of course, but no use knotting yourself
275 up in too tight. Must have an instinct about the man on the other side –
and the people on your own side too. What was it Foch† said? War
not an exact science, but a terrible and passionate drama? Something
like that. Fact is, marriage is rather like that too.'

'But surely that was what Widmerpool was trying to make it? To
280 some extent he seems to have succeeded. What happened sounded
terrible and dramatic enough in its own way.'

'I'll have to think about that,' said the General. 'I see what you mean.
I'll have to think about that.'

All the same, although I had raised this objection, I agreed with what
285 he said. Marriage was a subject upon which it was hard to obtain
accurate information. Its secrets, naturally, are those most jealously
guarded; never more deeply concealed than when apparently most
profusely exhibited in public. However true that might be, one could
still be sure that even those marriages which seem outwardly dull
290 enough are, at one time or another, full of the characteristics of which
he spoke. Was it possible to guess, for example, what lay behind the
curtain of his own experience? As I had never before conceived of
exchanging such a conversation with General Conyers, I thought this
an opportunity to enquire about a matter that had always played some
295 part in my imagination since mentioned years earlier by Uncle Giles.
The moment particularly recommended itself, because the General
rarely spoke either of the practice or theory of war. The transient

---

Barnes in Surrey
Foch Ferdinand Foch (1851–1929), French general

reference he had just made to Foch now caused the question I wanted
to ask to sound less inept.

300   'Talking of the army,' I said. 'What did it feel like when you were in
the charge?'

'In where?'

'The charge – after French's cavalry brigades crossed the Modder
River.'†

305   The General looked perplexed for a moment. Then his expression
altered. He grasped the substance of my enquiry.

'Ah, yes,' he said. 'When the whole cavalry division charged. Unusual
operation. Doubted the wisdom of it at the time. However it came off
all right. Extraordinary that you should have known about it. That was

310   the occasion you mean? Of course, of course. What was it like? Just
have to think for a moment. Long time ago, you know. Have to collect
my thoughts. Well, I think I can tell you exactly. The fact was there
had been some difficulty in mounting me, as I wasn't officially attached
to the formation. Can't remember why not at this length of time. Some

315   technicality. Ride rather heavy, you know. As far as I can remember, I
had the greatest difficulty in getting my pony out of a trot. I'm sure
that was what happened. Later on in the day, I shot a Boer in the shin.
But why do you ask?'

'I don't know. I've always wanted to ask, for some reason. Infantilism,

320   perhaps. A primordial image.'

The General agreed, cordially.

'You are an introvert, of course,' he said.

'I think undoubtedly.'

'Introverted intuitive type, do you think? I shouldn't wonder.'

325   'Possibly.'

'Anyway,' said the General, 'keep an eye on not overcompensating.
I've been glad to tell that story about Widmerpool to someone who can
appreciate the circumstances. Haven't made up my own mind about it
yet. I've got a slow reactive rapidity. No doubt about that. Just as well

330   to recognise your own limitations. Can't help wondering about the
inhibiting action of the incest barrier though – among other things.'

He moved his leg once more, at the same time shifting the weight of
his body, as he pondered this riddle. The angle of his knee and ankle
emphasised the beauty of his patent leather boots.

335   'Well, I mustn't keep you up here away from the others any longer,'
he said. 'Lots of people you ought to be meeting. You are going to be a
very lucky young man, I am sure. What do you want for a wedding
present?'

French's . . . river   J. D. P. French (1852–
1925), British general. British forces suffered
two severe defeats at the Modder River,

Orange Free State, in 1899, early in the Boer
War

340 The change in his voice announced that our fantasy life together was over. We had returned to the world of everyday things. Perhaps it would be truer to say that our real life together was over, and we returned to the world of fantasy. Who can say?

1957

Samuel Beckett

1906–

Samuel Barclay Beckett was born at Foxrock, near Dublin, and was educated at Portora Royal School, Enniskillen, and Trinity College, Dublin – where he was briefly a lecturer (1930–1). He taught in Paris, in the late 1920s, and became a friend of James Joyce; he published an essay on Joyce in 1929, and translated part of *Finnegans Wake* into French. He has lived in France (where he was active in the wartime Resistance) since 1937. His trilogy of novels, *Molloy* (1951), *Malone Meurt* (1951) and *L'Innommable* (1953) were all written in French; Beckett later issued English renderings. His play *En attendant Godot* (1952) was performed in Paris in 1953; his English version, *Waiting for Godot* (1955) was, although controversial, a success in London, making Beckett well known in the English-speaking world, and influential as a playwright of the 'Absurd'. Later plays include *Fin de Parti* (1957) translated as *Endgame* (1958), *Krapp's Last Tape* (1958, published 1959), a monologue, and *Breath* (1969), a thirty-second *jeu d'esprit*. *Collected Poems in English and French* appeared in 1977. Beckett's blend of desperation and gaiety is unique, and he writes with strength and grace in both languages. He was awarded the Nobel Prize in 1969.

Early in the second of the two Acts of *Waiting for Godot*, the clownish-tramplike Vladimir and Estragon are still waiting beside their tree, passing the time in conversational 'canters'.

From WAITING FOR GODOT

[Magicians]

ESTRAGON:	That wasn't such a bad little canter.
VLADIMIR:	Yes, but now we'll have to find something else.
ESTRAGON:	Let me see.
	He takes off his hat, concentrates.
VLADIMIR:	Let me see. (*He takes off his hat, concentrates. Long*
	silence.) Ah!
	They put on their hats, relax.

5

	ESTRAGON:	Well?
	VLADIMIR:	What was I saying, we could go on from there.
	ESTRAGON:	What were you saying when?
	VLADIMIR:	At the very beginning.
10	ESTRAGON:	The beginning of WHAT?
	VLADIMIR:	This evening . . . I was saying . . . I was saying . . .
	ESTRAGON:	I'm not a historian.
	VLADIMIR:	Wait . . . we embraced . . . we were happy . . . happy . . . what do we do now that we're happy . . . go on waiting . . . waiting . . . let me think . . . it's coming . . . go on waiting . . . now that we're happy . . . let me see . . . ah! The tree!
15		
	ESTRAGON:	The tree?
	VLADIMIR:	Do you not remember?
20	ESTRAGON:	I'm tired.
	VLADIMIR:	Look at it.
		They look at the tree.
	ESTRAGON:	I see nothing.
	VLADIMIR:	But yesterday evening it was all black and bare. And now it's covered with leaves.
25	ESTRAGON:	Leaves?
	VLADIMIR:	In a single night.
	ESTRAGON:	It must be the Spring.
	VLADIMIR:	But in a single night!
	ESTRAGON:	I tell you we weren't here yesterday. Another of your nightmares.
30		
	VLADIMIR:	And where were we yesterday evening according to you?
	ESTRAGON:	How do I know? In another compartment. There's no lack of void.
35	VLADIMIR:	(*sure of himself*). Good. We weren't here yesterday evening. Now what did we do yesterday evening?
	ESTRAGON:	Do?
	VLADIMIR:	Try and remember.
	ESTRAGON:	Do . . . I suppose we blathered.
40	VLADIMIR:	(*controlling himself*). About what?
	ESTRAGON:	Oh . . . this and that, I suppose, nothing in particular. (*With assurance.*) Yes, now I remember, yesterday evening we spent blathering about nothing in particular. That's been going on now for half a century.
45	VLADIMIR:	You don't remember any fact, any circumstance?
	ESTRAGON:	(*weary*). Don't torment me, Didi.
	VLADIMIR:	The sun. The moon. Do you not remember?
	ESTRAGON:	They must have been there, as usual.

	VLADIMIR:	You didn't notice anything out of the ordinary?
50	ESTRAGON:	Alas!
	VLADIMIR:	And Pozzo?[†] And Lucky?[†]
	ESTRAGON:	Pozzo?
	VLADIMIR:	The bones.
	ESTRAGON:	They were like fishbones.
55	VLADIMIR:	It was Pozzo gave them to you.
	ESTRAGON:	I don't know.
	VLADIMIR:	And the kick.
	ESTRAGON:	That's right, someone gave me a kick.
	VLADIMIR:	It was Lucky gave it to you.
60	ESTRAGON:	And all that was yesterday?
	VLADIMIR:	Show your leg.
	ESTRAGON:	Which?
	VLADIMIR:	Both. Pull up your trousers. (*Estragon gives a leg to Vladimir, staggers. Vladimir takes the leg. They stagger.*) Pull up your trousers.
65	ESTRAGON:	I can't.
		Vladimir pulls up the trousers, looks at the leg, lets it go. Estragon almost falls.
	VLADIMIR:	The other. (*Estragon gives the same leg.*) The other, pig! (*Estragon gives the other leg. Triumphantly.*) There's the wound! Beginning to fester!
	ESTRAGON:	And what about it?
70	VLADIMIR:	(*letting go the leg*). Where are your boots?
	ESTRAGON:	I must have thrown them away.
	VLADIMIR:	When?
	ESTRAGON:	I don't know.
	VLADIMIR:	Why?
75	ESTRAGON:	(*exasperated*). I don't know why I don't know!
	VLADIMIR:	No, I mean why did you throw them away?
	ESTRAGON:	(*exasperated*). Because they were hurting me!
	VLADIMIR:	(*triumphantly, pointing to the boots*). There they are! (*Estragon looks at the boots.*) At the very spot where
80		you left them yesterday!
		Estragon goes towards the boots, inspects them closely.
	ESTRAGON:	They're not mine.
	VLADIMIR:	(*stupefied*). Not yours!
	ESTRAGON:	Mine were black. These are brown.
	VLADIMIR:	You're sure yours were black?

Pozzo . . . Lucky two grotesque figures who visit Vladimir and Estragon in both Acts. Pozzo is pronounced Po'dzo. Beckett has said that there is no significance in any of the characters' names

85	ESTRAGON:	Well, they were a kind of grey.
	VLADIMIR:	And these are brown? Show.
	ESTRAGON:	(*picking up a boot*). Well, they're a kind of green.
	VLADIMIR:	Show. (*Estragon hands him the boot. Vladimir inspects it, throws it down angrily.*) Well of all the –
90	ESTRAGON:	You see, all that's a lot of bloody –
	VLADIMIR:	Ah! I see what it is. Yes, I see what's happened.
	ESTRAGON:	All that's a lot of bloody –
	VLADIMIR:	It's elementary. Someone came and took yours and left you his.
95	ESTRAGON:	Why?
	VLADIMIR:	His were too tight for him, so he took yours.
	ESTRAGON:	But mine were too tight.
	VLADIMIR:	For you. Not for him.
	ESTRAGON:	(*having tried in vain to work it out*). I'm tired! (*Pause.*)
100		Let's go.
	VLADIMIR:	We can't.
	ESTRAGON:	Why not?
	VLADIMIR:	We're waiting for Godot.
	ESTRAGON:	Ah! (*Pause. Despairing.*) What'll we do, what'll we do!
105	VLADIMIR:	There's nothing we can do.
	ESTRAGON:	But I can't go on like this!
	VLADIMIR:	Would you like a radish?
	ESTRAGON:	Is that all there is?
	VLADIMIR:	There are radishes and turnips.
110	ESTRAGON:	Are there no carrots?
	VLADIMIR:	No. Anyway you overdo it with your carrots.
	ESTRAGON:	Then give me a radish. (*Vladimir fumbles in his pockets, finds nothing but turnips, finally brings out a radish and hands it to Estragon, who examines it, sniffs it.*) It's
115		black!
	VLADIMIR:	It's a radish.
	ESTRAGON:	I only like the pink ones you know that!
	VLADIMIR:	Then you don't want it?
	ESTRAGON:	I only like the pink ones!
	VLADIMIR:	Then give it back to me.
		Estragon gives it back.
120	ESTRAGON:	I'll go and get a carrot.
		He does not move.
	VLADIMIR:	This is becoming really insignificant.
	ESTRAGON:	Not enough.
		Silence.
	VLADIMIR:	What about trying them?
	ESTRAGON:	I've tried everything.

125	VLADIMIR:	No, I mean the boots.
	ESTRAGON:	Would that be a good thing?
	VLADIMIR:	It'd pass the time. (*Estragon hesitates.*) I assure you, it'd be an occupation.
	ESTRAGON:	A relaxation.
130	VLADIMIR:	A recreation.
	ESTRAGON:	A relaxation.
	VLADIMIR:	Try.
	ESTRAGON:	You'll help me?
	VLADIMIR:	I will of course.
135	ESTRAGON:	We don't manage too badly, eh Didi, between the two of us?
	VLADIMIR:	Yes yes. Come on, we'll try the left first.
	ESTRAGON:	We always find something, eh Didi, to give us the impression we exist?
140	VLADIMIR:	(*impatiently*). Yes yes, we're magicians. But let us persevere in what we have resolved, before we forget. (*He picks up a boot.*) Come on, give me your foot. (*Estragon raises his foot.*) The other, hog! (*Estragon raises the other foot.*) Higher! (*Wreathed together they stagger about the stage. Vladimir succeeds finally in getting on the boot.*) Try and walk. (*Estragon walks*) Well?
145		
	ESTRAGON:	It fits.
	VLADIMIR:	(*taking string from his pocket*). We'll try and lace it.
	ESTRAGON:	(*vehemently*). No no, no laces, no laces!
150	VLADIMIR:	You'll be sorry. Let's try the other. (*As before.*) Well?
	ESTRAGON:	(*grudgingly*). It fits too.
	VLADIMIR:	They don't hurt you?
	ESTRAGON:	Not yet.
155	VLADIMIR:	Then you can keep them.
	ESTRAGON:	They're too big.
	VLADIMIR:	Perhaps you'll have socks some day.
	ESTRAGON:	True.
	VLADIMIR:	Then you'll keep them?
160	ESTRAGON:	That's enough about these boots.
	VLADIMIR:	Yes, but —
	ESTRAGON:	(*violently*). Enough! (*Silence.*) I suppose I might as well sit down.
		He looks for a place to sit down, then goes and sits down on the mound.
	VLADIMIR:	That's where you were sitting yesterday evening.
165	ESTRAGON:	If I could only sleep.

VLADIMIR:	Yesterday you slept.
ESTRAGON:	I'll try.
	He resumes his foetal posture, his head between his knees.
VLADIMIR:	Wait. (*He goes over and sits down beside Estragon and begins to sing in a loud voice.*)
	Bye bye bye bye
170	Bye bye –
ESTRAGON:	(*looking up angrily*). Not so loud!
VLADIMIR:	(*softly*).
	Bye bye bye bye
	Bye bye bye bye
	Bye bye bye bye
175	Bye bye . . .
	(*Estragon sleeps. Vladimir gets up softly, takes off his coat and lays it across Estragon's shoulders, then starts walking up and down, swinging his arms to keep himself warm. Estragon wakes with a start, jumps up, casts about wildly. Vladimir runs to him, puts his arms round him.*) There . . . there . . . Didi is there . . . don't be afraid . . .
ESTRAGON:	Ah!
VLADIMIR:	There . . . there . . . it's all over.
180 ESTRAGON:	I was falling –
VLADIMIR:	It's all over it's all over.
ESTRAGON:	I was on top of a –
VLADIMIR:	Don't tell me! Come, we'll walk it off.
	He takes Estragon by the arm and walks him up and down until Estragon refuses to go any further.
ESTRAGON:	That's enough. I'm tired.
185 VLADIMIR:	You'd rather be stuck there doing nothing?
ESTRAGON:	Yes.
VLADIMIR:	Please yourself.
	He releases Estragon, picks up his coat and puts it on.
ESTRAGON:	Let's go.
VLADIMIR:	We can't.
190 ESTRAGON:	Why not?
VLADIMIR:	We're waiting for Godot.

1947/8   1952

John Betjeman
1906–84

Sir John Betjeman was born in Highgate and educated at Highgate School, Marlborough College and Magdalen College, Oxford. In 1931, after a brief spell as a schoolmaster, he started writing for the *Architectural Review*; architecture was to be a lifelong interest. His first book of verse, *Mount Zion* (1931), was followed by further collections, and Betjeman gradually became known to a larger public than most poets have been able to reach. *Collected Poems* (1958, revised 1962) and *Summoned by Bells* (1960), a verse account of the author's school and university days, were very successful. Academic critics have underrated Betjeman's light, urbane verses about suburban mores and Anglican churchgoing, but Auden and Larkin, among other poets, acknowledged the subtlety and variety of his art. John Betjeman was knighted in 1969 and became Poet Laureate in 1972.

IN WESTMINSTER ABBEY

Let me take this other glove off
   As the *vox humana*† swells,
And the beauteous fields of Eden
   Bask beneath the Abbey bells.
5 Here, where England's statesmen lie,
Listen to a lady's cry.

Gracious Lord, oh bomb the Germans.
   Spare their women for Thy Sake,
And if that is not too easy
10   We will pardon Thy Mistake.
But, gracious Lord, whate'er shall be,
Don't let anyone bomb me.

Keep our Empire undismembered
   Guide our Forces by Thy Hand,

---

vox humana   (Latin) human voice, a throbbing organ stop

15   Gallant blacks from far Jamaica,
       Honduras and Togoland;
    Protect them Lord in all their fights,
    And, even more, protect the whites.

    Think of what our Nation stands for,
20   Books from Boots† and country lanes,
    Free speech, free passes, class distinction,
      Democracy and proper drains.
    Lord, put beneath Thy special care
    One-eighty-nine Cadogan Square.

25   Although dear Lord I am a sinner,
      I have done no major crime;
    Now I'll come to Evening Service
      Whensoever I have the time.
    So, Lord, reserve for me a crown,
30   And do not let my shares go down.

    I will labour for Thy Kingdom,
      Help our lads to win the war,
    Send white feathers to the cowards
      Join the Women's Army Corps,
35   Then wash the Steps around Thy Throne
    In the Eternal Safety Zone.

    Now I feel a little better,
      What a treat to hear Thy Word,
    Where the bones of leading statesmen,
40   Have so often been interr'd.
    And now, dear Lord, I cannot wait
    Because I have a luncheon date.

1940   1940

Books from Boots' Boots' shops offered a
  'Booklovers' Library', on subscription, from 1899 to 1966

SENEX

[Old Man]

Oh would I could subdue the flesh
   Which sadly troubles me!
And then perhaps could view the flesh
As though I never knew the flesh
5   And merry misery.

To see the golden hiking girl
   With wind about her hair,
The tennis-playing, biking girl,
The wholly-to-my-liking girl,
10   To see and not to care.

At sundown on my tricycle
   I tour the Borough's edge,
And icy as an icicle
See bicycle by bicycle
15   Stacked waiting in the hedge.

Get down from me! I thunder there
   You spaniels! Shut your jaws!
Your teeth are stuffed with underwear,
Suspenders torn asunder there
20   And buttocks in your paws!

Oh whip the dogs away, my Lord,
   They make me ill with lust.
Bend bare knees down to pray, my Lord,
Teach sulky lips to say, my Lord,
25   That flaxen hair is dust.

1940

MAY-DAY SONG FOR NORTH OXFORD

(Annie Laurie Tune)

Belbroughton Road[†] is bonny, and pinkly bursts the spray
Of prunus and forsythia across the public way,
For a full spring-tide of blossom seethed and departed hence,
Leaving land-locked pools of jonquils by sunny garden fence.

5   And a constant sound of flushing runneth from windows where
The toothbrush too is airing in this new North Oxford air
From Summerfields to Lynam's,[†] the thirsty tarmac dries,
And a Cherwell[†] mist dissolveth on elm-discovering skies.

Oh! well-bound Wells and Bridges![†] Oh! earnest ethical search
10 For the wide high-table[†] λογος[†] of St C. S. Lewis's Church.
This diamond-eyed Spring morning my soul soars up the slope
Of a right good rough-cast buttress on the housewall of my hope.

And open-necked and freckled, where once there grazed the cows,
Emancipated children swing on old apple boughs,
15 And pastel-shaded book rooms bring New Ideas to birth
As the whitening hawthorn only hears the heart beat of the earth.

1945

SUNDAY MORNING, KING'S CAMBRIDGE

File into yellow candle light, fair choristers of King's
   Lost in the shadowy silence of canopied Renaissance[†] stalls
In blazing glass above the dark glow skies and throne and wings

Belbroughton Road   in the residential area of North Oxford, built in the later nineteenth century for academic families
Summerfields to Lynam's   boys' preparatory schools. Lynam's is the Dragon School
Cherwell   a modest tributary of the Thames
Bridges   the poet Robert Bridges (1844–1930)
high-table . . . Church   academic staff dine at 'high table' in Oxford college halls. C. S. Lewis (1898–1963), the popular theologian, taught English and was a prominent lay Anglican
λογος   (Greek) the Word
Renaissance   King's College chapel was built 1446–1515

Blue, ruby, gold and green between the whiteness of the walls
5 And with what rich precision the stonework soars and springs
To fountain out a spreading vault – a shower that never falls.

The white of windy Cambridge courts, the cobbles brown and dry,
The gold of plaster Gothic and ivy overgrown,
The apple-red, the silver fronts, the wide green flats and high.
10 The yellowing elm-trees circled out on islands of their own –
Oh, here behold all colours change that catch the flying sky
To waves of pearly light that heave along the shafted stone.

In far East Anglian churches, the clasped hands lying long
Recumbent on sepulchral slabs or effigied in brass
15 Buttress with prayer this vaulted roof so white and light and strong
And countless congregations as the generations pass
Join choir and great crowned organ case, in centuries of song
To praise Eternity contained in Time and coloured glass.

1954

W. H. Auden

1907–73

Wystan Hugh Auden was born in York and educated at Gresham's School, Holt, and Christ Church, Oxford. His first books of verse, *Poems* (1930), *The Orators* (1932), and *Look, Stranger!* (1936), established him as the ablest and most influential poet of his generation, a metrical genius, achieving, in elegant colloquial verse, a voice which impressed readers of the 1930s as a civilised reply to the stridency of fascism. Auden travelled in Germany, Iceland, China and, in 1937, Spain (in the Republican cause). His writings of this period were fashionably left-wing. He often worked in collaboration: with Christopher Isherwood (1904–85), on plays, *The Dog Beneath the Skin* (1935), *The Ascent of F 6* (1936) and *On the Frontier* (1938), and an account of their visit to China, *Journey to a War* (1939); he wrote *Letters from Iceland* (1937) with Louis MacNeice (1907–63); Benjamin Britten set his verse to music and based his first opera, *Paul Bunyan* (1941), on Auden's script. Auden went to America early in 1939 and became an American citizen in 1946. A new collection of poems, *Another Time*, was published in 1940. *New Year Letter* (1941), an essay in verse which ends with a prayer, was the beginning of the Christian outlook of his increasingly complex post-war verse. *For the Time Being: A Christmas Oratorio* and *The Sea and the Mirror* (dramatic monologues based on Shakespeare's *The Tempest*) appeared in 1944, *The Age of Anxiety: A Baroque Eclogue* in 1948, *The Shield of Achilles* in 1955. His post-war criticism includes *The Enchafèd Flood* (New York, 1950), *The Dyer's Hand* (New York, 1962), and *Secondary Worlds* (1968). E. Mendelson edited *Collected Poems* (1976).

THIS LUNAR BEAUTY

This lunar beauty
Has no history,
Is complete and early;
If beauty later

5   Bear any feature,
    It had a lover
    And is another.

    This like a dream
    Keeps other time,
10 And daytime is
    The loss of this;
    For time is inches
    And the heart's changes,
    Where ghost has haunted
15 Lost and wanted.

    But this was never
    A ghost's endeavour
    Nor, finished this,
    Was ghost at ease;
20 And till it pass
    Love shall not near
    The sweetness here,
    Nor sorrow take
    His endless look.

April 1930   1930

ON THIS ISLAND

    Look, stranger, on this island now
    The leaping light for your delight discovers,
    Stand stable here
    And silent be,
5   That through the channels of the ear
    May wander like a river
    The swaying sound of the sea.

    Here at the small field's ending pause
    When the chalk wall falls to the foam and its tall ledges
10 Oppose the pluck
    And knock of the tide,
    And the shingle scrambles after the sucking surf,
    And the gull lodges
    A moment on its sheer side.

15 Far off like floating seeds the ships
    Diverge on urgent voluntary errands,
    And the full view
    Indeed may enter
    And move in memory as now these clouds do,
20 That pass the harbour mirror
    And all the summer through the water saunter.

1935   1936

LULLABY

    Lay your sleeping head, my love,
    Human on my faithless arm;
    Time and fevers burn away
    Individual beauty from
5   Thoughtful children, and the grave
    Proves the child ephemeral:
    But in my arms till break of day
    Let the living creature lie,
    Mortal, guilty, but to me
10 The entirely beautiful.

    Soul and body have no bounds:
    To lovers as they lie upon
    Her tolerant enchanted slope
    In their ordinary swoon,
15 Grave the vision Venus sends
    Of supernatural sympathy,
    Universal love and hope;
    While an abstract insight wakes
    Among the glaciers and the rocks
20 The hermit's carnal ecstasy.

    Certainty, fidelity
    On the stroke of midnight pass
    Like vibrations of a bell
    And fashionable madmen raise
25 Their pedantic boring cry:

Every farthing of the cost,
All the dreaded cards foretell,
Shall be paid, but from this night
Not a whisper, not a thought,
30   Not a kiss nor look be lost.

Beauty, midnight, vision dies:
Let the winds of dawn that blow
Softly round your dreaming head
Such a day of welcome show
35   Eye and knocking heart may bless,
Find our mortal world enough;
Noons of dryness find you fed
By the involuntary powers,
Nights of insult let you pass
40   Watched by every human love.

January 1937   1940

GARE DU MIDI†

A nondescript express in from the South,
Crowds round the ticket barrier, a face
To welcome which the mayor has not contrived
Bugles or braid: something about the mouth
5   Distracts the stray look with alarm and pity.
Snow is falling. Clutching a little case,
He walks out briskly to infect a city
Whose terrible future may have just arrived.

December 1938   1940

MUSÉE DES BEAUX ARTS

About suffering they were never wrong,
The Old Masters: how well they understood

Gare du Midi   the railway station for the South in Paris

Its human position; how it takes place
While someone else is eating or opening a window or just walking dully
5   along;
How, when the aged are reverently, passionately waiting
For the miraculous birth, there always must be
Children who did not specially want it to happen, skating
On a pond at the edge of the wood:
10   They never forgot
That even the dreadful martyrdom must run its course
Anyhow in a corner, some untidy spot
Where the dogs go on with their doggy life and the torturer's horse
Scratches its innocent behind on a tree.

15   In Breughel's *Icarus*,[†] for instance: how everything turns away
Quite leisurely from the disaster; the ploughman may
Have heard the splash, the forsaken cry,
But for him it was not an important failure; the sun shone
As it had to on the white legs disappearing into the green
20   Water; and the expensive delicate ship that must have seen
Something amazing, a boy falling out of the sky,
Had somewhere to get to and sailed calmly on.

December 1938   1940

IN MEMORY OF W. B. YEATS
(d. Jan. 1939)

I

He disappeared[†] in the dead of winter:
The brooks were frozen, the airports almost deserted,
And snow disfigured the public statues;
The mercury[†] sank in the mouth of the dying day.
5   What instruments we have agree
The day of his death was a dark cold day.

Breughel's Icarus   The Fall of Icarus by Peter Breughel (*c.* 1525–69); this painting is in the Musées Royaux des Beaux Arts (Royal Museums of Fine Arts), Brussels. Icarus, a boy flying on wings attached by wax, fell to his death when he flew too near the sun
He disappeared   Yeats died in Roquebrune in the south of France 28 January 1939
mercury   in the thermometer

Far from his illness
The wolves ran on through the evergreen forests,
The peasant river was untempted by the fashionable quays;
10   By mourning tongues
The death of the poet was kept from his poems.

But for him it was his last afternoon as himself,
An afternoon of nurses and rumours;
The provinces of his body revolted,
15   The squares of his mind were empty,
Silence invaded the suburbs,
The current of his feeling failed; he became his admirers.

Now he is scattered among a hundred cities
And wholly given over to unfamiliar affections,
20   To find his happiness in another kind of wood
And be punished under a foreign code of conscience.
The words of a dead man
Are modified in the guts of the living.

But in the importance of noise of to-morrow
25   When the brokers are roaring like beasts on the floor of the Bourse,[†]
And the poor have the sufferings to which they are fairly accustomed,
And each in the cell of himself is almost convinced of his freedom,
A few thousand will think of this day
As one thinks of a day when one did something slightly unusual.
30   What instruments we have agree
The day of his death was a dark cold day.

II

You were silly like us; your gift survived it all:
The parish of rich women, physical decay,
Yourself. Mad Ireland hurt you into poetry.
35   Now Ireland has her madness and her weather still,
For poetry makes nothing happen: it survives
In the valley of its making where executives
Would never want to tamper, flows on south
From ranches of isolation and the busy griefs,
40   Raw towns that we believe and die in; it survives,
A way of happening, a mouth.

Bourse the Paris stock-exchange

III

Earth, receive an honoured guest:
William Yeats is laid to rest.
Let the Irish vessel lie
45   Emptied of its poetry.

In the nightmare of the dark
All the dogs of Europe bark,
And the living nations wait,
Each sequestered in its hate;

50   Intellectual disgrace
Stares from every human face,
And the seas of pity lie
Locked and frozen in each eye.

Follow, poet, follow right
55   To the bottom of the night,
With your unconstraining voice
Still persuade us to rejoice;

With the farming of a verse
Make a vineyard of the curse,
60   Sing of human unsuccess
In a rapture of distress;

In the deserts of the heart
Let the healing fountain start,
In the prison of his days
65   Teach the free man how to praise.

February 1939   1940

LAW LIKE LOVE

Law, say the gardeners, is the sun,
Law is the one
All gardeners obey
To-morrow, yesterday, to-day.

5   Law is the wisdom of the old,
     The impotent grandfathers feebly scold;
     The grandchildren put out a treble tongue,
     Law is the senses of the young.

     Law, says the priest with a priestly look,
10   Expounding to an unpriestly people,
     Law is the words in my priestly book,
     Law is my pulpit and my steeple.
     Law, says the judge as he looks down his nose,
     Speaking clearly and most severely,
15   Law is as I've told you before,
     Law is as you know I suppose,
     Law is but let me explain it once more,
     Law is The Law.

     Yet law-abiding scholars write:
20   Law is neither wrong nor right,
     Law is only crimes
     Punished by places and by times,
     Law is the clothes men wear
     Anytime, anywhere,
25   Law is Good morning and Good night.

     Others say, Law is our Fate;
     Others say, Law is our State;
     Others say, others say
     Law is no more,
30   Law has gone away.

     And always the loud angry crowd,
     Very angry and very loud,
     Law is We,
     And always the soft idiot softly Me.

35   If we, dear, know we know no more
     Than they about the Law,
     If I no more than you
     Know that we should and should not do
     Except that all agree
40   Gladly or miserably
     That the Law is
     And that all know this,

If therefore thinking it absurd
To identify Law with some other word,
45 Unlike so many men
I cannot say Law is again,
No more than they can we suppress
The universal wish to guess
Or slip out of our own position
50 Into an unconcerned condition.
Although I can at least confine
Your vanity and mine
To stating timidly
A timid similarity,
55 We shall boast anyway:
Like love I say.

Like love we don't know where or why,
Like love we can't compel or fly,
Love love we often weep,
60 Like love we seldom keep.

September 1939   1940

THE SHIELD OF ACHILLES†

She looked over his shoulder
    For vines and olive trees,
Marble well-governed cities
    And ships upon untamed seas,
5 But there on the shining metal
    His hands had put instead
An artificial wilderness
    And a sky like lead.

A plain without a feature, bare and brown,
10 No blade of grass, no sign of neighbourhood,
Nothing to eat and nowhere to sit down,
    Yet, congregated on its blankness, stood
    An unintelligible multitude,
A million eyes, a million boots in line,
15 Without expression, waiting for a sign.

The Shield of Achilles Achilles's mother Thetis asked the god Hephaestos to replace the armour he lost at Troy; Hephaestos made a shield of gold and other rare metals on which the world and the doings of mankind were portrayed. See Homer's *Iliad* XVIII, 478–608

Out of the air a voice without a face
  Proved by statistics that some cause was just
In tones as dry and level as the place:
  No one was cheered and nothing was discussed;
20   Column by column in a cloud of dust
They marched away enduring a belief
Whose logic brought them, somewhere else, to grief.

         She looked over his shoulder
             For ritual pieties,
25   White flower-garlanded heifers,
             Libation and sacrifice,
         But there on the shining metal
             Where the altar should have been,
         She saw by his flickering forge-light
30   Quite another scene.

Barbed wire enclosed an arbitrary spot
  Where bored officials lounged (one cracked a joke)
And sentries sweated for the day was hot:
  A crowd of ordinary decent folk
35   Watched from without and neither moved nor spoke
As three pale figures were led forth and bound
To three posts driven upright in the ground.

The mass and majesty of this world, all
  That carries weight and always weighs the same
40 Lay in the hands of others; they were small
  And could not hope for help and no help came:
What their foes liked to do was done, their shame
Was all the worst could wish; they lost their pride
And died as men before their bodies died.

45   She looked over his shoulder
             For athletes at their games,
         Men and women in a dance
             Moving their sweet limbs
             Quick, quick, to music,
50   But there on the shining shield
         His hands had set no dancing-floor
             But a weed-choked field.

A ragged urchin, aimless and alone,
  Loitered about that vacancy; a bird

55 Flew up to safety from his well-aimed stone:
    That girls are raped, that two boys knife a third,
    Were axioms to him, who'd never heard
Of any world where promises were kept,
Or one could weep because another wept.

60   The thin-lipped armourer,
                Hephaestos, hobbled away,
            Thetis of the shining breasts
                Cried out in dismay
            At what the god had wrought
65   To please her son, the strong
            Iron-hearted man-slaying Achilles
                Who would not live long.

1952   1955

ET IN ARCADIA EGO[†]

Who, now, seeing Her so
Happily married,
Housewife, helpmate to Man,

Can imagine the screeching
5 Virago, the Amazon,
Earth Mother was?

Her jungle growths
Are abated, Her exorbitant
Monsters abashed,

10 Her soil mumbled,
Where crops, aligned precisely,
Will soon be orient:

Levant or couchant,[†]
Well-daunted thoroughbreds
15 Graze on mead and pasture,

Et in Arcadia Ego   two possible meanings: 'I
too was in Arcady' or 'Even in Arcady I am
there'; Arcady being a region of innocent joy.
This saying, which is not classical, is often
found on tombstones. Erwin Panofsky deals
with it in *Philosophy and History* (1936)
levant or couchant   in heraldry (from French),
of animals standing or lying with head raised

A church clock subdivides the day,
Up the lane at sundown
Geese podge† home.

As for Him:
20   What has happened to the Brute
Epics and nightmares tell of?

No bishops pursue
Their archdeacons with axes,
In the crumbling lair

25   Of a robber baron
Sightseers picnic
Who carry no daggers.

I well might think myself
A humanist,
30   Could I manage not to see

How the autobahn
Thwarts the landscape
In godless Roman arrogance,

The farmer's children
35   Tiptoe past the shed
Where the gelding knife is kept.

1964   1965

---

podge   makes a verb of the noun *podge*, a fat square creature

William Empson
1908–84

Sir William Empson was born in Yorkshire and educated at Winchester College and Magdalene College, Cambridge, where he turned to English studies from mathematics and wrote the first draft of *Seven Types of Ambiguity* (1930) while still a pupil of I. A. Richards (1893–1979). He held professorships in China and Japan, and was Professor of English at the University of Sheffield from 1953 to 1971. *Some Versions of Pastoral* (1935), *The Structure of Complex Words* (1951) and *Milton's God* (1961) are, with *Seven Types*, among the most stimulating modern works of literary criticism. Empson's verse, in *Poems* (1935), *The Gathering Storm* (1940) and *Collected Poems* (1955), is deliberately puzzling but worth the time and thought he expects of his readers.

TO AN OLD LADY

Ripeness is all; her in her cooling planet
Revere; do not presume to think her wasted.
Project her no projectile, plan nor man it;
Gods cool in turn, by the sun long outlasted.

5   Our earth alone given no name of god
Gives, too, no hold for such a leap to aid her;
Landing, you break some palace and seem odd;
Bees sting their need, the keeper's queen invader.

No, to your telescope; spy out the land;
10   Watch while her ritual is still to see,
Still stand her temples emptying in the sand
Whose waves o'erthrew their crumbled tracery;

Still stand uncalled-on her soul's appanage;
Much social detail whose successor fades,
15   Wit used to run a house and to play Bridge,
And tragic fervour, to dismiss her maids.

Years her precession do not throw from gear.
She reads a compass certain of her pole;
Confident, finds no confines on her sphere,
20   Whose failing crops are in her sole control.

Stars how much further from me fill my night,
Strange that she too should be inaccessible,
Who shares my sun. He curtains her from sight,
And but in darkness is she visible.

1929   1935

HOMAGE TO THE BRITISH MUSEUM

There is a Supreme God in the ethnological section;
A hollow toad shape, faced with a blank shield.
He needs his belly to include the Pantheon,[†]
Which is inserted through a hole behind.
5   At the navel, at the points formally stressed, at the organs of sense,
Lice glue themselves, dolls, local deities,
His smooth wood creeps with all the creeds of the world.

Attending there let us absorb the cultures of nations
And dissolve into our judgement all their codes.
10   Then, being clogged with a natural hesitation
(People are continually asking one the way out),
Let us stand here and admit that we have no road.
Being everything, let us admit that is to be something,
Or give ourselves the benefit of the doubt;
15   Let us offer our pinch of dust all to this God,
And grant his reign over the entire building.

1932   1935

Pantheon   temple for all the gods

MISSING DATES

Slowly the poison the whole blood stream fills.
It is not the effort nor the failure tires.
The waste remains, the waste remains and kills.

It is not your system or clear sight that mills
5   Down small to the consequence a life requires;
Slowly the poison the whole blood stream fills.

They bled an old dog dry yet the exchange rills
Of young dog blood gave but a month's desires
The waste remains, the waste remains and kills.

10   It is the Chinese tombs and the slag hills
Usurp the soil, and not the soil retires.
Slowly the poison the whole blood stream fills.

Not to have fire is to be a skin that shrills.
The complete fire is death. From partial fires
15   The waste remains, the waste remains and kills.

It is the poems you have lost, the ills
From missing dates, at which the heart expires.
Slowly the poison the whole blood stream fills.
The waste remains, the waste remains and kills.

1937   1940

Kathleen Raine

1908–

Kathleen Jessie Raine was born in London and educated at the County High School, Ilford, and at Girton College, Cambridge, where she was a research fellow from 1955 to 1961. Her marriage to the left-wing poet Charles Madge (1912–) was dissolved. Scotland is the background to many of her poems which show a keen awareness of nature and, she says, 'of the sacred'. *Collected Poems* appeared in 1981. She has published critical work on William Blake.

SHELLS

Reaching down arm-deep into bright water
I gathered on white sand under waves
Shells, drifted up on beaches where I alone
Inhabit a finite world of years and days.
5 I reached my arm down a myriad years
To gather treasure from the yester-millennial sea-floor,
Held in my fingers forms shaped on the day of creation.

Building their beauty in the three dimensions
Over which the world recedes away from us,
10 And in the fourth, that takes away ourselves
From moment to moment and from year to year
From first to last they remain in their continuous present.
The helix revolves like a timeless thought,
Instantaneous from apex to rim,
15 Like a dance whose figure is limpet or murex,* cowrie or   whelk
    golden winkle.

They sleep on the ocean floor like humming-tops
Whose music is the mother-of-pearl octave of the rainbow,
Harmonious shells that whisper for ever in our ears,
'The world that you inhabit has not yet been created.'

ROCK

There is stone in me that knows stone,
Substance of rock that remembers the unending unending
Simplicity of rest
While scorching suns and ice ages
5 Pass over rock-face swiftly as days.
In the longest time of all come the rock's changes,
Slowest of all rhythms, the pulsations
That raise from the planet's core the mountain ranges
And weather them down to sand on the sea-floor.

10 Remains in me record of rock's duration.
My ephemeral substance was still in the veins of the earth from the
        beginning,
Patient for its release, not questioning
When, when will come the flowering, the flowing,
The pulsing, the awakening, the taking wing,
15 The long longed-for night of the bridegroom's coming.

There is stone in me that knows stone,
Whose sole state is stasis
While the slow cycle of the stars whirls a world of rock
Through light-years where in nightmare I fall crying
20 'Must I travel fathomless distance for ever and ever?'
All that is in me of the rock, replies
'For ever, if it must be: be, and be still; endure.'

1952

Stephen Spender
1909–

Sir Stephen Harold Spender was born in London and educated at University College School, London, and University College, Oxford, where he met W. H. Auden. He held left-wing views during the 1930s and worked on Republican propaganda during the Spanish Civil War; he was in the National Fire Service from 1941 to 1944. He co-edited the magazines *Horizon* (with Cyril Connolly, 1939–41) and *Encounter* (1953–66). He held many visiting professorships in America during the 1950s and 1960s and was Professor of English Literature at University College, London, from 1970 to 1977. Spender has published criticism, political reflections and translations from Spanish and German poetry as well as many volumes of verse. *Collected Poems 1928–1953* appeared in 1955.

THE TRULY GREAT

I think continually of those who were truly great.
Who, from the womb, remembered the soul's history
Through corridors of light where the hours are suns,
Endless and singing. Whose lovely ambition
5   Was that their lips, still touched with fire,
Should tell of the Spirit, clothed from head to foot in song.
And who hoarded from the Spring branches
The desires falling across their bodies like blossoms.

What is precious, is never to forget
10   The essential delight of the blood drawn from ageless springs
Breaking through rocks in worlds before our earth.
Never to deny its pleasure in the morning simple light
Nor its grave evening demand for love.
Never to allow gradually the traffic to smother
15   With noise and fog, the flowering of the Spirit.

Near the snow, near the sun, in the highest fields,
See how these names are fêted by the waving grass
And by the streamers of white cloud

And whispers of wind in the listening sky.
20 The names of those who in their lives fought for life,
Who wore at their hearts the fire's centre.
Born of the sun, they travelled a short while toward the sun
And left the vivid air signed with their honour.

1933

AN ELEMENTARY SCHOOL CLASSROOM IN A SLUM

Far far from gusty waves these children's faces.
Like rootless weeds, the hair torn round their pallor.
The tall girl with her weighed-down head. The paper-
seeming boy, with rat's eyes. The stunted, unlucky heir
5 Of twisted bones, reciting a father's gnarled disease,
His lesson from his desk. At back of the dim class
One unnoted, sweet and young. His eyes live in a dream
Of squirrel's game, in tree room, other than this.

On sour cream walls, donations. Shakespeare's head,
10 Cloudless at dawn, civilized dome riding all cities.
Belled, flowery, Tyrolese valley. Open-handed map
Awarding the world its world. And yet, for these
Children, these windows, not this world, are world,
Where all their future's painted with a fog,
15 A narrow street sealed in with a lead sky,
Far far from rivers, capes, and stars of words.

Surely, Shakespeare is wicked, the map a bad example
With ships and sun and love tempting them to steal —
For lives that slyly turn in their cramped holes
20 From fog to endless night? On their slag heap, these children
Wear skins peeped through by bones and spectacles of steel
With mended glass, like bottle bits on stones.
All of their time and space are foggy slum.
So blot their maps with slums as big as doom.

25 Unless, governor, teacher, inspector, visitor,
This map becomes their window and these windows
That shut upon their lives like catacombs,

Break O break open till they break the town
And show the children to green fields, and make their world
30   Run azure on gold sands, and let their tongues
Run naked into books, the white and green leaves open
History theirs whose language is the sun.

1939

Norman MacCaig
1910–

Norman Alexander MacCaig was born in Edinburgh and educated there at the Royal High School and the University. He was a schoolmaster and, briefly, a headmaster, before teaching English at the University of Stirling. *Far Cry* (1943) was the first of many books of poems. His *Poems* was published in 1971. Many but not all MacCaig's poems treat the landscapes and people of Scotland.

FEEDING DUCKS

One duck stood on my toes.
The others made watery rushes after bread
Thrown by my momentary hand; instead,
She stood duck-still and got far more than those.

5   An invisible drone boomed by
With a beetle in it; the neighbour's yearning bull
Bugled across five fields. And an evening full
Of other evenings quietly began to die.

And my everlasting hand
10   Dropped on my hypocrite duck her grace of bread.
And I thought, 'The first to be fattened, the first to be dead',
Till my gestures enlarged, wide over the darkening land.

1960

NUDE IN A FOUNTAIN

Clip-clop go water-drops and bridles ring –
Or, visually, a gauze of water, blown
About and falling and blown about, discloses
Pudicity herself in shameless stone,
5   In an unlikely world of shells and roses.

On shaven grass a summer's litter lies
Of paper bags and people. One o'clock
Booms on the leaves with which the trees are quilted
And wades away through air, making it rock
10   On flowerbeds that have blazed and dazed and wilted.

Light perches, preening, on the handle of a pram
And gasps on paths and runs along a rail
And whitely, brightly in a soft diffusion
Veils and unveils the naked figure, pale
15   As marble in her stone and stilled confusion.

And nothing moves except one dog that runs,
A red rag in a black rag, round and round
And that long helmet-plume of water waving,
In which the four elements, hoisted from the ground,
20   Become this grace, the form of their enslaving.

Meeting and marrying in the midmost air
Is mineral assurance of them all;
White doldrum on blue sky; a pose of meaning
Whose pose is what is explicit; a miracle
25   Made, and made bearable, by the water's screening.

The drops sigh, singing, and, still sighing, sing
Gently a leaning song. She makes no sound.
They veil her, not with shadows, but with brightness;
Till, gleam within a glitter, they expound
30   What a tall shadow is when it is whiteness.

A perpetual modification of itself
Going on around her is her; her hand is curled
Round more than a stone breast; and she discloses
The more than likely in an unlikely world
35   Of dogs and people and stone shells and roses.

1960

CELTIC CROSS

The implicated† generations made
This symbol of their lives, a stone made light
By what is carved on it.
                    The plaiting† masks,
But not with involutions of a shade,
5   What a stone says and what a stone cross asks.

Something that is not mirrored by nor trapped
In webs of water or bag-nets of cloud;
The tangled mesh of weed
                      lets it go by.
Only men's minds could ever have unmapped
10 Into abstraction such a territory.

No green bay going yellow over sand
Is written on by winds to tell a tale
Of death-dishevelled gull
                    or heron, stiff
As a cruel clerk with gaunt writs in his hand
15 – Or even of light, that makes its depths a cliff.

Singing responses order otherwise.
The tangled generations ravelled out
In links of song whose sweet
                   strong choruses
Are these stone involutions to the eyes
20 Given to the ear in abstract vocables.

The stone remains, and the cross, to let us know
Their unjust, hard demands, as symbols do.
But on them twine and grow
                 beneath the dove
Serpents of wisdom whose cool statements show
25 Such understanding that it seems like love.

1960

---

implicated   because Christian   in a style reminiscent of the plaiting of hair
plaiting   the stone of Celtic crosses is carved   or braid

William Golding
1911–

William Golding, born at St Columb Minor in Cornwall, was educated at Marlborough Grammar School and Brasenose College, Oxford. He worked in the theatre and then became a schoolmaster. In the Royal Navy during the Second World War, he commanded a rocket ship. *Lord of the Flies* (1954), his first novel, has been very successful indeed. *The Inheritors* (1955), whose characters are Neanderthals, and *The Spire* (1964), which has a medieval setting, are less accessible but perhaps more rewarding. Golding's other novels are *Pincher Martin* (1956), *Free Fall* (1959), *The Pyramid* (1967), *Darkness Visible* (1979), *Rites of Passage* (1980), and *The Paper Men* (1984). He has also published stories (*The Scorpion God*, 1971), essays (*The Hot Gates*, 1965) and a play (*The Brass Butterfly*, 1958). His theme is the fallen, cruel nature of man; his settings are varied and usually removed from familiar social milieux; symbolism and fable are conspicuous features of his work. Golding was awarded the Nobel Prize for Literature in 1983.

In this passage a group of Neanderthals struggle not only to survive but also to find meaning in their own sensations and memories and in their experience of Nature (Oa). Mal is the oldest of the tribe and Lok represents the new generation.

From THE INHERITORS

[Pictures]

At that the people talked again excitedly. They hurried into the hollow. Mal crouched down between the fire and the recess and spread out his hands, while Fa and Nil brought more wood and placed it ready. Liku brought a branch and gave it to the old woman. Ha squatted against
5 the rock and shuffled his back till it fitted. His right hand found a stone and picked it up. He showed it to the people.

'I have a picture of this stone. Mal used it to cut a branch. See! Here is the part that cuts.'

Mal took the stone from Ha, felt the weight, frowned a moment,
10   then smiled at them.

'This is the stone I used,' he said. 'See! Here I put my thumb and
here my hand fits round the thickness.'

He held up the stone, miming Mal cutting a branch.

'The stone is a good stone,' said Lok. 'It has not gone away. It has
15   stayed by the fire until Mal came back to it.'

He stood up and peered over the earth and stones down the slope.
The river had not gone away either or the mountains. The overhang
had waited for them. Quite suddenly he was swept up by a tide of
happiness and exultation. Everything had waited for them: Oa had
20   waited for them. Even now she was pushing up the spikes of the bulbs,
fattening the grubs, reeking the smells out of the earth, bulging the fat
buds out of every crevice and bough. He danced onto the terrace by
the river, his arms spread wide.

'Oa!'

25   Mal moved a little way from the fire and examined the back of the
overhang. He peered at the surface and swept a few dried leaves and
droppings from the earth at the base of the pillar. He squatted and
shrugged his shoulders into place.

'And this is where Mal sits.'

30   He touched the rock gently as Lok or Ha might touch Fa.

'We are home!'

Lok came in from the terrace. He looked at the old woman. Freed
from the burden of the fire she seemed a little less remote, a little more
like one of them. He could look her in the eye now and speak to her,
35   perhaps even be answered. Bsides, he felt the need to speak, to hide
from the others the unease that the flames always called forth in him.

'Now the fire sits on the hearth. Do you feel warm Liku?'

Liku took the little Oa from her mouth.

'I am hungry.'

40   'To-morrow we shall find food for all the people.'

Liku held up the little Oa.

'She is hungry too.'

'She shall go with you and eat.'

He laughed round at the others.

45   'I have a picture –'

Then the people laughed too because this was Lok's picture, almost
the only one he had, and they knew it as well as he did.

'– a picture of finding the little Oa.'

Fantastically the old root was twisted and bulged and smoothed away
50   by age into the likeness of a great-bellied woman.

'– I am standing among the trees. I feel. With this foot I feel –' He mimed for them. His weight was on his left foot and his right was searching in the ground. '– I feel. What do I feel? A bulb? A stick? A bone?' His right foot seized something and passed it up to his right
55 hand. He looked. 'It is the little Oa!' Triumphantly he sunned himself before them. 'And now where Liku is there is the little Oa.'

The people applauded him, grinning, half at Lok, half at the story. Secure in their applause, Lok settled himself by the fire and the people were silent, gazing into the flames.
60 The sun dropped into the river and light left the overhang. Now the fire was more than ever central, white ash, a spot of red and one flame wavering upwards. The old woman moved softly, pushing in more wood so that the red spot ate and the flame grew strong. The people watched, their faces seeming to quiver in the unsteady light. Their
65 freckled skins were ruddy and the deep caverns beneath their brows were each inhabited by replicas of the fire and all their fires danced together. As they persuaded themselves of the warmth they relaxed limbs and drew the reek into their nostrils gratefully. They flexed their toes and stretched their arms, even leaning away from the fire. One of
70 the deep silences fell on them, that seemed so much more natural than speech, a timeless silence in which there were at first many minds in the overhang; and then perhaps no mind at all. So fully discounted was the roar of the water that the soft touch of the wind on the rocks became audible. Their ears as if endowed with separate life sorted the
75 tangle of tiny sounds and accepted them, the sound of breathing, the sound of wet clay flaking and ashes falling in.

Then Mal spoke with unusual diffidence.

'It is cold?'

Called back into their individual skulls they turned to him. He was
80 no longer wet and his hair curled. He moved forward decisively and knelt so that his knees were on the clay, his arms as supports on either side and the full heat beating on his chest. Then the spring wind flicked at the fire and sent the thin column of smoke straight into his open mouth. He choked and coughed. He went on and on, the coughs
85 seeming to come out of his chest without warning or consultation. They threw his body about and all the time he gaped for his breath. He fell over sideways and his body began to shake. They could see his tongue and the fright in his eyes.

The old woman spoke.
90 'This is the cold of the water where the log was.'

She came and knelt by him and rubbed his chest with her hands and kneaded the muscles of his neck. She took his head on her knees and shielded him from the wind till his coughing was done and he lay still, shivering slightly. The new one woke up and scrambled down from

95 Fa's back. He crawled among the stretched legs with his red thatch
glistening in the light. He saw the fire, slipped under Lok's raised knee,
took hold of Mal's ankle and pulled himself upright. Two little fires lit
in his eyes and he stayed, leaning forward, holding on to the shaking
leg. The people divided their attention between him and Mal. Then a

100 branch burst so that Lok jumped and sparks shot out into the darkness.
The new one was on all fours before the sparks landed. He scuttled
among the legs, climbed Nil's arm and hid himself in the hair of her
back and neck. Then one of the little fires appeared by her left ear, an
unwinking fire that watched warily. Nil moved her face sideways and

105 rubbed her cheek gently up and down on the baby's head. The new
one was enclosed again. His own thatch and his mother's curls made a
cave for him. Her mop hung down and sheltered him. Presently the
tiny point of fire by her ear went out.

Mal pulled himself up so that he sat leaning against the old woman.
110 He looked at each of them in turn. Liku opened her mouth to speak
but Fa hushed her quickly.

Now Mal spoke.

'There was the great Oa. She brought forth the earth from her belly.
She gave suck. The earth brought forth woman and the woman brought
115 forth the first man out of her belly.'

They listened to him in silence. They waited for more, for all that
Mal knew. There was the picture of the time when there had been many
people, the story that they all liked so much of the time when it was
summer all year round and the flowers and fruit hung on the same
120 branch. There was also a long list of names that began at Mal and went
back choosing always the oldest man of the people at that time: but
now he said nothing more.

Lok sat between him and the wind.

'You are hungry, Mal. A man who is hungry is a cold man.'
125 Ha lifted up his mouth.

'When the sun comes back we will get food. Stay by the fire, Mal,
and we will bring you food and you will be strong and warm.'

Then Fa came and leaned her body against Mal so that three of them
shut him in against the fire. He spoke to them between coughs.
130 'I have a picture of what is to be done.'

He bowed his head and looked into the ashes. The people waited.
They could see how his life had stripped him. The long hairs on the
brow were scanty and the curls that should have swept down over the
slope of his skull had receded till there was a finger's-breadth of naked
135 and wrinkled skin above his brows. Under them the great eye-hollows
were deep and dark and the eyes in them dull and full of pain. Now he
held up a hand and inspected the fingers closely.

'People must find food. People must find wood.'

He held his left fingers with the other hand; he gripped them tightly
140 as though the pressure would keep the ideas inside and under control.
'A finger for wood. A finger for food.'
He jerked his head and started again.
'A finger for Ha. For Ha. For Nil. For Liku –'
He came to the end of his fingers and looked at the other hand,
145 coughing softly. Ha stirred where he sat but said nothing. Then Mal
relaxed his brow and gave up. He bowed down his head and clasped
his hands in the grey hair at the back of his neck. They heard in his
voice how tired he was.
'Ha shall get wood from the forest. Nil will go with him, and the
150 new one.' Ha stirred again and Fa moved her arm from the old man's
shoulders, but Mal went on speaking.
'Lok will get food with Fa and Liku.'
Ha spoke:
'Liku is too little to go on the mountain and out on the plain!'
155 Liku cried out:
'I will go with Lok!'
Mal muttered under his knees:
'I have spoken.'
Now the thing was settled the people became restless. They knew in
160 their bodies that something was wrong, yet the word had been said.
When the word had been said it was as though the action was already
alive in performance and they worried. Ha clicked a stone aimlessly
against the rock of the overhang and Nil was moaning softly again.
Only Lok, who had fewest pictures, remembered the blinding pictures
165 of Oa and her bounty that had set him dancing on the terrace. He
jumped up and faced the people and the night air shook his curls.
'I shall bring back food in my arms' – he gestured hugely – 'so much
food that I stagger – so!'
Fa grinned at him.
170 'There is not as much food as that in the world.'
He squatted.
'Now I have a picture in my head. Lok is coming back to the fall.
He runs along the side of the mountain. He carries a deer. A cat has
killed the deer and sucked its blood, so there is no blame. So. Under
175 this left arm. And under this right one' – he held it out – 'the quarters
of a cow.'
He staggered up and down in front of the overhang under the load
of meat. The people laughed with him, then at him. Only Ha sat silent,
smiling a little until the people noticed him and looked from him to
180 Lok.
Lok blustered:
'That is a true picture!'

Ha said nothing with his mouth but continued to smile. Then as they watched him, he moved both ears round, slowly and solemnly aiming them at Lok so that they said as clearly as if he had spoken: I hear you! Lok opened his mouth and his hair rose. He began to gibber wordlessly at the cynical ears and the half-smile.

Fa interrupted them.

'Let be. Ha has many pictures and few words. Lok has a mouthful of words and no pictures.'

At that Ha shouted with laughter and wagged his feet at Lok and Liku laughed without knowing why. Lok yearned suddenly for the mindless peace of their accord. He put his fit of temper on one side and crept back to the fire, pretending to be very miserable so that they pretended to comfort him. Then there was silence again and one mind or no mind in the overhang.

Quite without warning, all the people shared a picture inside their heads. This was a picture of Mal, seeming a little removed from them, illuminated, sharply defined in all his gaunt misery. They saw not only Mal's body but the slow pictures that were waxing and waning in his head. One above all was displacing the others, dawning through the cloudy arguments and doubts and conjectures until they knew what it was he was thinking with such dull conviction.

'To-morrow or the day after, I shall die.'

The people became separate again. Lok stretched out his hand and touched Mal. But Mal did not feel the touch in his pain and under the woman's sheltering hair. The old woman glanced at Fa.

'It is the cold of the water.'

She bent and whispered in Mal's ear:

'To-morrow there will be food. Now sleep.'

Ha stood up.

'There will be more wood too. Will you not give the fire more to eat?'

The old woman went to a recess and chose wood. She fitted these pieces cunningly together till wherever the flames rose they found dry wood to bite on. Soon the flames were beating at the air and the people moved back into the overhang. This enlarged the semicircle and Liku slipped into it. Hair crinkled in warning and the people smiled at each other in delight. Then they began to yawn widely. They arranged themselves round Mal, huddling in, holding him in a cradle of warm flesh with the fire in front of him. They shuffled and muttered. Mal coughed a little, then he too was asleep.

Lok squatted to one side and looked out over the dark waters. There had been no conscious decision but he was on watch. He yawned too and examined the pain in his belly. He thought of good food and

dribbled a little and was about to speak but then he remembered that they were all asleep. He stood up instead and scratched the close curls under his lip. Fa was within reach and suddenly he desired her again; but this desire was easy to forget because most of his mind preferred to
230   think about food instead. He remembered the hyenas and padded along the terrace until he could look down the slope to the forest. Miles of darkness and sooty blots stretched away to the grey bar that was the sea; nearer, the river shone dispersedly in swamps and meanders. He looked up at the sky and saw that it was clear except where layers of
235   fleecy cloud lay above the sea. As he watched and the after-image of the fire faded he saw a star prick open. Then there were others, a scatter, fields of quivering lights from horizon to horizon. His eyes considered the stars without blinking, while his nose searched for the hyenas and told him that they were nowhere near. He clambered over
240   the rocks and looked down at the fall. There was always light where the river fell into its basin. The smoky spray seemed to trap whatever light there was and to dispense it subtly. Yet this light illumined nothing but the spray so that the island was total darkness. Lok gazed without thought at the black trees and rocks that loomed through the dull
245   whiteness. The island was like the whole leg of a seated giant, whose knee, tufted with trees and bushes, interrupted the glimmering sill of the waterfall and whose ungainly foot was splayed out down there, spread, lost likeness and joined the dark wilderness. The giant's thigh that should have supported a body like a mountain, lay in the sliding
250   water of the gap and diminished till it ended in disjointed rocks that curved to within a few men's lengths of the terrace. Lok considered the giant's thigh as he might have considered the moon: something so remote that it had no connection with life as he knew it. To reach the island the people would have to leap that gap between the terrace and
255   the rocks across water that was eager to snatch them over the fall. Only some creature more agile and frightened would dare that leap. So the island remained unvisited.

A picture came to him in his relaxation of the cave by the sea and he turned to look down river. He saw the meanders as pools that glistened
260   dully in the darkness. Odd pictures came to him of the trail that led all the way from the sea to the terrace through the gloom below him. He looked and grew confused at the thought that the trail was really there where he was looking. This part of the country with its confusion of rocks that seemed to be arrested at the most tempestuous moment of
265   swirling, and that river down there split among the forest were too complicated for his head to grasp, though his senses could find a devious path across them. He abandoned thought with relief. Instead he flared his nostrils, and searched for the hyenas but they were gone. He pattered down to the edge of the rock and made water into the river. Then he

270   went back softly and squatted to one side of the fire. He yawned once, desired Fa again, scratched himself. There were eyes watching him from the cliffs, eyes even, on the island, but nothing would come nearer while the ashes of the fire still glowed. As though she were conscious of his thought the old woman woke, put on a little wood and began to rake

275   the ashes together with a flat stone. Mal coughed dryly in his sleep so that the others stirred. The old woman settled again and Lok put his palms into the hollows of his eyes and rubbed them sleepily. Green spots from the pressure floated across the river. He blinked to the left where the waterfall thundered so monotonously that already he could

280   no longer hear it. The wind moved on the water, hovered; and then came strongly up from the forest and through the gap. The sharp line of the horizon blurred and the forest lightened. There was a cloud rising over the waterfall, mist stealing up from the sculptured basin, the pounded river water being thrown back by the wind. The island

285   dimmed, the wet mist stole towards the terrace, hung under the arch of the overhang and enveloped the people in drops that were too small to be felt and could only be seen in numbers. Lok's nose opened automatically and sampled the complex of odours that came with the mist.

290   He squatted, puzzled and quivering. He cupped his hands over his nostrils and examined the trapped air. Eyes shut, straining attention, he concentrated on the touch of the warming air, seemed for a moment on the very brink of revelation; then the scent dried away like water, dislimned like a far-off small thing when the tears of effort drown it.

295   He let the air go and opened his eyes. The mist of the fall was drifting away with a change of wind and the smell of the night was ordinary.

     He frowned at the island and the dark water that slid towards the lip, then yawned. He could not hold a new thought when there seemed no danger in it. The fire was sinking to a red eye that lit nothing but

300   itself and the people were still and rock-coloured. He settled down and leaned forward to sleep, pressing his nostrils in with one hand so that the stream of cold air was diminished. He drew his knees to his chest and presented the least possible surface to the night air. His left arm stole up and insinuated the fingers in the hair at the back of his neck.

305   His mouth sank on his knees.

     Over the sea in a bed of cloud there was a dull orange light that expanded. The arms of the clouds turned to gold and the rim of the moon nearly at the full pushed up among them. The sill of the fall glittered, lights ran to and fro along the edge or leapt in a sudden

310   sparkle. The trees on the island acquired definition, the birch trunk that overtopped them was suddenly silver and white. Across the water on the other side of the gap the cliff still harboured the darkness but everywhere else the mountains exhibited their high snow and ice. Lok

slept, balanced on his hams. A hint of danger would have sent him
315 flying across the terrace like a sprinter from his mark. Frost twinkled
on him like the twinkling ice of the mountain. The fire was a blunted
cone containing a handful of red over which blue flames wandered and
plucked at the unburnt ends of branches and logs.

The moon rose slowly and almost vertically into a sky where there
320 was nothing but a few spilled traces of cloud. The light crawled down
the island and made the pillars of spray full of brightness. It was
watched by green eyes, it discovered grey forms that slid and twisted
from light to shadow or ran swiftly across the open spaces on the sides
of the mountain. It fell on the trees of the forest so that a scatter of
325 faint ivory patches moved over the rotting leaves and earth. It lay on
the river and the wavering weed-tails; and the water was full of tinsel
loops and circles and eddies of liquid cold fire. There came a noise from
the foot of the fall, a noise that the thunder robbed of echo and
resonance, the form of a noise. Lok's ears twitched in the moonlight so
330 that the frost that lay along their upper edges shivered. Lok's ears spoke
to Lok.

'?'

But Lok was asleep.

1955

Roy Fuller
1912–

Roy Fuller was born in Failsworth in Lancashire and was educated at Blackpool High School. He practised as a solicitor from 1933, except for a period of service in the Royal Navy from 1941–6, working for many years with a building society. In 1969 he became Vice-President of the Building Societies Association. *Poems* (1939) echoes the left-wing 1930s verse of Auden, Spender and Day-Lewis. His later books of verse are distinguished by careful, increasingly experimental craft, and greater interest in the individual, and by a personal voice. *Collected Poems 1936–61* (1962) was followed by *From the Junk Shop* (1975) and *The Reign of Sparrows* (1980). His novel *Image of a Society* was published in 1956. His lectures at Oxford, where he was Professor of Poetry from 1968–73, were published in *Owls and Artificers* (1971) and *Professors and Gods* (1973).

THE BARBER

Reading the shorthand on a barber's sheet
In a warm and chromium basement in Cannon Street
I discovered again the message of the city,
That without power there is no place for pity.

5   The barber with a flat and scented hand
Moved the dummy's head in its collar band.
'What will you do with the discarded hair?'

The mirror showed a John the Baptist's face,
Detached and sideways. 'Can you tell me how,'
10   It said, 'I may recover grace?

'Make me a merchant, make me a manager,'
His scissors mournfully declined the task.
'Will you do nothing that I ask?'

'It is no use,' he said, 'I cannot speak
15 To you as one in a similar position.
For me you are the stern employer,
Of wealth the accumulator.
I must ignore your singular disposition.'

He brushed my shoulders and under his practised touch
20 I knew his words were only a deceit.
'You spoke to me according to the rules
Laid down for dealing with madmen and with fools.'

'I do my best,' he said, 'my best is sufficient.
If I have offended it is because
25 I never formulate the ideal action
Which depends on observation.'

'And do you never observe and never feel
Regret at the destruction of wealth by war?
Do you never sharpen your razor on your heel
30 And draw it across selected throats?'

He smiled and turned away to the row of coats.
'This is your mackintosh,' he said, 'you had no hat.
Turn left for the station and remember the barber.
There is just time enough for that.'

1939   1942

THE FAMILY CAT

This cat was bought upon the day
That marked the Japanese defeat;
He was anonymous and gay,
But timorous and not discreet.

5 Although three years have gone, he shows
Fresh sides of his uneven mind:
To us – fond, lenient – he grows
Still more eccentric and defined.

He is a grey, white-chested cat,
10 And barred with black along the grey;

Not large, and the reverse of fat,
His profile good from either way.

The poet buys especial fish,
Which is made ready by his wife;
15 The poet's son holds out the dish:
They thus maintain the creature's life.

It's not his anniversary
Alone that's his significance:
In any case mortality
20 May not be thought of in his presence.

For brief as are our lives, more brief
Exist. Our stroking hides the bones,
Which none the less cry out in grief
Beneath the mocking, loving tones.

1949

AT A WARWICKSHIRE MANSION

Mad world, mad kings, mad composition† – KING JOHN

Cycles of ulcers, insomnia, poetry –
Badges of office; wished, detested tensions.
Seeing the parsley-like autumnal trees
Unmoving in the mist, I long to be
5 The marvellous painter who with art could freeze
Their transitory look: the vast dissensions
Between the human and his world arise
And plead with me to sew the hurt with eyes.

Horn calls on ostinato† strings: the birds
10 Sweep level out of the umbrageous wood.
The sun towards the unconsidered west
Floats red, enormous, still. For these the words
Come pat, but for society possessed

Mad world . . . composition Shakespeare,
King John II.1.561; *composition*, political
settlement

ostinato ground bass

With frontal lobes for evil, rear for good,
15   They are incongruous as the poisoner's
Remorse or as anaemia in furs.

In the dank garden of the ugly house
A group of leaden statuary perspires;
Moss grows between the ideal rumps and paps
20   Cast by the dead Victorian; the mouse
Starves behind massive panels; paths relapse
Like moral principles; the surrounding shires
Darken beneath the bombers' crawling wings.
The terrible simplifiers jerk the strings.

25   But art is never innocent although
It dreams it may be; and the red in caves
Is left by cripples of the happy hunt.
Between the action and the song I know
Too well the sleight of hand which points the blunt,
30   Compresses, lies. The schizophrenic craves
Magic and mystery, the rest the sane
Reject: what force and audience remain?

The house is dark upon the darkening sky:
I note the blue for which I never shall
35   Find the equivalent. I have been acting
The poet's role for quite as long as I
Can, at a stretch, without it being exacting:
I must return to less ephemeral
Affairs — to those controlled by love and power;
40   Builders of realms, their tenants for an hour.

1957

F. T. Prince

1912–

Frank Templeton Prince, born at Kimberley, Cape Province, South Africa, was educated in Kimberley and at Balliol College, Oxford, and at Princeton. He was Professor of English at Southampton University from 1957 to 1974. His books of poems include *Soldiers Bathing and Other Poems* (1954); his *Collected Poems* was published in 1979.

SOLDIERS BATHING

The sea at evening moves across the sand.
Under a reddening sky I watch the freedom of a band
Of soldiers who belong to me. Stripped bare
For bathing in the sea, they shout and run in the warm air;
5   Their flesh worn by the trade of war, revives
And my mind towards the meaning of it strives.

All's pathos now. The body that was gross,
Rank, ravenous, disgusting in the act or in repose,
All fever, filth and sweat, its bestial strength
10   And bestial decay, by pain and labour grows at length
Fragile and luminous. 'Poor bare forked animal,'[†]
Conscious of his desires and needs and flesh that rise and fall,
Stands in the soft air, tasting after toil
The sweetness of his nakedness: letting the sea-waves coil
15   Their frothy tongues about his feet, forgets
His hatred of the war, its terrible pressure that begets
A machinery of death and slavery,
Each being a slave and making slaves of others: finds that he
Remembers his old freedom in a game
20   Mocking himself, and comically mimics fear and shame.

He plays with death and animality;
And reading in the shadows of his pallid flesh, I see
The idea of Michelangelo's cartoon[†]

Poor . . . animal   King Lear III.4.110
Michelangelo's cartoon   the paper sketch or

cartoon for his *Bathers* by Michelangelo
Buonarroti (1475–1564)

Of soldiers bathing, breaking off before they were half done
25   At some sortie of the enemy, an episode
Of the Pisan wars with Florence. I remember how he showed
Their muscular limbs that clamber from the water,
And heads that turn across the shoulder, eager for the slaughter,
Forgetful of their bodies that are bare,
30   And hot to buckle on and use the weapons lying there.

  – And I think too of the theme another found
When, shadowing men's bodies on a sinister red ground,
Another Florentine, Pollaiuolo,[†]
Painted a naked battle: warriors, straddled, hacked the foe,
35   Dug their bare toes into the ground and slew
The brother-naked man who lay between their feet and drew
His lips back from his teeth in a grimace.

They were Italians who knew war's sorrow and disgrace
And showed the thing suspended, stripped: a theme
40   Born out of the experience of war's horrible extreme
Beneath a sky where even the air flows
With *lacrimae Christi*.[†] For that rage, that bitterness, those blows,
That hatred of the slain, what could they be
But indirectly or directly a commentary
45   On the Crucifixion? And the picture burns
With indignation and pity and despair by turns,
Because it is the obverse of the scene
Where Christ hangs murdered, stripped, upon the Cross. I mean,
That is the explanation of its rage.

50   And we too have our bitterness and pity that engage
Blood, spirit, in this war. But night begins,
Night of the mind: who nowadays is conscious of our sins?
Though every human deed concerns our blood,
And even we must know, what nobody has understood,
55   That some great love is over all we do,
And that is what has driven us to this fury, for so few
Can suffer all the terror of that love:
The terror of that love has set us spinning in this groove
Greased with our blood.

Pollaiuolo   Antonio Pollaiuolo (*c.* 1432–
1498), whose engraving *Battle of the Naked*   *Men* is described here
                                                    lacrimae Christi   (Latin) Christ's tears

60   These dry themselves and dress,
Combing their hair, forget the fear and shame of nakedness.
Because to love is frightening we prefer
The freedom of our crimes. Yet, as I drink the dusky air,
I feel a strange delight that fills me full,
65 Strange gratitude, as if evil itself were beautiful,
And kiss the wound in thought, while in the west
I watch a streak of red that might have issued from Christ's breast.

1954

R. S. Thomas

1913–

Ronald Stuart Thomas was born in Cardiff and educated at University College, Bangor, and St Michael's College, Llandaff. He was ordained deacon in 1936, priest 1937, in the Church of Wales. He was, in turn, rector of Monafon (1942–54), vicar of Eglwysfach (1952–4), and vicar of St Hywyn, Aberdaron (1954–78). He has published several volumes of verse; *Selected Poems 1946–68* appeared in 1973. Thomas writes about the people of his rural Welsh parishes, dwelling on the poverty of their lives. He edited *The Penguin Book of Religious Verse* (1963).

EVANS

    Evans? Yes, many a time
    I came down his bare flight
    Of stairs into the gaunt kitchen
    With its wood fire, where crickets sang
5   Accompaniment to the black kettle's
    Whine, and so into the cold
    Dark to smother in the thick tide
    Of night that drifted about the walls
    Of his stark farm on the hill ridge.

10 It was not the dark filling my eyes
    And mouth appalled me; not even the drip
    Of rain like blood from the one tree
    Weather-tortured. It was the dark
    Silting the veins of that sick man
15 I left stranded upon the vast
    And lonely shore of his bleak bed.

1958

A WELSH TESTAMENT

All right, I was Welsh. Does it matter
I spoke the tongue that was passed on
To me in the place I happened to be,
A place huddled between grey walls
5   Of cloud for at least half the year.
My word for heaven was not yours.
The word for hell had a sharp edge
Put on it by the hand of the wind
Honing, honing with a shrill sound
10   Day and night. Nothing that Glyn Dŵr†
Knew was armour against the rain's
Missiles. What was descent from him?

Even God had a Welsh name:
We spoke to him in the old language;
15   He was to have a peculiar care
For the Welsh people. History showed us
He was too big to be nailed to the wall
Of a stone chapel, yet still we crammed him
Between the boards of a black book.

20   Yet men sought us despite this.
My high cheek-bones, my length of skull
Drew them as to a rare portrait
By a dead master. I saw them stare
From their long cars, as I passed knee-deep
25   In ewes and wethers. I saw them stand
By the thorn hedges, watching me string
The far flocks on a shrill whistle.
And always there was their eyes' strong
Pressure on me: You are Welsh, they said;
30   Speak to us so; keep your fields free
Of the smell of petrol, the loud roar
Of hot tractors; we must have peace
And quietness.

          Is a museum
35   Peace? I asked. Am I the keeper
Of the heart's relics, blowing the dust

Glyn Dŵr Owen Glendower (*c.* 1339–
c. 1416), Welsh leader against the English under Henry IV

In my own eyes? I am a man;
I never wanted the drab rôle
Life assigned me, an actor playing
40   To the past's audience upon a stage
Of earth and stone; the absurd label
Of birth, of race hanging askew
About my shoulders. I was in prison
Until you came; your voice was a key
45   Turning in the enormous lock
Of hopelessness. Did the door open
To let me out of yourselves in?

1961

Henry Reed

1914–86

Henry Reed was born in Birmingham and educated there at King Edward VI School and at the University. He worked as a broadcaster from 1945 and published collections of his plays for radio: *The Streets of Pompeii* (verse dramas, 1971) and *Hilda Tablet and Others* (1971). *A Map of Verona* (1946) is his only book of verse.

NAMING OF PARTS

To-day we have naming of parts. Yesterday,
We had daily cleaning. And to-morrow morning,
We shall have what to do after firing. But to-day,
To-day we have naming of parts, Japonica
5 Glistens like coral in all of the neighbouring gardens,
     And to-day we have naming of parts.

This is the lower sling swivel. And this
Is the upper sling swivel, whose use you will see,
When you are given your slings. And this is the piling swivel,
10 Which in your case you have not got. The branches
Hold in the gardens their silent, eloquent gestures,
     Which in our case we have not got.

This is the safety-catch, which is always released
With an easy flick of the thumb. And please do not let me
15 See anyone using his finger. You can do it quite easy
If you have any strength in your thumb. The blossoms
Are fragile and motionless, never letting anyone see
     Any of them using their finger.

And this you can see is the bolt. The purpose of this
20 Is to open the breech, as you see. We can slide it
Rapidly backwards and forwards: we call this
Easing the spring. And rapidly backwards and forwards
The early bees are assaulting and fumbling the flowers:
     They call it easing the Spring.

25 They call it easing the Spring: it is perfectly easy
    If you have any strength in your thumb: like the bolt,
    And the breech, and the cocking-piece, and the point of balance,
    Which in our case we have not got; and the almond-blossom
    Silent in all of the gardens and the bees going backwards and forwards,
30   For to-day we have naming of parts.

1946

CHARD WHITLOW

(*Mr Eliot's Sunday Evening Postscript*)

As we get older we do not get any younger.
Seasons return, and to-day I am fifty-five,
And this time last year I was fifty-four,
And this time next year I shall be sixty-two.
5   And I cannot say I should care (to speak for myself)
    To see my time over again – if you can call it time,
    Fidgeting uneasily under a draughty stair,
    Or counting sleepless nights in the crowded Tube.

There are certain precautions – though none of them very reliable –
10 Against the blast from bombs, or the flying splinter,
    But not against the blast from Heaven, *vento dei venti*,[†]
    The wind within a wind, unable to speak for wind;
    And the frigid burnings of purgatory will not be touched
    By any emollient.
15   I think you will find this put,
    Far better than I could ever hope to express it,
    In the words of Kharma.[†] 'It is, we believe,
    Idle to hope that the simple stirrup-pump
    Can extinguish hell.'

20   Oh, listeners,
    And you especially who have switched off the wireless,
    And sit in Stoke or Basingstoke, listening appreciatively to the silence
    (Which is also the silence of hell), pray not for yourselves but your
    souls.

---

vento dei venti   (Italian) wind of winds   Buddhist *Karma* theory of inevitability
Kharma   a made-up name, in allusion to the

And pray for me also under the draughty stair.
25   As we get older we do not get any younger.

And pray for Kharma under the holy mountain.

1946

Dylan Thomas
1914–53

Dylan Marlais Thomas was born in Swansea and educated at Swansea Grammar School where his father was the English master. He worked as a journalist and broadcaster. His first book of poems *Eighteen Poems* (1934) was followed by several more; *Deaths and Entrances* (1946) made his name, as a modern 'bard', romantic and rhetorical. Tales of his reckless way of life and heavy drinking added to his fame. Among his prose works are the autobiographical stories of *Portrait of the Artist as a Young Dog* (1955) and the prose-poetry play for radio, *Under Milk Wood*, on which he was working when he died. *Collected Poems 1934–52* (1952) was reprinted twelve times during the 1950s. A new edition, *The Poems of Dylan Thomas*, was published in 1971.

THE FORCE THAT THROUGH THE GREEN FUSE DRIVES THE FLOWER

The force that through the green fuse drives the flower
Drives my green age; that blasts the roots of trees
Is my destroyer.
And I am dumb to tell the crooked rose
5   My youth is bent by the same wintry fever.

The force that drives the water through the rocks
Drives my red blood; that dries the mouthing streams
Turns mine to wax.
And I am dumb to mouth unto my veins
10 How at the mountain spring the same mouth sucks.

The hand that whirls the water in the pool
Stirs the quicksand; that ropes the blowing wind
Hauls my shroud sail.
And I am dumb to tell the hanging man
15 How of my clay is made the hangman's lime.

The lips of time leech to the fountain head;
Love drips and gathers but the fallen blood
Shall calm her sores.
And I am dumb to tell a weather's wind
20   How time has ticked a heaven round the stars.

And I am dumb to tell the lover's tomb
How at my sheet goes the same crooked worm.

1933   1934

AND DEATH SHALL HAVE NO DOMINION

And death shall have no dominion.[†]
Dead men naked they shall be one
With the man in the wind and the west moon;
When their bones are picked clean and the clean bones gone,
5   They shall have stars at elbow and foot;
Though they go mad they shall be sane;
Though they sink through the sea they shall rise again;
Though lovers be lost love shall not;
And death shall have no dominion.

10   And death shall have no dominion.
Under the windings of the sea
They lying long shall not die windily;
Twisting on racks when sinews give way,
Strapped to a wheel, yet they shall not break;
15   Faith in their hands shall snap in two,
And the unicorn evils run them through;
Split all ends up they shan't crack;
And death shall have no dominion.

And death shall have no dominion.
20   No more may gulls cry at their ears
Or waves break loud on the seashores;
Where blew a flower may a flower no more
Lift its head to the blows of the rain;

And Death ... Dominion   Romans 6. 19

Though they be mad and dead as nails,
25   Heads of the characters hammer through daisies;
Break in the sun till the sun breaks down,
And death shall have no dominion.

1933   1936

FERN HILL†

Now as I was young and easy under the apple boughs
About the lilting house and happy as the grass was green,
    The night above the dingle starry,
      Time let me hail and climb
5   Golden in the heydays of his eyes,
And honoured among wagons I was prince of the apple towns
And once below a time I lordly had the trees and leaves
    Trail with daisies and barley
    Down the rivers of the windfall light.

10   And as I was green and carefree, famous among the barns
About the happy yard and singing as the farm was home,
    In the sun that is young once only,
      Time let me play and be
    Golden in the mercy of his means,
15   And green and golden I was huntsman and herdsman, the calves
Sang to my horn, the foxes on the hills barked clear and cold,
      And the sabbath rang slowly
    In the pebbles of the holy streams.

All the sun long it was running, it was lovely, the hay
20   Fields high as the house, the tunes from the chimneys, it was air
    And playing, lovely and watery
      And fire green as grass.
    And nightly under the simple stars
As I rode to sleep the owls were bearing the farm away,
25   All the moon long I heard, blessed among stables the night-jars
    Flying with the ricks, and the horses
      Flashing into the dark.

Fern Hill   the house in the Welsh countryside where Thomas spent holidays when a boy

And then to awake, and the farm, like a wanderer white
With the dew, come back, the cock on his shoulder: it was all
30   Shining, it was Adam and maiden,
        The sky gathered again
     And the sun grew round that very day.
So it must have been after the birth of the simple light
In the first, spinning place, the spellbound horses walking warm
35   Out of the whinnying green stable
        On to the fields of praise.

And honoured among foxes and pheasants by the gay house
Under the new made clouds and happy as the heart was long,
     In the sun born over and over,
40   I ran my heedless ways,
     My wishes raced through the house high hay
And nothing I cared, at my sky blue trades, that time allows
In all his tuneful turning so few and such morning songs
     Before the children green and golden
45   Follow him out of grace,

Nothing I cared, in the lamb white days, that time would take me
Up to the swallow thronged loft by the shadow of my hand,
     In the moon that is always rising,
       Nor that riding to sleep
50   I should hear him fly with the high fields
And wake to the farm forever fled from the childless land.
Oh as I was young and easy in the mercy of his means,
      Time held me green and dying
     Though I sang in my chains like the sea.

1946

Charles Causley
1917–

Charles Causley was born in Launceston, Cornwall, and educated at Launceston College and Peterborough Training College. He has taught in Cornwall since 1947. He has published several volumes of verse since his first, *Farewell, Aggie Weston* (1951), and plays, short stories and books for children. His very lively, simple poems are influenced by modern ballads; he edited *Modern Folk Ballads* (1966). *Collected Poems* appeared in 1975.

TIMOTHY WINTERS

Timothy Winters comes to school
With eyes as wide as a football pool,
Ears like bombs and teeth like splinters:
A blitz of a boy is Timothy Winters.

5   His belly is white, his neck is dark,
And his hair is an exclamation mark.
His clothes are enough to scare a crow
And through his britches the blue winds blow.

When teacher talks he won't hear a word
10   And he shoots down dead the arithmetic-bird,
He licks the patterns off his plate
And he's not even heard of the Welfare State.

Timothy Winters has bloody feet
And he lives in a house on Suez Street,
15   He sleeps in a sack on the kitchen floor
And they say there aren't boys like him any more.

Old Man Winters likes his beer
And his missus ran off with a bombardier,
Grandma sits in the grate with a gin
20   And Timothy's dosed with an aspirin.

The Welfare Worker lies awake
But the law's as tricky as a ten-foot snake,
So Timothy Winters drinks his cup
And slowly goes on growing up.

25   At Morning Prayers the Master helves†
For children less fortunate than ourselves,
And the loudest response in the room is when
Timothy Winters roars 'Amen!'

So come one angel, come on ten:
30   Timothy Winters says 'Amen
Amen amen amen amen.'
Timothy Winters, Lord.
                              Amen.

1957

---

helves   (*Cornish dialect*) lows like cattle alarmed

John Heath-Stubbs
1918–

John Francis Alexander Heath-Stubbs, born in London, was educated at Bembridge School, Worcester College for the Blind, and The Queen's College, Oxford. He has taught at universities in England, America and Egypt. Heath-Stubbs is primarily a poet but also a critic, editor, translator, historian and antiquary; he is a gifted public reader of poetry. He has published many volumes of poems since *Wounded Thammuz* (1942), including an Arthurian epic, *Artorius* (1972). A collection, *Naming the Beasts*, appeared in 1982.

NOT BEING OEDIPUS

Not being Oedipus he did not question the Sphinx,†
Nor allow it to question him. He thought it expedient
To make friends and try to influence it.
In this he entirely succeeded,

5   And continued his journey to Thebes.† The abominable thing
Now tame as a kitten (though he was not unaware
That its destructive claws were merely sheathed)
Lolloped along beside him –

To the consternation of the Reception Committee.
10   It posed a nice problem: he had certainly overcome
But not destroyed the creature – was he or was he not
Entitled to the hand of the Princess

Dowager Jocasta? Not being Oedipus
He saw it as a problem too. For frankly he was not
15   By natural instinct at all attracted to her.
The question was soon solved –

---

the Sphinx when Oedipus, in Greek legend and drama, solved the Sphinx's riddle it killed itself

Thebes here Oedipus in ignorance killed his father, King Laius, and married his mother, Queen Jocasta

Solved itself, you might say; for while they argued
The hungry Sphinx, which had not been fed all day,
Sneaked off unobserved, penetrated the royal apartments,
20   And softly consumed the lady.

So he ascended the important throne of Cadmus,[†]
Beginning a distinguished and uneventful reign.
Celibate, he had nothing to fear from ambitious sons;
Although he was lonely at nights,

25   With only the Sphinx, curled up upon his eiderdown.
Its body exuded a sort of unearthly warmth
(Though in fact cold-blooded) but its capacity
For affection was strictly limited.

Granted, after his death it was inconsolable,
30   And froze into its own stone effigy
Upon his tomb. But this was self-love, really –
It felt it had failed in its mission.

While Thebes, by common consent of the people, adopted
His extremely liberal and reasonable constitution,
35   Which should have enshrined his name – but not being Oedipus,
It vanished from history, as from legend.

1939

TO A POET A THOUSAND YEARS HENCE[†]

I who am dead a thousand years
And wrote this crabbed post-classic screed
Transmit it to you – though with doubts
That you possess the skill to read,

5   Who, with your pink, mutated eyes,
Crouched in the radioactive swamp,
Beneath a leaking shelter, scan
These lines beside a flickering lamp;

Cadmus   Phoenician founder of Thebes   *To a Poet*   see p. 292

Or in some plastic paradise
10   Of pointless gadgets, if you dwell,
And finding all your wants supplied
Do not suspect it may be Hell.

But does our art of words survive –
Do bards within that swamp rehearse
15   Tales of the twentieth century,
Nostalgic, in rude epic verse?

Or do computers churn it out –
In lieu of songs of War and Love,
Neat slogans by the State endorsed
20   And prayers to *Them*, who sit above?

How shall we conquer? – all our pride
Fades like a summer sunset's glow:
Who will read me when I am gone –
For who reads Elroy Flecker now?

25   Unless, dear poet, you were born,
Like me, a deal behind your time,
There is no reason you should read,
And much less understand, this rhyme.

1978

HORNBILLS IN NORTHERN NIGERIA

(*To Hilary Fry*)

As if their great bone-spongey beaks were too heavy,
A party of Grey Hornbills flops overhead
Through the hot, humid air. These are on migration –
('Well, you tell me where,' the zoologist said) –

5   They emit high, whining, almost gull-like cries,
Seeming, someone remarks, as if they were mass-produced
Off the production-line of an inferior factory.
But this is not apt. Has it not been deduced

The grotesque Hornbill stems from an ancient race
10   By the fossil testimony of a small, stony word,
Petrified bone-fragment in alluvial clay?
Look again, you witness a prehistoric bird;

On miocene and pliocene landscapes has gazed
The cold, saurian, humanly eyelashed eye,
15   Which looks out now over the airfield,
Where forms of camels – not incongruous – stray.

And ceremonial trumpets welcome the guest who comes
By Comet or Viscount,[†] out of the modern century;
The place is not distant from the mediaeval walls,
20   Nor the satellite-tracking station (Project Mercury).

Here unashamed, anthropomorphic gods send rain;
And dawn, like history, flames a violent birth,
Out of a night with crickets and toads articulate,
For black bodies pushing ground-nuts into the red earth.

1964   1979

Comet or Viscount   aeroplanes for long journeys

Iris Murdoch
1919–

Iris Jean Murdoch was born in Dublin and educated at Badminton College and Somerville College, Oxford. She was an Assistant Principal at the Treasury during the War. From 1948 to 1961 she was Fellow and philosophy tutor at St Anne's College, Oxford. She married the critic John Bayley in 1956. *Sartre: Romantic Rationalist* (1953) was her first book. *Under the Net* (1954) was the first of more than twenty thoughtful and entertaining novels. *The Bell* (1958) has been the most popular. *The Fire and the Sun: Why Plato Banished the Artists* (1977), based on her Romanes Lecture in 1976, shows the authority and charm with which she can present ideas.

From THE FIRE AND THE SUN
[Praising Art to Plato]

Art is about the pilgrimage from appearance to reality (the subject of every good play and novel) and exemplifies in spite of Plato what his philosophy teaches concerning the therapy of the soul. This is the 'universal', the high concern which Tolstoy said was the proper province
5 of the artist. The divine (intelligent) cause persuades the necessary cause so as to bring about the best possible. It is the task of mortals (as artists and as men) to understand the necessary for the sake of the intelligible, to see in a pure just light the hardness of the real properties of the world, the effects of the wandering causes, why good purposes are
10 checked and where the mystery of the random has to be accepted. It is not easy to do justice to this hardness and this randomness without either smoothing them over with fantasy or exaggerating them into (cynical) absurdity. Indeed 'the absurd' in art, often emerging as an attempt to defeat easy fantasy, may merely provide it with a sophisticated
15 disguise. The great artist, while showing us what is not saved, implicitly shows us what salvation means. Of course the Demiurge† is attempting against insuperable difficulties to create a harmonious and just world. The (good) human artist, whom Plato regards as such a base caricature,

---

the Demiurge   the Creator in Plato's theology

is trying to portray the partially failed world as it is, and in doing so to
20   produce something pleasing and beautiful. This involves an intelligent
disciplined understanding of what may be called the structural problems
of the Demiurge. There is a 'sublime absurd', comic or tragic, which
depends on this insight into where the 'faults' come. (Both *2 Henry IV*
III.ii and *King Lear* v.iii.) Forgivably or unforgivably, there is a partly
25   intelligible causality of sin. The good artist helps us to see the place of
necessity in human life, what must be endured, what makes and breaks,
and to purify our imagination so as to contemplate the real world
(usually veiled by anxiety and fantasy) including what is terrible and
absurd. Plato said at *Republic*[†] 395a that no one can write both comedy
30   and tragedy. As the *Symposium*[†] ends Socrates is telling Agathon and
Aristophanes[†] that this can be done. One would like to have an account
of this conversation. Plato, with a perverse negligence, never favours
us with any serious literary criticism.

Moral philosophers, attempting to analyse human frailty, have
35   produced some pretty unrealistic schemata, usually because they were
trying to do too many things at the same time. The contemporary
philosopher is in this respect more modest. The question, at what level
of generality am I to operate? is of course one which faces both the
artist and the philosopher. Great discoveries are made at great levels of
40   generality, as when Plato subjects the profound idea that no one errs
willingly to a number of transformations within a general picture of
the human soul as knower and agent. On the other hand, the lack of
detail can leave the reader unconvinced that he is really seeing 'human
life' and not the 'ghostly ballet of bloodless categories', the vision of
45   which haunted another and more recent Platonist, F. H. Bradley.[†] To
take one example, Plato, wishing to make the different levels of the
soul correspond to different tasks in society and different types of
state, connects his concept of θγμοειδές [lit.: soul-image], the central
transformational region of the soul, especially with honour and
50   ambition, and thereby oversimplifies a concept which is essential to his
analysis of moral change. The *Republic*, like many other great ethical
treatises, is deficient in an account of positive evil. The 'tyrannical man'
has to prove too much. A portrayal of moral reflection and moral

---

Republic Plato's treatise of government. Iris
Murdoch is considering its argument that
artists, including creative writers, should be
excluded from the ideal city-state. Her title
comes from *Republic* VII where the knowledge
of this world is compared to cave shadows
cast by a fire
Symposium . . . Aristophanes Socrates (469–
399 BC) taught philosophy to Plato (*c.* 428–
c. 348 BC). Plato wrote *Dialogues* in which

Socrates debates philosophy with friends.
The *Symposium* ('The Banquet' – given in
honour of the tragedian Agathon) is a
discussion of love. Other *Dialogues*
mentioned in this extract are *Philebus*,
Timaeus, *Theaetetus* and *Phaedrus*.
Aristophanes (448–*c.* 380 BC) was the great
Athenian comic dramatist
F. H. Bradley (1846–1924), metaphysician;
author of *Appearance and Reality* (1893)

change (degeneration, improvement) is the most important part of any
55   system of ethics. The explanation of our fallibility in such matters as
seeing the worse as the better is more informatively (though of course
less systematically) carried out by poets, playwrights, and novelists. It
has taken philosophy a long time to acknowledge this: the famous
'quarrel' is indeed of long standing, and the suspicion that art is
60   fundamentally frivolous. It is only comparatively recently that moral
philosophers have condescended to enlist the aid of literature as a mode
of explanation.

The sight of evil is confusing, and it is a subject on which it is hard
to generalize because any analysis demands such a battery of value
65   judgements. One would like to think that the just man sees the unjust
man clearly. ('God sees him clearly'.) Art is (often too) jauntily at home
with evil and quick to beautify it. Arguably however, good literature is
uniquely able publicly to clarify evil, and emulate the just man's private
vision without, such is his privilege, the artist having to be just except
70   in his art. That this separation is possible seems a fact of experience.
Art accepts and enjoys the ambiguity of the whole man, and great
artists can seem to 'use' their own vices for creative purposes without
apparent damage to their art. This mystery belongs indeed to the region
of the unmeasured and unlimited. Plato understands what criticism
75   must be constantly aware of, how the bad side of human nature is
secretly, precariously, at work in art. There is a lot of secret cruelty
there and if the art is good enough (consider Dante, or Dostoevsky) it
may be hard to decide when the disciplined 'indulgence' of the cruelty
damages the merit of the work or harms the client. But to see misery
80   and evil justly is one of the heights of aesthetic endeavour and one
which is surely sometimes reached. How this becomes beautiful is a
mystery which may seem very close to some of the central and most
lively obscurities in Plato's own thought. (The divine cause is always
touching the necessary cause.) Shakespeare makes not only splendour
85   but beauty out of the malevolence of Iago and the intolerable death of
Cordelia, as Homer does out of the miseries of a pointless war and the
stylish ruthlessness of Achilles. Art can rarely, but without authority,
show how we learn from pain, swept by the violence of divine grace
toward an unwilling wisdom, as described in the first chorus of the
90   *Agamemnon* in words which somehow remind us of Plato, who
remained (it appears) so scandalously indifferent to the merits of
Aeschylus.[†] (A case of envy?) And of course art can reveal without
explaining and its justice can also be playful. The docility of necessity

---

Aeschylus (525–456 BC) the earliest of the
great Athenian dramatists; his *Agamemnon*,
following the allusions to *King Lear* and
Othello, and to Homer's *Iliad*, is a reminder
that Plato was familiar with art of the highest
order

to intelligence may be as vividly evident in non-mimetic non-conceptual
95 art ('pure contraption' and 'absolute gift'), which fleetingly illuminates
deep structures of reality, as if the artist could indeed penetrate the
creative reverie of the Demiurge where truth and play mysteriously,
inextricably mingle.

One might, in praising art to Plato, even add that if there is, as an
100 effective persuasion, an ontological proof (Plato's main idea after all),
art provides a very plausible version of it. Perhaps in general art *proves*
more than philosophy can. Familiarity with an art form and the
development of taste is an education in the beautiful which involves
the often largely instinctive, increasingly confident sorting out of what
105 is good, what is pure, what is profoundly and justly imagined, what
rings true, from what is trivial or shallow or in some way fake, self-
indulgent, pretentious, sentimental, meretriciously obscure, and so on.
Most derogatory critical terms impute some kind of falsehood, and on
the other hand (Keats) 'what the imagination seizes as beauty must be
110 truth.' Bad art is a lie about the world, and what is by contrast seen as
good is in some important evident sense seen as *ipso facto* [by that very
fact] true and as expressive of reality: the sense in which Seurat[†] is
better than Burne-Jones,[†] Keats than Swinburne, Dickens than Wilkie
Collins,[†] etc. etc. Plato says in the *Philebus* that an experience of
115 pleasure may be infected with falsity. Learning to detect the false in art
and enjoy the true is part of a life-long education in moral discernment.
This does not mean living in an aesthetic cloister. Good art, however
complex, presents an evident combination of purity and realism: and if
we think at once of moral teachings which do the same (the Gospels,
120 St Augustine, Julian of Norwich,[†] parts of Plato), it has to be admitted
that these too are in their own perfectly natural way art. The development
of any skill increases our sense of (necessity) reality. Learning an art is
learning all sorts of strange tricks, but fundamentally it is learning how
to make a formal utterance of a perceived truth and render it splendidly
125 worthy of a trained purified attention without falsifying it in the process.
When Plato says (*Philebus* 48d) that to enjoy the ridiculous is to obey
the command: do not know thyself, he is using (though perversely) an
important principle of literary criticism: that which militates against
self-knowledge is suspect. To know oneself *in the world* (as part of it,
130 subject to it, connected with it) is to have the firmest grasp of the real.
This is the humble 'sense of proportion' which Plato connects with
virtue. Strong agile realism, which is of course not photographic
naturalism, the non-sentimental, non-meanly-personal imaginative grasp

---

Seurat ... Collins the painter Sir Edward
Burne-Jones (1833–98) is as obviously
inferior to the French Impressionist Georges
Seurat (1859–91) as the novelist Wilkie

Collins (1824–89) is to Dickens; Swinburne's
poetry is out of fashion
Julian of Norwich mystical writer of the
fourteenth century

of the subject-matter is something which can be recognized as value in
135   all the arts, and it is this which gives that special unillusioned pleasure
which is the liberating whiff of reality; when in high free play the
clarified imaginative attention of the creative mind is fixed upon its
object. Of course art is playful, but its play is serious. τῆς σποτδῆς
ἀδελφή παιδιά [play is the sister of earnestness]. Freud says that the
140   opposite of play is not work but reality. This may be true of fantasy
play but not of the playfulness of good art which delightedly seeks and
reveals the real. Thus in practice we increasingly relate one concept to
another, and see beauty as the artful use of form to illuminate truth,
and celebrate reality; and we can then experience what Plato spoke of
145   but wished to separate from art: the way in to desire the beautiful is to
desire the real and the good.

It may be tempting here to say that the disciplined understanding,
the just discernment, of the good artist must depend (if one wants to
play further with the *Timaeus* myth) upon some kind of *separate* moral
150   certainty. Again the metaphor of vision: a source of light. However it
is difficult to press the idea beyond the status of a tautology. Good
artists can be bad men; the virtue may, as I said earlier, reside entirely
in the work, the just vision be attainable only there. After all, however
much we idolize each other, we are limited specialized animals.
155   Moreover, even the work itself may be less perfect than it seems. We
are creatures of a day, nothing much. We do not understand ourselves,
we lack reality, what we have and know is not ὄντως ὄν [the really
real], but merely ὄν πῶς [the seeming real]. We are cast in the roles of
Shallow and Silence;† and must not, in favour of art or philosophy,
160   protest too much. (The best in this kind are but shadows, and the worst
are no worse, if imagination amend them.†) Because of the instinctive
completing activity of the client's mind, its 'unlimited' cooperation with
the artist, we often do not see how unfinished even great work may be;
and if the artist presses this upon our attention we are shocked since
165   we so much want to believe in perfection. Great works of art often do
seem like perfect particulars, and we seem here to enjoy that 'extra'
knowledge which is denied to us at the end of the *Theaetetus*. But
because of the muddle of human life and the ambiguity and playfulness
of aesthetic form, art can at best only explain partly, only reveal almost;
170   and of course any complex work contains impurities and accidents
which we choose to ignore. Even the Demiurge will never entirely
understand. Although art can be so good for us, it does contain some
of those elements of illusion out of which its detractors make so much
of their case. The pierced structure of the art object whereby its sense

---

Shallow and Silence   2 Henry IV iii,2
The best . . . amend them   A Midsummer Night's Dream v.1.213

175   flows into life is an essential part of its mortal nature. Even at its most
       exquisite art is incomplete. Simone Weil,[†] that admirable Platonist, said
       that a poem is beautiful in so far as the poet's thought is fixed upon
       the ineffable. Art, like (in Plato's view) philosophy, hovers about in the
       very fine air which we breathe just beyond what has been expressed.
180   One need not, however, enter into metaphysical or psychological
       arguments to diminish art or to defend it either. Its simpler solider
       merits are obvious: a free art is an essential aspect of a free society, as
       a degraded lying art is a function of a tyrannical one. Art as the great
       general universal informant is an obvious rival, not necessarily a hostile
185   one, to philosophy and indeed to science, and Plato never did justice to
       the unique truth-conveying capacities of art. The good or even decent
       writer does not just 'imitate doctors' talk', but attempts to understand
       and portray the doctors' 'world', and these pictures, however modest,
       of other 'worlds' are interesting and valuable. The spiritual ambiguity
190   of art, its connection with the 'limitless' unconscious, its use of irony,
       its interest in evil, worried Plato. But the very ambiguity and voracious
       ubiquitousness of art is its characteristic freedom. Art, especially
       literature, is a great hall of reflection where we can all meet and where
       everything under the sun can be examined and considered. For this
195   reason it is feared and attacked by dictators, and by authoritarian
       moralists such as the one under discussion. The artist is a great
       informant, at least a gossip, at best a sage, and much loved in both
       roles. He lends to the elusive particular a local habitation and a name.[†]
       He sets the world in order and gives us hypothetical hierarchies and
200   intermediate images: like the dialectician he mediates between the one
       and the many; and though he may artfully confuse us, on the whole he
       instructs us. Art is far and away the most educational thing we have,
       far more so than its rivals, philosophy and theology and science. The
       pierced nature of the work of art, its limitless connection with ordinary
205   life, even its defencelessness against its client, are part of its characteristic
       availability and freedom. The demands of science and philosophy and
       ultimately of religion are extremely rigorous. It is just as well that there
       is a high substitute for the spiritual and the speculative life: that few
       get to the top morally or intellectually is no less than the truth. Art is a
210   great international human language, it is for all. Of course art has no
       formal 'social role' and artists ought not to feel that they must 'serve
       their society'. They will automatically serve it if they attend to truth
       and try to produce the best art (make the most beautiful things) of
       which they are capable. The connection of truth with beauty means
215   that art which succeeds in being for itself also succeeds in being for

---

Simone Weil (1909–43) French philosopher   a local habitation . . . name   A Midsummer
and moralist   Night's Dream v.1.17

everybody. And even without the guarantee of a Platonic aesthetic, art need not be too humble. Hear the words of Jane Austen (*Northanger Abbey*, Chapter V). ' "And what are you reading Miss ——?" "Oh, it is only a novel", replies the young lady; while she lays down her book
220   with affected indifference, or momentary shame. – "It is only Cecilia, or Camilla, or Belinda";[†] or, in short, only some work in which the greatest powers of the mind are displayed, in which the most thorough knowledge of human nature, the happiest delineation of its varieties, the liveliest effusion of wit and humour are conveyed to the world in
225   the best chosen language.'

The most obvious paradox in the problem under consideration is that Plato is a great artist. It is not perhaps to be imagined that the paradox troubled him too much. Scholars in the land of posterity assemble the work and invent the problems. Plato had other troubles,
230   many of them political. He fought a long battle against sophistry and magic, yet produced some of the most memorable images in European philosophy: the Cave, the charioteer, the cunning homeless Eros, the Demiurge cutting the *Anima Mundi* [Soul of the World] into strips and stretching it out crosswise. He kept emphasizing the imageless
235   remoteness of the Good, yet kept returning in his exposition to the most elaborate uses of art. The dialogue form itself is artful and indirect and abounds in ironical and playful devices. Of course the statements made by art escape into the free ambiguity of human life. Art cheats the religious vocation at the last moment and is inimical to philosophical
240   categories. Yet neither philosophy nor theology can do without it; there has to be a pact between them, like the pact in the *Philebus* between reason and pleasure.

Plato says (*Phaedrus*, Letter VIII) that no sensible man will commit his thought to words and that a man's thoughts are likely to be better
245   than his writings. Without raising philosophical problems about what a man's thoughts *are*, one may reply that the discipline of committing oneself to clarified public form is proper and rewarding: the final and best discoveries are often made in the actual formulation of the statement. The careful responsible skilful use of words is our highest
250   instrument of thought and one of our highest modes of being: an idea which might seem obvious but is not now by any means universally accepted. There may in theoretical studies, as in art, be so-called ultra-verbal insights at any level; but to call ultimate truth ineffable is to utter a quasi-religious principle which should not be turned round
255   against the careful verbalization of humbler truths. Nor did Plato in

---

Cecilia . . . Belinda Jane Austen admired the novelists Fanny Burney (1752–1840), author of *Cecilia* (1782) and *Camilla* (1796), and Maria Edgeworth (1768–1849), author of *Belinda* (1801)

practice do this. He wanted what he more than once mentions, immortality through art; he felt and indulged the artist's desire to produce unified, separable, formal, durable objects. He was also the master, indeed, the inventor, of a pure calm relaxed mode of philosophi-
260 cal exposition which is a high literary form and a model forever. Of course he used metaphor, but philosophy needs metaphor and metaphor is basic; how basic is the most basic philosophical question. Plato also had no doubt a strong personal motive which prompted him to write. Socrates (*Theaetetus* 210c) called himself a barren midwife. Plato often
265 uses imagines of paternity. Art launches philosophy as it launches religion; and it was necessary for Plato, as it was for the evangelists, to write if the Word was not to be sterile and the issue of the Father was to be recognized as legitimate.

Plato feared the consolations of art. He did not offer a consoling
270 theology. His psychological realism depicted God as subjecting mankind to a judgement as relentless as that of the old Zeus,[†] although more just. A finely meshed moral causality determines the fate of the soul. That the movement of the saving of Eros is toward an impersonal pictureless void is one of the paradoxes of a complete religion. To
275 present the idea of God at all, even as myth, is a consolation, since it is impossible to defend this image against the prettifying attentions of art. Art will mediate and adorn, and develop magical structures to conceal the absence of God or his distance. We live now amid the collapse of many such structures, and as religion and metaphysics in the West
280 withdraw from the embraces of art, we are it might seem being forced to become mystics through the lack of any imagery which could satisfy the mind. Sophistry and magic break down at intervals, but they never go away and there is no end to their collusion with art and to the consolations which, perhaps fortunately for the human race, they can
285 provide; and art, like writing and like Eros,[†] goes on existing for better and for worse.

1976   1977

---

the old Zeus principal deity of traditional
  Greek pantheism
Eros Divine Love. Iris Murdoch writes earlier

in the essay, 'Plato's Eros is a principle which connects the commonest human desire to the highest morality'

D. J. Enright

1920–

Dennis Joseph Enright was born in Leamington and educated at Leamington College and Downing College, Cambridge. *Memoirs of a Mendicant Professor* (1969) is an entertaining account of his career as a teacher of English literature overseas; he taught in Egypt, Spain and West Berlin, and held Chairs in Bangkok (1957–9) and Singapore (1960–70). His *Collected Poems* appeared in 1981.

UNIVERSITY EXAMINATIONS IN EGYPT

The air is thick with nerves and smoke: pens tremble in sweating hands:
Domestic police flit in and out, with smelling salts and aspirin:
And servants, grave-faced but dirty, pace the aisles,
With coffee, Players and Coca-Cola.

5   Was it like this in my day, at my place? Memory boggles
Between the aggressive fly and curious ant – but did I really
Pause in my painful flight to light a cigarette or swallow drugs?

The nervous eye, patrolling these hot unhappy victims,
Flinches at the symptoms of a year's hard teaching –
10   'Falstaff indulged in drinking and sexcess', and then,
'Doolittle was a dusty man' and 'Dr Jonson edited the Yellow Book.'

Culture and aspirin: the urgent diploma, the straining brain – all in the
    evening fall
To tric-trac[†] in the café, to Hollywood in the picture-house:
15   Behind, like tourist posters, the glamour of laws and committees,
Wars for freedom, cheap textbooks, national aspirations –

---

tric-trac   a game like backgammon

And, further still and very faint, the foreign ghost of happy Shakespeare,
Keats who really loved things, Akhenaton[†] who adored the Sun,
And Goethe who never thought of Thought.

1953

HISTORY OF WORLD LANGUAGES

They spoke the loveliest of languages.
Their tongues entwined in Persian, ran
And fused. Words kissed, a phrase embraced,
Verbs conjugated sweetly. Verse began.
5   So Eve and Adam lapped each other up
The livelong day, the lyric night.

Of all known tongues most suasive
Was the Snake's. His oratory was Arabic,
Whose simile and rhetoric seduced her
10   ('Sovran of creatures, universal dame').
So potent its appeal –
The apple asked for eating,
To eat it she was game.

Now Gabriel turned up, the scholars say,
15   Shouting in Turkish. Harsh and menacing,
But late. And sounds like swords were swung.
Fault was underlined, and crime defined.
The gate slammed with the clangour of his tongue.

Eden was gone. A lot of other things
20   Were won. Or done. Or suffered.
Thorns and thistles, dust and dearth.
The words were all before them, which to choose.
Their tongues now turned to English,
With its colonies of twangs.
25   And they were down to earth.

1978

Akhenaton Amenhotep IV, a Pharaoh of the
eighteenth dynasty, believed in one god
    manifested in the sun and took the name
Akhenaton ('Good to Aten, the sun')

Keith Douglas
1920–44

Keith Castellan Douglas, born in Tunbridge Wells and educated at Christ's Hospital and Merton College, Oxford, was the most gifted poet of the Second World War. *Selected Poems* (1943) was the only book published in his lifetime. His prose narrative *From Alamein to Zem Zem* appeared in 1946 and *Collected Poems* in 1951; Desmond Graham edited *The Complete Poems* (1979). Douglas was killed in Normandy.

ON A RETURN FROM EGYPT

To stand here in the wings of Europe
disheartened, I have come away
from the sick land where in the sun lay
the gentle sloe-eyed murderers
5   of themselves, exquisites under a curse;
here to exercise my depleted fury.

For the heart is a coal, growing colder
when jewelled cerulean seas change
into grey rocks, grey water-fringe,
10   sea and sky altering like a cloth
till colour and sheen are gone both:
cold is an opiate of the soldier.

And all my endeavours are unlucky explorers
come back, abandoning the expedition;
15   the specimens, the lilies of ambition
still spring in their climate, still unpicked:
but time, time is all I lacked
to find them, as the great collectors before me.

The next month, then, is a window
20   and with a crash I'll split the glass.
Behind it stands one I must kiss,
person of love or death

a person or a wraith,
I fear what I shall find.

March–April 1944   1946

SIMPLIFY ME WHEN I'M DEAD

Remember me when I am dead
and simplify me when I'm dead.

As the processes of earth
strip off the colour and the skin
5   take the brown hair and blue eye

and leave me simpler than at birth,
when hairless I came howling in
as the moon came in the cold sky.

Of my skeleton perhaps
10   so stripped, a learned man will say
'He was of such a type and intelligence,' no more.

Thus when in a year collapse
particular memories, you may
deduce, from the long pain I bore

15   the opinions I held, who was my foe
and what I left, even my appearance
but incidents will be no guide.

Time's wrong-way telescope will show
a minute man ten years hence
20   and by distance simplified.

Through that lens see if I seem
substance or nothing: of the world
deserving mention of charitable oblivion

not by momentary spleen
25   or love into decision hurled,
leisurely arrive at an opinion.

Remember me when I am dead
and simplify me when I'm dead.

May 1941   1951

VERGISSMEINNICHT†

Three weeks gone and the combatants gone
returning over the nightmare ground
we found the place again, and found
the soldier sprawling in the sun.

5   The frowning barrel of his gun
overshadowing. As we came on
that day, he hit my tank with one
like the entry of a demon.

Look. Here in the gunpit spoil
10   the dishonoured picture of his girl
who has put: *Steffi.*† *Vergissmeinnicht*
in a copybook gothic script.

We see him almost with content,
abased, and seeming to have paid
15   and mocked at by his own equipment
that's hard and good when he's decayed.

But she would weep to see today
how on his skin the swart flies move;
the dust upon the paper eye
20   and the burst stomach like a cave.

For here the lover and killer are mingled
who had one body and one heart.
And death who had the soldier singled
has done the lover mortal hurt.

May–June 1943 Tunisia   1951

Vergissmeinnicht   (German) Forget-me-not   *Steffi*   a girl's name

Kingsley Amis
1922–

Born in Clapham, Kingsley Amis attended the City of London School and read English at St John's College, Oxford. He taught English, at University College, Swansea, and then at Peterhouse, Cambridge, until 1963. He made his name as an irreverent 'angry young man' with his very funny first novel, *Lucky Jim* (1954), set in a provincial university. Since then he has published more than a dozen novels. Many are vituperative satires on modern English folly and pretentiousness: *Take a Girl Like You* (1960), *Girl 20* (1971) and *Jake's Thing* (1978) are among the best of these. But Amis has written successfully in several genres. *Colonel Sun* (under the pseudonym 'Robert Markham', 1968) is a James Bond story. *The Green Man* (1969) mixes social satire and supernatural invention. *The Riverside Villas Murder* (1973) is an 'armchair mystery' set in the 1930s. *The Alteration* (1976) creates a twentieth-century world in which Europe is still ruled by the Catholic Church. *Russian Hide and Seek* (1980) shows us England fifty years after the Soviet Conquest. *The Old Devils* (1986) won the Booker Prize for fiction. Amis is also a poet of craft, clarity and colloquial vigour (*Collected Poems 1944–1979*, 1979), an editor (*The New Oxford Book of Light Verse*, 1978), and a decisive critic, scornful of fashion. *What Became of Jane Austen? and Other Questions* (1970), a collection of reviews, treats various new trends in literature to spirited derision.

In this extract the young history lecturer, Jim Dixon, has been invited to spend a musical weekend at the home of Welch, his professor.

From LUCKY JIM

[Ordeal by Music]

'Of course, this sort of music's not intended for an audience, you see,' Welch said as he handed the copies round. 'The fun's all in the singing. Everybody's got a real tune to sing – a real tune,' he repeated violently. 'You could say, really, that polyphony got to its highest point, its peak,

5   at that period, and has been on the decline ever since. You've only got
       to look at the part-writing in things like, well, *Onward, Christian
       Soldiers*, the hymn, which is a typical . . . a typical . . .'
       'We're all waiting, Ned,' Mrs Welch said from the piano. She played
       a slow arpeggio, sustaining it with the pedal. 'All right, everybody?'
10   A soporific droning filled the air round Dixon as the singers hummed
       their notes to one another. Mrs Welch rejoined them on the low
       platform that had been built at one end of the music-room, taking up
       her stand by Margaret, the other soprano. A small bullied-looking
       woman with unabundant brown hair was the only contralto. Next to
15   Dixon was Cecil Goldsmith, a colleague of his in the College History
       Department, whose tenor voice held enough savage power, especially
       above middle C, to obliterate whatever noises Dixon might feel himself
       impelled to make. Behind him and to one side were three basses, one a
       local composer, another an amateur violinist occasionally summoned
20   at need by the city orchestra, the third Evan Johns.
           Dixon ran his eye along the lines of black dots, which seemed to go
       up and down a good deal, and was able to assure himself that everyone
       was going to have to sing all the time. He'd had a bad setback twenty
       minutes ago in some Brahms rubbish which began with ten seconds or
25   so of unsupported tenor – more accurately, of unsupported Goldsmith,
       who'd twice dried up in face of a tricky interval and left him opening
       and shutting his mouth in silence. He now cautiously reproduced the
       note Goldsmith was humming and found the effect pleasing rather than
       the reverse. Why hadn't they had the decency to ask him if he'd like to
30   join in, instead of driving him up on to this platform arrangement and
       forcing sheets of paper into his hand?
           The madrigal began at the bidding of Welch's arthritic forefinger.
       Dixon kept his head down, moved his mouth as little as possible
       consistent with being unmistakably seen to move it, and looked through
35   the words the others were singing. 'When from my love I looked for
       love, and kind affections due,' he read, 'too well I found her vows to
       prove most faithless and untrue. But when I did ask her why . . .' He
       looked over at Margaret, who was singing away happily enough – she
       turned out regularly during the winter with the choir of the local
40   Conservative Association – and wondered what changes in their
       circumstances and temperaments would be necessary to make the words
       of the madrigal apply, however remotely, to himself and her. She'd
       made vows to him, or avowals anyway, which was perhaps all the
       writer had meant. But if he'd meant what he seemed to mean by 'kind
45   affections due', then Dixon had never 'looked for' any of these from
       Margaret. Perhaps he should: after all, people were doing it all the
       time. It was a pity she wasn't a bit better-looking. One of these days,
       though, he would try, and see what happened.

'Yet by, and by, they'll arl, deny, arnd say 'twas *bart* in jast,'
50   Goldsmith sang tremulously and very loudly. It was the last phrase;
Dixon kept his mouth open while Welch's finger remained aloft, then
shut it with a little flick of the head he'd seen singers use as the finger
swept sideways. All seemed pleased with the performance and anxious
for another of the same sort. 'Yes, well, this next one's what they called
55   a ballet. Of course, they didn't mean what we mean by the similar . . .
Rather a well-known one, this. It's called *Now is the Month of Maying*.
Now if you'll all just . . .'
A bursting snuffle of laughter came from Dixon's left rear. He glanced
round to see Johns's pallor rent by a grin. The large short-lashed eyes
60   were fixed on him. 'What's the joke?' he asked. If Johns were laughing
at Welch, Dixon was prepared to come in on Welch's side.
'You'll see,' Johns said. He went on looking at Dixon. 'You'll see,'
he added, grinning.
In less than a minute Dixon did see, and clearly. Instead of the
65   customary four parts, this piece employed five. The third and fourth
lines of music from the top had *Tenor I* and *Tenor II* written against
them; moreover, there was some infantile fa-la-la-la stuff on the second
page with numerous gaps in the individual parts. Even Welch's ear
might be expected to record the complete absence of one of the parts
70   in such circumstances. It was much too late now for Dixon to explain
that he hadn't really meant it when he'd said, half an hour before, that
he could read music 'after a fashion'; much too late to transfer allegiance
to the basses. Nothing short of an epileptic fit could get him out of this.
'You'd better take first tenor, Jim,' Goldsmith said; 'the second's a
75   bit tricky.'
Dixon nodded bemusedly, hardly hearing further laughter from Johns.
Before he could cry out, they were past the piano-ritual and the droning
and into the piece. He flapped his lips to: 'Each with his bonny lass, a-
a-seated on the grass: fa-la-la la, fa-la-la-la-la-la la la-la . . .' but Welch
80   had stopped waving his finger, was holding it stationary in the air. 'The
singing died. 'Oh, tenors,' Welch began; 'I didn't seem to hear . . .'
An irregular knocking on the door at the far end of the room was at
once followed by the bursting-open of this door and the entry of a tall
man wearing a lemon-yellow sportscoat, all three buttons of which
85   were fastened, and displaying a large beard which came down further
on one side than on the other, half-hiding a vine-patterned tie. Dixon
guessed with surging exultation that this must be the pacifist painting
Bertrand whose arrival with his girl had been heralded, with typical
clangour, by Welch every few minutes since tea-time. It was an arrival
90   which must surely prove an irritant sooner or later, but for the moment
it served as the best possible counter-irritant to the disastrous madrigals.
Even as Dixon thought this, the senior Welches left their posts and

went to greet their son, followed more slowly by the others who, perhaps finding the chance of a break not completely unwelcome, broke
95   into conversation as they moved. Dixon delightedly lit a cigarette, finding himself alone: the amateur violinist had got hold of Margaret; Goldsmith and the local composer were talking to Carol, Goldsmith's wife, who'd refused, with enviable firmness, to do more than sit and listen to the singing from an armchair near the fireplace; Johns was
100 doing something technical at the piano. Dixon moved down the room through the company and leaned against the wall at the end by the door where the bookshelves were. Placed here, savouring his cigarette, he was in a good position to observe Bertrand's girl when she came in, slowly and hesitantly, a few seconds later, and stood unnoticed, except
105 by him, just inside the room.

In a few more seconds Dixon had noticed all he needed to notice about this girl: the combination of fair hair, straight and cut short, with brown eyes and no lipstick, the strict set of the mouth and the square shoulders, the large breasts and the narrow waist, the
110 premeditated simplicity of the wine-coloured corduroy skirt and the unornamented white linen blouse. The sight of her seemed an irresistible attack on his own habits, standards, and ambitions: something designed to put him in his place for good. The notion that women like this were never on view except as the property of men like Bertrand was so
115 familiar to him that it had long since ceased to appear an injustice. The huge class that contained Margaret was destined to provide his own womenfolk: those in whom the intention of being attractive could sometimes be made to get itself confused with performance; those with whom a too-tight skirt, a wrong-coloured, or no, lipstick, even an ill-
120 executed smile could instantly discredit that illusion beyond apparent hope of renewal. But renewal always came: a new sweater would somehow scale down the large feet, generosity revivify the brittle hair, a couple of pints site positive charm in talk of the London stage or French food.
125 The girl turned her head and found Dixon staring at her. His diaphragm contracted with fright; she drew herself up with a jerk like a soldier standing easy called to the stand-at-ease position. They looked at each other for a moment, until, just as Dixon's scalp was beginning to tingle, a high, baying voice called 'Ah, there you are, darling; step
130 this way, if you please, and be introduced to the throng' and Bertrand strode up the room to meet her, throwing Dixon a brief hostile glance. Dixon didn't like him doing that; the only action he required from Bertrand was an apology, humbly offered, for his personal appearance.

Dixon had been too distressed at the sight of Bertrand's girl to want
135 to be introduced to her, and kept out of the way for a time; then he moved down and started talking to Margaret and the amateur violinist.

Bertrand dominated the central group, doing a lot of laughing as he
told some lengthy story; his girl watched him intently, as if he might
ask her later to summarize its drift. Coffee and cakes, intended to
140 replace an evening meal, were brought in, and getting enough of
these for himself and Margaret kept Dixon fully occupied. Then
Welch came up to him and said, inexplicably enough: 'Ah, Dixon,
come along now. I want you to meet my son Bertrand and his . . .
his . . . Come along.'
145 With Margaret at his side, Dixon was soon confronted by the two
people Welch wanted him to meet and by Evan Johns. 'This is Mr
Dixon and Miss Peel,' Welch said, and drew the Goldsmiths away.
Before a silence could fall, Margaret said 'Are you down here for
long, Mr Welch?' and Dixon felt grateful to her for being there and for
150 always having something to say.
Bertrand's jaws snatched successfully at a piece of food which had
been within an ace of eluding them. He went on chewing for a moment,
pondering. 'I doubt it,' he said at last. 'Upon consideration I feel it
incumbent upon me to doubt it. I have miscellaneous concerns in
155 London that need my guiding hand.' He smiled among his beard, from
which he now began brushing crumbs. 'But it's very pleasant to come
down here and to know that the torch of culture is still in a state of
combustion in the provinces. Profoundly reassuring, too.'
'And how's your work going?' Margaret asked.
160 Bertrand laughed at this, turning towards his girl, who also laughed,
a clear, musical sound not unlike Margaret's tiny silver bells. 'My
work?' Bertrand echoed. 'You make it sound like missionary activity.
Not that some of our friends would dissent from that description of
their labours. Fred, for instance,' he said to his girl.
165 'Yes, or Otto possibly,' she replied.
'Most assuredly Otto. He certainly looks like a missionary, even if
he doesn't behave like one.' He laughed again. So did his girl.
'What work do you do?' Dixon asked flatly.
'I am a painter. Not, alas, a painter of houses, or I should have been
170 able to make my pile and retire by now. No no; I paint pictures. Not,
alas again, pictures of trade unionists or town halls or naked women,
or I should now be squatting on an even larger pile. No no; just pictures,
mere pictures, pictures *tout court*, or, as our American cousins would
say, pictures period. And what work do you do? always provided, of
175 course, that I have permission to ask.'
Dixon hesitated; Bertrand's speech, which, except for its peroration,
had clearly been delivered before, had annoyed him in more ways
than he'd have believed possible. Bertrand's girl was looking at him
interrogatively; her eyebrows, which were darker than her hair, were
180 raised, and she now said, in her rather deep voice: 'Do gratify our

curiosity.' Bertrand's eyes, which seemed to lack the convexity of the normal eyeball, were also fixed to him.

'I'm one of your father's underlings,' Dixon said to Bertrand, deciding he mustn't be offensive; 'I cover the medieval angle for the History
185   Department here.'

'Charming, charming,' Bertrand said, and his girl said: 'You enjoy doing that, do you?'

Welch, Dixon noticed, had rejoined the group and was looking from face to face, obviously in quest of a point of entry into the conversation.
190   Dixon resolved to deny him this at all costs. He said, quietly but quickly: 'Well, of course, it has its own appeal. I can quite see that it hasn't the sort of glamour of', he turned to the girl, 'your line of country.' He must show Bertrand that he wasn't below including her in the conversation.

195   She looked perplexedly up at Bertrand. 'But I haven't noticed much glamour knocking about in . . .'

'But surely,' Dixon said, 'I know there must be a lot of hard work and exercise attached to it, but the ballet, well,' he disregarded a nudge from Margaret, 'there must be plenty of glamour there. So I've always
200   understood, anyway.' As he spoke, he gave Bertrand a smile of polite, comradely envy, and stirred his coffee with civilized fingers, splaying them a good deal on the handle of the spoon.

Bertrand was going red in the face and was leaning towards him, struggling to swallow half a bridge roll and speak. The girl repeated
205   with genuine bewilderment: 'The ballet? But I work in a bookshop. Whatever made you think I . . .?' Johns was grinning. Even Welch had obviously taken in what he'd said. What had he done? He was attacked, simultaneously by a pang of fear and the speculation that 'ballet' might be a private Welch synonym for 'sexual intercourse'.

210   'Look here, Dickinson or whatever your name is,' Bertrand began, 'perhaps you think you're being funny, but I'd as soon you cut it out, if you don't mind. Don't want to make a thing of it, do we?'

The baying quality of his voice, especially in the final query, together with a blurring of certain consonants, made Dixon want to call attention
215   to its defects, also, perhaps, to the peculiarity of his eyes. This might make Bertrand assail him physically – splendid: he was confident of winning any such encounter with an artist – or would Bertrand's pacifism stop him? But in the ensuing silence Dixon swiftly decided to back down. He'd made some mistake about the girl; he mustn't make
220   things any worse. 'I'm terribly sorry if I've made a mistake, but I was under the impression that Miss Loosmore here had something to do with . . .'

He turned to Margaret for aid, but before she could speak Welch, of all people, had come in loudly with: 'Poor old Dixon, ma-ha-ha, must

225 have been confusing this . . . this young lady with Sonia Loosmore, a
friend of Bertrand's who let us all down rather badly some time ago. I
think Bertrand must have thought you were . . . twitting him or
something, Dixon; ba-ha-ha.'

'Well, if he'd taken the trouble to be introduced, this wouldn't have
230 happened,' Bertrand said, still flushed. 'Instead of which, he . . .'

'Don't worry about it, Mr Dixon,' the girl cut in. 'It was only a silly
little misunderstanding. I can quite see how it happened. My name's
Christine Callaghan. Altogether different, you see.'

'Well, I'm . . . thanks very much for taking it like that. I'm very sorry
235 about it, really I am.'

'No no, don't let it get you down, Dixon,' Bertrand said, with a
glance at his girl. 'If you'll excuse us, I think we might circulate round
the company.'

They moved off, followed at a distance by Johns, towards the
240 Goldsmith group, and Dixon was left alone with Margaret.

'Here, have a cigarette,' she said. 'You must be needing one. God,
what a swine Bertrand is. He might have realized . . .'

'It was my fault, really,' Dixon said, grateful for nicotine and support.
'I should have been there to be introduced.'

245 'Yes, why weren't you? But he needn't have made it worse. But that's
typical of him, as far as I can gather.'

'I sort of couldn't face meeting him. How often have you met him?'

'He came down once before, with the Loosmore girl. I say, it is rather
queer, isn't it? He was going to marry the Loosmore then, and now
250 here he is with a new piece. Yes, of course; Neddy gave me a long
harangue about when the Loosmore wedding was coming off, and so
on, only a couple of days ago. So as far as he knew . . .'

'Look, Margaret, can't we go out for a drink? I need one, and we
shan't get one here. It's only just eight; we could be back . . .'

255 Margaret laughed, so that he could see a large number of her teeth, one
canine flecked with lipstick. She always made up just a little too heavily.
'Oh, James, you're incorrigible,' she said. 'Whatever next? Of course we
can't go out; what do you suppose the Neddies would think? Just as their
brilliant son's arrived? You'd get a week's notice like a shot.'

260 'Yes, you're right, I admit. But I'd give anything for three quick pints.
I've had nothing since the one I had down the road yesterday evening,
before I showed up here.'

'Much better for your pocket not to have them.' She began to laugh
again. 'You were wonderful in the madrigals. Your best performance yet.'

265 'Don't remind me, please.'

'Even better than your rendering of the Anouilh† tough. Your accent

---

Anouilh   Jean Anouilh (1910–), French dramatist

made it sound so frightfully sinister. What was it? "*La rigolade, c'est autre chose*" [Fun – that's different]? Very powerful, I thought.'

Dixon screamed softly from a tightened throat. 'Stop it. I can't bear
270 it. Why couldn't they have chosen an English play? All right, I know.
Don't explain to me. Look, what's going to happen now?'

'Recorders, I think.'

'Well, that lets me out, anyway. No disgrace in not playing them.
I'm only a lay brother, after all. Oh, but isn't it horrible, Margaret.
275 Isn't it horrible? How many of the bloody things do you have going at
once?'

She laughed again, glancing quickly round the room. This was a
reliable sign that she was enjoying herself. 'Oh, any number can play,
as far as I know.'

280 Dixon laughed too, trying to forget about beer. It was true that he
had only three pounds left in his tin box to last until pay-day, which
was nine days off. In the bank he had twenty-eight pounds, but this
was a fund he'd started against the chance of being sacked.

'Pretty girl, that Christine Whatshername,' Margaret said.

285 'Yes, isn't she?'

'Wonderful figure she's got, hasn't she?'

'Yes.'

'Not often you get a figure as good as that with a good-looking face.'

'No,' Dixon tensed himself for the inevitable qualification.

290 'Pity she's so refained, though.' Margaret hesitated, then decided to
gloss this epithet. 'I don't like women of that age who try to act the
gracious lady. Bit of a prig, too.'

Dixon, who'd arrived at similar conclusions already, found he didn't
much want to have them confirmed in this way. 'Oh, I don't know,' he
295 said. 'Can't really tell at this stage.'

This was greeted with the tinkle of tiny bells. 'Ah, you always were
one for a pretty face, weren't you? Covers a multitude is what I always
say.'

He thought this profoundly true and, debarred from saying so, was
300 at a loss what to reply. They looked anxiously at each other, as if
whatever either might say next must be an insult. Finally Dixon said:
'She does seem rather as if she's tarred with the same brush as Bertrand.'

She gave him a curious sardonic smile. 'I should say they've got a lot
in common.'

305 'I imagine so.'

A maidservant was now collecting the used crockery, and the company
was moving about. The next stage of the evening was clearly imminent.
Bertrand and his girl had disappeared, possibly to unpack. At Welch's
summons, Dixon left Margaret to help arrange some chairs. 'What's
310 the next item on the programme, Professor?' he asked.

Welch's heavy features had settled into their depressive look after the manic phase of the last hour and a half. He gave Dixon a mutinous glare. 'Just one or two instrumental items.'

'Oh, that'll be nice. Who's first on the list?'

315 The other brooded, his slab-like hands on the back of a ludicrously low chair that resembled an inefficently converted hassock. In a moment he disclosed that the local composer and the amateur violinist were going to 'tackle' a violin sonata by some Teutonic bore, that an unstated number of recorders would then perform some suitable item, and that 320 at some later time Johns might be expected to produce music from his oboe. Dixon nodded as if pleased.

He returned to Margaret to find her in conversation with Carol Goldsmith. This woman, aged about forty, thin, with long straight brown hair, Dixon regarded as one of his allies, though sometimes she 325 overawed him a little with her mature air.

'Hallo, Jim, how's it going?' she asked in her abnormally clear voice.

'Badly. There's at least an hour of scraping and blowing in front of us.'

'Yes, that's badly all right, isn't it? Why do we come to this sort of 330 thing? Well, I know why you come, Jim, and poor Margaret's living here. I suppose what I mean is why the hell do I come.'

'Oh, wifely support for your spouse, I take it,' Margaret said.

'Something in that, I suppose. But why does he come? There aren't even any drinks.'

335 'James has already noticed that.'

'It would hardly be worth coming just to meet the great painter, would it?' Dixon said, meaning to start a conversation that might diminish his retrospective embarrassment over the recent Loosmore–Callaghan *imbroglio*.

340 For a reason he didn't then understand, the reception of this remark was perceptibly unfavourable. Margaret looked at him with lifted chin as if ready to reprove some indiscretion, but to her any sort of adverse remark about anybody was, unless they were alone, indiscreet enough. Carol half-closed her eyes and smoothed her straight hair. 'What makes 345 you say that?' she said.

'Well, nothing really,' Dixon said in alarm. 'I had a little brush with him just now, that's all. I got into some mix-up over his girl's name, and he was a bit offensive, I thought. Nothing drastic.'

'Oh, that's quite typical,' Carol said. 'He always thinks he's being 350 got at. He often is, too.'

1951/2   1954

Donald Davie

1922–

Donald Alfred Davie was born in Barnsley and educated at Barnsley Grammar School and St Catherine's College, Cambridge. After serving in the Royal Navy (1941–6) he held several academic appointments including Chairs of English at Essex and Stanford; since 1978 he has been Professor of Humanities at Vanderbilt University. *Purity of Diction in English Verse* (1951) was followed by many critical and scholarly books. His first collection of poems was *Brides of Reason* (1955); his *Collected Poems* appeared in 1972, and *Collected Poems 1971–1983* in 1983. Davie writes witty, ingenious, technically skilful verse, with a critic's awareness of his own art; detractors have complained that he is too cerebral and deliberate.

THE GARDEN PARTY

Above a stretch of still unravaged weald
In our Black Country,[†] in a cedar-shade,
I found, shared out in tennis courts, a field
Where children of the local magnates played.

5   And I grew envious of their moneyed ease
In Scott Fitzgerald's unembarrassed vein.
Let prigs, I thought, fool others as they please,
I only wish I had my time again.

To crown a situation as contrived
10   As any in 'The Beautiful and Damned',[†]
The phantom of my earliest love arrived;
I shook absurdly as I shook her hand.

Black Country the industrial Midlands of
  England
'The Beautiful and the Damned' the novel of
this title (1942) about a rich, doomed
marriage, by the American novelist F. Scott
Fitzgerald (1896–1940)

As dusk drew in on cultivated cries,
Faces hung pearls upon a cedar-bough;
15 And gin could blur the glitter of her eyes,
But it's too late to learn to tango now.

My father, of a more submissive school,
Remarks the rich themselves are always sad.
There is that sort of equalizing rule;
20 But theirs is all the youth we might have had.

1955

Philip Larkin
1922–85

Philip Arthur Larkin was born in Coventry and educated at the King
Henry VIII School, Coventry, and (with Kingsley Amis) at St John's
College, Oxford. He became a librarian in 1943; from 1955 he was
Librarian of the Brynmor Jones Library, University of Hull. From
1961 to 1971 he was jazz-critic for the *Daily Telegraph* and a collection
of essays, *All That Jazz*, appeared in 1970. He was a Visiting Fellow
at All Souls College, Oxford (1970–1), while he worked on his
(controversial) anthology, *The Oxford Book of Twentieth Century
English Verse* (1973). His first collection of poems, *The North Ship*,
was published in 1945. The publishers Faber and Faber encouraged
him to persist with poetry. *The Less Deceived* (1955), *The Whitsun
Weddings* (1964), and *High Windows* (1974), are slim volumes of
fine poems. Larkin's verse matches colloquial rhythms to subtle
versification, varies literary and vulgar phrasing, and observes modern
England with mixed affection and disdain. His novels, *Jill* (1946) and
A Girl in Winter (1947) deserve to be better known. A collection of
prose, *Required Writing: Miscellaneous Pieces 1955–82*, was published in 1983. He was made a Companion of Honour in 1985.

CHURCH GOING

Once I am sure there's nothing going on
I step inside, letting the door thud shut.
Another church: matting, seats, and stone,
And little books; sprawlings of flowers, cut
5   For Sunday, brownish now; some brass and stuff
Up at the holy end; the small neat organ;
And a tense, musty, unignorable silence,
Brewed God knows how long. Hatless, I take off
My cycle-clips in awkward reverence,

10   Move forward, run my hand around the font.
From where I stand, the roof looks almost new –
Cleaned, or restored? Someone would know: I don't.

Mounting the lectern, I peruse a few
Hectoring large-scale verses, and pronounce
15 'Here endeth' much more loudly than I'd meant.
The echoes snigger briefly. Back at the door
I sign the book, donate an Irish sixpence,
Reflect the place was not worth stopping for.

Yet stop I did: in fact I often do,
20 And always end much at a loss like this,
Wondering what to look for; wondering, too,
When churches fall completely out of use
What we shall turn them into, if we shall keep
A few cathedrals chronically on show,
25 Their parchment, plate and pyx† in locked cases,
And let the rest rent-free to rain and sheep.
Shall we avoid them as unlucky places?

Or, after dark, will dubious women come
To make their children touch a particular stone;
30 Pick simples† for a cancer; or on some
Advised night see walking a dead one?
Power of some sort or other will go on
In games, in riddles, seemingly at random;
But superstition, like belief, must die,
35 And what remains when disbelief has gone?
Grass, weedy pavement, brambles, buttress, sky,

A shape less recognisable each week,
A purpose more obscure. I wonder who
Will be the last, the very last, to seek
40 This place for what it was; one of the crew
That tap and jot and know what rood-lofts* were?   galleries
Some ruin-bibber,* randy for antique,   drinker
Or Christmas-addict, counting on a whiff
Of gown-and-bands and organ-pipes and myrrh?
45 Or will he be my representative,

Bored, uninformed, knowing the ghostly silt
Dispersed, yet tending to this cross of ground
Through suburb scrub because it held unspilt
So long and equably what since is found
50 Only in separation – marriage, and birth,

pyx box for Communion wafers   *simples* medical herbs

And death, and thoughts of these – for which was built
This special shell? For, though I've no idea
What this accoutred frowsty barn is worth,
It pleases me to stand in silence here;

55   A serious house on serious earth it is,
      In whose blent air all our compulsions meet,
      Are recognised, and robed as destinies.
      And that much never can be obsolete,
      Since someone will forever be surprising
60   A hunger in himself to be more serious,
      And gravitating with it to this ground,
      Which, he once heard, was proper to grow wise in,
      If only that so many dead lie round.

                                                    1955

LINES ON A YOUNG LADY'S PHOTOGRAPH ALBUM

At last you yielded up the album, which,
Once open, sent me distracted. All your ages
Matt and glossy on the thick black pages!
Too much confectionery, too rich:
5   I choke on such nutritious images.

My swivel eye hungers from pose to pose –
In pigtails, clutching a reluctant cat;
Or furred yourself, a sweet girl-graduate;
Or lifting a heavy-headed rose
10   Beneath a trellis, or in a trilby hat

(Faintly disturbing, that, in several ways) –
From every side you strike at my control,
Not least through these disquieting chaps who loll
At ease about your earlier days:
15   Not quite your class, I'd say, dear, on the whole.

But o, photography! as no art is,
Faithful and disappointing! that records
Dull days as dull, and hold-it smiles as frauds,

And will not censor blemishes
20 Like washing-lines, and Hall's-Distemper boards,†

But shows the cat as disinclined, and shades
A chin as doubled when it is, what grace
Your candour thus confers upon her face!
How overwhelmingly persuades
25 That this is a real girl in a real place,

In every sense empirically true!
Or is it just *the past*? Those flowers, that gate,
These misty parks and motors, lacerate
Simply by being over; you
30 Contract my heart by looking out of date.

Yes, true; but in the end, surely, we cry
Not only at exclusion, but because
It leaves us free to cry. We know *what was*
Won't call on us to justify
35 Our grief, however hard we yowl across

The gap from eye to page. So I am left
To mourn (without a chance of consequence)
You, balanced on a bike against a fence;
To wonder if you'd spot the theft
40 Of this one of you bathing; to condense,

In short, a past that no one now can share,
No matter whose your future; calm and dry,
It holds you like a heaven, and you lie
Unvariably lovely there,
45 Smaller and clearer as the years go by.

1955

TOADS

Why should I let the toad *work*
    Squat on my life?
Can't I use my wit as a pitchfork
    And drive the brute off?

Hall's-Distemper boards hoardings for advertisements

5   Six days of the week it soils
        With its sickening poison –
    Just for paying a few bills!
        That's out of proportion.

    Lots of folk live on their wits:
10   Lecturers, lispers,
    Losels, loblolly-men,* louts –   louts
        They don't end as paupers;

    Lots of folk live up lanes
        With fires in a bucket,
15   Eat windfalls and tinned sardines –
        They seem to like it.

    Their nippers have got bare feet,
        Their unspeakable wives
    Are skinny as whippets – and yet
20   No one actually *starves*.

    Ah, were I courageous enough
        To shout *Stuff your pension*!
    But I know, all too well, that's the stuff
        That dreams are made on:†

25   For something sufficiently toad-like
        Squats in me, too;
    Its hunkers are heavy as hard luck,
        And cold as snow,

    And will never allow me to blarney
30   My way to getting
    The fame and the girl and the money
        All at one sitting.

    I don't say, one bodies the other
        One's spiritual truth;
35   But I do say it's hard to lose either,
        When you have both.

1955

---

the stuff . . . made on In Shakespeare's *The Tempest*, IV. 1. 156, Prospero says, 'We are such stuff / As dreams are made on, and our little life / Is rounded with a sleep'

AT GRASS

The eye can hardly pick them out
From the cold shade they shelter in;
Till wind distresses tail and mane;
Then one crops grass, and moves about
5   – The other seeming to look on –
And stands anonymous again.

Yet fifteen years ago, perhaps
Two dozen distances sufficed
To fable them: faint afternoons
10   Of Cups and Stakes and Handicaps,
Whereby their names were artificed
To inlay faded, classic Junes –

Silks at the start: against the sky
Numbers and parasols: outside,
15   Squadrons of empty cars, and heat,
And littered grass: then the long cry
Hanging unhushed till it subside
To stop-press columns on the street.

Do memories plague their ears like flies?
20   They shake their heads. Dusk brims the shadows.
Summer by summer all stole away,
The starting-gates the crowds and cries –
All but the unmolesting meadows.
Almanacked,[†] their names live; they

25   Have slipped their names, and stand at ease,
Or gallop for what must be joy,
And not a fieldglass sees them home,
Or curious stop-watch prophesies:
Only the groom, and the groom's boy,
30   With bridles in the evening come.

1955

Almanacked   winners of the main events in the
racing calendar are recorded each year in
Racehorses of the Year, Directory of the Turf,
Whitaker's Almanack and other reference
books

TOADS REVISITED

Walking around in the park
Should feel better than work:
The lake, the sunshine,
The grass to lie on,

5   Blurred playground noises
Beyond black-stockinged nurses –
Not a bad place to be.
Yet it doesn't suit me,

Being one of the men
10   You meet of an afternoon:
Palsied old step-takers,
Hare-eyed clerks with the jitters,

Waxed-fleshed out-patients
Still vague from accidents,
15   And characters in long coats
Deep in the litter-baskets –

All dodging the toad work
By being stupid or weak.
Think of being them!
20   Hearing the hours chime,

Watching the bread delivered,
The sun by clouds covered,
The children going home;
Think of being them,

25   Turning over their failures
By some bed of lobelias,
Nowhere to go but indoors,
No friends but empty chairs –

No, give me my in-tray,
30   My loaf-haired secretary,
My shall-I-keep-the-call-in-Sir:
What else can I answer,

When the lights come on at four
At the end of another year?
35   Give me your arm, old toad;
Help me down Cemetery Road.

1964

THE WHITSUN WEDDINGS

That Whitsun, I was late getting away:
     Not till about
One-twenty on the sunlit Saturday
Did my three-quarters-empty train pull out,
5   All windows down, all cushions hot, all sense
Of being in a hurry gone. We ran
Behind the backs of houses, crossed a street
Of blinding windscreens, smelt the fish-dock; thence
The river's level drifting breadth began,
10   Where sky and Lincolnshire and water meet.

All afternoon, through the tall heat that slept
     For miles inland,
A slow and stopping curve southwards we kept.
Wide farms went by, short-shadowed cattle, and
15   Canals with floatings of industrial froth;
A hothouse flashed uniquely: hedges dipped
And rose: and now and then a smell of grass
Displaced the reek of buttoned carriage-cloth
Until the next town, new and nondescript,
20   Approached with acres of dismantled cars.

At first, I didn't notice what a noise
     The weddings made
Each station that we stopped at: sun destroys

The interest of what's happening in the shade,
25   And down the long cool platforms whoops and skirls
I took for porters larking with the mails,
And went on reading. Once we started, though,
We passed them, grinning and pomaded, girls
In parodies of fashion, heels and veils,
30   All posed irresolutely, watching us go,

As if out on the end of an event
    Waving goodbye
To something that survived it. Struck, I leant
More promptly out next time, more curiously,
35   And saw it all again in different terms:
The fathers with broad belts under their suits
And seamy foreheads; mothers loud and fat;
And uncle shouting smut; and then the perms,
The nylon gloves and jewellery-substitutes,
40   The lemons, mauves and olive-ochres that

Marked off the girls unreally from the rest.
    Yes, from cafés
And banquet-halls up yards, and bunting-dressed
Coach-party annexes, the wedding-days
45   Were coming to an end. All down the line
Fresh couples climbed aboard: the rest stood round;
The last confetti and advice were thrown,
And, as we moved, each face seemed to define
Just what it saw departing: children frowned
50   At something dull; fathers had never known

Success so huge and wholly farcical;
    The women shared
The secret like a happy funeral;
While girls, gripping their handbags tighter, stared
55   At a religious wounding. Free at last,
And loaded with the sum of all they saw,
We hurried towards London, shuffling gouts of steam.
Now fields were building-plots, and poplars cast
Long shadows over major roads, and for
60   Some fifty minutes, that in time would seem

Just long enough to settle hats and say
    I nearly died,
A dozen marriages got under way.

They watched the landscape, sitting side by side
65 – An Odeon went past, a cooling tower,
And someone running up to bowl – and none
Thought of the others they would never meet
Or how their lives would all contain this hour.
I thought of London spread out in the sun,
70 Its postal districts packed like squares of wheat:

There we were aimed. And as we raced across
    Bright knots of rail
Past standing Pullmans,† walls of blackened moss
Came close, and it was nearly done, this frail
75 Travelling coincidence; and what it held
Stood ready to be loosed with all the power
That being changed can give. We slowed again,
And as the tightened brakes took hold, there swelled
A sense of falling, like an arrow-shower
80 Sent out of sight, somewhere becoming rain.

                                        1964

Vers de Société

[Society Verse]

My wife and I have asked a crowd of craps
To come and waste their time and ours: perhaps
You'd care to join us? In a pig's arse, friend.
Day comes to an end.
5 The gas fire breathes, the trees are darkly swayed.
And so *Dear Warlock-Williams: I'm afraid –*

Funny how hard it is to be alone.
I could spend half my evenings, if I wanted,
Holding a glass of washing sherry, canted
10 Over to catch the drivel of some bitch
Who's read nothing but *Which*;
Just think of all the spare time that has flown

Pullmans railway coaches for which an extra   Pullman (1831–97), their American inventor
amount was charged, called after George M.

Straight into nothingness by being filled
With forks and faces, rather than repaid
15   Under a lamp, hearing the noise of wind,
And looking out to see the moon thinned
To an air-sharpened blade.
A life, and yet how sternly it's instilled

All solitude is selfish. No one now
20   Believes the hermit with his gown and dish
Talking to God (who's gone too); the big wish
Is to have people nice to you, which means
Doing it back somehow.
Virtue is social. Are, then, these routines

25   Playing at goodness, like going to church?
Something that bores us, something we don't do well
(Asking that ass about his fool research)
But try to feel, because, however crudely,
It shows us what should be?
30   Too subtle, that. Too decent, too. Oh hell,

Only the young can be alone freely.
The time is shorter now for company,
And sitting by a lamp more often brings
Not peace, but other things.
35   Beyond the light stand failure and remorse
Whispering *Dear Warlock-Williams: Why, of course* –

1974

THE EXPLOSION

On the day of the explosion
Shadows pointed towards the pithead:
In the sun the slagheap slept.

Down the lane came men in pitboots
5   Coughing oath-edged talk and pipe-smoke,
Shouldering off the freshened silence.

One chased after rabbits; lost them;
Came back with a nest of lark's eggs;
Showed them; lodged them in the grasses.

10   So they passed in beards and moleskins,
Fathers, brothers, nicknames, laughter,
Through the tall gates standing open.

At noon, there came a tremor; cows
Stopped chewing for a second; sun,
15   Scarfed as in a heat-haze, dimmed.

The dead go on before us, they
Are sitting in God's house in comfort,
We shall see them face to face –

Plain as lettering in the chapels
20   It was said, and for a second
Wives saw men of the explosion

Larger than in life they managed –
Gold as on a coin, or walking
Somehow from the sun towards them,

25   One showing the eggs unbroken.

1974

James Kirkup

1923–

James Falconer Kirkup was born in South Shields, Durham; he was educated at the High School there, and at Durham University. Professor Kirkup has held senior university posts in English Literature, in Japan, America and elsewhere, and is a distinguished translator. His books of poems include *A Correct Compassion* (1952), *The Descent into the Cave* (1957), *Paper Windows* (1968), and *A Bewick Bestiary* (1971). In 1977 the editor of *Gay News* was successfully prosecuted on a charge that Kirkup's poem 'The love that dares to speak its name', which had been published in the magazine, was a blasphemous libel.

RUGBY LEAGUE GAME

Sport is absurd, and sad.
Those grown men, just look,
In those dreary long blue shorts,
Those ringed stockings, Edwardian,
5   Balding pates, and huge
Fat knees that ought to be heroes'.

Grappling, hooking, gallantly tackling –
It all this courage really necessary? –
Taking their good clean fun
10   So solemnly, they run each other down
With earnest keenness, for the honour of
Virility, the cap, the county side.

Like great boys they roll each other
In the mud of public Saturdays,
15   Groping their blind way back
To noble youth, away from the bank,
The wife, the pram, the spin drier,
Back to the spartan freedom of the field.

Back, back to the days when boys
20   Were men, still hopeful, and untamed.

That was then: a gay
And golden age ago.
Now, in vain, domesticated,
Men try to be boys again.

1963

John Mortimer

1923–

John Clifford Mortimer was born in London and educated at Harrow School and Brasenose College, Oxford. As a barrister he has been a notable opponent of censorship. His first play, *The Dock Brief*, was broadcast on radio and television in 1957 (published 1958). His later writing for television includes the series about Rumpole of the Bailey. *A Voyage Round My Father* (performed 1970; published 1971) is a tribute to his father, Clifford Mortimer, a blind barrister.

The concluding episodes in Act One of this play offer to the son, and to the audience, some wry observations on the human condition, with sharp, sardonic comment by the father.

From A VOYAGE ROUND MY FATHER

[Words into the Darkness]

MISS COX. I could've kissed you when you came in to our shop.
SON. Could you really?
MISS BAKER. And actually bought a book!
MISS COX. Most people come in for pamphlets. A hundred things to do
5   with dried egg† – published by the Ministry of Food ...

> *The radio stops playing 'La Vie en Rose'. A* BBC ANNOUNCER *speaks cheerily.*

ANNOUNCER'S VOICE. 'What do I do if I come across German or Italian broadcasts when tuning my wireless? I say to myself: "Now this blighter wants me to listen to him. Am I going to do what this blighter wants?"'
10 MISS BAKER (*switches the radio off*). We'll have to give up that shop.
SON. Why will you?
MISS COX. Bill's going to be called up.
SON. Who's Bill?
MISS BAKER I'm Bill. (*She picks up a bit of bread and butter and waves it*
15   *at* MISS COX.) She's Daphne ... (*She goes to the macaw's cage, prods*

---

dried egg a feature of Second World War rationing

a piece of bread and butter through the cage bars.) . . . This bloody bird gets half my butter ration . . .

MISS COX. They're putting Bill on the land . . .

MISS BAKER. I'll probably ruin the crops.

20 MISS COX. I'll send you off in the morning darling . . . with a meat pie and a little bottle of cold tea.

MISS BAKER. Thank you very much!

MISS COX. It's the war, Bill! We all have to make sacrifices. (*To* SON.) Bill doesn't much care for this war. We were more keen on the war in

25 Spain.

MISS BAKER. And in the evenings, I suppose you'll wash me down in front of the fire (*To the macaw.*) Eat up, Miss Garbo!

MISS COX. Nonsense. They're not sending you down the mines! (*To the* SON.) All our friends were awfully keen on the war in Spain; Stephen

30 Spender and all that jolly collection . . . I expect you'll go into the Fire Service . . .?

SON. Why?

MISS COX. All our friends go into the Fire Service.

MISS BAKER. They get a lot of time for writing, waiting about between

35 fires . . .

SON. My father says I should avoid the temptation to do anything heroic . . .

Change of light, projection of a darker garden upstage. The MOTHER *comes in, leading the* FATHER, *carrying his camp stool and a bucket. She sits him down in front of a plant with inverted flower pots on a stick around it. Then she leaves him. He begins to feel for the pots and empty them in the bucket.*

MISS COX. We've never actually met your father . . .

MISS BAKER. We looked over the gate one evening and shouted – but he

40 was busy in the garden doing something.

SON. Probably the earwigs.

MISS BAKER. What?

SON. He drowns the earwigs every night.

MISS COX. How most extraordinary . . .

She gets up and starts putting things back on the tea tray.

45 The Fire Service! That's where you'll end up. It gives everyone far more time to write.

MISS BAKER. Is that what you're going to be then – a writer?

Pause. Change of light. The light fades on MISS COX *and* MISS BAKER'S *part of the stage, and increases on the* FATHER *as the* SON *leaves the two ladies, and walks across to join the* FATHER. *On his way he collects a camp stool and puts it up and sits beside the* FATHER. *He starts to help him with the earwig traps, taking off the inverted flower pots and emptying the earwigs that have gone in there for warmth and shelter, into the bucket of water to drown miserably.* MISS BAKER *and* MISS COX *go.*

FATHER. Is that you?

SON. Yes, it's me.

50 FATHER. What're you doing?

SON. Helping you.

FATHER. Consider the persistence of the earwig! Each afternoon, it feasts on the dahlia blooms. Each night it crawls into your flower pots to sleep. Each morning, we empty the flower pots and drown the earwigs
55 ... but still they come! Nature's remorseless.

SON. I may be a writer ...

FATHER. If we did this for one million years all over the world, could we make some small dent in the pattern of evolution? Would we produce an earwig that could swim? (*Pause.*) You'd be better off in the
60 law ...

SON. I'd like to write ...

FATHER. You'll have plenty of spare time! My first five years in Chambers, I did nothing but *The Times* crossword puzzle. Besides which, if you were only a writer, who would you rub shoulders with? (*With*
65 *contempt.*) Other writers? You'll be far better off in the law.

SON. I don't know ...

FATHER. No brilliance is needed in the law. Nothing but common sense, and relatively clean finger nails. Another thing, if you were a writer, think of your poor, unfortunate wife ...

70 SON. What?

FATHER. She'd have you at home every day! In carpet slippers ... Drinking tea and stumped for words! You'd be far better off down the tube each morning and off to the Law Courts ... How many have we bagged today?

75 SON (*looking down into the bucket*). About a hundred.

FATHER. A moderate bag, I'd say. Merely moderate. You know, the law of husband and wife might seem idiotic at first sight. But when you get to know it, you'll find it can exercise a vague medieval charm. Learn a little law, won't you? Just to please me ...

The MOTHER *enters. She goes up to the* FATHER, *touches him.*

80 MOTHER. Your bath's ready.

FATHER. What?

MOTHER. I said your bath water's nice and hot.

He gets up, takes her arm. She starts to lead him off the stage.

I suppose there isn't an easier way of getting rid of earwigs?

FATHER. An easier way! Sometimes I wonder if women understand
85   anything.

They go. The SON *stands, then moves down towards the audience.*
The light changes and the garden fades on the back-cloth, to be
replaced by a pattern of Gothic arches. The SON *speaks to the*
audience, downstage right.

SON. It was my father's way to offer the law to me – the great stone
column of authority which has been dragged by an adulterous,
careless, negligent and half criminal humanity down the ages – as if
it were a small mechanical toy which might occupy half an hour on
90   a rainy afternoon.

Upstage a Judge's chair with a coat of arms, a witness box. A JUDGE
enters, and takes his place: from offstage left, the sound of footsteps
on a stone passage and the tapping of a stick. Then the FATHER *and*
MOTHER enter downstage left. The FATHER *is now wearing a black*
jacket and a winged collar and bow tie. The MOTHER *stations the*
FATHER by one of the cubes on which a mirror is hanging. She goes
out and returns with his wig, gown and white bands to take the
place of his tie, and helps him to change. The opposing barrister,
MR BOUSTEAD, robed, but carrying his wig, comes and starts to comb
his hair in front of the mirror.

SON (*to the audience*). He never used a white stick – but his clouded
malacca was heard daily, tapping the cold stone corridors of the Law
Courts. He had no use for dogs, therapy, training, nor did he adapt
himself to his condition. He simply pretended that nothing had
95   happened. (*The* SON *goes*.)
BOUSTEAD. Good morning.
FATHER. Who's that?
MOTHER. It's Mr Boustead, dear . . . He's for the husband.
FATHER. Agin me, Bulstrode. Are you agin me?
100   BOUSTEAD. Boustead.
FATHER. Excuse me. Boustead of course. Where are you?
BOUSTEAD. Here, I'm here . . .
FATHER. I have studied your case pretty closely and I have a suggestion
to make which you might find helpful.
105   BOUSTEAD. Really?
FATHER. What I was suggesting, entirely for your assistance of course –
is that you might like – my dear boy – to throw in your hand . . .
Now, is that a help to you . . . ?
BOUSTEAD. Certainly not! I'd say we have some pretty valuable evi-
110   dence . . .

Light change. In the witness box appears MR THONG, *a private detective of a crafty appearance, wearing a brown suit and a cycling club badge on his lapel.* BOUSTEAD *moves to upstage right, stands questioning him. The* MOTHER *leads the* FATHER *to his seat left and sits behind him.*

BOUSTEAD. Now from the vantage point which you have described, Mr Thong, will you tell my Lord and the Jury exactly what you saw?

The FATHER *turns and speaks in a loud stage whisper to the* MOTHER.

FATHER. Throat spray!

The MOTHER *puts a small throat spray into the* FATHER'S *hand.* THONG *consults his notebook.*

BOUSTEAD. Yes, Mr Thong, in your own words.

115 FATHER. (*loud whisper*). Thanks.

THONG (*monotonously, reading his notebook*). From my point of vantage, I was quite clearly able to see inside the kitchen window . . .

BOUSTEAD. Yes?

THONG. And –

The FATHER *opens his mouth and starts, very loudly, to spray his throat.*

120 JUDGE. Speak up, Mr Thong, I can't hear you.

THONG. My Lord. I was able to distinguish clearly the Respondent . . .

JUDGE (*writing carefully*). Yes . . .

THONG. In the act of . . . (*His mumble is again drowned by the* FATHER'S *work with the throat spray.*) . . . with a man distinguishable only by

125 a small moustache . . . I now recognize him as the Co-Respondent, Dacres.

BOUSTEAD. In the act of what, Mr Thong?

THONG. The act of . . . (*The* FATHER *works the throat spray very loudly.*

BOUSTEAD. If my learned friend would allow us to hear the evidence . . .

130 FATHER (*puts down the throat spray and whispers deafeningly to* BOUSTEAD). I'm so sorry. My dear boy, if *this* is the valuable evidence you told me about, I shall be quiet – as the tomb . . .!

BOUSTEAD (*firmly*). Mr Thong.

FATHER. (*half rising to address the* JUDGE). By all means, my Lord. Let us

135 hear this *valuable* evidence.

JUDGE. Very well.

THONG. I distinctly saw them . . .

JUDGE. Distinctly saw them what?

THONG. Kissing and cuddling, my Lord.

140 BOUSTEAD. And then . . .

THONG. The light was extinguished . . .

BOUSTEAD. Where?

THONG. In the kitchen.

BOUSTEAD. And a further light appeared?

145 THONG. In the bedroom.

JUDGE. For a moment?

THONG. Merely momentarily, my Lord.

BOUSTEAD. So . . .

THONG. The house was shrouded in darkness. And the Co-Respondent,

150   this is the point that struck us, had not emerged.

BOUSTEAD. And you kept up observation until . . .

THONG. Approximately, dawn.

BOUSTEAD (*very satisfied, as he sits down*). Thank you, Mr Thong.

> *The FATHER rises, clattering. Folds his hands on his stomach, gazes sightlessly at MR THONG and then allows a long pause during which MR THONG stirs uncomfortably. Then he starts quietly, slowly working himself up into a climax.*

FATHER. Mr Thong, what price did you put on this valuable evidence?

155 THONG. I don't know what you mean . . .

FATHER. You have been paid, haven't you, to give it?

THONG. I'm a private enquiry agent . . .

FATHER. A professional witness?

THONG. Charging the usual fee.

160 FATHER. Thirty pieces of silver?†

BOUSTEAD (*rises, indignant*). My Lord, I object. This is outrageous.

JUDGE. Perhaps that was not entirely relevant. (BOUSTEAD *subsides.*)

FATHER. Then let me ask you something which is very relevant. Which goes straight to the secret heart of this wretched little conspiracy.

165   Where was this lady's husband during your observations?

THONG. Captain Waring?

FATHER. Yes. Captain Waring.

THONG. He had accompanied me . . .

FATHER. Why?

170 THONG. For the purpose of . . .

FATHER. For the purpose of what . . .?

THONG. Identification . . .

FATHER. And how long did he remain with you?

THONG. As long as observation continued . . .

175 FATHER. Till dawn . . .?

THONG. Until approximately 5.30 a.m.

FATHER. And did he not storm the house? Did he not beat upon the door? Did he not seize his wife's paramour by the throat and hurl him into the gutter?

---

thirty pieces of silver   the sum paid to Judas when he betrayed Christ

180   THONG. According to my notebook. No.

FATHER. And according to my notebook, was he enjoying himself?

BOUSTEAD (*driven beyond endurance, rises to protest*). Really . . .!

FATHER. Please, Mr Bulstrode! I've sat here for three days! Like patience on a monument! Whilst a series of spiteful, mean, petty, trumped-up

185   sickening and small-minded charges are tediously paraded against the unfortunate woman I represent. And now, when I rise to cross-examine . . . *I will not be interrupted!*

JUDGE. Gentlemen! Please, gentlemen. (*To* FATHER.) What was your question?

190   FATHER. I've forgotten it. My learned friend's interruption has had the effect he no doubt intended and I have forgotten my question!

BOUSTEAD. This is quite intolerable . . .

FATHER. Ah . . . Now I've remembered it again. Did he enjoy the night, Thong, in this field . . . from which he was magically able to overlook

195   his own kitchen . . .?

THONG. This plot of waste ground . . .

FATHER. Up a tree, was he?

THONG. What?

FATHER. Was he perched upon a tree?

200   THONG. We had stepped up, into the lower branches.

FATHER. Was it the naked eye?

THONG. Pardon?

FATHER. Was he viewing this distressing scene by aid of the naked eye?

THONG. Captain Waring had brought a pair of field glasses.

205   FATHER. His racing glasses . . .?

THONG. I . . .

JUDGE. Speak up, Mr Thong.

THONG. I imagine he used them for racing, my Lord.

FATHER. You see Captain Waring has given evidence in this Court.

210   BOUSTEAD (*ironic*). On the subject of his racing glasses?

FATHER (*his voice filled with passion*). No, Mr Bulstrode. On the subject of love. He has told us that he was deeply, sincerely in love with his wife.

THONG. I don't know anything about that.

215   FATHER. Exactly, Mr Thong! You are hardly an expert witness, are you, on the subject of love?

> *Light change.* MR THONG *leaves the witness box.* BOUSTEAD *leaves also. The* FATHER *is standing as if addressing the Jury.*

May it please you, my Lord, Members of the Jury. Love has driven men and women in the course of history to curious extremes. Love tempted Leander to plunge in and swim the raging Hellespont. It led

220   Juliet to feign death and Ophelia to madness. No doubt it complicated

the serenity of the Garden of Eden and started the Trojan War: but surely there is no more curious example of the mysterious effects of the passion than the spectacle of Captain Waring of the Royal Engineers, roosted in a tree, complacently viewing the seduction of
225 his beloved through a pair of strong racing binoculars . . .

The light fades altogether on the back of the upstage areas. The FATHER'S *voice comes out of the shadows.*

Is not the whole story, Members of the Jury, an improbable and impertinent tissue of falsehood . . .?

The SON *is lit downstage as in the upstage darkness, the* JUDGE, *the* FATHER, *and the* MOTHER *go and the Courtroom furniture is moved away.*

SON (*to the audience*). He sent words out into the darkness, like soldiers sent off to battle, and was never short of reinforcements. In the Law
230 Courts he gave his public performance. At home he returned to his private ritual, the potting shed, the crossword puzzle and, when I was at home, the afternoon walk.

Projection of trees as the upstage area becomes slowly lighter.

The woods were dark and full of flies. We picked bracken leaves to swat them, and when I was a child he told me we carried cutlasses
235 to hack our way through the jungle. I used to shut my eyes at dead rats, or magpies gibbeted on the trees: sights his blindness spared him. He walked with his hand on my arm. A small hand, with loose brown skin. From time to time, I had an urge to pull away from him, to run into the trees and hide . . . to leave him alone, lost in perpetual
240 darkness. But then his hand would tighten on my sleeve; he was very persistent . . .

The SON *walks behind a cube and emerges with the* FATHER *who is wearing a tweed jacket and his straw hat and is holding the* SON'S *arm tightly as they walk round the stage, slowly towards a raised platform upstage . . .*

FATHER. I've had a good deal of fun . . . out of the law.
SON. Have you ever been to the South of France?
FATHER. Once or twice. It's all right, except for the dreadful greasy food
245 they can't stop talking about.
SON. Bill and Daphne say the worst of the War is that they can't get to the South of France.
FATHER. Who're they?
SON. Two ladies from the book shop.
250 FATHER. Where you had to go, as a visitor?

SON. That's right.

FATHER. My heart bled for you on that occasion.

SON. Daphne's Miss Cox.

FATHER. And Bill ...?

255 SON. ... Bill's Miss Baker.

FATHER. Damned rum!

SON. Before the War they practically lived in Cannes. They met Cocteau† ...

FATHER. Who?

260 SON. He smoked opium. Have you ever smoked opium?

FATHER. Certainly not! Gives you constipation. Dreadful binding effect. Ever seen those pictures of the wretched poet Coleridge? Green around the gills. And a stranger to the lavatory. Avoid opium.

SON. They may find me a war job.

265 FATHER. Who?

SON. Miss Baker and Miss Cox.

FATHER. Why, is 'Bill' on the General Staff?

SON. They have a friend who makes propaganda films for the government. He needs an assistant.

270 FATHER. You're thinking of entering the film world?

SON. Just ... for the duration.

FATHER. Well! At least there's nothing heroic about it.

SON. No.

FATHER. Rum sort of world, isn't it – the film world?

275 SON. I expect so.

FATHER. Don't they wear their caps *back to front* in the film world?

SON. You're thinking of the silent days.

FATHER. Am I? Perhaps I am. Your mother and I went to a silent film once. In Glastonbury.

280 SON. Did you?

FATHER. We were staying there in an hotel. Damn dull. Nothing to do in the evenings. So we sallied forth, to see this silent film. The point was, I invariably dressed for dinner, when in Glastonbury. Follow?

SON. I follow.

285 FATHER. And when your mother and I entered this picture palace – in evening dress – the whole audience burst into spontaneous applause! I believe they took us for part of the entertainment! ... Rum kind of world I must say. Where are we?

SON. At the bottom of Stonor Hill.

290 FATHER. I'll rest for a moment. Then we'll go up to the top.

    The SON *moves him to the right of the platform and sits him down.*

Cocteau Jean Cocteau (1889–1963), versatile French writer and film director

SON. Will we?

FATHER. Of course we will! You can see the three counties from the top of Stonor Hill. Don't you want to see three counties . . .?

SON. All right.

295 FATHER. See everything. Everything in Nature . . . That's the instinct of the May beetle. Twenty-four hours to live, so spend it . . . looking around.

SON. We've got more time . . .

FATHER. Don't you believe it! It's short . . . but enjoyable! You know

300 what? If they ever say to you – 'your old Father, he couldn't have enjoyed life much. Overdrawn at the Bank and bad-tempered and people didn't often visit him . . .' 'Nonsense' you can say. 'He enjoyed every minute of it . . .'

SON. Do you want to go on now?

305 FATHER. When you consider the embryo of the liver fluke, born in sheeps' droppings, searching the world for a shell to bore into for the sake of living in a snail until it becomes tadpole-like and leaves its host – and then gets swallowed up by a sheep again! When you consider that – complicated persistence, well, of course, I've clung on for sixty

310 five years. It's the instinct – that's all. The irresistible instinct! All right. We'll go up . . . Watch carefully and you'll see three counties . . .

He puts out his hand, the SON *pulls him up. They walk off behind a cube. Light change. The projection of trees changes to blue sky and small clouds. On the platform,* MISS COX *and* MISS BAKER *are sunbathing: wearing bathing suits, lying on a rug, their arms around each other. They are kissing as the* FATHER *and* SON *re-appear breathless after their climb. The* SON *says nothing.* MISS BAKER *puts a hand over* MISS COX's *mouth.*

What can you see?

SON. Three counties . . .

315 FATHER. Be my eyes then. Paint me the picture . . .

SON (*pause*). We can just see three counties. Stretched out. That's all we can see.

FATHER. A fine prospect?

SON. Yes. A fine prospect.

320 FATHER. We've bagged a good many sights today! What've we seen?

SON. We saw a hare. Oh, and that butterfly.

FATHER. Danaius Chrysippus! The one that flaunts a large type of powder puff. You described it to me. You painted me the picture.

SON. Shall we go home now?

325 FATHER. We saw a lot today.

As the SON *moves back towards the door the* FATHER *moves with him.*

We saw a good deal – of the monstrous persistence of Nature . . .

The FATHER *and the* SON *move away,* MISS BAKER *takes her hand off* MISS COX's *mouth releasing a cascade of giggles as the light fades.*

1970   1971

Patricia Beer
1924–

Patricia Beer was born in Exmouth, Devon, and educated at Exmouth
Grammar School, Exeter University, and St Hugh's College, Oxford.
She worked in Italy from 1946 to 1953, and was Senior Lecturer at
Goldsmith's College, London, from 1962 to 1968. Her books of
poems include *The Loss of the Magyar* (1959) and *Spanish Balcony*
(1973). *Selected Poems* came out in 1980. *Mrs Beer's House* (1968) is
her autobiography; *Moon's Ottery* (1978), her only novel, is set in
sixteenth-century Devon.

SPANISH BALCONY

The trains that have been howling
Out on the plain all night
Have gone quiet or away.
Ordinary noises have come back to the town
5   And light to the balcony
Where today's batch of morning glories
Have begun to stir.

The moon remains, uselessly, in the smooth sky
White and rumpled like a vaccination mark.

10   Someone puts a melon into a patch of sun
To ripen for this evening. On the pavement
Stands a basket of pig's trotters
Not divisible by four.

Twenty morning glories have come out by now
15   More than any day this year.
They ride on the heat.

All the clocks in the town are wrong.
Light lowers and one roof leads to another.
This is the time of day when in the churches
20   Every Madonna dressed in party clothes
Begins to look less out of place.

Twenty blue morning glories have shut for ever.
They lie beside tomorrow's lot,
The same shape, dead or sleeping,
25   But there is no doubt which is which.

The golden melon has been taken in.
The moon has more point now.
Somewhere the trains are getting ready to howl.

1973

Elizabeth Jennings
1926–

Elizabeth Joan Jennings was born in Boston, Lincolnshire, and educated at Oxford High School and St Anne's College, Oxford. She worked in the Oxford City Library from 1950 to 1958, was a publisher's reader from 1958 to 1960, and became a freelance writer in 1961. Visits to Italy, and a Catholic faith which has sustained her through periods of mental breakdown, are reflected in her honest, moving poems. Her *Collected Poems* (1967) drew on several earlier books. *Moments of Grace* was published in 1979.

40 SAN PAOLO† FUORI LE MURA, ROME

It is the stone makes stillness here. I think
There could not be so much silence if
The columns were not set there rank on rank,
For silence needs a shape in which to sink
5   And stillness needs these shadows for its life.

My darkness throws so little space before
My body where it stands, and yet my mind
Needs the large echoing churches and the roar
Of streets outside its own calm place to find
10   Where the soft doves of peace withdraw, withdraw.

The alabaster windows here permit
Only suggestions of the sun to slide
Into the church and make a glow in it;
The battering daylight leaps at large outside
15   Though what slips here through jewels seems most fit.

And here one might in his discovered calm
Feel the great building draw away from him,
His head bent closely down upon his arm,
With all the sun subsiding to a dim
20   Past-dreamt-of peace, a kind of coming home.

San Paolo   (Church of) Saint Paul Outside the Walls (Italian)

For me the senses still have their full sway
Even where prayer comes quicker than an act.
I cannot quite forget the blazing day,
The alabaster windows or the way
25   The light refuses to be called abstract.

1958

THE NOVICE

She turns her head demurely. In a year
Or two she will
Be able to smile openly at all
She once enjoyed so much. Now there's a wall,
5   Also a grille.
Only the narrow, indoor things are clear.

She is not certain yet if she will stay.
She watches those
Who have been living here for many years.
10   No doubt upon each timeless face appears.
These stayed and chose
And in their suffering learnt how to pray.

Upon her window-sill two turtle doves
Gently demur.
15   All of the noisy world is here brought low
To these quiet birds who come and go
And seem to her
So far removed from all she hates and loves.

1967

William Trevor

1928–

William Trevor (William Trevor Cox) was born in County Cork and educated at Trinity College, Dublin. His novels include *The Old Boys* (1964), *Elizabeth Alone* (1973) and *Fools of Fortune* (1983). Volumes of short stories include *The Day We Got Drunk on Cake* (1969), *Angels at the Ritz* (1975), *Beyond the Pale* (1981) and *The News from Ireland* (1986). He has lived in Ireland for most of his life. Many of his settings are Irish but he writes convincingly about England and the English, 'I don't know who now has the most right to claim Mr Trevor,' the novelist John Fowles has said, 'England or Ireland, nor do I much care, since it is clear to me that his excellence comes from a happy marriage of central values in both traditions.'

From LUNCH IN WINTER

The Bayeux Lounge

That evening she sat in her usual corner of the Bayeux Lounge,† sipping vodka and tonic and thinking about the day. She'd been terrible; if she knew poor Fitz's number she'd ring him now from the booth in the passage and say she was sorry. 'Wine goes to your head, Nancy,' Laurie
5 Henderson used to say and it was true. A few glasses of red wine in the Trattoria San Michele† and she was pawing at a waiter who was young enough to be her son. And Fitz politely sat there, officer and gentleman still written all over him, saying he'd sell his house up and come to London. The waiter'd probably thought she was after his body.
10   Not that it mattered what he thought, because he and the Trattoria San Michele already belonged in Memory Lane. She'd never been there until that lunchtime six months ago when old Fitz had said, 'Let's turn in here.' No word would come from him, she sensed that also: never again on a Thursday would she hurry along to the Trattoria San Michele
15 and say she was sorry she was late.

    I'll be around, no matter how you treat me now . . . She'd seen him

---

Bayeux Lounge in a hotel in Putney, London
Trattoria San Michele Italian restaurant, in London

first when they'd sung that number the grand finale; she'd suddenly
noticed him, three rows from the front. She'd seen him looking at her
and had wondered while she danced if he was Mr R. R.[†] Well, of
20   course, he had been in a way. He'd stood up for her to his awful
relations, he'd kissed away her tears, saying he would die for her. And
then the first thing she'd done when he'd married her after all that fuss,
when he'd gone back after his leave, was to imagine that that stupid
boy with a tubercular chest was the be-all and end-all. And when the
25   boy had proved beyond a shadow of doubt that he was no such thing
there was the new one they'd taken on for his tap-dancing.
       She smiled in the Bayeux Lounge, remembering the laughter and the
applause when the back legs of Jack and the Beanstalk's Dobbin
surprised everyone by breaking into that elegant tap-dance, and how
30   Jack and his mother had stood there with their mouths comically open.
She'd told Fitz about it a few lunches ago because, of course, she hadn't
been able to tell him at the time on account of the thing she'd had with
the back legs. He had nodded solemnly, poor Fitz, not really amused,
you could see, but pleased because she was happy to remember. A right
35   little trouble-maker that tap-dancer had turned out to be, and a right
little scrounge, begging every penny he could lay his hands on, with no
intention of paying a farthing back.
       If she'd run out of hope, she thought, she could have said yes, let's
try again. She could have admitted, because it was only fair to, that
40   she'd never be like the responsible woman who'd gone and died on
him. She could have pointed out that she'd never acquire the class of
his mother and his sister because she wasn't that sort of person. She'd
thought all that out a few weeks ago, knowing what he was getting
around to. She'd thought it was awful for him to be going to a bureau
45   place and have women telling him about how the heat affected their
feet. She'd imagined saying yes and then humming something special,
probably *Love is the Sweetest Thing*,[†] and leaning her face towards
him across the table, waiting for his kiss again. But of course you
couldn't live in fantasies you couldn't just pretend.
50   'Ready for your second, Nancy?' the barmaid called across the empty
lounge, and she said yes she thought she was.
       You gave up hope if you just agreed because it sounded cosy. When
he'd swept her off her feet all those years ago everything had sounded
lovely: being with him in some nice place when the War was over,
55   never again being short, the flowers he brought her. 'No need to come
to London, Fitz,' she might have said today. 'Let's just go and live in
your house by the sea.' And he'd have been delighted and relieved,

---

Mr R. R.   Mr 'Robin Right' – an imaginary,   *Love is the Sweetest Thing*   dance tune,
         ideal husband   popular in the 1930s

because he'd only mentioned selling up in order to show her that he
would if she wanted him to. But all hope would be gone if she'd agreed.

60 She sighed, sorry for him, imagining him in the house he talked
about. He'd have arrived there by now, and she imagined him turning
the light on and everything coming to life. You could tell from the way
he talked that there were memories there for him, that the woman he'd
married was still all over the place: it wasn't because he'd finished

65 making a stone wall in the garden that he wanted to move on. He'd
probably pour himself a drink and sit down to watch the television;
he'd open a tin later on. She imagined him putting a match to the fire
and pulling over the curtains. Probably in a drawer somewhere he had
a photo of her as a sunflower. He'd maybe sit with it in his hand, with

70 his drink and the television. 'Dear, it's a fantasy,' she murmured. 'It
couldn't ever have worked second time round, no more'n it did before.'

'Warm your bones, Nancy,' the barmaid said, placing her second
vodka and tonic on a cardboard mat on the table where she sat. 'Freeze
you tonight, it would.'

75 'Yes, it's very cold.'

She hadn't returned to the flat after the visit to the Trattoria San
Michele; somehow she hadn't felt like it. She'd walked about during
the couple of hours that had to pass before the Bayeux Lounge opened.
She'd looked in the shop windows, and looked at the young people

80 with their peculiarly coloured hair. Two boys in Eastern robes, with no
hair at all, had tried to sell her a record. She hadn't been keen to go
back to the flat because she wanted to save up the hope that something
might have come on the second post, an offer of a part. If she saved it
up it would still hover in her mind while she sat in the Bayeux Lounge –

85 just a chance in a million but that was how chances always were. It
was more likely, when her luck changed, that the telephone would ring,
but even so you could never rule out a letter. You never should. You
should never rule out anything.

She wished now she'd tried to tell him all that, even though he might

90 not ever have understood. She wished she'd explained that it was all to
do with not giving up hope. She'd felt the same when Eddie had got
the children, even though one of them wasn't his, and when they'd gone
on so about neglect. All she'd been doing was hoping then too, not
wanting to be defeated, not wanting to give in to what they demanded

95 where the children were concerned. Eddie had married someone else,
some woman who probably thought she was an awful kind of person
because she'd let her children go. But one day the children would write,
she knew that inside her somewhere; one day there'd be that letter
waiting for her, too.

100 She sipped more vodka and tonic. She knew as well that one day Mr
R. R. would suddenly be there to make up for every single thing. He'd

make up for all the disappointment, for Simpson and Eddie and Laurie
Henderson, for treating badly the one man who'd been good to you.
He'd make up for scrounging tap-dancers and waiters you wanted to
105 be with because there was sadness in their faces, and the dear old
Trattoria San Michele gone for ever into Memory Lane. You couldn't
give up on Mr R. R., might as well walk out and throw yourself down
into the river; like giving up on yourself it would be.

'I think of you only,' she murmured in her soft whisper, feeling much
110 better now because of the vodka and tonic, 'only wishing, wishing you
were by my side.' When she'd come in at half-past five she'd noticed a
chap booking in at the reception, some kind of foreign commercial
traveller since the tennis people naturally didn't come in winter; fiftyish,
handsome-ish, not badly dressed. She was glad they hadn't turned on
115 the television yet. From the corner where she sat she could see the stairs,
where sooner or later the chap would appear. He'd buy a drink and
then he'd look around and then she'd be.

1986

John Osborne

1929–

John James Osborne, born in London and educated at Belmont College, Devon, became an actor in repertory theatre and started writing plays in the early 1950s. The London success of *Look Back in Anger* (published 1957) in 1956, whose abusive protagonist Jimmie Porter pours scorn on stuffy 'Edwardian' values, made Osborne's name, helped to give vogue to the term 'angry young man', and encouraged theatre companies to stage new types of drama by young playwrights. Osborne's later plays include *The Entertainer* (1957), *Inadmissible Evidence* (1964), *A Patriot for Me* (1965), and *West of Suez* (1971). Osborne has become a combative, splenetic writer on public issues. His 'Damn You England' letter in *Tribune* remains the most famous of his newspaper pronouncements.

The opening scene of *Look Back in Anger* establishes the relationship between Jimmie Porter, his wife and his partner, and shows something of the tensions which will drive Porter to his famous attack upon the Establishment and the Empire.

From LOOK BACK IN ANGER

[Damn Then All]   Act I

Standing L., *below the food cupboard, is* ALISON. *She is leaning over an ironing board. Beside her is a pile of clothes. Hers is the most elusive personality to catch in the uneasy polyphony of these three people. She is tuned in a different key, a key of well-bred malaise that is often drowned in the robust orchestration of the other two. Hanging over the grubby, but expensive, skirt she is wearing is a cherry-red shirt of* JIMMY'S, *but she manages somehow to look quite elegant in it. She is roughly the same age as the men. Somehow, their combined physical oddity makes her beauty more striking than it really is. She is tall, slim, dark. The bones of her face are long and delicate. There is a surprising reservation about her eyes, which are so large and deep they should make equivocation impossible. The room is still, smoke filled. The only sound is the occasional thud of* ALISON's *iron on the board. It is one of those chilly spring evenings, all cloud and shadows. Presently,* JIMMY *throws his paper down.*

JIMMY. Why do I do this every Sunday? Even the book reviews seem to be the same as last week's. Different books – same reviews. Have you finished that one yet?

CLIFF. Not yet.

5 JIMMY. I've just read three whole columns on the English Novel. Half of it's in French. Do the Sunday papers make *you* feel ignorant?

CLIFF. Not 'arf.

JIMMY. Well, you *are* ignorant. You're just a peasant.   (*To* ALISON.) What about you? You're not a peasant are you?

10 ALISON (*absently*). What's that?

JIMMY. I said do the papers make you feel you're not so brilliant after all?

ALISON. Oh – I haven't read them yet.

JIMMY. I didn't ask you that. I said –

15 CLIFF. Leave the poor girlie alone. She's busy.

JIMMY. Well, she can talk, can't she? You can talk, can't you? You can express an opinion. Or does the White Woman's Burden make it impossible to think?

ALISON. I'm sorry. I wasn't listening properly.

20 JIMMY. You bet you weren't listening. Old Porter talks, and everyone turns over and goes to sleep. And Mrs Porter gets 'em all going with the first yawn.

CLIFF. Leave her alone, I said.

JIMMY (*shouting*). All right, dear. Go back to sleep. It was only me
25 talking. You know? Talking? Remember? I'm sorry.

CLIFF. Stop yelling. I'm trying to read.

JIMMY. Why do you bother? You can't understand a word of it.

CLIFF. Uh huh.

JIMMY. You're too ignorant.

30 CLIFF. Yes, and uneducated. Now shut up, will you?

JIMMY. Why don't you get my wife to explain it to you? She's educated. (*To her.*) That's right, isn't it?

CLIFF (*kicking out at him from behind his paper*). Leave her alone, I said.

JIMMY. Do that again, you Welsh ruffian, and I'll pull your ears off.
         (*He bangs* CLIFF's *paper out of his hands.*)

35 CLIFF (*leaning forward*). Listen – I'm trying to better myself. Let me get on with it, you big, horrible man. Give it me. (*Puts his hand out for paper.*)

ALISON. Oh, give it to him, Jimmy, for heaven's sake! I can't think!

CLIFF. Yes, come on, give me the paper. She can't think.

JIMMY. Can't think! (*Throws the paper back at him.*) She hasn't had a
40   thought for years! Have you?

ALISON. No.

JIMMY (*picks up a weekly*). I'm getting hungry.

ALISON. Oh, no, not already!

CLIFF. He's a bloody pig.

45   JIMMY. I'm not a pig. I just like food – that's all.

CLIFF. Like it! You're like a sexual maniac – only with you it's food.
       You'll end up in the *News of the World*, boyo, you wait. James
       Porter, aged twenty-five was bound over last week after pleading
       guilty to interfering with a small cabbage and two tins of beans on
50   his way home from the Builders' Arms. The accused said he hadn't
       been feeling well for some time, and had been having black-outs. He
       asked for his good record as an air-raid warden, second class, to be
       taken into account.

JIMMY (*grins*). Oh, yes, yes, yes. I like to eat. I'd like to live too. Do you
55   mind?

CLIFF. Don't see any use in your eating at all. You never get any fatter.

JIMMY. People like me don't get fat. I've tried to tell you before. We just
       burn everything up. Now shut up while I read. You can make me
       some more tea.

60   CLIFF. Good God, you've just had a great pot-ful! I only had one cup.

JIMMY. Like hell! Make some more.

CLIFF (*to* ALISON). Isn't that right? Didn't I only have one cup?

ALISON (*without looking up*). That's right.

CLIFF. There you are. And she only had one cup, too. I saw her. You
65   guzzled the lot.

JIMMY (*reading his weekly*). Put the kettle on.

CLIFF. Put it on yourself. You've creased up my paper.

JIMMY. I'm the only one who knows how to treat a paper, or anything
       else, in this house. (*Picks up another paper.*) Girl here wants to know
70   whether her boy friend will lose all respect for her if she gives him
       what he asks for. Stupid bitch.

CLIFF. Just let me get at her, that's all.

JIMMY. Who buys this damned thing? (*Throws it down.*) Haven't you
       read the other posh paper yet?

75   CLIFF. Which?

JIMMY. Well, there are only two posh papers on a Sunday – the one
       you're reading, and this one. Come on, let me have that one, and
       you take this.

CLIFF. Oh, all right.

                            (*They exchange.*)

80   I was only reading the Bishop of Bromley. (*Puts out his hand to*
       ALISON.) How are you, dullin'?

ALISON. All right thank you, dear.

CLIFF (*grasping her hand*). Why don't you leave all that, and sit down for a bit? You look tired.

85   ALISON (*smiling*). I haven't much more to do.

CLIFF (*kisses her hand, and puts her fingers in his mouth*). She's a beautiful girl, isn't she?

JIMMY. That's what they all tell me. (*His eyes meet* ALISON'S.)

CLIFF. It's a lovely, delicious paw you've got. Ummmmm. I'm going to
90   bite it off.

ALISON. Don't! I'll burn his shirt.

JIMMY. Give her her finger back, and don't be so sickening. What's the Bishop of Bromley say?

CLIFF (*letting go of* ALISON). Oh, it says here that he makes a very moving
95   appeal to all Christians to do all they can to assist in the manufacture of the H-bomb.

JIMMY. Yes, well, that's quite moving, I suppose. (*To* ALISON.) Are you moved, my darling?

ALISON. Well, naturally.

100   JIMMY. There you are: even my wife is moved. I ought to send the Bishop a subscription. Let's see. What else does he say? Dumdidumdidumdi-dum. Ah yes. He's upset because someone has suggested that he supports the rich against the poor. He says he denies the difference of class distinctions. 'This idea has been persistently and wickedly
105   fostered by – the working-classes!' Well!

(*He looks up at both of them for reaction, but* CLIFF *is reading, and* ALISON *is intent on her ironing.*)

JIMMY (*to* CLIFF). Did you read that bit?

CLIFF. Um?

(*He has lost them, and he knows it, but he won't leave it.*)

JIMMY (*to* ALISON). You don't suppose your father could have written it, do you?

110   ALISON. Written what?

JIMMY. What I just read out, of course.

ALISON. Why should my father have written it?

JIMMY. Sounds rather like Daddy, don't you think?

ALISON. Does it?

115   JIMMY. Is the Bishop of Bromley his *nom de plume* [pen-name], do you think?

CLIFF. Don't take any notice of him. He's being offensive. And it's so easy for him.

JIMMY (*quickly*). Did you read about the woman who went to the mass
120   meeting of a certain American evangelist at Earls Court? She went forward, to declare herself for love or whatever it is, and, in the rush of converts to get to the front, she broke four ribs and got kicked in

the head. She was yelling her head off in agony but, with fifty-
thousand people putting all they'd got into 'Onward Christian
125   Soldiers', nobody even knew she was there.

(*He looks up sharply for a response, but there isn't any.*)

Sometimes, I wonder if there isn't something wrong with me. What
about that tea?

CLIFF (*still behind paper*). What tea?

JIMMY. Put the kettle on.

(ALISON *looks at him.*)

130   ALISON. Do you want some more tea?

JIMMY. I don't know. No, I don't think so.

ALISON. Do you want some, Cliff?

JIMMY. No, he doesn't. How much longer will you be doing that?

ALISON. Won't be long.

135   JIMMY. God, how I hate Sundays! It's always so depressing, always the
same. We never seem to get any farther, do we? Always the same
ritual. Reading the papers, drinking tea, ironing. A few more hours,
and another week gone. Our youth is slipping away. Do you know
that?

140   CLIFF (*throws down paper*). What's that?

JIMMY (*casually*). Oh, nothing, nothing. Damn you, damn both of you,
damn them all.

CLIFF. Let's go to the pictures. (*To* ALISON.) What do you say, lovely?

ALISON. I don't think I'll be able to. Perhaps Jimmy would like to go.

145   (*To* JIMMY.) Would you like to?

JIMMY. And have my enjoyment ruined by the Sunday night yobs in the
front row? No thank you. (*Pause.*) Did you read [J.B.] Priestley's
piece this week? Why on earth I ask, I don't know. I know damned
well you haven't. Why do I spend ninepence on that damned paper

150   every week? Nobody reads it except me. Nobody can be bothered.
No one can raise themselves out of their delicious sloth. You two
will drive me round the bend soon – I know it, as sure as I'm sitting
here. I know you're going to drive me mad. Oh heavens, how I long
for a little ordinary human enthusiasm. Just enthusiasm – that's all. I

155   want to hear a warm, thrilling voice cry out Hallelujah! (*He bangs
his breast theatrically.*) Hallelujah! I'm alive! I've an idea. Why don't
we have a little game? Let's pretend that we're human beings, and
that we're actually alive. Just for a while. What do you say? Let's
pretend we're human. (*He looks from one to the other.*) Oh, brother,

160   it's such a long time since I was with anyone who got enthusiastic
about anything.

CLIFF. What did he say?

JIMMY (*resentful of being dragged away from his pursuit of* ALISON). What
did who say?

165   CLIFF. Mr Priestley.

    JIMMY. What he always says, I suppose. He's like Daddy – still casting
        well-fed glances back to the Edwardian twilight from his comfortable,
        disenfranchised wilderness. What the devil have you done to those
        trousers?

170   CLIFF. Done?

    JIMMY. Are they the ones you bought last week-end? Look at them. Do
        you see what he's done to those new trousers?

    ALISON. You are naughty, Cliff. They look dreadful.

    JIMMY. You spent good money on a new pair of trousers, and then
175   sprawl about in them like a savage. What do you think you're going
        to do when I'm not around to look after you? Well, what are you
        going to do? Tell me.

    CLIFF (grinning). I don't know. (To ALISON.) What am I going to do,
        lovely?

180   ALISON. You'd better take them off.

    JIMMY. Yes, go on. Take 'em off. And I'll kick your behind for you.

    ALISON. I'll give them a press while I've got the iron on.

    CLIFF. O.K. (Starts taking them off.) I'll just empty the pockets. (Takes
        out keys, matches, handkerchief.)

    JIMMY. Give me those matches, will you?

185   CLIFF. Oh, you're not going to start up that old pipe again, are you? It
        stinks the place out. (To ALISON.) Doesn't it smell awful?

                    (JIMMY grabs the matches and lights up.)

    ALISON. I don't mind it. I've got used to it.

    JIMMY. She's a great one for getting used to things. If she were to die,
        and wake up in paradise – after the first five minutes, she'd have got
190   used to it.

    CLIFF (hands her the trousers). Thank you, lovely. Give me a cigarette,
        will you?

    JIMMY. Don't give him one.

    CLIFF. I can't stand the stink of that old pipe any longer. I must have a
195   cigarette.

    JIMMY. I thought the doctor said no cigarettes?

    CLIFF. Oh, why doesn't he shut up?

    JIMMY. All right. They're your ulcers. Go ahead, and have a bellyache,
        if that's what you want. I give up. I give up. I'm sick of doing things
200   for people. And all for what?

                (ALISON gives CLIFF a cigarette. They both light up, and she goes on
                    with her ironing.)

    Nobody thinks, nobody cares. No beliefs, no convictions, and no
    enthusiasm. Just another Sunday evening.

                (CLIFF sits down again, in his pullover and shorts.)

    Perhaps there's a concert on. (Picks up Radio Times.) Ah. (Nudges

CLIFF *with his foot.*) Make some more tea.
(CLIFF *grunts. He is reading again.*)
205 Oh, yes. There's a Vaughan Williams.† Well, that's something, anyway. Something strong, something simple, something English. I suppose people like me aren't supposed to be very patriotic. Somebody said – what was it? – We get our cooking from Paris. (*That's a laugh.*) Our politics from Moscow, and our morals from Port Said. Something
210 like that, anyway. Who was it? (*Pause.*) Well, you wouldn't know anyway. I hate to admit it, but I think I can understand how her Daddy must have felt when he came back from India, after all those years away. The old Edwardian brigade do make their brief little world look pretty tempting. All home-made cakes and croquet, bright
215 ideas, bright uniforms. Always the same picture: high summer, the long days in the sun, slim volumes of verse, crisp linen, the smell of starch. What a romantic picture. Phoney, too, of course. It must have rained sometimes. Still, even I regret it somehow, phoney or not. If you've no world of your own, it's rather pleasant to regret the passing
220 of someone else's. I must be getting sentimental. But I must say it's pretty dreary living in the American Age – unless you're an American of course. Perhaps all our children will be Americans. That's a thought, isn't it?
(*He gives* CLIFF *a kick, and shouts at him.*)
I said, that's a thought!
225 CLIFF. You did?
JIMMY. You sit there like a lump of dough. I thought you were going to make me some tea.
(CLIFF *groans.* JIMMY *turns to* ALISON.)
Is your friend Webster coming tonight?
ALISON. He might drop in. You know what he is.
230 JIMMY. Well, I hope he doesn't. I don't think I could take Webster tonight.
ALISON. I thought you said he was the only person who spoke your language.
JIMMY. So he is. Different dialect but same language. I like him. He's
235 got bite, edge, drive –
ALISON. Enthusiasm.
JIMMY. You've got it. When he comes here, I begin to feel exhilarated. He doesn't like me, but he gives me something, which is more than I get from most people. Not since –
240 ALISON. Yes, we know. Not since you were living with Madeline.

---

a Vaughan Williams music by the English
composer Ralph Vaughan Williams (1872–1958)

(*She folds some of the clothes she has already ironed, and crosses to the bed with them.*)

CLIFF (*behind paper again*). Who's Madeline?

ALISON. Oh, wake up, dear. You've heard about Madeline enough times. She was his mistress. Remember? When he was fourteen. Or was it thirteen?

245 JIMMY. Eighteen.

ALISON. He owes just about everything to Madeline.

CLIFF. I get mixed up with all your women. Was she the one all those years older than you?

JIMMY. Ten years.

250 CLIFF. Proper little Marchbanks, you are!

JIMMY. What time's that concert on? (*Checks paper.*)

CLIFF (*yawns*). Oh, I feel so sleepy. Don't feel like standing behind that blinking sweet-stall again tomorrow. Why don't you do it on your own, and let me sleep in?

255 JIMMY. I've got to be at the factory first thing, to get some more stock, so you'll have to put it up on your own. Another five minutes.

(ALISON *has returned to her ironing board. She stands with her arms folded, smoking, staring thoughtfully.*)

She had more animation in her little finger than you two put together.

CLIFF. Who did?

ALISON. Madeline.

260 JIMMY. Her curiosity about things, and about people was staggering. It wasn't just a naïve nosiness. With her, it was simply the delight of being awake, and watching.

(ALISON *starts to press* CLIFF'S *trousers.*)

CLIFF (*behind paper*). Perhaps I will make some tea, after all.

JIMMY (*quietly*). Just to be with her was an adventure. Even to sit on the
265 top of a bus with her was like setting out with Ulysses.

CLIFF. Wouldn't have said Webster was much like Ulysses. He's an ugly little devil.

JIMMY. I'm not talking about Webster, stupid. He's all right though, in his way. A sort of female Emily Brontë. He's the only one of your
270 friends (*To* ALISON.) who's worth tuppence, anyway. I'm surprised you get on with him.

ALISON. So is he, I think.

JIMMY (*rising to window* R., *and looking out*). He's not only got guts, but sensitivity as well. That's about the rarest combination I can
275 think of. None of your other friends have got either.

ALISON (*very quietly and earnestly*). Jimmy, please – don't go on.

(JIMMY *turns and looks at* ALISON. *The tired appeal in her voice has*

*pulled him up suddenly. But he soon gathers himself for a new
assault. He walks* C., *behind* CLIFF, *and stands, looking down at his
head.*)

JIMMY. Your friends – there's a shower for you.

CLIFF (*mumbling*). Dry up. Let her get on with my trousers.

JIMMY (*musingly*). Don't think I could provoke her. Nothing I could do
280   would provoke her. Not even if I were to drop dead.

CLIFF. Then drop dead.

JIMMY. They're either militant – like her Mummy and Daddy – militant,
arrogant and full of malice, or vague. She's somewhere between the
two.

285   CLIFF. Why don't you listen to that concert of yours? And don't stand
behind me. That blooming droning on behind me gives me a funny
feeling down the spine.

(JIMMY *gives his ears a twist and* CLIFF *roars with pain.* JIMMY *grins
back at him.*)

That hurt, you rotten sadist! (*To* ALISON.) I wish you'd kick his head
in for him.

290   JIMMY (*moving in between them*). Have you ever seen her brother?
Brother Nigel? The straight-backed, chinless wonder from Sandhurst?
I only met him once myself. He asked me to step outside when I told
his mother she was evil-minded.

CLIFF. And did you?

295   JIMMY. Certainly not. He's a big chap. Well, you've never heard so many
well-bred commonplaces come from beneath the same bowler hat.
The Platitude from Outer Space – that's brother Nigel. He'll end up
in the Cabinet one day, make no mistake. But somewhere at the back
of that mind is the vague knowledge that he and his pals have been
300   plundering and fooling everybody for generations. (*Going* U.S., *and
turning.*) Now Nigel is just about as vague as you can get without
being actually invisible. And invisible politicians aren't much use to
anyone – not even to *his* supporters! And nothing is more vague
about Nigel than his knowledge. His knowledge of life and ordinary
305   human beings is so hazy, he really deserves some sort of decoration
for it – a medal inscribed 'For Vaguery in the Field'. But it wouldn't
do for him to be troubled by any stabs of conscience, however vague.
(*Moving* D. *again.*) Besides, he's a patriot and an Englishman, and he
doesn't like the idea that he may have been selling out his countryman
310   all these years, so what does he do? The only thing he *can* do – seek
sanctuary in his own stupidity. The only way to keep things as much
like they always have been possible, is to make any alternative too
much for your poor, tiny brain to grasp. It takes some doing
nowadays. It really does. But they knew all about character building
315   at Nigel's school, and he'll make it all right. Don't you worry, he'll

make it. And, what's more, he'll do it better than anybody else!

(*There is no sound, only the plod of* ALISON's *iron. Her eyes are fixed on what she is doing.* CLIFF *stares at the floor. His cheerfulness has deserted him for the moment.* JIMMY *is rather shakily triumphant. He cannot allow himself to look at either of them to catch their response to his rhetoric, so he moves across to the window, to recover himself, and look out.*)

It's started to rain. That's all it needs. This room and the rain.

(*He's been cheated out of his response, but he's got to draw blood somehow.*)

(*Conversationally.*) Yes, that's the little woman's family. You know Mummy and Daddy, of course. And don't let the Marquess of Queensberry manner fool you. They'll kick you in the groin while you're handing your hat to the maid. As for Nigel and Alison – (*In a reverent, Stuart Hibberd voice.*) Nigel and Alison. They're what they sound like: sycophantic, phlegmatic and pusillanimous.

CLIFF. I'll bet that concert's started by now. Shall I put it on?

JIMMY. I looked up that word the other day. It's one of those words I've never been quite sure of, but always thought I knew.

CLIFF. What was that?

JIMMY. I told you – pusillanimous. Do you know what it means?

(CLIFF *shakes his head.*)

Neither did I really. All this time, I have been married to this woman, this monument to non-attachment, and suddenly I discover that there is actually a word that sums her up. Not just an adjective in the English language to describe her with – it's her name! Pusillanimous! It sounds like some fleshy Roman matron, doesn't it? The Lady Pusillanimous seen here with her husband Sextus, on their way to the Games.

(CLIFF *looks troubled, and glances uneasily at* ALISON.)

Poor old Sextus! If he were put into a Hollywood film, he's so unimpressive, they'd make some poor British actor play the part. He doesn't know it, but those beefcake Christians will make off with his wife in the wonder of stereophonic sound before the picture's over.

(ALISON *leans against the board, and closes her eyes.*)

The Lady Pusillanimous has been promised a brighter easier world than old Sextus can ever offer her. Hi, Pusey! What say we get the hell down to the Arena, and maybe feed ourselves to a couple of lions, huh?

ALISON. God help me, if he doesn't stop, I'll go out of my mind in a minute.

JIMMY. Why don't you? That would be something, anyway. (*Crosses to chest of drawers* R.) But I haven't told you what it means yet, have I? (*Picks up dictionary.*) I don't have to tell her – she knows. In fact, if

350 my pronunciation is at fault, she'll probably wait for a suitably public
moment to correct it. Here it is. I quote: 'Pusillanimous. Adjective.
Wanting of firmness of mind, of small courage, having a little mind,
mean spirited, cowardly, timidity of mind. From the Latin pusillus,
very little, and animus, the mind.' (*Slams the book shut.*) That's my
wife! That's *her* isn't it? Behold the Lady Pusillanimous. (*Shouting*
355 *hoarsely.*) Hi, Pusey! When's your next picture?

(JIMMY *watches her, waiting for her to break. For no more than a*
flash, ALISON's *face seems to contort, and it looks as though she*
might throw her head back, and scream. But it passes in a moment.
She is used to these carefully rehearsed attacks, and it doesn't look
as though he will get his triumph tonight. She carries on with her
ironing. JIMMY *crosses, and switches on the radio. The Vaughan*
Williams concert has started. He goes back to his chair, leans back
in it, and closes his eyes.)

ALISON (*handing* CLIFF *his trousers.*) There you are, dear. They're not very
good, but they'll do for now.

(CLIFF *gets up and puts them on.*)

CLIFF. Oh, that's lovely.

ALISON. Now try and look after them. I'll give them a real press later
360 on.

CLIFF. Thank you, you beautiful, darling girl.

1956   1957

Ted Hughes
1930–

Edward James Hughes was born in Mytholmroyd, Yorkshire, and educated at Mexborough Grammar School and Pembroke College, Cambridge. He married the poet Sylvia Plath, whom he met at Cambridge, in 1956. His first book of poems, *The Hawk in the Rain* (1957), reflects his fascination with beauty and cruelty in nature. The sequence of poems in *Crow* (1970) was praised by some reviewers as original and powerful but castigated by critics associated with 'the Movement' who found it verbally slack and self-indulgent in its emphasis on violence. Hughes has published many verse collections, poems and plays for children, and an adaptation of Seneca's *Oedipus* (1968). He succeeded Betjeman as Poet Laureate in 1984.

THE JAGUAR

The apes yawn and adore their fleas in the sun.
The parrots shriek as if they were on fire, or strut
Like cheap tarts to attract the stroller with the nut.
Fatigued with indolence, tiger and lion

5   Lie still as the sun. The boa-constrictor's coil
Is a fossil. Cage after cage seems empty, or
Stinks of sleepers from the breathing straw.
It might be painted on a nursery wall.

But who runs like the rest past these arrives
10   At a cage where the crowd stands, stares, mesmerized.
As a child at a dream, at a jaguar hurrying enraged
Through prison darkness after the drills of his eyes

On a short fierce fuse. Not in boredom –
The eye satisfied to be blind in fire,
15   By the bang of blood in the brain deaf the ear –
He spins from the bars, but there's no cage to him

More than to the visionary his cell:
His stride is wildernesses of freedom:
The world rolls under the long thrust of his heel.
20   Over the cage floor the horizons come.

1954   1957

PIKE

Pike, three inches long, perfect
Pike in all parts, green tigering the gold.
Killers from the egg: the malevolent aged grin.
They dance on the surface among the flies.

5   Or move, stunned by their own grandeur
Over a bed of emerald, silhouette
Of submarine delicacy and horror.
A hundred feet long in their world.

In ponds, under the heat-struck lily pads –
10   Gloom of their stillness:
Logged on last year's black leaves, watching upwards.
Or hung in an amber cavern of weeds

The jaws' hooked clamp and fangs
Not to be changed at this date;
15   A life subdued to its instrument;
The gills kneading quietly, and the pectorals.

Three we kept behind glass,
Jungled in weed: three inches, four,
And four and a half: fed fry to them –
20   Suddenly there were two. Finally one.

With a sag belly and the grin it was born with.
And indeed they spare nobody.
Two, six pounds each, over two feet long,
High and dry and dead in the willow-herb –

25   One jammed past its gills down the other's gullet:
The outside eye stared: as a vice locks –

The same iron in this eye
Though its film shrank in death.

A pond I fished, fifty yards across,
30   Whose lilies and muscular tench
Had outlasted every visible stone
Of the monastery that planted them —

Stilled legendary depth:
It was as deep as England. It held
35   Pike too immense to stir, so immense and old
That past nightfall I dared not cast

But silently cast and fished
With the hair frozen on my head
For what might move, for what eye might move.
40   The still splashes on the dark pond,

Owls hushing the floating woods
Frail on my ear against the dream
Darkness beneath night's darkness had freed,
That rose slowly towards me, watching.

1959   1960

Harold Pinter
1930–

Harold Pinter was born in the East End of London and educated at Hackney Downs Grammar School. *The Room*, his first play, written while he was a repertory actor, was performed in 1957. *The Birthday Party* (1958) and *The Caretaker* (1960) established his reputation as a playwright. In these and later plays, notably *The Homecoming* (1965), he captured the absurdities and inadequacies of real-life speech and dialogue. Pinter has also written for radio and television; among his screen plays, his script for Joseph Losey's *The Go-Between*, based on the novel by L. P. Hartley (1895–1972), is especially successful.

In Act Two of *The Caretaker*, Davies, the old tramp who has been provided with shelter, and the offer of a job as caretaker, by the rather odd Aston, is now consulted about Aston by his brother, Mick.

From THE CARETAKER

[Worries]

MICK. I had a bit of beetroot somewhere. Must have mislaid it.

Pause.

DAVIES *chews the sandwich.* MICK *watches him eat. He then rises and strolls downstage.*

Uuh . . . listen . . . can I ask your advice? I mean, you're a man of the world. Can I ask your advice about something?

DAVIES. You go right ahead.

5   MICK. Well, what it is, you see, I'm . . . I'm a bit worried about my brother.

DAVIES. Your brother?

MICK. Yes . . . you see, his trouble is . . .

DAVIES. What?

10   MICK. Well, it's not a very nice thing to say . . .

DAVIES (*rising, coming downstage*). Go on now, you say it.

MICK *looks at him.*

MICK. He doesn't like work.

Pause.

DAVIES. Go on!

MICK. No, he just doesn't like work, that's his trouble.

15   DAVIES. Is that a fact?

MICK. It's a terrible thing to have to say about your own brother.

DAVIES. Ay.

MICK. He's just shy of it. Very shy of it.

DAVIES. I know that sort.

20   MICK. You know the type?

DAVIES. I've met them.

MICK. I mean, I want to get him going in the world.

DAVIES. Stands to reason, man.

MICK. If you got an older brother you want to push him on, you want

25   to see him make his way. Can't have him idle, he's only doing himself
harm. That's what I say.

DAVIES. Yes.

MICK. But he won't buckle down to the job.

DAVIES. He don't like work.

30   MICK. Work shy.

DAVIES. Sounds like it to me.

MICK. You've met the type, have you?

DAVIES. Me? I know the sort.

MICK. Yes.

35   DAVIES. I know that sort. I've met them.

MICK. Causing me great anxiety. You see, I'm a working man: I'm a
tradesman. I've got my own van.

DAVIES. Is that a fact?

MICK. He's supposed to be doing a little job for me . . . I keep him here

40   to do a little job . . . but I don't know . . . I'm coming to the
conclusion he's a slow worker.

Pause.

What would your advice be?

DAVIES. Well . . . he's a funny bloke, your brother.

MICK. What?

45   DAVIES. I was saying, he's . . . he's a bit of a funny bloke, your brother.

MICK *stares at him.*

MICK. Funny? Why?

DAVIES. Well . . . he's funny. . . .

MICK. What's funny about him?

Pause.

DAVIES. Not liking work.

50 MICK. What's funny about that?

DAVIES. Nothing.

Pause.

MICK. I don't call it funny.

DAVIES. Nor me.

MICK. You don't want to start getting hypercritical.

55 DAVIES. No, no, I wasn't that, I wasn't . . . I was only saying . . .

MICK. Don't get too glib.

DAVIES. Look, all I meant was –

MICK. Cut it! (*Briskly.*) Look! I got a proposition to make to you. I'm thinking of taking over the running of this place, you see? I think it

60 could be run a bit more efficiently. I got a lot of ideas, a lot of plans. (*He eyes* DAVIES.) How would you like to stay on here, as caretaker?

DAVIES. What?

MICK. I'll be quite open with you. I could rely on a man like you around the place, keeping an eye on things.

65 DAVIES. Well now . . . wait a minute . . . I . . . I ain't never done no caretaking before, you know. . . .

MICK. Doesn't matter about that. It's just that you look a capable sort of man to me.

DAVIES. I am a capable sort of man. I mean to say, I've had plenty offers

70 in my time, you know, there's no getting away from that.

MICK. Well, I could see before, when you took out that knife, that you wouldn't let anyone mess you about.

DAVIES. No one messes me about, man.

MICK. I mean, you've been in the services, haven't you?

75 DAVIES. The what?

MICK. You been in the services. You can tell by your stance.

DAVIES. Oh . . . yes. Spent half my life there, man. Overseas . . . like . . . serving . . . I was.

MICK. In the colonies, weren't you?

80 DAVIES. I was over there. I was one of the first over there.

MICK. That's it. You're just the man I been looking for.

DAVIES. What for?

MICK. Caretaker.

DAVIES. Yes, well . . . look . . . listen . . . who's the landlord here, him

85 or you?

MICK. Me. I am. I got deeds to prove it.

DAVIES. Ah . . . (*Decisively.*) Well listen, I don't mind doing a bit of caretaking, I wouldn't mind looking after the place for you.

MICK. Of course, we'd come to a small financial agreement, mutually

90 beneficial.

DAVIES. I leave you to reckon that out, like.

MICK. Thanks. There's only one thing.

DAVIES. What's that?

MICK. Can you give me any references?

95   DAVIES. Eh?

MICK. Just to satisfy my solicitor.

DAVIES. I got plenty of references. All I got to do is to go down to Sidcup†
tomorrow. I got all the references I want down there.

MICK. Where's that?

100   DAVIES. Sidcup. He ain't only got my references down there, he got all
my papers down there. I know that place like the back of my hand.
I'm going down there anyway, see what I mean, I got to get down
there, or I'm done.

MICK. So we can always get hold of these references if we want them.

105   DAVIES. I'll be down there any day, I tell you. I was going down today,
but I'm . . . I'm waiting for the weather to break.

MICK. Ah.

DAVIES. Listen. You can't pick me up a pair of good shoes, can you? I
got a bad need for a good pair of shoes. I can't get anywhere without
110   a pair of good shoes, see? Do you think there's any chance of you
being able to pick me up a pair?

THE LIGHTS FADE TO BLACKOUT.

LIGHTS UP. *Morning.*

ASTON *is pulling on his trousers over long underwear. A slight
grimace. He looks around at the head of his bed, takes a towel
from the rail and waves it about. He pulls it down, goes to* DAVIES
and wakes him. DAVIES *sits up abruptly.*

ASTON. You said you wanted me to get you up.

DAVIES. What for?

ASTON. You said you were thinking of going to Sidcup.

115   DAVIES. Ay, that'd be a good thing, if I got there.

ASTON. Doesn't look much of a day.

DAVIES. Ay, well, that's shot it, en't it?

ASTON. I . . . I didn't have a very good night again.

DAVIES. I slept terrible.

Pause.

120   ASTON. You were making. . . .

DAVIES. Terrible. Had a bit of rain in the night, didn't it?

ASTON. Just a bit.

*He goes to his bed, picks up a small plank and begins to sandpaper
it.*

Sidcup   in Kent

DAVIES. Thought so. Come in on my head.

Pause.

Draught's blowing right in on my head, anyway.

Pause.

125 Can't you close that window behind that sack?

ASTON. You could.

DAVIES. Well then, what about it, then? The rain's coming right in on my head.

ASTON. Got to have a bit of air.

DAVIES *gets out of bed. He is wearing his trousers, waistcoat and vest.*

130 DAVIES (*putting on his sandals*). Listen. I've lived all my life in the air, boy. You don't have to tell me about air. What I'm saying is, there's too much air coming in that window when I'm asleep.

ASTON. Gets very stuffy in here without that window open.

ASTON *crosses to the chair, puts the plank on it, and continues sandpapering.*

DAVIES. Yes, but listen, you don't know what I'm telling you. That bloody
135 rain, man, come right in on my head. Spoils my sleep. I could catch my death of cold with it, with that draught. That's all I'm saying. Just shut that window and no one's going to catch any colds, that's all I'm saying.

Pause.

ASTON. I couldn't sleep in here without that window open.

140 DAVIES. Yes, but what about me? What . . . what you got to say about my position?

ASTON. Why don't you sleep the other way round?

DAVIES. What do you mean?

ASTON. Sleep with your feet to the window.

145 DAVIES. What good would that do?

ASTON. The rain wouldn't come in on your head.

DAVIES. No, I couldn't do that. I couldn't do that.

Pause.

I mean, I got used to sleeping this way. It isn't me has to change, it's that window. You see, it's raining now. Look at it. It's coming down
150 now.

Pause.

ASTON. I think I'll have a walk down to Goldhawk Road. I got talking to a man there. He had a saw bench. It looked in pretty good condition to me. Don't think it's much good to him.

Pause.

Have a walk down there, I think.

155   DAVIES. Listen to that. That's done my trip to Sidcup. Eh, what about closing that window now? It'll be coming in here.

ASTON. Close it for the time being.

DAVIES *closes the window and looks out.*

DAVIES. What's all that under that tarpaulin out there?

ASTON. Wood.

160   DAVIES. What for?

ASTON. To build my shed.

DAVIES *sits on his bed.*

DAVIES. You haven't come across that pair of shoes you was going to look out for me, have you?

ASTON. Oh. No, I'll see if I can pick some up today.

165   DAVIES. I can't go out in this with these, can I? I can't even go out and get a cup of tea.

ASTON. There's a café just along the road.

DAVIES. There may be, mate.

During ASTON'S *speech the room grows darker.*
By the close of the speech only ASTON *can be seen clearly.* DAVIES
and all the other objects are in the shadow. The fadedown of the
light must be as gradual, as protracted and as unobtrusive as
possible.

ASTON. I used to go there quite a bit. Oh, years ago now. But I stopped.

170   I used to like that place. Spent quite a bit of time in there. That was before I went away. Just before. I think that . . . place had a lot to do with it. They were all . . . a good bit older than me. But they always used to listen. I thought . . . they understood what I said. I mean I used to talk to them. I talked too much. That was my mistake.

175   The same in the factory. Standing there, or in the breaks, I used to . . . talk about things. And these men, they used to listen, whenever I . . . had anything to say. It was all right. The trouble was, I used to have kind of hallucinations. They weren't hallucinations, they . . . I used to get the feeling I could see things . . . very clearly . . . everything

180   . . . was so clear . . . everything used . . . everything used to get very quiet . . . everything got very quiet . . . all this . . . quiet . . . and . . . this clear sight . . . it was . . . but maybe I was wrong. Anyway,

someone must have said something. I didn't know anything about it. And ... some kind of lie must have got around. And this lie went round. I thought people started being funny. In that café. The factory. I couldn't understand it. Then one day they took me to a hospital, right outside London. They ... got me there. I didn't want to go. Anyway ... I tried to get out, quite a few times. But ... it wasn't very easy. They asked me questions, in there. Got me in and asked me all sorts of questions. Well, I told them ... when they wanted to know ... what my thoughts were. Hmmnn. Then one day ... this man ... doctor, I suppose ... the head one ... he was quite a man of ... distinction ... although I wasn't so sure about that. He called me in. He said ... he told me I had something. He said they'd concluded their examination. That's what he said. And he showed me a pile of papers and he said that I'd got something, some complaint. He said ... he just said that, you see. You've got ... this thing. That's your complaint. And we've decided, he said, that in your interests there's only one course we can take. He said ... but I can't ... exactly remember ... how he put it ... he said, we're going to do something to your brain. He said ... if we don't, you'll be in here for the rest of your life, but if we do, you stand a chance. You can go out, he said, and live like the others. What do you want to do to my brain, I said to him. But he just repeated what he'd said. Well, I wasn't a fool. I knew I was a minor. I knew he couldn't do anything to me without getting permission. I knew he had to get permission from my mother. So I wrote to her and told her what they were trying to do. But she signed their form, you see, giving them permission. I know that because he showed me her signature when I brought it up. Well, that night I tried to escape, that night. I spent five hours sawing at one of the bars on the window in this ward. Right throughout the dark. They used to shine a torch over the beds every half hour. So I timed it just right. And then it was nearly done, and a man had a ... he had a fit, right next to me. And they caught me, anyway. About a week later they started to come round and do this thing to the brain. We were all supposed to have it done, in this ward. And they came round and did it one at a time. One a night. I was one of the last. And I could see quite clearly what they did to the others. They used to come round with these ... I don't know what they were ... they looked like big pincers, with wires on, the wires were attached to a little machine. It was electric. They used to hold the man down, and this chief ... the chief doctor, used to fit the pincers, something like earphones, he used to fit them on either side of the man's skull. There was a man holding the machine, you see, and he'd ... turn it on, and the chief would just press these pincers on either side of the skull and keep them there.

Then he'd take them off. They'd cover the man up ... and they wouldn't touch him again until later on. Some used to put up a fight, but most of them didn't. They just lay there. Well, they were coming
230 round to me, and the night they came I got up and stood against the wall. They told me to get on the bed, and I knew they had to get me on the bed because if they did it while I was standing up they might break my spine. So I stood up and then one or two of them came for me, well, I was younger then, I was much stronger than I am now, I
235 was quite strong then, I laid one of them out and I had another one round the throat, and then suddenly this chief had these pincers on my skull and I knew he wasn't supposed to do it while I was standing up, that's why I ... anyway, he did it. So I did get out. I got out of the place ... but I couldn't walk very well. I don't think my spine
240 was damaged. That was perfectly all right. The trouble was ... my thoughts ... had become very slow ... I couldn't think at all ... I couldn't ... get ... my thoughts ... together ... uuuhh ... I could ... never quite get it ... together. The trouble was, I couldn't hear what people were saying. I couldn't look to the right or the left, I
245 had to look straight in front of me, because if I turned my head round ... I couldn't keep ... upright. And I had these headaches. I used to sit in my room. That was when I lived with my mother. And my brother. He was younger than me. And I laid everything out, in order, in my room, all the things I knew were mine, but I didn't die. The
250 thing is, I should have been dead. I should have died. Anyway, I feel much better now. But I don't talk to people now. I steer clear of places like that café. I never go into them now. I don't talk to anyone ... like that. I've often thought of going back and trying to find the man who did that to me. But I want to do something first. I want to
255 build that shed out in the garden.

1957   1960

Geoffrey Hill

1932–

Geoffrey Hill, born in Bromsgrove, Worcestershire, was educated at the High School there and at Keble College, Oxford. He taught in the School of English at Leeds University (Professor, 1976–80) and has been a Fellow of Emmanuel College, Cambridge, since 1981. His books of verse include *For the Unfallen* (the first, 1959), *King Log* (1968) and *Tenebrae* (1978). *Mercian Hymns* (1971) is a collection of prose poems in praise of Offa, the eighth-century Anglo-Saxon King of Mercia. *The Mystery of the Charity of Charles Péguy* (1983) is a long poem on the life of the French Catholic poet and mystic. Geoffrey Hill's verse is erudite and tough; his themes are often historical and religious.

GENESIS

I

Against the burly air I strode,
Where the tight ocean heaves its load,
Crying the miracles of God.

And first I brought the sea to bear
5   Upon the dead weight of the land;
And the waves flourished at my prayer,
The rivers spawned their sand.

And where the streams were salt and full
The tough pig-headed salmon strove,
10 Curbing the ebb and the tide's pull,
To reach the steady hills above.

II

The second day I stood and saw
The osprey plunge with triggered claw,
Feathering blood along the shore,
15 To lay the living sinew bare.

And the third day I cried: 'Beware
The soft-voiced owl, the ferret's smile,
The hawk's deliberate stoop in air,
Cold eyes, and bodies hooped in steel,
20   Forever bent upon the kill.'

III

And I renounced, on the fourth day,
This fierce and unregenerate clay,

Building as a huge myth for man
The watery Leviathan,[†]

25   And made the glove-winged albatross
Scour the ashes of the sea
Where Capricorn and Zero cross,[†]
A brooding immortality –
Such as the charmed phoenix has
30   In the unwithering tree.

IV

The phoenix burns as cold as frost;
And, like a legendary ghost,
The phantom-bird goes wild and lost,
Upon a pointless ocean tossed.

35   So, the fifth day, I turned again
To flesh and blood and the blood's pain.

V

On the sixth day, as I rode
In haste about the works of God,
With spurs I plucked the horse's blood.

40   By blood we live, the hot, the cold,
To ravage and redeem the world:
There is no bloodless myth will hold.

And by Christ's blood are men made free
Though in close shrouds their bodies lie
45   Under the rough pelt of the sea;

Leviathan   See Job 4. 1
Capricorn . . . cross   where the tropic of Capricorn crosses 0° Longitude

Though Earth has rolled beneath her weight
The bones that cannot bear the light.

1952   1959

CANTICLE† FOR GOOD FRIDAY

The cross staggered him. At the cliff-top
Thomas, beneath its burden, stood
While the dulled wood
Spat on the stones each drop
5   Of deliberate blood.

A clamping, cold-figured day
Thomas (not transfigured) stamped, crouched,
Watched
Smelt vinegar and blood. He,
10   As yet unsearched, unscratched,

And suffered to remain
At such near distance
(A slight miracle might cleanse
His brain
15   Of all attachments, claw-roots of sense)

In unaccountable darkness moved away,
The strange flesh untouched, carrion-sustenance
Of staunchest love, choicest defiance,
Creation's issue congealing (and one woman's).

1956   1959

Canticle   a non-metrical hymn

'DOMAINE PUBLIC'

[Public Domain]
i.m. Robert Desnos, died Terezin Camp,† 1945

For reading I can recommend
   the Fathers.† How they
cultivate the corrupting flesh:

    toothsome contemplation: cleanly
5   maggots churning spleen
to milk. For exercise, prolonged

suppression of much improper
   speech from proper tombs.
If the ground opens, should men's mouths

10   open also? 'I am nothing
    if not saved now!' or
'Christ, what a pantomime!' The days

of the week are seven pits. Look,
   Seigneur,† again we
15   resurrect and the judges come.

1964

Terezin Camp   a notorious concentration
   camp, mainly for Jews, established by the
   Germans in Czechoslovakia during the
Second World War
the Fathers   eminent early Christian writers
Seigneur   Lord

Tony Harrison

1937–

Tony Harrison was born in Leeds and educated at Leeds Grammar School and the University of Leeds, where he studied classics. His poems have been published in *Loiners* (1970), *The School of Eloquence* (1978) and *Continuous* (1981). He has also written verse translations of French classical and Ancient Greek dramas. *Selected Poems* appeared in 1984.

A KUMQUAT[†] FOR JOHN KEATS

Today I found the right fruit for my prime,
not orange, not tangelo, and not lime,
nor moon-like globes of grapefruit that now hang
outside our bedroom, nor tart lemon's tang
5 (though last year full of bile and self-defeat
I wanted to believe no life was sweet)
nor the tangible sunshine of the tangerine,
and no incongruous citrus ever seen
at greengrocers' in Newcastle or Leeds
10 mis-spelt by the spuds and mud-caked swedes,
a fruit an older poet might substitute
for the grape John Keats thought fit to be Joy's fruit,[†]
when, two years before he died, he tried to write
how Melancholy dwelled inside Delight,
15 and if he'd known the citrus that I mean
that's not orange, lemon, lime or tangerine,
I'm pretty sure that Keats, though he had heard
'of candied apple, quince and plum and gourd'[†]
instead of 'grape against the palate fine'
20 would have, if he'd known it, plumped for mine,
this Eastern citrus scarcely cherry size

Kumquat small fruit akin to an orange
Joy's fruit John Keats (1795–1821) wrote in the third stanza of 'Ode on Melancholy' (1819): 'Ay in the very temple of delight / Veil'd Melancholy has her sovran shrine, / Though seen of none save him whose strenuous tongue / Can burst Joy's grape against his palate fine;'
of candied . . . gourd Keats's 'Eve of St Agnes', l. 265

he'd bite just once and then apostrophize
and pen one stanza how the fruit had all
the qualities of fruit before the Fall,
25   but in the next few lines be forced to write
how Eve's apple tasted at the second bite,
and if John Keats had only lived to be,
because of extra years, in need like me,
at 42 he'd help me celebrate
30   that Micanopy† kumquat that I ate
whole, straight off the tree, sweet pulp and sour skin –
or was it sweet outside, and sour within?
For however many kumquats that I eat
I'm not sure if it's flesh or rind that's sweet,
35   and being a man of doubt at life's mid-way
I'd offer Keats some kumquats and I'd say:
*You'll find that one part's sweet and one part's tart:
say where the sweetness or the sourness start.*

I find I can't, as if one couldn't say
40   exactly where the night became the day,
which makes for me the kumquat taken whole
best fruit, and metaphor, to fit the soul
of one in Florida at 42 with Keats
crunching kumquats, thinking, as he eats
45   the flesh, the juice, the pith, the pips, the peel,
that this is how a full life ought to feel,
its perishable relish prick the tongue,
when the man who savours life's no longer young,
the fruits that were his futures far behind.
50   Then it's the kumquat fruit expresses best
how days have darkness round them like a rind,
life has a skin of death that keeps its zest.
History, a life, the heart, the brain
flow to the taste buds and flow back again.
55   That decade or more past Keats's span
makes me an older not a wiser man,
who knows that it's too late for dying young,
but since youth leaves some sweetnesses unsung,
he's granted days and kumquats to express
60   Man's Being ripened by his Nothingness.
And it isn't just the gap of sixteen years,
a bigger crop of terrors, hopes and fears,

Micanopy   a small town in Florida

but a century of history on this earth
between John Keats's death and my own birth –
65   years like an open crater, gory, grim,
with bloody bubbles leering at the rim;[†]
a thing no bigger than an urn explodes
and ravishes all silence,[†] and all odes,
Flora[†] asphyxiated by foul air
70   unknown to either Keats or Lemprière,[†]
dehydrated Naiads, Dryad[†] amputees
dragging themselves through slagscapes with no trees,
a shirt of Nessus[†] fire that gnaws and eats
children half the age of dying Keats . . .

75   Now were you twenty five or six years old[†]
when that fevered brow at last grew cold?
I've got no books to hand to check the dates.
My grudging but glad spirit celebrates
that all I've got to hand's the kumquats, John,
80   the fruit I'd love to have your verdict on,
but dead men don't eat kumquats, or drink wine,
they shiver in the arms of Proserpine,[†]
not warm in bed beside their Fanny Brawne,[†]
nor watch her pick ripe grapefruit in the dawn
85   as I did, waking, when I saw her twist,
with one deft movement of a sunburnt wrist,
the moon, that feebly lit our last night's walk
past alligator swampland, off its stalk.
I thought of moon-juice juleps[†] when I saw,
90   as if I'd never seen the moon before,
the planet glow among the fruit, and its pale light
make each citrus on the tree its satellite.

Each evening when I reach to draw the blind
stars seem the light zest squeezed through night's black rind;

---

bloody bubbles . . . rim in Keats's 'Ode to a
Nightingale' (1819) a beaker of wine has
'beaded bubbles winking at the brim'
an urn . . . silence an allusion to Keats's 'Ode
on a Grecian Urn' (1819), where the urn is
addressed in the first line as 'Thou still
unravish'd bride of quietness,'
Flora the Roman goddess of Fertility,
mentioned in the 'Ode to a Nightingale'
Lemprière Keats made use of the *Classical
Dictionary* (1788) of John Lemprière (1765–
1824)

Naiads, Dryad naiads, water nymphs in
classical mythology, and dryads, tree
nymphs, often figure in Keats's poems
a shirt of Nessus a shirt steeped in poisoned
blood which, in classical mythology, killed
Hercules
twenty five . . . old Keats died at the age of
twenty-five years and four months
Proserpine Queen of Hades
Fanny Brawne the girl Keats loved
juleps a julep is a sweet, minty American drink

95   the night's peeled fruit the sun, juiced of its rays,
      first stains, then streaks, then floods the world with days,
      days, when the very sunlight made me weep,
      days, spent like the nights in deep, drugged sleep,
      days in Newcastle by my daughter's bed,
100   wondering if she, or I, weren't better dead,
      days in Leeds, grey days, my first dark suit,
      my mother's wreaths stacked next to Christmas fruit,
      and days, like this in Micanopy. Days!

      As strong sun burns away the dawn's grey haze
105   I pick a kumquat and the branches spray
      cold dew in my face to start the day.
      The dawn's molasses make the citrus gleam
      still in the orchards of the groves of dream.

      The limes, like Galway after weeks of rain,
110   glow with a greenness that is close to pain,
      the dew-cooled surfaces of fruit that spent
      all last night flaming in the firmament.
      The new day dawns. O days! My spirit greets
      the kumquat with the spirit of John Keats.
115   O kumquat, comfort for not dying young,
      both sweet and bitter, bless the poet's tongue!
      I burst the whole fruit chilled by morning dew
      against my palate. Fine, for 42!

      I search for buzzards as the air grows clear
120   and see them ride fresh thermals overhead.
      Their bleak cries were the first sound I could hear
      when I stepped at the start of sunrise out of doors,
      and a noise like last night's bedsprings on our bed
      from Mr Fowler sharpening farmers' saws.

1979   1981

BRINGING UP

      It was a library copy otherwise
      you'd've flung it in the fire in disgust.
      Even cremation can't have dried the eyes
      that wept for weeks about my 'sordid lust'.

5   The undertaker would have thought me odd
    or I'd've put my book in your stiff hand.
    You'd've been embarrassed though to meet your God
    clutching those poems of mine that you'd like banned.

    I thought you could hold my *Loiners*, and both burn!

10 And there together in the well wrought urn,
    what's left of you, the poems of your child,
    devoured by one flame, unreconciled,
    like soots on washing, black on bone-ash white.

    Maybe you see them in a better light!

15 But I still see you weeping, your hurt looks:

    You weren't brought up to write such mucky books!

                                                    1981

Gillian Clarke
1937–

Gillian Clarke was born in Cardiff and educated at St Clare's Convent, Porthcawl, and at University College, Cardiff. She has published two major collections of verse, *The Sundial* (1978) and *Letter from a Far Country* (1982). Her clear and sensitive poems are often inspired by family life in rural Wales. A part-time lecturer, she edits the *Anglo-Welsh Review*.

THE SUNDIAL

Owain was ill today. In the night
He was delirious, shouting of lions
In the sleepless heat. Today, dry
And pale, he took a paper circle,
5   Laid it on the grass which held it
With curling fingers. In the still
Centre he pushed the broken bean
Stick, gathering twelve fragments
Of stone, placed them at measured
10 Distances. Then he crouched, slightly
Trembling with fever, calculating
The mathematics of sunshine.

He looked up, his eyes dark,
Intelligently adult as though
15 The wave of fever taught silence
And immobility for the first time.
Here, in his enforced rest, he found
Deliberation, and the slow finger
Of light, quieter than night lions
20 More worthy of his concentration
All day he told the time to me.

All day we felt and watched the sun
Caged in its white diurnal heat,
Pointing at us with its black stick.

1978

PLUMS

When their time comes they fall
without wind, without rain.
They seep through the trees' muslin
in a slow fermentation.

5   Daily the low sun warms them
in a late love that is sweeter
than summer. In bed at night
we hear heartbeat of fruitfall.

The secretive slugs crawl home
10   to the burst honeys, are found
in the morning mouth on mouth,
inseparable.

We spread patchwork counterpanes
for a clean catch. Baskets fill,
15   never before such harvest,
such a hunters' moon burning

the hawthorns, drunk on syrups
that are richer by night
when spiders pitch
20   tents in the wet grass.

This morning the red sun
is opening like a rose
on our white wall, prints there
the fishbone shadow of a fern.

25   The early blackbirds fly
guilty from a dawn haul
of fallen fruit. We too
breakfast on sweetnesses.

Soon plum trees will be bone,
30   grown delicate with frost's
formalities. Their black
angles will tear the snow.

1982

Tom Stoppard
1937–

Tom Stoppard was born in Zlin in Czechoslovakia, the son of Dr Eugene Straussley. His family went to Singapore in 1939; his father was killed there, and Tom took his stepfather's name when he came to England in 1946. He worked as a journalist in Bristol from 1954 to 1963. His first play, *A Walk on the Water*, was televised in 1963. *Rosencrantz and Guildenstern are Dead* (1966) made his name. Since then he has written a series of very successful, witty and thoughtful plays, for stage and for television, including *The Real Inspector Hound* (1968), *Jumpers* (1972), *Travesties* (1974) and *Undiscovered Country* (1980). Stoppard writes intellectual comedies. *Every Good Boy Deserves Favour* (1977), about the ordeals of dissidents in Russia, and *Professional Foul* (1978), a television play about a Cambridge philosopher who visits a former pupil in Prague, show his concern for freedom of thought. His novel *Lord Malquist and Mr Moon* was published in 1965.

In *Jumpers*, George Moore, a philosopher, is struggling gamely – and word-gamely – to reconcile a belief in the existence of God with his experience of a chaotic environment. As the Second Act begins, a dead gymnast having been disposed of, Mrs Moore, the murderess, is about to be visited by her psychiatrist, Archie.

From JUMPERS
[What to Believe?]

> The Bedroom is blacked out, but music still comes from it – presumably the next track on the album [The song 'Forget Yesterday', composed by Marc Wilkinson with lyrics by Tom Stoppard]. Only a minute or two have passed.
> BONES appears from the Kitchen entrance. He is pushing a well-laden dinner-trolley in front of him. It has on it a covered casserole dish, a bottle of wine in an ice bucket, two glasses, two plates, two of everything . . . dinner for two in fact, and very elegant.

He is followed by GEORGE *holding a couple of lettuce leaves and a carrot, which he nibbles absently.*

GEORGE: What do you mean, 'What does he look like?' He looks like a rabbit with long legs.

(*But* BONES *has stopped, listening to Dotty's voice, rather as a man might pause in St Peter's on hearing choristers. . . .*)

BONES: That was it. . . . That was the one she was singing. . . . I remember how her voice faltered, I saw the tears spring into her eyes,
5   the sobs shaking her breast . . . and that awful laughing scream as they brought the curtains down on the first lady of the musical stage – never to rise again! Oh yes, there are many stars in the West End night, but there's only ever been one Dorothy Moore. . . .

GEORGE: Yes, I must say I envy her that. There have not been so many
10   philosophers, but *two* of them have been George Moore,[†] and it tends to dissipate the impact of one's name. But for that, I think my book *Conceptual Problems of Knowledge and Mind* would have caused quite a stir.

BONES: Any chance of a come-back, sir?

15   GEORGE: Well, I'm still hoping to find a publisher for it. I have also made a collection of my essays under the title, *Language, Truth and God.* An American publisher has expressed an interest but he wants to edit it himself and change the title to *You Better Believe It.* . . . I suppose it would be no worse than benefiting from my wife's gramophone
20   records.

BONES: A consummate artist, sir. I felt it deeply when she retired.

GEORGE: Unfortunately she retired from consummation about the same time as she retired from artistry.

BONES: It was a personal loss, really.

25   GEORGE: Quite. She just went off it. I don't know why.

BONES (*coming round to him at last*): You don't have to explain to me, sir. You can't keep much from her hard-core fans. Actually, I had a brother who had a nervous breakdown. It's a terrible thing. It's the pressure, you know. The appalling pressure of being a star.

30   GEORGE: Was your brother a star?

BONES: No, he was an osteopath. Bones the Bones, they called him. Every patient had to make a little joke. It drove him mad, finally.

(*They have been approaching the Bedroom door, but* BONES *suddenly abandons the trolley and takes* GEORGE *downstage.*)

(*Earnestly.*) You see, Dorothy is a delicate creature, like a lustrous-

---

two . . . *George Moore*   George E. Moore   was author of *Principia Ethica* (1903)
(1873–1958), the Cambridge philosopher,

eyed little bird you could hold in your hand, feeling its little brittle
35   bones through its velvety skin – vulnerable, you understand; highly
strung. No wonder she broke under the strain. And you don't get
over it, just like that. It can go on for years, the effect, afterwards –
building up again, underneath, until, one day – *Snap!* – do something
violent perhaps, quite out of character, you know what I mean? It
40   would be like a blackout. She wouldn't know what she was doing.
(*He grips* GEORGE's *elbow.*) And I should think that any competent
or, better still, eminent psychiatric expert witness would be prepared
to say so. Of course, he wouldn't be cheap, but it can be done, do
you follow me?

45   GEORGE (*puzzled*): I'm not sure that I do.

BONES: Well, your wife says you can explain everything, and you say
you are wholly responsible, but –

GEORGE: Are you still going on about that? – for goodness sake, I just
lost my temper for a moment, that's all, and took matters into my
50   own hands.

BONES: Because of the noise?

GEORGE: Exactly.

BONES: Don't you think it was a bit extreme?

GEORGE: Yes, yes, I suppose it was a bit.

55   BONES: Won't wash, Wilfred. I believe you are trying to shield her.

GEORGE: Shield who?

BONES: It's quite understandable. Is there a man who could stand aside
when this fair creature is in trouble –

GEORGE: Aren't you getting a little carried away? The point is, surely
60   that I'm the householder and I must be held responsible for what
happens in my house.

BONES: I don't think the burden of being a householder extends to
responsibility for any crime committed on the premises.

GEORGE: Crime? You call that a crime?

65   BONES (*with more heat*): Well, what would you call it?

GEORGE: It was just a bit of *fun*! Where's you sense of humour, man?

BONES (*staggered*): I don't know, you bloody philosophers are all the
same, aren't you? A man is dead and you're as cool as you like. Your
wife begged me with tears in her eyes to go easy on you, and I don't
70   mind admitting I was deeply moved –

GEORGE: Excuse me –

BONES (*angrily*): But you're wasted on her, mate. What on earth made
her marry *you*, I'll never know, when there are so many better men –
decent, strong, protective, understanding, sensitive –

75   GEORGE: Did you say somebody was dead?

BONES: Stone dead, in the bedroom.

GEORGE: Don't be ridiculous.

BONES: The body is lying on the floor!

GEORGE (*going to Door*): You have obviously take leave of your senses.

80 BONES: Don't touch it! – it will have to be examined for fingerprints.

GEORGE: If there is a body on the floor, it will have my *footprints* on it.

(*He opens the Bedroom door. In the Bedroom, no one is in view. The drapes – or screens – are round the bed. The ambiguous machine – the dermatograph – is set up so that it peers with its lens through the drapes. The camera-lights are in position round the bed, shining down over the drapes into the bed. The TV set is connected by a lead to the dermatograph.*

GEORGE *pauses in the doorway.*)

ARCHIE (*within*): . . . There . . .

DOTTY (*within*): . . . Yes . . .

ARCHIE: There . . . there . . .

85 DOTTY: Yes . . .

ARCHIE: . . . and there . . .

DOTTY: Yes . . . yes.

(*These sounds are consistent with a proper doctor–patient relationship. If* DOTTY *has a tendency to gasp slightly it is probably because the stethoscope is cold.* ARCHIE *on the other hand, might be getting rather overheated under the blaze of the dermatograph lights.*)

ARCHIE (*within*): Excuse me . . .

(ARCHIE'*s coat comes sailing over the drapes.* GEORGE *retreats, closing the door.*)

GEORGE: Well, he's very much alive now.

90 BONES: Sir?

GEORGE: My wife's doctor.

BONES: Really? On the floor?

GEORGE: He's a psychiatrist, notorious for his methods. And for much else.

(*On this bitter note,* GEORGE *goes into the Study.* BONES, *with the trolley, cautiously enters the Bedroom. No one is in view.* BONES *pauses. One of* ARCHIE'*s shoes comes over the drapes and falls on the floor. Another pause. The second shoe comes over, falling into* BONES'*s hands. The absence of a thump brings* ARCHIE'*s head into view, popping up over the drapes.*)

95 ARCHIE: Ah! Good morning!

(ARCHIE *moves to come out from the bed. Meanwhile* DOTTY *looks over the top.*)

DOTTY: Lunch! And Bonesy!

(ARCHIE *picks his coat up and hands it to* BONES, *and then readies himself to put his arms in the sleeves, as though* BONES *were a manservant.*)

ARCHIE (*slipping on his coat*): Thank you so much. Rather warm in there. The lights, you know.

DOTTY: Isn't he sweet?

100 ARCHIE: Charming. What happened to Mrs Whatsername?

DOTTY: No, no, it's Bonesy!

BONES: Inspector Bones, C.I.D.

DOTTY (*disappearing*): Excuse me!

ARCHIE: Bones . . ? I had a patient named Bones. I wonder if he was

105 any relation? an osteopath.

BONES: My brother!

ARCHIE: Remember the case well. Cognomen Syndrome. My advice to him was to take his wife's maiden name of Foot and carry on from there.

110 BONES: He took your advice but unfortunately he got interested in chiropody. He is now in an asylum near Uxbridge.

ARCHIE: Isn't that interesting? I must write him up. The Cognomen Syndrome is my baby, you know.

BONES: You discovered it?

115 ARCHIE: I've got it. Jumper's the name – my card.

BONES (*reading off card*): 'Sir Archibald Jumper, M.D., D.Phil., D.Litt., L.D., D.P.M., D.P.T. (*Gym*)' . . . What's all that?

ARCHIE: I'm a doctor of medicine, philosophy, literature and law, with diplomas in psychological medicine and P.T. including gym.

120 BONES (*handing back the card*): I see that you are the Vice-Chancellor of Professor Moore's university.

ARCHIE: Not a bad record, is it? And I can still jump over seven feet.

BONES: High jump?

ARCHIE: Long jump. My main interest, however, is the trampoline.

125 BONES: Mine is show business generally.

ARCHIE: Really? Well, nowadays, of course, I do more theory than practice, but if trampoline acts appeal to you at all, a vacancy has lately occurred in a little team I run, mainly for our own amusement with a few social engagements thrown in –

130 BONES: Just a minute, just a minute! – what happened to Professor McFee?

ARCHIE: Exactly. I regret to tell you he is dead.

BONES: I realize he is *dead* –

ARCHIE: Shocking tragedy. I am entirely to blame.

135 BONES: You, too, sir?

ARCHIE: Yes, Inspector.

BONES: Very chivalrous, sir, but I'm afraid it won't wash.

(*He addresses the drapes, loudly.*) Miss Moore, is there anything you wish to say at this stage?

DOTTY (*her head appearing*): Sorry?

BONES: My dear – we are all *sorry* –

(DOTTY *disappears.*)

140   ARCHIE: Just a moment! I will not have a patient of mine browbeaten by the police.

BONES (*thoughtfully*): Patient . . .

ARCHIE: Yes. As you can see I have been taking a dermatographical reading.

145   BONES (*indicating the dermatograph*): This? What does it do?

ARCHIE: It reads the skin, electronically; hence dermatograph.

BONES: Why is it connected to the television set?

ARCHIE: We'll get the read-back on the screen. All kinds of disturbances under the skin show up on the surface, if we can learn to read it, and

150   we are learning.

BONES: Disturbances? Mental disturbances?

ARCHIE: Among other things.

BONES (*a new intimacy*): Sir Jim –

ARCHIE: Archie –

155   BONES: Sir Archie, might I have a word with you, in private?

ARCHIE: Just what I was about to suggest. (*He opens the Bedroom door.*) Shall we step outside . . .?

(BONES *steps into the Hall.*)

DOTTY: . . . Things don't seem so bad after all. So to speak.

(ARCHIE *follows* BONES *into the Hall. Fade out on Bedroom.* ARCHIE *and* BONES *move towards Kitchen exit.*)

BONES: This is just between you and me, Sigmund. I understand your

160   feelings only too well. What decent man could stand aside while that beautiful, frail creature –

(*In the Study,* GEORGE *has resumed . . .*)

GEORGE: The study of moral philosophy is an attempt to determine what we mean when we say that something is good and that something else is bad. Not all value judgements, however, are the proper study

165   of the moral philosopher. Language is a finite instrument crudely applied to an infinity of ideas, and one consequence of the failure to take account of this is that modern philosophy has made itself

ridiculous by analysing such statements as, 'This is a good bacon
sandwich,' or, 'Bedser had a good wicket.' *(The* SECRETARY *raises her*
170 *head at 'Bedser'.)* Bedser! – Good God, B-E-D-S . . .

(Fade on Study.
ARCHIE *and* BONES *re-enter.)*

ARCHIE: Please come to the point, Inspector. The plain facts are that
while performing some modest acrobatics for the entertainment of
Miss Moore's party-guests, Professor McFee was killed by a bullet
fired from the outer darkness. We all saw him shot, but none of us
175 saw who shot him. With the possible exception of McFee's fellow
gymnasts, anybody could have fired the shot, and anybody could
have had a reason for doing so, including, incidentally, myself.
BONES: And what might *your* motive be, sir?
ARCHIE: Who knows? Perhaps McFee, my faithful protégé, had secretly
180 turned against me, gone off the rails and decided that he was St Paul
to Moore's Messiah.
BONES: Doesn't seem much of a reason.
ARCHIE: It depends. Moore himself is not important – he is our tame
believer, pointed out to visitors in much the same spirit as we point
185 out the magnificent stained glass in what is now the gymnasium. But
McFee was the guardian and figurehead of philosophical orthodoxy,
and if he threatened to start calling on his masters to return to the
true path, then I'm afraid it would certainly have been an ice-pick in
the back of the skull.
190 DOTTY *(off)*: Darling!
ARCHIE: And then again, perhaps it was Dorothy. Or someone.
(Smiles.)
DOTTY *(off)*: Darling!
BONES: My advice to you is, number one, get her lawyer over here –
ARCHIE: That will not be necessary. I am Miss Moore's legal adviser.
195 BONES: Number two, completely off the record, get her off on expert
evidence – nervous strain, appalling pressure, and one day – snap!
blackout, can't remember a thing. Put her in the box and you're half-
way there. The other half is, get something on Mad Jock McFee, and
if you don't get a Scottish judge it'll be three years probation and the
200 sympathy of the court.
ARCHIE: This is most civil of you, Inspector, but a court appearance
would be most embarrassing to my client and patient; and three
years' probation is not an insignificant curtailment of a person's
liberty.
205 BONES: For God's sake, man, we're talking about a murder charge.
ARCHIE: You are. What I had in mind is that McFee, suffering from
nervous strain brought on by the appalling pressure of overwork –

for which I blame myself entirely – left here last night in a mood of
deep depression, and wandered into the park, where he crawled into
210   a large plastic bag and shot himself . . .

(*Pause.* BONES *opens his mouth to speak.*)

. . . leaving this note . . . (ARCHIE *produces it from his pocket.*) . . .
which was found in the bag together with his body by some gymnasts
on an early morning keep-fit run.

(*Pause.* BONES *opens his mouth to speak.*)

Here is the coroner's certificate.

(ARCHIE *produces another note, which* BONES *takes from him.* BONES
reads it.)

215   BONES: Is this genuine?

ARCHIE: (*testily*): Of course it's genuine. I'm a coroner, not a forger.

(BONES *hands the certificate back, and almost comes to attention.*)

BONES: Sir Archibald Bouncer –

ARCHIE: Jumper.

BONES: Sir Archibald Jumper, I must –

220   ARCHIE: Now, I judge from your curiously formal and somewhat dated
attitude, that you are deaf to offers of large sums of money for
favours rendered.

BONES: I didn't hear that.

ARCHIE: Exactly. On the other hand, I think you are a man who feels
225   that his worth has not been recognized. Other men have got on –
younger men, flashier men . . . Superintendents . . . Commis-
sioners . . .

BONES: There may be something in that.

ARCHIE: I dare say your ambitions do not stop with the Police Force,
230   even.

BONES: Oh?

ARCHIE: Inspector, my patronage is not extensive, but it is select. I can
offer prestige, the respect of your peers and almost unlimited credit
among the local shopkeepers – in short, the Chair of Divinity is yours
235   for the asking.

BONES: The Chair of Divinity?

ARCHIE: Not perhaps, the Chair which is in the eye of the hurricane
nowadays, but a professorship will still be regarded as a distinction
come the day – early next week, in all probability – when the Police
240   Force will be thinned out to a ceremonial front for the peace-keeping
activities of the Army.

BONES: I see. Well, until that happens, I should still like to know – if

McFee shot himself inside a plastic bag, where is the gun?

ARCHIE (*awed*): Very good thinking indeed! On consideration I can give
245   you the Chair of Logic, but that is my last offer.

BONES: This is a British murder enquiry and some degree of justice must
be seen to be more or less done.

ARCHIE: I must say I find your attitude lacking in flexibility. What makes
you so sure that it *was* Miss Moore who shot McFee?

250 BONES: I have a nose for these things.

ARCHIE: With the best will in the world I can't give the Chair of Logic
to a man who relies on nasal intuition.

DOTTY (*off*): Help!

    (BONES *reacts.* ARCHIE *restrains him.*)

ARCHIE: It's all right – just exhibitionism: what we psychiatrists call 'a
255   cry for help'.

BONES: But it *was* a cry for help.

ARCHIE: Perhaps I'm not making myself clear. *All* exhibitionism is a cry
for help, but a cry for help *as such* is only exhibitionism.

DOTTY (*off*): MURDER!

    (BONES *rushes to the Bedroom, which remains dark.* ARCHIE *looks at
his watch and leaves towards the Kitchen.
In the Study,* GEORGE *resumes.*)

260 GEORGE: . . . whereas a spell with the heavy roller would improve it
from Bradman's point of view and worsen it from Bedser's . . .

Likewise, to say that this is a good bacon sandwich is only to say
that by the criteria applied by like-minded lovers of bacon sandwiches,
this one is worthy of approbation. The word good is reducible to
265   other properties such as crisp, lean and unadulterated by tomato
sauce. You will have seen at once that to a man who likes his bacon
sandwiches underdone, fatty and smothered in ketchup, this would
be a rather *poor* bacon sandwich. By subjecting any given example
to similar analysis, the modern school, in which this university has
270   played so lamentable a part, has satisfied itself that all statements
implying goodness or badness, whether in conduct or in bacon
sandwiches, are not statements of *fact* but merely expressions of
feeling, taste or vested interest.

But when we say that the Good Samaritan acted well, we are surely
275   expressing more than a circular prejudice about behaviour. We mean
he acted kindly – selflessly – *well*. And what is our approval of
kindness based on if not on the intuition that kindness is simply good
in itself and cruelty is not. A man who sees that he is about to put
his foot down on a beetle in his path, decides to step on it or not to.
280   Why? What process is at work? And what is that quick blind mindless

connection suddenly made and lost by the man who didn't see the beetle but only heard the crunch?

(*Towards the end of this speech,* ARCHIE *re-enters and quietly lets himself into the Study.*)

It is ironic that the school which denies the claims of the institution to know good when it sees it, is itself the product of the pioneer
285 work set out in his *Principia Ethica* by the late G. E. Moore, an intuitionist philosopher whom I respected from afar but who, for reasons which will be found adequate by logical spirits, was never in when I called. Moore did not believe in God, but I do not hold that against him – for of all forms of wishful thinking, humanism demands
290 the greatest sympathy – and at least by insisting that goodness was a fact, and on his right to recognize it when he saw it, Moore avoided the moral limbo devised by his successors, who are in the unhappy position of having to admit that one man's idea of good is no more meaningful than another man's whether he be St Francis or – Vice-
295 Chancellor!

(*For he has noticed* ARCHIE *in the mirror.* ARCHIE *comes forward.*)

ARCHIE: An inept comparison, if I may say so. I'm very fond of animals. (*He picks up* PAT.) What do you call it?
GEORGE: Pat.
ARCHIE: Pat! . . . what a lovely name.
300 GEORGE: It's a good name for a tortoise, being sexually ambiguous. I also have a hare called Thumper, somewhere. . . . By the way, I wasn't really comparing *you* with –
ARCHIE: Quite understand. You were going to say Hitler or Stalin or Nero . . . the argument always gets back to some lunatic tyrant, the
305 *reductio ad absurdum* of the new ethics, and the dog-eared trump card of the intuitionists.
GEORGE: (*rising to that*): Well, why not? When I push *my* convictions to absurdity, *I* arrive at God – which is at least as embarrassing nowadays. (*Pause.*) All I know is that I think that I know that I know
310 that nothing can be created out of nothing, that my moral conscience is different from the rules of my tribe, and that there is more in me than meets the microscope – and because of *that* I'm lumbered with this incredible, indescribable and definitely shifty *God*, the trump card of atheism.
315 ARCHIE: It's always been a mystery to me why religious faith and atheism should be thought of as opposing attitudes.
GEORGE: Always?
ARCHIE: It just occurred to me.

GEORGE: It occurred to you that belief in God and the conviction that
320   God doesn't exist amount to much the same thing?

ARCHIE: It gains from careful phrasing. Religious faith and atheism differ
mainly about God; about Man they are in accord: Man is the highest
form of life, he has duties he has rights, etcetera, and it is usually
better to be kind than cruel. Even if there is some inscrutable divinity
325   behind it all, our condition for good or ill is apparently determined
by our choice of actions, and choosing seems to be a genuine human
possibility. Indeed, it is surely religious zeal rather than atheism which
is historically notorious in the fortunes of mankind.

GEORGE: I'm not at all sure that the God of religious observance is the
330   object of my faith. Do you suppose it would be presumptuous to
coin a deity?

ARCHIE: I don't see the point. If he caught on, you'd kill for him, too.
(*Suddenly remembering.*) Ah! – I knew there was something! –
McFee's dead.

335   GEORGE: What?!!

ARCHIE: Shot himself this morning, in the park, in a plastic bag.

GEORGE: My God! Why?

ARCHIE: It's hard to say. He was always tidy.

GEORGE: But to shoot himself . . .

340   ARCHIE: Oh, he could be very violent, you know . . . In fact we had a
furious row last night – perhaps the Inspector had asked you about
that . . .?

GEORGE: No . . .

ARCHIE: It was a purely trivial matter. He took offence at my description
345   of Edinburgh as the Reykjavik of the South.

(GEORGE *is not listening.*)

GEORGE: . . . Where did he find the despair . . .? I thought the whole
point of denying the Absolute was to reduce the scale, instantly,
to the inconsequential behaviour of inconsequential animals; that
nothing could ever be that important . . .

350   ARCHIE: Including, I suppose, death . . . It's an interesting view of
atheism, as a sort of *crutch* for those who can't bear the reality of
God . . .

GEORGE: (*still away*): I wonder if McFee was afraid of death? And if he
was, what was it that he would have been afraid of: surely not the
355   chemical change in the material that was his body. I suppose he
would have said, as so many do, that it is only the dying he feared,
yes, the physical process of giving out. But it's not the dying with
me – one knows about pain. It's *death* that I'm afraid of.

(*Pause.*)

ARCHIE: Incidentally, since his paper has of course been circulated to
360   everyone, it must remain the basis of the symposium.

GEORGE: Yes, indeed, I have spent weeks preparing my commentary on
it.

ARCHIE: We shall begin with a two-minute silence. That will give me a
chance to prepare mine.

365   GEORGE: You will be replying, Vice-Chancellor?

ARCHIE: At such short notice I don't see who else could stand in. I'll
relinquish the chair, of course, and we'll get a new chairman, someone
of good standing; he won't have to know much philosophy. Just
enough for a tribute to Duncan.

370   GEORGE: Poor Duncan . . . I like to think he'll be there in spirit.

ARCHIE: If only to make sure the materialistic argument is properly
represented.

DOTTY (off): Darling!

(*Both men respond automatically, and both halt and look at each
other.*)

GEORGE &
ARCHIE: } How is she?

375   GEORGE: How do I know? You're the doctor.

ARCHIE: That's true.

(ARCHIE *moves out of the Study,* GEORGE *with him; into the Hall.*)

I naturally try to get her to open up, but one can't assume she tells
me everything, or even that it's the truth.

GEORGE: Well, I don't know what's the matter with her. She's like a cat
380   on hot bricks, and doesn't emerge from her room. All she says is,
she's all right in bed.

ARCHIE: Yes, well there's something in that.

GEORGE (*restraining his going; edgily*): What exactly do you do in there?

ARCHIE: Therapy takes many forms.

385   GEORGE: I had no idea you were still practising.

ARCHIE: Oh yes . . . a bit of law, a bit of philosophy, a bit of medicine,
a bit of gym. . . . A bit of one and then a bit of the other.

GEORGE: You examine her?

ARCHIE: Oh yes, I like to keep my hand in. You must understand, my
390   dear Moore, that when I'm examining Dorothy I'm not a lawyer or
a philosopher. Or a gymnast, of course. Oh, I know, my dear fellow –
you think that when I'm examining Dorothy I see her eyes as
cornflowers, her lips as rubies, her skin as soft and warm as velvet –
you think that when I run my hands over her back I am carried away
395   by the delicate contours that flow like a sea-shore from shoulder to

heel – oh yes, you think my mind turns to ripe pears as soon as I press –

GEORGE (*viciously*): No, I don't!

ARCHIE: But to us medical men, the human body is just an imperfect
400   machine. As it is to most of us philosophers. And to us gymnasts, of course.

DOTTY (*off; urgently*): Rape! (*Pause.*) Ra——!

(ARCHIE *smiles at* GEORGE, *and quickly lets himself into the Bedroom, closing the door behind him.*
The Bedroom lights up. The dermatograph and the lights have been put away. The bed is revealed as before. DOTTY *is sobbing across the bed.*
BONES *standing by as though paralysed. A wild slow smile spreads over his face as he turns to* ARCHIE, *the smile of a man pleading, 'It's not what you think.'* ARCHIE *moves in slowly.*)

ARCHIE: Tsk tsk . . . Inspector, I am shocked . . . deeply shocked. What a tragic end to an incorruptible career . . .

405   BONES: . . . I never touched her –

ARCHIE: Do not despair. I'm sure we can come to some arrangement. . . .

(GEORGE *has returned to the study.*)

GEORGE: How the hell does one know what to believe?

(*Fade out on Bedroom, to* BLACKOUT.
The SECRETARY *has taken down the last sentence.*)

GEORGE: No, no – (*Changes mind.*) Well, all right. (*Dictating.*) How does one know what it is one believes when it's so difficult to know what
410   it is one knows.

1972

Ian Hamilton
1938–

Robert Ian Hamilton was born in King's Lynn and educated at Darlington Grammar School and Keble College, Oxford. He founded and edited the poetry magazines *The Review* (1962–9) and *The New Review* (1974–9). His books of subtle and humane verse include *Pretending Not to Sleep: Poems* (1964), *The Visit: Poems* (1970), and *Anniversary and Vigil* (1971).

PRETENDING NOT TO SLEEP

The waiting rooms are full of 'characters'
Pretending not to sleep.
Your eyes are open
But you're far away,
5   At home, *am Rhein*,† with mother and the cats.
Your hair grazes my wrist.
My cold hand surprises you.

The porters yawn against the slot-machines
And watch contentedly; they know I've lost.
10   The last train
Is simmering outside, and overhead
Steam flowers in the station rafters.
Soft flecks of soot begin to settle
On your suddenly outstretched palms.
15   Your mouth is dry, excited, going home;

The velvet curtains,
Father dead, the road up to the village,

---

am Rhein (*German*) on the Rhine

Your hands tightening in the thick fur
Of your mother's Persian, your dreams
20 Moving through Belgium now, full of your trip.

                                    1964

NOW AND THEN

The white walls of the Institution
Overlook a strip of thriving meadowland.
On clear days, we can walk there
And look back upon your 'second home'
5 From the green shelter
Of this wild, top-heavy tree.

It all seems so long ago. This afternoon
A gentle sun
Smiles on the tidy avenues, the lawns,
10 The miniature allotments,
On the barred windows of the brand new
Chronic block, 'our pride and joy'.
At the main gate
Pale visitors are hurrying from cars.

15 It all seems so far away. This afternoon
The smoke from our abandoned cigarettes
Climbs in a single column to the sky.
A gentle sun
Smiles on the dark, afflicted heads
20 Of young men who have come to nothing.

                                    1964

Seamus Heaney
1939–

Seamus Justin Heaney was born in Castledawson, County Derry, and educated at St Columb's College, Derry, and Queen's University, Belfast. He has taught English at Queen's and in California and is at present a professor at Harvard University. *Eleven Poems* (1965) was followed by *Death of a Naturalist* (1966) and *Door into the Dark* (1969). Recent volumes of verse include *North* (1975), *Field Work* (1979) and *Station Island* (1984). *Preoccupations: Selected Prose 1968–78* was published in 1980.

THE OTTER

When you plunged
The light of Tuscany wavered
And swung through the pool
From top to bottom.

5   I loved your wet head and smashing crawl,
Your fine swimmer's back and shoulders
Surfacing and surfacing again
This year and every year since.

I sat dry-throated on the warm stones.
10 You were beyond me.
The mellowed clarities, the grape-deep air
Thinned and disappointed.

Thank God for the slow loadening,
When I hold you now
15 We are close and deep
As the atmosphere on water.

My two hands are plumbed water.
You are my palpable, lithe
Otter of memory
20 In the pool of the moment,

Turning to swim on your back,
Each silent, thigh-shaking kick
Re-tilting the light,
Heaving the cool at your neck.

25 And suddenly you're out,
Back again, intent as ever,
Heavy and frisky in your freshened pelt,
Printing the stones.

1979

THE SKUNK

Up, black, striped and damasked like the chasuble
At a funeral mass, the skunk's tail
Paraded the skunk. Night after night
I expected her like a visitor.

5   The refrigerator whinnied into silence.
My desk light softened beyond the verandah.
Small oranges loomed in the orange tree.
I began to be tense as a voyeur.

After eleven years I was composing
10 Love-letters again, broaching the word 'wife'
Like a stored cask, as if its slender vowel
Had mutated into the night earth and air

Of California. The beautiful, useless
Tang of eucalyptus spelt your absence.
15 The aftermath of a mouthful of wine
Was like inhaling you off a cold pillow.

And there she was, the intent and glamorous,
Ordinary, mysterious skunk,
Mythologized, demythologized,
20 Snuffing the boards five feet beyond me.

It all came back to me last night, stirred
By the sootfall of your things at bedtime,

Your head-down, tail-up hunt in a bottom drawer
For the black plunge-line nightdress.

1979

HOLLY

It rained when it should have snowed.
When we went to gather holly

the ditches were swimming, we were wet
to the knees, our hands were all jags

5   and water ran up our sleeves.
There should have been berries

but the sprigs we brought into the house
gleamed like smashed bottle-glass.

Now here I am, in a room that is decked
10   with the red-berried, waxy-leafed stuff,

and I almost forget what it's like
to be wet to the skin or longing for snow.

I reach for a book like a doubter
and want it to flare round my hand,

15   a black-letter bush, a glittering shield-wall
cutting as holly and ice.

1984

Douglas Dunn

1942–

Douglas Eaglesham Dunn was born in Inchinnan, near Glasgow, and educated at Renfrew High School, at Camphill, Paisley, and at the Scottish School of Librarianship and the University of Hull. His first collection of verse, *Terry Street* (1969), was widely admired and enjoyed. Several volumes followed. *Elegies* (1985) was written after the death of Dunn's wife in March 1981.

THE CLEAR DAY

Sunlight gathers in the leaves, dripping
Invisible syrups. Long afternoons
Have been reduced to this significant
Table, melodious ice cubes shaken in
5   A blue tumbler, lazily tipped vermouth
And a hand measuring it, a propped elbow,
A languid eye, while a reflection on
A leaf turns into everything called summer.
The heat haze ripples through the far away
10 Gardens of strangers, acquaintances, of those
I can put a face to. With my eyes shut,
Squeezing the soft salts of their sweat, I see
Beyond my body, nerves, cells, brain, and leisure.
Blue coastal persons walk out of the haze.
15 They have outflown the wind, outswum the sea.
I think, and feel, and do, but do not know
All that I am, all that I have been, once,
Or what I could be could I think of it.
These blue pedestrians bruise the edge of me
20 To a benign remorse, with my lessons.
With my eyes shut, I walk through a wet maze
Following a thread of sounds – birdsong in
Several cadences, children, a dog-bark,
The traffic roaring against silence as
25 A struck match drowns it out, simple tunes of
An amateur pianist, a vulgar shout,

A bottle tapped against a thirsty glass,
The burst of its pouring, and the slip
When the chilled glass wets a wet lower lip.
30 I could not guess at what the pictures are
In the eyes of a friend turned round to watch
Shrub shadows dapple a few yards of lawn
As his smoke clings to his thoughtful posture.
Tonight, I shall look out at the dark trees,
35 Writing this in the muddle of lost tenses
At an o'clock of flowers turned colourless.
Then, as always, the soul plays over mind
With radiantly painful speculations.
I shall sieve through our twenty years, until
40 I almost reach the sob in the intellect,
The truth that waits for me with its loud grief,
Sensible, commonplace, beyond understanding.

1985

A SUMMER NIGHT

Dusk softens round the leaf and cools the West.
Rhythmical fragrances, wind, grass and leaves,
Fly in and out on scented cadences.
I go into the bedroom of the world,
5 Discovering the long night of my life.
This telephone is electronic lies,
Ringing with calls, with farewells of the dead
Paid for on credit. Nocturnal postmen ring
My doorbell; I refuse to let them in.
10 My birch trees have their own two lives to lead
Without our love, although we named them us.
They play inside the aromatic wind
That is their house for ever. Outside time,
On the sensation of a memory
15 I walk through the dark house, remembering.
I meet the seasons on the stairs, breathing
Their pulchritudes, their four degrees of heat,
Four shades of day, shade on shade, shade on shade.
I have gone through a year, in at one end,
20 Out at the same way in. Same every year,

But that year was different. I counted days
As Francis counted sparrows, being kind to them.
They were not kind to me. My floating life
Borrows its fortitude from a cool silence
25   Composed of green, from two trees, from the tingle
That was the touch of us against the world.
It left its lived heat everywhere we'd been,
A small white cry, one last wild, stubborn rose.

1985

James Fenton
1949–

James Fenton was born in Lincoln and educated at Repton School and Magdalen College, Oxford. He has worked as a newspaper reporter and theatre reviewer. *Terminal Moraine*, his first volume of poems, was published in 1972. *The Memory of War* (1982) attracted wide critical acclaim.

THE KILLER SNAILS

The killer snails
Have slung their silver trails
Along the doormat, out across the lawn,
Under the bushes
5   Where the alarming thrushes
Give night its notice, making way for dawn,
And the obliging lizards drop their tails.

On webs of dew
The spiders stir their pots of glue
10   And drag their quartered victims to the shade.
Soaked in their rugs
Of grass and moss the slugs
Wind up another night of sluggish trade
And young ingredients get into a stew.

15   The sorrel bends.
The path fades out but never ends
Where brambles clutch and bracken wipes your feet.
It goes in rings.
Its mind's on other things.
20   Its way and its intentions never meet.
Meeting of friends?
It gives no undertaking. It depends.

Further Reading

Allen, Walter, *Tradition and Dream: The English and American Novel from the Twenties to Our Time* (London: Phoenix House, 1964); as *The Modern Novel in Britain and the United States* (New York: Dutton, 1964).

Bergonzi, Bernard, *The Myth of Modernism and Twentieth Century English Literature* (Brighton: Harvester, 1986).

——, *The Situation of the Novel* (London: Macmillan, 1970; revised 1979).

Blamires, Harry, *Twentieth-Century English Literature*, in the 'Macmillan History of Literature' (London: Macmillan, 1982).

Bradbury, Malcolm, *The Social Context of Modern English Literature* (Oxford: Basil Blackwell; New York: Shocken Books, 1971).

Connolly, Cyril, *Enemies of Promise* (London: Deutsch, 1939).

Ford, Boris (ed.), *The Present*, vol. 8 of 'The New Pelican Guide to English Literature' (Harmondsworth: Penguin Books, 1983).

Fraser, G. S., *The Modern Writer and his World* (London: Verschoyle, 1953; New York: Criterion Books, 1955; revised, London: Deutsch, 1964; New York: Praeger, 1965).

Fussell, Paul, *The Great War and Modern Memory* (London and New York: Oxford University Press, 1975).

Gillie, C., *Movements in English Literature (1900–1940)* (London: Cambridge University Press, 1975).

Harrison, John R., *The Reactionaries* (London: Gollancz, 1966). Preface by William Empson.

Hynes, Samuel, *The Auden Generation: Literature and Politics in England in the 1930s* (London: Bodley Head, 1976).

Johnstone, J. K., *The Bloomsbury Group* (London: Secker & Warburg, 1954).

Karl, Frederick R., *A Reader's Guide to the Contemporary English Novel* (London: Thames & Hudson, 1961).

Leavis, F. R., *New Bearings in English Poetry* (London: Chatto & Windus, 1932; new edn, 1950).

McEwan, Neil, *The Survival of the Novel: British Fiction in the Later Twentieth Century* (London: Macmillan, 1981).

Maxwell, D. E. S., *Poets of the Thirties* (London: Routledge & Kegan Paul, 1969).

Morrison, Blake, *The Movement: English Poetry and Fiction of the 1950s* (Oxford: Oxford University Press, 1980).

O'Faolain, Sean, *The Vanishing Hero: Studies in Novelists of the Twenties* (London: Eyre & Spottiswoode, 1956).

Orr, Peter (ed.), *The Poet Speaks: Interviews with Contemporary Poets* (London: Routledge & Kegan Paul, 1966).

Powell, Anthony, *To Set the Ball Rolling: The Memoirs of Anthony Powell* (Harmondsworth: Penguin Books, 1983). An abridged and revised edition of four volumes published by Heinemann, London: *Infants of the Spring* (1976), *Messengers of Day* (1978), *Faces in My Time* (1980), *The Strangers All Are Gone* (1982).

Press, John, *A Map of Modern English Verse* (London and New York: Oxford University Press, 1969).

Robson, W. W., *Modern English Literature* (London: Oxford University Press, 1970).

Schmidt, Michael and Lindop, Grevel, *British Poetry Since 1960* (Oxford: Carcanet Press, 1972).

Scully, James (ed.), *Modern Poets on Modern Poetry* (London: Fontana, 1977).

Silkin, Jon, *Out of Battle: Poetry of the Great War* (London and New York: Oxford University Press, 1972).

Sisson, C. H., *English Poetry 1900–1950: An Assessment* (London: Hart Davis, 1971).

Spender, Stephen, *World Within World: The Autobiography of Stephen Spender* (London: Hamish Hamilton; New York: Harcourt Brace, 1951).

Stewart, J. I. M., *Eight Modern Writers*, vol. XII of the 'Oxford History of English Literature' (Oxford: Clarendon Press, 1963).

Taylor, John Russell, *Anger and After: A Guide to the New British Drama* (London: Methuen, 1962).

Thwaite, Anthony, *Poetry Today: 1960–1973* (London: Longman, 1973).

Index of First Lines

About suffering they were never wrong,   444
Above a stretch of still unravaged weald   518
Against the burly air I strode,   575
All right, I was Welsh. Does it matter   481
Although I can see him still,   86
And death shall have no dominion.   487
A nondescript express in from the South,   444
Apeneck Sweeney spreads his knees   342
As I drive to the junction of lane and highway,   10
As if their great bone-spongey beaks were too heavy,   494
A snake came to my water-trough   304
As the team's head brass flashed out on the turn   212
A sudden blow: the great wings beating still   89
As we get older we do not get any younger.   484
A thrush in the syringa sings   384
At last you yielded up the album, which,   522

Bald heads forgetful of their sins,   86
Barely a twelvemonth after   326
Beautiful lofty things: O'Leary's noble head;   98
Belbroughton Road is bonny, and pinkly bursts the spray   439
Bent double, like old beggars under sacks,   364
'But that was nothing to what things came out   375

Children are dumb to say how hot the day is,   374
Christmas Eve, and twelve of the clock.   11
Cities and Thrones and Powers   129
Clip-clop go water-drops and bridles ring –   461
Close up the casement, draw the blind,   4
Cole, that unwearied prince of Colchester   198
Could man be drunk for ever   77
Cycles of ulcers, insomnia, poetry –   475

Down by the salley gardens my love and I did meet;   82
Downhill I came, hungry, and yet not starved;   211
Down the blue night the unending columns press   321
Dusk softens round the leaf and cools the West.   606

Ere Mor the Peacock flutters, ere the Monkey People cry,   124
Evans? Yes, many a time   480
Everyone suddenly burst out singing   319

Far, far from gusty waves these children's faces.   459
File into yellow candle light, fair choristers of King's   439
Fish (fly-replete, in depth of June,   320

For reading I can recommend   578
From prehistoric distance, beyond clocks,   217
From shadows of rich oaks outpeer   379

God gave all men all earth to love,   126
God of our fathers, known of old,   125
Gone to hunt; and my brothers   384
Good morning, Algernon, Good morning, Percy.   181
'Good morning; Good morning!' the General said   317
Good-night; ensured release,   80

He disappeared in the dead of winter: 445
He does not think that I haunt here nightly: 7
Here they went with smock and crook,   380
Hereto I come to view a voiceless ghost;   9
How do you know that the pilgrim track   6

I drip, drip here   16
If I should die, think only this of me: 323
If it's ever spring again,   15
If you can keep your head when all about you   130
I had this thought a while ago   85
I have come to the borders of sleep,   213
I have heard that hysterical women say   96
I have seen old ships sail like swans asleep   293
I heard the graybird bathing in the rill,   382
I know that I shall meet my fate   88
I leant upon a coppice gate   2
I made my song a coat   86
I must go down to the seas again, to the lonely sea and the sky, 208
In the northern hemisphere   309
In the time of old sin without sadness   200
In valleys green and still   79
I pitched my day's leazings in Crimmercrock Lane,   3
I said to Love   1
I sought a theme and sought for it in vain,   99
I think continually of those who were truly great.   458
It is the stone makes stillness here. I think   547
It rained when it should have snowed,   604
It seemed that out of battle I escaped   365
It was a library copy otherwise   582
It was a little captive cat   386
It were a proud God-guiling, to allure   350
I walk through the long schoolroom questioning;   91
I went by the Druid stone   14
I who am dead a thousand years (Flecker)   292
I who am dead a thousand years (Heath-Stubbs)   493
I will arise and go now, and go to Innisfree,   83

Lady, when your lovely head   181
Law, say the gardeners, is the sun,   447
Lay your sleeping head, my love,   443
Let me take this other glove off   436
Let us go then, you and I,   338
Look, stranger, on this island now   442
Lord Lundy from his earliest years   178

Me clairvoyant   200
Midwinter spring is its own season   343
My love looks like a girl tonight,   304
My spirit will not haunt the mound   6
My wife and I have asked a crowd of craps   529

Never give all the heart, for love   84
Nobody heard him, the dead man,   387
Not being Oedipus he did not question the Sphinx,   492
Not every man has gentians in his house   316
Not the end: but there's nothing more.   214
Now as I was young and easy under the apple boughs   488
Now, God be thanked Who has matched us with His hour,   322
Now it is autumn and the falling fruit   312
Nudes – stark and glistening,   352

Of an old King in a story   199
Oh what a pity, Oh! don't you agree   311
Oh would I could subdue the flesh   438
Old King Cole was a merry old soul,   198
O Love, be fed with apples while you may,   375
Once I am sure there's nothing going on   520
One duck stood on my toes.   461
On the day of the explosion   530
On Wenlock Edge the wood's in trouble;   75
Others, I am not the first,   74
Owain was ill today. In the night   584

Pike, three inches long, perfect   565

Quinquireme of Nineveh from distant Ophir   209

Reaching down arm-deep into bright water   456
Reading the shorthand on a barber's sheet   473
Remember me when I am dead   507
Ripeness is all; her in her cooling planet   453

She looked over his shoulder   449
She sped through the door   13
She turns her head demurely. In a year   548

Since I emerged that day from the labyrinth,   324
Slow bleak awakening from the morning dream   218
Slowly the poison the whole blood stream fills.   455
Smile at us, pay us, pass us; but do not quite forget;   195
Sombre the night is.   352
Sport is absurd, and sad.   532
Stars, I have seen them fall,   80
Still falls the Rain –   329
Sunlight gathers in the leaves, dripping   605
Swear by what the sages spoke   101
Swift has sailed into his rest;   93

That day when oats were reaped, and wheat was ripe, and barley
    ripening   17
That is no country for old men. The young   90
That Whitsun, I was late getting away: 527
The accursed power which stands on Privilege   181
The air is thick with nerves and smoke: pens tremble in sweating
    hands;   504
The apes yawn and adore their fleas in the sun.   564
The chestnut casts his flambeaux, and the flowers   75
The covenant of god and animal,   324
The cross staggered him. At the cliff-top   577
The darkness crumbles away.   351
The Devil, having nothing else to do,   180
The eye can hardly pick them out   525
The force that through the green fuse drives the flower   486
The Garden called Gethsemane   134
The hop-poles stand in cones,   381
The implicated generations made   463
The killer snails   608
The old professor of Zoology   291
The orchards half the way   78
The plunging limbers over the shattered track   353
There are the Alps. What is there to say about them?   383
There fared a mother driven forth   197
There is a Supreme God in the ethnological section;   454
There is a wind where the rose was   182
There is stone in me that knows stone,   457
The sea at evening moves across the sand.   477
These hearts were woven of human joys and cares,   322
The skylarks are far behind that sang over the down;   215
The trains that have been howling   545
The unpurged images of day recede;   93
The waiting rooms are full of 'characters'   600
The white walls of the Institution   601
They have taken the gable from the roof of clay   211
They sing their dearest songs   12

They spoke the loveliest of languages.   505
This cat was bought upon the day   474
This lunar beauty   441
Three Michaelmas daisies   384
Three picture-drawn people stepped out of their frames –   18
Three weeks gone and the combatants gone.   508
Timothy Winters comes to school   490
Tis mute, the word they went to hear on high Dodona mountain   76
Today I found the right fruit for my prime,   579
To-day we have naming of parts. Yesterday   483
To stand here in the wings of Europe   506
Turning and turning in the widening gyre   88

Under my window-ledge the waters race   95
Up, black, striped and damasked like the chasuble   603

Very old are the woods;   182

Walking around in the park   526
Well, how are things in Heaven? I wish you'd say,   317
Well, World, you have kept faith with me,   17
What is a woman that you forsake her,   129
'What of vile dust?' the preacher said.   194
What passing-bells for those who die as cattle?   363
When did you start your tricks,   307
When I play on my fiddle in Dooney   83
When I returned at sunset,   216
When I set out for Lyonnesse,   5
When I would muse in boyhood   79
When Julius Fabricius, Sub-Prefect of the Weald,   131
When their time comes they fall   585
When the Present has latched its postern behind my tremulous stay,   15
When we are dead, some Hunting-boy will pass   181
When you plunged   602
When you see millions of the mouthless dead   377
'Who knocks?' 'I, who was beautiful,   183
Who now, seeing Her so   451
Who smoke-snorts toasts o' My Lady Nicotine,   199
Why did you give no hint that night   8
Why should I blame her that she filled my days   85
Why should I let the toad *work*   523
Why should not old men be mad?   98

Yes, I remember Adlestrop –   210
You are blind like us. Your hurt no man designed,   377
You idiot! What makes you think decay will   385

Index of Authors

Amis, Kingsley   509
Auden, W. H.   441

Beckett, Samuel   430
Beer, Patricia   545
Belloc, Hilaire   178
Bennett, Arnold   147
Betjeman, John   436
Blunden, Edmund   379
Brooke, Rupert   320
Bunting, Basil   383

Causley, Charles   490
Chesterton, G. K.   194
Churchill, Winston   201
Clarke, Gillian   584
Compton-Burnett, Ivy   356
Conrad, Joseph   49

Davie, Donald   518
de la Mare, Walter   182
Douglas, Keith   506
Dunn, Douglas   605

Eliot, T. S.   337
Empson, William   453
Enright, D. J.   504

Fenton, James   608
Flecker, James Elroy   291
Ford, Ford Madox   185
Forster, E. M.   220
Fuller, Roy   473

Galsworthy, John   162
Golding, William   464
Graves, Robert   374
Greene, Graham   408

Hamilton, Ian   600
Hardy, Thomas   1
Harrison, Tony   579
Heaney, Seamus   602
Heath-Stubbs, John   492
Hill, Geoffrey   575
Housman, A. E.   74
Hughes, Ted   564
Huxley, Aldous   367

James, Henry   20
Jennings, Elizabeth   547
Joyce, James   269

Kipling, Rudyard   104
Kirkup, James   532

Larkin, Philip   520
Lawrence, D. H.   294
Lawrence, T. E.   331

MacCaig, Norman   461
Masefield, John   208
Monro, Harold   216
Mortimer, John   534
Muir, Edwin   324
Munro, H. H.   173
Murdoch, Iris   496

Orwell, George   398
Osborne, John   553
Owen, Wilfred   363

Pinter, Harold   567
Powell, Anthony   420
Prince, F. T.   477

Raine, Kathleen   456
Reed, Henry   483
Rosenberg, Isaac   350

Sassoon, Siegfried   317
Shaw, George Bernard   38
Sitwell, Edith   329
Smith, Stevie   386

Sorley, Charles   377
Spender, Stephen   458
Stoppard, Tom   587
Strachey, Lytton   229

Thomas, Dylan   486
Thomas, Edward   210
Thomas, R. S.   480
Trevor, William   549

Waugh, Evelyn   388
Wells, H. G.   135
Wodehouse, P. G.   241
Woolf, Virginia   257

Yeats, W. B.   82

Source List

(Excluding those listed in the Acknowledgements)

Arnold Bennett, *The Old Wives' Tale,* edited by John Wain (Penguin, Harmondsworth, 1983); **Rupert Brooke,** *Collected Poems* (Sidgwick & Jackson, London, 1979); **G. K. Chesterton,** *The Collected Poems* (Methuen, London, 1959); **Joseph Conrad,** *Typhoon and The Shadow Line* (Dent, London, 1979); **Joseph Conrad,** *The Secret Agent* (Penguin, Harmondsworth, 1969); **J. Elroy Flecker,** *Collected Poems* (Secker & Warburg, London, 1946); **John Galsworthy,** *Strife* (Duckworth, London, 1977); **Thomas Hardy,** *The Complete Poems of Thomas Hardy,* New Wessex Edition, edited by James Gibson (Macmillan, London, 1976); **A. E. Housman,** *The Collected Poems* (Cape, London, 1960); **Henry James,** *The Complete Tales,* edited by Leon Edel, 12 vols (Rupert Hart-Davis, London, 1962–4), vol. 12; **Rudyard Kipling,** *Kim* (Macmillan, London, 1961); **Rudyard Kipling,** *Rudyard Kipling's Verse,* Definitive Edition (Hodder & Stoughton, London, 1940); **D. H. Lawrence,** *Women in Love* (Penguin, Harmondsworth, 1969); **D. H. Lawrence,** *The Complete Poems,* edited by Vivian de Sola Pinto and Warren Roberts (Heinemann, London, 1964); **T. E. Lawrence,** *Seven Pillars of Wisdom: A Triumph* (Cape, London, 1976); **Harold Monro,** *Collected Poems,* edited by Alida Monro (Duckworth, London, 1970); **'Saki': H. H. Munro,** *The Complete Works of Saki* (The Bodley Head, London, 1980); **Wilfred Owen,** *Collected Poems,* edited by C. Day Lewis (Chatto & Windus, London, 1963); **Isaac Rosenberg,** *The Collected Poems,* edited by Gordon Bottomley and Denys Harding (Chatto & Windus, London, 1974); **Charles H. Sorley,** *Marlborough and Other Poems* (Cambridge University Press, Cambridge, 1932); **Lytton Strachey,** *Eminent Victorians* (Chatto & Windus, London, 1979); **Edward Thomas,** *Collected Poems,* edited by R. G. Thomas (Oxford University Press, Oxford, 1978).